The Dramatic
Imagination of
Robert Browning

The Dramatic Imagination of *Robert Browning*

A LITERARY LIFE

Richard S. Kennedy
and
Donald S. Hair

University of Missouri Press
Columbia and London

Library of Congress Cataloging-in-Publication Data

Kennedy, Richard S.
   The dramatic imagination of Robert Browning : a literary life / Richard S. Kennedy and
Donald S. Hair.
       p.   cm.
   Includes bibliographical references (p.   ) and index.
   ISBN-13: 978-0-8262-1691-5 (hard cover : alk. paper)
   ISBN-10: 0-8262-1691-9 (hard cover : alk. paper)
   1. Browning, Robert, 1812–1889.   2. Browning, Robert, 1812–1889—Friends and
associates.   3. Browning, Elizabeth Barrett, 1806–1861.   4. Browning, Elizabeth Barrett,
1806–1861—Friends and associates.   5. Poets, English—19th century—Biography.
6. Married people—Great Britain—Biography.   I. Hair, Donald S.   II. Title.
   PR4231.K36 2007
   821'.809—dc22
   [B]   2006100678

Designer: *foleydesign*
Typesetter: BookComp, Inc.
Printer and binder: Thomson-Shore, Inc.
Typefaces: Adobe Jenson and Cochin

The University of Missouri Press gratefully acknowledges the Smallman Fund
of the University of Western Ontario for a contribution in support
of the publication of this book.

Contents

Preface

When Dick Kennedy died in December 2002, he had written about two-thirds of this critical biography, his twenty-six chapters telling the story of Robert Browning's life to 1856 and providing critical commentary on his works and their reception to *Men and Women*. He also left, in longhand, an account of Elizabeth Barrett Browning's death in 1861, which now makes up the final pages of chapter 27. His work on Browning, anticipated by his book on *Asolando* after a scholarly career devoted largely to Thomas Wolfe and E. E. Cummings, became an absorbing retirement project for him, but ill health eventually impeded its progress, and he began to fear, as early as the fall of 1999, that he might be unable to finish it. He and I had met at the Armstrong Browning Library four years earlier, and our long and enjoyable conversations about the poet made us friends then and later led him to ask me to carry on with the project if he were unable to. That is how my name has come to be linked with his in the writing of this book, to which I have contributed the final eight chapters. I note a sad fact about Browning biographies: two of the standard ones—Griffin and Minchin's (1910) and Irvine and Honan's (1974)—have two authors because the scholars who started the works did not live to finish them.

Two authors means two voices in the book, and although Dick had written to me saying that "I want you to feel that this is our book brought into being by the two of us," death has made impossible one kind of collaboration: continuing discussions, the reading and revising of each other's drafts, the settling on our versions of events in the life and approaches to the works. Dick, with his characteristic generosity of spirit, foresaw his collaborator's situation, and when he sketched his plans for the chapters he knew he would be unable to write, he concluded by saying that "you, of course, should handle all this in any way your professional judgment guides you." Then he went even further: "I wish you to feel free to make any changes, cuts, or revisions in the 26 chapters I pass on to you, including revisions of my critical opinions." To make the book a manageable length and to meet the suggestions of its publisher, I have cut, and while I have revised some of Dick's critical opinions or substituted my own for his, I have retained nearly everything that has to do with his chief critical approach to Browning: that a "dramatic imagination" characterizes this Victorian poet, and that a theory of classification of the poems—set out in chapter 9, Dick's central critical chapter—will illuminate the ways and directions in which a "dramatic imagination" expresses itself.

One may guess how Dick might have written the final sections of this critical biography by looking at the concluding chapter—"Epilogue to an 'Epilogue'"—in his book on *Asolando*. There he outlines Browning's whole career as a poet. I have departed from that outline, not thinking that after *The Ring and the Book* Browning's "creative powers went into decline" but rather that they developed in directions neglected by all but a few critics. Those directions have intellectual interests and excitements of their own for Browning's readers, and I have tried to indicate why those later poems are well worth critical attention, and why they are evidence for Bishop Blougram's (and his creator's) dictum "Never leave growing."

Browning himself set the agenda—reluctantly but realistically—for the biographers who, he knew, would inevitably tackle his life and works by saying, in the poem called "House" in his 1876 *Pacchiarotto* volume, that they must bring to the evidence, both factual and textual, their "spirit-sense." In chapter 33 I explain what that is. I have tried to meet the poet's criterion, and Dick, an experienced biographer, certainly tried to do so, too. How well we have succeeded must be left to others to judge. Still, we were aware that every critical biography is the product of its particular time in literary history, and Janus-like, looks both backward and forward. We have looked back to, and are indebted to, Browning's many editors and biographers, but at the same time we knew that new materials would be coming to light and would make future biographies different from ours. Had Dick's collaborator world enough and time, he would dearly love to make use of the Armstrong Browning Library's recent acquisitions: letters between Browning and Julia Wedgwood, and the papers and letters in the Joseph Milsand Archive. Others will relish the excitement of using those materials, and I can only quote Hamm's line in Beckett's *Endgame:* "We do what we can."

Dick did extensive primary research for this biography in libraries and in special collections in the United States, Britain, and elsewhere, and the many people who helped him ought to be named and thanked here. Unfortunately, the papers and files he left with me do not include acknowledgments, but I do know that both of us owe a great deal to scholarly friends at the Armstrong Browning Library at Baylor University: to Philip Kelley, to Cyndie Burgess, to Rita Patteson, and to Christi Klempnauer. I also know that Dick would have wanted to thank Mary Rose Sullivan, who read, and commented on, his chapters in the year before his death. Dick's collaborator is grateful to Brian Corman, the chair of the Department of English at the University of Toronto, for making available to him the 1954 master's thesis of Leo Anthony Hetzler, and he is particularly grateful to Kathleen Okruhlik, Dean of the Faculty of Arts and Humanities at the University of Western Ontario, for approving a subvention in aid of publication from the Smallman Fund; she and Douglas Kneale, the chair of the Department of English at Western, also provided office space when I most needed it. The University of Toronto Press kindly allowed me to use some of my materials on *Balaustion's Adventure* and *Aristophanes' Apology* from my earlier book, *Robert Browning's Language*, and the University of Missouri Press gave me permission to use some of Dick Kennedy's sentences from his earlier *Robert Browning's* Asolando. The Provost and Fellows of Eton College (who hold the copyright for the Brownings), through the generosity of Michael Meredith, granted permission to quote from unpublished letters of both Brownings, and I am also grateful for permission granted by the British Library (for materials in the W. Hall Griffin collection and for the typescript prepared by Frederic G. Kenyon for his edition of EBB's letters). An 1855 letter from RB to John Kenyon (Autograph File, B) is used by permission of the Houghton Library, Harvard University. For permission to use parts of Dick Kennedy's article on Browning's ancestry (first published in *Browning Society Notes* in 2000) I am grateful to the Hon. Secretary of the Browning Society of London, Pamela Neville-Sington. Special thanks are due to Lindsay Stainton, the curator of the Camellia Collection, Linton Park, Kent, who not only gave us permission to quote from unpublished letters by EBB but also carefully checked the transcripts against the originals. Finally, both of us—Dick in the past and I in the present—are grateful to the editorial and production staff at the University of Missouri Press, and particularly to its director and editor in chief, Beverly Jarrett. Working with her and her team has been a pleasure.

One word more: Dick's "spirit-sense" as a biographer was always shaped and energized by his partner in life and art, Ella Dickinson Kennedy. Had he lived to complete the biography, he would inevitably have acknowledged her, as he did in his other biographies, as his best critic, and so it is only appropriate that Dick's collaborator, grateful both for her help and for her patience while he was writing, dedicate the completed work to her.

Donald S. Hair
London Ontario
October 2006

Abbreviations

AB	Arabella Barrett
ABL	Armstrong Browning Library, Baylor University, Waco, Texas
American Friends	*Browning to His American Friends: Letters between the Brownings, the Storys and James Russell Lowell 1841–1890,* edited by Gertrude Reese Hudson. London: Bowes and Bowes, 1965.
BC	*The Brownings' Correspondence,* edited by Philip Kelley and Ronald Hudson (vols. 1–8) and Philip Kelley and Scott Lewis (vols. 9–14). Winfield, KS: Wedgestone, 1984–.
BL-KT	British Library–Kenyon Typescript: British Library Add. Ms. 42229–42231, the typescript prepared by Frederic G. Kenyon for his edition of EBB's letters
Browning's Trumpeter	*Browning's Trumpeter: The Correspondence of Robert Browning and Frederick J. Furnivall 1872–1889,* edited by William S. Peterson. Washington, D.C.: Decatur House, 1979.
BSN	*Browning Society Notes*
BSP	*Papers of the Browning Society, 1881–1891.* 3 vols. Nendeln, Liechtenstein: Kraus Reprint, 1966.
Collections	Kelley, Philip, and Betty A. Coley. *The Browning Collections: A Reconstruction with Other Memorabilia.*

Winfield, KS: Armstrong Browning Library, Browning Institute, Mansell, Wedgestone, 1984.

Dearest Isa *Dearest Isa: Robert Browning's Letters to Isabella Blagden*, edited by Edward C. McAleer. Austin: University of Texas Press, 1951.

DeVane DeVane, William Clyde. *A Browning Handbook*. 2nd ed. New York: Appleton-Century-Crofts, 1955.

Domett *The Diary of Alfred Domett 1872–1885*, edited by E. A. Horsman. London: Oxford University Press, 1953.

EBB Elizabeth Barrett Browning

EBB *Arabella* *The Letters of Elizabeth Barrett Browning to Her Sister Arabella*, edited by Scott Lewis. 2 vols. Waco, TX: Wedgestone Press, 2002.

EBB *Diary* *Diary by E.B.B. The Unpublished Diary of Elizabeth Barrett Barrett, 1831–1832*, edited by Philip Kelley and Ronald Hudson. Athens: Ohio University Press, 1969.

EBB *Letters* *The Letters of Elizabeth Barrett Browning*, edited by Frederic G. Kenyon. 2 vols. New York: Macmillan, 1898.

EBB *Mitford* *The Letters of Elizabeth Barrett Browning to Mary Russell Mitford 1836–1854*, edited by Meredith B. Raymond and Mary Rose Sullivan. 3 vols. Winfield, KS: Armstrong Browning Library, Browning Institute, Wedgestone Press, Wellesley College, 1983.

EBB *Ogilvy* *Elizabeth Barrett Browning's Letters to Mrs. David Ogilvy 1849–1861*, edited by Peter N. Heydon and Philip Kelley. New York: Quadrangle/New York Times and Browning Institute, 1973.

EBB *Works* *The Complete Works of Elizabeth Barrett Browning*, edited by Charlotte Porter and Helen A. Clarke. 1900. Reprint, New York: AMS, 1973.

FJF Frederick J. Furnivall

GB   George Barrett

George Barrett   *Letters of the Brownings to George Barrett*, edited by
                            Paul Landis. Urbana: University of Illinois Press,
                            1958.

Griffin and Minchin   Griffin, W. Hall, and Harry Christopher Minchin.
                           *The Life of Robert Browning, with Notices of His Writ-
                           ings, His Family, and His Friends*. 1910. Reprint,
                           Hamden, CT: Archon Books, 1966 (reprint of 3rd
                           ed. 1938).

HB   Henrietta Barrett (Mrs. Surtees Cook)

Hood   *Letters of Robert Browning Collected by Thomas J. Wise*,
                           edited by Thurman L. Hood. London: John Mur-
                           ray, 1933.

Huxley   *Elizabeth Barrett Browning: Letters to Her Sister,
                           1846–1859*, edited by Leonard Huxley. London:
                           John Murray, 1931.

IB   Isabella Blagden

KB   Katharine de Kay Bronson

Learned Lady   *Learned Lady: Letters from Robert Browning to Mrs.
                           Thomas FitzGerald 1876–1889*, edited by Edward C.
                           McAleer. Cambridge: Harvard University Press,
                           1966.

Macready   *The Diaries of William Charles Macready 1833–1851*,
                           edited by William Toynbee. 2 vols. London: Chap-
                           man and Hall, 1912.

Mason   Mason, Cyrus. *The Poet Robert Browning and His
                           Kinsfolk by His Cousin Cyrus Mason*, edited by
                           W. Craig Turner. Waco: Baylor University Press,
                           1983.

Maynard   Maynard, John. *Browning's Youth*. Cambridge: Har-
                           vard University Press, 1977.

Miller   Miller, Betty. *Robert Browning, a Portrait*. London:
                           Murray, 1952.

More than Friend	*More than Friend: The Letters of Robert Browning to Katharine de Kay Bronson*, edited by Michael Meredith. Waco, TX: Armstrong Browning Library; Winfield, KS: Wedgestone Press, 1985.
MRM	Mary Russell Mitford
New Letters	*New Letters of Robert Browning*, edited by William Clyde DeVane and Kenneth Leslie Knickerbocker. London: John Murray, 1951.
Orr	Orr, Mrs. Sutherland. *Life and Letters of Robert Browning*. 2nd ed. London: Smith, Elder, 1891.
Pettigrew and Collins	*Robert Browning: The Poems*, edited by John Pettigrew and Thomas J. Collins. 2 vols. Harmondsworth: Penguin, 1981.
RB	Robert Browning
RBAD	*Robert Browning and Alfred Domett*, edited by Frederic G. Kenyon. London: Smith, Elder, 1906.
SB	Sarianna Browning
Sharp	Sharp, William. *Life of Robert Browning*. London: Walter Scott, 1890.
TTUL	*Twenty-Two Unpublished Letters of Elizabeth Barrett Browning and Robert Browning Addressed to Henrietta and Arabella Moulton-Barrett*. 1935. Reprint, New York: Haskell House, 1971.
Wedgwood	*Robert Browning and Julia Wedgwood: A Broken Friendship as Revealed in Their Letters*, edited by Richard Curle. London: John Murray, 1937.
Woolford and Karlin	*The Poems of Browning*, edited by John Woolford and Daniel Karlin. 2 vols. Longman Annotated English Poets. London: Longman, 1991.

*The Dramatic
Imagination of*
Robert Browning

Mesmerism

"And a cat's in the water-butt." —Robert Browning

AYE you're a man that! ye old mesmerizer
Tyin' your meanin' in seventy swadelin's,
One must of needs be a hang'd early riser
To catch you at worm turning. Holy Odd's bodykins!

"Cat's i' the water butt!" Thought's in your verse-barrel,
Tell us this thing rather, then we'll believe you,
You, Master Bob Browning, spite your apparel
Jump to your sense and give praise as we'd lief do.

You wheeze as a head-cold long-tonsilled Calliope,
But God! what a sight you ha' got o' our in'ards,
Mad as a hatter but surely no Myope,
Broad as all ocean and leanin' man-kin'ards.

Heart that was big as the bowels of Vesuvius,
Words that were wing'd as her sparks in eruption,
Eagled and thundered as Jupiter Pluvius,
Sound in your wind past all signs o' corruption.

Here's to you, Old Hippety-Hop o' the accents,
True to the Truth's sake and crafty dissector,
You grabbed at the gold sure; had no need to pack cents
Into your versicles.
     Clear sight's elector!

        —Ezra Pound

Chapter 1

Signposts Unregarded

For more reasons than one, Robert Browning called W. J. Fox, the Unitarian minister of the South Place Chapel, "my literary father."[1] But among them surely was Fox's publication of Browning's first excursions into short monodramatic verse. In the mid-1830s, Fox, as editor of the *Monthly Repository*, was trying to move his periodical away from identification with Unitarianism and make it a more general literary and political magazine.[2] When he asked his young friend Browning to contribute some poems, Robert riffled through his "portfolio" of working papers—poems in progress, literary ideas and plans, experiments with form—and drew out five poems, including lyrics that were later to appear in *Pippa Passes* (1841) and "James Lee's Wife" (1864) but also including two dramatic poems that were the earliest examples of what later became his most characteristic work. Both were short poems, spoken not by the voice of the poet but by that of a character in an earlier historical period or a remote setting; both were ironical; both were in standard rhyme and meter yet in run-on lines, loose rhythm, and in diction that reflected what Wordsworth called "the real language of men."[3] One, in the Gothic vein, was highly melodramatic; the other had theological doctrine for its material. Neither bore Browning's name as author: they were merely signed "Z" (perhaps because Fox signed his literary articles in various periodicals "A").

The first of the pair, "Porphyria," published in the January 1836 issue, is set on a landed estate (England? Italy?). The speaker, a servant in love with Porphyria, the daughter of the proprietor, recounts the events of a rainy, gusty night when Porphyria slipped away from the festivities at the great hall to visit the speaker at his humble cottage. She sits by the fireside embracing him tenderly and declaring her love. But this romantic story, reminiscent of the grand opera stage, takes a sudden turn as the speaker tries to think how he can hold her love forever at this passionate peak—and Browning's simple diction, when the speaker reveals what happened, stands in stark ironic contrast to the horror of the outcome:

> That moment she was mine, mine, fair,
> Perfectly pure and good: I found
> A thing to do, and all her hair
> In one long yellow string I wound
> Three times her little throat around,
> And strangled her. (36–41)

The jolt the reader feels is intensified by the additional irony of the speaker's smug delusion of divinely granted impunity:

> And thus we sit together now,
> And all night long we have not stirred,
> And yet God has not said a word! (58–60)

Its companion poem, "Johannes Agricola" (also January 1836), has a grim satirical edge, this time directed even more sharply against religious self-righteousness. The speaker, Johannes Agricola, as Browning pointed out in a note, was a sixteenth-century German and founder of the Antinomians, a sect who believed that God predestined a select group of human beings to heavenly salvation, no matter what the quality of their lives, and condemned all others to eternal damnation despite their innocence or good deeds. There is no action in the poem. The speaker's mind merely roams idly through a course of thought about sin, grace, good works, and divine judgment. The irony turns on his immense self-satisfaction as he sweetly expresses faith in his effortless salvation and in the damnation of some who have striven to lead sanctified lives.

> For as I lie, smiled on, full fed
> With unexhausted blessedness,—
> I gaze below on Hell's fierce bed,
> And those its waves of flame oppress,
> Swarming in ghastly wretchedness,
> Whose like on earth aspired to be
> One altar-smoke,—so pure!—to win
> If not love like God's love to me,

At least to keep his anger in . . .
And all their striving turned to sin! (41–50; text of 1836)

Browning appears to have chosen the poems especially for Fox's Unitarian readers, who would respond to these particular religious ironies, and especially to "Johannes Agricola," for they felt scorn for Calvinistic doctrines, similar to Johannes's theological beliefs, about the power of faith and the inadequacy of good works and about God's predestination of a heavenly reward for a chosen few. Later, when Browning published these two poems in *Dramatic Lyrics* (1842), he guided the interpretation for a broader group of readers by pairing them under the title "Madhouse Cells."

Although both poems are examples of soliloquy, the simplest form of poetic monodrama, and although they are not powerful performances, they are ventures into a form of verse that Browning continued to explore and to vary until he became the unsurpassed master of it, the model for poets of his own age and the teacher of those of a later and less grateful time.

What is surprising is the fact that he seemed to regard the poems as efforts by the left hand, mere exercises that he had tossed off and then set aside in his portfolio. He was now twenty-three years old, one of the most learned (although irregularly educated) young men in England. He had been consciously pursuing a career as a poet for five years and, as a follower of Shelley, Byron, and Goethe, composing book-length poems of uneven quality, parts of them unrelentingly tedious. Yet he still did not regard this new form of short dramatic poem as worth much consideration.

He was still at work on *Sordello*, his most ambitious and complex work, written, alas, in an elliptical and allusive style that was to baffle its readers for generations to come. Next, he was to become a follower of Shakespeare, seeking the immediate gratification of fame by writing verse plays for the stage, none of which brought him that satisfaction.

The road to fame led in a direction he could not see during these years, but, undeterred, he continued to write, taking encouragement from friends and family members, who had stood behind him loyally ever since he broke off his studies at the London University, as it was then called, during his first year and declared his intention to dedicate his life to becoming a poet. Indeed, his life had tended in this direction from an early age while he grew up in the quiet of London suburbs across the Thames. Even so, he would be over thirty years old before he again published poems of the sort upon which his reputation now stands.

Chapter 2

The Brownings of Southampton Street

R obert Browning derived a double benefit from the place of his birth and upbringing. Camberwell was a middle-class suburb south of London that was still quite rural. In nearby pastures, cattle grazed; in nearby fields, farmers grew vegetables for the London market. The Surrey Canal, through which barges were drawn by drowsy horses on the tow path, cut through the village: a windmill stood near it in Blackhorse Field. In neighboring Dulwich, he could see creatures of the woods and hear the soothing murmur of brooks.[1] Yet he was within an hour's walk of London with all of its cultural richness and burgeoning urban complexity. Fellow villagers commuted to the city easily, for three coaches ran daily between Camberwell and Fleet Street.[2] Thus Browning's Wordsworthian response to the green world was as natural to him as his mingling in social and literary circles when he was a young man.

He was born on May 7, 1812, to parents of modest means in Rainbow Cottage on Southampton Street, a winding tree-shaded lane (formerly Rainbow Lane) near Cottage Green, the village center, and baptized on June 14, 1812, at the York Street (Independent) Chapel in nearby Walworth.[3] Indeed, the suburban areas south of London—Walworth, Camberwell, Peckham, Herne Hill, Denmark Hill, and Clapham—were well populated with Nonconformists and members of the Church of England who leaned toward the church party known as Evangelical. There were thirteen Nonconformist chapels in the area surrounding Camberwell, in addition to five churches and four Episcopal chapels. These religious centers provided the prevailing social and religious atmosphere of Robert Browning's early years.

Yet all was not hymns and sermons in Camberwell. Every August, a fair was held on the village green for three weeks that was known for feasting and drinking, mirth and lively entertainment. Here young Robert could see puppet shows, performing dogs, acrobats, dancing bears, and theatrical performances by itinerant players presenting everything from scratched-together Shakespeare to current melodrama with interludes of music and dance. In 1827 the vestry of St. Giles Church tried to have the fairs at Camberwell and adjacent Peckham suppressed—but without success. There was also the village conviviality at the local taverns, the Hen and Chickens and, especially, the Rosemary Branch in Peckham, the latter renowned for its extensive sporting grounds for cricket, pigeon-shooting, and horse-racing. Here the landlord rang a bell and made an announcement in the neighborhood whenever he tapped a new barrel of beer. This was, he proclaimed, "an establishment which has no suburban rival."[4]

Browning's mother, Sarah Anna Wiedemann, born June 13, 1772, a Scottish woman of Germanic descent, was the daughter of a sugar processor and small shipowner in Dundee.[5] In her quiet way, she was the dominant spirit of the Browning household. No one ever described her as a beauty. She had "the *squarest* head & forehead I almost ever saw in a human being," recalled Alfred Domett, one of Robert's lifelong friends, "putting me in mind . . . of a tea-chest or tea-caddy."[6] But everyone attested to her gentle, loving nature. At some point in the late 1700s, she and her sister Christina, probably with their widowed father, moved from Scotland to the area south of London. She joined the Lock's Fields Meeting House—later called the York Street Chapel—in Walworth, attracted no doubt by its "Rule," which was Congregationalist and followed the (Calvinistic) Westminster Confession of Faith.[7] She was listed as number seventy-eight on the chapel register when its new minister, the Reverend George Clayton, arrived in 1804, and was identified as living in Peckham.

She did not marry until she was thirty-eight, when she met Mr. Robert Browning, a quiet, self-effacing man of scholarly inclinations who had quarreled with his father about his future course of life and was now a clerk at the Bank of England. It did not augur well for their courtship when Mr. Browning's choleric father sought out Miss Wiedemann's uncle, with whom she was then living, to tell him that she "would be thrown away on a man so evidently born to be hanged."[8] But the couple persevered and were married at Robert Browning's parish church of St. Giles in Camberwell on February 9, 1811. Even though Mrs. Browning's ties to the York Street Chapel were to dominate the religious life of the family, a church wedding was necessary, for only marriages solemnized by the Church of England were legal. Some years later she persuaded her amiable husband to become a member of her Independent Chapel.

Few facts are known about her life. She was an active contributor to the missionary fund of the chapel, and she taught Sunday school there. A few of her books survive; they underscore her religious outlook as well as her gentleness of temper. Besides her biblical concordance, which she later gave to Robert, there are two religious books that she had owned before her marriage, both of which counseled the practice of good human relations: one was Elisha Coles's *A Practical Discourse of Effectual Calling and of Perseverance* (1677), a work of guidance in approaching Calvinistic theology; the other was a book of short homilies entitled *Spiritual Gleanings* (1808), which recommended daily Bible reading and the reading of good books, especially the poems of Milton and Cowper, as well as cultivating habits of doing good to others and exercising restraint on hasty words that might trouble one's neighbor.[9] Her literary tastes were compatible with her religious tendencies. She had a copy of William Cowper's *The Task*, that mild didactic favorite of nineteenth-century Evangelical readers, and a seventeenth-century edition of George Herbert's *The Temple*, perhaps a gift from her husband, for it had long been a provider of spiritual comfort to members of the Church of England.[10] She loved birds and animals and was said to have a special talent for attracting them.[11] She was an industrious gardener whose plants produced an abundance of fruits and flowers. She took delight in music and enjoyed playing the piano, especially at twilight. One afternoon while at the keyboard she heard a sound behind her and turned to see the child Robert listening, enrapt. He rushed into her arms, sobbing and whispering over and over, "Play! play!"[12] She suffered greatly from neuralgia in her later years and was further weakened by anaemia. Nevertheless, she brought a cheerful spirit to her domestic tasks and provided a warm atmosphere for the Browning home.

Two years after her son, Robert, was born, Sarah Anna bore a daughter whose name became a compressed version of her own, Sarianna. For years, the girl was the constant companion and confidant of her brother and grew up to be a lively, witty young woman. "She is marvelously clever," another of Robert's friends, Joseph Arnould, remarked, "such fine clear animal spirits—talks much and well, and yet withal so simply and deeply good-hearted that it is a real pleasure to be with her."[13] Yet she never sought a husband; she remained at home taking care of her mother until Sarah Anna's death in 1849. At that time Elizabeth Barrett Browning, writing to her sister Henrietta, described Sarianna as "a most devoted daughter, giving up all Society (for which her accomplishments peculiarly fit her) and refusing to marry—all, that her invalid mother might not miss a comfort she could offer. Her mother was the beginning and ending of life."[14] But Sarianna was equally devoted to her father, whom she looked after until his death in 1866. Thereafter she lived and traveled with her brother Robert for the remainder of his life.

The poet's father, Robert Browning, born July 6, 1782, was ten years younger than his wife. Of Dorsetshire background, he was the son of Robert Browning (who called himself "Rob"[15]), a clerk who rose to higher position in the Bank of England, and of Margaret Tittle, from St. Kitts in the West Indies, whose descent harbors some elements of mystery. Hints of a strain of Negro ancestry in her background were first offered by F. J. Furnivall, who recorded a secondhand report from a friend at the bank that it was understood that Miss Tittle had "a strain of Negro blood, a dash of the tar brush."[16] It would be interesting to consider that some exotic invigoration of the gene pool contributed to the emergence of poetic genius in the Browning family, but the evidence is insufficient. Furnivall based his conclusion about the Brownings' racial mixture on hearsay and confusion, and he maintained his view through stubborn-mindedness. He had begun his inquiries outside the family, talking first to two people at the Bank of England; one of them, H. G. Bowen, an accountant, who had never met any of the Browning family, first made the suggestion of mixed race. Bowen's view was substantiated only by a family anecdote and a brief description from a cousin, R. Shergold Browning, who had seen the poet only once in his life. As for Margaret Tittle, Jeannette Marks, in her 1938 book *The Family of the Barrett*, speculates on the reasons for Margaret's presumed father, John Tittle, being cut out of his stepmother's will: he may have been of mixed race. Or he may simply have been illegitimate.[17] Yet as seen in letters and other documents, John Tittle does not seem to have led the life of a Jamaican person of color in the eighteenth century.[18] Such speculations aside, Margaret died April 17, 1789, after bearing one son, the father of the poet, and one daughter. Her husband, Rob Browning, remarried and fathered nine more children.

When Margaret's son, Robert Browning, was twenty years old, he was sent to St. Kitts to claim his share of his deceased mother's plantation holdings and to make his fortune. He was, however, so horrified by the barbarities of the slavery system that (as his son later told Elizabeth Barrett) the young legatee "relinquished every prospect—supported himself while there, in some other capacity, and came back, while yet a boy, to his father's profound astonishment and rage."[19] Because of the young man's principled stand, he and his father became estranged, although they continued to live near each other in Camberwell.[20] In later years he would never talk about his period in St. Kitts: "—if you question him about it," Robert told Elizabeth, "he shuts his eyes involuntarily and shows exactly the same marks of loathing that may be noticed while a piece of cruelty is mentioned—and the *word* 'blood,' even, makes him change colour." Partly as a consequence of this experience, he took care to exhibit kindness toward his fellow beings and tolerance toward their ways. He was extremely chivalrous to all women: "There is no service which the ugliest, oldest, crossest woman in the world might not exact of him."[21]

As these reports indicate, he was in personality an extraordinarily genial man. Cousin Mason remembers that "his countenance carried continually a sort of sedate cheerfulness as if enjoying a little chat with himself."[22] This air of preoccupation lent a dreamy quality to his manner so that he was thought by many friends and family members to have a childlike naïveté or a tinge of eccentricity.[23]

Mr. Browning had considerable artistic skill. He could dash off a caricature anywhere with a few quick strokes. He would use the mantelpiece or the back of a chair or a book he was reading for these rapid sketches, all the while "sedately smiling." If he pleased, he would color them afterward and add below a comic statement from the figure he was characterizing, as if it were a visual parody of a Theophrastian "character." He kept hundreds of them in portfolios. Many visitors, especially children, delighted in his work, but Sarah Anna and Sarianna disapproved of his burlesque style, which they considered "ungenteel."[24]

In his youth he had hoped to follow a career in art or perhaps in literature, but the quarrel with his father killed all hopes for a university education or further training in art and made it necessary for him to earn a living without parental support or encouragement, although he did have a small family inheritance from his mother's side of the family.[25] He managed to secure, by his own efforts, a clerkship in the Bank of England, work that he "detested" in spite of his diligence and his record of punctuality. He held this post for almost fifty years.

His happiness in life came from a blissful marriage and immense satisfaction in a quiet family life and his individual pursuit of learning. He had income sufficient to indulge his passion for old and rare books, which he hunted down zealously. His half-brother Reuben remarked that "old books were his delight, and by his continued search after them he not only knew all the old bookstalls in London, but their contents."[26] Over the years he managed to acquire a library of about six thousand books.

In this way, Mr. Browning provided the intellectual and educational environment in the Camberwell home for the childhood and youth of his son and daughter. In the years before going to St. Kitts, he had obtained a solid classical education at the Reverend Mr. Bell's School in Cheshunt, with some instruction in French as well.[27] His schoolmate John Kenyon remembers that he organized play-battles between the Trojans and the Achaeans with wooden swords and schoolroom slates used as shields.[28] His knack for languages was such that he knew by heart the first book of Homer's *Iliad* and all the odes of Horace.[29] Nor did his learning stop with the classics. He acquired Hebrew in later years through his own study, and as years passed, he developed an extensive knowledge of English, French, Italian, and Spanish literatures, plus an extraordinary amount of curious intellectual and cultural knowledge so that he came to be regarded as a walking encyclopedia.

This facility with language and interest in history seemed to run in the family. A few of old Rob Browning's books that remain point in this direction.[30] His two other sons, Mr. Browning's half-brothers, both of whom held banking positions, were also very literary in their tastes and tendencies. Reuben Browning was the author of several books on finance and maintained scholarly and cultural interests. William Shergold Browning was the author of a *History of the Huguenots* and two historical novels as well as being a contributor of articles to the *Gentleman's Magazine*.[31]

Mr. Browning's continuing interest in art led him to build "a choice collection" of drawings and engravings, especially of his favorite, William Hogarth, and of the Dutch and Flemish masters. His son, Robert, told Elizabeth that his father's taste in art was different from his own, that he liked the earthy scenes of such artists as Adriaen Brouwer, Adriaen van Ostade, and David Teniers: "he would turn from the Sistine Altar piece to these."[32]

In middle age, Mr. Browning is remembered as a "fresh-coloured," blue-eyed man, somewhat "undersized" and "rather reserved," very proud of his son as the author of some perplexing long poems, whom he now regarded as "beyond him." He was a man content in presiding over a serene household. In Alfred Domett's words, "Altogether, father, mother, only son and only daughter formed a most suited, harmonious and intellectual family."[33] This spirit of harmony and reasonableness resulted, to some extent, from the combination of Mrs. Browning's liberal bending away from the strictness of attitude that was held by most Nonconformist chapelgoers and Mr. Browning's temperament of tolerance. Unlike others in the York Street Chapel congregation, this was not a family that frowned on the pleasures of dancing, smoking, wine-drinking, and theater-going. Indeed, when Robert was a young man, he was given dancing lessons and encouraged to attend the opera and the theater as part of his cultural development. Among his friends, he enjoyed a bottle of wine and a good cigar, although he gave up smoking when he married Elizabeth Barrett.

A word must be added here about Mr. Browning's library of six thousand books, which, because of its looming presence in the Browning home, seemed like another member of the family. Most of the books have disappeared during the last century and a half, but a record of about six hundred of them is preserved in *The Browning Collections: A Reconstruction* (1984), edited by Philip Kelley and Betty Coley. A few additional volumes were seen by W. Hall Griffin in the early 1900s when a remnant was still in the possession of Pen Browning, Robert's son. But judging from what remains as a representative sample, one can say that Mr. Browning's library was a miscellaneous collection, comprising books of varying quality that displayed broad interests.

Some were valuable items, such as a copy of Thomas More's *Utopia* (1548), or many seventeenth-century editions, such as a "Breeches" Bible (1615), a Ben Jonson First Folio (1616), the *Eikon Basilike* attributed to Charles I (1649), Henry More's *Philosophicall Poems* (1647), Robert Howard's *Life and Reign of King Richard the Second* (1681), Sir Thomas Browne's *Works* (1686), and a first edition of both Milton's *Poems on Several Occasions* (1673) and his *Paradise Regain'd* (1680).[34] But some of his books were chance purchases of little value, for Mr. Browning was always indiscriminately ready to acquire any bound printed pages. He often would pick up bargains in odd volumes of broken sets such as volume 2 of a *Bibliotheca Classica* (no date), or volume 1 of D. E. Williams's *Life of Sir Thomas Lawrence* (1831). Or he would stumble on important works in poor condition, with missing title pages and front matter. The first edition of Defoe's *Robinson Crusoe* (1719) that he found for his son lacked the concluding pages.[35]

The diversity of Mr. Browning's choices shows curiosity that led down many byways. He had several books on the eighteenth-century political polemicist "Junius" or on attempts to establish his identity. He had many items on the English Civil War and the trial and execution of Charles I. Several books in the library reflect his fascination with questions of historical chronology. His copy of J. Lempriere's *Classical Dictionary* (1804) begins with a chronological table that sets down dates for such events as the Creation, the Deluge, the building of the Tower of Babel, the expedition of the Argonauts, the fall of Troy and so on, up to the fall of Constantinople in 1453. His copy of the Reverend Arthur Bedford's *Animadversions upon Sir Isaac Newton's Book Intitled the Chronology of Ancient Kingdoms Amended* (1728) attempts to "demonstrate the chronology of the world history by reference to the Scripture." Alphonse des-Vignoles's *Chronologie de L'Histoire Sainte et des Histoires Estrangeres* (1737) devotes about 800 pages of a quarto volume to a chronology that runs from the biblical Patriarchs and the Exodus from Egypt through the reigns of the kings of Israel and Judah and the kings of

Tyre, Syria, Egypt, and Babylon on up through the Greeks and Romans, drawing upon the Bible, Herodotus, Ctesias, Josephus, and others.[36]

He was also drawn to quirky writers like John Hardouin, a French Jesuit whose folio volume of 970 pages, *Opera Selecta* (1709), in double columns of Latin, argued that the principal writings of the classical authors were really modern forgeries; for example, that the *Aeneid* and the *Odes* of Horace were written by thirteenth-century monks and that the New Testament was originally written in Latin. He owned Sir Kenelm Digby's copy of the works in Latin of the sixteenth-century occult philosopher Henry Cornelius Agrippa von Nettesheim which had been read until it was falling apart. He also managed to secure a copy of Agrippa's *De Scientiis* (1622), essays on diverse subjects from grammar to alchemy. He also spent much time over his two-volume enlarged edition of *Winged Words* (1829) by the eighteenth-century philologist and wit John Horne Tooke, a strange discourse on language, grammar, and the expression of abstractions.[37]

His accumulation of eccentric books matched his taste for historical works that were encyclopedic assemblies of fact, such as John Stow's *Chronicle of England* (1604); P. Heylyn's *A Help to English History* (1680), a big volume choked with details about the English kings, the princes of Wales, the lords of Man and the Isle of Wight, the bishops and their cathedrals, the aristocracy—from dukes down to baronets—with their coats of arms and descriptions of their seats; and Bevill Higgons's *A Short View of the English History* (1788), that follows the English kings, reign by reign, from William I to James II, giving "their Characters and Manners . . . and all other Remarkable Incidents" up to the revolution of 1688. To his son, Robert, he presented Sir Walter Raleigh's *History of the World* (1614), which begins in the Garden of Eden, and Nathaniel Wanley's *Wonders of the Little World* (1678)[38], a fantastic miscellany of extraordinary occurrences, persons, and customs drawn from classical and medieval history, literature, and folklore that was inspired by a suggestion in Bacon's *The Advancement of Learning* of a need for a collection of "The Ultimaties . . . or Summits . . . of Human Nature."[39] Wanley's unique work became an important source for Robert Browning's poems, as will be indicated in future chapters.

Many of the books on religious matters in this eclectic library take an historical approach. Mr. Browning was an avid reader of works that compared the doctrines and beliefs of the Church of England and the Church of Rome and provided historical background for the sixteenth-century development of Protestantism in England. Nathaniel Spinckes's *The Case Stated between the Church of Rome and the Church of England* (1713) was in dialogue form and "shewed that the Doubt and Danger is in the Former and Safety is in the

Latter Communion." In his notes written in Edward Stone's *Remarks upon the History of the Life of Reginald Pole* (1766), Mr. Browning makes clear his extensive knowledge of Reformation controversy; and other notes in Horace Walpole's *Historic Doubts on the Life and Reign of Richard III* (1822) reflect his ready familiarity with John Foxe's *Actes and Monuments* (1563; "The Book of Martyrs") and its Protestant outlook. Other books in the library show his historical knowledge of the corruptions of the papacy in Renaissance times: Étienne Michel Masse's *Histoire du Pape Alexandre VI, et de César Borgia* (1830), and Gregorio Leti's *History of the Pope's Nephews from the Time of Sixtus the IV to the Death of the last Pope Alexandre VI* (1669). Still other books deal with doctrinal questions, such as Thomas Burnet's *Treatise Concerning the State of Departed Souls before, and at, and after the Resurrection* (1739), and John Hurrion's *The Proper Divinity, Real Personality, and External and Extraordinary Works of the Holy Spirit* (1823).[40] All these are in addition to the many Bibles and commentaries on Scripture.

Works of literature constituted a large proportion of the library. Besides standard works by the Greek and Roman poets, historians and dramatists, both in the original and in translation, the literature of England is represented in quantity. Samuel Bagster's sixty-two volume set of the English poets (1807),[41] as well as shelves of titles by individual authors from the medieval period up to a first edition of Wordsworth's *The Waggoner* (1819),[42] lined the walls of the Browning household on Southampton Street.

This extensive gathering of solid learning and curious lore provided the intellectual milieu for the young Browning during his growing-up years in London's green suburb of Camberwell. It was accessible for hours of concentrated reading and, more important, for browsing and laying up a store of scattered facts, stories, anecdotes, myths, quotations, and bits of worldly wisdom that the future poet could draw upon for narratives, images, and allusions in his work. Above all, it was there like an always-available teacher of immense diversity and breadth, abetted by a parent who could point to a source, back up a statement, find an answer to a question, and offer a guide to further study.

Chapter 3

The Education of a Would-Be Poet

Robert Browning was a hyperactive, fiery-tempered child, closely watched over by his mother. Mrs. Orr relates an anecdote about his jealous resentment of an elderly lady who was visiting his mother. Young Robert, playing the role of what he conceived to be a devil, attached a tail to his body and streaked naked through the room in order to frighten her.[1] He followed his mother in his fondness for animals. He was even attracted to such creatures of the garden as frogs, newts, and snakes. He had a pet toad who would emerge from a tree root and allow Robert to scratch his head. He once rescued an injured cat and persuaded his mother to sew up its wound, then nursed it back to health. In stories that were read to him, he did not like those that included the death of animals.[2]

Guided by his mother, he was "passionately religious" in childhood.[3] The family regularly attended the York Street Chapel, a large brick structure with a mansard roof and arched windows, its portico with pillars in front making it look more like a theater than a church. Inside, its most desirable pews stood in rows between walls of puritanical plainness, above which was a large gallery that held the less expensive pews extending in a horseshoe curve, its arms reaching far up toward the front of the chapel. The Browning pew was the foremost on the left side of the gallery on a level with and close to the Reverend George Clayton as he preached in his pulpit. Young Robert Browning was in full view of the other chapelgoers: "It was the most wonderful face in the whole congregation—pale, somewhat mysterious—and shaded with black flowing hair, but a face whose expression you remember through a lifetime," one of the members recalled.[4] For many years a plaque on the wall marked the place: "Baptized in this building, June 4, 1812 / Robert Browning / worshipped in his boyhood and youth below this spot."[5] York Street Chapel drew a fashionable South London congregation. Clayton himself robed at home, drove to the chapel in his gown and was ushered to the pulpit "by a footman in white gloves."[6]

As a child Robert was amazingly precocious in his command of language. He not only learned to read early, but as far back as he could remember, he composed rhymes. He wrote "verses at six,"[7] he told Elizabeth, possibly the imitation of Macpherson's *Ossian* that he later described to her as "the first *composition* I ever was guilty of" and that he "laid up for posterity under the cushion of a great arm-chair."[8] Encouraged by this facility with sound and rhythm, his father taught him Latin declensions by means of rhyme. For a short period he attended a dame school kept by a Mrs. Reader and her daughter Anne. Browning's experience there yielded a story on which he dined out years later. "One regular ceremony at the school was the weekly combing out and oiling of the hair of the pupils," Browning told the Reverend Boyd Carpenter in the early 1880s. "Mrs. Reader was fond of hymns, and was wont to sing them as opportunity offered. The weekly hairdressing was such an opportunity, and so it went on to the accompaniment of the hymn 'Sweet is the Work, my God and King.' This was sung to the tune known as Portugal New." "In telling this," Carpenter recorded,

> Browning vividly illustrated the whole procedure. The head to be treated was held in Mrs. Reader's hands as the hymn began—"Sweet is the Work." The comb was applied to the hair and tugged through the tangled locks as the hymn went on—"But fools can never rise so high. Like brutes" (tug at the hair) "they live—like brutes" (further tug at the hair) "they die." Then came the preparation for the final anointing of the head, while the singer continued—
>
> > "But I shall share a glorious part,
> > When grace hath well refined my heart."
>
> By this time the dame's hands were ready with the oil, and as she smeared it over the head she continued triumphantly—
>
> > "While countless blessings on me shed
> > Like holy oil upon my head."
>
> While telling us this tale Browning was full of mirth. The memory of his infant experiences was given with such a keen sense of the comedy of it all.[9]

What he thought about it at the time we do not know: he was sent to the dame school for exercise in reading and writing, but he was soon sent home because his skills were far beyond those of other pupils.[10] Thus, his earliest education took place under the guidance of his parents.

Much of it had a religious tinge. He passed from Bible stories learned from his mother to John Fellows's *History of the Holy Bible* in two volumes (1811) given to him by his father when he was seven years old.[11] He also became familiar with what Isaac Watts had done to render the Psalms into "common metre" in the well-thumbed family copy of *Psalms and Hymns* (1812),[12] although it was a less dignified form of English than the King James version that he had already heard. One of the special favorites of these early years was Francis Quarles's *Emblems*, which he was able to read in the first edition of 1634, illustrated by charming woodcuts.[13] The somewhat naive quality of Quarles's verse, addressed to the common reader, was ideal for the seven-year-old boy, and so well did he remember these verses that he was able to cite a peculiarity of Quarles's rhyming—"the most emphatic close of any verse I ever read"—in the last years of his life.[14] Another favorite was a big volume, full of engravings, by Gerard de Lairesse, *The Art of Painting* (1778), of which he recalled in later life, "I read this book more often and with greater delight, when I was a child, than any other: and still remember the main of it most gratefully for the good I seem to have got by the prints, and wondrous text."[15] Lairesse became the subject of one of the most nostalgic of Browning's *Parleyings with Certain People of Importance in Their Day* in 1887.

Also available were some volumes of Bohn's *Classical Library* to introduce the boy, in translations, to some of the Greek and Roman writers very early, before he became, at the age of eight or nine, a weekly boarder at the Reverend Thomas Ready's School in nearby Peckham. Here he received the standard instruction in Latin and, a bit later, in Greek. He possibly was also introduced to mathematics and French. He was soon so far ahead of his schoolmates that some of them resented his accomplishments and teased him because of his superiority. Alfred Domett's two brothers remember him at school, where they would set him against some of the older boys in a "'chaffing' match" to see the "little bright-eyed fellow's skill at repartee."[16]

Robert wrote playlets at school and organized his fellows in school productions. He also revived the play *The Royal Convert* (1707) by the former poet laureate Nicholas Rowe and acted the part of "Aribert" himself. He may also have considered staging Nathaniel Lee's tragedy *Caesar Borgia* ("the first play I ever read").[17] In the ceremonies at the end of the term one year, he delivered a rhymed address to the assembled parents.[18] He remained at

Mr. Ready's school until he was fourteen, but since he regarded the Latin and Greek drills as tedious, he was withdrawn in order to continue further studies at home. In later years, he said that "they taught him nothing there" and that he was bullied by the older boys. When he and Domett were passing by the site of the school one day, Browning improvised an epigram:

> Within these walls and near that house of glass,
> Did I, three (?) years of hapless childhood pass—
> Damned undiluted misery it was![19]

In spite of this condemnation, his sister, Sarianna, testified that it was a well-regarded school for the quality of its instruction and that the pupils were always kindly treated.[20]

Now at home, Robert had the Latin poets readily available, and whatever Greek he learned at Mr. Ready's was supplemented by what his father taught him. According to Browning's reminiscent poem "Development," his father had introduced him to Homer's *Iliad* through Pope's translation and later led him to the original Greek through Heyne's edition (1802).[21] Mr. Browning's enthusiasm for Homer was a helpful stimulant that drove Robert through the whole of Homer's work, including even work attributed to him like *The Battle of the Frogs and Mice*, which the family library had in a 1622 edition of Homer's complete works with a Latin translation on the pages facing the Greek.[22]

Over the next few years, Mr. Browning devoted all his leisure time to his son's education.[23] Although the emphasis was on Latin and Greek, Robert still had time for reading on his own in the family library. We do not know exactly where his desire led him, but we can glean some knowledge about it, depending upon books that bear his own name or upon hints that emerge from anecdotes or later references in letters. It was probably at this time that he read that favorite book of the Nonconformists, John Bunyan's *Pilgrim's Progress*.[24] He probably also explored his father's books on the English Civil War and received then his copy ("from my father") of Milton's *Ikonoklastes, in Answer to a Book Intitul'd Eikon Basilike* (1690).[25] It was a time too when he could browse through the miscellaneous contents of such works as Otto Melander's *Jocoseria* (1597? "a gift from my father when I was young")[26] with its assemblage in Latin of anecdotes, poems, and folktales, including a version of the Pied Piper of Hamelin story; or *The Polyanthea* in two volumes (1804), a mishmash containing jokes, a collection of amusing epitaphs, anecdotes of Dr. Sheridan, examples of sectarian zeal in the House of Commons during the Puritan ascendancy, a report on Icelandic witches, a description of the Bristol Slave Market, biographies of such diverse figures as the mar-tyred Thomas More, the raucous John Wilmot, Earl of Rochester, the actress Mrs. Pilkington, and the Methodist preacher Mr. Whitfield, an account of famous regicides, and a collection of famous letters, including one from the Earl of Strafford to King Charles I from the Tower of London; and the heavy oversize volumes (1701) of Jeremy Collier's *The Great Histori-cal, Geographical Genealogical and Poetical Dictionary, Being a Curious Miscellany of Sacred and Profane History containing, in Short, The Lives and Most Remarkable Actions of the Patriarchs, Judges, and Kings of the Jews; of Popes, Cardinals, Bishops, etc. Of the Heresiarchs and Schismatics, with an Account of Their Principal Doc-trines; of Emperors, Kings, Illustrious Princes, and Great Generals; Of Ancient and Modern Authors; of Philosophers, Inventors of Arts, and all those who have com-mended themselves to the World, by their Valour, Virtue, Learning, or Some Notable Circumstance of their Lives. Together with the Establishment and Progress both of Religious and Military Orders, and the Lives of their Founders. As also, The Fabulous History of the Heathen Gods and Heroes* (1701).[27] So frequently did the Brown-ing father and son consult this book that Mr. Browning found another copy of volume 1 for Robert in 1837, which he read to pieces as the years passed. It also contained a version of the Pied Piper story, under the entry "Hamlen."

But best of all was Nathaniel Wanley's *Wonders of the Little World, or A General and Complete History of Man* (1678; "Robert Browning, the gift of his father Novr. 1825")[28] which contained a dazzling mixture of the most het-erogeneous material to stimulate young Robert's imagination: instances of strange phenomena about the human body (e.g., "Chapter III Of such women whose children have been petrified and turned to Stone in their Wombs"), others about human emotions; stories illustrating the Virtues, others of Wickedness (of Atheists, Bad Parents, Bad Children, Bad Wives, Bad Husbands, Unnatural Brothers and Sisters, Barbarous Cruelty of Some Men, Bitter Revenges, of Great Eaters and Drinkers, "Voluptuous and Effeminate Persons"); Thumbnail sketches of Roman Emperors, Popes,[29] Poets, Painters, Magicians, Witches, Fathers of the Church; a medley of accounts of Dreams, Predictions, Presages, Sudden Changes of Fortunes, Long Sleeps, Trances, Finders of Hidden Treasure, Great Mistakes of Men; tales about the Apparitions of Demons and Spectres—one of which led to his poem "The Cardinal and the Dog." And, again, the book had a version of the Pied Piper of Hamelin.

Works of this sort not only built up the clutter of odd bits of information that found their way into the narratives and the imagery of Browning's poetry over the next sixty years, but they also developed his taste for the grotesque and the sensational that would mark his work from first to last.

Moreover, they contributed disparate elements to the figures of speech that he often produced, a feature that he shares with the Metaphysical poets of the seventeenth century, especially John Donne.

During this period, contemporary poetry fell into Robert's hands too. As early as his twelfth year, Byron had become a favorite and inspired him to put together a volume of verses that he entitled, with self-depreciation, *Incondita* (disordered or unformed works).

His early biographer, Mrs. Sutherland Orr, records that Robert hoped to see the collection in print but that no publisher would take it. Mrs. Browning, however, showed her son's manuscript to a friend, Eliza Flower, daughter of the radical journalist Benjamin Flower, editor of the *Cambridge Intelligencer*.[30] Miss Flower admired the poems so much that she copied them out and showed them to her father's friend W. J. Fox, a Unitarian minister who had many connections with publishers. Fox praised the work and "ventured to prophesy a splendid future,"[31] but he convinced Robert that it was not worthy of publication.[32]

The last sight of this boyhood collection of poems was given, by chance, to F. J. Furnivall, the president of the Browning Society, and T. J. Wise, the book collector, one afternoon in 1884 when they witnessed, with feelings of distress, the aged Browning feeding letters and personal papers to the fire—among them was the copy of *Incondita* that Eliza Flower had taken pains to preserve.[33] Fox had kept the verses for years, and after his death, his daughter returned them to Browning, only to have them fall victim to his archival destruction.

This acquaintance with Eliza and with her younger sister, Sarah, two charming, free-spirited young women who became wards of Fox after their father's death and lived with him in Finsbury, was a refreshing experience for young Robert, and he developed a boyhood crush on Eliza, who was nine years older than he. Her "fragile sylph-like"[34] figure and her gentle, breathy conversation were like nothing that he had ever encountered in Camberwell. Sarah, the more emotional of the pair, was almost as attractive. Both were accomplished musicians who played and sang together at Fox's South Place (Unitarian) Chapel. Eliza was a gifted composer, whom Browning later hoped might provide musical settings for the songs in *Pippa Passes*. Sarah was a poet and would-be actress. One hymn that she wrote, "Nearer My God to Thee," is known today throughout the Christian world.[35]

Browning continued to visit the Flower sisters and send verses to them for their encouraging comment. Two of these poems survive, the earliest specimens of Browning's juvenilia.[36] They were enclosed in a letter that Sarah Flower sent to Fox with some playful yet admiring words about "that Genius's poetry"—"shall I tell you whose *mine* these gems come from?—and yet I wish they were *mine* with all my soul—and I'm sure it would be worth all *my* soul if they were. . . . They are 'the boy' Browning's *Aet. 14*."[37]

A reader is struck immediately by the fact that neither poem is a lyric but is a dramatic rendering spoken by a narrator or by characters. "The First-Born of Egypt" is an eyewitness account, in blank verse, of the tenth plague that fell on Pharaoh's Egypt when Moses was struggling to free the Israelites; the language throughout is clear and concrete. The second poem, "The Dance of Death," sets forth, in tetrameter couplets, a series of allegorical speakers: Fever, Pestilence, Ague, Madness, and Consumption, each in rivalry boasting of its power with grim sadistic pride as they claim their victims. The diction and syntax in the poem are again clear and uncomplicated, but the tone is more hectic than in "The First-Born of Egypt" and the phrasing lapses into occasional clichés. Although commentators have seen some likeness to Coleridge's "Fire, Famine, and Slaughter,"[38] the likeness is in the dark allegorical mode, not in the style or form, of Coleridge's dramatic dialogue. Although these poems are admirable examples of what Browning was capable of at this age, it is more important to recognize that, even in his early teens, he had the imaginative tendency to dramatize, to create characters who presented the scene, action, or feeling in the poem.

ℛ ℛ ℛ

About this time, an event occurred that brought about a complete change in Browning's poetic style. His cousin James Silverthorne presented him with a volume of *Miscellaneous Poems* by Shelley, a pirated edition that contained almost all the shorter poems.[39] Although Shelley is one of the greatest lyric poets in English literature, this introduction was a dubious blessing for young Robert. Shelley's poetic vigor was a clear inspiration for Browning to move beyond Byron in intensity of expression; yet the excesses of Shelley's unbounded idealism and his readiness to "fall upon the thorns of life and bleed" were a damaging influence for Browning's first long poems, *Pauline*, *Paracelsus*, and *Sordello*.

His enthusiasm for Shelley's poetry led him to beg his mother for more work by this new favorite as a birthday gift. She obligingly sought out booksellers for other volumes—not an easy task, since Shelley's poetry still had a limited readership. Eventually, however, she brought home for her son what she could find: first editions of *Prometheus Unbound*, *Rosalind and Helen*, *Epipsychidion*, *Adonais* (the scarce Pisa edition), *The Revolt of Islam*, and the second edition of *The Cenci*. Upon the recommendation of a bookseller, she also bought three volumes of Keats's poems, including *Endymion* and one of the great books of nineteenth-century publication, *Lamia, Isabella, The Eve of St. Agnes and Other Poems.* The work of these two poets "came to him as the two nightingales which, he told some friends, sang together in the May night which closed this eventful day: one in the laburnum [tree] in his father's garden, the other in a copper beech which stood on adjoining ground … The two new human voices sounded from what were to him … unknown heights and depths of the imaginative world."[40] Browning, age fifteen, now began to immerse himself in the glories of his Romantic predecessors.

One result of this new enthusiasm must have been very distressing for Sarah Anna Browning. Robert's reading of Shelley's *Queen Mab,* which he had also acquired,[41] led him to espouse atheism and vegetarianism. The atheism was of a qualified sort, a romantic rejection of belief in the God of the Bible. Shelley's long note on the phrase "There is no God" explains at the beginning, "This negation must be understood solely to affect a creative Deity. The hypothesis of a pervading Spirit co-eternal with the universe remains unshaken."[42]

He gave vegetarianism up after two years when he found that it affected his health, but the skeptical beliefs had a greater impact. Although he later stated that his period of disbelief "was an access of boyish folly,"[43] he never returned to the kind of theology that was preached in the York Street Chapel but rather developed his own form of Christian optimism as years went by. One immediate consequence, however, was his shaking the belief of Sarah Flower in the authority of the Bible. In a letter to W. J. Fox, November 23, 1827, she described her crisis of faith (she was at the time twenty-two years old; Robert was fifteen):

> My mind has been wandering for a long time, and now it seems to have lost sight of that only invulnerable hold against the assaults of this war-ring world, a firm belief in the genuineness of the Scriptures … I do believe in the existence of an All-wise and Omnipotent Being—and that, involving as it does the conviction that everything is working together for good, brings with it comfort I would not resign for worlds. Still I would fain go to my Bible as I used to—but I cannot. The cloud has come over me gradually, and I did not discover the darkness in which my soul was shrouded until in seeking to give light to others, my own gloomy state became too settled to admit of doubt. It was in answering Robert Browning that my mind refused to bring forth argument, turned recreant, and sided with the enemy.[44]

Robert's shift in religious belief came at a period of tension in the Browning household brought about by his general adolescent rebelliousness. As Mrs.

Orr reports, this precocious teenager "set the judgments of those about him at defiance, and gratuitously proclaimed himself everything that he was, and some things that he was not."[45]

Robert was still attending chapel to please his parents but was very restless in his response to the Reverend George Clayton's sermons. It must have been about this time that he was publicly rebuked for his inattention during the services.[46] Clayton was a competent but uninspiring preacher, and we can know something of the mild Calvinism that he offered to his congregation from the course of sermons he preached on "Faith and Practice" a few years later, 1838–1839,[47] which included the standard Calvinistic views of "the depravity and sinfulness of man" and the need for the "justifying righteousness" of a redeemer to save him. He did not stress the perils of Hell with colorful threat; rather, he exhorted his hearers to follow the gospel, for "they who neglect it have not the remotest prospect of escape from the utter and hopeless ruin which such neglect inevitably involves." Browning, enthralled by Shelley's idealism, was in no mood for Clayton's Christian pessimism delivered with rhetorical flatness.

When Robert was about eighteen, he began occasionally to attend Camden Chapel, a Church of England proprietary in Peckham that had been established when a group of dissatisfied parishioners had broken off from St. Giles Church.[48] Here the new minister was a golden-tongued young divine named Henry Melvill, whose preaching style appealed to Robert's literary tastes. Soon both he and Sarianna were attending York Street Chapel in the morning and Camden Chapel in the evening.[49] As an adolescent, Robert was ready to vibrate in response to the oratorical pitch from the pulpit, and Melvill was capable of sounding it with Shelleyan intensity. As an example, one of his sermons, "The Impossibility of Creature-Merit," reveals vigorously his own form of Calvinism and his substantial rhetorical skills in repetition, suspension, and rhythmical variations:

> [God] asks your heart; give it to him; it is his own. He asks your intellect; give it to him; it is his own. He asks your money; give it to him; it is his own. Remember the words of the Apostle, "Ye are not your own; ye are bought with a price." Ye are not your own. Ye are bought even if ye perish. Your bodies are not your own, though you may enslave them to lust; they are God's, to be thrown on the rock. Your souls are not your own, though you may hide, and tarnish, and degrade their immortality; they are God's, to be chained down to the rock, that the waves of wrath may dash and break over them. Oh, we want you; nay, the spirits of the just want you; and the holy angels want you; and the Father, and the Son, and the Holy Ghost want you; all but the devil and ruined souls

want you, to leave off defrauding the Almighty, and to give them *his own*, yourselves, his by creation, his doubly by redemption. I must give God the body, I must give God the soul. I give him the body, if I clothe my tongue with his praises, if I yield not my members as instruments of unrighteousness; if I suffer not the fires of unhallowed passion to light up mine eye, nor the vampire of envy to suck the color from my cheek; if I profane not my hands with the gains of ungodliness; if I turn away mine ear from the scoffer, and keep under every appetite, and wrestle with every lust; making it palpable that I consider each limb as not destined to corruption, but intended for illustrious service, when, at the trumpet-blast of the resurrection, the earth's sepulchres shall be riven.[50]

In theology Melvill was alternately sophisticated and fundamentalist. He was skeptical about the doctrine of the Trinity, saying that the Scripture was "silent as the grave" on this question; so he would wait until afterlife to see the problem resolved. He faced up to the central contradiction of Calvinism by declaring, "We have Scriptural warranty of God's election; and we have also Scriptural warranty of man's free agency. . . . Scripture reveals but does not reconcile the two."[51] His response was to accept both and to preach both and not to attempt an explanation. He did believe in a real operative "Satanic influence" in the world and in the literalness of the Garden of Eden story. He was not much different from Clayton in this regard. He accepted the dark view of the Fall of Man and its effect on human reason: that humankind existed in a "state of natural corruption" and suffered from a consequent "disorganized mind." He recommended reading of the Bible for "strengthening of the mind."[52]

These were the kinds of preaching young Robert Browning was listening to in the two chapels on Sundays. The liberalization of his religious outlook was several years in the future.

ॐ ॐ ॐ

The Browning family by now had moved to Hanover Cottage, a newly built semidetached house with trees in front and soon to be covered with vines, still on Southampton Street (a portion later named Wellington Street) at the corner of Grove Lane.[53] The new home had more room for books, a larger garden, and stables for York, Uncle Reuben's horse, which Robert exercised during the week.

After he left Ready's school, Robert not only studied under his father's guidance but he also began to receive a "gentleman's education," which included boxing, fencing, dancing, riding, singing and playing musical instruments.[54] One imagines him like Pip in Dickens's *Great Expectations* being prepared to assume a place in a higher sphere of society. Indeed, when he later married "Elizabeth Barrett Moulton Barrett, Spinster," he did not hesitate to sign the marriage certificate "Robert Browning, Gentleman."

Since he loved music, he responded eagerly to his music teachers and learned to play the violin, the cello, and the piano (and sometime later, he also mastered the organ). His instructor in harmony and counterpoint was "Great John Relfe" (as he called him in the autobiographical poem "Parleying with Charles Avison"), "master of mine, learned, redoubtable" (81–82), with whom he learned to compose. He set to music John Donne's "Go and Catch a Falling Star" besides poems of Thomas Hood and Thomas Love Peacock.[55] During this time he had four singing masters; the greatest of them was Isaac Nathan, the composer of *Hebrew Melodies*. The technical skill he acquired not only gave him the confidence to develop his own style in poetry but also showed itself in his ability to render musical experience in linguistic terms when he wrote poems about musicians, "A Toccata of Galuppi's," "Abt Vogler," or "Master Hugues of Saxe-Gotha," or even when he tried to depict the player practicing his lessons in "Flute Music—with Accompaniment."[56]

More systematic than his study of classical languages were Browning's two years of instruction in French, which he and Sarianna received from their tutor, Auguste Loradoux. Robert mastered the language well enough to read French literature with ease for the rest of his life and to write and converse whenever he had need. He also helped Loradoux with a textbook translation of LeSage's *Gil Blas* in an abridged version for schools.[57] On the shelves of the family library he had available the fifty volumes of the *Biographie Universelle*, which he frequently consulted and which, in the future, yielded him materials for *Paracelsus, Sordello*, several of his plays, and many of his poems.

In those two years, from age fourteen to sixteen, Browning's zeal for learning increased so much that he yearned for a university education. But as a conscientious Nonconformist, he was barred from Oxford and Cambridge, both of which required students to subscribe to the Thirty-Nine articles of the Church of England, and he knew that the attendance at a Scottish university or a university on the Continent would be very costly.

Fortunately his desire ripened just as plans for a new university in London were coming into being. Since 1825, a group of Whig leaders and Nonconformists, under the leadership of Henry (later Lord) Brougham, had been developing a proposal "to bring the means of a complete Scientific and Literary Education home to the doors of the individuals of the Metropolis, so that they may be enabled to educate their sons at a very moderate expense."[58] Their prospectus pointed out that, whereas education at Oxford or Cambridge cost £200 to £250 or more per year, the student attending the London University would have expenses of only £25 to £30 per year, for it was to be a nonresidential institution.

The new university was to be a serious venture into higher education. It did not envision a tutorial system. Students would attend regular classes as at the German universities. Rigorous oversight of student progress would be exercised: each class period was to consist of one hour of lecture and one hour of examination of students. Written examinations were required every week for every class. The general plan was to offer instruction in languages, mathematics, "mental and moral sciences" (i.e., philosophy, logic, economics, political economy), history, medicine, and law. But not theology: this was to be a secular institution with no religious tests for entrance.

The council of governors was a distinguished group: among them were members of Parliament, such as J. C. Hobhouse, Charles Calvert, and Joseph Hume; the poet Thomas Campbell; and other intellectuals and political leaders, such as James Mill, Henry Hallam, George Grote, and Lord John Russell. The founders sold shares, as in a stock company, to acquire funds. They purchased seven acres of land near the British Museum and erected new buildings designed by William Wilkins (the architect of the National Gallery) in 1827. His Royal Highness, the Duke of Sussex, laid the cornerstone. Among the shareholders was Robert Browning, Senior, who was eager to provide for his son the higher education that he himself had been denied.

The new university suffered a good deal of derision from conservative quarters. *John Bull*, the ultra-Tory magazine, called it "a humbug joint-stock company subscription school for Cockney boys,"[59] and printed derogatory verses entitled "The Cockney University" and "The Cockney College," with such stanzas as these:

> Each Dustman shall speak, both in Latin and Greek,
> And Tinkers beat Bishops in knowledge—
> If the opulent tribe will consent to subscribe
> To build up a new Cockney College.[60]

Criticism abounded from Oxford and Cambridge universities at the rise of this upstart urban rival, and the Royal College of Physicians, which had a monopoly on the licensing of physicians in England, jealously found fault with the proposed university education in medicine, because the Royal College favored the present system of educating physicians by lecture-demonstrations at the hospitals plus a kind of apprenticeship to older physicians and "walking the wards."[61] The loudest voices of opposition came from the church, especially the Evangelical wing, which deplored the secular emphasis of the new university. For example, the Reverend T. W. Lancaster attacked the curriculum, declaring that "Religion is the only part of education essentially *needful* to society."[62] One concession that the council made to the religious critics was to rule that the boardinghouses in the neighborhood must require that students produce proof of "correctness of character, with regard to religious habits and morals" and that they "be regular in attending public houses of worship."[63]

In contrast to the brief glimpses that are available of Robert Browning's early development, the period that he spent at London University provides the first detailed picture of his intellectual milieu. His association with the university began with his father's letter, April 22, 1828, to Mr. Coates the secretary, requesting admission for his son and assuring the secretary of Robert's "unwearied application for the last 6 years to the Greek, Latin, and French languages."[64] This statement answered the university requirement that entering students were expected to be able "to read Latin verse and prose such as Caesar's *Commentaries*"; in Greek "to construe Xenophon's *Anabasis*"; in French to read "an easy French author."[65] In October Robert enrolled for classes in Greek, daily, 9:30 to 11:30; in Latin, daily, 12:00 to 2:00; and, new for him, in German, Tuesday and Thursday, 2:30 to 4:00, and Saturday, 9:30 to 11:00.

Although he first took lodgings on Bedford Square, he found them unnecessary, and perhaps uncongenial, and returned home after a week to continue his studies over the next months by commuting to London like his father. Betty Miller has contended that he left his lodgings because he could not bear to be away from his mother.[66] A simpler and more reasonable explanation is that Browning, who had already boarded away from home at Mr. Ready's school, had arranged to live at Bedford Square because his Greek class started at 8:30 a.m.; then, before the term began, the university council changed the schedule to 9:30 so that students in the villages surrounding London would not be inconvenienced.[67] Browning, seeing that he no longer had need to live near the university, very sensibly spared his father additional expense by moving back home.

His experience during the following months meant an exposure to professional scholarship at a very high level from his classics professors, George Long in Greek and Thomas Hewitt Key in Latin, both of whom had been educated at Trinity College, Cambridge, and earned A.M. degrees and, coincidentally, both of whom had held positions on the faculty of the University of Virginia in the United States. In the preliminary outline of his course, Professor Long presented an extravagant plan for two years of study that would cover Greek history and culture through readings in Herodotus (portions of nine books), Plutarch (selected "Lives"), readings in Thucydides, Xenophon, Aristotle's *Politics*, and Polybius, plus additional readings in the Attic orators and Arrian that would carry the history of Athens and Sparta to the time of Alexander. A play by Aeschylus and one by Sophocles would illustrate the development of Greek drama, and "several plays of Aristophanes" would be read in connection with the Peloponnesian War. Finally, the Homeric poems would be studied toward the end of the second year.[68]

Problems arose, however, both because of Long's overambitious program of study and because of the lack of preparation that the London University students brought to their study of Greek. By December, he was forced to revise his plans and, indeed, divide his two class levels into three, each according to student proficiency. Now, the most advanced class, the one in which Browning probably was enrolled, was to deal only with Herodotus, Book 1, in the first term and Aeschylus' *Prometheus Bound* in the second.[69]

Professor Key likewise had to climb down from his grandiose two-year plan for Latin study, in which he had planned to cover, in the first three months, Caesar's *Gallic Wars*, "2 or 3 books of the *Aeneid*," and "a few Odes of Horace," and then go on to Cicero, Terence, Ovid, and Livy for the rest of the year. His second year was to be equally burdensome—ending the last three months with Tacitus (the most difficult of the Roman historians), Juvenal, and Martial.[70] By Christmas of Browning's year of study, Key had to reduce even the most advanced of his classes to a first-year study merely of Livy and Roman history.[71]

Browning's professor of German language and literature, Ludwig von Muhlenfels, who held a doctorate from Heidelberg, had an admirable vision of a two-year course for beginners that included lectures on German literature and culture, but even at the beginning of the term, he had to bring it down to the realities of the limitations of his English students. Most of the year was spent on grammar, etymology, and analysis of words. He postponed all lectures on literature until January.[72]

The scaling back of elaborate plans probably disappointed Browning in his university studies. Certainly he found that his classics courses did not place the emphasis on literature that he had hoped for. Professor Long, an expert on Herodotus and Xenophon (he later published books on each of them), took the position that "the extant historians and orators form the most valuable portion of Grecian literature," and he felt that they should receive "a greater share of the student's attention."[73] Beyond this, he devoted a great deal of time to geography, etymology, the formation of word compounds, and working at the blackboard. Professor Key, who was said to be a very good teacher, was nevertheless also said to be a zealot in philological minutiae. Two of his students, Walter Bagehot and R. H. Hutton, remember him as "overreaching" in his search for etymological origins and relations.[74] All of this must have seemed uninspiring to a would-be poet, especially one who had recently immersed himself in Byron and Shelley and who had access to an excellent home library.

Even so, the Greek dramatists so appealed to Browning's imagination that the study of Aeschylus' *Prometheus*, which he pursued under Professor Long, contributed to the lifelong study and reading of Greek drama that his career later exhibited, both in his literary interchanges with Elizabeth Barrett and in his publication of three volumes of poetry drawing upon the Greek drama: *Balaustion's Adventure*, *Aristophanes' Apology*, and *The Agamemnon of Aeschylus*.[75]

Yet it is possible that Browning profited most from the time he spent in the classes of Professor Muhlenfels. Since this was his first exposure to a Germanic language, the daily drills in grammar must have been more of a chore for him than responding to the beauties of Marot and Ronsard under his former French tutor, Loradoux. Yet this professor, who was a friend of Felix Mendelssohn's and was steeped in German Romanticism, managed to instill such a feeling for the German language in one year that Browning continued reading on his own, beginning with Schlegel and Tieck's translations of Shakespeare's plays, as his letters to Alfred Domett attest.[76] Later his sense of German culture was sufficiently strong that he was able to evoke it in works as diverse as *Paracelsus*, "Abt Vogler," and "Master Hugues of Saxe-Gotha." Even so, he never developed the love for the German language that he did for French and Italian.

In May 1829, toward the end of his first year of study, a few days before his seventeenth birthday, Robert decided to withdraw from the London University. There is no question of his not doing well in his studies or of the challenge being too much for him. One of his classmates remembers that "bright handsome youth, with long black hair falling over his shoulders" in Professor Long's Greek class and adds, "I well recollect the esteem and regard in which he was held by his fellow students."[77] As the months had passed, he had apparently become aware that the instruction in language was offered from the perspective of professional scholars and that his inclinations were different both from those of his professors and those of his fellow students, who were training themselves for law, medicine, or mercantile affairs. He himself had youthful ambitions to be a poet. His father's wish for him to become a lawyer had long since been set aside. Nor was clerkship in a bank, the common career choice for members of the Browning family, urged on him, for Robert Browning, Senior, regarded this form of work as deadening. When his father asked him what he wanted to do, Robert appealed to him to be allowed to "cultivate the powers of his mind"[78] on his own, so that he could devote his talents to poetry. How long the elder Browning hesitated in this situation we do not know. Not long, according to Gosse's notes on the poet's recollections, for "so great was the confidence of the father in the genius of the son" that the ever-indulgent father "at once acquiesced in the proposal."[79] It was a genuine career decision and a risky one, a decision that for several years Robert Browning would not be able to prove was right.

Chapter 4

Filling the Reservoir

Very little is known about the next four years of Robert Browning's life, during which he followed a program of self-education. We are told that he began to prepare himself for a literary career by reading through Johnson's *Dictionary* in an attempt to engorge language wholesale, and since he was blessed with an unusually retentive memory—"I . . . can forget nothing (but names and the date of the Battle of Waterloo)"[1]—the project may not have been a presumptuous mistake. It has been estimated that Browning's poems show that he had a working vocabulary of forty thousand words, far more than that of most English writers.[2] During this period he engaged in prodigious feats of reading in both classical and modern literature, with the preponderance of it in the traditional English writers. The intensity of this effort tapered off after he began to publish in 1833, but until he married in 1846 at age thirty-four, he continued to surround himself with books and to indulge his Faustian habits of delving into them. We can pick up hints about which writers he spent time on in the earlier portion of his premarital period from items in the Browning library that still remain, from references in his letters to Alfred Domett, Amédée de Ripert-Monclar, and Elizabeth Barrett, and from allusions in his early poems.

He turned first, one may be sure, to improving his knowledge of Greek. As he told his friend Ripert-Monclar, he had concentrated his efforts there long ago, beginning with the first years after he left Mr. Ready's school: "I betook myself to music again and to general study, particularly of Greek literature for which I have always had a passion."[3]

This love of Greek literature spurred him now to further reading in the Greek drama that he had begun under Professor Long. Aeschylus' *Agamemnon*, which he came to know even more thoroughly after his discussions of it with Elizabeth, was very likely the first work he chose. He even published a peculiar translation of it in the later part of his career. Aeschylus' *Choephori, Eumenides, Septem Contra Thebas*, and Sophocles' *Ajax, Antigone*, and *Electra*, the Browning copy of which has been read to pieces, were probably studied at this time too.[4] It is also likely that his attraction to Euripides, who became his favorite Greek dramatist, began in this period. An eighteenth-century edition of the *Cyclops*[5] was in the family library, and there must have been others, perhaps the complete tragedies, for in his letters to Elizabeth and to Domett, Robert mentions the *Troades* and *Hippolytus*,[6] and he alludes to the *Bacchae* in *Sordello* and to both *Iphigeneia in Aulis* and *Iphigeneia in Tauris* in his poem "Waring." At some point, he even tried his hand at a tragedy on the Hippolytus theme. Only a fragment of the unfinished work remains, which he published under the title "Artemis Prologizes" in 1842.[7] How much further he read in the Greek dramatists at this time we cannot say for sure.[8]

If he had not studied Xenophon, Aesop, Hesiod, and Anacreon (the *Carmina* [1783] was his father's schoolbook)[9] in the years after he left Mr. Ready, he did so now. He alludes to Lucian's satiric *Dialogues of the Dead* later in *Pippa Passes*. A gift of Epictetus' *Enchiridion* (1748) from his Uncle Reuben, March 8, 1830,[10] helps to place his reading of this basic manual of Stoic philosophy. At the same time, he made his way through *The Republic* and the best-known dialogues of Plato, perhaps inspired by Shelley's translations. He struggled with Aristotle's *Ethics*, and in his poem "Development" implies that it was hard going. Even so, Browning developed a facility with Greek during these years so that he read it as easily as Latin or French.

For Latin literature, he may have taken his cue from Professor Key's elaborate outline of study to choose the poets and dramatists that he would spend time with. He had on hand an anthology of selections from Terence, Ovid, Virgil, Horace, Juvenal, and Persius in two volumes.[11] He had encountered Horace much earlier when his Uncle Reuben had sent him an edition of *The Works of Horace* translated by Christopher Smart,[12] a favorite poet of Robert's youth, whom he included at the end of his career in *Parleyings with Certain People of Importance in Their Day*. Echoes from Ovid's *Metamorphoses, Fasti*, and *Heroides* are heard in *Pauline* and *Sordello*. He had studied parts of Virgil's *Aeneid* with Mr. Ready; he covered the rest of it, plus the *Georgics*, now. Seneca's tragedies (1656), purchased in 1836,[13] Petronius' *Satyricon* in a 1700 edition,[14] and a translation of Suetonius' *Lives of the First*

Twelve Caesars (1796)[15]—all were available on the family shelves. He even coped with Lucretius' *De Rerum Natura*.[16]

He continued the reading in French literature that he had begun under Monsieur Loradoux. There is evidence that he was familiar with the plays of Corneille[17] and Racine,[18] the poems of Ronsard and Marot,[19] the *Gargantua and Pantagruel* of Rabelais,[20] the *Essais* of Montaigne,[21] *Du Contrat Social* of Rousseau[22] and the novels of Balzac, Frédéric Soulié, George Sand, and Alfred de Musset.[23] He did not regard Dumas' *Le Comte de Monte Cristo* highly,[24] but he was favorably impressed by Hugo's *Nôtre-Dame de Paris*.[25] Most important, he spent time browsing the complete works of Voltaire,[26] who was instrumental in liberalizing Browning's religious views. Voltaire's attractiveness lay in the fact that his ideas were presented in very readable philosophical romances as well as in his witty and stylistically lucid *Lettres Philosophiques* and *Dictionnaire Philosophique*. Contrary to the popular notion that Voltaire was an atheist, he was in fact a Deist who looked on God as the Creator of the universe, arguing that the existence of a watch implied a watchmaker, but rejecting the idea that God concerned himself about the lives and behavior of human beings. He took a scientific view of the world and became a popularizer of Locke's philosophy, which had laid the groundwork for destroying the doctrine of original sin and the theology of Calvin that depended upon it. Voltaire was hostile to organized Christianity, both Catholic and Protestant, because of the persecutions that the leaders had carried out in upholding their authority. Browning took his religious tolerance from his father but had it reinforced by Voltaire. His belief in God had begun to take on a new sophistication, if we can take seriously his quoting Voltaire to Elizabeth in a well-known aphorism, "si Dieu n'existait pas, il faudrait l'inventer."[27]

After Robert had left the London University, Mr. Browning arranged for a course of study in Italian for both Robert and Sarianna under the guidance of a tutor, Angelo Cerutti, an Italian grammarian who had migrated to England and who believed in teaching the language by exposure to the best writers.[28] Although he introduced Browning to Dante, Petrarch, Tasso, Pulci, Ariosto, and Boccaccio, he used his own edition of Daniello Bartoli's *De' Simboli Trasportati al Morale* (London: C. Armand, [1830]) as a textbook for beginners. Both Robert and Sarianna are listed in the book as subscribers.[29] Its chapters discuss a great many ancient monuments in the Near East and the Mediterranean area and point to a "moral" to be drawn from them. Browning brought his copy along on both of his voyages to Italy, in 1838 and 1844, as a sample of the best Tuscan style but also perhaps because of the sites and monuments it referred to. His copy also tells us the occasion of two of his early poems, for he wrote on the endpaper in ink:"'The Ride to Ghent' was originally written in pencil on this and part of the next page at sea, off the African coast. RB ('Home Thoughts from Abroad' also written here)." The penciled poems (written on the 1844 voyage) have, unfortunately, been erased, so we cannot know what variations his first drafts contained.

This experience of study under Signor Cerutti was the beginning of Browning's fascination with Italian culture. It encouraged him toward a later and more thorough study of Dante and Petrarch[30] and a reading of Vittorio Alfieri's tragedies that imitated the Greek form.[31] It drew him twice to Italy, the expatriate land of Shelley and Byron, before he eventually chose to make his home there with his wife, Elizabeth Barrett. Italy and Italian literature served as an inspirational spring for his poetry from *Sordello* in 1840 to *Asolando* in 1889.

During this early period, his companion in his studies was his sister, Sarianna. Mr. Browning had provided her with a better education than was common for young women in the mid-nineteenth century. She had earlier been sent to Miss Goodson's school in Camberwell, where she had first been a pupil of Cerutti.[32] Only a hint about her studies there has survived, a small book, *Geographical Questions and Exercises, blended with Historical and Biographical Information and an Appendix containing questions on Astronomy* by Richard Chambers.[33] She must have excelled at geography, for she won as a prize *Polar Scenes, exhibited in the Voyages of Heemskerk and Barenz* with thirty-six engravings ("My first prize—S. B.").[34] Another prize came later: a copy of Thomson's *The Seasons* from Miss Goodson herself.[35] As we have seen, she was given lessons in modern languages and she may have had some training in Latin through her father, but she apparently did not learn to read Greek, for among her books the only item in Greek literature is a collection of abridged translations of Aeschylus' seven tragedies, subtitled *Popular Specimens of the Greek Dramatic Poets*, with introductory essays and notes.[36]

As Browning strove to complete his education on his own, he placed the greatest emphasis on English writers, especially the poets and dramatists. His range stretched from Chaucer up to then-current writers. The books at hand in the family home and the references and allusions in letters and early poems indicate that he had read Chaucer thoroughly and was familiar with Sidney, Spenser (plus the great work of scholarly criticism in his father's first edition, Thomas Warton's *Observations on the Faerie Queene of Spenser* 1754),[37] Donne, Herbert, and Crashaw—as well as the soaring prose of Sir Thomas Browne and the moral severity of Joseph Hall. His references to Shakespeare show that he knew not only the major plays but also *Love's Labour's Lost*[38] and *Henry VIII*[39]—and even that sensational item that was once attributed to Shakespeare, *The Yorkshire Tragedy*.[40] Among the other Elizabethan dramatists, he read Marlowe, Jonson, Chapman, Beaumont and Fletcher, Ford, Webster, and Shirley. Browning's religious background combined with his love of poetry to lead him to a serious study of all of Milton's poetical works, for which he made full use of his father's collection of early editions. Dryden and Congreve represented for him the Restoration drama, but he came to know the period best, and the conditions of the English stage, from Colley Cibber's *An Apology for the Life of Mr. Colley Cibber*.[41] Samuel Butler's *Hudibras*[42] was another work he enjoyed and one that invited him to be free and irregular in his meter when he was taking a light tone in poems of his own.

Eighteenth-century writers seemed close to him because of his father's perspective. He read Addison, Swift, Pope (and Joseph Warton's monumental study, *An Essay on the Genius and Writings of Pope* in two volumes, his father's revised edition, 1782),[43] Johnson's *Lives of the English Poets*[44] as well as his verse, Goldsmith, both poems and plays, Thomson, Gray, Churchill, Cowper, Garrick's comedies as well as Sheridan's. He read through Chatterton's Rowley poems (Robert had actually discovered the source for one of Chatterton's plagiarisms in a sermon of John Hurrion's in *Works of the Holy Spirit*[45]), Mandeville's *Fable of the Bees*,[46] Chesterfield's *Letters*,[47] and Smollett's *Humphry Clinker*,[48] although he did not care much for English novelists, especially those who published in his own century.

One item in his library must be lingered over here, a volume originally published in 1646 by his old favorite, Francis Quarles, *Judgment and Mercy for Afflicted Souls, or Meditations, Soliloquies and Prayers* in an edition of 1837,[49] a time in which Browning was beginning to compose short poems in monologue form. The work is a series of dramatized characterizations of types of wicked men, for example, the Liar, the Sensual Man, the Drunkard, the Vain-Glorious Man, the Oppressor, the Hypocrite, the Covetous Man, and so on.[50] Each one, as he speaks, exults in his way of life and offers arguments to support it; then he hears a voice whisper a scriptural text in his ear. There follows a soliloquy, consisting of a meditation on his sinful state and a presentation of penitent thoughts. One is struck immediately by the resemblance that these apologies bear to some of Browning's monodramatic poems, whether they be the ironical self-justifications of his Johannes Agricola or the special pleadings of his dukes and bishops. Here, for instance, is Quarles's "The Oppressor's Plea," which gives us a merchant who is defending the demands he makes upon a debtor, that he get "my utmost farthing, or his bones":

> The commodity was good enough, as wares went then; and he possest but a thriving wit, with the necessary help of a good merchantable conscience, he might have gained, perchance, as much as now he lost:

however, gain or not gain, I must have my money. . . . Come tell me not of a good conscience; a good conscience is no parcel of my trade; it hath made more bankrupts than all the loose wives in the city. My conscience is no fool; it tells me that my own's my own, and that a well filled bag is no deceitful friend, but will stick close to me when all my friends forsake me. If to gain a good estate out of nothing, and to regain a desperate debt which is as good as nothing, be the fruits and sign of a bad conscience, God help the good. Tell me not of griping and oppression: the world is hard, and he that hopes to thrive, must grip hard. What I give, I give, and what I lend, I lend. If the way to heaven be to turn beggar upon earth, let them take it that like it, I know not what ye call oppression. . . . (7)

One can hear echoes of the proud assertions of a Guido Franceschini with his harsh demands about his marriage bargain.

Then there is "The Hypocrite's Prevarication," which begins in this way:

There is no such stuff to make a cloak of as religion: nothing so fashionable—nothing so profitable: it is a livery wherein a wise man may serve two masters, God and the world, and make a gainful service by either: I serve both, and in both, myself—by prevaricating with both. Before man, none serves his God with more severe devotion; for which, among the best of men, I work my own ends, and serve myself. In private, I serve the world, not with such strict devotion; but with more delight, where in fulfilling her servant's lusts, I work my ends and serve myself. (20)

Here one detects a voice like Browning's Mr. Sludge, the medium, describing his use of spiritualism for profit.

In this book, Quarles has created prose monologues for his ironhearted speakers with persuasive brilliance. Dramatized character sketches like these could encourage Browning in his dramatic attempts to enter warped or evil minds, as was his wont, and could stand as models for him down through the years. We cannot say for certain when—or even if—Browning studied this work that occupied a place in the family library. But it seems likely it was a guide to him because Quarles was a writer he had cherished from childhood and because the Quarles monologues seem in conception to resemble so many of Browning's dramatic creations. Indeed, the clearest likeness between Quarles's book and one of Browning's works is in the plot mechanism that draws together the scenes of Browning's play *Pippa Passes*, in which Pippa's songs fall upon the ears of the evil or wavering characters to bring about a critical change in their actions. Her songs function in the same way as the whispers that turn Quarles's scoundrels to penitence.

After steeping himself in the literature of the past, Robert Browning was able to feel a quickened response to the work of his more recent contemporaries, Wordsworth, Coleridge, Southey, Shelley, Keats, and Byron, plus lesser lights such as Charles Lamb, Leigh Hunt, Thomas Moore, Samuel Rogers, and Thomas Campbell. Indeed, in the late 1830s and early 1840s, his reading among nineteenth-century writers occupied more of his time as he began to think of himself as a practising poet among fellow poets. He not only discovered Landor and Tennyson—and a "Miss Barrett," whose poetry drew his increasing admiration—but he also read whoever was being read and discussed at the time, poets whose names are now forgotten, such as Laman Blanchard and Sir John Hanmer, poets now being read again, such as "L. E. L." (Letitia Elizabeth Landon) and Felicia Hemans, and playwrights such as Thomas Noon Talfourd, "Barry Cornwall" (Bryan Waller Procter), Douglas Jerrold, and Henry Taylor. He even eased his scorn for English novels and began to read the early Dickens up to *Martin Chuzzlewit*,[51] perhaps because of the humor. Disraeli's *Vivian Grey* captured his interest,[52] and perhaps *Sibyl* as well.[53] He approved of Bulwer-Lytton's *The Last Days of Pompeii*, but he judged *The Last of the Barons* to be "a poor affair," from the excerpts he encountered.[54] Whatever he saw reviewed in the *Athenaeum* or the *Morning Chronicle* seemed to be part of a world he wished to enter.

℮ ℮ ℮

This period while Browning was equipping himself for his career (and trying out verses that he showed to no one) finds him forming some early and local friendships that were important to his maturing years. The Browning family was a close-knit unit, perhaps holding together more closely because they were Nonconformists in a nation that upheld an Established Church. They maintained, however, a warm relationship with Mrs. Browning's sister Christina's family, the Silverthornes, who had three sons, all of whom were said to be musical and somewhat wild.[55] The eldest, Jim, was Robert's companion sometimes in attending plays or operas in London. Later, he was Robert's best man at his wedding. His early death was the occasion for Browning's poem "May and Death." The Brownings also kept cordial relations with Mr. Browning's half brothers and sisters. Reuben Browning, only nine years older than Robert, was a financial officer in the House of Rothschild. The other brother, William Shergold Browning, associated with the Parisian branch of the Rothschild Bank, provided a link with French culture for the Camberwell Brownings, yet because of the distance, Robert saw little of his Uncle William.

This seems to be the limit of their intimacy with blood relatives. Grandfather Rob Browning's second wife, Jane, was said to be cold to her two stepchildren, Robert and Margaret, and to have been instrumental in having Rob Browning move his second family out of Camberwell to Islington in north London.[56] If we can believe cousin Cyrus Mason, who always took a sour view of the Robert Browning family, some members of the second family felt that the Camberwell Brownings held aloof from them, and Mason himself expressed resentment toward the Brownings' inwardness and sense of privacy. He describes their suburban contentment in the mid-1840s as "constantly self-absorbed, Uncle Robert intently studying some learned book or amusing himself by making grotesque drawings; Aunt Robert ever mindful of her garden or busy arranging some household punctillios; Cousin Sarianna absorbed in her own importance or considering matters connected with the chapel she attended; the Poet so pre-occupied, by his love affair [with Miss Barrett], that he found no opportunity to show much attention to Kinsfolk."[57]

Young Robert did find time for friends beyond Camberwell through a Captain James Pritchard, an old friend of the family who introduced him to a circle of young men in Limehouse, all associated with the shipping business, who formed a group called "The Colloquials."[58] Captain Pritchard appears to have been more like a character out of Dickens who might hobnob with Dan Peggotty rather than associate with young poets and theatergoers. He was "a little white-haired sailor with a squint who told delightful stories of adventures."[59] A bachelor, he had the peculiarity of never letting anyone know where he lived. But he was a lover of literature and learning, as his gifts of books to Robert attest. He brought him a Lyon edition of the *Essais* of Montaigne (1593),[60] and a presentation copy from Charles I, *Reliquiae Sacrae Carolinae* (1650).[61]

Through Captain Pritchard, Browning came to know Chris Dowson, whose family owned Bridge Dock in Limehouse, which was at that time a quiet Thames-side village. Chris and his brother Joseph were poets and interested in all things literary. Although they never published, the semidormant literary seed finally grew and blossomed in Chris Dowson's grandson, who became the well-known decadent poet of the 1890s, Ernest Dowson. The treasurer of the little Literary Society, Frederick Young, Chris Dowson's partner in the Ship Biscuit Bakery in Limehouse, was intensely interested in the theater and knew much of Shakespeare by heart. He was later one of the "Claquers" in the audience when Browning's play *Strafford* was staged at Covent Garden, May 1, 1837.[62] Captain Pritchard was the cousin of Dr. James Blundell, lecturer at Guy's Hospital in Midwifery, and arranged for

Browning to attend the lectures, an opportunity that expanded his knowledge of female anatomy and sex.[63] Blundell's nephew, Bezer, was another
member of the Colloquials. Less is known about other members of this little "Debating Society,"[64] as Frederick Young's sister called it.[65]

Early on, the group met at the Youngs' house, but later they would have
evenings at the British Coffee Tavern or at the Artichoke near the West
India Docks. Browning is remembered at this time as being "pale, thin, and
rather delicate looking,"[66] "with dark curls,"[67] and whiskers that extended
from his lower cheeks to the area under his chin. These gatherings provided
him with his first opportunity outside his family to discuss poetry, drama,
and philosophy and, over claret and cigars, to discover a little more sophistication than he had found in Camberwell. In this company he seems to have
been a bit awkward and perhaps unsure of himself, for Joseph Arnould said
later that "we remember him as hardly doing justice to himself in society" —
in his conversation, that is — "but now" (Arnould was writing in the 1840s)
"it is quite the reverse," and "from the habit of good and extensive society he
has improved in this respect wonderfully." Arnould characterized his mature
conversation as "remarkably good": "anecdotical, vigorous, showing great
thought and reading, but in his language most simple, energetic, and accurate."[68] The Colloquials that fostered this change did more than discuss
poetry and new books and plays. Robert joined with Chris Dowson to produce an amateur musical comedy, *Olla Podrida*, about which nothing is
known except that Emily Dowson, daughter of Chris, saw it performed
when she was a child.[69] In 1833–1834, the Colloquials published a periodical, *The Trifler*, a jumble of verse and prose worthy of the title. In February
1833, Browning contributed an article signed "Z," a reply to an essay on debt
in the previous issue. It was a rather labored exercise of wit, with a conscious
attempt to display learning.[70]

As time went on, Robert's association with the Colloquials served him
well. Not only did it take him out of the rather restrictive atmosphere of
Camberwell, but it also led to the formation of the two most important
friendships of his early life with Alfred Domett and Joseph Arnould.

☙ ☙ ☙

During Browning's youth, he lived "just a green half hour's walk" from the
only art gallery in England that was open to the public.[71] Earlier, he had
learned something about the world of art from books and from his father's
collection of prints and engravings. But in a neighboring village, in the Dulwich College Picture Gallery, Robert had available the real thing. Tickets of

admission were free; however, they were unobtainable in Dulwich. They could only be secured at certain London booksellers. Mr. Browning, who was in the city daily and usually stopping by bookshops, picked up tickets frequently, and by this means he introduced Robert to the glories of European art when he was younger than fourteen, the required age for admission.

This excellent collection, housed in a building designed by John Soane, had originally been assembled for King Stanislaus of Poland, but by a series of fortunate accidents it was eventually bequeathed to Dulwich College, an institution established in 1619 for the education of needy boys.[72] The gallery had a rich assembly of works by Dutch and Flemish artists, including paintings by Rembrandt, Rubens, Hobbema, the Ruysdaels, the Teniers, Cuyp, Dou, Both, Van Dyck, and Wouwerman. It also had several Murillos, and representative paintings by Italian, French, and English masters. In a tone of nostalgic exaltation, Robert recalled for Elizabeth his rapt response to its aesthetic excellence: "that Gallery I so love . . . those two Guidos, the wonderful Rembrandt of Jacob's vision, such a Watteau, the triumphant three Murillo pictures, a Giorgione music-lesson group, all the Poussins with the 'Armida' and 'Jupiter's nursing'—and—no end to 'ands'—I have sate before one, some *one* of those pictures I had predetermined to see,—a good hour and then gone away."[73]

Here Browning's taste in art was formed. One may note that the pictures he mentions favor narrative painting, mostly depicting biblical stories or classical mythology. One of the Murillos is an appealing Madonna and child, the model a realistic young mother; one of the Poussins is David carrying the giant head of Goliath in a triumphant procession; one of the Guido Reni works is St. John preaching in the wilderness; the two Poussins that he specifically mentions are, first, a picture of Tasso's Rinaldo asleep being discovered by Armida, and the second, a representation of the child Jupiter being nursed by a goat, surrounded by classically idealized immortals in a pastoral scene. There is an uplifting spirituality about some of those that he listed for Elizabeth, especially the one attributed to Rembrandt,[74] Jacob's vision of two shining angels on high. The only exception is the Watteau (later identified as by Lancret), "Fête Champêtre," a scene of elegant court ladies picnicking with their attendants in a clearing in the woods.

A few other features of this collection should not be overlooked. Here Browning saw his first Andrea del Sartos, a "Virgin and Child with St. John" and a "Holy Family." Beyond this, one might note two distinguishing characteristics of the collection: first, that the emphasis is on landscape painting with many figures wandering in forests, on roads inquiring the way, or in settings with ancient ruins or blasted trees; second, that there are many paintings of peasants, beggars, or common folk inside or outside taverns—realistic scenes that he might not want to mention to Elizabeth, especially one by Andriaen Brouwer, "Interior of an Ale-House," with figures of men smoking their pipes vigorously and tipping up huge ale pots, another devouring a herring held high over his mouth, another fondling the ale wife, and one pissing against a post. Indeed, the collection represents life in all its diversity, scenes spiritual and vulgar, nature idealized and threatening, human beings in their multiplicity of roles from king to swineherd.[75]

This overview of Browning's self-education in a formative period of his life has necessarily been sketchy and speculative because of the scarcity of the usual biographical evidence. There are no diaries, no notebooks, no travel journals. There is only one biased memoir by cousin Cyrus Mason, plus a few remembrances that W. Hall Griffin drew from Sarianna or from Robert's friends and acquaintances in their old age. There are only five letters before 1835 and a sparse and unsatisfactory scattering of others before the seven letters to Ripert-Monclar in the late 1830s, the fourteen letters to Alfred Domett in the early 1840s, and the correspondence with Elizabeth that began in 1845, when he was thirty-three years old. Thus one is forced to rely on circumstantial evidence that may be found in the existing books that can be identified as being within his reach and in oblique references that appear in his subsequent correspondence or peep forth from his poems, most of which are dramatic.

In order to try to fill in the biographical portrait, then, we have gone chronologically too far and must now return to the time in which his public activity is observable: when he began to publish in 1833.

Chapter 5

Browning Aspires to Be Shelley

The ambitions of youth are grandiose, and a young man of romantic inclinations, twenty years old, a passionate enthusiast for the aetherial flights of Shelley, can be filled with the divine afflatus. On an October night in 1832, while Robert Browning was returning on foot from Richmond where he had gone to see the great Edmund Kean in *Richard III*,[1] he formed an elaborate scheme for "a series of monodramatic epics," as he later told Edmund Gosse.[2] This plan, he wrote in a penciled note of 1833, would enable him "to assume and realize I know not how many characters." The world was not to guess that the various works—poem, opera, novel, speech—were all written by one author. He would intrigue the literary world as the great unknown author of *Waverley* had done. The first work was to be by "the *Poet* of the batch who would have been more legitimately *myself* than most of the others."[3] This first work became *Pauline: A Fragment of a Confession*, which Browning wrote in secret and published in March 1833, and which was dated at the end "Richmond, 22 October 1832." Only Sarianna, who made a fair copy for the printer, knew of its authorship. Aunt Christina Silverthorne heard about the book, however, perhaps from her son Jim, who often accompanied Robert to performances in London and may have been his companion on the night that the extravagant literary plan was conceived. She offered Robert £30 toward the cost of publication.

Browning's first venture into print seemed almost furtive. This long Romantic poem bore no author's name. The dating of the work was used "purposely as a blind," Sarianna later explained: "[we] never lived at Richmond." The authorship was "a strict secret, except from myself."[4] The poem was preceded by a long epigraph in Latin by the occult philosopher Cornelius Agrippa von Nettesheim, which warned away hostile readers and welcomed friendly ones with an apology for the author's youthful indiscretions.

The confession referred to in the subtitle points to the substance of the poem and to the sense in which the poem is dramatic. The substance consists of reiterated statements by the speaker to Pauline that he has succumbed to a self-centeredness that inhibits his powers as a poet. This state also causes him to lose the ability to love and brings about the temporary loss of his belief in God. As the speaker describes his early life, he recalls that the figure of Shelley was an inspiration to him, which he then lost, falling into disillusion and cynicism. His confession of all this to Pauline seems motivated by the hope that he will recover his poetic powers and will be sustained by the renewed love of God and the love of Pauline, with whom he fancies a withdrawal from the world into a womblike seclusion. The sense in which the confession is dramatic is best described by W. J. Fox, the poem's earliest reviewer. He quotes Channing, the well-known American Unitarian, as saying that "the great revelation which man now needs is a revelation of man to himself," a revelation of "the mystery within ourselves." The author of *Pauline* has undertaken that move from outer to inner: "The confessions have nothing in them which needs names: the external world is only reflected in them in its faintest shades; its influences are only described after they have penetrated into the intellect." The dramatic action is entirely within, and the feelings and emotions are the characters that propel it: "The scenery is in the chambers of thought; the agencies are powers and passions; the events are transitions from one state of spiritual existence to another."[5]

Despite the presence of many linguistically brilliant passages, the poem is a prime example of Shelley's bad influence on the young Robert Browning. The fevered intensity is reminiscent of the narrative about the unnamed "Poet" in Shelley's *Alastor*; even the misleading hints of the speaker's impending demise were perhaps inspired by the decline of Shelley's Poet, who comes to his death without discernible cause. It was an undeserved stroke of good fortune for Browning's reputation that the book did not sell and was scarcely noticed by the literary press.

Not that Browning did not do the best he could to get the book reviewed. In March 1833 he wrote a rather mannered letter to his old acquaintance W. J. Fox, who had offered him encouraging words about *Incondita*, for he knew Fox wrote for the *Westminster Review*.[6] Fox's reply probably told Browning that he would do what he could to draw critical attention to the book because by return post Browning sent him twelve copies, plus Shelley's *Rosalind and Helen* for the Flower sisters to read.[7] Fox, ever-helpful to a new talent, wrote a laudatory review for his young suppliant—not in the *Westminster Review* but in his own periodical, the *Monthly Repository*, for April 1833. His treatment was that of welcoming a new poet to the public and overlooking the limitations of a "hasty and imperfect sketch" in order to acknowledge that it had "truth and life in it." He perceptively defined the kind of dramatic poem the anonymous author was undertaking; he singled out for praise the "Suntreader" passage—the speaker's apostrophe to Shelley—and quoted a good part of it. Finally, he called upon his readers to recognize a fresh poetic voice in their midst and likened himself to Archimedes who, in reacting to discovery, "gave a glorious leap and shouted *Eureka!*"[8]

As for *Rosalind and Helen*, Eliza Flower lost it on a picnic, which occasion allowed the kindly Fox to imagine it planted and sprouting new works when in a later notice in his magazine he wrote, "This spring some one found a delicate exotic-looking plant, growing wild . . . with *Pauline* hanging from its slender stalk. Unripe fruit it may be, but of a pleasant flavour and promise, and a mellower produce, it may be hoped, will follow."[9]

The *Athenaeum* thought the poem showed hope for the future ("fine things abound") and quoted two long passages.[10] But the rest of Fox's efforts to publicize his young friend's work did no good. Other periodicals ignored it—or gave it abrupt, abrasive dismissal such as the one in the *Literary Gazette* that described it as "somewhat mystical, somewhat poetical, somewhat sensual, and not a little unintelligible"[11] or the one in *Tait's Edinburgh Magazine*, which gave it only a phrase: "a piece of pure bewilderment."[12] Browning later declared that, to the best of his knowledge, not one copy was sold. Also later, he complained to Fox that the printing costs were paid to the publisher for a "stipulated" number of copies and "from that time to this I have been unable to ascertain whether a dozen have been disposed of or two dozen really printed—but *this* I *did* ascertain, from more quarters than one, that several well-disposed folks actually sought copies & found none—& that so exorbitant a price was affixed to a trifle of a few pages, as to keep it out of the hands of everybody but a critic."[13] Still later he reported to Elizabeth that he had a "whole bale" of the printed sheets of *Pauline* that had been returned to him by the publisher.[14]

But this was not the end of critical response to the poem. Fox had sent a copy to John Stuart Mill, asking him to review it. Mill's review, which he tried unsuccessfully to have printed in the *Examiner* and *Tait's*, has been lost, but his marked and annotated copy of *Pauline* has survived. He returned it to Fox, who sent it on to Browning for his edification. Mill's markings and his frequent marginal comments, "beautiful," along with his question marks and statements about obscurity indicate that he would have given it the "beauties and faults" treatment that was common in nineteenth-century reviews.[15]

But Browning's attention focused only on Mill's negative remarks or queries, and some of the replies he wrote in the margins of the book show that, like most new authors under such circumstances, he felt unjustly treated. He defended himself against Mill's objection to the use of "so" to mean "accordingly" by quoting ten passages from *Paradise Lost*; he countered Mill's failure to recognize three of his allusions to Greek tragedies by quoting the sources in Greek—in the *Agamemnon* and *Choephori* of Aeschylus and the *Ajax* of Sophocles. But what really must have stung him was the summarizing judgment that Mill wrote on the flyleaf at the end, apparently a draft of the conclusion that Mill wrote for his review. It is the kind of commonsense approach that one might expect from a reader who sees the speaker in the poem as a real person, not the Romantic persona that Browning had created in the Shelleyean mode. It begins, "With considerable poetic powers, the writer seems to me possessed with a more intense and morbid self-consciousness than I ever knew in any sane human being," a statement that Browning later quoted to Elizabeth in an ambiguous way, as if he were not certain whether to feel pride or shame in such an assessment. Pauline, Mill said, "is evidently a mere phantom." The speaker "neither loves her nor fancies he loves her, yet insists upon *talking* love to her. If she *existed* and loved him, he treats her most ungenerously and unfeelingly . . . then he *pays her off* toward the end by a piece of flummery, amounting to the modest request that she will love him and live with him and give herself up to him *without* his *loving her*. . . . I know not what to wish for him but that he may meet with a *real* Pauline."[16]

There is a long tradition among commentators on Browning's career that Mill's sharp strictures on *Pauline* as an autobiographical poem made Browning resolve, in William DeVane's words, that "henceforth his poetry would be 'dramatic in principle.'"[17] But as we have seen, his readiness to speak through dramatic characters was present as early as age fourteen, when he wrote "The First-Born of Egypt" and "The Dance of Death." Even his grand plan for a series of anonymous works was to call for a variety of dramatic voices.

In response to Mill's harsh words, however, Browning abandoned his multivolume project and further development of the *Alastor*-like poet in *Pauline*, of whom he said, "I had planned a very delicious and romantic life for him." The reviews, and Mill, changed his outlook: "Thereupon I got sick of my scheme, destroyed 'Pauline, Part 2,' and some other works written in pursuance of it, and set about a genuine work of my own."[18] That work eventually became another kind of dramatic poem composed by his Romantic predecessors—a poem in dramatic dialogue or a closet drama like Shelley's *Rosalind and Helen* and Byron's *Manfred*—but a form Browning attempted to treat in a new and different way.

&ct; &ct; &ct;

By the autumn of 1833, Browning had been studying at home and working intermittently at verse for four years, and his chosen career seemed to be going nowhere. One can imagine a growing restlessness in spite of his security in the midst of a loving family. Sarianna said of this time that his home life seemed to him confining and that he felt his social surroundings were narrow: "He chafed under them."[19] But in the winter of 1833–1834 a welcome change offered itself when he came to know, perhaps through one of his uncles, the Russian consul general, Chevalier George de Benkhausen, who invited him to be his secretary on a mission to St. Petersburg. We know almost nothing about this sudden widening of horizons, for even though Robert wrote diarylike letters home to his sister, he destroyed all of them toward the end of his life when he methodically burned his early letters to his family. Sarianna remembered a few details, and over the years Robert dropped occasional remarks about his experiences. With this little information to go on, it is possible to discern only the barest outline of his three-month sojourn.

On March 1, 1834, Browning departed from London to sail to Ostend. As he left, his mother gave him a Bible to take on his journey.[20] His passport describes him of "medium" height, with dark brown hair and eyebrows, gray eyes, "oval" face, and a round chin.[21] From Ostend the party traveled by carriage, drawn by six post-horses, day and night through Rotterdam, Castle Ravenstein, Cleves, and Aix-la-Chapelle across Germany and Poland to St. Petersburg. He reported impressions of their galloping through pine forests covered with snow. He suffered a series of bad headaches in Russia, whether from the cold weather or the pounding journey across northern Europe, we do not know. He recalled the spring thaw and break-up of the ice on the River Neva and the annual ceremony of the czar drinking the first glass of water from it.[22] With his quickness to acquire languages, Browning learned some Russian, including folk songs that he remembered all his life: he was still able to sing them for the Russian Prince Gagarin in Venice during his last years.[23]

He returned to London in June 1834 and seemed refreshed by his travels. He was soon at work on poems short and long, including a start on a narrative poem about the thirteenth-century troubador Sordello, which he broke off to write *Paracelsus*, a dramatic poem about the sixteenth-century physician and alchemist who is often called "the father of chemistry." This subject was suggested to him by Count Amédée de Ripert-Monclar, a young French Royalist who was temporarily on diplomatic duty in London. He had come to Camberwell with a letter of introduction from William Shergold Browning in Paris, and he and Robert soon became close friends.[24]

For information on Paracelsus, Browning drew principally upon his father's edition of Paracelsus' *Opera Omnia* (1658), edited by Frederick Bitiskius (and later—on December 29, 1835—given to him by his father).[25] W. Hall Griffin has pointed out that Browning's approach to the character of Paracelsus came from Bitiskius's preface, where he defended the physician's reputation from charges that he was a charlatan and praised him for his desire to know all the secrets of Nature, but Griffin also makes clear that Browning used very little of the five volumes aside from the preface. The preponderance of the material in the poem is Browning's own creation.[26]

So is his treatment of the poetic form. The preface of 1835, which Browning excluded from subsequent printings of the text, has as its subject the nature of the "Dramatic Poem" as written in his own day. Such a text is designed for reading, not for stage representation, and yet Browning expresses surprise that writers of dramatic poems retain in their texts the conventions of writing for the stage. "I do not very well understand," he says, "what is called a Dramatic Poem, wherein all those restrictions only submitted to on account of compensating good in the original scheme are scrupulously retained, as though for some special fitness in themselves—and all new facilities placed at an author's disposal by the vehicle he selects, as pertinaciously rejected." Browning was determined to make the most of those "new facilities," and in particular to make them serve a new dramatic purpose: the playing out of the inner life of his central character. He knew only too well how "stage representation" conventionally suggested "any phenomenon of the mind or the passions," which was by outward and visible means, "the operation of persons and events." His purpose was different: "I have ventured to display somewhat minutely the mood itself in its rise and progress." By "mood" he meant (as the Old English origin of the word indicates) "mind" in the sense of "intention." Browning uses dialogue to propel this inner action (unlike his procedure in *Pauline*), and the other characters, who are more sharply defined than the shadowy eponymous heroine of his earlier poem, serve to evoke the speeches which "display somewhat minutely the mood itself."

Browning's dramatic poem has five sections, but the poet pointedly calls them "parts" rather than "acts," and their titles—"Paracelsus Aspires,"

"Paracelsus Attains," "Paracelsus," "Paracelsus Aspires," "Paracelsus Attains"—indicate the shape of the dramatic action, the "rise and progress" of the "mood," though in a puzzling way which, as Browning says in his preface, requires the "co-operating fancy" of the reader if he or she is to grasp the shape and significance of the whole. Paracelsus aspires to know all—"the secret of the world, / Of man, and man's true purpose, path, and fate" (1.276–77)—and he fails in that "mood" or purpose. His struggle to understand that failure plays itself out in his responses to his loyal and caring friends, Festus and Michal, and especially in his responses to his counterpart, Aprile, whose desire to "LOVE infinitely" (2. 385) parallels Paracelsus' Faustian aspiration to "KNOW" (2. 384) and seems to supply something missing in Paracelsus' exclusively cognitive purpose, for by "love" Aprile means "the loveliness of life" (2. 485), beauty as embodied in the arts (sculpture, painting, oratory—including the oral delivery of poetry—and music), and his purpose is aesthetic and affective. He too has failed. His death, which Paracelsus misreads and which seems like the demise-without-discernible-cause of Shelley's Poet in *Alastor*, in fact points to part 5, where Paracelsus, himself dying, voices ideas which would become characteristic of Browning's thinking, and which Browning here sets out for the first time. Those ideas revolve around the pattern of aspiration and failure: what is the significance of human reaching up, of human desire for more than one can realize? Paracelsus gives an answer to that question in the best-known section of the poem, his last great speech in part 5, in which he describes development and progress as the governing pattern of all creation, human aspirations as evidence of that pattern, and the imperfect (etymologically the incomplete) as the promise of perfection. Browning would return to these ideas again and again, and would later insist, long after the 1859 publication of *Origin of Species*, that "all that seems *proved* in Darwin's scheme was a conception familiar to me from the beginning: see in *Paracelsus* the progressive development from senseless matter to organized, until man's appearance (*Part v.*)."[27] Though the poet was confusing two distinct and different ideas—evolution and progress—his pointing to that speech indicates its importance in his thinking. It is also the denouement of the inner action of this dramatic poem. The full shape of that action, of the sequence of five "parts," has been best summarized by F. E. L. Priestley: "true aspiration and ironic attainment followed by ironic or false aspiration and true attainment."[28] "True attainment" is the recognition of one's role in the governing pattern of all creation.   .

In *Paracelsus*, Browning felt that he had created something unique, "a sort of dramatic poem," he told W. J. Fox, "made after rules of my own, on a subject of my own, in a manner of my own, & I have put forth my whole strength, such as it is . . . I do think I have some right to ask people to listen this time."[29]

$$\text{do} \quad \text{do} \quad \text{do}$$

The young poet had begun to spend more time with Fox and his wards, the Flower sisters. As chance would have it, a friend of Eliza Flower, Catherine Bromley, kept a diary that affords a few remembrances of Browning during this period, although they are colored by Catherine's intense jealousy because of Browning's attentions to Eliza. Indeed it was Robert's attraction to Eliza that made his visits to the Fox household more frequent. As one of Catherine's relatives commented to her in a letter, "There is no doubt that Robert Browning fell under the sway of Miss Flower, the universal fascinator. It was not so much her beauty, as the thousand times more dangerous magnetism of her personality. No one could withstand her."[30] But he found himself in the midst of an unusual situation. Fox and his wife had separated, and when Fox left home to set up a new household at 5 Craven Hill in Bayswater, the angelic Eliza Flower appeared to be its domestic head, overseeing the care of Fox's daughter Elizabeth ("Tottie") and his deaf son, Florance. Although Fox declared that there were no grounds for scandal and that Eliza's position as his ward was unaltered, Mrs. Fox had begun whispering complaints to some of the members of the South Place Chapel, a campaign that brought about a call for Fox's resignation as the minister. As a consequence, a split developed in this Unitarian congregation, and when Fox refused to resign, about one third of the members withdrew. Old friends rallied to Fox's support, however, and continued to keep up social relations. Among them were Mary and Charles Cowden Clarke, Shakespearean popularizers who were neighbors; John Stuart Mill, whose close relations with Mrs. Harriet Taylor were causing troubles of their own; John Forster, lawyer and chief theatrical critic for the *Examiner*; William C. Macready, the actor-manager of Covent Garden Theater; Thomas Noon Talfourd, serjeant-at-law, poet, and playwright; Harriet Martineau, journalist and novelist; and Robert Browning.[31]

In his visits to the Fox household, Browning was exposed to all the progressive religious, political, and social ideas of the mid-nineteenth century. Although Fox had always been a social and political radical, he was now liberalizing his religious beliefs too. His sermons and writings reveal his critical questioning of the authority of the Bible and his growing acceptance of Universalism—that is, the disbelief in hell and damnation and the belief that God intends salvation for every human being. Over a decade he gradually secularized his pulpit.

Drawn to Fox and his liberal religious views, Browning often attended the services at the South Place Chapel,[32] and as his poems later reveal, he began to take on a religious optimism himself that led eventually as far as universalism. His social horizons broadened too. All around him in Fox's drawing room, he encountered zeal for the causes Fox espoused—anti-Corn-Law legislation, educational reform, women's rights, freedom of religious opinion, antislavery, and support for the working class.

The place was a cultural center where Fox and his guests conducted Shakespearean readings or discussed poetry. Fox was ready to talk about the books he was reviewing, works by Tennyson, Landor, Leigh Hunt, and Richard Hengist Horne. When Talfourd was in the group he was always eager to offer anecdotes about his old friends Lamb and Coleridge. Song was ever-present, too, from Eliza or from next-door-neighbor Clara Novello, who was soon to make her name in sacred oratorio.[33]

Browning also made his contributions to these gatherings. Catherine Bromley describes one occasion on which he recited, from memory, stanzas from an Italian poem that someone had mentioned. When Eliza brought forth a book that contained the poem, Robert proceeded to translate it fluently "into exquisite English."[34] On another occasion at tea, "he read some splendid scenes from Victor Hugo's 'Tribould' and 'Lucretia Borgia,'" translating as he went along.[35] In later years Catherine remembered how both she and Eliza were overwhelmed by Browning's genius: "To meet this plain-looking boy, to listen to his silvery voice, to marvel at his easy translations from many tongues, became to us both a recurring intellectual treat."[36] It was in Fox's sitting room one afternoon that Browning read *Paracelsus* aloud to Fox and discussed its ideas.

Once again he was turning to Fox ("my Chiron," he called him) for help with his literary projects. For the publication of *Paracelsus*, Fox's friend Charles Sturtevant wrote Browning a letter of introduction and sent him to John Murray, but without success. ("No go," as Browning told Sarah Flower.)[37] Fox then had him try Edward Moxon, but Moxon complained that poetry did not pay these days (look at Tennyson: "of 800 copies which were printed of his last, some 300 only have gone off"[38]). Not even Saunders and Otley, the publishers of *Pauline*, would touch it. Eventually, one of Fox's friends, the radical reformer Effingham Wilson, agreed to publish, but Robert's father had to bear the costs.[39]

When the book appeared in August 1835, reviewers were, on the whole, kind to it and continued to be so over the next couple of years. Browning was gratified to see his long-postponed ambitions fulfilled. He became recognized as a poet who had a career ahead of him. The response, however, was rather slow at the beginning. The first published notices were hasty judgments that appeared on the day of publication and the one in the *Athenaeum*, which he had eagerly awaited, was only a short squib that came out a week later. All of them were balanced in condemnation and grudging praise. The *Athenaeum*, for example, found "talent" in the poem but pronounced it "dreamy and obscure."[40] Eventually good luck arrived for the anxious author when a long review by John Forster appeared in the *Examiner* on September 6. This carefully developed critical assessment turned the tide of literary judgment in Browning's favor and pushed *Paracelsus* toward a critical success among readers who took poetry seriously. Forster's copy of the book shows that he had read it carefully. Marginal marks and underlinings are frequent, and toward the end, several of Paracelsus' speeches are both marked and underscored. Forster's only written judgment comes in a brief penciled remark at the conclusion, "a true poem."[41] Translated into a three-column review, this became a series of praises for "poetic genius" and "general intellectual power," plus quotations of long passages and the prediction of a "brilliant career."[42]

Then in November, Fox came through with a review-article in the *Monthly Repository* that summarized Browning's ideas in the poem about striving for knowledge, the necessity of love, and the divine plan for meliorism in developing the higher moral being of humanity.[43] Clearly both Forster and Fox were pleased to see a link between their time and the Romantic decades at the beginning of the century, and for them Browning's idealism forged it.

Forster's laudatory words had opened up literary interest in *Paracelsus*, and even though the big quarterlies ignored the poem, minor periodicals continued to give it favorable notice over the decade. For Victorians who were feeling inner turmoil about the increasing changes in their social and intellectual world, Browning's poem spoke to their need for spiritual assurance. And one must add with regret that for poets who wished to express uplift and to probe metaphysical questions in the language of poetry, it became a model—poets who were later derided as forming the "Spasmodic School of Poetry."

Browning Aspires to Be Shakespeare

William Charles Macready was an occasional guest at W. J. Fox's home at Craven Hill near Kensington Gardens. It was a peaceful place to spend an afternoon. The scent of roses and clematis and of flowering lime trees drifted into the house; in the distance, cattle grazed.[1] Since he was engaged in an effort to restore "the true Shakespeare" to the London stage, after the many adaptations and revisions the plays had undergone in the last century and a half, Macready enjoyed coming to a home where Shakespeare was loved. Sarah Flower, now married to Thomas Bridges Adams, a railway engineer, would organize play readings with family and friends in the Fox sitting room, where she could play Constance in *King John* or Portia in *The Merchant of Venice*, probably with the Cowden Clarkes as part of the cast. She herself was at work on the play that a few years later became *Viva Perpetua*, about the martyrdom of a Christian noblewoman in Carthage.

One evening in November 1835, after Macready had dined with Fox, Robert Browning dropped in. "I was very much pleased to meet him," Macready recorded in his diary. "His face is full of intelligence. My time passed most agreeably. . . . I took Mr. Browning on, and requested to be allowed to improve my acquaintance with him. He expressed himself warmly . . . wished to send me his book; we exchanged cards and parted."[2] Browning was ecstatic. Here was the greatest Shakespearean actor of his day desiring to know him. He soon sent a copy of *Paracelsus*, which Macready read and found to be "a work of great daring, starred with poetry of thought, feeling, and diction, but occasionally obscure: the writer can scarcely fail to be a leading spirit of his time."[3]

Here began an association that was central to Browning's career for the next eight years. Macready's diary reveals that he felt a genuinely warm regard for the young poet and a respect for his talent. For Browning, to have the friendship of this great tragic actor was an extraordinary privilege. But Macready was more than a man of the stage. He was a man of culture and taste who read widely in history and poetry as well as in plays and novels. His life was dedicated to reviving the plays of Elizabethan and Restoration dramatists, especially Shakespeare, in accurate texts and with appropriate costumes. No more would Macbeth appear before the witches in powdered wig and knee breeches, as Garrick portrayed him. Moreover, Macready was a dignified and gracious man, a good host, a friend of writers, painters, and singers. But he was also a man of strong feelings and an explosive temper, characteristics that would eventually bring him into clashes with Browning, who in spite of his amiability could be stubborn-minded and egoistic.

In December of that year, Macready invited Browning to a New Year's Eve party at Elm Place in the village of Elstree, his country home. While changing coaches at a pub called The Blue Posts on the way, Browning by chance met John Forster, who was also bound for Macready's party. Upon learning Browning's name, this stockily built stranger with a somewhat loud voice inquired, "Did you see a little notice of you I wrote in the *Examiner*?"[4]

Browning and Forster, almost exactly the same age, would become life-long friends in a close but touchy relationship marked by several quarrels. Forster was an attorney who had turned his back on the law to engage in literary pursuits. He had made himself a protégé of Leigh Hunt and Charles Lamb and, through them, gained access to London's literary periodicals. Although he had once published a book of verse, his time was now largely occupied with literary journalism, and his present post was that of theatrical critic for the *Examiner*, a literary weekly for which he wrote reviews of plays and books of poetry. Since Forster had thrust his way into the literary world through the patronage of older, more established figures, he now seemed to wish to reverse this pattern and to combine patronage with friendship in his association with Browning even though he was only one month older than he. He began immediately to promote Browning's career.[5] Macready's diary indicates that Forster's treatment of Browning as if he were a protégé was under way a month after their first meeting: "Forster was talking much of Browning who is his present *all-in-all*."[6] From this point on, the aspiring young dramatist and the pushy young critic are to be found in tandem throughout Browning's attempt to write for the stage.

The New Year's Eve invitation from Macready led to more than Browning's friendship with Forster. It set in motion a series of ripples that carried him into the whirl of theatrical and literary acquaintance. Very soon he came to know Dickens and often attended the theater, rehearsals, or readings where he was present. The list of new friends is long: Edward Bulwer, the novelist whose *Eugene Aram* was currently popular and who was soon to have his play *The Lady of Lyons* produced by Macready; Thomas Noon Talfourd, the successful barrister usually known as Serjeant Talfourd, who was the friend and biographer of Charles Lamb and the author of *Ion*, a verse tragedy that Macready was about to stage; Bryan Procter, poet and play-wright who published under the name "Barry Cornwall" and who was to become one of Browning's closest friends; Walter Savage Landor, the epic poet and satirist, author of the brilliant series *Imaginary Conversations*; Mary Russell Mitford, the poet and dramatist, now best known for her sequence of stories *Our Village*, who was a close friend of Elizabeth Barrett; Henry Chorley, literary and music critic for the influential cultural review the *Athenaeum*; Richard Hengist Horne, poet and man of letters, whose epic poem *Orion* was priced at one farthing in order to bring it into the hands of ordinary people (only one copy was allowed for each purchaser); Harrison Ainsworth, author of the "Newgate" novels about famous criminals, *Rook-wood* and *Jack Sheppard*; Alexander Dyce, scholar of the Elizabethan drama, especially Shakespeare; Richard Monckton Milnes, Member of Parliament, poet, wit, and dilettante of letters; the painters Edwin Landseer, whose land-scapes—especially those involving animals—were widely popular, and Daniel Maclise, whose picture "The Serenade" stimulated Browning's imag-ination and inspired him to compose "In a Gondola."

Browning's presence at the New Year's Eve celebration was a sample of the social impression that he made in the midst of literary gatherings. As Macready recorded it, "Mr. Browning was very popular with the whole party; his simple and enthusiastic manner engaged attention and won opin-ions from all present; he looks and speaks more like a youthful poet than any man I ever saw."[7] Robert had moved into a new and dazzling world far beyond Camberwell and Limehouse.

The most memorable of such occasions for Browning took place the fol-lowing May at the supper that was held to celebrate the first-night success of Talfourd's *Ion*, a tragedy about a Greek youth who sets out to kill a tyrant whose fatal destruction has been prophesied. When the king is slain by someone else, the youth discovers that the king was his father and that the hereditary curse has now descended upon him. After cutting and revising Talfourd's published text, Macready put it on the stage, acting the leading role to great applause. On May 26, 1836, Talfourd invited about sixty notables of the literary world to a supper at his elegant townhouse on Russell Square.

Browning found himself seated opposite Macready, who sat between Wordsworth and Landor. During an evening of many toasts, Talfourd at one point proposed one to "the Poets of England," and after a tribute to Wordsworth and Landor, directed his words to Browning, "the author of *Paracelsus*," as the youngest of the poets. Flattered, Browning rose and replied "with grace and modesty" and, according to Miss Mitford, the twenty-four-year-old poet "looked still younger than he was."[8] When Browning was leaving the party, Macready stopped him to say, "Write a play, Browning, and keep me from going to America."[9] Two days later, Browning wrote to praise Macready's contributions to the English theater and promised to give his "whole heart & soul to the writing a Tragedy" as soon as he completed another project. He pledged to put the play into Macready's hands by November 1, 1836.[10]

Macready had previously turned down a proposal from Browning (supported by Forster) to write a verse play about Narses, a sixth-century Roman general, the victor in the battle of Capua. But he was pleased with the young man's enterprise and recorded in his diary his hopes that he awakened in Browning "a spirit of poetry whose influence would elevate, ennoble, and adorn our degraded drama."[11] By the following August, Macready was enthusiastic about Forster's report that Browning was planning a tragedy about the Earl of Strafford, the chief counselor of Charles I, who had been impeached by Parliament and executed for treason under a bill of attainder signed by the ungrateful king.[12] Since Browning had been helping Forster to write a short biography of Strafford in the "Statesmen of the Commonwealth" series, it is probable that Forster had a hand in choosing the subject for the tragedy. In any case, Macready's response to this historical subject encouraged and excited Browning: perhaps he would achieve the renown that had come to Talfourd for *Ion*.

Browning was unable to meet the deadline he had set for himself of November 1, but, urged on and encouraged by Forster, he was able to give Macready the first three acts plus a summary of the remainder by November 20. Macready was "greatly pleased" by what he hastily read, and when he gave his tentative approval along with some suggestions for change, Browning was gratified—"agreeing in my objections," wrote Macready, "and promising to do everything needful."[13] But when Macready sat down to read the play "*very attentively*," he had misgivings: "I find more grounds for exception than I had anticipated. I had been too much carried away by the truth of character to observe the meanness of plot, and occasional obscurity."[14]

Macready's seesawing back and forth between satisfaction and worry about the success of *Strafford* for the stage was to continue over the next year.

Browning completed the play and conscientiously worked over the material to satisfy Macready's criticisms. By March 1837 he thought he had cleared up all the problems. When the still doubtful Macready read it to Osbaldiston, the manager of Covent Garden Theater, where Macready was now under contract, Osbaldiston "caught at it with avidity." He agreed to produce it "without delay on his part, and to give the author £12 per night for twenty-five nights, and £10 per night for ten nights beyond."[15] This would mean a considerable sum for Browning, a final vindication of his father's faith in his son's genius. Meanwhile, the ever-aggressive Forster had arranged for Longman's to publish *Strafford*. When Browning asked permission of Macready to dedicate the printed version of the play to him, Macready replied graciously that he would be honored.

Yet all was not well in the progress of *Strafford* toward performance. The events of the next month show, in the interchanges and difficulties that Browning had with Macready, how unsuited he was to be a dramatist writing for the stage. The successful playwright is a member of a team. He must work with and listen to directors, actors, and stage technicians and adapt his script to their needs. Browning was unable creatively to provide the modifications that Macready called for and unable temperamentally to be as cooperative as a real professional must be.

On April 2, after an outstanding performance of *Richard III*, Browning and Forster came with friends to Macready's dressing room to offer congratulations. After the others left, Macready called for two bottles of champagne and the three of them went through the script of *Strafford* critically. Browning took notes on the alterations that were still needed. But Macready, sensing some unwillingness in Browning to make the necessary changes, called for Forster two days later, and in Browning's absence "we went over the play of *Strafford*, altered, omitted, and made up one new scene."[16] They worked from 11:00 A.M. until 4:00 P.M. but found that they still required the hand of the author.

When Browning turned up on April 7, the passages he had promised to supply were, in Macready's judgment, "very feebly written."[17] Browning did not really want to make changes in his play. When he saw the cuts and revisions that Macready had made, he was dismayed by the way his play was being taken over by others and deeply offended by Forster's arrogance in presuming to act as his surrogate.

In this unpleasant atmosphere, *Strafford* moved toward production. During the next week, Macready and Forster worked through the play twice, and Forster was supposed to convince Browning of the absolute necessity for revision. The result was a quarrelsome scene, with Forster in his bullying manner showing a good deal more ill temper than the aggrieved author, who was angry about the collusion of Macready and Forster against him. Right from the beginning of their relationship, Forster had taken a patronizing attitude toward Browning as if he, the successful theatrical expert, were helping to mold Browning's career,[18] and by now he had come to feel some proprietary rights about the play he had cheered Browning on to write. Macready tried to mediate between the two men: "There were mutual complaints—much temper—sullenness, I should say, on the part of Forster, who was very much out of humour with Browning, who said and did all that man could do to expiate any offence he might have given."[19] At length, Browning agreed to revise and rewrite, even to supply a trial scene that seemed to his advisors to be necessary.

On April 14, they all met at Forster's sumptuous chambers. But Browning, who was losing heart, brought to the meeting only "some scraps of paper with hints and unconnected lines—the full amount of his labour upon the alterations agreed on."[20] The three men went over the play again. Browning departed with discouraged spirit to try once more. Later that night he returned to Macready and expressed his wish to withdraw the play. Macready was torn between his own adverse judgment on the possible success of *Strafford* and his desire to see Browning's labors on the play come to some sort of fruition. Forster, having come this far with Browning's play, was loathe to see his brainchild aborted. The three argued "the pros and cons" of production. Finally, Macready agreed to produce the play in its present state.[21]

Rehearsals went forward. Browning was appalled at the ignorance of the actors, who thought the word *impeachment* meant "poaching,"[22] but he was heartened by Macready's acting in the title role at the final rehearsal. He had seen, he told Macready, "his utmost hopes of character perfectly embodied."[23] Forster was certain the play would be a success, and Mr. Dow, a close friend of Macready and Forster, was planning a party to celebrate after the performance. Browning was confident enough now, despite some pretended predictions of disaster to friends. On opening night, he brought his father backstage to shake hands with Macready. He also had supporters in the audience for the first night. The Colloquials were to be "clacquers" for him.[24]

The play in the form that Browning published it before its performance is a dramatic failure for a number of reasons. For one thing, its historical complexity is bewildering. The English audience could be expected to be familiar with many aspects of the Civil War, such as the conflicts between King Charles and Parliament over ship money or the inflexibility of Archbishop Laud in his attempts to impose the canons and rituals of the Church of England upon Scotland. The audience was familiar, too, with such historical figures as Pym and Hampden, and with the main dramatic action, the king's betrayal of his loyal counselor and military leader, Strafford. But ordinary theatergoers could not be expected to be knowledgeable about all the details of the historical situation or the identity of obscure political figures such as Rudyard, Saville, Fiennes, and Holland. As the early acts of Browning's play drag through long stretches of historical exposition, the basic conflicts between the king and parliamentary leaders are clogged with details and with oblique references that are not made dramatically clear. In addition, the many minor characters who come and go are not sufficiently distinctive. As Macready said when he first read through the work, the play "I fear is too historical."[25] Browning as playwright lacked an understanding of what an audience could absorb.

Further, the dialogue itself hindered comprehension. The characters keep interrupting one another and themselves, with the result that in the first half of the play too much of the dialogue sputters forth in abrupt fragments of speech and unfinished thoughts. (One of the reviewers compared it to the staccato outbursts of Alfred Jingle in Dickens's *Pickwick Papers*.)[26] In addition, the main causes of the action are sometimes introduced suddenly and without explanation, such as the evidence that leads to Strafford's arrest. It is not surprising that Macready in his diary entries complained of "the want of connection in the scenes of Browning's play."[27]

The alterations that Macready carried out while the script was in progress must have resolved some of these problems. In later life, Browning recalled that about one-third of his material had been deleted for stage production.[28] It is also true that good actors can help enormously to convey meaning to an audience. This is probably what Macready had in mind when he jotted in his diary during rehearsals that *Strafford* "might *pass muster*—not more—if it were equally and respectably acted" and hoped the acting would "carry it to the end without disapprobation."[29]

Strafford opened on May 1, 1837, before a huge, restless audience. The poet William Bell Scott has left an account of his own attempt to help it succeed:

> My admiration for "Paracelsus" was so great I determined to go [to the performance of *Strafford*] and applaud without rhyme or reason; and so I did, in front of the pit. From the first scene it became plain that applause was not the order. The speakers had every one of them orations to deliver, and no action of any kind to perform. The scene changed, another door opened, and another half-dozen gentlemen entered as long-winded as the last. Still, I kept applauding with some few others, till the howling was too overpowering and the disturbance so consider-

able that for a few minutes I lost my hat. The truth was that the talk was too much the same and too much in quantity; it was no use continuing to hope something would turn up to surprise the house.[30]

Yet so great was the commanding presence of Macready as an actor that when he took the stage in scene 2, the play began to pick up, and he dominated the performance for the remainder of the evening. As a consequence—and to Macready's surprise—the production was a success, and some of the reviewers were generous. The critic from the *Morning Chronicle*, for example, had read the play in its published form and was disappointed because of Browning's lack of dramatic power, yet he changed his mind during the performance: "We entered the theatre with this unfavourable impression, but as the play proceeded it wore gradually away, and when the curtain fell we were convinced that we had done the author injustice." He remarked on the avoiding of "those sparkling poetic passages which may charm in the closet, but which fall monotonously upon the ear when drawled forth by a second-rate actor"—perhaps a reference to Macready's cuts—and he praised Macready's performance as "noble and touching." He singled out act 5, where Strafford, then a prisoner in the Tower and awaiting execution, hears his children singing, as "a triumph of histrionic art," "only equalled, but not surpassed, by the final scene with the vacillating and unworthy *Charles*."[31]

Since the first performance was a benefit night for Macready, he had many loyal followers who were on hand to supply the applause at the close of each act and at the final curtain when he was "called for." In truth, the energy and dignity of Macready as Strafford and the tenderness of Helen Faucit, a new actress at the beginning of a brilliant career, as the Countess of Carlisle, carried the play. The rest of the principals were very poor, especially Mr. Dale, who was rather deaf, as King Charles. If we can believe Forster, who genuinely hoped for a triumph, Dale was so bad that "some one should have stepped out of the pit and thrust Mr. Dale from the stage."[32]

The play ran for five performances and might have continued further. A review in the *Morning Herald* after the second performance gave the opinion that "*Strafford* is *by far* the best tragedy that has been produced on this, or any other of our great theatres, for many years."[33] But the play closed because Mr. Vanderhoff, who played Pym, withdrew from the cast to accept another engagement. By this time, Macready felt he had done his duty by Browning for the play he had commissioned. He did not find a replacement for Vanderhoff. Nor did he ever revive *Strafford*. He thought that he had borne enough when on May 22 he received a letter from Browning proposing to add a speech in act 2 and to restore an entire scene in act 4. His diary entry shows his exasperation:"Such a selfish, absurd, and useless imposition to lay on me could scarcely have entered into anyone's imagination." "I was surprised and annoyed; as if I had done nothing for him." But the wave of chagrin passed. He realized that the novice playwright "did not know what he required me to do . . . 'so let him pass, a blessing on his head!'"[34]

Browning himself felt ill-used. He was upset at his friend Forster for writing an honest review rather than a laudatory one. Most of all, he carried a heavy grievance about all the haggling with Macready and Forster over the script. He told Eliza Flower that he was "annoyed at the go of things behind the scenes"[35] and declared that he would never write a play again. Browning did not disown the play, but he seemed somewhat ashamed of it. He did not reprint it in his *Collected Works* of 1849, although he finally and reluctantly included it in the edition of 1863. Even so, the creative energy that he expended on *Strafford* was not entirely wasted. The five performances brought him £60, the first money that he had ever earned through his writing. More important, he was discovering, painfully, whether or not the demands of writing for the stage could be reconciled with his interests as a dramatic poet.

Chapter 7

A Literary Disaster

Since the renewal of his visits to the W. J. Fox household, Browning had declined in Eliza Flower's favor. She thought the grown-up Robert less attractive than the youngster she had known. She found him too full of self-esteem, now that he had achieved some recognition, as well as too intellectual, saying in a letter to Catherine Bromley, "If he had not got the habit of talking of head and heart as two independent existences, one would say he was born without a heart."[1] Perhaps it was common knowledge that Browning had her in mind as Pauline,[2] and she was shying away from any acknowledgment of this. In any case, she was now the mistress of Fox's domain, much more out of Browning's reach than ever. In 1834 he had composed a sonnet that seems more of a personal expression of his feeling about Eliza Flower than anything in *Pauline*:

> Eyes, calm beside thee, (Lady couldst thou know!)
>   May turn away thick with fast-gathering tears:
> I glance not where all gaze: thrilling and low
>   Their passionate praises reach thee—my cheek wears
> Alone no wonder when thou passest by;
> Thy tremulous lids bent and suffused reply
> To the irrepressible homage which doth glow
>   On every lip but mine: if in thine ears
> Their accents linger—and thou dost recall
>   Me as I stood, still, guarded, very pale,
> Beside each votarist whose lighted brow
> Wore worship like an aureole, "O'er them all

My beauty," thou wilt murmur, "did prevail
Save that one only":—Lady couldst thou know!

It was the first poem that he sent to Fox for publication in the *Monthly Repository*.[3] Did he place this chivalric declaration there for her, especially, to see?

But Browning had met another fascinating young woman in his visits to Macready's house in Elstree. She was Euphrasia Fanny Haworth, a versifier as well as a painter and a neighbor of Macready's who lived in the manor house at Bartram Lodge. Like Eliza Flower, she was about a decade older than Robert.[4] She became the recipient of some of the earliest letters of Browning that have survived, letters that were mannered and allusive in Browning's characteristic epistolary style when he wanted either to be playful or to impress someone with learned nonchalance. In 1836 she published two "Sonnets to the author of *Paracelsus*" in the *New Monthly Magazine*, the first poetic tributes ever addressed to him.[5] Fanny Haworth provided an attraction for Browning that was not dimmed until Elizabeth Barrett came into his life, after which time she became a firm friend of both poets.

Because of the chance survival of some travel notes and also a letter to Miss Haworth, we know the details of Browning's itinerary when he traveled to Italy in 1838 to gather some authentic detail for his next project, a poem about the thirteenth-century poet Sordello. We do not know how this journey came about. Perhaps a ship's passage was arranged through one of his uncles' commercial connections. In any case, he sailed on April 13, as the only passenger aboard a merchant vessel, the *Norham Castle*, bound for Trieste. Sarianna's memory of Robert's letters, which are no longer extant, tells us that he spent two weeks below deck prostrate with seasickness. Captain Davidson helped him up on deck to view the passage through the Strait of Gibraltar, but he improved when the ship passed into the calmer waters of the Mediterranean Sea.[6]

One morning, off the Algerian coast, they sighted a wreck that turned out to be a capsized smuggler, a victim of corsairs. Six dead bodies were aboard and a partial cargo of cloth, tobacco, and cigars. After the crew of the *Norham Castle* had heaved the dead bodies overboard, they looted the ship of cigars. Robert, with his more romantic tastes, preferred to take two cutlasses and a dagger—in spite of the macabre sight of mutilated bodies.[7]

The ship arrived at Trieste after a six-week voyage, and Browning boarded a ferry for Venice because the purpose of his voyage was to explore Italian sites and settings to enrich *Sordello*, the poem he had been working on. He had begun composition even before *Paracelsus*, but interruptions and digressions had postponed his progress until now. The hero of his poem, Sordello, a Provençal troubador, lover, and soldier, had been active in the conflicts between the Guelfs and the Ghibellines in northern Italy. Browning had hoped to complete the poem while on the ground that Sordello had trod, but, as he told Fanny Haworth, he wrote only four lines during his travels, two of them addressed to her as his English "Eyebright" (his translation of her first name, Euphrasia; the lines are 967–68 in book 3 of the completed poem). Instead of composing couplets, he absorbed Italy.

First, he spent two weeks in Venice, staying near the Piazza San Marco at the Casa Stefani, Calle Giacomuzzi, S. Moise 1139.[8] During this time the incident which he records at the end of book 3 of *Sordello* took place: he breaks off his story, muses "on a ruined palace-step / At Venice" (3. 676–77), and catches sight of a peasant girl who approaches and begs him for money. "Into one face / The many faces crowd" (3. 754–55), and he sees in her the spirit of all suffering humanity—and his inspiration for the poem. The chance meeting leads to his theorizing on the nature, purpose, and effect of poetry in the last four hundred lines of book 3, and hence was an important milestone in Browning's development as a poet.

From Venice he began a walking tour north, along a route dotted with Palladian villas, to Treviso,[9] "the Venice of the North," with its canals and frescoed casas; thence to the walled and moated stronghold of Castelfranco; and on to the town of Bassano with its ancient covered bridge over the rushing river Brenta and its fine view of Mount Grappa. From here he was diverted up to the mountain town of Asolo, one of the most charming spots in the most picturesque country in the world. He stayed four days in its peaceful arcaded streets and drew inspiration that later led him to set *Pippa Passes* there.

He wandered around the region—to Possagno (where he watched an old woman light a candle for divine protection when the thunder rolled, put it out when it stopped, relight it with each thunder clap);[10] to San Zeno, where he talked with a priest who had seen the Ghibelline warrior Alberic's skeleton unearthed from a barrow only five years back;[11] then a return to the quiet beauty of Asolo in June.

No longer on foot, he headed south to Vicenza, the home of Palladio and the center for many buildings he had designed. Here Browning bought a guide book, dated it "June 24, 1838,"[12] and used it for his visits to the secular "basilica" in the Piazza dei Signori, the clock tower, the Olympic Theater, the cathedral, and to identify the many art works that he viewed. He went next down to Padua, where he could marvel at Giotto's frescos in the Scrovegni Chapel. Unable to leave the region quite yet, he returned to Venice once more to linger under its spell. Sarianna declared that she was certain he visited Mantua and perhaps Goito, but Browning made no mention of them in his travel notes or his letter to Fanny Haworth.

Traveling by stagecoach, he headed west to Verona, the rose-ochre city caught in its loop of the river Adige, where amid other sights Browning saw his first major monument dating back to ancient Rome, the amphitheater, one of the largest in the Roman world. He now turned north to leave Italy, passing by Trent on through the Brenner Pass to Innsbruck in the Austrian Tyrol. By July he was as far north as Munich. He then took a jog in his course over to Salzburg, headed back west to Frankfurt, and finally reached Mainz on the Rhine. He now had the lazy luxury of a Rhine journey as far as Cologne, floating past memorable castles. At this point he turned west for a visit to Charlemagne's capital, Aix-la-Chapelle. From there, he traveled through Liège and eventually up to the busy port of Antwerp, where he caught a vessel home and arrived in mid-July.

He had experienced a small lifetime of wonders in three months. Although he had set out to gather material for the completion of *Sordello*, his plans to write were overwhelmed by his daily impressions of foreign cultures, especially the glories of Renaissance Italy. This journey through Italy, Austria, Germany, and the Low Countries was the beginning of a career that made him, eventually, the most international of the English writers of the Victorian era.

&ð &ð &ð

Robert Browning was brimming with life on his return from Europe. Fox's daughter Elizabeth ("Tottie"), who was then a young girl, has merged two memories of him, in May and July of this year, into a description of one day when he came to call while she was practising her drawing:

> Mr. Browning entered the little drawing-room, with a quick light step; and on hearing from me that my father was out, . . . he said: "It's my birthday today; I'll wait till they come in," and sitting down to the piano, he added: "If it won't disturb you, I'll play till they do." . . . He was then slim and dark, and very handsome; and—may I hint it—just a trifle of a dandy, addicted to lemon-coloured kid gloves and such things: quite the "glass of fashion and the mould of form." But full of ambition, eager for success, eager for fame and what's more determined to conquer fame and to achieve success.[13]

Browning had many stories with which to dazzle the Colloquials. But one of the new members, Alfred Domett, was even more traveled than he. Not only had Domett been to Italy and the Tyrol, but he had also traveled across Canada and the United States. Domett, a young lawyer who had left St. John's College, Cambridge, without taking his degree, lived in Camberwell, although Browning did not know him until about this time. He was a remote cousin of Chris Dowson who became more closely connected when his sister Mary became Chris's wife. One of Domett's earliest friends in Camberwell was Joseph Arnould, a lawyer and graduate of Wadham College, Oxford, with whom he briefly shared chambers and whom he now drew into the circle of the Colloquials. Both men were serious poets. Domett had issued a pamphlet entitled *Poems* in 1833, and his long poem *Venice* would be published in 1839. Arnould had won the Newdigate Prize at Oxford with his poem "The Hospice of St. Bernard." Browning's new friends encouraged him in his early trials of poetry and offered useful criticism of his work. Within the Colloquials, Chris and Joe Dowson, Captain Pritchard, Alfred Domett, Joseph Arnould, and Robert Browning formed a close association that Chris referred to as "our set."[14]

Alfred Domett appears to have become Browning's closest friend during the years 1840 to 1842, at which point Domett emigrated from England to New Zealand, England's newly annexed colony in the empire, going out with the settlers of the New Zealand Company to Nelson.[15] Browning maintained a continuing correspondence with him until the time of his own marriage to Elizabeth in 1846. Because of these circumstances, the letters to Domett provide the most intimate picture of Browning, his interests and aspirations, that we have of his earlier years. Browning's letters always contained the latest literary news from London colored by his own views of what was being published by Tennyson, Carlyle, Dickens, Bulwer, Macaulay, Patmore, "Miss Barrett," and others. More than this, he revealed to Domett his responses to the reviews he received as he continued to publish and showed a humble acceptance of Domett's criticism and advice about his own work. His first note to Domett, however, was a brief one, dated "St. Perpetua's Day" (March 7) in 1840, presenting him with a copy of his latest publication.[16]

ॐ ॐ ॐ

Robert Browning's third long poem, *Sordello*, was a major effort, one that he hoped would establish him as more than a "promising young poet" among his contemporaries. Epic in scope, it is the story of poetic genius surrounded by the grandeur of historical event; its subject is the conjunction of poetry, society, and politics; and its materials are the conventional materials of romance, if romance be understood in its most basic literary sense, as a tale of adventures in love and war: the hero, conventionally "Knight, Bard, Gallant" (6: 828) is (supposedly) an orphan with extraordinary powers as a poet and troubadour; Palma, his love interest, is torn between him and an aristocrat; Sordello attempts to bring his art to bear on society and politics; and he turns out to be the son of the leader of one of the warring factions, the revelation of his paternity being the climax of the story. Such materials explain why Browning's earliest recorded reference to the poem, in a letter to Fox in April 1835, is to "another affair on hand, rather of a more popular nature."[17] Readers familiar with the popular romances of Scott and Byron, for instance, would expect the story to be the main interest and the rapidity of the narrative to be the chief claim on their attention, like the "flying story" with which Sordello defeats his rival Eglamor: "the lay could barely keep / Pace with the action visibly rushing past" (2: 86–87). Browning establishes such conventions only to reject them: Sordello says in book 5 that "my art intends / New structure from the ancient" (5: 642–43), and certainly that is his creator's purpose as well. He subordinates the story to an exploration of Sordello's inner life, and in so doing he brings the conventional rapidity of the external action to a near standstill. Readers may be forgiven for having some sympathy with Naddo, whose criticism of Sordello could be applied to his creator as well:

> "the man can't stoop
> To sing us out," quoth he, "a mere romance;
> He'd fain do better than the best, enhance
> The subjects' rarity, work problems out
> Therewith." (2: 784–88)

The "problems" include the questions (as in *Paracelsus*) of what to make of Sordello's aspirations and failures, of how to judge the decisions he comes to, of how to understand and interpret the shifts and changes in his thinking and emotions. When in 1863 Browning defined the "problems" more explicitly in a new preface he wrote for the poem, he referred to them as "incidents in the development of a soul," and he dismissed the history as "decoration" and "of no more importance than a background requires." The soul, in his view, does grow—that is the purpose of its life on earth—and it does so when the mind assesses its situation, makes choices of which it cannot know the outcome, and proceeds until failure or adversity makes necessary more choices. And although Browning the narrator promises in the early lines of the poem (1: 25–31) to comment and explain, to be the reader's guide through the difficulties of the story (the conventional role of the speaker in narrative poetry), he also expects (as he had in *Paracelsus*) the "co-operating fancy" of the reader to make sense of the poem, which he designs as a do-it-yourself kit rather than a fully finished consumer product. At the end of book 3 Browning says that his purpose is to be a "Maker-see" (3: 928) rather than a tell-all; and in the middle of book 2 he says of Sordello's language that its audience must "clutch / And reconstruct" while "his office [is] to diffuse, / Destroy" (2: 598–600). Browning shared that view of poetic language, and his chief instrument in fulfilling his "office" of "Maker-see" is his verse form, the heroic couplet.

Browning well knew that rhyming iambic pentameter lines had been considered especially appropriate for narrative poems, largely because of Pope's use of them in his translations of Homer, where the form was praised as clear, vigorous, flexible, and rapid in movement. Browning deliberately set out to counter those (by now) conventional effects of the couplet and to deconstruct it so radically that readers would have to struggle just to be aware of the repeated sounds among the bewildering syntax of phrase piled upon phrase, clause upon clause, parenthesis interrupted by parenthesis, and pronoun references with uncertain antecedents in sentences so long that readers have to go back through them again and again to sort them out. Even the rhythm of his syntax works against the rhyme. His lines are usually enjambed rather than end-stopped; the rhyme word is frequently one not naturally stressed or sometimes one less important semantically. Closure is the conventional effect of the reader's experience of the repeated rhyme; Browning frustrates that expectation and makes his reader's experience open-ended and tentative. He was asking a great deal of his readers, and for nearly all of them it was too much. *Sordello* became the most notoriously obscure poem of the nineteenth century.

When *Sordello* was published by Edward Moxon in 1840 (subsidized once again by the ever-generous Robert Browning, Senior) reviewers were bewildered by it. Some attempted large parts of it but could not finish it; others read no more than a few pages and then dismissed it in anger or scorn; a few studied it carefully but still were dazed or discouraged by its forbidding style. Browning must have been devastated by its reception. Here is a representative sample of English literary opinion. The *Spectator* for March 14, 1840, complains, "What this poem may be in its extent we are unable to say, for we *cannot* read it . . . it is so overlaid . . . by digression, affectation, obscurity. . . ."[18] The *Atlas* for March 28 recorded disappointment after the promise of *Paracelsus*: "The whole structure is faulty, not only in its entire outline, but in its minutest details." Then, after quoting a long passage, the reviewer comments, "Here we have the same pitching, hysterical, and broken sobs of sentences—the same excisions of words—the same *indications* of power—imperfect grouping of thoughts and images—and hurried, exclamatory, and obscure utterance of things that would, probably, be very fine if we could get them in their full meaning, but which, in this bubbling and tumult of the verse, are hardly intelligible. . . ."[19] The reviewer for the *Athenaeum* took time to try to accustom himself to the style and did not write until May 30, but he finally reported, regretfully, "The song of the bard falls dull and muffled on the ear, as from a fog; and if, at times, a breath of purer inspiration sweeps off the vapours, letting his voice come articulately to the understanding, it is but for a moment."[20]

Anecdotes abound about the reaction of some of Browning's literary friends and well-wishers to the syntactic puzzles and the bombardment of historical references. Harriet Martineau gave up her attempt to read it: "I was so wholly unable to understand it that I supposed myself ill."[21] Douglas Jerrold, who tried to read it when he was convalescing from an illness, thought he had lost his mind.[22] Tennyson declared, "There were only two lines in it that I understood, and they were both lies; they were '*Who will may hear Sordello's story told*' and '*Who would has heard Sordello's story told!*'" (the opening and closing lines of the poem).[23] Jane Carlyle read through the work "without being able to make out whether 'Sordello' was a man, or a city, or a book."[24] Thomas Carlyle himself was kinder to his young friend. Commenting on both *Pippa Passes* and *Sordello*, he said, "You seem to possess a rare spiritual gift, poetical, pictorial, intellectual," but he added a wish "that your next work were written in prose."[25]

However crushed Robert must have felt by the judgments rendered on his poem, he kept up a good front. When Alfred Domett gave him back the presentation copy with questions written in the margins ("Who?" or "Whose?" or "Who says this?"),[26] Browning returned it to him with answers and revisions, which he incorporated into later editions. He was grateful to Fanny Haworth for some kind words about *Sordello*, even though she asked him to explain the passage he had addressed to her as "my English Eyebright." He reflected cheerfully on the critical abuse he had received: "You say roses and lilies and lilac-bunches and lemon-flowers about it while every body else pelts cabbage stump after potato-paring"—everyone save Carlyle, he added.[27]

More interesting in his letter to Miss Haworth is his drawing attention to the importance of the incident in Venice that brought him back to finishing his poem: "The sad disheveled form . . . that plucked and pointed, wherein I put, comprize, typify and figure to myself Mankind, the whole poor-devildom one sees cuffed and huffed from morn to midnight, that, so typi-

fied, she may come at times and keep my pact in mind, prick up my republi-
canism, . . . renewed me, gave me fresh spirit, made me after finishing Book
3d. commence Book 4th. . . ."[28] Moreover, he also gives a defense of his style:
he was not addressing the "miscellaneous public," as described by his friend
R. H. Horne, who "take up a poem by way of a little *relaxation*."[29] He revealed
to Miss Haworth that he did not like to explain his lines and gave an example of an editor, a certain "Watson," who translated Horace and filled in all
the ellipses and spelled out all the references in this ridiculous fashion: "O
Maecenas, descended from Kings (*Tuscan, that is Etrurian*) your Ancestors,
(*O You who have proved yourself to be*) both my patron (*since you kindly reconciled
me with Augustus*) and a sweet honor to me (*by your Quality and politeness to
poor me whose father was nothing but a Freedman*) &c. &c. &[c]."[30]

Fanny Haworth may not have been enlightened by his explanation.

&ð &ð &ð

No one reads *Sordello* now except for a few scholars, especially textual
scholars whose forced association with the text has made them like Byron's
prisoner of Chillon: "My very chains and I grew friends." John Pettigrew
referred to *Sordello* as "that superb disaster of a poem"[31] and Morse Peckham
called it "Browning's *Finnegan's Wake*."[32] Critics often use it, however, as a
document that can provide oblique evidence of Browning's own notions
about language, creativity, the soul and the unconscious, or his Platonic concepts of beauty, or his debt to the Romantic poets.[33] Indeed, even with its
vagaries, it serves those purposes well.

Yet one twentieth-century figure who refused to cast *Sordello* on the literary scrap heap was Ezra Pound, who was always interested in out-of-the-
way learning and especially the Provençal poets. He saw Browning as
different from the other Victorians, and he appreciated the stylistic experiment in *Sordello*. He affirmed that Browning was his literary father, and
while Browning was important to him throughout his life, his influence was
particularly so, George Bornstein has argued, "during the crucial decade or
so stretching from composition of the *A Lume Spento* poems (published
1908) to the appearance of *Three Cantos* in 1917." The *Three Cantos*, Pound
told his father, "start out with a barrel full of allusions to 'Sordello,'" and
among the poems in the *A Lume Spento* volume is "Mesmerism," which forms
the epigraph to this book. Bornstein has neatly summarized the things
Pound liked about Browning: he admired his "profundity ('Thought's in
your verse-barrel'), psychological insight ('But God! what a sight you ha' got
o' our in'ards') and breadth ('broad as all ocean')," his innovative metrics

("Old Hippety-Hop o' the accents"), and "his expansion of poetic diction to include 'unpoetic' phrases like 'cat's in the water-butt.'"[34] Browning had showed Pound how to "make it new."

Browning's three long poems at the outset of his career led him to be loosely associated in the mind of the reading public with the "Spasmodic Poets"—so labeled and ridiculed by William Edmondstoune Aytoun— such poets as Philip James Bailey, Alexander Smith, and Sydney Dobell.[35] Indeed, in an overview of Browning's early career, Edmund Gosse argued in 1881 that *Paracelsus* in its "shapeless" development and its emotional extravagance was the "parent . . . of a monstrous family of *Festuses* [Bailey] and *Balders* [Dobell] and *Life-Dramas* [Smith] only quite lately extirpated and never any more, it is to be hoped, to flourish above ground."[36] These now-forgotten literary figures, who had an extensive readership in their day (including Elizabeth Barrett), have been characterized by Jerome Buckley in this way:

> They had inherited from Byron and Shelley a view of art which the principal Victorians were seeking to disown, the concept of the poet as a divinely inspired creature with an inalienable right to eccentricity, a right to despise the conventions that bound other men and to indulge a brooding genius in studied self-absorption. . . . Uncertain of their ultimate design, [the Spasmodics] neglected over-all theme and action to magnify isolated emotion.[37]

Browning was now to move beyond his early excesses and experiments gradually, but only gradually, through some further ventures into drama. But probably it was the chastening he received from reviewers and the well-meant expressions of puzzlement he heard from friends that brought him to more sureness of structure and more clarity of style in his work. Still, the early poems made possible the strengths of the later ones. Could the skill with which Browning handles the heroic couplet in the 1842 "My Last Duchess," for instance, have developed without his experiment with the form in *Sordello*? So idiomatically and naturally does Browning match his rhyme with his syntax in the duke's dramatic speech that students coming to the poem for the first time think it is written in blank verse.

Browning as Dramatist for Closet and Stage

The friendship between Browning and Macready remained strong in spite of the strains it had undergone, because Browning was a young man with a sunny disposition and a longing for literary fame and Macready was a gentleman of tact and grace as well as an encourager of aspiring dramatists. Both were also able to curb a hot temper most of the time.

In the two years since *Strafford*, Browning had continued to frequent the theater and to drop in backstage after Macready's performances in *Macbeth*, *Othello*, Byron's *The Two Foscari*, or Beaumont and Fletcher's *The Maid's Tragedy*—usually with Forster, sometimes also with Dickens, Talfourd, Horne, Stanfield, or Procter. From time to time, Macready sent him "orders" (free tickets) to see him perform. In addition, Macready, a convivial host, invited Browning to dinners with varying groups that included Forster, Harriet Martineau, Lamon Blanchard (the poet), Helen Faucit, George Cattermole (the artist and illustrator), Percy Fitzgerald (the biographer and friend of Charles Lamb), and Erasmus Darwin (brother of the great evolutionist). On December 10, 1838, Macready invited Browning to dine and make one of "a select auditory" for a reading of Bulwer's new play, *Richelieu*.[1] The group, Browning, Forster (who fell asleep), Blanchard, Fox, T. J. Serle, the playwright, and others, were to take notes and pass judgment on the play.[2] Clearly, Macready valued Browning's friendship and still had respect for his literary talent.

As time went on, Browning came to know Macready's family, including his boy Willie, for whom he revised one of his short poems so that Willie could draw illustrations for it. Since it is an example of Browning's skill at impromptu versifying as well as a revelation of his lighter side, we should pause for a close look at this poem, slight though it may be.

The development took place in this way. In browsing through his copy of Nathaniel Wanley's *Wonders of the Little World*, Browning came upon the chapter "Of the Apparition of Demons and Spectres" and was intrigued by the legend of Cardinal Crescenzio, who was haunted by the vision of a huge black dog. He was the papal legate who had presided over five sessions of the Council of Trent, a tough-minded opponent of Protestantism and Church reform. In medieval tradition, a black dog was often an emissary of Satan charged to carry off a sinner to hell (a tradition also used by Goethe in *Faust*, where Mephistopheles first appears as a black dog). His Protestant sensibilities stirred, Browning tossed off a comic treatment of the story, scribbling it in the marginal spaces of the book. By placing the poem alongside Wanley's text, one can see clearly how Browning converted Wanley's phrasing into verse:[3]

Crescentius the Popes legate at the Council of *Trent* 1552. *March 25.* was busie writing of Letters to the Pope till it was far into the night, whence rising to refresh himself, he saw a black Dog of a vast bigness, flaming eyes, ears that hung down almost to the ground enter the room, which came directly towards him, and laid himself down under the table. Frighted at the sight, he called his Servants in the Antichamber, commanded them to look for the Dog, but they could find none. The Cardinal	Crescentius the Pope's Legate At Council High of Trent, Was (Fifteen Hundred fifty-two, March Twenty five,) intent

Writing of letters to the Pope   Till far 'twas in the night: Whence rising to refresh himself   He saw a monstrous sight.

A black dog of vast bigness,   And flaming eyes, and ears   That hung almost to the ground   Within the room appears.

A black Dog of vast bigness,   Eyes flaming, ears that hung Down to the very ground almost,   Into the chamber sprung;

Which came directly towards him   And laid himself down under The table where Crescentius wrote: He called in fear and wonder

His servants in the Antiroom— |

fell melancholy,	Commanded every one
thence sick, and	To look for and find out the Dog;
died at *Verona*: on	But looking they found none.
his death bed he	
cryed out to drive	The Cardinal fell melancholy,
away the Dog that	Thence sick, soon after died:
leaped upon his bed.	And at Verona as he lay
	On his death-bed he cried
	Aloud "to drive away the Dog
	That leapt on his bed-side."
	Done into Dog-rel,
	Febr. 27. 1841. R. B.

In May 1842, when Willie Macready was ill, Browning sought to amuse him by making a slight revision of his poem and sending it to the boy so that he could make drawings to illustrate parts of the story. At the end of his life, Browning revised the poem further and published it under the title "The Cardinal and the Dog" in *Asolando* (1889). He converted the ballad-stanza pattern into long seven-stress lines, but the most important change was the addition of a final line so that the poem concludes:

> he cried
> Aloud to drive away the Dog that leapt on his bed-side.
> Heaven keep us Protestants from harm: the rest . . . no ill betide!

This is the best comic touch in the poem, for Browning has added a pause after "the rest . . ." as if he had intended to say "can go to the devil." Instead Browning, the benevolent universalist, added "no ill betide!"

兊 兊 兊

Browning had by now taken plenty of time to absorb the lessons of *Strafford*. He had vowed never to write for the stage again, but he had an inclination to write another poem in dramatic form like *Paracelsus*, which had brought him so much celebrity. The idea for a new work came to him, he told Mrs. Orr, one day as he walked through the Dulwich woods alone: "The image flashed upon him of someone walking thus alone through life; one apparently too obscure to leave a trace of his or her passage, yet exercising a lasting though unconscious influence at every step of it; and the image shaped itself into the little silk-winder of Asolo, Felippa, or Pippa."[4]

The excitement of his experience in Italy was still fresh enough that he decided to set his new work in Asolo. What is more, he would avoid an historical setting and choose the contemporary world, making use of the peripheral glimpses of Italian life that had come to him when he had wandered through the Veneto in 1838: working girls in silk mills, art students in the piazzas, clerics with secular attitudes, political talk about the Austrian rule, casual chatter among street girls. Italy was a muse for him again but this time to inspire a poem that could reach the ordinary reader of verse and even provide some prose sequences fully equal to the dramatic interchange of the theater. Nothing could be more different from Browning's previous work than *Pippa Passes*. It is a well-executed series of short scenes linked by theme, not by probability. It has variety in stylistic expression, varying kinds of versification, diversity of mood, humor and banter as well as melodramatic tension. In a word, it has literary abundance, which was to become one of Browning's chief characteristics as an artist. Moreover, *Pippa Passes* has a governing theme related to this abundance: that the chance happenings of life are part of God's plan; life is not what it seems nor can it be what one expects.

Pippa Passes presents a day in the life of a working girl on holiday from the silk factory as she roams through Asolo imagining herself experiencing the lives of the four most fortunate people in the town, each representative of a form of love. Ottima, despite the presence of her elderly husband, is the object of the worship of Sebald, first her music teacher and now her lover; Phene is to be married that day to Jules, the sculptor; Luigi, a young patriot, is to bid good-bye to his mother before undertaking a special mission; and Monsignor the Bishop arrives from Rome to perform burial rites for his deceased brother. Romantic love, married love, filial and parental love, and God's love. Browning has thus arranged four disparate scenes in a carefully unified time scheme of morning, noon, evening, and night and has further wound in a subplot wherein Pippa is ironically ignorant of narrowly escaping a conspiracy to have her carried off to a degraded life in a Roman brothel.

But the principal irony lies in Pippa's being unaware that each of the happy personages is in the midst of a terrible crisis. Sebald has murdered Ottima's husband and, overcome with guilt, Sebald and Ottima will carry out a double suicide. Phene and Jules are caught up in a mock marriage instigated by a gang of vengeful art students. Luigi is planning to leave for Vienna to assassinate the Emperor of Austria. Monsignor the Bishop faces temptation: to allow the plot against Pippa to proceed, and so to gain his dead brother's estates, to which Pippa (unknowingly) has the prior claim.

Not only is the action well paced, but the style is surprisingly varied and vigorous. In her greeting to the morning with which the play opens, Pippa speaks in irregularly rhymed iambic lines pulsing with imagery and rhythmically varied to approximate colloquial speech; the line length itself varies as needed. The other principals are given blank-verse interchanges that move the action forward with good dramatic conflict. The interscenes that carry the subplot are in prose, balancing the higher level of language with effective earthiness. In fact, the scene in which the young prostitutes chat about their wishes is most unusual for a Victorian play, for they discuss their patrons—mostly of grandfatherly age—and the way they deal with them.

Four distinct features of *Pippa Passes* show that Browning was progressing toward the kind of work that made him a great English poet. First of all, the whole outlook on life that the play reflects is ironical, and this irony is displayed in the action. Each time Pippa passes one of her character groups, her song acts as a catalyst in their lives, spurring them into moral action. Further, this ironical view is used to create an ambiguous ending. For example, we do not know what will happen to Luigi in his assassination attempt— nor do we know if the bishop will act to change Pippa's life when he learns that she is his niece and the heiress to his brother's property. Ambiguous endings and unexplained motives are marks of the best dramatic monologues that Browning was later to write. Another look to his future work is inherent in the arrangement of the play in short dissimilar scenes, for Browning's reputation-to-be as a major poet would be based on an accumulation of short poems, mostly in monodramatic form. Most interesting of all considerations about the future is the fact that embedded in *Pippa Passes* was the first dramatic monologue Browning ever published. Strictly speaking, a dramatic monologue is a form of monodrama in which the speaker addresses an assumed listener or group of listeners. It differs from a soliloquy, which, according to the conventions of drama, reveals the inner thoughts of the speaker. In a dramatic monologue, however, the presence of an auditor forces the reader to see a nonprivate situation, in which no one ever knows if the speaker is telling the full truth; hence, ambiguity of meaning is possible, although rhetorical indicators may incline the reader toward accepting or doubting the truth of what the speaker is saying.

In the art students' scheme, Phene is supposed to remain silent until after the marriage ceremony. Thus when Jules brings her home, she still does not speak at first and stands dumb before him (like the statue of Pygmalion) when he expresses his ardor and devotion. He first looks at and praises her eyes, lips, and chin as a sculptor might, then tells her that his artistic work will probably suffer when she is present in the studio to distract him with her beauty. He next shows her the bundle of letters, well saved, that he has received from her. When her eyes roam about the room, he tells her about his books, hoping they will read Homer together. He speaks of his statues, of

Hippolyta, who drew the love of Theseus, as Phene drew his own, and of Harmodius who slew the tyrant Hipparchus. He tells of the way he sought to render ideal forms, and so on (2: 1–93), each point ironically pertinent to the plot against them, until she finally speaks. The whole monologue responds to her presence, moves with ease and poetic logic from point to point, and despite occasional obscurity, develops allusions and themes suitable to the situation, just as Browning's later dramatic monologues were to do.

Pippa Passes was Browning's first memorable literary achievement after a long apprenticeship. Yet he was still mesmerized by the stage. He did not know what a giant stride forward he had taken.

⪻ ⪻ ⪻

As he put together his new closet drama, Browning decided to write for the stage again in spite of what he had told Eliza Flower in a moment of chagrin. The instant gratification that comes to a dramatist when he sees an audience rapt by what he has created was still a temptation. On February 1, 1839, he had seen the young Queen Victoria and her entourage at a performance of Bulwer's *The Lady of Lyons* with Helen Faucit in the title role. What if a dramatic piece of his own were played before royalty?

The following summer Macready found Browning at his lodgings after a rehearsal. Although Browning at first indulged in a meandering conversation, he finally revealed what he had come for. He wanted to know if he wrote "a really good play," would Macready accept it?[5] He got the answer he wanted. Two weeks later, he handed Macready a manuscript. It was not *Pippa Passes*. It was another historical drama, *King Victor and King Charles*, a four-character play with a single setting (and thus cheap to produce) about a weak son in conflict with a strong father, the King of Sardinia, in the eighteenth century.[6] Although it focused on an abdication crisis, there was little action and even less motivation for the behavior of the characters. Its crowning weakness came at the end when Browning brought about the death of a major character by sudden collapse. After a quick reading, Macready declared it "*a great mistake*" and told Browning "most explicitly" why it would not do.[7]

Yet their friendly association did not waver. Browning continued to visit Macready at the theater. Macready frequently invited him to dine. They saw each other at Carlyle's lectures *On Heroes, Hero-Worship and the Heroic in History*. Browning proudly gave Macready a copy of *Sordello* when it was published in 1840.

Some years earlier, Browning had sought the advice of a woman for the subject of another tragedy. In a letter to Fanny Haworth, he explained that he wanted a story "of the most wild and passionate love . . . give me your notion of a thorough self-devotement, self-forgetting; should it be a woman who loves thus or a man?"[8] What he finally composed did not fit this formula, but it certainly had more romantic appeal than *Strafford* or the drab *King Victor and King Charles*.

The Return of the Druses, a play about an obscure Arab-Christian sect held captive by the Knights-Hospitallers of Rhodes, resembles the libretto of a grand opera, with all the extravagances of plot, exotic setting (the "Orientalism" of Greece and the Middle East), and thematic mixture of love and patriotism. Whether Browning thought it gave opportunity for the kind of spectacle that the taste of the period desired or he was merely exhibiting his own attraction to out-of-the-way subjects, one knows not.

Macready's first response to the play on July 31, 1840, was apprehensive: it "*does not look well.*"[9] His serious doubts about Browning's power to control his prolific pen seem to have begun earlier in the year when he tried, twice, to puzzle his way into *Sordello* and gave up: "It is *not* readable."[10] Now, after reading *The Return of the Druses*, he confided to his diary, "with the deepest concern I yield to the belief that he will *never write again*—to any purpose. I fear his intellect is not quite clear."[11] He returned it to Browning with a detailed set of reasons why it was unsuitable for performance. Undaunted, Browning replied in a long letter defending the play and later pursued him to his home, even while he was finishing his bath, with "his self-opinionated persuasions upon his *Return of the Druses*." Macready was exasperated: "he really *wearied* me."[12] But gracious as ever, he agreed to one more reading, only to conclude that it was "mystical, strange and heavy."[13]

Even though these two plays were turned down, Browning was indefatigable in his zeal for another stage production. He tried once again, this time a play without historical complexities or exotic setting. He seemed to be following some suggestions that Macready and Forster had given him, for he broke the news to Macready about his new work in terms that do not sound like Robert Browning of Camberwell: "'The luck of the third adventure' is proverbial—I have written a spick & span new Tragedy—(a sort of compromise between my own notion & yours—as I understand it, at least—) and will read it to you if you care to be bothered so far—there is *action* in it, drabbing [whoring], stabbing, et autre gentillesses,—who knows but the Gods may mean me good even yet?"[14] Forster was an enthusiastic backer of this new venture entitled *A Blot in the 'Scutcheon* and strongly urged Macready to give it a reading.

Despite his wariness of Browning's dramatic abilities, Macready accepted the play for production shortly before he took over the management of

Drury Lane Theater in December.[15] He must have been surprised by the quality of Browning's new verse tragedy, for in many respects the play is up to the level of *Pippa Passes* (which he had not seen), yet it is clearly written for the stage. It is full of conflict and action; it moves with probability from one point to the next; and the characters are fully developed and behave according to their place in the action. The only shortcomings (but, alas, they are major) are its thematic motif of a stain on the family honor through mistaken identity which preciptates the catastrophe, and the long speeches in the last act that impede the progress of the action to its tragic end.

A Blot in the 'Scutcheon, set somewhere vaguely in the recent past, presents the story of Mildred Tresham, a very young woman who yields to her fiancé, Lord Mertoun, before their marriage has been arranged. When her lover's visits are reported by an observant family retainer, her brother and guardian, the Earl of Tresham, confronts her with questions and accusations. She admits her guilt but refuses to disclose her lover's name. Incensed at the debaucher of his sister, Tresham lies in wait that night and mortally wounds Mertoun before he recognizes him. Tresham is filled with remorse over his hasty deed. But the dying Mertoun is now anguished that his death will be more than Mildred can bear and cries out, "What right was yours to set / The thoughtless foot upon her life and mine, / And then say, as we perish, 'Had I thought, / All had gone otherwise?'" (3. 1. 152–55). In the conclusion, Mildred expires with grief (once again, Browning's use of a stock Romantic demise), and Tresham poisons himself, calling out a warning against taking vengeance in defense of family honor.

Modern readers will find fault with the extended sentiments exchanged by the dying or distraught characters in the final scenes. But with some judicious cutting, this play could still be presented on a twenty-first-century stage effectively if the audience were willing to accept it as a period piece.

However that may be, Macready, after accepting Browning's play, was once more immobilized by doubts about it, especially when he remembered the difficulties he had undergone with the author during the production of *Strafford*. He was also concerned that the Lord Chamberlain's office, which oversaw the licenses of all theaters, might object more to the drabbing than the stabbing in Browning's play. Macready proposed a good many cuts in order to adapt it for performance and, no doubt with the Lord Chamberlain's office in mind, he made a great many alterations in the love scene in which Mertoun visits Mildred Tresham's bedchamber by night.[16] In fact, he cut so many lines that the scene scarcely makes clear that this was a sexual encounter. Browning agreed to these changes, apparently realizing that the Lord Chamberlain should not be challenged by a scene that was too passionate. All this, plus other changes made by both Macready and Browning himself in order to speed up the action, reduced *A Blot in the 'Scutcheon* from five acts to a three-act play.

Macready, still in doubt, was persuaded by Forster to have Dickens read the script and offer his judgment on the matter. The result was several months' delay before Dickens's verdict came in. It turned out to be a laudatory recommendation:

> Browning's play has thrown me into a perfect passion of sorrow. To say that there is anything in its subject save what is lovely, true, deeply affecting, full of the best emotion, the most earnest feeling, and the most true and tender source of interest, is to say that there is no light in the sun, and no heat in the blood. . . . And I swear it is a tragedy that MUST be played: and must be played, moreover, by Macready.[17]

Meanwhile, Macready had promised Browning a production, although he told him that two other new plays had to be presented before *A Blot in the 'Scutcheon* could be scheduled. The first of these, *Plighted Troth* by Charles Darley, turned out to be a failure. A discouraged Macready brought his theater season to an end, "shutting the house a month earlier than he had meant."[18]

The following theatrical season, from October 1, 1842, to June 15, 1843, was a brilliant one, presenting Macready's usual array of Shakespeare's comedies, histories, and tragedies, in addition to classic works by Dryden, Sheridan, Goldsmith, Congreve, Vanbrugh, and contemporary plays by Byron, Bulwer, Knowles, and five new plays, including *A Blot in the 'Scutcheon*.

Macready's halfheartedness about the play, however, got it off to a bad start. Since his days were filled with problems of management and his nights spent performing (four to five times a week), he asked Mr. Willmott, the head prompter, to carry out the first read-through for the cast. Wilmott, who was "a grotesque person with a red nose and a wooden leg, ill at ease in the love scenes,"[19] botched the reading. As Helen Faucit, who played Mildred Tresham, remembered it years later, "the delicate subtle lines were twisted, perverted, and sometimes made ridiculous in his hands. . . . [Mr. Elton] sat writhing and indignant, and tried by gentle asides to make me see the real meaning of the verse. But somehow the mischief proved irreparable. . . ."[20] The players laughed throughout at the tragedy they were to perform. When Browning heard of it he was furious, and Macready was able to mollify him only by conducting another reading for the cast himself. Still, he told Browning that the press of Drury Lane responsibility was such that he could not play the lead, and he assigned the part to Samuel Phelps, a rising young player. Although Browning did not realize it at the time, this placed the mark of death on *A Blot in the 'Scutcheon*. No new play ever succeeded, Forster later explained to him, without Macready in the principal role.[21]

As it turned out, however, Phelps fell ill with "English cholera," forcing Macready to become an emergency understudy. At length, having paced out and rehearsed the role, Macready decided to take it over for performance. But another turn of events occurred the day before the play was to open. Phelps, partly recovered, sent a note to Macready saying the he wished to play Tresham even if he "died for it."[22] Moreover, he met Browning at the stage door before the rehearsal and begged him to intercede for him. Foolish, chivalrous Browning then marched into the green room and told Macready in front of his players, "I find that Mr. Phelps, although he has been ill, feels himself quite able to take the part, and I shall be very glad to leave it in his hands."[23]

Macready, tired out and unwell, chagrined at the time he had spent learning the part, asserted angrily, "But do you understand that I, *I*, am going to act the part?" To which Browning doggedly replied, "I shall be very glad to intrust it to Mr. Phelps." Macready exploded. He rolled up the script and hurled it across the room.[24]

In spite of his outburst, Macready went ahead with the rehearsal, for he was still responsible for a Drury Lane calendar of performances. He offered his suggestions to Phelps about playing the part and recommended to Browning that the end of the play be changed so that Tresham would retire to a monastery rather then die by poisoning himself. He wrote the following two lines to be inserted in Tresham's final speech:

> Within a convent's shade in stranger lands
> Penance and prayer shall wear my life away.[25]

Browning refused, for he thought it weakened the tragic effect of the play. Besides, he felt that he had agreed to too much tampering with his script already. Macready's diary summarizes the tense situation: "Browning . . . in the worst taste, manner, and spirit, declined any further alterations, expressing himself perfectly satisfied with the manner in which Mr. Phelps executed Lord Tresham. I had no more to say. I could only think Mr. Browning a very disagreeable and offensively mannered person."[26]

Calm descended the next day, for performance is all-important to theatrical professionals. Macready directed the last rehearsal and "made many valuable improvements."[27] Browning apologized for his behavior the previous day, claiming that he was out-of-sorts because of a quarrel with Forster. Nevertheless, he had arranged with Moxon to have his play printed in twenty-four hours so that it could be offered to reviewers and sold to theatergoers in its original version without what he considered to be damaging cuts and changes.[28] His final disappointment with the plans for production came when he learned that no expenditure had been allowed to mount the play. Costumes and scenery from an earlier new play were made to do service once again.

In spite of Macready's misgivings, the opening night of *A Blot in the 'Scutcheon*, February 11, 1843, was a distinct success. The audience "raised a most deafening shout when the curtain fell."[29] Phelps was recalled several times. Helen Faucit was deeply appreciated for the tenderness and feeling she displayed as Mildred. There was "a great uproar" in a call for the author, but Browning chose to remain in his box, feeling somewhat scornful, "too sick and sorry at the whole treatment of his play" to come forward.[30]

Two reports from members of the audience survive, giving contrasting views. One comes from Cyrus Mason, the resentful cousin, who came to see the play with another cousin, both of them ready, in a patronizing way, "to be generous towards it's [sic] faults and bestow our applause freely for the sake of the family." They found the action "lethargic" and observed that the dialogue was for many members of the audience "beyond their comprehension." They described one scene as causing laughter and impatient foot-shuffling when Lord Mertoun sang a serenade to Mildred while climbing a ladder somewhat precariously toward her window.[31] The other account comes from one of Browning's fellow members of the Colloquials, Joseph Arnould, who wrote to Alfred Domett in New Zealand:

> The first night was magnificent . . . and there could be no mistake at all about the honest enthusiasm of the audience. The gallery . . . took all the points quite as quickly as the pit, and entered into the general feeling and interest of the action far more than the boxes—some of whom took it upon themselves to be shocked at being betrayed into so much interest for a young woman who had behaved so improperly as Mildred. Altogether the first night was a triumph.

He returned the second night to witness an equally effective performance, but he reported that although the gallery was full and a scattering of people were with him in the pit, the boxes were mostly unoccupied. On the third night, he took box seats and brought his wife: "My own delight, and hers too, in the play was increased at this third representation, and would have gone on increasing to a thirtieth; but the miserable, great, chilly house, with its apathy and emptiness, produced on us both the painful sensation which made her exclaim that 'she could cry with vexation' at seeing so noble a play so basely marred." Yet in spite of his enthusiasm, Arnould could recognize that the final scenes were "a falling off from the second act." Even so, he knew Browning well enough that he was confident that, whether the play was "a failure or a partial success, the effect on him will be the same, viz. to make him still to work, work, work."[32]

Among the reviewers there was a consensus that the play was based on "a disagreeable subject" and that the final act was the weak point in the play. The *Literary Gazette* was the harshest on the "dying scene in which [Mertoun's] martyrdom of talking, after being mortally hurt, was enough to try the patience of Job. His conversation with his slayer, intermixed with groans and twistings, became almost ludicrous."[33] Beyond that, the opinions ranged widely. The *Morning Post* called it an "unequivocal success," "a work of genuine genius, conceived with an abundant and spirit stirring passion." Yet it had "grave absurdities of construction."[34] The *Times* found it "one of the most faulty dramas we ever beheld."[35] However, Forster came through in the *Examiner* with praise for Browning as "a man of genius and a true poet" and for the play: "In performance it was successful: a result which it had been hardly safe to predict of a work of so much rare beauty, and of such decisive originality."[36]

After the third night Macready withdrew the play, never to bring it back that season or any other. He had undergone enough wrangling with an author who did not understand the theater. In addition, he had received a letter of complaint from the Lord Chamberlain for his failure to obtain preliminary approval of the script.

Browning emerged from the experience with deeply felt grievances. By now, he had come to think of Macready as an antagonist who had done all he could to make his play fail, even suspecting that he had put out the word to reviewers to heap abuse on it.[37] "Macready has used me vilely," he told Domett.[38] But it was Browning himself who had thrown away its possible chances of success when he insisted that Phelps play the leading role.

However true that might have been, a more basic difficulty lay at the heart of Browning's failure in the theater. His own views on the drama ran completely counter to the realities of stage performance. Writing to Elizabeth later, he explained his ideas about tragedy and what he conceived the buildup of tragic inevitability to be. "It is all in long speeches—the *action, proper*, is in them—. . . in a drama of this kind, all the *events*, (and interest,) take place in the *minds* of the actors."[39] What he did not understand is that the essential requisite for drama is conflict, but if the conflicts are inner conflicts or scarcely perceptible conflicts of value and attitude that cannot be presented in action, then the play will have no theatrical life. Browning's strongly held views are those of one who desires to write closet drama like Shelley's *The Cenci*, Byron's *Manfred*, Wordsworth's *The Borderers*, or Landor's

Count Julian.[40] More important, those same views led to his successes in writing dramatic poems.

Macready had found more flexibility when he worked with other verse dramatists. When he took the privately published version of Talfourd's "sweet tragic poem of *Ion*" and reduced and reshaped it "into an acting form and dimensions," he expected "to find [Talfourd] refractory on some points—and where some of the most poetical passages are omitted, it is difficult to persuade an author that the effect of the whole is improved; but imagery and sentiment will not supply the place of action."[41] But Talfourd bowed to the wisdom of Macready's theatrical experience. Macready noted in his diary that "we went over the play, he not offering an objection to all my omissions."[42] Macready (and Forster too) worked the same way with Bulwer's blank-verse drama *Richelieu*.

Both Talfourd and Bulwer, far inferior to Browning as poets, went on to great success in the theater. Browning was temperamentally and creatively unable to take that path. He was the kind of artist who would move rapidly from first inspiration to completed work. Even in the "secondary creativity"[43] of revision he could only work alone toward his final version. He was unable to create in conjunction with others. In the drama, he could not alter his own conception of a play to that of someone else even though that person might be wise in the ways of the stage. He wrote three more plays—closet dramas—before abandoning the form, and he profited from the practice of hammering out dialogue and bringing character into being, but in the theater he was destined henceforth to be a spectator, not a practicing dramatist.

Varieties of Poetic Monodrama
Dramatic Lyrics

Early in 1841 the Browning family had moved a few miles east to New Cross, Hatcham, in the Borough of Deptford, a rural-suburban area with large estates and farms. The new home was in a former farmhouse situated on a lane south of the New Cross Road, on a site now occupied by the Haberdasher's Aske's Girls School on Jerningham Road. A tradition at the school holds that Browning once composed a poem while sitting under a chestnut tree located on the school playground.[1] Sarianna recalled that "the house had three stories including the ground floor. The upper story had large, though low, rooms, one of which was used as a book room and a study. There was a tradition that this room had formerly been fitted up as a chapel by a [Roman Catholic] family then living in the house."[2] There was a stable for Uncle Reuben's horse, which Robert still exercised, and a large garden and orchard for Mrs. Browning. The landlord provided a key to the gate opening onto the grounds and hills behind, and his pond was available for water to be pumped for the garden. Robert's "favourite toad lived under a white moss rosetree near the pump."[3]

The Deptford railway station was a short walk away so that Mr. Browning could travel to the City by rail in bad weather. Cyrus Mason remembered that the passengers rode standing, gripping a metal bar, in open cars that offered little protection from the soot or the rain.[4]

Robert's new friend, Thomas Carlyle, who was almost two decades older than he, rode his horse out to Hatcham to visit him. Carlyle enjoyed Mrs. Browning, whom he judged to be "the true type of a Scottish gentlewoman,"[5] and observed that both parents worshiped their talented son: "he was the very apple of their eyes."[6] Browning had probably become acquainted with Carlyle through Fox and, to improve the association, sent him a copy of *Paracelsus* and later *Sordello*. Carlyle did not fully appreciate Browning's poetry and, as we have seen, advised him to write prose—advice he also gave to other poets. But he liked the young man, found he had an original, unconventional mind, invited him to dine (although his wife, Jane, ever since *Sordello* cared for neither Browning's work nor his presence), and developed a fatherly attitude toward him. Browning returned the love with genuine filial feeling: "I dined with dear Carlyle and his wife," he wrote to Miss Haworth, "(catch me calling people 'dear,' in a hurry, except in letter-beginnings!) yesterday—I don't know any people like them."[7] The friendship lasted until Carlyle's death in his eighties.

ॐ ॐ ॐ

Soon after the move to New Cross, Browning began a new publishing venture. *Pippa Passes* had been finished in 1840,[8] but the dismal reception of *Sordello* seemed to discourage temporarily Browning's plans for publication. Or perhaps his dashed hopes for success made him think twice about putting his father to the expense of another printing and sale of a book. When he conferred with Moxon, who despite his valiant support of literature was always complaining about the slow market for poetry, Browning discovered that the publisher was issuing cheap reprints of the works of Shakespeare and other Elizabethan dramatists, the plays of Sheridan, Lamb's essays, and the poetry of Rogers, Campbell, and others. He learned that he could have a play published, using small print in double columns on a page, in a paper-bound pamphlet, for about £16. Copies would sell for six pence.

In this way in 1841, *Pippa Passes* became the first in a series that Browning called *Bells and Pomegranates*, an esoteric title alluding to a passage in the Book of Exodus. As Robert later explained to Elizabeth, "The Rabbis make Bells & Pomegranates symbolical of Pleasure and Profit, the Gay & the Grave, the Poetry & the Prose, Singing and Sermonizing."[9] In an "Advertisement" on the verso of the title page, he offered a defense of his publishing a new work in such a cheap format. He remarked that since the audience in the pit had applauded his play *Strafford*, he wished, in appreciation of their response, to seek a "pit audience" once more. He dedicated *Pippa Passes* to Serjeant Talfourd.

Reviewers treated this pamphlet publication seriously because it was the work of a poet of some reputation. In general, *Pippa's* "lyric outpourings" were appreciated, although complaints were uttered about some obscure passages, especially in the Jules and Phene scene. Beyond that, the reviews were decidedly mixed, although more positive than anything Browning had received since *Paracelsus*. Forster in the *Examiner* went to some length to praise *Pippa Passes*, and to print long extracts. He was particularly struck by the high quality of poetic expression in the play: "Its rich variety of verse, embodying the nicest shades of poetical and musical rhythm, flows in a full tide of harmony with each lightest change of sentiment."[10] But Thomas Kibble Hervey in the *Athenaeum* thought it deplorable that such a "remarkably beautiful" theme with such a "simple and healthy moral" was wrapped in language "nearly as obscure as ever."[11] Other reviewers, more conservative, objected to Browning's highly original concept and structure. Said one, this is "not a drama, but scenes in dialogue, without coherence or action."[12] Another wrote that the play was "a chaos of speeches, dialogues, and figures, in which we can discover neither coherency nor positive meaning."[13] Comments of this sort always embedded themselves deeply in Browning's resentful memory, but it is to be hoped that he took some comfort in the brief notice in the *Morning Herald*, which declared, "The scenes thus set forth are highly dramatic, glowing with strong and original conception, and combining the darker and the more gentle passions in vigorous contrast."[14]

Bells and Pomegranates, number two, published early in 1842, was the rejected *King Victor and King Charles*. Its "Advertisement" described the historical characters upon whom the play was based and the sources Browning used. Most reviewers did not bother to give the play any notice, but two who did were not overly pleased. The *Spectator* called it "a Dialogue of the Dead in blank verse,"[15] and the *Athenaeum* regretted that Browning was "cumbered" by his learning and his imagination and unable "to do justice to his own meanings," although he handled the plot and characterizations with skill.[16] Even Forster was sparing in support for his friend. He thought that the play was a product of "the wayward perverseness of a man of true genius," although it had many "beautiful, powerful, and pathetic passages."[17]

Whether Moxon thought the play rather dull or whether as the publisher of *Sordello* he feared that most of Browning's work was rather forbidding for the general reader, he made an excellent suggestion for the next number of *Bells and Pomegranates*. He recommended that "for popularity's sake" Browning issue a collection of short poems.[18] As publisher of Wordsworth, Campbell, Rogers, "Miss Barrett," and Tennyson, Moxon had a good sense of what sale was likely for poetry, and as the publisher of *Sordello* he may have wished for the sake of his young friend's reputation to publish something that was readily accessible for a large readership (and perhaps to take the taint of *Sordello* off Browning's current series of little books.) Browning dug into his portfolio for earlier work and even wrote one or two new poems that reflected his Italian journey of 1838, and late in 1842 he issued *Dramatic Lyrics* as the third number of his series.

In his "Advertisement" for *Pippa Passes,* Browning had indicated that he planned to use the series to publish his plays. Now in the collection of short poems he offered a brief "Advertisement" pointing out that the majority of the poems in the volume might properly come "under the head of 'Dramatic Pieces,'" that they were "for the most part Lyric in expression, always Dramatic in principle, and so many utterances of so many imaginary persons, not mine." Browning's definition of "dramatic" in 1842 is one he would insist upon again and again: that in his poems he was not speaking in his own voice. That psychological need to hide behind his creations had major consequences for English poetry.

The important feature of the pamphlet is that it collected and put before the public the first samples of a generic form, poetic monodrama, that Robert Browning was to develop fully for English literature and in which he was to surpass all other practitioners. Before turning to the poems themselves, we should digress for a moment to say a word or two about poetic monodrama and to establish some terminology that will make discussion more precise, because monodrama was to Victorian poetry as important and dominant a genre as blank verse drama was to the Elizabethan period.

Monodramatic verse was not new in the nineteenth century. B. W. Fuson[19] has reminded us that the form goes back to the ancients: that the method of role-playing is found in the Sicilian pastoral tradition and that the speaker's address to an audience was fully developed and popularized in Ovid's *Heroic Epistles.* Any number of other commentators point to the numerous examples in early English poetry, too, going back as far as "The Seafarer" and "The Wanderer."[20] In fact, the more loosely a term like dramatic lyric or dramatic monologue is defined, the more examples one can turn up in the past.

In the early nineteenth century, nevertheless, Arthur Hallam thought he had perceived a new development in poetry when he reviewed Tennyson's 1830 volume, *Poems, Chiefly Lyrical,* and found that "a considerable portion of this book is taken up with a very singular and very beautiful class of poems" which attempted to characterize individual minds. He continued,

> These expressions of character are brief and coherent; nothing extraneous to the dominant fact is admitted; nothing illustrative of it, and, as it were, growing out of it, is rejected. They are like summaries of mighty dramas. We do not say this method admits of such large luxuriance of power as that of our real dramatists; but we contend that it is a new species of poetry, a graft of the lyric on the dramatic, and Mr. Tennyson

deserves the laurel of an inventor, an enlarger of our modes of knowledge and power.[21]

These are extravagant words for Tennyson's modest achievement in his 1830
volume, but they accurately reflect the opinion held by critics down through
Hallam's century and the next,[22] that Tennyson and Browning and their followers were working in a new genre.

But the something new that they perceived did not mean they had forgotten Chaucer's Wife of Bath's "Prologue" or Pope's "Eloisa to Abelard." Rather,
they were aware that poets were manipulating the form in new ways. Poets
were creating greater aesthetic distance between the poet and the speaker in
the poem, frequently by using historical materials or foreign settings; they
were subtly allowing characterization to emerge, especially by oblique revelations of the inner being of the speaker; and they were accommodating the syntax and the rhythms of what Wordsworth had called "the real language of
men"[23] within the formal confinements of verse. Above all, they were filling a
need that the nineteenth-century theater ("our degraded drama" as Macready
had scornfully described it) was no longer able to supply. Certainly there is a
connection between the decline of vigorous new drama in nineteenth-century
England[24] and the development of new skills in the writing of dramatic
poems. These two facts of literary history are the twin marks of the inward
turning of the literary mind in the nineteenth century. Matthew Arnold, looking at the verse of his own time, called it the "dialogue of the mind with itself."[25]

I [RSK] use the general term "monodrama" for this "new genre" because
the term that has commonly been applied to Browning's work, "dramatic
monologue," has been used too loosely for the immense variety of dramatic
poems that he composed. For example, Robert Langbaum in his admirable
book *The Poetry of Experience: The Dramatic Monologue in Modern Literary Tradition* applies the term *dramatic monologue* not only to extraordinarily complex
poems like "The Tomb at St. Praxed's" but also to a simple soliloquy like
"Porphyria" and even to a direct didactic poem like "Rabbi Ben Ezra," which
has no indication other than the title that a rabbi is speaking.[26] We fail to
appreciate Browning's inventiveness and skill if we employ just this one term
to embrace all of Browning's dramatic poems when discussing his work, and
we are impeded from distinguishing his best work from that which is less
successful. Thus I wish to offer some additional terminology along with
explanatory working definitions, in order to allow us to perceive the immense possibilities of monodramatic verse that Browning was able to exploit
during his long career.

In reading through a series of definitions of the dramatic monologue in
literary handbooks as well as in critical studies of Browning's work, one may

be struck by the simple fact that they commonly include two features that are present in Browning's characteristic pieces: (1) the speaker dominates the work; and (2) the work is dramatic in form—in the sense that the speaker is more than a mere narrator; his words seem to have been written for performance by a single actor. For the purposes of discussing Browning's poems, I wish to take these two elements as the basis of the term *monodrama* and then to make distinctions among varieties of this form and label them soliloquy, dramatic narrative, dramatic monologue, and dramatic lyric. I use the general term *monodrama* because it was commonly used in the Victorian period and became widely known when Tennyson called his poem *Maud* a monodrama.[27] I use the other terms because they are similar to many that Browning used in titling his volumes or poems, even though he seemed uncertain exactly what he meant to suggest by the titles and groupings of his work as *Dramatic Romances, Dramatic Idyls, Dramatic Lyrics,* or simply *Men and Women.*[28] Since Browning never used the term *dramatic monologue* himself, it is odd that this became the label so frequently applied to the bulk of his work.[29]

Let us go back to Browning's starting place now—the drama. The three elements necessary for a play are characters, action, and audience. When Browning turned to monodrama, he began to produce work in which one character, the speaker, became all-important; in which the action could be a complicated narrative or perhaps just a series of evanescent, shifting moods; and in which the audience could be an implied listener, or a group of listeners, addressed by the speaker—or sometimes only the reader. What I want to point up is that Browning learned to vary the forms of monodrama by placing the chief emphasis on just one of the essential elements of drama— the speaker, the story that is told, or the presence of a listener—or sometimes even by holding them in a balanced proportion.

             撴 撴 撴

Browning's first collection of short pieces, *Dramatic Lyrics*, contains examples of these variations of monodramatic verse. Two are soliloquies. The first one was "Porphyria" (which is now known by the title that Browning later gave it, "Porphyria's Lover"), the poem Browning published back in 1836 in Fox's *Monthly Repository*. Its lack of subtlety in presenting its horrific story reveals that it is an early attempt at working with a dramatic speaker. Recognizing the bluntness of the tale his speaker has told, Browning now supplied the over-title "Madhouse Cells" for this poem, together with "Johannes Agricola," when he republished them in *Dramatic Lyrics*.

Whereas "Porphyria's Lover" describes an action that has already taken place, the second example of soliloquy, "Cloister (Spanish)"—now known by its later title, "Soliloquy of the Spanish Cloister"—brings us into an ongoing situation, which for the reader is closer to the experience of a stage presentation. We listen to a petty-minded monk revealing his hatred for Brother Lawrence, the mild-mannered gardener of the monastery. We follow him through his mockery of Lawrence's mincing table talk; his scorn for Lawrence's orderly care for his table ware and goblet; his suspicion that Lawrence was casting a lustful glance at "brown Dolores" outside the convent, washing her hair (in the 1842 text)

> Blue-black, lustrous, thick like horsehairs
> —Can't I see his dead eye grow
> Bright, as 'twere a Barbary corsair's?
> That is, if he'd let it show. (29–32)

He goes on to disclose his tricks to keep his brother monk's flowers from being double and his secret wish to entrap him into damnation by a heretical text in the Bible, by slipping him "my scrofulous French novel" (57), or by making a pact with Satan—all this Browning packs into flowing eight-line stanzas of casual phrasing, even working growls, "Gr-r-r," into the meter.

Like Porphyria's murderously jealous lover, the monk is self-deceiving. He reveals his own lasciviousness, and he takes religious pride in his own meaningless ritual acts in handling his knife and fork and goblet. Thus both soliloquies create their ironies, but they have quite different effects. The first one builds grotesque horror; the second, with its childish pranks tied into the malicious monk's schemes, is highly comic. Browning was already showing variety of tone in his experiment with form.

When there is less emphasis on speaker and more on action, we have what could be called a *Dramatic Narrative* (Browning's term, used rather loosely, is *Dramatic Romance*). The poem "Camp (French)," now known as "Incident of the French Camp," is a rather short example of this variation in the monodramatic form. The speaker tells of the day when "we French stormed Ratisbon" (1), and at a point when the battle is in doubt, a messenger boy rides up to Napoleon to report victory. As he gives his news, it is revealed that "his breast / Was all but shot in two" (23–24). The story of the mortally wounded boy takes up three and a half of the five stanzas in the poem, and its effect is to arouse feelings of mingled pity and admiration associated with those of loyalty and patriotism. But these feelings are enhanced by the function of the speaker. It is *his* voice that presents the action. It is *his* voice that describes Napoleon. It is *his* voice that interprets the commander's concern for the boy:

> The chief's eye flashed; but presently
>   Softened itself, as sheathes
> A film the mother-eagle's eye
>   When her bruised eaglet breathes;
> "You're wounded!" (33–37)

This poem is a compact and skillful handling of dramatic narrative. Browning was to compose many longer ones as his career went on.

When the third element, the listener (audience), is brought into a mono-dramatic poem, we have what has generally been regarded as its highest form, dramatic monologue.[30] "My Last Duchess," the outstanding work in *Dramatic Lyrics* (where it is entitled simply "Italy") is a classic example. Not only does it employ a dramatic speaker, a defined listener, and a developing action in the present, but it also has the gradual ironical revelation of the character of the speaker and the implication of another action in the past. It presents the situation of an arrogant duke showing off his artistic treasures to an envoy who has come to negotiate the dowry for the duke's coming marriage. The poem begins in the middle of the scene as the duke is unveiling a portrait of his former wife. While he describes it, hints emerge that he has done away with her because she did not sufficiently appreciate the noble name and person she had married.

The poem's success is partly due to the harmonious complex of the elements of character, action, and audience. The speaker makes frequent direct address to the listener ("Will't please you sit and look at her?" [5] "so not the first / Are you to turn and ask thus" [12–13], "Will't please you rise?" [47]) so that we are aware that the duke is controlling what he says to the envoy. The story of the duchess, and our developing sense of her appealing personality in contrast to that of the proud duke, is carried out entirely through the discussion of the portrait:

> Oh sir, she smiled, no doubt,
> Whene'er I passed her; but who passed without
> Much the same smile? This grew; I gave commands;
> Then all smiles stopped together. (43–46)

The revelation of the character of the duke becomes an accompaniment to our understanding the story of the duchess. Further, the whole action takes on a new ironical dimension when it becomes clear that the listener is an emissary for the arrangement of a new marriage. But there are other features, too, that intensify our experience of the work. The poem in its compactness makes every detail count. For example, the single statement that reveals the plan for a second marriage contains a reference to the dowry, thus drawing together at one stroke the whole discussion of artistic works and wives within a context of property. Again, the final artistic image sums up what has gone before: the discussion of art and possessions and the ironical disclosure of the relationship between the duke and duchess. As the duke and the envoy walk down the stairs, they pause:

> Notice Neptune, though,
> Taming a sea-horse, thought a rarity,
> Which Claus of Innsbruck cast in bronze for me! (54–56)

He was the powerful tamer, she the little sea horse. She was the rarity, which in his cold egoism he was unable to value.[31]

The style of the poem demands a comment. It is the first of Browning's monodramas in pentameter couplets, a form well adapted to the speech rhythm that Browning sought to reproduce. As he uses the form, the couplets flow so smoothly that they are scarcely discernible from blank verse, yet they still contribute those echoes of repeated sound pleasurable to the ear. Within the lines, too, we have the parenthetical phrase, the hesitation, the afterthought, the intruded question, and other marks of casual conversation—all the colloquial syntax merged with and playing against the pentameter pattern. "My Last Duchess" is such a high achievement, especially with the irony of the duke's unconscious self-revelation, that the genre seems new, even though Tennyson had preceded Browning in breathing new vigor into this favorite form of the Victorian era.

Almost as admirable is "Count Gismond" (in *Dramatic Lyrics* called simply "France"), a monodramatic poem that lies somewhere between a dramatic narrative and a dramatic monologue, for although it has an identified listener, the bulk of the poem is given over to the story of a tournament and a trial by combat that took place years ago. What makes the poem structurally interesting is Browning's handling of the two narrative threads, the story of the past played against the ongoing life of the present. The Countess Gismond in her court at Aix-en-Provence during late medieval times is telling her friend Adela about the crucial moment in her life when she as Queen of the Tournament was suddenly and publicly accused by Count Gauthier of being unchaste and thus unworthy of her rule over the ceremonies. But immediately her honor was defended by Count Gismond, who challenged Gauthier to a trial by combat to decide the truth of his accusations. Gismond slew

Gauthier, who confessed to his lie before he died. Gismond then chose the rescued heroine for his bride and carried her away to his castle. At this point of the present story, the countess begins to describe her two sons to Adela just as the count returns from hunting. She tells the count that she has been talking about her hunting bird and how much prey it had captured this year.

We can note some important examples of the way the two narrative lines are entwined by looking first at some instances of Browning's making the voice of the countess display some human variations to break the rather formal tale-telling that is going on. When she reaches the point where she must report the sudden accusation that was made against her, Browning makes her voice falter as she momentarily relives the shock:

> 'twas time I should present
> The victor with his ... there, 'twill last
> No long time ... the old mist again
> Blinds me ... but the true mist was rain. (45–48)

(These are the lines as they appeared in 1842.) At this point, Browning brings in the present-day activity. Gismond is seen at the gate with his two boys. The countess recovers herself and continues her story. Browning is thus able to suggest that Gismond's presence had bolstered her, rescued her once again. Later, another break in the narrative occurs when she reaches the point of Gismond's asking for her hand in marriage. It is a revelation, made dramatically, of how precious those words were to her:

> Then Gismond, kneeling to me, asked
>   —What safe my heart holds tho' no word
> Could I repeat now, if I tasked
>   My powers for ever, to a third
> Dear even as you are. Pass the rest
> Until I sank upon his breast. (103–8)

Browning has worked the manner of conversation into the formality of his six-line stanza as easily and skillfully as he handled the couplets in "My Last Duchess." This same casualness of manner is employed as he brings the poem to an end and at the same time manages to echo the opening stanza and to refer appropriately to the title of the poem. The countess is speaking of her children, who carry their father's features and imitate his bearing, when she breaks off suddenly. Her refusal to say directly what she had been talking about is balanced by the final image, which does reveal something, for Gismond, like her tercel, had struck for her:

Our elder boy has got the clear
    Great brow; tho' when his brother's black
Full eye shows scorn, it . . . Gismond here?
    And have you brought my tercel back?
I was just telling Adela
How many birds it struck since May. (121–26)

But this poem is not a soliloquy; it is a dramatic monologue that has a listener. A soliloquy, ever since the Elizabethan period, has been understood
by its audience to reveal the true inner thoughts of the speaker. A dramatic
monologue, on the other hand, is a more complex form of monodrama, for
the speaker is presenting him or herself as he or she wishes to be seen by the
listener. The reader does not know whether the truth is being told because
one cannot see into the mind of the speaker and, therefore, the form allows
for ambiguity of meaning. Thus controversy has arisen over the interpretation of "Count Gismond."

John Hagopian has challenged the common reading of the poem as a
romantic tale. He sees the countess as a deceptive woman because she lies to
the count when she declares that she has been telling Adela about her hunting bird.[32] John W. Tilton and R. Dale Tuttle have also seen the countess as
a questionable figure.[33] Was she really Gauthier's mistress as he claimed?
Although she says that Gauthier confessed to the lie before he died, we hear
only her version of the events. Does her change of subject when Count Gismond returns mean that her version embroiders upon the facts, or is she
only sparing him a revisit to that bloody episode? These and many other
questions are possible because of the dramatic form and Browning's subtle
handling of it. Ambiguity of meaning makes this poem more complex and
psychologically interesting than it first seems.

But what about a poem in which the speaker is not characterized in detail,
no listener is established, and the action is not developed but rather the mood
of the speaker is revealed as he allows his mind to follow a stream of mixed
thought and feeling? Such a poem, which had formerly been published in
Fox's *Monthly Repository* and which now is known by the title Browning later
gave it, "Johannes Agricola in Meditation," could truly be called a "dramatic
lyric." The speaker is an historical figure. There is no action, only the presentation of Johannes's theological musings. This dramatic lyric differs from the
two soliloquies we have examined earlier: the words seem scarcely to be spoken but rather to rise from the mind and flow in an expression of feeling.
Obviously a dramatic lyric differs little from an ordinary lyric poem in which
a *persona* of the poet speaks, giving utterance to thought and feeling. Browning's special touch in this poem is to introduce an ironical contrast between

how the speaker sees himself and how the reader sees him. Johannes Agricola's smug certainty of salvation is disclosed in his theological justification for it. But his cruel theological satisfaction in thinking that people of goodwill and good works will suffer the pangs of hell marks him as a despicable wretch—and also provides a withering judgment on his theology.

As far back as we can know—that is, as early as the poems copied out by Sarah Flower, "The First-Born of Egypt" and "The Dance of Death"—Browning had a bent toward writing dramatically. His first two long poems display this readiness to speak through characters, both in the rambling, scarcely dramatic, monologue, *Pauline*, and in the dramatic poem *Paracelsus*. His plays for the stage seem to indicate that full-length dramatic works designed for theatrical production were not suitable creative vehicles for his particular talent. Only *Pippa Passes*, which was a series of short dramatic episodes, was aesthetically under control. It appears that, at this point of his career, his efforts at short dramatic works were to be his greatest successes.

Since the mid-1830s, he had been experimenting with short poems, most of them dramatic, and keeping them in his portfolio. This activity was further stimulated in mid-1842 by Tennyson's new volume of poems. Writing to Domett on July 13, he gave special praise to two of Tennyson's fully developed monodramatic poems. He called "St. Simeon Stylites" "perfect" and his "Locksley Hall" "noble."[34] Although he did not mention it, Tennyson's "Ulysses" appeared in that same volume. Now in November of the same year, when he published *Dramatic Lyrics*, he revealed what he himself could do with monodramatic verse. Browning had found his form, although he still was not ready to commit his full creative energies to it. He was to go on to explore and develop his control of it over the next decade until finally, in 1855, in *Men and Women*, he demonstrated that he was the unsurpassed master of this new genre that he had helped to create.

∽ ∽ ∽

Dramatic Lyrics contains more than the examples of monodrama we have discussed in the previous pages. What is amazing about this little collection is the variety of meters, stanza forms, exotic settings (Italy, Spain, Provence, Germany, Greece, and Algeria), and the range of tones, from the formality of "Artemis Prologizes" to the colloquial language of "Waring." There is a short opera libretto, "In a Gondola," that had been inspired by Daniel Maclise's painting of a Venetian serenade. It had its origin on a day when Forster asked Browning to jot a few lines "on the instant" to serve as a motto for the picture.[35] Browning then took the 8 lines he had hastily scribbled off for

Forster and expanded them to 232 lines, a lyric dialogue telling a story of a love intrigue that led to tragic death.[36] Another series of three poems, "Cavalier Tunes," presents a marching song, a drinking song, and a riding song for Cavalier troopers—all set in the Civil War period.

Other poems include a courtly love tribute by the troubadour Rudel set in twelfth-century Provence ("Rudel and the Lady of Tripoli"[37]); a poem set in Algiers, which demonstrates that a single rhyme could be sustained throughout forty lines and joined to the rhythm of riding ("Through the Metidja to Abd-el-Kadr—1842");[38] a fragment of an unfinished play in the Greek manner, telling the story of Phaedra and Hippolytus ("Artemis Prologizes");[39] and a meditation on love, spoken by a courtier of Queen Cristina of Spain in the nineteenth century ("Cristina"), which was Browning's first expression of the romantic theme of unwavering devotion after love's arrow has struck its mark. This last poem was paired with "Rudel" under the overall title "Queen-Worship."

The two remaining poems need fuller comment. "Waring" is a poem inspired by Alfred Domett's departure for New Zealand, although Browning has highly fictionalized the details and the character ("so many utterances of so many imaginary persons, not mine"). It is the speaker's lament for a lost friend, Waring, who suddenly left London to go wandering over the world and an expression of regret that Waring has not fulfilled the promise of his great talent:

> "True, but there were sundry jottings,
> Stray-leaves, fragments, blurs and blottings,
> Certain first steps were achieved
> Already which"—(is that your meaning?)
> "Had well borne out whoe'er believed
> In more to come!" (32–37)

The speaker muses on Waring's multiple gifts: his abilities in painting, music, stage performance, anonymous pamphleteering in political polemics like Junius, and highly imaginative versifying like Chatterton. He moves on to deplore the loss of Waring to England during a time of little men and meager achievements, but he returns to express his love for his former comrade, his envy of his travels, and his expectation for Waring's future attainment and fame: "Oh, never star / Was lost here but it rose afar! / Look East, where whole new thousands are! / In Vishnu-land what Avatar?" (254–57).

One of the most attractive features of "Waring" is in the casualness of phrasing and tone, making it a true Victorian sample of the new realism in verse. The colloquial phrases are slipped easily into the meter: "What's become of Waring / Since he gave us all the slip?"; "He was prouder than the Devil"; "Who'd have guessed it from his lip / Or his brow's accustomed bearing?" "I left his arm that night myself / For what's-his-name's, the new prose-poet." In addition, Browning has developed the whole 262-line poem in irregular rhyming and in line lengths that vary from four to nine syllables. The work is thus in a form highly appropriate for a nostalgic expression of friendship, a wistful mixture of regret and well-wishing.

When Moxon's printer had set the sheaf of poems that Browning had given him, there was still ample room for two or three more. Browning chose to fill the space with a longer work of over 300 lines, another poem that he had written for Willie Macready to illustrate: "The Pied Piper of Hamelin."[40] The story had long been a favorite of Browning's, one that he knew in varying versions, including a prose summary in Wanley's *Wonders of the Little World* and one in Jeremy Collier's *Great Historical, Geographical, Genealogical and Poetical Dictionary* and a Latin version in Otto Melander's *Jocoseria*.[41] Browning's poem has delighted children of all ages, telling the story of how the piper rid the town of Hamelin of its plague of rats by enticing them with his magic piping to drown in the River Weser. When the town council refused to pay the piper his fee, he played a tune that made all the children follow him until they vanished through a magical entrance into a mountainside, never to return.

In this unique poem that Browning subtitled "A Child's Story," his play with language gives life and vigor to the old legend. The story bounces along with irregular rhymes, frequently including unusual combinations of sound to produce comic rhymes. Browning has created a rollicking rhythm by using short, tetrameter lines and giving them additional lilt by including many three-syllable feet and by tacking on frequent feminine endings. He added speed occasionally by thrusting in a pair of three-stress lines or some internal rhymes.

> Rats!
> They fought the dogs and killed the cats,
>   And bit the babies in the cradles,
> And ate the cheeses out of the vats,
>   And licked the soup from the cooks' own ladles,
> Split open the kegs of salted sprats,
> Made nests inside men's Sunday hats,
> And even spoiled the women's chats,
>   By drowning their speaking
>   With shrieking and squeaking
> In fifty different sharps and flats. (10–20)

Browning picked up a detail from a version of the story[42] that told of a little lame boy who could not keep up with the other children and was thus left behind when the entrance to the mountain closed. In an imaginative way, he created the boy's testimony of what the piper's magical lure seemed to mean for the children. It was a promise of a children's land of Cockaigne, and further, for the boy, the fulfillment of his dearest wish, a cure for his lameness:

> For he led us, he said, to a joyous land,
> Joining the town and just at hand,
> Where waters gushed and fruit-trees grew,
> And flowers put forth a fairer hue,
> And everything was strange and new;
> The sparrows were brighter than peacocks here,
> And their dogs outran our fallow deer,
> And honey-bees had lost their stings,
> And horses were born with eagles' wings;
> And just as I became assured
> My lame foot would be speedily cured,
> The music stopped and I stood still,
> And found myself outside the Hill. (233–45)

But the most imaginative touch of all was Browning's supplying an account by one of the rats, who had escaped drowning and who described a rats' vision of an earthly paradise that the piper's tune held out to them:

> At the first shrill notes of the pipe,
> I heard a sound as of scraping tripe,
> And putting apples, wondrous ripe,
> Into a cider-press's gripe:
> And a moving away of pickle-tub-boards,
> And a leaving ajar of conserve-cupboards,
> And a drawing the corks of train-oil-flasks,
> And a breaking the hoops of butter-casks;
> And it seemed as if a voice
> (Sweeter than by harp or by psaltery
> Is breathed) called out, "Oh rats, rejoice!
> The world is grown to one vast drysaltery!" (text of 1842; 121–32)

Browning's kindly gift for Willie Macready has been savored by readers for the last century and a half.

The immense variety in *Dramatic Lyrics* was the result of Browning's personal enjoyment of experimenting with form over the years and trying out his linguistic and metrical play on unusual subjects. The subjects he chose reflect his own taste for the unique and the unfashionable. The characters that speak his lines come from that library of both standard and out-of-the-way volumes collected by his father that he pored over during his years of self-education or from his eye-opening tour of Italy in 1838. None of his contemporaries could have created such a gallery—Civil War cavaliers, a proud, heartless Italian duke, a hate-filled Spanish monk, a determined Arabian warrior, a love-struck Provençal poet, a German theologian, a courtier prostrate with devotion for his queen, a Venetian serenader, a murderous household servant, a Greek goddess who speaks with a healing tone, a countess for whom a trial by combat was fought, and a rat who dreamed of an inexhaustible larder.

This sixteen-page pamphlet was worth a hundred *Sordellos*.

Chapter 10

Another Duchess and a Dying Bishop

While Browning was still in the grip of theater fever, he was approached in the spring of 1843 by Charles Kean, Macready's current rival on the London stage, to write a play for him. Tempted once more, he composed *Colombe's Birthday*, a historical drama set in the seventeenth century that centered on the conflicting claims for the rule of the Duchy of Juliers. Although the work has neither the innovative structure nor the imaginative vigor of *Pippa Passes*, it is much more compact and coherent than any of the four plays he wrote for Macready. In March 1844 he read the finished play to Kean and his wife, Ellen Tree, who accepted it for production but could not promise performance until the following spring. Kean also laid down a troubling condition: Browning was not to publish *Colombe's Birthday* in the interval.[1] Nor did he pay the two or three hundred pounds that Browning expected. Remembering Macready's postponements and hesitations about the two earlier productions, Browning nursed some serious misgivings: put not your trust in actors and managers. In spite of Kean's stipulation, he decided to publish the play—he had sent the copy to the printer on the same day as he read the play to Kean—and it appeared about five weeks later, as the next number of his *Bells and Pomegranates* series. His intention was to keep his name before the public. (The play was eventually produced in 1853 through the influence of Helen Faucit, who played the Duchess of Cleves and Juliers.)[2]

In *Colombe's Birthday*, Browning finally brought into action the theme that he had long ago described to Fanny Haworth of a love that was "a thorough self-devotement, a self-forgetting."[3] The hero, the young advocate, Valence, a "pale fiery young man," who is seeking to redress the wrongs done to the people of Cleves, adores the Duchess Colombe and has won her love, but he selflessly refuses to pursue his advantage, for he had learned that if she marries below her rank, she must forfeit her right to the duchy. Meanwhile, she has received an offer of marriage from Prince Berthold, the claimant to her duchy, who has made his offer as a gesture of political goodwill. The play ends happily, however, when Colombe voluntarily relinquishes her duchy to marry Valence.

Taken with the two poems on "Queen Worship," the "Sonnet" to Eliza Flower, "In a Gondola," and "Count Gismond," this play exhibits a romantic attitude toward love that recurs persistently in Browning's poetry. This romantic idea holds that true love, which begins at first sight, is single and intense in its direction, extreme in its expression, and everlasting in its devotion. Love in this manifestation is a secular form of religion, wherein the lover sees the beloved as an object of worship for whom he will endure danger, hardship, or humiliation—or even maintain a lifelong silence about his love if his beloved is out of reach. It is derived from the courtly love tradition of the medieval chivalric romances, with which Browning had become thoroughly familiar in his youthful reading. In the chivalric romances, the knight will go on impossible quests or take foolhardy risks in battle in order to prove himself worthy of his beloved. In lyric poetry, this romantic idea of love was treated fully by Dante and Petrarch, two of Browning's favorite poets. It seems clear that this is a concept of love that was shaped and developed by literary tradition rather than by life.[4]

As a young man, Robert Browning held to this romantic view of love in his personal life, too. Although he was thirty-two years old, his emotional life was still at an immature stage. Since he lived at home with his parents and had no means of livelihood, he seemed in this respect frozen in the role of a contented but overgrown adolescent. His repressed sexual feelings were sublimated into his studies and his creative work and thus fell easily into the imaginative patterns of chivalry. Mounted on the wall before him as he sat in his third-floor study at New Cross was a print taken from a fresco by Polidoro da Caravaggio of Perseus rescuing Andromeda from the dragon.[5] It is an erotic rendering of the nude and helpless Andromeda and an armor-clad Perseus raising his sword against a coiled dragon, who symbolizes lustful aggression. With his eyes on the picture, Browning had described her in *Pauline*:

> —so beautiful
> With her dark eyes, earnest and still, and hair
> Lifted and spread by the salt-sweeping breeze;

> And one red beam, all the storm leaves in heaven,
> Resting upon her eyes and face and hair,
> As she awaits the snake on the wet beach,
> By the dark rock, and the white wave just breaking
> At her feet; quite naked and alone.... (658–65; text of 1833)

During his early years, Browning had very little experience with the opposite sex outside the family household. He had responded to the universal charmer Eliza Flower, and he had been attracted to the artistic Fanny Haworth, both of whom were a decade older than he, a situation that discouraged any steps toward intimacy. His social life thus far had been largely confined to his male companions among the Colloquials and to the literary set that frequented the theater. Any intensity of feeling at this immature stage of his development would seem to have been directed more toward Alfred Domett and John Forster than toward Eliza or Fanny—or even Helen Faucit, who had brought his heroines to life on the stage. His devotion to his calling as a poet did not allow for any plans for marriage: financially dependent upon his father, with no immediate prospects for an income of his own, he was in no position to support a wife and family. (He had before him the terrible example of the debt-ridden Leigh Hunt, reduced to hackwork and to frequent sponging off his friends.) Robert Browning seemed destined to lead a bachelor's celibate life.

ↂ ↂ ↂ

Meanwhile, Browning's reputation as a poet was growing because of his persistent efforts at publication over the years. In October of 1842, R. H. Horne wrote a lengthy article on Browning's work, from *Paracelsus* up through *King Victor and King Charles*, which he published in the *Church of England Quarterly Review*.[6] In this overview, Horne set Browning before the public as a contemporary poet worthy to stand beside Tennyson. He dismissed *Strafford* as a "maimed thing" for the stage but called *Sordello* "the richest puzzle to all lovers of poetry which was ever given to the world." He recognized Browning as a poet of great promise and even urged him to revise and clarify *Sordello* because of its profundity and the many beautiful passages that made it a work deserving a wider readership. The Ottima and Sebald scene in *Pippa Passes*, in Horne's opinion, "for profound tragic emotion surpasses anything of a like nature in the modern acted drama." He likened the character of Ottima to Lady Macbeth and the Duchess of Malfi. Horne judged that Browning's *Paracelsus* had built a reputation among the critics "who regard poetry of a superior kind as a thing to be respected and studied." He recommended that "Professors of poetry should decypher and comment upon a few lines [of *Sordello*] every morning before breakfast" and that young students should be drilled upon it.

This was heady material for Browning to find in print, and he hastened to send a clipping to Domett, telling him that he had heard that the "sharp bits" in the article had been inserted by a subeditor in order to balance the general enthusiasm of the critic.[7]

Some of the reviews of *Dramatic Lyrics* had been encouraging, too, even though the big quarterlies still ignored Browning's poetry. Forster in the *Examiner*[8] found proof in the collection that Browning showed a "firmer march and steadier control" as he continued to publish. He especially appreciated Browning's technique, declaring that "in the art of versification he must be called a master" and (no doubt thinking of "The Pied Piper") that "for the neatness of his rhymes in his lighter efforts, we think that Butler would have hugged him." The critic in the *Morning Herald*[9] felt that the "Camp (French)" demonstrates "how masterly a hand he throws across his lyre." The reviewer in the *Monthly Magazine* was now ready to say that there could be no denial that "Mr. Browning is a great poet."[10] The critic for the *Church of England Quarterly Review*[11] (possibly R. H. Horne once more) gave a long, perceptive review in which he quoted "My Last Duchess" and offered a commentary indicating that he recognized the subtlety of Browning's gradual revelation of the duke's character. He then chose "Artemis Prologizes" for special praise: "the whole reads like the finest possible translation of some noble Greek poem."

Most of the reviews quoted extensively from the volume, printing such items as "Cloister (Spanish)," "My Last Duchess," "In a Gondola," extracts from "The Pied Piper," and one of the "Cavalier Tunes." It is historically interesting to note that some of the reviewers regarded the monodramatic form as new or unusual, and a few did not know how to read these dramatic pieces or at least were bewildered by Browning's handling of the form. Even Horne (if indeed it were he) commented that Browning wrote "sometimes by delicate insinuation" that went beyond the reach of ordinary readers.[12]

ॐ ॐ ॐ

One of the great punsters of the early nineteenth century, Thomas Hood, the lighthearted parodist and social satirist, was dying of tuberculosis. Browning had known of him both as a neighbor in Peckham and as a struggling fellow poet, although he had never met him. An assistant editor of

Hood's Magazine, F. O. Ward, called upon friends to help Hood out in his last year by contributing their work to be published in the magazine. When he asked Browning if he had anything on hand that would be a filler, Browning replied, "I will this minute set about transcribing the best of whatever I can find in my desk likely to suit you—and will send it in the course of the day . . . morning, I hope."[13] What he found he entitled "The Laboratory (Ancien Régime)," and Ward published it in the June 1844 issue.

It is a horrific dramatic monologue set in late-seventeenth-century France, spoken by a court lady who takes excited delight in her plans to poison the rival who had stolen her lover.[14] Speaking to an aged creator of poisons in his laboratory, she relishes watching him mix the deadly concoction that she will slip into her rival's drink. The final lines of the poem add a perverse touch as she bids the poison-maker seal their bargain:

> You may kiss me, old man, on my mouth if you will!
> But brush this dust off me, lest horror there springs
> Ere I know it—next moment I dance at the King's! ([46–48]
>   text of 1844)

There is a similar frisson in "Claret" which, along with "Tokay," appeared in the same issue of *Hood's*. The speaker, when tossing an empty claret flask into a pond, offers a grim simile:

> Our laughing little flask, compelled
>   Through depth to depth more bleak and shady;
> As when, both arms beside her held,
>   Feet straightened out, some gay French lady
> Is caught up from life's light and motion,
> And dropped into death's silent ocean! (7–12)

This is a side of Browning reflecting a fascination with the powers of darkness and with evil and resulting in his interest in getting inside the minds of murderers and lunatics as well as of slightly deranged, obsessive human beings. Further, there was a dark streak in Browning's tastes and personality too, nurtured perhaps by his father's interests in murder cases and by his reading in some of the eccentric books in his father's library. In his third-floor study, he had on his desk two skulls, in one of which he watched a pet spider weaving its web in the hollow of the jaw.[15] This kind of Gothic desk decoration is physical evidence of Browning's taste for the macabre, like the daggers he looted from the shipwreck with its mutilated corpses, off the coast of Algiers. This side of Browning was either a psychic balance to the idealistic side of his nature or a reaction to the repressive life he lived surrounded by the churchgoing quietude of the middle-class communities of Camberwell and New Cross.[16] In either case, its manifestation in his published work thrust before readers scenes and characters that shocked or repelled many reviewers, who denounced him for breaches of taste or decorum.

&⅜ &⅜ &⅜

Browning was buoyed up by the recent responses to *Dramatic Lyrics*. Writing to Domett, he confessed, "I feel myself so much stronger, if flattery not deceive." He indicated that he was taking an interest in writing short monodramatic poems now, and he postponed work on the two additional plays that he had planned to publish in his *Bells and Pomegranates* series. "I really seem to have something fresh to say. In all probability, however, I shall go to Italy first,—(Naples & Rome—) for my head is dizzy and wants change."[17]

This second trip to Italy in the autumn of 1844 confirmed and intensified Browning's love for Italy and began the long parade of poems reflecting his keen observation and his fine sensibility as they drew upon the sights and sounds of this un-English Mediterranean nation. We have no record of his itinerary this time, but we can piece together a general outline and a few details from comments in letters or in allusions that crop up in his poems, plus one page of dates that he had jotted down in the early part of the trip.[18]

On August 12, 1844, Browning sailed for Italy on the merchant ship *Ariadne*, a passage that cost him about £10. As the ship rounded the Iberian peninsula, he was moved by what he saw and began writing verse. On September 5, in the endpapers of Bartoli's *De Simboli Trasporti al Morale*, he set down in pencil the poem later entitled "Home Thoughts from the Sea,"[19] a splendid patriotic tribute to Nelson's victory, seven long lines with a single rhyme, drawing together the view of the sunset—"one glorious blood-red, reeking into Cadiz Bay" (2)—and the memory of the glorious sea battle that destroyed the French and Spanish fleet in 1805. About the same time he probably wrote "Here's to Nelson's memory!" a lively toast which closes with an anecdote about Nelson told to Browning by *Ariadne's* captain, R. Crozier, presented with the same jaunty wordplay that had enlivened "The Pied Piper":

> He [Crozier] says that at Greenwich they point the beholder
> To Nelson's coat, "still with tar on the shoulder:
> For he used to lean with one shoulder digging,
> Jigging, as it were, and zig-zag-zigging
> Up against the mizen-rigging!"

Further along on the voyage, as the ship was sailing from Sicily to Naples, he scribbled another poem in his copy of Bartoli,[20] "How They Brought the Good News from Ghent to Aix." It was a curious place to write an historical poem that reflected the revolt of the Low Countries against Spanish oppression in the late sixteenth century, but since Browning later received many inquiries about the occasion of the ride and what the "good news" was, we know more about the writing of the poem than is usual with a Browning work. The weather was hot, the sea was calm, he remembers: "I had a good horse at home in my stables, and I thought to myself how much I should like a breezy gallop. As I could not ride on board ship, I determined to enjoy a ride in imagination."[21] He drew upon his memory of galloping in a coach through Flanders on his way to St. Petersburg and of his reading in Reformation history, and produced a breathtaking story of three messengers galloping night and day to carry word to a besieged town that help was on the way.[22] There is an urgency and speed from the very opening of the poem, and the galloping anapests and trochees of the four-beat lines speed us through to the end of the journey sixty lines later.[23] This poem became one of Browning's most popular dramatic narratives, read and recited by schoolchildren throughout the English-speaking world for the next century and a half.

Nearing Naples, Browning asked Captain Crozier to wake him as they passed Capri: he wanted to see the villa where Tiberius Caesar had spent his last days. On September 26, the ship arrived at Naples, whose setting on the bay, with Mount Vesuvius in the background, has never failed to fill a traveler with wonder. Using a guidebook that B. W. Procter had given him, *Notes on Naples and Its Environs*,[24] Browning explored the vicinity for about three weeks. He loved the vivacity of the Neapolitan people and the diversity of the city scene—palace, castles, churches, the steep hills, the narrow medieval streets, sometimes with washing hanging on lines high above, the music and song. He enjoyed the city so much that he later considered it as a haven when he and Elizabeth were planning to leave London.

On the day he arrived, he discovered that an opera house was presenting one act of an opera *Sordello* that very night. He attended and never had to look once at the libretto. He wandered over to nearby Sorrento with its peaceful walks high on the cliffs above Naples Bay. On October 4 he visited the nearby Galli Islands, where legend placed the Sirens who sang to Odysseus. He picked up a shell from the beach to bring home as a souvenir.[25] He climbed Mount Vesuvius; he prowled among the ruins of Pompeii.[26]

By good fortune, he became friends with a young Neapolitan, a Signor Scotti, who not only became his guide in Naples but also accompanied him to Rome, acting as a sort of courier, making travel and hotel arrangements and doing the necessary bargaining. In Rome they spent many evenings with an acquaintance of Browning's father, the Countess Carducci.[27]

In the Protestant cemetery Browning paid homage to the grave of Keats and to the grave-site where Trelawney had buried Shelley's heart. He may have plucked a flower from Keats's grave as he did on a later visit in 1859, or a tendril of ivy from Shelley's.[28] He ventured out into the Campagna along the Via Appia Antiqua to visit the grotto of Egeria, a spot celebrated by Byron's lines on love in *Childe Harold's Pilgrimage*.[29] Here he collected some fennel seeds, but when he planted them at home, they turned out to be hemlock.[30]

On a memorable day he visited the Piazza Santa Maria Maggiore, where he must have paid a visit to the basilica, for this fifth-century church is one of the great pilgrimage goals in Rome. But we do know that he stepped into Santa Prassede, a small ninth-century parish church with a plain brick façade, across the piazza. It is typical of Browning that he would take more interest in this humble structure than he would in the great center of pilgrimage on the opposite side of the piazza. Yet when a traveler enters Santa Prassede, he sees a jewel box of mosaic decoration. Georgina Masson has called it "the most exquisite mosaic-decorated chapel in Rome, whose medieval name 'the garden of paradise' is easily understood."[31] It is also typical of Browning that his attention fastened less on the gorgeous mosaics than on two burial monuments: one highly decorated and embellished with motifs from classical and Christian sources, the sepulchre of Cardinal Alain Cetine de Taillebour; the other the rather plain tomb of Cardinal Panteleone Anchier de Troyes. The contrast between the two tombs struck a creative spark in Browning that later developed into his poem "The Tomb at Saint Praxed's" (subsequently entitled "The Bishop Orders His Tomb at Saint Praxed's Church").

In late October Browning traveled to Florence. He later told Elizabeth that he did not care for the atmosphere of the city because it was overrun with English residents and tourists. His guide book also warned him that the drinking water in the city was unsafe, except for that from a fountain near Santa Croce.[32] Nevertheless he sought out the principal sights. Later remarks show that he paid more than one visit to the Uffizi Gallery, where he was able to view its unsurpassable collection of major works by the master painters of the Italian Renaissance. He specifically mentioned the Tribune Room (where he heard too many English voices[33]), which is renowned for its Medici portraits by Pontormo and Bronzino. He also mentioned seeing, in the Medici Church of San Lorenzo, Michelangelo's statue of Lorenzo de Medici seated, which is sometimes called "Il Pensiero."[34] Since he made his way to the Duomo, he probably also stepped over to the nearby baptistry to study Ghiberti's bronze doors with scenes from the Old Testament and then went inside to admire the overpowering mosaics.

Pisa was his next stop. Here he judged the cathedral with its alternating colors of marble to be more impressive than that in Florence. Its Romanesque bronze doors with scenes from both Old and New Testaments must certainly have caught his eye. The whole assembly of great religious monuments in the Piazza del Duomo—the cathedral, baptistry, and the leaning campanile— with "the green grass round,"[35] he found especially memorable.

Most of the cities he had visited on this trip were associated with Shelley, and he now came in even closer contact when he traveled to Leghorn to meet Edward Trelawney, friend of both Byron and Shelley, who had been present at the funeral pyre when Shelley's body was burned and who had snatched Shelley's heart from the smoldering embers. Browning did not record what Trelawney told him about the two poets, but he did say that during the interview Trelawney was having a surgeon remove a bullet that had long been lodged in his leg.[36]

In early December he returned home by a route much like that he followed in 1838, over the Alps, down the Rhine, and through Flanders to a channel port. His travels had planted his heart in the European past, especially the Italian Renaissance. He was now prepared to become England's new international poet.

Browning arrived home in mid-December, Joseph Arnould reported, "full of Venice, Rome, Naples, & enthusiasm, with restored health, increased spirits & I hope a successful poem or two inpetto."[37]

The chief poem to emerge, "The Tomb at Saint Praxed's (Rome 15_)," was the most important poem that Browning had yet created. On February 18, 1845, he sent it off to *Hood's*, where it was published in March. It reappeared soon in the next issue of *Bells and Pomegranates*. This dramatic monologue reflects that feature of the form that Arthur Hallam had noted about Tennyson's monodramatic work: it seems like the shortened version of a play. All the action is in the present; any previous happenings are implied or described. The splendid ironies of the bishop's monologue make up much of its appeal: the mixing of the spiritual and the material, the religious and the secular, Christian and pagan, this life and the afterlife. Ruskin's praise of the poem for its embodiment of the inconsistencies of the Renaissance spirit is well known, and for more recent critics the text, with all its concrete suggestiveness, raises questions about the nature of representation and of action-inducing language, presents a drama of homosocial conflict (for the bishop defines himself by his rivalry with Gandolf and subordinates his mistress to that ongoing struggle), and obliquely embodies a critique of contemporary Victorian culture, for Browning told the subeditor of *Hood's*, F. O. Ward, that he was satirizing, indirectly, the Oxford Movement and the Camden Society (which advocated a return to the vestments and ritual of the Roman Church). The poem, he said, was "a pet of mine, and just the thing for the time—what with the Oxford business, and Camden society and other embroilments."[38]

⚵ ⚵ ⚵

One evening in the mid-1830s when Robert Browning was dining at Serjeant Talfourd's elegant townhouse on Russell Square, he had been approached by a genial elderly man wearing a pair of round spectacles, who asked him if his father's name was Robert and if he had attended Mr. Bell's School in Cheshunt. The man introduced himself as John Kenyon, who had been Robert's father's old schoolmate and good friend.[39] It was not until May 1837 that Robert arranged a meeting between the two,[40] but in the meantime he had become more acquainted with Kenyon, who was frequently found in the literary circles to which Browning had been introduced through Macready and Forster.

John Kenyon had been born in Jamaica in 1784 and brought to England when he was about five years old. He was a remote cousin of the poet Elizabeth Barrett and had known her father at Trinity College, Cambridge, in the early 1800s. A poet himself, he knew Wordsworth, Southey, Landor, and all of the literary figures of Robert's generation. Wordsworth frequently stayed with Kenyon when he came to London, where Browning developed an acquaintance with him. Kenyon had been instrumental in introducing Elizabeth Barrett to Wordsworth and Landor and to Mary Russell Mitford, who became one of her closest friends and correspondents.[41]

In the early 1840s Kenyon tried to arrange a meeting between Robert and Elizabeth, but the shy Miss Barrett held him off. Yet when Robert returned from Italy he discovered, through a copy of Elizabeth's recent two-volume *Poems*, which Kenyon had sent to Sarianna, that she was an admirer of his work. In her poem "Lady Geraldine's Courtship," the young poet Bertram reads aloud to Lady Geraldine passages from Spenser and Petrarch:

> Or at times a modern volume,—Wordsworth's
>   solemn-thoughted idyl,
> Howitt's ballad-verse, or Tennyson's enchanted reverie,—
> Or from Browning some 'Pomegranate,' which, if cut deep down the
>   middle,
> Shows a heart within blood-tinctured, of a veined humanity. (161–64)

She had been an enthusiastic reader of Browning's work for some time. She had been enthralled by *Paracelsus*, although she did not approve of the roughness of his meters, "the defect in harmony," as she called it.[42] She was a great admirer of his plays, especially *Pippa Passes*, which she defended against Mary Russell Mitford's criticism.[43] She liked most of the *Dramatic Lyrics*, although she "sighed over" his "vain jangling with rhymes."[44] The obscurity in his work troubled her too, but she bore with him as a "riddle-maker"[45] because she regarded him as "a master in clenched passion . . . concentrated passion . . . burning through the metallic fissures of language."[46] Also she felt drawn beyond the everyday world by this intensity: "I like, I do like, the 'heart of a mystery' when it beats moderate time! I like a twilight of mysticism— when the sun & moon both shine together!"[47] She discussed his work in letters to "Orion" Horne, to her brother George, to the poet Thomas West- wood, and repeatedly in letters to Miss Mitford. She recognized him, along with Tennyson, as "original" because he was "strong enough to express his own individuality."[48] Altogether she thought him "a true soul-piercing poet."[49] But she was afraid to meet him in person when Kenyon proposed it.

The ebullient Robert, who had always eagerly taken opportunities to meet the literary celebrities of his day, now had a pretext to write to her and express his admiration for her new volumes, which he had told Domett con- tained "some divine things."[50] After he consulted with Kenyon, who strongly urged him to write, he began his letter by blurting out a personal response: "I love your verses with all my heart, dear Miss Barrett—and this is no off- hand complimentary letter that I shall write." And indeed this praise came in gushes of his own enthusiasm: "part of me has it become, this great living poetry of yours, not a flower of which but took root and grew." He embraced her work because of "the fresh strange music, the affluent language, the exquisite pathos and true new brave thought." All the chivalric yearning toward a lady whose colors he might wear in jousting with the world now seemed to burst forth in this first letter: "I do, as I say, love these Books with all my heart—and I love you too."[51] Here was the beginning of the most cel- ebrated courtship of the nineteenth century.

Chapter 11

A Worthy Fellow Poet

Writing to her old friend and former neighbor Julia Martin on January 11, 1845, Elizabeth Barrett reported the surprise that the mail had brought her. "I had a letter from Browning the poet last night which threw me into ecstasies."[1] Being diffident herself, she was not used to sudden revelations of feeling, but Browning's openheartedness did not scare her away. Indeed, it appealed to her vulnerability. Replying the next day, she thanked him profusely for the praises that had tumbled out of his letter. "Sympathy is dear—very dear to me: but the sympathy of a poet & of such a poet, is the quintessence of sympathy to me!" She quickly admitted that she was a "devout admirer & student of your works," and she expressed her regret that she had lost the chance to meet him three years ago. She suggested perhaps in the spring they could arrange it.[2]

Browning was not long in writing again with a hasty, scattered series of references to his travels in Rome and Naples, to Tasso and Titian, and finally a declaration that her poetry meant far more to him than his could possibly mean to her. He then gave his reasons and steered his compliments into professional chat, "for you *do* what I always wanted, hoped to do . . . you speak out, *you*,—I only make men & women speak,—give you truth broken into prismatic hues, and fear the pure white light, even if it is in me."[3]

Her answering letter was in a comfortable informal vein, which she confessed was characteristic of her, what her Italian teacher had called "headlong." The letter rambled on about their common friend Richard Hengist Horne's travels in Germany, but it soon turned to literary talk about striving after the expression of that inner-felt truth: "What no mere critic sees, but what you, an artist, know, is the difference between the thing desired & the thing attained, between the idea in the writer's mind, & the ειδωλον cast off in his work." She closed with an appreciation of "the delight of your friendship."[4]

Very quickly each of the two poets had recognized a fellow spirit, and they were now launched into an extended exchange of ideas, plans, and hopes, along with personal revelations that Elizabeth had encouraged when she expressed her readiness to add Robert to her select group of regular correspondents, but urged, "Only *dont* let us have any constraint, any ceremony! *Dont* be civil to me when you feel rude,—nor loquacious, when you incline to silence,—nor yielding in the manners, when you are perverse in the mind."[5]

Who was this new literary friend whom Robert was so eager to know? Elizabeth Barrett had recently attained a sudden celebrity with her *Poems* in two volumes, 1844, a body of work that made her preeminent among contemporary women poets, now that Felicia Hemans and L. E. L. (Letitia Elizabeth Landon) were no longer among the living. Her new publication had received high praise for its principal work, "A Drama of Exile," a verse play quite worthy of its Miltonic inspiration, in which Adam and Eve, after the Fall, repent their transgression against God, contend once more with Lucifer outside Eden, but are drawn out of their despair by an apparition of Christ, who prophesies that Eve will bear the seed whereby evil and sin will be overcome. Another religious poem was "The Dead Pan," an answer to Schiller's "Götter Griechenlands," which had bemoaned the passing of the Greek gods and all the power and beauty they represented. Barrett's poem took an opposing view as it celebrated Christianity's triumph over the "vain false gods of Hellas." Her volumes also presented an admirable gathering of lyrics, sonnets, meditations, narratives, plus "A Vision of Poets," a literary catalogue of tributes to the great, from Homer down to Coleridge, all of whom had produced art out of suffering.

Her poetic success had a long development behind it. She had been, like Browning, a rhymester since childhood, hiding her verses "between the mattrasses [*sic*] of my crib—a little mahogany crib."[6] At age eight, she produced some lines on virtue and for them received from her father a letter addressed to the "Poet Laureat [*sic*] of Hope End" (her childhood home in Herefordshire).[7] After Elizabeth checked the dictionary to find out what laureate meant, she undertook a laureate's duty and over the years produced birthday odes for all members of the family and verses for holidays and special occasions. She wrote plays for the Barrett children to perform. Sitting in her little "house," a retreat under the sideboard, she composed, between the ages of nine and eleven, a series of short epic poems,[8] culminating when she was twelve in *The Battle of Marathon*, a highly creditable imitation of Pope's style in his Homeric translations. Her father had fifty copies printed for private circulation in 1820.

Her remarkable creativity continued to flow, and six years later, at age twenty, Barrett published *An Essay on Mind* (1826), another imitation of Pope in heroic couplets, which displayed an impressive range of learning and an easy familiarity with the history of ideas and with the major writers of both English and classical literature. This work caught the attention of a local classical scholar, Hugh Stuart Boyd, with whom she then developed an extensive correspondence, which led to her study of Greek under his tutelage for four years. Indeed she developed a girlish crush on Boyd, who was married, blind, and twenty-five years her senior. Elizabeth was still in her early twenties when she finally met Boyd in person, and her attachment to him lasted until he left the area and the Barretts moved to Sidmouth in 1832, although she continued correspondence with him and her feelings gradually became more filial. As a result of Boyd's scholarly stimulus, she undertook a verse translation of Aeschylus' *Prometheus Bound* and arranged for its publication in 1833.

These published volumes had each included short poems of varying interest and maturity, but Barrett took further steps forward in the next few years, placing many short poems worthy of publication in the *Athenaeum*, the *New Monthly Magazine*, and Mary Russell Mitford's annual, *Finden's Tableaux*. This accumulation of poems was reprinted in her next volume, *The Seraphim and Other Poems*, 1838, in which for the first time she allowed her name to be placed on the title page. The title poem, "The Seraphim," which she called "a dramatic lyric, rather than a lyrical drama,"[9] was an intensely religious work on the crucifixion of Christ as witnessed by the angels of heaven and by allegorical spirits of earth. In the preface she maintained that "had Aeschylus lived after the incarnation and crucifixion of our Lord Jesus Christ, he might have turned" to this subject.[10] Encouraged by the response to this volume, she had rededicated herself to "this divine art of poetry"[11] and over the next few years had produced a mature body of work that had brought her to her present standing in the literary world.

At the end of January 1845, Elizabeth wrote again to Mrs. Martin with the news "I am getting deeper & deeper into correspondence with Robert Browning, poet & mystic,—& we are growing to be the truest of friends."[12] Indeed, she began to feel both a professional and personal association with him. She had spoken with critical discernment of his monodramatic experiments in *Dramatic Lyrics*, which she understood were "not dramatic in the strict sense" although "a great dramatic power may develop itself otherwise than in the formal drama." Yet she hoped for work that would be more revealing of his own ideas and feelings. She wished that he would "give the public a poem unassociated directly or indirectly with the stage, for a trial on the popular heart."[13]

She began quite ingenuously to lure Robert by her open admiration of his work. No reviewer had ever shown such appreciation and understanding of what he was doing. No friend, neither Domett nor Forster, had commented with the detailed critical response that Elizabeth was capable of expressing. She praised the range of his work, "from those high faint notes of the mystics . . . to dramatic impersonations, gruff with nature, 'gr-r— you swine.'" As a poet, she could be especially delighted to see these diverse elements "thrown into harmony," as in *Pippa Passes*.[14]

She thrust herself imaginatively into his creative life in a desire to be part of it. She pictured his top-floor room with the *Bells and Pomegranates* poems lying about, with her own volumes of poems beside them, a proof "of your caring for them so much beyond the tide-mark of my hopes. . . . Overjoyed I am with this cordial sympathy."[15] She told him she wanted to know all about him—what books he read, what hours he wrote in, what writers influenced his early work, and how his tastes had changed over time.

Robert was not quite ready to be so open about his literary practices. He admitted that "what I have printed gives *no* knowledge of me." "I never have begun, even, what I hope I was born to begin and end,—'R. B. a poem.'" If what she had read of his work so far seemed a "sadly imperfect demonstration" of his ability, "these scenes and song-scraps *are* such mere and very escapes of my inner power."[16] His letters so far did not give much more. From thickets of good-natured verbiage about publishers and critics came only some indications that he wrote out of a sense of "duty"; then he veered off into talk about reviewers. But Elizabeth was persistent. She had her poet in an epistolary dock, and she wanted some answers. If she could not know him from his printed works then "teach me yourself . . . you." In the correspondence so far, "your rays fall obliquely rather than directly straight. . . . Do tell me all of yourself that you can & will . . . before the R. B. poem comes out."[17] She particularly wanted to know about his habits as a writer, about his personal surroundings as he spun out his dramatic verses. What about those two skulls that Horne had told her about?

Robert obliged by allowing her a glimpse into his study. He described the skulls and the spiders that he had domesticated, one "a great fellow that housed himself, with real gusto, in the jaws of a great scull [*sic*], whence he watched me as I wrote." He revealed the presence of his print of Andromeda and the dragon. He told her of his plans for his play in progress, *Luria*, and his accumulated cluster of "Romances and Lyrics, all dramatic," a "dancing ring of men & women," and his hopes for his personal poem: "*Now*—I call it . . . what is to be done *now*, believed *now*,—so far as it has been revealed to me—solemn words, truly,—and to find myself writing them to anyone else! Enough now."[18] This was a more intimate peep into his literary workshop than he had ever allowed anyone—even sister Sarianna, his confidante in New Cross.

His disclosure prompted Elizabeth to describe her own plans and literary ambitions. She told him about her *Prometheus Bound*, the remaining copies of which she had demanded that her father lock up in his wardrobe, for she was ashamed of the unpoetic literalness of her translation, and about her intention to undertake a retranslation. She would include her reissue of it with a companion work, "a monodram [*sic*] of my own—not a long poem, . . but a monologue of Aeschylus as he sate a blind exile on the flats of Sicily and recounted the past to his own soul, just before the eagle cracked his great massy skull with a stone."[19] But more surprising, she revealed her resolve to write a bold and unfeminine "novel-poem." It was to startle the middle-class reading public, "running into the midst of our conventions, & rushing into drawing rooms . . . & so, meeting face to face & without mask, the Humanity of the age, & speaking the truth as I conceive of it, out plainly."[20] This was the first glimmer of the major work of Elizabeth Barrett's later career, *Aurora Leigh*.

Robert was enthusiastic about her proposed novel-poem, "the *only* Poem to be undertaken now by you or anyone that *is* a Poet at all."[21] But he had much more to say about her *Prometheus* translation. He even recommended that she create a complete prelude to it, a replacement of the lost Aeschylean work that was part of the trilogy. *Prometheus Firebearer* he called it and outlined the plot of a play that he once had thought to compose himself.

As he scribbled along, he joked about the peculiarities of his enigmatic style when he had tried to express what her friendship meant to him: "the language with which I talk to myself of these matters is spiritual Attic and 'loves contractions' as grammarians say,—but I read it myself, and well know what it means."[22] Elizabeth was pleased, in any case, about what he had tried to say. She finally told Mary Russell Mitford, who was jealous of any intimate correspondent of Elizabeth's, about their recent letter exchange: "Mr. Browning & I have grown to be devoted friends. . . . And then he writes letters to me with Attic contractions, saying he '*loves*' me. Who can resist *that*—?—." She found him "quite heart-moving & irresistible."[23] She confessed her resolve to grant him his wish to meet with her when the summer began.

As the weeks went by, Robert had come to realize that Elizabeth was not only a poet but also an intellectual of extensive learning and scholarly inclination, in fact someone whose experience of study and omnivorous reading was not unlike his own. This was evident in the allusions and quotations in her letters but especially in the prefaces to her books of poetry. She had also published essays in the *Athenaeum*: first, a series in four installments, "Some Account of the Greek Christian Poets" (February 26 to March 19, 1842); second, and most impressive, a series in five installments (June 4 to August 13, 1842), "The Book of the Poets," a review that became a short history of English poetry from Chaucer, Langland, and Gower up to Wordsworth and a brief mention of her contemporaries, "the Tennysons and Brownings."[24]

This display of learning reflected Barrett's continual study from her earliest years. She had been precocious in every way that was associated with language. She read "very prettily"[25] by the time of her fourth birthday and wrote coherent letters by age five and a half. Her earliest reading went from fairy tales and *The Seven Champions of Christiandom* to children's histories of England and of Rome. Her lessons were supervised by her mother, who led her, at age eight, through Pope's *Iliad*, passages from Milton's *Paradise Lost*, Shakespeare's *The Tempest*, *Othello*, and some history plays. The Barrett family visited France when Elizabeth was nine years old, and they remained in Boulogne for seven months, during which time, under French tutors, she learned to speak French fluently. Later at home she learned to read and write French under her French governess, Rosa Gordin. At age ten, when her younger brother Edward (called "Bro") began study with a Latin master, Mr. McSwinney, she joined him and soon surpassed him, especially when they started to learn Greek the following year.

This first grappling with Greek was "rather guessing & stammering and tottering through parts of Homer & extracts from Zenophon [*sic*], than reading,"[26] but her love for Homer drove her to study Greek by herself after Bro went to Charterhouse in London for his formal education. By May 1839, when she was thirteen, she could claim a working knowledge of Greek grammar and syntax and could put together acceptable sentences.

She read widely during her teens—all the major English poets up to Byron and Wordsworth, who were her favorites among the moderns. By dint of hard study of the English, European, and classical historians and philosophers, she acquired, over time, an enviable foundation for her later career. In the preface to *An Essay on Mind* (1826) she made references to books that Henry Cary said "no young man of his day at Oxford had ever looked into."[27]

At the time she began her association with Hugh Boyd, she told him, "My classical studies have been very solitary & unassisted."[28] Yet she was giving daily lessons in Greek to her younger brothers George and Charles John (called "Stormie"), taking them through passages in Homer and Xenophon.

When she began reading Aeschylus' *Septem Contra Thebas* under Boyd in 1831, he found her grammar "slovenly." He marveled that she could "read so fluently & *be* so ignorant [of] . . . 'Ladye Gramar'"[29] (as she later told Kenyon), and he began drilling her on all the forms of τυπτω and the μι verbs. But grammar or no, her skill in writing poetry was so far advanced that she could translate Aeschylus' choral odes into English verse easily. Her scholarly determination was so relentless during her early twenties that she read through all the tragedies of Aeschylus, Sophocles, and Euripides; several comedies of Aristophanes, the Odes of Pindar, Epictetus' *Enchiridion*, Theophrastus' *Characters*, all the dialogues of Plato except the *Laws*; Aristotle's *Poetics*, *Rhetoric*, and *Ethics*; Herodotus, Xenophon, Thucydides, Theocritus, Bion, Anacreon, and many minor Greek writers. In addition, Boyd had taken her through a wearying series of the poems and sermons of the Greek Christian writers, St. Gregory Nazianzen, St. John Chrysostom, St. Basil, and Synesius of Cyrene. She had already read the major Latin writers. She found Hebrew a simpler language than Greek and was able to learn it on her own. In 1832 she read through the complete Hebrew Bible. Earlier, of course, she had gone through the whole of the New Testament in Greek, and she frequently reread the Gospels. For relaxation from her studies, she devoured novels both in English and French. She had mastered Italian in her teens. In her thirties she was beginning German and soon reading Schiller and Goethe, but she did not respond with pleasure to the German language as such.

Since references in Elizabeth's letters ranged up and down the whole of European literature with wit and wordplay, Robert Browning was charmed by her intellectual agility as well as by her cultural breadth. He began to feel within his deepest being that he had discovered another self but of a female kind, someone whose life was dedicated to poetry but who had also striven on her own to grasp all knowledge. Further, he had learned from Kenyon that she was an invalid, though he knew nothing of the cause of her condition, only that she was largely confined to her room and that her health was fragile. His romantic inclinations toward chivalrous rescue were stirred.

In the past, he had never let anyone see his work until it was published, except for Sarianna, his amanuensis who made fair copies for the printer. But this fellow feeling toward Elizabeth made him want to open up his workshop to her, both to show off his talents in process and to gain by her critical overview of his poems in their early state. He went so far as to say he would like her to look over "Saul," a poem he was having difficulty finishing. In her reply, Elizabeth wondered if he hinted that he would show her the work in his portfolio. She had been intrigued by the first part of "The Flight of the Duchess," which he had published in *Hood's,* and she expressed her wish to see the remainder if it were completed. Surprisingly Robert was ready to let her see the present versions of everything that he had in progress. He declared that he would welcome her criticism of his "new Romances and Lyrics, and Lays & Plays" and asked her to "read them and heed them and end them and mend them!"[30]

He grew restless waiting for the invitation she had held out to him that he might visit in the spring, and he urged her strongly to grant it as the month of May came on. But Elizabeth, open and intimate in letters, was shy and apprehensive about a personal visit and began to procrastinate: Spring is late this year; she has not yet been downstairs;[31] she cannot admit visitors "in a general way"; "there is nothing to see in me,—nor to hear in me"; "if my poetry is worth anything to any eye,—it is the flower of me ... the rest of me is nothing but a root, fit for the ground & the dark."[32] But she yielded at last and agreed to let him call on May 20, 1845.

Because of the many details in Elizabeth's letters both before and after the event, we can re-create much of what Robert observed on that appointed day he turned off Marylebone Road to approach the Barrett home at 50 Wimpole Street. He saw a narrow street lined on both sides by attached Georgian houses of dark red brick with "high star-raking chimneys."[33] Elizabeth had remarked that the walls "look so much like Newgate's turned inside out."[34] The Barrett house was five stories high, the top story showing low-ceilinged rooms designed for servants' quarters, where some of the youngest Barrett sons also slept (Octavius was two stories above Elizabeth).

Robert was not received in the drawing room. Arabella Barrett escorted him up three flights to Elizabeth's room, a large bedroom disguised as a sitting room, at one end "the bed, like a sofa & no bed."[35] In the middle was a sofa with an armchair opposite, also a large table piled with books and papers. Since the room was at the back of the house, it was dark, although it had five windows, three of which formed a bay window. Elizabeth, in a feeble attempt to suggest rural life, had planted nasturtiums and scarlet runners in a deep window box, and from it a network of branching ivy climbed high up to be fastened at sister Henrietta's window above. She had a transparent blind in the window that showed, when illuminated by the sun, a castle, peasants, and groves of trees.[36]

Elizabeth tried her best to import what she could to suggest the outdoors: her favorite color for draperies and carpeting was green, "that I might so live in an everlasting sort of forest shadow."[37]

But the room had a distinct literary appearance. Shelves lined with books, her favorite kind of furniture, stood on the chest of drawers, and on shelves over the washstand there was a bust of Chaucer above the volumes of English poetry and one of Homer above Greek literature. Three other literary busts stared down from the top of the wardrobe. Framed portraits of Browning, Tennyson, Wordsworth, Carlyle, and Harriet Martineau usually adorned the walls, but in preparation for Robert's visit Elizabeth had removed his picture "in a fit of shyness" and also one of Tennyson "in a fit of justice."[38]

The man whom Arabella introduced was short and slim, with a brisk step and a sun-bright smile. He had a head of dark brown hair that fell in waves down to his collar and a clipped, curling ruff of beard that led down his cheeks and under his chin, just like the portrait Elizabeth had taken off the wall, but with his dark, laughing eyes and regal nose, he looked more handsome. His personality was so striking that she was at first frightened of him. She sensed he had "power" over her in some way. She felt he could read her thoughts.[39]

The woman Robert saw before him was a diminutive sylph dressed in a black silk gown with a white lace collar and reclining on a sofa with an embroidered coverlet over her feet. She had silky dark brown hair arranged in long curls cascading down to her shoulders, framing an appealing face of dark complexion. Her large, widely spaced brown eyes and wide, modestly smiling mouth dominated her face. She spoke in a voice scarcely above a whisper. Indeed, Robert feared that his own voice was too loud. Since she did not rise to greet him, he assumed that she suffered from a spinal injury of some sort. Her dog, Flush, the King Charles spaniel given to her by Mary Russell Mitford, was probably not present, for Robert did not mention him in his follow-up letter that day.

Elizabeth expressed more than once her appreciation of how kind he had been in responding to her letter. They chatted politely but amiably about their impressions of each other after so long an exchange of letters and probably too about literary matters. But however polite their conversation may have been, the meeting touched Robert to the core of his romantic being, for he fell in love with this incarnation of his sparkling correspondent. In fact, he later confessed that he had come ready to fall in love with whomever he might find.[40] Elizabeth was flattered, almost unbelieving, when her brilliant new caller asked if he might be allowed to become a regular visitor.

Robert's next follow-up letter to Elizabeth no longer exists, for he destroyed it after it was returned to him. But other evidence allows us to speculate that he impulsively made a proposal of marriage. It seems not to have been an orthodox one, for he understood her to be an invalid. It was perhaps a proposal that they share a life together and live to inspire each other to create poetic works.

Elizabeth was alarmed and distressed by Robert's impetuous letter,—alarmed by the mere thought of a totally new and intimate connection with someone outside her immediate family and distressed that her relationship with this fascinating poet who seemed to share her inmost feelings might have to be broken off. She suffered "pain & agitation." She could not sleep. She was afraid that her fevered condition might cause her to talk deleriously and give away this harbored secret.[41] She tried twice to reply and could not. Finally, two days later, she wrote to admonish him for "speaking so wildly" and saying "some intemperate things," which "you will not say over again, nor unsay, but *forget at once, & for ever, having said at all.* . . . Now, if there shd. be one word of answer attempted to this,—or of reference,—I *must not*—I WILL *not* SEE YOU *again.*"[42]

And yet, she did want to see him again and to renew that developing friendship and the epistolary intimacy that had served to relieve her emotional drought. She did not wish to lose this new relationship that had offered such possibilities: here was the poet with a greater future than anyone in her literary world, and he might become the chief figure in her life. In language that unconsciously suggested how closely she had embraced the spirit of his presence in their correspondence, she begged him to "spare me the sadness of having to break through an intercourse just as it is promising pleasure to me,—to me who have so many sadnesses & so few pleasures. . . . Your friendship & sympathy will be dear & precious to me all my life. . . . Your mistakes in me . . which I cannot mistake . . . I put away gently, & with grateful tears in my eyes." The whole matter was then thrust out of mind, and she proceeded to write about his reading of her new work the next time he called ("bring a tomahawk & do the criticism"), and she asked about his offer to let her help with the unfinished "Saul" and to see the last part of "The Flight of the Duchess."[43]

Robert was in utter consternation. He probably wrote and tore up several replies, but the next day he did manage to send off a puzzling letter full of apologies and obfuscation. He pretended that she had misunderstood his meaning. He said that whenever he attempted to communicate something from his inner self, he bungled it. He claimed that he was only expressing his gratitude to her for her sympathy and his hope for her assistance and frankness in discussing his future work. He had dedicated himself "to be a Poet, if not *the* Poet" and sometimes his vanity and ambition overcame his powers of expression, as in the letter he had written to her. He asked to have it returned.[44]

Now it was Elizabeth's turn to pretend. She wrote to apologize for her "over-seriousness" in response to his "indefinite compliments." She had misread his letter because of its stylistic peculiarities: "a good deal of what is called obscurity in you, arises from a habit of very subtle association." She agreed to return the letter, asking him to burn it and never to mention it again "TO ME OR ANOTHER." But she tempered her strictures with sincere reassurance: "I will reverence you both as 'a poet' & as '*the* poet'—because it is no false 'ambition' but a right you have."[45]

The roiled waters were calm again, and the two poets resumed their professional roles both in their correspondence and their now weekly tête-à-têtes.

❧ ❧ ❧

Over the next few months the exchange of letters between Robert and Elizabeth grew more frequent, with a good deal of exploration of each other's feelings as well as discussion of the procedures they followed in creating their poetic works. Elizabeth was interested in methods of versification and in creating "music" in poetry at which Tennyson, whose work she greatly admired, was so successful. Robert was more ready to speculate about how poems came to be written in the first place. He wrote,

> The more one sits and thinks over the creative process, the more it confirms itself as "inspiration" nothing more nor less—Or, at worst, you write down old inspirations, what you remember of them—but with *that* it begins: "Reflection" is exactly what it names itself—a *re*-presentation, in scattered rays from every angle of incidence, of what first of all became present in a great light, a whole one. So tell me how these lights are born, if you can!

"The mechanical part of the art" was easy: "I can tell anybody how to make melodious verses—let him do it therefore—it should be exacted of all writers."[46] A clear indication of his defiant recognition that portions of his work were far from "melodious."

Elizabeth thought the creative process hard to express, and she tried to articulate the transcendent reach that was so often the goal in her religious poems. She felt the experience was an approach toward the capture of an ultimate reality: "far beyond any work of *reflection* . . . appears that gathering of light on light . . . as you go (in composition) step by step, till you get intimately near to things, & see them in a fulness & clearness, & an intense trust in the truth of them . . . but which you have *then* . . & . struggle to communicate."[47] Trust and truth were key words for Elizabeth whenever she spoke earnestly about what was deeply important to her.

Robert brought her many of the poems in progress from his portfolio and told her about an aborted play entitled "Only a Player Girl" that he had found there, a play set in St. Petersburg at a fair on the River Neva. Elizabeth showed him her revised translation of *Prometheus Bound*, which led to his providing seven and a half pages of criticism plus general praise for what she had done ("it is all magnificently rendered"[48]). She, in turn, went well beyond her promise to give him *"all my impressions"*[49] of his new poems. Over the next three months she provided forty-two pages of suggestions for revision of sixteen of the poems that later appeared in *Dramatic Romances and Lyrics*.[50]

"The Flight of the Duchess" was the first work Robert brought to her. Whether he genuinely wanted the scrutiny of another eye on his recently completed poem or whether he was inviting this critique to draw her into further intimacy, we cannot be certain. In either case, he received a fully detailed set of notes and suggestions for revision.

He had begun the poem perhaps as early as spring 1842, preparing to tell the story of an unhappily married duchess who runs off with the gypsies—to "a *real* life—not an unreal one like that with the Duke."[51] He planned to include all the subsequent "wild adventures" with her gypsy lover in a romantic tale in the Byronic manner. The poem remained a fragment in his portfolio for two years.

What is fascinating to consider is that when Browning took up the poem once more, he altered his original conception. He no longer emphasized the lady's new freedom in the gypsy world but was drawn instead toward his favorite theme of a damsel in need of rescue, the theme that had invigorated "My Last Duchess," "Count Gismond," and *Colombe's Birthday*. The work was still incomplete in 1845 when F. O. Ward urgently asked him for a contribution to help keep *Hood's Magazine* afloat. Browning sent him the first 215 lines of "The Flight of the Duchess" for the April issue. The remainder was either in draft or still undeveloped when Elizabeth, fascinated by what she had read in *Hood's*, asked to see the rest. Robert hastily completed the poem and brought it along on one of his visits to Wimpole Street in early July.

The poem that he presented for Elizabeth's reading is a dramatic narrative in four-beat lines, irregularly rhymed, although couplets occur most frequently. Additional unstressed syllables in the lines provide variations in the meter, and this free metrical play gives the poem a colloquial tone, quickens the pace of the narrative, and enlivens the descriptions. As a poem of 915 lines it is Browning's first return to narrative length since *Sordello*, yet a totally new venture in form and tone, and with some suggestions of Browning's personal situation. When the duke's huntsman, who is the speaker in the poem, describes the duchess, the lines may point to Elizabeth:

> She was the smallest Lady alive,
> Made, in a piece of Nature's madness,
> Too small, almost, for the life and gladness
> That over-filled her. . . . (135–38)

And the crone-turned-gypsy-queen who lures the duchess to join their band speaks in terms of a lover, for she bids the duchess to fall

> Into our arms for evermore;
> And thou shalt know, those arms once curled
> About thee, what we knew before,
> How love is the only good in the world.
> Henceforth be loved as heart can love,
> Or brain devise, or hand approve!
> Stand up, look below,
> It is our life at thy feet we throw
> To step with into light and joy. (612–20)

Elizabeth was immensely pleased with "The Flight of the Duchess," finding it "a very singular & striking poem, full of power."[52] It seems that Robert's lines had cast their spell on her, for she provided more notes with suggestions for revision in this work than for any other poem. Most of her comments reflected her own predilection for regularity in rhythm, but additionally she tried from time to time to introduce clarity of meaning. For example, she observed, about the words (in line 287) "if that were worth aught": "there is something clogged in the sound. And, in the next line, why not read . . . for clearness . . . 'Of the weight by day & the watch by night—'?"[53] She was tactful in her criticisms and frequently suggested that Robert had omitted a word by a slip of the pen. She was careful, too, when she recommended that he expand some of his elliptical phrasings, warning that he might otherwise invite the charge of obscurity that reviewers were prepared to bring. For instance, about line 228, "Oh, and the old books they knew the way of it," she wrote, "All this is quite clear to *me*—& I like the abruptness. Still people are sure to say, from the break in the narrative, that it's obscure—& *so* little a change (of a word or two) would allow them to read on without thinking!!"[54] Other suggestions were distinct improvements for Robert's hastily completed poem. For some lines she was able to find more suitable phrasing; for others she was able to eliminate an overstrained rhyme.

But the bulk of her commentary was focused on versification. The roughness of Browning's metrical variations had always troubled her. His poetry was often "defective in *harmony*," she had said to Mary Russell Mitford.[55]

Now she had an opportunity to offer some corrections. She revised his lines, suggesting "a word here & there"[56] for rhythmic regularity. She especially liked to supply extra words, a "that," an "and," or an interjection like "well," when Browning had omitted a syllable from a metrical foot.[57] In one place (line 572) she wished to alter the accent and to introduce an anapest when she suggested, "And art ready to say & do" should become "And all thou art ready to say & do."[58] In another (line 658) she changed a syncopated iambus into an anapest when she suggested that "Shame to feel & pride to show" might be "'With our shame to feel,' &c."[59] Not all of this was helpful for the characterization of the speaker. She seemed to ignore the fact that the roughness of Browning's lines was more appropriate for the huntsman than her own suggestions for the "music" of metrical regularity. The poem Browning had presented to her had a tumbling rhythm and more lines full of extra syllables and unusual rhymes than anything he had written since "The Pied Piper." Even so, it appears that Browning set out to produce a narrative poem in the Barrett manner. He had recently been steeping himself in such poems as "The Romaunt of Margret," "The Romaunt of the Page," and "The Lay of the Brown Rosary," and he had been drawn especially to the poem that had mentioned him by name, "Lady Geraldine's Courtship." Browning's poem bears more likeness to these works than anything he had written before.

Robert and Elizabeth's comradely interchange of helpful criticism during the summer of 1845 and the continued meetings in the privacy of Elizabeth's room drew them into a bond that quickened Robert's hopes. Elizabeth offered her thanks not only for his considerate comments and suggestions about her *Prometheus Bound* but also for the time and attention he had devoted to her. In late July, she expressed her appreciation in a passionate tone that had not appeared in earlier letters: "As long as I live & to the last moment of life, I shall remember with an emotion which cannot change its character, all the generous interest & feeling you have spent on me. . . . I never shall forget these things, my dearest friend."[60] Robert, in turn, expressed a deeply felt gratitude for her willingness to spend time on his poem and told her that he accepted all her suggestions and had adopted all of "the improvements."[61] As a result, "The Flight of the Duchess" is a unique specimen among Browning's works. He felt that with Elizabeth's touch it was a partial collaboration, and as such it became for him a creative step toward the union he so fervently desired.

Chapter 12

Miss Barrett's Mysterious Illness

During this early summer interchange of ideas and professional collaboration, Robert had already detected a warmer note developing in Elizabeth's letters and saw it as an opportunity to act. In mid-July 1845 he expressed his frustration at being bound to silence about continuing his courtship—which he had not really abandoned—and offered a straightforward protest: "I am yours *ever*, and not till summer ends & my nails fall out, and my breath breaks the bubbles,—ought you to write thus having restricted me as you once did, and do still?"[1] Elizabeth too sensed the change that was creeping into their relationship, and she wished to keep it their secret. She admonished him not to speak to John Kenyon about her or about his frequent visits.

Later in July, Elizabeth revealed a feature of her life that was central to her private self, the essentials of her religious belief. She offered first the fact that she was "one of those schismatiques of Amsterdam," using John Donne's phrase for members of Reformed Churches. She told him that she used to go to "the nearest dissenting chapel of the congregationalists" with her father. She was referring to a time when she was a young woman living at Hope End in Herefordshire and it was the family custom to attend religious service twice on Sundays, going to St. James's Church in the village of Colwall in the morning and in the afternoon to the small "School House" Chapel outside the entrance gate of Hope End. Elizabeth did not like "state churches." The Church of England was too authoritarian for her with its established liturgy and its set ceremonies. She liked "the simplicity of that praying & speaking without books." Even in those early days she would frequently refuse to attend church in the morning, staying at home to read the Bible or a religious treatise and then in the afternoon walk with her father to the nearby chapel, where the most frequent preacher was the local Baptist minister from Ledbury.[2]

Robert was surprised and delighted to find they had one more thing in common. He reported that on that very morning his parents worshiped at an "Independent Chapel," the one where he had been baptized.[3] He neglected to mention that he himself went to hear the Reverend Henry Melvill preach at the Church of England chapel in Peckham. Always seeking to knit their lives together, the love-smitten Robert began to amalgamate his religious views with Elizabeth's. He no longer exhibited interest in the Unitarian liberalism of his early mentor, W. J. Fox, and his circle, especially once he became aware that Elizabeth looked upon "the ice-bound unitarians"[4] as not truly religious. Yet there was one radical belief that they both shared with Fox, his universalism, for Elizabeth, during some theological debates with Hugh Boyd, had come upon a passage in the Epistle of Paul to the Romans that favored the doctrine of general redemption, and after some discussion of the point with others, she accepted it.[5]

It was true that she declared herself "a Congregational Christian"[6] in her private opinions, but she was quite tolerant in her attitude toward all the Protestant sects, although she seemed at times uncomfortable among her fellow dissenters. She thought them narrow in their tastes and disliked their suspicious or even forbidding opinions about literature and the arts.[7] She found "an arid, grey Puritanism in the clefts of their souls," yet she judged that these nonconformists knew, as she asserted to Robert, "what the 'liberty of Christ' *means*, far better than those do who call themselves 'churchmen.'"[8] Her beliefs were simple: faith in the teachings of Jesus in the gospels "and hope [for salvation] by His death!"[9] For living her life, she felt the truest religious practice could be summed up in the words, "We were placed on this earth to love each other,"[10] and she was ready to give voice to it in her poetry too. "That seventeenth chapter of John's Gospel" and all the love expressed in it were, she declared, "my system of divinity."[11] Over and over, she included views of this sort in her letters to Robert.

ಹಿ ಹಿ ಹಿ

Since an increasing openness developed during Robert's twice-weekly visits to Wimpole Street, he came to know more not only about her religious outlook, but also about all aspects of her early life, especially the history of her health problems. Elizabeth Barrett was born March 6, 1806, at Coxhoe Hall near Durham in Northumberland, the first child of Edward Barrett

Moulton-Barrett and Mary Graham-Clarke, both of them from families of sugar planters in Jamaica. Elizabeth was baptized two years later,[12] on February 10, along with her baby brother, Edward Moulton-Barrett, nicknamed "Bro," who became the dearest to her of her eight brothers.

In 1810, Mr. Moulton-Barrett moved his growing family to Hope End,[13] a 475-acre estate near Malvern in the region near the Welsh border. Here Elizabeth grew up in the midst of a loving family.[14] She roamed over the Malvern hills with her dog, Hannah, and at times with Bro or her sisters Henrietta and Arabella, or she rode her pony, Moses. She wandered in the Hope End deer park, dabbled her feet in the pool formed by the dammed-up stream, watched her brothers, Bro, Sam, George, and the stuttering Stormie, play cricket with their father. In summers she made extended visits to the seashore with the family. Her mother was her first teacher, giving lessons in reading and writing and supervising her religious instruction. Later, tutors took over for French, Latin, Greek, Italian, and music. With her brothers and sisters she organized theatricals for which she wrote scripts in both English and French. All the children drew and sketched, and composed verses for birthdays. Laughter and creative play enlivened the nursery and schoolroom, with Elizabeth as the dominant figure.

The blissfulness of these early years was interrupted when Elizabeth was fifteen, for she was stricken with an illness that baffled her doctors. She suffered headache and fever, later, painful muscle spasms ("paroxysms . . . accompanied by convulsive twitches of the muscles") in the back and shoulder, together with "loss of locomotive power."[15] "I nearly died," she later told R. H. Horne.[16] She was sent for treatment to the Spa Hotel in Gloucester, where she remained for a year. Most biographers have accepted the opinion of Dr. D. J. Davis of the University of Illinois Medical School that she was suffering from an early onset of tuberculosis.[17] However that may be, one must point out that an affliction of the lungs did not occur until eleven years later. It is possible that her early illness was a case of poliomyelitis, a disease unknown at the time. One of her legs was affected for the next three years.[18]

As time went on, Elizabeth continued in fragile health. Her appetite was poor; she was thin and easily exhausted by exercise; she fainted from too much exertion.[19] In July 1832, four years after her mother's death, when Elizabeth was twenty-six, she suffered a severe cold that lasted for months, followed by a "disagreeable cough"[20] that she could not shake off. It became less persistent after the family moved from Hope End to Sidmouth on the Channel coast in late August.

Elizabeth was then in her mid-twenties. Her emotional needs seemed to steer her toward older men, preferably ones who were safely married. In

Sidmouth, she became attracted to the Reverend George Barrett Hunter (not a relative) of the March Independent Chapel, drawn by his eloquent preaching and his scholarly and literary interests. He had a wife, who was mentally ill and under private care, and a ten-year-old daughter, who became a favorite with the Barrett sisters. Since Mr. Barrett looked with favor on Hunter's religious views, he invited him to call and, after Hunter's wife died, allowed him to visit Elizabeth. Although Hunter professed to admire Elizabeth's poetry, he was imperiously critical of her publishing poems in magazines and newspapers. But she tolerated his dominating manner with amusement for the sake of literary discussion.

Elizabeth's lungs were badly damaged by her long respiratory affliction. She may also have begun to suffer from an asthmatic condition at this time, having inherited the tendency from her father.[21] In any case, her condition, which had improved during the three years that the family lived in Sidmouth, took a turn for the worse at the end of 1835 when they moved to London, with its pervasive smog and damp and with coal fires burning in every room during the cold weather, to heat their new home at 74 Gloucester Place. The cough returned. Elizabeth's situation was no better when Mr. Barrett moved the family once again to more spacious quarters at 50 Wimpole Street, where she looked out on those prisonlike walls and could not see "even a leaf or a sparrow without soot on it."[22]

"A common cough striking on an *insubstantial* frame began my bodily troubles," she later wrote to Horne in an account of her health problems.[23] When the Barretts were finally settled in London, her father arranged for the best medical help he could find to deal with the cough and its complications. He engaged Dr. William Chambers, the physician to Queen Victoria, to attend Elizabeth. Dr. Chambers told her that her condition was not a disease but "an irritability of chest" that he called "*bilious fever.*"[24] He prescribed opium to help her sleep and, following the barbarous practice of the time, bled her by means of leeches for her feverish spells. When she came down with a bad cold the following summer, she began to spit up blood. She was frequently feverish and required digitalis to slow a rapid pulse. It seems likely that she had contracted tuberculosis. Dr. Chambers recommended that she be sent to a Mediterranean climate before the cold weather came on, but since Mr. Barrett objected to such a distance from the family, they compromised by deciding on the south of England.

Torquay on the Channel coast, with its mild temperatures, long-blooming flowers, and cliffs offering protection from the east wind, was the chosen place. Elizabeth, too weak to travel overland, sailed from London with Bro and her sisters. Her Aunt Jane and Uncle Robert Hedley, who were living temporarily in Torquay, were to look after her, along with Henrietta and Arabella, who were to stay one at a time to help care for her. Her favorite aunt, Arabel, called "Bummy" by the young Barretts, arrived some weeks later. Mr. Barrett also hired a maid, the young Elizabeth Crow, to attend to Elizabeth's needs.

Her new physician in Torquay, Dr. Robert Barry, who was an athletic out-doorsman, insisted on getting Elizabeth up by ten and sending her for an outing every day in a "Bath chair," dressed in flannel waistcoats up to her chin. Although she was exhausted by this activity every day, she began to improve. But Dr. Barry's application of hot "blisters" and use of leeches kept her weak. He was additionally cruel in forbidding her to read or write poetry, which, he warned, would excite her too much and send her pulse rac-ing. With the onset of cold weather, her old symptoms returned—cough, spitting up blood, increased pulse, fatigue, and general weakness. In midwin-ter her life "seemed to hang by a thread."[25] For months she remained in bed or reclined on a sofa wrapped in shawls and cloaks. Feverish at night, she was unable to sleep without an opiate.

The next year, 1839–1840, the same pattern recurred: recovery in warm weather; decline and debility in winter. Despite her condition, Elizabeth was strong-willed and ready to take heart at any bright report that the doctors might give her. In November 1839 she wrote to Mrs. Martin that although her new physician, Dr. William Scully, thought her case "in the highest degree precarious, yet knowing how much I bore last winter & understand-ing from him that the worst *tubercular* symptoms have not actually appeared, I am willing to think it may be God's will to keep me here still longer."[26] Actually, her doctors had never agreed about her illness. Some diagnosed tuberculosis; others called it a "*congestion of the heart.*"[27] Dr. Chambers judged that a broken blood vessel in her lung was taking a long time to heal. She accepted his medical opinion and continued to report it in letters to friends.[28] She pushed away any suggestion that she was tubercular.

Elizabeth had pleaded with her father to allow Bro to stay with her in Torquay and finally persuaded him. Now in a house of their own with both sisters and dearest "Bummy," plus Miss Crow, the Barrett mini-household by the sea provided warm family comfort and devoted care for her. Yet the win-ter had left her "lamentably weak"[29] even as late as May 1840, and she wrote her brother George in June that she had never been so weak or so ill.

She was still sunk in these depths when the cruelest blow of all befell her. Her beloved Bro, out sailing with friends on July 11, 1840, was caught by a squall and drowned when the boat capsized. Elizabeth, remembering too piercingly how she had begged her father to allow him to remain with her in

Torquay, was devastated by guilt combined with grief. She became delirious and was only half-conscious for days. She had a "spasmodic action in the throat"[30] that kept her from swallowing food. Because she was unable to sleep, Dr. Scully prescribed a double dose of opium mixed with brandy and water. Arabella and Miss Crow spelled each other sitting up during the night to make sure she did not stop breathing. At length they could feed her spoonfuls of wine and of jelly, followed by a little macaroni. News of the death of her next oldest brother, Sam, from a tropical fever in Jamaica added further pain. As she later remembered this period, she lived "completely dead to hope of any kind . . . absolutely indifferent to the me which is in every human being."[31] She was suffering from what modern medical opinion calls "posttraumatic stress disorder."

Haunting her memory were Bro's words to her, ten days before the boating accident, as he held her hand and said that he "'loved me better than them all & that he *would not* leave me . . . till I was well.'"[32] When over a year later she struggled to recount to her closest friend, Mary Russell Mitford, what had happened, she recognized that she was not directly responsible for Bro's death but could not stop thinking it was God's punishment for her selfishness:

> I cannot write of these things . . . I have never spoken—not one word—not to Papa—never named that name anymore. . . . & because he loved me too well to leave me I am thus—& he is thus. . . . It was not I in a sense. I wd. have laid down this worthless life ten times, & thanked God—but the sacrifice was unacceptable. On the contrary, I was used, I & my love were used as the wretched ever miserable instruments of crushing ourselves in another.[33]

A fortuitous gift helped to distract her from her sorrows. Miss Mitford presented her with a puppy, a King Charles spaniel named Flush, who soon became the center of Elizabeth's existence. Flush spent the day on a cushioned chair by her side, slept with her at night, was fed by hand—buttered muffins (he preferred marmalade) or morsels of breast of partridge.

Gradually, she recovered, as if waking from a nightmare, and struggled back "from the edge of the chasm."[34] She now wanted to flee Torquay and its bitter associations. Once she had loved her seaside resort, but now she looked on it as a ghoulish place. Almost every family had someone ill or dying; yet it was a popular spa and, as such, a "dancing, fiddling cardplaying gossipping place." She shuddered at the "ghastliness of the collision there between life & death, merriment & wailing."[35] The greatest horror of all was the proximity of their house to the sea: "These walls—& the sound of what is very fearful a few yards from them—that perpetual dashing sound, have preyed on me."[36] Although she was still too feeble to walk and had to be carried from her bed to the sofa, she pleaded with her doctor and her father to let her return to London and the bosom of her whole family.

When Dr. Scully finally permitted her to travel, she was conveyed to London in September 1841 by "one of the patent carriages with a thousand springs"[37] that was fitted with a mattress so that she did not have to sit up. The journey took ten days.

Back home in the populous Barrett household at 50 Wimpole Street, she gradually regained strength over the next four years, despite the relapses in winter that imprisoned her in an oxygen-depleted room sealed off against the cold air and never dusted until spring. Her description suggests the grotesque situation of Miss Haversham in Dickens's *Great Expectations:* "The consequence of living through the winter in one room, with a fire, day & night, & every crevice sealed close" is, she explained to Miss Mitford, that "at last we come to walk upon a substance like white sand, & if we dont lift our feet gently up & put them gently down, we act Simoom, & stir up the sand into a cloud. . . . The spiders have grown tame—& their webs are a part of our own domestic oeconomy,—Flush eschews walking under the bed."[38] Her father's room adjoined her own, and late every evening he came through the connecting doors to pray with her and for the restoration of her health, his hands enfolded with hers.

It was not just renewed family life but poetry that saved her. "I . . . sate here alone . . . so weary of my own being that to take interest in my very poems I had to lift them up by an effort & separate them from myself & cast them out from me into the sunshine where I was not."[39] Yet as her creative powers returned, she increased her contributions to the periodicals and gift albums. She undertook her series on the Greek Christian poets and the one on the history of English poetry. She assisted Richard Hengist Horne in the preparation of his two-volume study of the literary figures of their time, *A New Spirit of the Age.* She accumulated enough new poems for her two-volume *Poems* of 1844. Literary associations were reestablished too. She deepened her friendship with Mary Russell Mitford. She received frequent visits from John Kenyon, who became her new mentor, offering critical readings of her new poems as well as supplying her with the gossip of literary London.

Yet Elizabeth seemed to be settling into a mood of resignation, looking upon herself as a permanent invalid. Withdrawn from public activity and knowing she had missed so many of life's experiences, she likened herself to Homer, "a *blind poet.*"[40] Her daily existence she compared to "an oyster's life."[41] This was her situation near to the time when Robert Browning's first words of praise dropped through the mail slot at 50 Wimpole Street.[42]

ళ ళ ళ

As Robert learned about Elizabeth's illness and her great sorrows, he sensed that he had been allowed an additional privilege of confidence. The love that he continued to nurture now began to include a growing desire to rescue her. For her part, she responded with a trusting warmth in this intriguing friendship and felt her spirits lift as they had not for years. Evidence of her restoration to life shines from her letters. "I have been growing & growing just like the trees," she exulted in early summer 1845, "—it is miraculous, the feeling of sprouting life in me & out of me."[43] Her fitful sleeping pattern began to smooth out. She was on her feet walking, with the help of a guiding arm. By July she was able to walk a short distance with confidence and sit in an armchair rather than recline on a sofa. She began to contemplate the possibility of a sea voyage to a warm climate as the autumn came on.

Aunt Jane Hedley, observing how Elizabeth flourished in the warm summer air, urged Mr. Barrett to send her to the Mediterranean area for the winter. Malta and Alexandria were discussed among the younger Barretts, and Elizabeth took courage to agree to the journey. Dr. Chambers was consulted about her ability to withstand such a trip. After using his stethoscope as he examined her thoroughly, he stated that only "a very slight affection of the left lung was observable, & which threatened no serious result whatever, if I did but take precautions . . . & that the long struggle of the morbid part of the constitution to set up an incurable form of consumption was coming to an end, & leaving the life to triumph . . . and he not merely *advised* but ENJOINED the trial of a warm climate, . . *naming Pisa*."[44]

As plans went forward in early September 1845 for Arabella and Stormie to accompany Elizabeth during a winter sojourn in Pisa, Robert, rejoicing over the doctor's decision, set about making his own arrangements for travel to Italy. But Mr. Barrett in his enigmatic way remained silent about giving his consent. Days passed and, at length pushed to a decision, Mr. Barrett wrote a formal letter to Elizabeth, who was in the next room, grudgingly permitting his thirty-seven-year-old daughter to seek the Italian sun for recovery of her health, but only with his "extreme displeasure."[45] After a few days, Elizabeth confronted him, with her brothers and sisters there as witnesses, and asked him to withdraw his displeasure, but he would not yield. Indeed, over the next few days he refused even to speak of Pisa when he paced silently back and forth across her room. Under these circumstances, Elizabeth's hope for a smoke-free, fog-free winter in the Italian sunshine was effectively blocked. She could not bring herself to go without her father's willing consent.

She no doubt remembered the time when she had begged him to allow Bro to stay in Torquay, and he had agreed but wrote in reply that "he considered it to be very *wrong in* [her] TO EXACT SUCH A THING."[46] Now, five years of heartbreak and guilt later, what if Arabella or Stormie were to fall mortally ill in Pisa? Or if she herself were to become stricken with malaria in mosquito-plagued Pisa and become a further burden to the household? Even though Arabella was quite willing to invoke her father's ill will by accompanying her, Elizabeth would not permit it.

The cancellation of the Pisa trip was as devastating to Robert as to Elizabeth. Not only had he counted on her escape from the danger of another London winter, but the two of them had reached a new understanding in the last three weeks. Emboldened by the thought that his own trip to Italy could include a stay in Pisa, he had decided to renew his pursuit of her hand in marriage and skirt her ban that he never refer to the subject again. What is curious about his mating dance is that it was carried out by mail rather than in person during his calls at Wimpole Street. If he were to bring up the subject in her presence, she might stop him immediately, but in written words he could plead his cause to its full extent.

On August 30, although he had visited her only days before, he offered by letter an unguarded declaration of love that still managed to avoid the word *marriage*, which she had forbidden him to speak. "I believe in *you* absolutely, utterly—I believe that when you bade me, that time, be silent,—that such *was* your bidding, and I was silent. . . . Let me say now—*this only once*—that I loved you from my soul, and gave you my life, so much of it is as you would take,—and all that is *done*, not to be altered now." His present situation, his having gained her firm friendship and her permission to visit her privately, "make the truest, deepest joy of my life." He declared that his "supreme happiness" would be in what he could only hint at here—"however distant."[47]

The fervor of his declaration convinced Elizabeth of what she had slowly come to realize about the sincerity of his earlier proposal. At that time, she had mistakenly thought that his impulsive offer was made only because of her "infirmities." She thought "that you cared for me only because your chivalry touched them with a silver sound."[48] Her reply now was a forthright statement of her true regard for him. "I am confident that no human being ever stood higher or purer in the eyes of another, than you do in mine." But she revealed something she had not disclosed to him before. She explained that when she bade him be silent, it was for his sake: she did not want him to waste his life on her, a confirmed invalid. "Your life? . . if you gave it to me & I put my whole heart into it, what should I put but anxiety, & more sadness than you were born to? What could I give you, which it would not be ungenerous to give?—Therefore we must leave this subject . . . without one word more."[49]

Since he now knew how deeply she felt about him, Robert was ready to speak once again of uniting their lives, but he gave her, as well as himself, a little more time before writing his reply. He sent a note two days later saying that he would answer her letter before she left for Pisa. But he closed the note with "Dearest friend—I am yours ever."[50]

How many drafts of that answer he scribbled out we do not know, but he waited eleven more days, and in the meantime visited her twice, before he put his heart on paper and mailed the letter. He began by addressing her as "dearest" and went on to say that "I never dreamed of winning your *love*." But since she now acknowledged it, he wanted her to put aside any thought that she could ever be a burden and an anxiety to his life. "I *know*, if one may know any thing, that to make that life yours and increase it by the union with yours, would render me *supremely happy*." He explained that he had formerly resolved merely to live frugally and be a writer, without plans to marry, but now he was ready to write for money or take other work for income, and go to her at Pisa where one could live for £100 a year. He exudes a chivalric attitude throughout his exuberant proposal that they join their lives. "'Tell me what I have a claim to hear': I can hear it . . . your friendship is my pride and happiness. If you told me your love was already bestowed elsewhere, and that it was in my power to serve you *there*, to serve you there would still be my pride and happiness . . . I submit to you and will obey . . . what I am able to conceive of your least desire, much more of your expressed wish." He was willing to alter his whole scheme of life just to be with her: "Take sense of all this, I beseech you, dearest—all you shall say will be best—I am yours. Yes—Yours ever."[51]

Despite these avowals, Elizabeth maintained her position that "we may be friends always . . . & cannot be . . . separated,"[52] but she asked him to forget her, as she euphemistically expressed it, "in one relation."[53] Still Robert would not be deterred, even after the plans for Pisa were scratched. When she resigned herself to trust in God, hoping for a mild winter in London, and urged him to go to Italy by himself, he refused. For the first time he exhibited some proprietary feelings about her in this conflict with her father about Pisa, even though he felt powerless to act on her behalf. He put forth strong arguments for her not to submit. He even used a religious argument, reminding her that God required that Man exercise free will and reject "the direction of an infallible church, or the private judgment of another. . . . In your case I do think you are called upon to do your duty to yourself,—that is, to God in the end." He even went beyond the constraints of her forbidding him to be explicit about marriage: "you are in . . . the veriest slavery— and I who *could* free you from it, I am here scarcely daring to write. . . . I would marry you now and thus—I would come when you let me, and go when you bade me—I would be no more than one of your brothers—*no more*," but he would be able to be in her company always.[54]

His urgings were to no avail, but he did extract from her a promise fulfilling his long-held wish, for in her reply she gave him her word, hedged only by a simple condition, improvement in her health. "You have touched me more profoundly than I thought even *you* could have touched me . . . Henceforward I am yours for everything but to do you harm. . . . a promise goes to you in it that none except God & your will, shall interpose between you & me,—I mean, that if He should free me within a moderate time from the trailing chain of this weakness, I will then be to you whatever at that hour you shall choose . . . whether friend or more than friend . . . a friend to the last in any case."[55] Robert had achieved his dream. However qualified, their engagement was set.

Monodramatic Developments

Dramatic Romances and Lyrics

At this same time, Robert Browning was preparing to publish his next issues of *Bells and Pomegranates*. He told Elizabeth that he wished to clear his portfolio of accumulated poems and finish the work on his two remaining plays so that he could move into a new stage of his career: to begin at last the personal poem that she had encouraged him to write.

Since she had gone beyond expectations in her comment on the material from *Hood's*, he now passed on to her the rest of the poems intended for *Bells and Pomegranates*, number seven, which he had decided to call *Dramatic Romances and Lyrics*. He was grateful for her further suggestions, even though they were not as extensive as those for "The Flight of the Duchess." They improved clarity in some places and rhythm in others. Later while the book was in press, he asked her to look over the proofs, which contained a few more poems she had not seen. Now that the threads of their personal lives had become interwoven, he enjoyed the idea that their literary lives could be intertwined as well.

Browning had planned this new number carefully. Going further with the device of pairing poems by subject or theme, as he had done with a few in *Dramatic Lyrics*, he arranged most of his new poems in groups of two or three, setting up themes for comparison and contrast or coupling poems that were alike in form or setting. As a result, there were pairs of love poems, of garden poems, a trio of patriotic poems, a pair of Gothic horror stories, and so on.[1] More telling for reverberations between poems was the thematic grouping: two poems on disappointments ("The Lost Leader" and "The

Lost Mistress"), two on ironies of love and fame (gathered under the title "Earth's Immortalities"), two poems spoken by national exiles ("Italy in England" and "England in Italy"), and two more with speakers of contrasting temperaments, one heroically vigorous, the other timorously withdrawn. Most important, however, Browning was presenting a showcase of what could be achieved by the monodramatic form, its possibilities for revealing character and feeling, for irony of effect, for complexity of motif and image, and in a variety of styles and structures.

Dramatic Romances and Lyrics begins with a plunge into action carrying the riders of "How They Brought the Good News from Ghent to Aix" to the success of their mission. This work is followed by the first of Browning's great painter poems, "Pictor Ignotus, Florence, 15—." Scholars have tried to identify him with Fra Angelico or Fra Bartolommeo,[2] but it is more reasonable to think that Browning had in mind the many unknown painters whose work he had seen in churches and monasteries all over Italy. Browning renders this soliloquy in his best conversational style, five-stress, rhythmically free lines that rhyme alternately yet run on so fluidly that they seem almost to be blank verse. The quiet meditative presentation changes only when its tone shifts to show the tug of inner conflict or when it becomes shrill with an outburst revealing fear. Browning created a character enviously resentful and torn by tension, representative of all the self-deceiving artists and writers who refuse to take risks but offer as a defense their scorn of stooping to seek public approval. At the end the poem has made clear the meaning of its title. We can speculate whether Browning's own desire for fame invigorated his poem.

The companion pieces "Italy in England" and "England in Italy" are both tributes to Italy, one to its revolutionary movement for freedom from Austrian rule, the other to the beauties of the Italian landscape and the charm of Italian customs. Although thus linked, the two poems are extremely different in tone and genre. "Italy in England," a dramatic monologue addressed to an unidentified listener, is partly a romantic adventure narrative of patriotic efforts on behalf of Italian independence and partly the speaker's wistful memories of the peasant woman who aided him in his need. When the poem was published, Giuseppe Mazzini, the Italian leader in the movement for Italian unification, who was an exile in London, wrote to Browning about his fervent response to the poem and told him, "Ho letto, riletto, e fatto leggere a miei amici l'Italy in England'" [I read, reread, and have read to my friends "Italy in England"].[3] Browning had met Mazzini at Carlyle's house sometime earlier. He was gratified to have touched the Italian heart so deeply. Highly contrasting in tone, "England in Italy, Piano di Sorrento" is a jolly dramatic monologue that becomes a description of the kind that had been popularized by Samuel Rogers's leisurely travel poem *Italy* (1822–1828). Elizabeth delighted in its evocative details and images. Immobilized in England, confined to her room, she visualized the scenes with pleasurable longing. "For giving the *sense of Italy*," she told Robert, "it is worth a whole library of travel books."[4]

Two short love poems, "Night" and "Morning," are not only complementary but together they present a compact dramatic narrative reflecting a decidedly masculine attitude toward love. In "Night" two stanzas convey the speaker's anticipation of a lover's tryst as his boat comes ashore and he crosses the beach to the cottage where his beloved awaits. The imagery of the scene carries powerful sexual suggestion: the waves leap

> In fiery ringlets from their sleep,
> As I gain the cove with pushing prow,
> And quench its speed i' the slushy sand.

Details of stealth and secrecy continue the action: "A tap at the pane, the quick sharp scratch / And blue spurt of a lighted match." The whispered voice of the beloved one is even softer than "two hearts beating each to each." Browning's urgent love for Elizabeth had led him to write the most sensual poem he had yet created. "Morning," only one four-line stanza long, spoken in retrospect, brings a different temper. The satisfied lover is eager to depart and get about the business of the day. Love may be pursued in darkness and isolation, but dawn brings sunlight and time for the purposeful activities of society, "The need of a world of men for me." Elizabeth was resilient enough not to object. Her only comment was "how beautiful that 'Night & Morning.'"[5]

Readers recognized that the attack in "The Lost Leader" was directed against Wordsworth. Browning, like other of his contemporaries, disapproved of Wordsworth's deserting liberal politics and turning Tory. Also, since he did not admire Wordsworth's poetry, he was perhaps exhibiting some resentment at Wordsworth's appointment as poet laureate in 1843. In any case, the poem's opening lines, with their allusion to Judas, show an unwarranted mean-spiritedness:

> Just for a handful of silver he left us,[6]
> Just for a riband to stick in his coat . . .

In later years Browning expressed regret for singling out Wordsworth's political shift as the sole ground for condemnation, and overlooking his "moral and intellectual superiority."[7]

This unusual assembly of monodramatic experiments is brought to a close by a blithe, witty monologue, "The Glove," spoken by the French poet Pierre Ronsard, telling of an incident at the court of Francis I. The poem is Browning's variation on Leigh Hunt's short poem, "The Glove and the Lions," in which the king and his courtiers are spectators at a fight between two of the royal lions. While they watch, the Count de Lorge's ladylove drops her glove into the lion pit as a challenge to her lover to demonstrate his devotion by retrieving it. De Lorge leaps down and picks it up, only to return and throw it in her face. The king and his courtiers applaud his action.[8] Browning continues the story and, characteristically, allows the lady to offer her views on the matter. He has Ronsard follow her and question her motive. She then explains to him that so often had de Lorge avowed his readiness to risk death for her love in order to entice her to succumb to his desires that she decided to test him. Browning, in a further twist to Hunt's story, adds an ironical sequel to the story of the lady, and in a further twist on his characterization of Ronsard, has the poet marry and—constantly and uncomplainingly—fetch his wife's gloves. Elizabeth was delighted by Robert's additions to Hunt's version: "All women should be grateful. . . . And then, with what a 'curious felicity' you turn the subject 'glove' to another use & strike de Lorge's blow back on him with it." She enjoyed "the chivalry of the interpretation . . . so plainly yours."[9]

۶ ۶ ۶

Dramatic Romances and Lyrics, coming after a decade of publication, finally secured Browning's reputation as an important, if controversial, poet of his time. The reviews both in England and from America, stretching over the next two years, acknowledged the place his name had won in the literary world, even though there were some of the usual cavils. By now Browning had many warm adherents, but he still had not taught the average literary commentator how to read him. Even as intelligent a critic as G. H. Lewes found few of the poems he could praise unstintingly and in general was so put off by the ruggedness of Browning's versification and the abruptness of his syntax that he, like Carlyle, recommended Browning try writing in prose.[10] Most reviewers, however, welcomed *Dramatic Romances and Lyrics* as evidence of the maturity of his always promising genius. Forster was the earliest to comment, and he set a standard of praise for the poet whom he still regarded as his protégé. In the *Examiner* (November 15, 1845), he rejoiced that Browning was "freeing himself" from metaphysics, observing that "the analytic and the imaginative powers never yet worked well together. . . .

Nothing but this retarded his advance." Forster then went on dutifully with some general laudatory assertions that identified the main features that the other reviewers, on the whole, recognized. "His writing has always the stamp and freshness of originality. . . . In all its most poetical and most musical varieties, he is a master. . . . [This book is] proof of a very affluent as well as original genius."[11]

Margaret Fuller, in a long review-essay in the *New York Daily Tribune* (April 1, 1846), followed the entire development of Robert Browning's career and found the "more masterly clearness in expression" in this latest publication. After copious extracts from his work, she urged American readers to become familiar with him and to take time to absorb what they read "of his delicate sheaths of meaning within meaning which must be opened slowly, petal by petal, as we seek the heart of a flower, and the spirit-like distant breathings of his lute, familiar with the secrets of shores distant and enchanted."[12]

There were frequent warnings that Browning's work required time to become acquainted with and enjoyed. "He is one of those," assured the reviewer for the *Critic* (December 27, 1845), "whom the more you read, the better you love." He hoped that *Dramatic Romances and Lyrics* would make Browning more widely known.[13] Words like "fresh," "refreshing," "original," and "daring" were common in the reviews, indicating a recognition of the uniqueness of Browning's creative powers. Camilla Toulmin, writing in the *New Monthly Belle Assemblée* for June 1846, praised "passages of great power—the power of a fresh coinage, stamping some truth which we instantly recognize in the glowing words which make it Poetry."[14] In an omnibus review of several publications in the *English Review* (December 1845), Eliot Warburton remarked that moving from the religiosity of Elizabeth Barrett's poems to those of Browning was like coming out of a cathedral and stepping into the open air, "nature's own wide temple,—fresh, genial, invigorating, and free."[15] Likewise, Browning's breadth and variety were recognized by reviewers. Henry Chorley, in the *Athenaeum* (January 17, 1846), commented that "few of his contemporaries . . . embrace so wide a field of subjects; be they of thought, or description, or passion, or character,"[16] and again in the *People's Journal* (July 18, 1846), he pointed out that the poems drew upon "almost every clime, and country, and emotion."[17]

Curiously enough, none of the reviewers commented on the distinctiveness of Browning's monodramatic forms. No matter. A fellow poet seemed to respond with full understanding to what he had accomplished. On November 19, 1845, Browning received, with breathtaking surprise and pleasure, a message of congratulation from Walter Savage Landor, who was now living in Italy. It was an unrhymed sonnet, placing Browning among the great poets of the English tradition and urging him to come to Italy and fulfill his poetic destiny:

> To Robert Browning
>
> There is delight in singing, though none hear
> Beside the singer; and there is delight
> In praising, tho' the praiser sit alone
> And see the praised far off him, far above.
> Shakespeare is not *our* poet, but the world's,
> Therefore on him no speech; and short for thee,
> Browning! Since Chaucer was alive and hale,
> No man hath walked along our roads with step
> So active, so inquiring eye, or tongue
> So varied in discourse. But warmer climes
> Give brighter plumage, stronger wing; the breeze
> Of Alpine heights thou playest with, borne on
> Beyond Sorrento and Amalfi, where
> The Siren waits thee, singing song for song.[18]

Browning sent a copy to his publisher, Edward Moxon, to share his jubilation, hoping, one assumes, that Moxon would give it wider circulation.[19] Moxon passed it on to the *Morning Chronicle*, which published it on November 22, 1846. After seeing the newspaper, Robert Browning, Senior, glowed with satisfaction over his son's newly acquired fame. His belief in his son's genius now vindicated, the proud father had a printer run off copies of the Landor sonnet for distribution to relatives and friends all over London.

Some Surprises about the Barrett Household

Robert Browning had learned something about the peculiar behavior and attitudes of Edward Moulton-Barrett shortly before the Pisa incident. When he visited Elizabeth on August 12, 1845, she had felt it necessary to tell him about the restrictions on her "liberty" imposed by her father.

In a follow-up letter she included a supplementary explanation of Mr. Barrett's strict rule over his household, which must have seemed to Robert to resemble that of a West Indian plantation master. When she described its effect on all the younger Barretts, she pointed out that his requirements of obedience and permissions led to "concealments . . . & then, the disengenuousness—the cowardice—the 'vices of slaves'!—And everyone you see . . . all my brothers, . . . constrained *bodily* into submission . . . apparent submission at least . . . by that worst & most dishonoring of necessities, the necessity of *living* . . . everyone of them all, except myself, being dependent in money-matters on the inflexible will."[1] She described, in a metaphor of animal training, how they had all become disciplined to accept their situation: "it is possible to get used to the harness & run easily in it at last—& there is a side-world to hide one's thoughts in." For her the retreat was the world of literature. She was free to read whatever she wished, including French novels that were frowned on by the English public, and she relished this as a privilege. It was a "real liberty which is never enquired into." She hastened to add that Mr. Barrett really had a "deep tender affection behind & below all those patriarchal ideas of governing grownup children 'in the way they *must* go!'" He sincerely loved them all, she testified. "The evil is in the system—& he simply takes it to be his duty to rule . . . like the Kings of Christendom, by divine right."[2]

Elizabeth's statement suggests what was at the bottom of Mr. Barrett's monomaniacal dominance of his family. The "system" was his fundamental- ist reading of the Bible as God's prescriptive commands, which Mr. Barrett interpreted, choosing those that suited his own wilfullness. It also suggests Elizabeth's readiness to regard her father as godlike in his power and behav- ior. Other phrases, as we shall see, liken him to Jove, the Thunderer.

Still Elizabeth acknowledged to Robert a love and understanding of her father, especially because he had been so "patient & forbearing" all through her illness, and most of all because he had never reproached her once about Bro's death. She was heavily bound to him by her sense of guilt, her feeling "that if it had not been for *me*, the crown of his house wd. not have fallen." She then revealed to Robert the full story of her stay at Torquay and the drowning of her beloved brother, adding, "I have never said so much to a liv- ing being."[3]

A month later, when Robert was earnestly renewing his courtship, she felt obliged to disclose a powerful reason why she could not marry him: if her father knew that he had written his proposal to her and that she had responded, avowing her love, he "would not forgive me at the end of ten years . . . for the singular reason that he never *does* tolerate in his family (sons or daughters) the development of one class of feelings."[4]

Robert was appalled. As he saw it, "the jewel is not being over guarded, but ruined, cast away."[5] With all of his own personal philosophy of activism aroused, he counseled her, as we have seen, against passive obedience, declar- ing that was not what God required of human beings. As the months went by, he came to know more and more about this peculiar father and to realize what a problem he had to overcome in order to make Elizabeth his wife, espe- cially when she showed so little sign of contesting her father's power over her.

&⁶ &⁶ &⁶

Edward Barrett Moulton was born in Jamaica on May 28, 1785. He was the eldest son of Charles Moulton, a shipping merchant and slave trader, and Eliz- abeth Barrett Moulton, daughter of a wealthy plantation owner. He had an older sister, Sarah, nicknamed "Pinkie,"[6] and a younger brother, Samuel. Their parents' marriage came apart when Charles Moulton deserted his wife and became a slave trader in the United States and later a landowner in England. Edward's mother sent her children to England in 1795 so that her sons could have an English education and perhaps to shake off the memory of Charles

Moulton. After she joined them, the family settled in Coxhoe Hall, a country estate in Northumberland, near Durham. Young Edward was enrolled at Harrow for his schooling but was withdrawn shortly afterward, following an incident in which he was severely beaten by an older student for whom he was fagging (a punishment for "burning the toast"[7]). He was thereafter educated by tutors at home.

Shortly afterward, his grandfather, Samuel Barrett, whose three sons had died in their maturity, willed his wealth and property not to his daughter, Elizabeth, but to her sons, Edward and Samuel, provided that they would adopt the surname Barrett, for he wished to preserve the family name. Young Edward Moulton, now Barrett by royal license,[8] had also inherited £30,000 from his bachelor uncle, George Goodin Barrett. In 1801 he entered Trinity College, Cambridge, but left without taking a degree when, in 1805, he married Mary Graham-Clarke, daughter of a leading merchant of Newcastle-on-Tyne, a shipowner and proprietor of sugar plantations in Jamaica. Edward and Mary established themselves at Coxhoe Hall with Elizabeth Barrett Moulton, her lively companion, Mary Trepsack (a mulatto ward of the family, "Treppy," who was to become dear to the next generation of young Barretts), and his brother, Sam.

Edward was at this time an immensely wealthy young man, just twenty years old, the lord of estates of more than ten thousand acres in Jamaica, worked by Negro slaves. Proud and self-willed by temperament and by Jamaican planter culture, he determined to remain in England as an absentee landlord and to establish a family dynasty. In 1809 after his first two children were born, he purchased Hope End, a country estate in Herefordshire, including a deer park, a stream and waterfall, and an extensive woodland—price about £25,000.[9] He modified the existing house at Hope End to become the stables of a mansion that he built "in the Turkish style," an architectural monstrosity displaying domes with spires and minarets with crescents as its most distinctive features.[10] Here he brought up his family, which grew over the years to include eight sons and four daughters, one of whom died at the age of three. He became a leading citizen in the community, was twice appointed a sheriff of the county, and founded a Bible society in Malvern.

Edward Moulton-Barrett was devoutly religious, held formal morning and evening prayers with the family and servants, and insisted on strict observance of the Sabbath—no games, no reading, except the Bible or religious treatises, no pleasurable activity. He held a Puritan prejudice against the theater, and family members were forbidden to see plays or hear operas. The Barretts attended St. James's Church in the nearby town of Colwall on Sunday mornings, even though Mr. Barrett dissented from church gover-

nance by the state. In the afternoon he went to hear the preaching at the
Independent Chapel outside the gate of Hope End. He was also active in
the Methodist meeting in the area.

His position as a Dissenter bade him to be a member of the Whig Party,
and thus a supporter of the Reform Bill of 1832 and even of the Bill for the
Abolition of Slavery in the Colonies in 1833. He was later elected to the
Reform Club in London. He appears to have been a loving father to his children when they were young, but after the death of his wife, Mary, in 1828
(Elizabeth was then twenty-two), the atmosphere of the household underwent a change. Mary was no longer present to lighten the self-righteousness
of his demeanor. He no longer entertained anyone at dinner except close relatives—not even John Kenyon, whose cousinship was apparently considered too far removed.

He was a highly self-disciplined man, who rose at four or five o'clock in
the morning, feeling that it was "both a moral & religious sin not to get up
before the second cock crowing."[11] Like an ancient Roman stoic, he never
displayed weakness under stress. He controlled his grief at the loss of loved
ones and his feelings of distress over his severe financial losses, such as the
decline of his fortune after the emancipation of the Jamaican slaves or a disastrous court judgment against him in a long-standing lawsuit over some
slaves and cattle in Jamaica. This firm self-possession caused him to be very
secretive in his behavior—for example, he never discussed, even with his
grown sons, the sale of Hope End after his financial reverses, nor did he let
anyone in the family know where they were going to move until his decision
was made. (They had all feared that they were to leave England and return
to the family estates in the West Indies.) His patriarchal rule had been distressing to his wife, Mary, who was "very tender," Elizabeth wrote, "but of a
nature harrowed up into some furrows by the pressure of circumstances . . .
a sweet gentle nature, which the thunder a little turned from its sweetness—
as when it turns milk—One of those women who never can resist,—but, in
submitting & bowing on themselves, make a mark, a plait, within, . . a sign of
suffering. Too womanly she was—it was her only fault."[12]

What was most humiliating for all of the younger Barretts was their
father's continuing to treat them like children. Although Elizabeth had
inherited money from her mother, which Mr. Barrett invested for her, she
still, at age twenty-five at Hope End, had to ask him for a shilling for the toll-
gate when she visited Mr. Boyd at Malvern for her Greek lesson. Later, in
1846, when she was thirty-nine, she heard an account from her sisters of an
evening in the drawing room that filled them all with chagrin. Mr. Barrett
had been discoursing to the assembled family, plus their cousin Capt. Surtees

Cook on "passive obedience, & particularly in respect to marriage." One by one, her brothers left the room until Captain Cook was the only man remaining to listen. After these pronouncements, Cook was emboldened to ask "if children were to be considered slaves?" In holding such views, Elizabeth wrote of her father, "he *sees* the law & the gospel on his side."[13]

After the family moved to London, he seemed to withdraw from society, perhaps because of his sense of loss and failure, and to retire into his domain at 50 Wimpole Street, although by day he was an active City merchant and shipowner in the West Indian trade and still involved in the oversight of his sugar plantations, which were now managed by his brother, Samuel.[14] In his London retreat, he became absorbed in his financial struggles and his personal griefs. His stern authoritarian ways increased, and he even frowned on his children enjoying social activities outside the family home. On one occasion the Barrett brothers and sisters, plus some admirers of Henrietta's, were invited to a picnic at Mary Russell Mitford's cottage in the village of Three Mile Cross (Elizabeth was still too weak to go). They had a glorious time but did so without telling Papa, who somehow would have found fault with their innocent pleasure party. Thus, during the afternoon, Elizabeth, waiting in her sickroom, was "in a complete terror" for fear Papa would come home from the City before they returned, and was "in an agony" when she heard him enter the house. Shortly afterward, to her relief, Arabella appeared in her room: the younger Barretts had come back from their excursion in time. "There is an excess of strictness," she explained to Miss Mitford. "Too much is found objectionable. And the result is that everything that *can* be done in an aside, *is* done. . . . But dear Papa's wishes wd. be consulted more tenderly, if his commands were less straight & absolute."[15]

Mr. Barrett may have offered his views on "filial obedience" with respect to marriage when Captain Cook was present, because he sensed that the captain had a tender interest in his daughter Henrietta. But in truth his irrational attitudes would have prevented his consent to any marriage. Elizabeth's grim jest to her sisters was that "if a prince of Eldorado should come, with a pedigree of lineal descent from some signory in the moon in one hand, & a ticket of good behaviour from the nearest Independent Chapel, in the other—'Why even *then*,' said my sister Arabel, 'it would not *do*.' . . . & one laughs at it till the turn comes for crying."[16]

One can guess that Mr. Barrett had a fear of and a revulsion toward sex even in the married state. It appears that he had entered into his union with Mary Graham-Clarke only in order to continue the Barrett line, as his grandfather would have wished his heir to do, but found consummation of the marriage so repellant that he continued intermittent sexual relations with his wife only because God in the Book of Genesis had enjoined man and wife to increase and multiply. These unnatural feelings led him to guard his grown children, especially his daughters, from entering into a marriage contract that would compel them to fulfill their "marital duty." He had a special reverence for Elizabeth, whom he regarded as "the purest woman he ever knew." Because of her invalid condition, she "had not troubled him with the iniquity of love-affairs, or any impropriety of seeming to think about being married."[17]

The Reverend George Barrett Hunter, who had recently moved to London, where he took in pupils for tutoring, was back on the scene once more in the Barrett household. But Mr. Barrett apparently did not regard him as a suitor when he called upon Elizabeth every Saturday. Hunter had, by now, formed a serious attachment to Elizabeth and looked upon Robert with jealous hostility. He made it clear to Elizabeth that he wished her "to have no friend, no praiser, except himself."[18] He sneered at Robert's coming from an unfashionable suburb. He dubbed him her "New Cross Knight." One day in October 1845, when Robert called upon Elizabeth, Hunter followed him up the stairs, "white with passion," as Elizabeth's maid reported.[19] When Hunter later that same day visited Elizabeth, he exploded with such jealous complaints that she had to rebuke him for his behavior. Subdued, Hunter offered his apologies.

After Robert and Elizabeth reached their conditional engagement, Robert wanted to approach Mr. Barrett directly about his intentions, but Elizabeth, terrified, forbade it. She warned him that if her father knew of their exchange of promises, Robert would be blocked from seeing her, and any letters addressed to her would be "stopped & destroyed—if not opened." She recounted to him the dreadful ordeal that Henrietta had been subject to a few years earlier because she dared to have a suitor. "I look back shuddering to the dreadful scenes in which poor Henrietta was involved who never offended as I have offended. . . . Yet how she was made to suffer . . . I hear how her knees were made to ring upon the floor, now! she was carried out of the room in strong hysterics, & I . . . fell flat down upon my face in a fainting-fit." This all happened, she pointed out to Robert, "because she had seemed to feel a little." Papa maintained, she added in lame excuse, "an eccentricity—or something beyond . . . on one class of subjects."[20] Indeed, Papa did not understand love "any more than he understands Chaldee."[21]

Nor did Mr. Barrett's mania apply only to his daughters. His beloved eldest son, Bro, had a love interest that he had discussed with Elizabeth shortly before the fatal accident. He felt helpless to defy his father because he had no financial independence. Elizabeth offered to sign over to him her accumulated investments but was unable to do so. "My hands were siezed [sic] & tied," she explained enigmatically to Robert.[22]

Feeling the secrecy placed him in a dishonorable position, Robert wished to send Elizabeth a sealed letter, presumably addressed to Mr. Barrett, in which he stated clearly their plans to marry when her health allowed. Then, if a situation arose wherein Mr. Barrett discovered that Robert was more than a literary friend who made frequent visits, the letter could be produced. But Elizabeth would not allow even this safeguard. She insisted that their pretence continue and that they "both must submit to God's necessity."[23]

⁝ ⁝ ⁝

Thus the winter of 1845–1846 wore on. The intensity of Robert's love did not diminish, nor did the stress of his frustration. The headaches to which he was prone because of his unusual eyesight (one eye was farsighted, the other nearsighted)[24] became more frequent under the increasing tension. But a number of distractions punctuated the next few months and helped the time to pass. The two plays that had sat unfinished for the last two years were finally published in April 1846, in the last issue of *Bells and Pomegranates*.

In the earliest and shortest of these, *A Soul's Tragedy*, Browning created a complex and puzzling character, Chiappino. He is not really a tragic figure but rather the central character in an age-old comic plot of "the biter bit." *A Soul's Tragedy* has its own significance in Browning's career as his first extensive use of special pleading, a legalistic procedure that he no doubt learned about from friends like Forster, Talfourd, and Arnould, who were lawyers. Chiappino and the wily Ogniben are the precursors of such special pleaders as Bishop Blougram, Mr. Sludge the medium, Guido Franceschini in *The Ring and the Book*, and Don Juan in *Fifine at the Fair*. The play is also of interest for its stylistic experiment. Browning uses blank verse for act 1, which depicts Chiappino's heroic behavior, and prose for act 2, which shows his lapse into corruption and falsity. The second play, *Luria*, is a confusing, ill-plotted work that Browning had great difficulty in completing, even though he was very fond of his central Othello-like character.

Admirers of Browning's new directions in his short monodramatic poems must have felt relieved to see him abandon his pretensions to be a dramatist for either stage or closet. Although their appearance kept his name before the public, these plays did nothing to help his reputation.

Chapter 15

Robert Awakes without a Headache

To Anna Jameson, Elizabeth wrote on December 1, 1845, "I am as well as anyone can be who has heard the prison-door shut for a whole winter at least, & knows it to be the only English alternative of a grave."[1] Dr. Chambers had warned her that both of her lungs were "very weak & sensitive to changes of temperature"[2] and were especially prone to respiratory problems during the winter months. Thus she was once more languishing in the sealed room on Wimpole Street. But "I *will not* be beaten down," she told Robert. She was now better able to endure her "cage."[3] Both of them thought of their present situation in terms of folktales: she with hope, for Robert had freed her from a "lampless dungeon" and set her on "the pinnacle of a mountain"; he with chagrin, for Mr. Barrett erected "the strange hedge round the Sleeping Palace keeping the world off."[4]

But the winter proved mild, and that, aided by Elizabeth's confidence in Robert's love, warded off any bad symptoms. Indeed, she seemed to continue the improved health of the previous summer. In mid-January she was walking downstairs by herself, and at the end of February, she managed to go up as well as down stairs, proving, she boasted, her "gigantic strength."[5] Robert kept offering cheery enticements of their seeing Italy together the following autumn.

Along with other encouragements, Robert hoped to draw her away from her daily use of opium. By now, Elizabeth had acquired a real dependence. Sleep, she told him, "will not easily come near me except in a red hood of poppies."[6] Years earlier, Dr. Chambers in London and Dr. Scully in Torquay had prescribed opiates, first in the form of laudanum, an alcoholic tincture of opium, and, later, in a stronger form, a muriate (a hydrochloric solution) of morphine, both of which were measured by drops into ether and sometimes a little brandy and water.[7] Her usual dose was now forty drops a day, and Dr. Chambers told her she "could not do with less."[8] She enjoyed its euphoric as well as its analgesic effect, for it made her feel young and lighthearted. She described it to Mary Russell Mitford, who had not had success with laudanum as a sleeping potion.

> I venture to suggest another attempt [with opium] by way of *morphine*. The muriate of morphine is what I take—what I call my elixir, & I take it in combination with ëther & something else . . . do try it, if it is not advised against. My elixir . . . quiets my mind, calms my pulse—warms my feet—spirits away any stray headache—gives me an appetite—relieves my chest—to say nothing of the bestowment of those sudden pleasant feelings belonging by right to better health & extreme youth.[9]

Of the £40 that her father allowed her every quarter from her investments, her "greatest personal expense" was morphine.[10]

She met Robert's worries defensively. She reassured him that "I dont take it for 'my spirits' in the usual sense,—you must not think such a thing. . . . Also I do not suffer from it in any way, as people usually do who take opium."[11] Nevertheless, he urged her to decrease her intake "slowly and gradually,"[12] and she agreed to try. By the end of February, she reported "less need for the opium,"[13] but she was never able to free herself from it completely.

As spring came on, she was able to go out for carriage rides, and in May she stepped out of the carriage in Regent's Park, feeling the earth under her feet for the first time in years. In June she was writing letters downstairs in the drawing room and walking by herself to the nearby post office to mail them.

More than the weather, her joy in the new life that Robert had brought her strengthened both her body and her will. She confided to her old friend Fanny Dowglass, "I never knew the taste of happiness until the last year."[14] She asked Robert to call her by her family nickname, for no one who loved her had ever called her Elizabeth, only "Ba." She herself gathered courage to go beyond the formality of "Mr. Browning," and early in the year he had become "dearest," "beloved," and "my Robert." Some months before, they had exchanged locks of hair, visible tokens of their commitment. She gave him hers encased in a ring; she wore his in a locket. Within her new and transformed self, a spring of creativity began to bubble: she secretly began work on some sonnets, a poetic chronicle of her rescue from the grasp of death, by love.[15]

In late June, she was able to go out with a new friend, Anna Jameson, to see the art collection of the poet Samuel Rogers (Raphael, Titian, Tintoretto, Guido Reni, Mantegna, Rubens, and a Rembrandt self-portrait). Mrs. Jameson was an Irishwoman who had separated from her husband and thereafter supported herself by writing travel books and art criticism.[16] She became an expert in the art of the Italian Renaissance. After her work gained recognition and respect, she was accepted into the London literary circle and came to know Robert Browning and John Kenyon and to admire the poetry of Elizabeth Barrett. In later 1844, she became one of the privileged few who were allowed to call on Miss Barrett. Hearing about her need to spend the winter in a warm climate, she offered to accompany her to Italy, not knowing anything of Robert Browning's presence in Elizabeth's life nor of their plans for an escape to the Mediterranean area.

As Robert observed Elizabeth's slow return to better health, he began to push for those plans to go forward, but he found that despite her sincere promises and fervent avowals ("My future belongs to you";[17] "I am as wholly yours as if you held me in your hand"[18]) she harbored a reluctance to make specific choices, and she hesitated over steps that needed to be taken. It was as if she enjoyed basking in a blissful present without thinking of the future. She had deep inner conflicts about the experience of real life that lay ahead.

Indeed, she had reason to be ambivalent about the direction her life with Robert would take. She had led a sheltered, even coddled life from which she would be uprooted. She would be leaving England, leaving the great cultural capital where John Kenyon and Anna Jameson brought her weekly the literary gossip of London; leaving the place where she had won recognition for her work. She would be parting from her sisters, who had shared her confidences and cared for her in her invalid condition, going out of that warm center of family life with its jolly crew of brothers whom she had helped to educate in their earlier years. Most of all, she would be betraying the confidence of her father, whose rule had guided the family destiny and who had, with prayer and medical oversight, nursed her back from the edge of the grave. As someone who had been taught to care about others and their welfare, Elizabeth felt guilt at looking now to her own wishes and desires. There can be no doubt that she wondered whether or not she was ready for her new life.

Robert wished her to agree to a specific time for their marriage and departure, "say, at the summer's end,"[19] and she promised that if her health allowed it, he could make the decision at that time. Yet she told him that she worried still about what his life might become once he was married to an invalid. She did not want to see his love sacrificed to duty. But such doubts only brought forth Robert's exasperated reply, "Do not for God's sake intro-duce an element of uncertainty and restlessness and dissatisfaction into the feeling whereon *my* life lies,"[20] and filled the pages of his letter with reassurances that his life would be worthless without her.

Her doubts also took the form of suggesting the postponement of the marriage for a year. Robert replied declaring his willingness to wait for twenty years if he was convinced their lives would be bettered by it but then spoke as plainly as he dared. He deemed such an idea "altogether intolerable!"[21] She returned then to the terms of their long-standing agreement, saying that she was only speculating, wanting him to take responsibility for their schedule. She would no longer talk of delay.

Three weeks later, he reminded her of their plan to leave "at the Summer's end,"[22] only to find that she interpreted this to be at the end of September. He pointed out, in reply, that some cold weather might set in before that. She countered that the longer the delay, the stronger she would be. But when he gave in to let her decide, she concluded, "Let it be September then."[23] Even so, he was ready to compromise further if need be—to make it October, "if your convenience is attained thereby."[24] This was the pattern of their exchanges during the summer: his optimistic hopes and urgings, met by her hesitations and uncertainties, which were answered by concessions and reassurances, followed by her reaffirmations—all embedded in expressions of love and devotion that gave clear evidence that their lives were bound together.

It is curious that so much of their planning took place in letters at a time when they were meeting twice a week for two or three hours. Perhaps the heightened thrill of being alone together, seeing, hearing, touching, was so important that such precious moments could not be wasted on the business of ordinary arrangements, or perhaps as literary people they found it more natural to put their thoughts on paper rather than letting them disappear into the evanescence of mere talk. Generations of readers have been the beneficiaries.

One mundane matter that needed discussion was money. Robert's travels in Italy had made him aware of how cheaply they could live there. The experience of his frugal practices led him to think they could live on as little as £100 a year, until he learned that even Elizabeth's expenses for morphine would come to about £80. In January she assured him that she would have enough income for them to live on, either in England or in Italy, and forbade him to discuss their finances any further because such talk was premature. After a few months, however, the improvement in her health made her realize that their dream was going to come true. Robert asked her to prepare to live simply and cheaply, as he was wont to do, reminding her that she was coming to live with him, not he with her. She agreed; she had already assured

him that she relished the prospect of the bohemian life wherein "all the conventions of society cut so close & thin, that the soul can see through . . .
beyond . . . above."[25] They must be oblivious to the opinions of others, especially about which of them had the money to support their mode of living.
But she revealed she had one important necessity that would involve some
expense. Although she did not expect carriages and fine houses, she did need
to take her maid, Elizabeth Wilson, with them. This was the shy, gentle,
young woman from Newcastle who had replaced Miss Crow. Elizabeth said
she would feel "helpless & impotent"[26] without Wilson.

Robert was penniless. He planned to borrow £100 from his father for the
journey to Italy. Beyond that, he had only naive notions about earning a
living—to go into the diplomatic service (he remembered his secretarial position in St. Petersburg) or somehow to obtain a government post. But Elizabeth was opposed. Such an appointment might lead to his being ordered to a
place like Russia, where she could not endure the cold. Besides she reminded
him that he was a poet and that his vocation required him to devote all his
energies to turning out volumes of verses. This said, she laid out the details of
her financial situation.

She owned shares in the merchant ship *David Lyon*, a gift from her Uncle
Samuel. This "ship money," as she called it, produced about £200 a year,
although it was not guaranteed. She also had about £8000 invested in government funds, which yielded £180 or more annually.[27] This, plus the little
they would each earn from publication, could provide ample means for their
living and for travel. She was full of optimism about the comfortable life
they would share.

Since she regarded all of her financial assets as "God's gifts . . . given perhaps in order to this very end,"[28] she also drew up a memorandum assigning
all of her property to Robert in the event of her death; should he not survive
her, it would go to her sisters and after their deaths to "such of my surviving
brothers as most shall need it."[29] When Robert received her signed document, he reminded her that outside the members of the Barrett family, there
might even be "a *claimant* . . . who knows?"[30] referring for the first time to the
sexual relations attendant upon marriage.

In equally delicate terms, Robert assured Elizabeth of her privacy after
they were married. In an age of washstands and chamber pots in the bedroom, he was aware that a woman of Elizabeth's background would want a
room of her own in which to dress and attend to her needs. As they discussed their future, he sought to reassure her about these matters by "begging a separate room from yours—I could never brush my hair and wash my
face, I do think, before my own father: I could not, I am sure, take off my

coat before you *now*—why should I ever?"[31] They lived in a time of excessive modesty and were of a class that insisted on behavior that respected it.

As September approached, Robert continued his visits, bringing baskets of midsummer flowers from his mother's garden, but he also carried a nagging worry that Mr. Barrett might perceive the quickened interest that Elizabeth displayed in her literary visitor. The tension caused him to suffer repeated headaches. The many references in Elizabeth's letters expressing her concerns about their recurrence make it seem that he, not she, was the ailing one.

Elizabeth had warned Robert some time ago that the frequency of his visits to Wimpole Street might arouse her father's suspicions. Indeed, she reported that he had been "not altogether pleased"[32] to find Robert there on one occasion when he came home early. Now, another episode took place to remind her of what had happened to poor Henrietta.

One day, a heavy afternoon thunderstorm caused Robert to delay his departure from her room until very late in the day. Elizabeth was terrified lest her father appear on the scene to find them still together. Then, just after Robert had left, Mr. Barrett entered her room to find her in her dressing gown. As Elizabeth recounted the story, "He looked a little as if the thunder had passed into him, & said, 'Has this been your costume since the morning, pray?' 'Oh no'—I answered—'only just now, because of the heat.' 'Well,' he resumed, with a still graver aspect . . . 'it appears, Ba, that *that man* has spent the whole day with you.'" She explained that Robert had several times tried to depart but was trapped by the rain. Since Elizabeth's longtime fear of thunder was well known in the family, Mr. Barrett later spoke to Arabella about his displeasure, stating that Elizabeth might have been made ill by the thunderclaps, "'& only Mr. Browning in the room!!!'" This kind of situation, he ruled, "was not to be permitted."[33]

More and more, Elizabeth revealed openly the details of her father's tyranny over the household, but her deep daughterly attachment to him always required her to defend him. Back in March, she had placed "the root of the evil" in his "miserable misconception of the limits & character of parental rights," but she had excused it as "a mistake of the intellect rather than of the heart." Then, in a contradictory way, she explained that "after using one's children as one's chattels for a time, the children drop lower & lower toward the level of the chattels, & the duties of human sympathy to them become difficult in proportion. And, (it seems strange to say it, yet it is true) *love*, he does not conceive of at all."[34]

Robert, of course, bristled at this whole bewildering picture of family injustice, but he had difficulty responding to this argument without upsetting Elizabeth by his frankness. He only said, with evident self-restraint, "I dare say I am unjust, . . . but all faults are such inasmuch as they are 'mistakes of the intellect' . . . but if I ever see it right, exercising my intellect, to treat any human beings like my 'chattels,'—I shall pay for that mistake one day or another, I am convinced."[35] His real feeling is revealed in a letter that Joseph Arnould wrote to Alfred Domett when reporting about Robert's marriage. Arnould described Mr. Barrett in terms that Robert probably used when he told Arnould about the Wimpole Street atmosphere: "[Miss Barrett] ha[s] been for some years an invalid, leading a very secluded life in a sick room in the household of one of those tyrannical, arbitrary, puritanical rascals who go sleekly about the world, canting Calvinism abroad, and acting despotism at home."[36]

Back in June, Robert had wished to tell the secret of their engagement to John Kenyon and to Anna Jameson, but Elizabeth forbade it. She feared that the word would get back to her father and as a result she would be "thrown out of the window."[37] (This was the third time in their letters that she referred to a parental punishment of being "thrown out of the window or its equivalent."[38]) She even denied Robert's request for her to meet his mother and father or to have Sarianna pay a call on her. She felt that his parents should be protected against blame for not discussing the marriage with Mr. Barrett. Or worse yet, Robert Browning, Senior, might feel obliged to call on Mr. Barrett, which would bring the whole structure of their plans crashing down. Robert acquiesced. The secret of their engagement was "*your* secret and not mine."[39] His parents would be understanding. After all, Mr. Browning had had difficulties with his own father at the time of his marriage.

Elizabeth dared not tell her own brothers, even George, upon whom she had leaned for help and advice during the Pisa crisis. But she did confide in her sisters. Indeed, Henrietta was plotting her own future with Capt. Surtees Cook, and Arabella was unconditionally loyal to Elizabeth in whatever she might venture. As for everyone else, Elizabeth was distressed about having to indulge in "pure lying" in order to go forward with the marriage, but she accepted the fact that they must risk the criticism of "affectionate friends" and carry on with the deceptions.[40]

All summer long, plans for travel were exchanged. They weighed the advantages of a voyage by sea, which would not require many changes and stopovers, but which might encounter rough weather. On the other hand, an overland journey would be much more tiring but would be less expensive and would allow many opportunities to rest. Besides, it would be more picturesque. They finally settled on a Southampton crossing to Le Havre and travel by coach and by rail to Paris, thence to Orléans and down to Lyon.

From Lyon, they would float down the Rhône River to Avignon, travel on to Marseilles by coach or rail, and then embark on a short sea voyage to Leghorn (Livorno).

The choice of their ultimate destination in Italy took much discussion. They considered Naples, Amalfi, Sorrento, Vietri (near Salerno), Florence, Pisa, Ravenna, and even Palermo in Sicily. They consulted guidebooks and discreetly inquired about the experiences of friends. They ruled out Florence because it was the haunt of too many English parvenus, decided against Ravenna because of bad water, passed up southern Italy because of possible unhealthful conditions, and finally decided once more on Pisa, known for its truly Mediterranean mildness in winter and blessed by its association with Byron and Shelley. One more detail had to be assured. Elizabeth must take Flush with them. "Because," she worried, "if I leave him behind, he will be hanged for my sins in this house."[41]

Robert's heartbeat quickened as they came finally to discuss the marriage ceremony itself. Although both were Dissenters, law required that the marriage be performed by a Church of England clergyman. Elizabeth had no objection. She preferred the "solemn & beautiful things in the Ch. of England Marriage-service"[42]—but without any High Church liturgical additions. They did not need to have an announcement of the banns; they could be married by license.

On August 29, a momentary unpleasantness took place when Robert encountered the Reverend George Barrett Hunter on the front steps of 50 Wimpole Street. The two exchanged some sharp words, for Robert reported to Elizabeth that he was guilty of some "silliness." Hunter may even have guessed what was afoot, for in his letter Robert referred enigmatically to Hunter's indignation at "this marriage you talk of."[43] But nothing further seems to have come of this confrontation, and their secret was not revealed to Elizabeth's father.

As the letters flew back and forth (the London postal system provided four deliveries a day), a sudden disruption in their plans occurred. On September 1, Flush was kidnapped by a gang of dog-stealers and held for a ransom of six and a half guineas, plus an extra guinea for the go-between, "the archfiend, Taylor."[44] It was the third time the gang had snatched him. Previously, brother Henry had met with Taylor and paid the ransom, bringing back Flush, dirty and panting with thirst. This time, however, Mr. Barrett refused when Henry asked him for the money and ordered him not to tell Ba. He wanted to hold out for a lower payment. Elizabeth's next letter misled Robert into thinking that Flush had been returned, and he indulged himself in some bluster about how he would have handled the matter:

refused payment and threatened vengeance to the death if the dog were harmed. Elizabeth, who had now found out the reason for the delay in Flush's return, was anxious and angry. The two men she loved most were both ready to sacrifice Flush to a little male stubbornness and self-aggrandizing. Called to account, Robert covered himself with apologies and with explanations that his headache had made him cross. Meanwhile, Elizabeth offered to pay the ransom with her own money, but now Henry was afraid to act against his father's wishes. Thwarted, Elizabeth girded her loins to go down near the East London docks herself to ransom her dog.

Demonstrating not only the power of her will but the degree to which she had regained her physical strength, she took Wilson with her in a cab down to Shoreditch, inquired as to the whereabouts of Taylor from a group of men at a public house, and got out of the cab (while Wilson tried to dissuade her by warnings of robbery and murder) and arranged with Mrs. Taylor to have the archfiend come to Wimpole Street for the ransom. Back at home, Elizabeth sent down the money when Taylor appeared, but the transaction was interrupted by brother Alfred, who happened to come upon the scene and denounce the man as a scoundrel in general and a liar and a thief in particular, whereupon Taylor departed with threats of Flush's permanent disappearance. Once more, the fate of Elizabeth's dog was jeopardized by male posturing. After an angry excoriation of Alfred, Elizabeth managed to persuade brother Septimus to go down to the Limehouse area and behave diplomatically in order to make the conclusive arrangements with Taylor. Flush was returned, dirty and whimpering, but soon pampered into calm repose. Elizabeth's mind then returned to her own personal affairs and dilemmas. With resolution, she went out and bought herself a pair of boots for Italy.[45]

Planning for the marriage continued, although Robert was undergoing a three-day series of severe headaches caused by the ever-present threat that somehow Mr. Barrett would manage to interfere. Suddenly, however, unexpected news on September 9 brought Robert's campaign to a climax. Mr. Barrett decreed that the family must vacate their home for a month while the house was being cleaned, repaired, and painted. Robert thought it "the intervention of Providence."[46] They could be married immediately and leave for Italy as soon as possible afterward. All of Elizabeth's packing and preparation for departure would be masked by the disruption of the household while everyone was making ready to leave for the temporary residence. Robert swung into action and within three days had got a license, received the wedding ring from Elizabeth, sought out his cousin Jim Silverthorne to be witness and best man at the wedding, arranged for Thomas Goldhawk, the curate of nearby St. Marylebone Church, to officiate, and solidified plans with Elizabeth for the ceremony.

She made an appointment to call on Mr. Boyd in St. John's Wood on the afternoon of September 12, but in the morning she and the faithful Wilson, who had been informed of the sudden decision only the night before, set out for the cabstand on Marylebone Road. Since the excitement made Elizabeth feel faint, they stopped at a chemist's for some sal volatile (smelling salts), which restored her. They then took a cab to the church, where Robert Browning, Gentleman, and Elizabeth Barrett Moulton Barrett, Spinster, both "Of Full age," were married.[47] Elizabeth remembered it as "our dreary marriage."[48] Robert said later that she looked "more dead than alive,"[49] but she managed to get through it without fainting. After the ceremony, she tried three times to sign her name on the marriage certificate but "could not form a letter."[50] She succeeded finally when someone gave her a glass of water. Wilson and Jim Silverthorne were the only witnesses in the big, empty church. Robert distributed money generously to the curate and the other officials, all of whom sensed that there was something furtive about the marriage. On the church steps, the pew opener stood "mouth wide open in mute surprise"[51] as he watched the bride and bridegroom part with joy and tears and leave in separate cabs.

Elizabeth and Wilson were to return home telling no one, not even Henrietta and Arabella. They went first to Mr. Boyd's, who had been informed a few days earlier of the planned marriage. While resting, Elizabeth sent Wilson home to summon her sisters to come. She drove with them to Hampstead Heath, bursting with momentous news but managing to behave as if it were a normal day. During the days that followed, she was in an agony over keeping her secret from her beloved confidantes. She was shielding them from anxiety and a responsibility that might later redound to their standing in Mr. Barrett's household. As it was, Elizabeth learned later that Arabella had perceived a distinct difference in her demeanor during the week but discreetly kept her suspicions to herself. The ebullient Henrietta probably would have been unable to do so.

Robert was not to call at Wimpole Street again. He could no longer ask to see Miss Barrett, for she was now Mrs. Browning. He awoke the next morning, he wrote to her, "*quite well*—quite free from the sensation in the head—I have not woke *so*, for two years."[52]

Notes and letters flew back and forth as they made the final arrangements for departure. Elizabeth and Wilson were to take as little luggage as possible. She was not to take her little writing desk; he would bring a larger one. He was leaving all his literary papers at home with a thought to getting them on a return trip to England. They had long ago agreed to take only "enough [books] to live upon."[53] She would send her luggage ahead; he was to call for it at Vauxhall Station.

Elizabeth quailed at the thought of the letter she must leave for her father. Guilt still haunted her. Her former procrastination returned: perhaps she should leave from the new house instead of from Wimpole Street. Robert made her see the impracticality of that hesitation. Still she ordered him not to tell anyone she knew, especially Kenyon. If Mr. Barrett learned of the secret marriage, "I shall be *killed*—it will be so infinitely worse than you can have an idea."[54] Daily she trembled at the thought of a confrontation. Several days earlier she had apologized for the fact that "I belong to that pitiful order of weak women who cannot command their bodies . . . & who sink down in hysterical disorder when they ought to act & resist."[55] She had undergone a good trial of her stamina over the recent loss of Flush, but she wanted to take as few risks as possible.

She prepared very carefully for the delicate task of breaking the news to her family and her intimates in letters to be posted on the day they left London. Writing to brother George, she began by saying that "I throw myself on your affection for me" and pled for love and for forgiveness that she had kept him in the dark. She explained her secret marriage, recounting the story of her developing love for Robert and his selfless devotion to her, ready even to live with her "as one of my brothers might" if only he could sit by her side and share a life of love and work for the rest of his days. She explained Robert's rejection of her money until she convinced him that they must use her income for the sake of her health and her need for special care. She asked George to "[break] gently the news" to "dearest Papa"[56] and give him the enclosed letter she had written for him. George had interceded for her in the Pisa incident the previous year. She counted on him once more. She had separate letters for her sisters and possibly for other brothers.

Two other dear ones deserved to be informed immediately—John Kenyon and Mary Russell Mitford, to whom she confessed that she had been existing "in a sort of *stupour*" during the week but looked forward to a "quiet, simple, rational life" in Italy, "to write poems & read books, & try to live not in vain & not for vanities."[57] The rest of their friends were to learn of the marriage through the undated announcement that Robert and Elizabeth composed for the newspaper.

She finally agreed to Saturday, September 19, for her flight from Wimpole Street. There were some blunders and confusions about train schedules and times of steamship departures from Southampton, but finally all was set. Robert was to meet them at 4 P.M. at Hodgson's bookshop nearby.

The evening before departure, she scribbled a final wail of anguish to Robert: "Oh—if I loved you less . . . a little, little less—Why I should tell you that our marriage was invalid, or ought to be—& that you should by no means come for me tomorrow. It is dreadful . . . dreadful . . . to have to give pain here by a voluntary act—for the first time in my life—."[58] At the last minute, she could not bear to leave behind the letters he had sent her. She packed them in her luggage. They were a precious record to keep alongside her new sonnets, the final one of which she had dated and inscribed, "50 Wimpole Street: Married—September 12, 1846."[59]

Flight to Italy

Robert Browning was by temperament an optimist, but his optimism had also been developed at home. The Browning family nurtured a tradition that "a Browning can fail in nothing."[1] Now, for him to whisk Elizabeth Barrett out of her sickroom and plan to carry her across France and over the Ligurean Sea to Pisa was putting his optimism to its most rigorous test.

The passage across the English Channel on September 19, 1846, was rough, and all of his charges—Elizabeth, Wilson, and Flush—arrived at Le Havre exhausted. After a few hours' rest, the party traveled to Rouen by diligence, drawn by five, sometimes seven, spirited horses on a moonlight journey, a bouncing, phantasmagoric experience. At Rouen, the coupé of the diligence was placed aboard a railroad car for a smoother ride. When the train arrived at Paris in midmorning, Robert took his little family to the nearest hotel. Although he had not slept for two days, he went immediately to the Hotel de la Ville de Paris, where he sought out Anna Jameson as the first of their friends whom they could greet as a newly married couple. Because she was out, he left a note, "Come & see your friend & my wife EBB" and signed himself "RB." He returned to his hotel and collapsed into sleep. Mrs. Jameson was at first dumbfounded and then delighted by Robert's message. Hurrying over to the Brownings' hotel, she greeted Elizabeth with open arms: "You wild, dear creature! You dear, abominable poets! . . . I shall dance for joy both in earth & in heaven."[2]

But the rigors of the ordeal so far had cost Elizabeth. Mrs. Jameson saw that she was "nervous—frightened—ashamed[,] agitated[,] happy, miserable.

... She had a feverish desire to go *on on*—as if there was to be neither peace nor health till she was beyond the Alps."[3] Mrs. Jameson calmed her, sympathized, encouraged, and eventually persuaded her to rest in Paris for a few days. Seasoned traveler that she was, she took charge of the newly wedded couple's affairs and moved them over to a pleasant apartment above her own rooms at her hotel. She agreed to accompany them to Pisa in order to help Robert look after Ba.

A few days' rest restored Robert's invalid, and he was able to take her to visit some of the familiar sights in Paris, such as Notre Dame Cathedral and the Louvre. In the museum, he and Mrs. Jameson served as her guides, one on each side, explaining the special features of the paintings. She was breathless at "the divine Raphaels." But for the most part the newlyweds lived quietly, dining out, returning to "sit through the dusky evenings, watching the stars rise over the high Paris houses, & telling childish happy things, or making schemes for work & poetry."[4] The marriage was probably consummated in Paris. "Such a strange week, it was!" Elizabeth wrote to Mary Russell Mitford, "—altogether like a vision. Whether in the body or out of the body I cannot tell scarcely."[5] Her response to Robert's love and care ranged from soaring happiness to abject adoration. "I have done well, & received full compensation for the past sorrows of my life," she told Arabella. "He is *perfect*—far too good & too tender for me—far too high & gifted—To hear him say that he is happy because of me, overwhelms me with a mixture of wonder & of shame."[6] She fully appreciated too his willingness to abide by all of the conditions and demands for secrecy she had imposed on him throughout their plans before the marriage: "for the love of me . . . he has consented to occupy for a moment a questionable position."[7]

The traveling group, including Mrs. Jameson's niece Gerardine Bate ("Geddie"), left Paris by diligence on September 28 for Chartres, where Mrs. Jameson needed to visit the cathedral for the book she was preparing. But even a few hours in the diligence always "bruised [Elizabeth] all over."[8] They continued on by rail to Orléans, where a bundle of letters from home awaited them. When Robert brought them from the post office, Elizabeth sat with numb anticipation, growing paler and more distressed, unable to open hers. Then after a brief glance at Papa's letter, she was so frightened that she put it aside "to read at leisurely courage."[9] Nor would she do so until Robert agreed to leave her alone to face what she feared and expected.

Before she left London, she had posted the long letter to her brother George explaining that Robert had come to her when she had done with life and gradually drew her back to hope. With his help she was now acting to save her life and to recover her health in Italy. She asked George to be a messenger of intercession and to place an enclosed letter begging forgiveness into her father's hands.[10]

But all this was to no avail. Before George could give Mr. Barrett the letter, Henrietta blurted out the news to her father that Ba had fled the household to marry Robert Browning and travel to Italy. A rumor developed among the relatives and friends that Mr. Barrett had responded by knocking Henrietta down the stairs. The closest we can get to the actual scene is the report that "Rowland Grey" (Lilian K. Rowland-Brown) received in an interview with Elizabeth's youngest brother, Octavius, in his old age, who told her, "The fact of the matter was my old Dad was standing upon the staircase with a heavy book in his hand, he threw it down, or dropped it or something, and she slipped down in dodging it."[11]

The letters that Elizabeth now opened from Mr. Barrett and George devastated her. Neither letter is now extant, but Elizabeth's reports and brief quotations give us some evidence of their tone. In the irrationality of Mr. Barrett's response, he spoke as if she were criminally guilty of "a murder & forgery." He also struck a religious note in his accusation, Elizabeth reported: "I have sold my soul for *genius* . . . mere *genius*." More than that, he delivered what she called "my death warrant." He told her that he would forget her and think of her as dead.[12] George's letter hurt her even more, for he had been her supporter during the Pisa crisis. His words in the letter were like "a sword." He railed that she had "sacrificed all delicacy & honour." He treated her as if she had eloped without being married, saying that she left "the weight of sorrow & shame to be borne by my family."[13]

The letters of Arabella and Henrietta applied some balm to her bruised heart, and she responded with tears of joy and gratitude at their sisterly wishes for happiness in her new life. Nor did they express any resentment about the secrecy of her plans or disappointment at not being present at the wedding. They not only understood her position but also defended it to their brothers. A letter from John Kenyon helped too, when he told the Brownings, "I know no two persons so worthy of each other" and declared that they were justified in the action they had taken.[14] From this moment, Kenyon was to become more and more a father to Elizabeth to replace the one who had rejected her.

Robert returned to soothe her further. He laid her on the hotel bed and sat for hours by her side, uttering endearments, and since he felt some responsibility for her sorrow at the family denunciations, he vowed to win back the love of her father and brothers.

The journey from Orléans to Lyon by diligence was again hard on Elizabeth. Robert tried to keep everyone cheery. Elizabeth reported, "He amuses us from morning till night,—thinks of everybody's feelings, . . is witty & wise, . . (& foolish too in the right place) charms cross old women . . . talks latin to the priests . . . & forgets nothing & nobody . . . except himself. . . . He has won Wilson's heart."[15] The trip included a stopover at Bourges, where the delighted Brownings looked in wonderment at the glories of the stained glass windows of the cathedral.

Nevertheless, the travel was agonizing for Elizabeth and made her companions anxious for her welfare. According to Mrs. Jameson, she was "often fainting and often so tired that we have been obliged to remain a whole day to rest at some wretched place."[16] Robert, carrying her fainting from the carriage, had to insist on these reststops. He carried her everywhere whenever fatigue overcame her powers.

The trip down the Rhône by boat from Lyon should have been a welcome and happy relief, but a steady downpour took away the pleasure, except for occasional glimpses of "wild striking scenery . . . the fantastic rocks & ruined castles,"[17] and the confinement in a hot and dirty public cabin caused further misery for the traveling invalid. Skies brightened at Avignon. Elizabeth, full of sweetness and good humor despite her sufferings on the way, rested at the hotel while Robert and the others visited the Palais des Papes in all its grandeur. The next day both poets made a pilgrimage to the Fountain at Vaucluse, sacred to the memory of Petrarch and Laura. Elizabeth's resilience on this occasion startled everyone. From the bank of the River Sorgue, where she saw "the fountain, shut up in everlasting walls of rock" and "the little river flashing from it like a green singing-bird," she skipped out over a series of rocks into the middle of the stream. "Ba, are you losing your senses?" Robert called and followed her over the stones to make sure she would not tumble in. There, on a large rock in the middle of the bubbling stream, they sat while Mrs. Jameson sketched them. Poor Flush, who tried to join his mistress, splashed out toward them but was repelled by Robert, guarding Elizabeth from a wet dog-leap.[18]

On October 9 Robert engaged a *voiturier* to drive them from Avignon through Aix to Marseilles "in the very footsteps of the Troubadours."[19] On October 11 they boarded *l'Océan*, a comfortable French steamer, for Genoa, on a stormy voyage of twenty-six hours that left them all prostrate with the heat or seasickness. Although Elizabeth was too storm-tossed at first to visit the city, by the next day she had recovered enough for a short walk ashore with Robert through the narrow streets, looking at the palaces on the Via Aura,

all strange & noble, [and] into a gorgeous church where mass was going on—altar pressing by altar, every one of a shining marble encrusted with gold—Great columns of twisted porphyry . . . frescoed angels glancing from the roof—Glory upon glory it was . . . and on the marble pavement, knelt monks with brown serge & cord . . . nuns of various orders—& Genoese ladies dropping their fans from their fingers, as they prayed covered with the national veil.

She was captivated. "Beautiful Genoa—what a vision it is!—& our first sight of Italy beside."[20]

The final nighttime voyage to Leghorn was an even rougher passage. Everyone was ill—except Elizabeth! A short rail journey brought them to Pisa, October 14, the whole trip from Paris having taken seven days longer than Robert and Mrs. Jameson had planned. Elizabeth was happy and relieved to reach her new "home" at last. Despite their troubles, the members of the little band of travelers had enjoyed each other's company enormously. Young Geddie had quite fallen in love with the newly wedded poets. Robert and Elizabeth felt bound to "Aunt Nina" for the rest of their lives. Mrs. Jameson admired Elizabeth's endurance and thought of Robert as "full of spirit & good humour & his unselfishness—& his turn for making the best of every thing & his bright intelligence & his rare acquirements of every kind rendered him the very prince of traveling companions—but"—and here she expressed a concern about the future of the young couple in the practicalities of life—"he is in all the common things of this life the most impractical of men—the most uncalculating—rash—in short the worst *manager* I ever met with." Yet, writing to Lady Byron, Mrs. Jameson spoke of Kenyon's remark that he did not think any man would undertake to become "the constant slave" to take care of Elizabeth in her weakened physical condition. Mrs. Jameson chortled with gleeful rebuttal: "What would [Mr. Kenyon] say if he saw B—carrying his wife up & down two flights of stairs—hanging over her as if she were something spared to him for a while out of heaven!"[21]

Although prices were higher in Pisa than Robert had expected, by October 18 he had found an apartment for them in the Collegio di Ferdinando, a palazzo redesigned by Vasari, with "a grand marble entrance, marble steps & pillars & a bust over all of Ferdinando primo" (all this in high contrast to the grim façade of 50 Wimpole Street). It stood a few steps from the assembly of principal monuments, the baptistry, the cathedral, the Campo Santo, and the campanile (the noble Leaning Tower), which was itself visible from the entrance to the Collegio and from which a harmonious peal sounded every morning at 4 A.M., and as Elizabeth wrote to Hugh Boyd, "rang my dreams apart."[22]

The apartment was spacious and comfortable: dining room, sitting room, three bedrooms, all furnished including silverware, china, glassware, and linen. Total rent: a little over £4 a month. Also included was a servant who came in the morning to prepare breakfast, make up the beds, and do light housekeeping. Robert arranged with the landlord for bread, butter, rolls, eggs, sugar, and coffee for their little pantry. Dinner for three was ordered every day from a nearby trattoria—such fare as soup, roast chicken, boiled potatoes, a pudding, and a bottle of chianti—all for two shillings. There was enough left for a cold supper. "Viva la trattoria," cried Elizabeth, who was no housekeeper.[23] Oranges grew in the garden behind the Collegio. They each had one every day, a real treat for the English.

They spent quiet evenings before the fireplace, roasting chestnuts and sampling the local grapes (which Robert fed by hand to a reclining Elizabeth), and exchanging dream-plans for their future. Mrs. Jameson, who stayed close by for a month, was forced to revise her opinion of Robert's management. She commended them both for their "miraculous prudence & economy."[24]

The Mediterranean climate worked wonders for Elizabeth's health because the sun was out every day. She reported that she was "able to throw off most of my invalid habits." She was soon going for daily walks along the River Arno, very near the Collegio. Her ghostly pallor was gone; color appeared in her cheeks. Mrs. Jameson declared, "You are not *improved:* you are *transformed.*"[25] But Robert, taking no chances as November came on, pampered her anyway, continuing to carry her up even the modest four steps into the Collegio. He urged her to eat, to finish her morning egg or her evening chianti, which they drank from tumblers. He would sneak more into her glass when she was not looking (he accepted that Victorian notion that red wine was good for the blood) until she often felt dizzy by the end of dinner, when he carried her to an armchair for a nap.

Although a doting husband and a mild climate lifted her spirits, the severe attitudes of the male members of the Barrett family troubled her, especially as Christmas approached. Her sisters had given depressing reports about Mr. Barrett's mean-spiritedness. His suspicions of Arabella's complicity in Elizabeth's flight led to his banishing her to a fourth-floor bedroom without a fireplace and preventing her from attending Paddington Chapel, where the Reverend James Stratten's liberal social attitudes made him another suspect in siding with Elizabeth and Robert. Around the home he treated her coldly. He caused Elizabeth's very presence to be obliterated from 50 Wimpole Street. He put her books, her papers, and her clothes in storage, and he had her former room redecorated ("this painting out of one's footsteps in the old room,"[26] as Elizabeth interpreted it). She asked that her things be taken out of storage and sent to the Brownings at New Cross. She felt that the tokens of her presence would be welcomed by her new family.

In the midst of her troubles, Elizabeth had actually neglected the Brownings. She had, of course, forbidden Robert to let any of them visit her for fear of Mr. Barrett's discovery of their secret. But it was not until December 12 that she wrote to Sarianna, thanking her for her wedding gift of a portable writing desk and begging to be considered a "dear sister" in the future. She also asked her to convey her apologies to Robert's parents for the private marriage, promising that she would be a *real daughter* to them. She even offered a greeting from Flush to "Mother Puss," the Browning cat.[27]

Ever since John Kenyon's cordial message, the Brownings had been receiving best wishes from other rejoicing friends, most of whom expressed delighted surprise: Joseph Arnould of the Colloquials, Carlyle, W. J. Fox, Fanny Haworth, R. H. Horne, H. F. Chorley, B. W. Procter, Monckton-Milnes, and others from the literary world.[28] John Forster sent an affectionate letter but did not tell them that, at first, he had thought the newspaper announcement was a hoax and demanded to see the letter that passed the information to the editor; he was satisfied only after he recognized Sarianna's handwriting. Wordsworth sent no message, but he expressed his opinion to Moxon that it would be "a happy union" and assumed that "they will speak more intelligibly to each other than . . . they have yet done to the Public."[29] Mary Russell Mitford finally sent her good wishes to Elizabeth, but expressed to others her jealous resentment over Robert's "stealing her away."[30] Elizabeth's relatives, who disapproved of being informed of the marriage by public announcement in a newspaper, came around rather slowly, but since they understood the circumstances of the Barrett household, they were willing to resume the old relationship with her. Trippy even provided a postal delivery address for Elizabeth's letters to her sisters.

The cold air swept into Pisa by mid-December—early, the inhabitants said—and Elizabeth felt the cold in her throat. Robert rose early every morning to build up the fire in the sitting room. He then retreated to the cold bedroom and allowed Elizabeth to wash and be dressed in privacy.

In order to draw her out of her depressing thoughts about missing the Christmas gaiety of home, Robert persuaded her to participate in an Italian Christmas. He dressed her in shawls and furs, wrapped her in his cloak, and carried her to the duomo for midnight mass on Christmas Eve. The interior of the duomo, with its brilliant mosaics on the walls and the vaulted ceiling that glittered gloriously in the abundant illumination from candle-filled chandeliers, was an impressive sight, and Elizabeth was enthralled by the power of the organ music and the singing of the choir. But she soon had her anti-Catholic misgivings reinforced by the "want of all reverence & decency" in the members of the congregation, who were laughing and talking and promenading about. Even those who were kneeling on the stone floor were chatting back and forth. Nevertheless, when the sun came out the following day and the weather was actually "*hot*," her spirits were restored and her lungs soothed for an Italian Christmas Day.[31]

The Brownings led a secluded life in Pisa. They avoided the English expatriates in the community and accepted no invitations. Their only contact with Italian society was with Professor Ferrucci of the University of Pisa, who helped them get books from the library. They also subscribed to a circulating library which had a small holding of French novels, most of which Elizabeth had read before. Robert did not care for any of the contemporary novelists except Balzac, Stendahl, and George Sand. Both poets worked at their verses. Elizabeth completed "The Runaway Slave at Pilgrim's Point," a vigorous attack on American slavery that she sent to James Russell Lowell for the American Anti-Slavery Society. The slave's monologue in the poem revealed that she had been raped and impregnated by her white master and in her bitterness had killed her child, and Elizabeth was not sure that the society would publish so harsh and forthright an indictment. Robert was occupied by a revision of his poems and plays for a collected edition of his work that he was preparing for Moxon. *Pauline, Sordello,* and *Strafford* were to be omitted.

Early in their marriage plans, the Brownings had agreed that they would draw up a marriage settlement to arrange for the control of Elizabeth's financial holdings. Since English law decreed that at the time of marriage the property of a wife became the unrestricted possession of her husband, it took a legal document to make any alteration of that transfer. Consequently, since Robert did not want to be regarded as a fortune hunter seeking the wealth of an ailing woman, he wanted to have a settlement that would turn Elizabeth's investments over to her sisters, but she was wise enough to refuse. She realized that in an uncertain future she might need the income for her medical expenses alone. Robert then thought that the money should revert to the family in case of her death, but she resisted that too, preferring that the money go to Robert during his lifetime and then pass to her sisters. Upon these terms, then, she asked John Kenyon to prepare a marriage settlement in which she would retain her investments and to draw up her will. He was to act as trustee along with Joseph Arnould and H. F. Chorley, and Chorley was also to be executor of her will. Since money was the underlying sore point with all of the Barrett brothers, Elizabeth was glad to complete a marriage settlement and hoped it would patch up her relationship with the male Barretts. But sullen brother George would not even agree to be the executor of her will, and she had been vexed that she had to go outside the family and ask Chorley. John Kenyon now took on total management of her financial affairs, not only handling her investments but also dispensing the income every quarter to the Brownings for their living expenses. The settlement also specified a separate allowance for Elizabeth of £100 a year. Kenyon told her that he would take the place of father and brother to her.

Robert was pleased to see Elizabeth appearing so well, even in colder weather. Her color was good. Her voice was strengthened. She was eating two eggs a day now and at dinner showing an increase in her birdlike appetite, even though she had a revulsion toward the oil and garlic that were characteristic of some of the meals prepared by the trattoria. She became less dependent on personal care by her maid. When Wilson fell ill with stomach complaints, Elizabeth learned to comb and put up her own hair, to dress herself—even to lace and hook her own stays. Robert was constantly urging her to reduce her intake of morphine, and by February 1847 she had cut her dosage in half. Although he was merely following his commonsense instinct, these were important measures to take for a person in Elizabeth's precarious state of health because opium in any form suppresses the immune system.[32]

Howevermuch progress she had been making, Elizabeth suffered a major setback in late March. She and Robert were both astounded to discover that her sudden nighttime pains and bleeding were the results of a miscarriage. Both were so ignorant of sexual matters that they were unaware that Elizabeth had been pregnant for almost five months. Wilson had been somewhat suspicious of Elizabeth's recent symptoms of internal discomfort but had said nothing. Elizabeth's isolation from the intimate company of other women had left her totally without the advice and counsel that accumulated women's wisdom always provides. Robert wept like a child at the loss, somehow blaming himself for not taking better care of his frail wife. In the days following, he spent all his time by her bedside, feeding her, reading to her, talking to her, rubbing her back and limbs. In a few days she was walking a little, and by April she was recovered but weak.

They were soon back to their reading and writing routine. They had grown tired of Pisa, however. Both of them were missing the association with their friends, the cultural stimulation of London, and the literary gossip of the town. Robert discovered too that they had been overcharged for their apartment, and an English resident pointed out to them that they had been regularly overpaying every time they went to the market, for foreigners were considered "lawful prey."[33] They made plans, as soon as Elizabeth was strong enough, to move to Florence, a more cosmopolitan center where there was greater variety of life and where most things of interest were clustered in the center of the city and could be reached by walking.

On April 20, the little party of English exiles arrived in Florence. Still weak after her miscarriage, Elizabeth was exhausted and aching from the journey, but Robert soon found a pleasant set of rooms on the Via della Belle Donna, near the magnificent Church of Santa Maria Novella, and kept her off her feet as much as possible. Their apartment was grander and more spacious than the one in Pisa; it had a large drawing room, dining room, and three bed-rooms with high ceilings and Venetian blinds for relief from the summer heat, all furnished (including a piano) for four pounds and ten shillings a month. For six shillings a month, a *donna di facienda* came in every day to clean the rooms, make the beds, and wash the dishes. Robert again arranged with a nearby trattoria for its daily services—this time, and for a modest price, sumptuous dinners like the following: soup à la macaroni, a roast shoulder of lamb, a boiled chicken with peas, risolles of veal, fried potatoes, spinach, rice pudding, bread, and butter stamped with arms of the Medici. The cost: nine-teen shillings a week, wine to be purchased extra.

After a month Robert was able to take Elizabeth out to see the principal sights. First, they walked over to Santa Maria Novella, its chancel adorned with brilliant frescoes by Domenico Ghirlandaio of scenes from the life of the Virgin Mary on one side and the life of John the Baptist on the other, plus the fresco of the Trinity by Tommaso Masaccio in the left aisle, a land-mark in the history of Renaissance painting.

The next day he took her to see the baptistry and Ghiberti's bronze doors with scenes from the life of Jesus; the duomo, crowned by Brunelleschi's huge dome; and Giotto's campanile. She was thrilled by the massiveness of the duomo. Writing to Hugh Boyd, she tried to express how it surpassed the one in Pisa:

> At Pisa we say "How beautiful," . . here we say nothing . . . it is enough if we can breathe—The mountainous marble masses, overcome us as we look up—we feel the weight of them on the soul—Tesselated mar-bles, . . (the green treading its elaborate pattern into the dim yellow which gives the general hue of the structure) . . climb against the sky, self-crowned with that prodigy of marble domes. . . . It seemed to carry its theology out with it: it signified more than a mere building.[34]

Later, he took her to the Uffizi Gallery, where she was vigorous enough to walk up the four flights of stairs, refusing to be carried, and where he drew her attention to the "Venus di Medici," which disappointed her, although Robert assured her she would appreciate it in time. Her taste ran instead toward religious works. Her sight of the last work of Michaelangelo, "The Dead Christ and the Three Marys" in the duomo was "worth a hundred of such elaborated shining things as that Venus." He brought her to the Pitti Palace Gallery where, as in the Uffizi, she looked at so many paintings that it was like "not going at all." But in the rich blur she singled out the Raphaels and again proclaimed them "*Divine*"—"The Madonna della Seggiola—and the Madonna del Gran Duca, *my* madonna, which stood on my chimney-piece in Wimpole Street—Oh, that divine child, that infantine majesty ... Raffael understood better than all your theologians how God came in the flesh, 'yet without sin.'"[35] She was beginning to yearn for motherhood.

As the weather became hot, Robert hired a carriage on some evenings and drove her around Florence, sometimes stopping by a church such as Santa Croce, where they stood in reverence before Michaelangelo's tomb, or the Church of the Carmine, renowned for Masaccio's frescoes, especially "The Expulsion of Adam and Eve from Eden." Years hence, Masaccio was to serve as a notable reference ("hulking Tom") in Robert's "Fra Lippo Lippi." Then they would drive through the Cascine, a park, partly woodland, outside the city, along the Arno, where "the trees take hands over your head & perfectly shut out the sky ... but then, there are depths of wood, & ravishing glimpses of hills, & sometimes the shining river."[36]

Robert and Elizabeth agreed that, in retrospect, Pisa was dull compared to Florence. Florence, they concluded, was "the most beautiful of the cities devised by man!"[37] Although Robert had visited it in 1844, to live here was different. Life was a daily spiritual enrichment. Even the life of the Florentine people seemed extraordinary, something brought about by the absence of a rigid class system. "What helps to charm here," wrote Elizabeth, echoing Robert's poem "The Englishman in Italy,"

> is the innocent gaiety of the people, who, for ever at feast-day & holiday celebration, come & go along the streets, the women in elegant dresses & with glittering fans, shining away every thought of northern cares & taxes, such as make people grave in England. No little orphan on a house-step, but seems to inherit naturally his slice of water-melon & bunch of purple grapes: and the rich fraternize with the poor as we are unaccustomed to see them, listening to the same music & walking in the same gardens & looking at the same Raffaels even![38]

The Brownings participated, as well as they were able, in the festivals of the people. During the feast of San Giovanni in June, they bought seats at a window on the Arno to watch the fireworks, which exploded great spectacles in the air—grand temples, fantastic palaces, fountains of flame. They were gratified by the well-behaved crowd, no drunkenness descending into rowdyism as would be seen in London. They watched the chariot races in the piazza in front of Santa Maria Novella, reminiscent of the entertainments of ancient Rome.

But the summer heat in Florence was intense. To escape it, they made plans to spend two months at Vallombrosa, high in the chestnut forests in the nearby mountains. There at the monastery of the Vallombrosan Order, they would study and write and feel the spirit of John Milton hovering near to inspire them. When the local bishop granted permission, they set off in high spirits. All went well at first. After an hour of travel, they reached the point where roads stopped. Then for four hours, Elizabeth and Wilson, together with all the baggage, had to be dragged up the mountain on sledges pulled by oxen, to the aerie where the monastery was perched, while Robert rode alongside on horseback. The scenery was spectacular—precipices, ravines, tumbling mountain streams, pines, chestnut trees, waterfalls.

But when the party arrived, the new abbot refused to admit them because female presence was forbidden. The bishop's permission was not valid; it was only a recommendation. They would be allowed to stay only in the "House of Strangers" outside the monastery complex for three days. Robert's argument that his wife was a renowned scholar of the early Greek Fathers of the Church did no good at all, although two additional days were grudgingly added to the stay in the outside premises, where the accommodations were unsatisfactory and the food was not to Elizabeth's finicky taste. She was outraged, provoked into a feminist furor by the ungracious rejection and especially at the discovery that the abbot could not abide "anything impure & feminine to keep a stinking in his nostrils above three days." At the time of departure, when no one was looking, she put her foot through the iron gateway and "stamped on the gravel of their courtyard. . . . There, was profanation for them, poor men! The little Abbot will have had a visitation of Satan through it . . . after the manner of St Anthony." If it had not been for Robert, who prevented it, she would have run in through the gate "& opened the way for a troop of devils."[39]

They returned to the heat of Florence and a necessary search for a new apartment. As luck would have it, Robert found an excellent place in the Palazzo Guidi on the other side of the Arno near the grand duke's Palazzo Pitti, a first-floor suite of six rooms with tall ceilings and a grand entrance. There were three bedrooms—one of them a master bedroom for Elizabeth—a dining room, a very large drawing room, and a small kitchen, plus a charming little terrace (really no more than a balcony) extending along the three main rooms and overlooking the street. The back area of the apartment also had a balcony that looked down upon a pleasant green courtyard. The apartment had formerly been occupied by a Russian prince and was furnished accordingly—with crimson and white satin couches and armchairs, marble consoles, "noble mirrors," plus china and silver "fit for the entertainment of the court of Tuscany."[40] Their occupancy included the privilege of access to the Boboli Gardens behind the Palazzo Pitti. Moreover, the rent seemed cheap for such grandeur, a guinea a week, plus nine shillings a month for the porter who brought up water and lighted the marble staircase leading to their rooms.

Although they could not escape the summer heat, the rooms were cooler than those of their former apartment, for this one was shaded from the sun by the Church of San Felice across the narrow street. They lived on melons, cherries, grapes, and figs for hot-weather suppers, with eggs, rolls, coffee, macaroni and cheese, and very little meat for their other meals. They cooled themselves all day long by drinking ice water.

Mrs. Jameson need not have worried about Robert's ability to manage the household affairs. Early in life he had adapted himself to a frugal way of living as preparation for making his way as a poet. As we have seen, he and Elizabeth had agreed, early on, to use her income for a way of life that would restore her to health, for they recognized that a bohemian existence of near starvation in an attic would never do. Aside from that agreement, Robert had a horror "of having to apply ever to any human being for pecuniary help." Since Elizabeth knew nothing about handling money, he had taken over their domestic accounts as soon as they set up housekeeping. He kept track of all their expenditures in a notebook, down "to the uttermost farthing," and set money aside regularly "lest Ba shd. be ill."[41] His care with expenses soon paid off all the personal debts that Elizabeth had left behind, for he hated a debt "like a scorpion."[42] He had a solid middle-class dislike of people who ran up long-standing bills; his "sympathies always go with the butchers & bakers."[43]

Robert had reckoned that their expenses for the first six months of marriage, inclusive of travel from London and of the high costs of morphine, were £150 for three people. Thus they would have money left over for travel, although Elizabeth had long ago given up the thought of an early visit to England. He was rather proud of his financial management, but Elizabeth was amused at his penny-pinching and his worry about having enough money to take care of her. "He is given to hear Lions roar round corners," she told Sarianna, "and to see shadows of crocodiles dilated to the whole height

& depth of his imagination." Robert countered that she would never concern herself with money until disaster befell and she grew very hungry and that then, instead of striving to get bread, she "would snatch up a French novel to forget the hunger in." She admitted that was "rather *like me*."[44]

They settled into a contented life in the Palazzo Guidi. They read books from Vieusseux's circulating library and his newspapers from London and Paris. They occasionally turned to their poetry. Robert played for Elizabeth on a piano he had rented. Elizabeth enjoyed mothering Flush. At the end of the day they would walk on their little terrace—just wide enough for two small poets—hearing the organ playing or the choir singing over at San Felice and waiting for the moon to rise.

Florence was in an especially joyous state just as the Brownings' first wedding anniversary approached. During the past decade, the nationalistic stirrings in Europe had stimulated a renewed desire for the unification of Italy. Then the ascendancy of Pius IX to the papacy in 1846 had given heart to Italian patriots because, by his handling of affairs in the Papal States, he had acquired a reputation for liberalism. He had proclaimed amnesty for all political prisoners, granted freedom of the press, and set about reforming the government of his provinces. This new spirit spread to Tuscany, which had been under Austrian rule since the end of the Napoleonic Wars in 1815. Grand Duke Leopold II, the ruling representative in Tuscany, was himself an easygoing liberal in his leanings.

In the summer of 1847, just after the Brownings moved into the Palazzo Guidi, the grand duke allowed the establishment of a civic guard to exercise military duties in Tuscany in place of the Austrian troops. The populace of Florence responded ecstatically and ceremonially to the change, and the Brownings joined in their enthusiasm, especially since the ducal palace, the Palazzo Pitti, was right around the corner from their apartment. When the festivities began on September 12, they felt that all Florence was, in a symbolic way, celebrating their anniversary.

Forty thousand people crowded into Florence from all the Tuscan cities for the formal inauguration of the new civic guard. Ceremonies began in the duomo with the blessing of their banners and the singing of a "Te Deum." Following this, a three-hour procession marched to the ducal palace—magistrates, priests and monks, nobles, peasants, soldiers, and people from other Tuscan cities displaying their civic banners, even foreign residents from European states with their flags, accompanied by music and cheering throngs, through streets where flowers and laurel leaves rained down from the windows. Robert and Elizabeth were well situated to see all the pageantry and enthusiasm, viewing it from a window in the Palazzo Guidi that looked onto a small corner of the palace yard. Elizabeth sat on a pile of cushions and waved her handkerchief until her arm ached. At night they walked among the crowds to the Arno where there was a special "illumination." "The people were *embracing* for joy," Elizabeth wrote to her sisters. "It was a state of phrenzy or rapture, extending to the children of two years old, several of whom I heard lisping . . 'Vivas'. . . . So wasn't our day kept well for us?"[45]

She was entitled to rejoice. Their married year had been their personal triumph over daunting obstacles. They now lived in a climate that had restored her to nearly normal health. Breathing the balmy Italian air of spring, summer, and fall, she went out almost every day, and even on most days of winter she could take a little outdoor exercise, free at last from the smog and damp of London. She no longer had to be carried upstairs. She could walk up the hill in the Boboli Gardens. She could join Robert, the inveterate walker, whenever he wished to go out. Her cousin Arlette Butler Reynolds, who had last seen her in London and was visiting Florence at the end of 1847, found her "past recognition." The Brownings were living their life in a civilized center that "combine[d] art & nature" to their utmost desire. But most of all, their love had developed from the ecstatic surprise at a new plane of life into the deep satisfaction of daily entwined existence— "unclouded happiness," Elizabeth called it. Robert, writing to Mrs. Jameson, put it more quaintly: "We are as happy as two owls in a hole, two toads under a tree-stump . . . Ba is fat and rosy."[46] His dream had been fulfilled; his optimism had been justified.

Joys and Sorrows

Over the next two years Robert Browning's personality seemed to change. Bearing responsibility for Elizabeth's health and happiness made him less the vivacious spirit he had been in London and more the serious householder. A little cloud of guilt hung over him, too, about his situation of living on his wife's income. The blithe thoughts of an earlier day about finding himself a diplomatic or secretarial post had been merely fanciful. He began to face the reality that he was an impecunious poet and likely to remain so for some time. His dignity could be upheld, however, in the fact that he had rescued Elizabeth Barrett from oppression and, indeed, a threat to her very life. He could also be her responsible money manager. The careful handling of their income became almost an obsession for him.

Another worry arose because the slimness of the family purse made them postpone a return visit to England longer than they had hoped. They had found in Italy an ideal climate for Elizabeth's recovery, but it took a while for them to realize that their lives were bound to this paradise of mild weather and, except for short visits, they were severed from home and England for the rest of Elizabeth's life. Robert became aware of an unsettling drift to their lives. Their situation seemed to be a continual relocation from one set of furnished rooms to another. After losing their apartment in the Palazzo Guidi because of Robert's haggling over the price of a new lease, they changed to one on the shaded, palazzo-lined Via Maggio, only to find the rooms precariously cold for Elizabeth's well-being. After ten days, Robert forfeited the cost of their six-month lease and moved them to a sunny location on the Piazza Pitti in "little funny rabbit-hutch rooms."[1] Six months later they were back in the luxurious space of the Palazzo Guidi.[2] Some new thinking had taken place about their establishing a home.

Robert had devised a plan for them to reduce expenses and set aside enough money for travel to London. They would take the Palazzo Guidi rooms unfurnished, thereby lowering their annual rent from forty-eight to twenty-five guineas. They would use the £70 they had received over the last two years from royalties (mostly for Elizabeth's books) for furnishings. In a little more than two years, their savings would cover the cost of their investment. Further, the optimistic Robert calculated that furnishing the rooms with satin curtains and spring sofas would make the apartment more desirable and thus possible to sublet at a profit whenever they wished to travel or to spend the warm months of the year in England.

Robert roamed the cabinetmakers' workshops and storage rooms of Florence and soon had six chests of drawers (two for Elizabeth, one of walnut, the other of ebony, each inlaid with ivory), eight sofas, three armchairs (Elizabeth's favorite was "sybaritically soft," "like sitting in a cloud"[3]), antique drawing room chairs of dark carved wood, other chairs of white and gold frames with crimson upholstery, a mirror with a richly carved gilt frame, and large comfortable beds (Wilson's with curtains surrounding it). Elizabeth boasted that Robert was able to obtain everything at bargain prices—sofas "for a song," chairs "for love," and tables for "nothing at all."[4] Robert was willing to spend £8, however, for a drawing room carpet. In the process of refurbishing, they discovered a fresco on the ceiling of the little study ("A cloud full of angels looking down on you"[5]). Robert fancied it was a Tintoretto.

They arranged to have their books shipped from England and bought two huge bookcases to hold them, one of which was a dark, rococo creation of imposing height, with carved angels and demons. Elizabeth, feeling more and more at home, wanted to have her own things around her and asked Arabella to send immediately certain cartons of books and her jewelry box. They were no longer nomads. She began to call their new home "Casa Guidi."

As time went on, Robert continued his bargain hunting to include objets d'art. He was able to buy some paintings for "a few pauls each" that the art dealers had passed by. He became like his father in former days, haunting the bookshops of London. His greatest triumph was in finding five pictures in a corn shop five miles from Florence where a collector who faced financial difficulties had been forced to leave these works of art behind. They had been there for years and were now available to any buyer who would "pay the custom house dues, with the other expenses." When Robert showed the paintings to his English friend Seymour Kirkup, an eccentric connoisseur, Kirkup made some fantastic attributions. One painting was pronounced to be a Giottino, another a Ghirlandaio, a third, "a Christ with an open Greek gospel," a Cimabue. A fourth, "a crucifixion painted on a banner," was declared to be Giottesque, if not by Giotto, but unique because painted on linen. The fifth was a small Virgin and Child by "a Byzantine master." The most remarkable feature of Robert's discovery was that the so-called Ghirlandaio was seen to match the edges of two paintings of angels that he had bought some months earlier in Arezzo. The three paintings turned out to be an altarpiece of the "Eterno Padre," surrounded by angels, that had been sawn into pieces for the sale of the separate items.[6] Reconstituted, the whole splendid work took on new power when, hung over their marble mantelpiece, it dominated the Brownings' drawing room in "Casa Guidi."[7]

Unable to return to England during the summer of 1848, Robert and Elizabeth decided to escape the Florentine heat by traveling over the Apennines by moonlight in the diligence, through Urbino to Fano, a town on the Adriatic coast recommended by Murray's guidebook as a suitable summer retreat for the English. They found instead a sunbaked town, in no way a place to sojourn. It had many attractive churches, however, which they visited: in San Agostino they encountered a sentimental religious painting by Guercino, "The Guardian Angel," that captivated them.[8]

Three times they visited the church and drank in the message of the painting, which shows an angel standing beside a nude child of about three years old. The child crouches on a tomb, hands clasped in prayer. Both figures gaze heavenward toward a hovering cluster of putti. Elizabeth lost herself contemplating Guercino's creation: she yearned for a child of her own whom she might teach to pray. But Robert imagined himself a child again and saw the guardian angel figure as one who could lift the pressures of the world from his shoulders. They next traveled down to Ancona. There he wrote "The Guardian-Angel," about the painting. It was the first poem he had composed since his marriage.

This personal lyric, unusual for Browning, shows his first attempt to speak in his own voice, as he had told Elizabeth during their courtship he hoped to do in the future. His poetic confession of a need for succor may reflect his response to the role he had assumed as guardian and protector of Elizabeth. He calls out for some care and nurturing of himself, and addresses the angel as a kind of mother figure. Curiously enough, the poem ends with a remembrance of his old friend Alfred Domett, who had immigrated to New Zealand: it asks a question about his present condition and whereabouts. Browning may have recalled Domett because he remembered a painting, "The Guardian Angel," by an unknown French painter, which he had often seen in the Dulwich Gallery as a young man.[9] It is possible that

Browning and Domett visited the gallery together on one occasion. These concluding lines to Domett are the only ones in the poem that are not stilted and reminiscent of the annual "gift book" verse of the period. The poem was included later in *Men and Women*.

The Brownings spent a week in Ancona, "a striking sea-city,"[10] with houses built against the cliffs like outcroppings of the rock. The heat overwhelmed them and prevented sightseeing, but they were determined to make the most of their exploration of the Adriatic coast. Ba was holding up well during their wandering journey in spite of some weakness from a second miscarriage she had suffered in March. They went on to Loreto, where they probably viewed with skepticism the "Holy House" of Mary and the child Jesus, which was said to have been borne across the sea by angels from Nazareth and deposited in the nearby woods. They traveled back up the coast, stopping at Pesaro, Rimini, and eventually Ravenna with its magnificent mosaics in the ancient churches and its unendurable stench from the adjacent marshes. They paid obeisance to Dante's tomb, looking through the window of the house that contained it (no entrance without special permission). Back across the Apennines by day, they were thrilled by the deep ravines, cool pine scents, and an unbelievable variety of hills and mountains. On the Adriatic coast, they had found no freedom from the heat of their three-week circuit, but they reveled in the visits to ancient cities. Traveling is "the pleasure of pleasures to us,"[11] Elizabeth told her sister Henrietta.

❧ ❧ ❧

In the winter of 1848, Elizabeth began sewing little petticoats and other infant garments. Ever since they had discovered the pregnancy in October, Robert had urged her, for the baby's sake, to stop her daily draughts of morphine, and she had cut back valiantly. On March 9, 1849, Robert was able to report to the Barrett sisters, "thro' God's infinite goodness our blessed Ba gave birth to a fine, strong boy at a quarter past two." It had been a difficult twenty-one-hour labor, but she bore up without a cry or a tear. Robert hovered near the whole time, and whenever Dr. Henry Harding allowed him, he held her hand. He was full of praise for her "selfdenial and general rationality" in giving up morphine and her dutifulness in following proper diet over the past several months.[12] As her forty-third birthday approached, Elizabeth had worried whether or not her ravaged body could produce a healthy child. Also she feared some malformation "what with the morphine and a frightful fall which I had in the autumn"[13] when she tumbled over the back of an armchair, landed on her head, and also caused some internal bleeding.

But the baby was an admirable specimen of boychild, who soon had "double chins and rosy cheeks, and a great wide chest—undeniable lungs."[14] Elizabeth gave up nursing right away, "being only too glad that my baby had escaped my evil star up to that moment."[15] A cheery, motherly *balia* (wet nurse) was hired who supplied him with abundant milk. In a characteristically generous gesture, John Kenyon settled £100 on the Brownings as a celebration of the baby's birth. Elizabeth once again felt that he was the man she could look to as a true father.

Elizabeth was surprised at Robert's delight in the child. "He always used to tell me," she confided to Mrs. Jameson, "that he didn't believe he had the least touch in him of the parental instinct." When she suffered from a cold just before the birthing, Robert, in his concern for her well-being, "wished to heaven the living creature would exhale and disappear in some mystical way" without doing her harm.[16] But at the time of birth he wept with joy and proceeded to dote on the new member of the family. The child was baptized Robert Wiedemann Barrett Browning on June 26 at the French Evangelical Lutheran Church in Florence (the final "n" in Wiedemann was later dropped). By this name, Robert wanted to please his mother, whom he felt he had neglected by an absence from home of almost three years.

But such pleasure was not to be. Sarah Anna Wiedemann Browning died a few days later of "an unexpected disease, (ossification of the heart)," as it was called. Robert's letter to New Cross about the birth of his son arrived while she was in a near coma, and the attending physicians would not allow the letter to be read to her. As a means of softening the blow during his present joy, Robert's sister Sarianna had reported Sarah Anna's death only after first sending false messages that she was "unwell" or "was very ill." Finally she revealed to Robert that death had taken his mother.[17]

He was devastated by the news. His grief was intensified by the guilt he felt at having left his ever-indulgent parents and the center of their closely knit family so suddenly to seek his own happiness in marriage. Nor had the family members ever been allowed to meet his bride. The guilt was compounded by the irony that at the fatal moment he was experiencing a special joy in the birth of his child. "I never saw a man so bowed down in an extremity of sorrow—never," Elizabeth wrote to Mary Russell Mitford, remembering perhaps her father's stoic control when he lost his wife at Hope End, years ago. "Robert was too enraptured at my safety & with his little son, .. and the sudden reaction was terrible."[18] "I never saw a *man* so overcome & wrung to the soul," Elizabeth told her sister Arabella "—The bursts of convulsive weeping, the recapitulation of all her goodness & tenderness in words that made the heart ache, & then the recovery of composure with such a ghastly violence, that you wished the agitation back again—these things, I shall not try to describe."[19] All thought of travel to England the following summer was put aside: Robert felt he could not bear the return to New Cross. "He says," Elizabeth reported, "it would break his heart to see his mother's roses over the wall & the place where she used to lay her scissors & gloves." He suffered loss of appetite and loss of sleep and went about with a distracted air.[20]

Deep in his grief and guilt, he had to be pushed into action by Elizabeth to seek out a refuge from the summer heat for his family. They found both La Spezia, by the sea, and Scravezza, in the mountains, too expensive. They visited Lerici and saw the house where Shelley lived at the end of his short life. The seacoast there was too hot, and in addition it brought memories of death by drowning to Elizabeth. But when they passed through Bagni di Lucca, which Robert had formerly despised because of its casino and the idle frivolity of the English expatriates who summered there, they were charmed by the mountain setting and by the quietness—most members of the English colony had fled Italy, fearful of being caught in the developing revolutionary turmoil. They were also reassured because the Ogilvys, a Scottish couple who occupied the apartment above them in the Palazzo Guidi, were planning to spend the summer there. They rented a set of rooms in Bagni Caldi, the topmost village in Bagni di Lucca, where "the springs of hot water gush out of the rock close by us." From their second-floor apartment, they could look across the roof tiles of the highest house in Bagni Caldi to the nearby hills "covered with vines, olives, chestnut and corn" or down onto the rushing river in the valley far below.[21]

But Robert remained burdened by his loss. Every letter from home only deepened his depression. Writing to Sarianna, he confessed, somewhat overdramatically, "I am wholly tired of opening my eyes on the world now." He took long walks in the forest and further up the mountain as a "plain duty in taking exercise and trying to amuse myself and recover my spirits."[22] Elizabeth was inspired to think that she perhaps had the means to pull him out of his dejected mood. Long ago he had mentioned that he deplored the poetic practice of expressing one's deepest feeling in verse, but recently he had offered an opinion approving of poems that sincerely expressed one's feeling of love. Acting on this hint, Elizabeth decided to show him the sonnets she had written before their marriage. "Do you know I once wrote some poems about *you*?"[23] she said diffidently one morning as he stood brooding, gazing out of the window at a mimosa tree, and she pointed to "that book on the little table there if you care to see it."[24] Robert was "much touched & pleased," and thought "highly of the poetry," Elizabeth reported modestly.[25] Indeed, he must have been emotionally overwhelmed by a sonnet sequence that followed their courtship and the blossoming of Elizabeth's love for him. The poems are in the best tradition of the Elizabethan sonnet sequences but less artificial; hers were nineteenth-century lyrics that despite their classical and Christian allusions were grounded in realism. The sonnets are generally regarded as the best poems Elizabeth ever wrote. The discipline of the sonnet form curbed her tendency to continue on too long, and the sequence of the whole group, with their poetic record of a sensibility that was prepared for death but rescued by love, has deeply moved generations of readers.

Robert strongly urged that the sequence of poems not be kept from publication "simply because it glorified an undeserving person" and that the whole group be added to her forthcoming collected edition in 1850. Elizabeth insisted, however, on some sort of "veil" that would disguise their source. Robert "suggested the ambiguous title 'Sonnets *from* the Portuguese,' which seems to mean a translation from the Portuguese, but really referred to the verses of 'Caterina [*sic*] to Camoens,'" the poem that would precede the sonnet sequence. Robert had been "greatly impressed" with that poem before he met Elizabeth, and after he came to know her, he thought that in her precarious health she somewhat resembled Catarina, who died before her lover, Camoens, returned from the war against the Moors in North Africa.[26] "In a loving fancy," Elizabeth remembered, "he had always associated me with Catarina."[27] One more change was necessary to guard their secret: she must omit one sonnet that quoted a line from an early poem, "My future will not copy fair my past." In later editions, after their close friends, such as Forster and Chorley, had seen behind their "veil," the sonnet was restored as number forty-two.[28]

At Bagni di Lucca, Robert's mood lightened. The episode of grief had been a beneficial sobering of his being. It had provided him with a backward look at the cushioned life his parents had created for him, giving him years of private study to prepare himself for the career of a poet, which he had accepted as if it were his due. Then when the presence of Elizabeth Barrett drew him into a new complex of emotions, he had wrapped himself in her life and departed hastily from England without a thought to the deprivation he had caused at New Cross. The shock of his mother's loss gave him a new perspective on his life, prompting him to revaluate his early years and recent actions but at the same time pushing him into a self-indulgent guilt and causing him to neglect his new responsibilities. Elizabeth's revelation of the sonnets brought a change that restored a proper balance to his life. He saw anew that she had abandoned home and family for him, and peculiar and threatening to her existence though her act may have been, her whole world now revolved with his. Everything he had done in creating the new life for both of them seemed right at last, and best of all, the health of his beloved wife had been restored.

"I have been growing stronger & stronger," Elizabeth recorded, "& where it is to stop I cant tell really; I can do as much, or more, now, than at any point of my life since I arrived at woman's estate."[29] Her appetite was better than ever before: she confessed herself to be "carnivorous, herbivorous & voracious altogether."[30] Obviously her delight in motherhood made an enormous difference in her life. It helped that Wiedeman was a merry, sweet-tempered child, with strength and vigor for his age. He was a good traveler, too, able to go on a number of excursions with his parents and the servants. On one particular five-mile journey to an almost inaccessible volcano, Elizabeth, the nurse, and Wilson, holding Wiedeman, all rode donkeys. Robert and the guides rode horseback. "No horse or ass, untrained to the mountains," Elizabeth reported, "could have kept foot a moment where we penetrated." Up precipitous dry streambeds they climbed "with a palm's breadth between you and the headlong ravines." But the mountain scenery was "sublime," with rushing streams "tearing the ground to pieces under your feet."[31] They had a picnic on a grassy spot high on a shepherd's clearing. They continued to enjoy various jaunts like this until early October, when they returned to Florence.

෯ ෯ ෯

As the Brownings followed the routines of their life, new agitation for the unification of Italy had been spreading all over the peninsula but most rapidly in the north. The previous year, King Charles Albert of Sardinia (his territory included Savoy and Piedmont) took the lead in trying to drive the Austrians out of Italy. He had granted a constitution to his people that established a parliamentary democracy similar to that in England. There were uprisings against Austrian domination in Milan, Parma, Modena, and Venice, and Charles Albert, moving under a tricolor banner of red, white, and green that symbolized a united Italy, was prepared to assist the struggling people of Lombardy and Venice. But other regional and city groups were reluctant to serve under him, and the reorganized Austrians defeated him in July 1848 at the Battle of Custoza. In the south, the hated Austrian puppet ruler, Ferdinand II of the Kingdom of the Two Sicilies, put down popular stirrings, and in Rome, Pope Pius IX, now uneasy over the revolutionary movements, began to retreat from his liberal policies. When a popular insurrection erupted in Rome in September 1848, the pope fled the city, and the Romans formed a Constituent Assembly in which Giuseppe Mazzini was the principal director of policy. The flamboyant patriot Giuseppe Garibaldi and five hundred of his red-shirted volunteers then arrived in Rome to help defend the city against any encroachment by the Austrians.

In Tuscany, when Grand Duke Leopold II granted a constitution, the people were overjoyed, but since they had no traditions of democratic government, their legislative attempts at political reform were attended by factional conflicts and regional concerns. When the legislative chambers of the Tuscan government supported the unification of Italy and voted to send representatives to the Constituent Assembly in Rome in January 1849, the grand duke, in fear and protest, left Florence for Siena and later joined the pope in exile. In his absence, the Tuscan legislators established a provisional republic. Again the Florentines celebrated amid huzzahs, military music, and muskets fired in the air. They planted a liberty tree in the Piazza Pitti near the Palazzo Guidi, where the Brownings, three days after the birth of Wiedeman, watched the populace dance around it. But in March 1849, there was a breakdown of order following the defeat of Italian troops by the Austrians at the battle of Novara. Soldiers from Leghorn roamed into Florence, looted the shops, and commandeered food and drink in the cafés. The Florentines fought back, and, for the first time, Florentine residents were in danger. One day, in the midst of the conflict, Robert had difficulty finding a bridge to get home safely. Dr. Harding jumped into a stable just before four skirmishers fell dead against its door. Following these disorders, the Florentine Municipal Council withdrew from the Tuscan governmental structure, established its own provisional government, and invited Grand Duke Leopold to return to power. The liberty tree was torn out as the people danced and sang the praises of the grand duke. Robert and Elizabeth were disgusted by the fickleness of the local citizenry: "O heavens! how ignoble it all has been and is! A revolution made by boys and *vivas*, and unmade by boys and *vivas*!" Elizabeth wrote scornfully. "The counter-revolution was strictly *counter*, observe. I mean, that if the Leghornese troops here had paid their debts at the Florentine coffee houses, the Florentines would have let their beloved Grand Duke stay on at Gaeta [where the Pope was in exile] to the end of the world."[32]

The treacherous grand duke immediately resumed his Austrian titles and ordered the return of the Austrian army. A hush fell over Florence on May 3, 1849, as the Austrians, the hated "Tedeschi," as the Italians called them, entered the city. Robert and Elizabeth watched from their little terrace as the troops, artillery, and baggage wagons marched near the Palazzo Guidi headed for their garrison. Elizabeth's throat swelled "with grief and indignation."[33] The Florentines watched from behind closed doors and curtained windows. The Brownings were especially outraged at the ordinance issued in June: "All dogs found in the street to be killed straightway, lest they shd. interfere with the movements of the Austrian horse!"[34] Flush was in danger now.

In Rome, the bright hopes of the springtime had soon dimmed when a new enemy appeared to strike against Italian unity. Louis Napoleon, the recently elected president of the new republic of France, sent troops to overcome the now flourishing Roman republic. Although Garibaldi was able to beat back the first French attacks, a second French army of thirty thousand men arrived with siege artillery to overwhelm the defenders. By June 1849, the French had taken control of the city, and they then restored the pope to power. Only Venice now remained in revolutionary isolation against the forces of oppression, but an Austrian siege and bombardment brought about a Venetian surrender at the end of August. Thus the first phase of the Risorgimento ended in total defeat for the Italians in north, south, and central Italy.[35]

Robert and Elizabeth did not always see eye to eye in their judgment of the political affairs of France and Italy in 1848–1849. They were in agreement on most points, but, as Elizabeth expressed it, "here and there we have plenty of room for battles."[36] Robert was an ordinary unsophisticated liberal, a supporter of Whig reform in England and of lurches toward republican rule in France. As such poems as "The Italian in England" and *Pippa Passes* make clear, he sided with Mazzini and the early sporadic opposition to Austrian rule in Italy. Elizabeth was more volatile in her political allegiances. Although she was a Francophile by inclination and had called herself a radical when she and Mary Russell Mitford corresponded in the early 1840s, Elizabeth was, nevertheless, basically conservative in her criticism of the Second French Republic in 1848, disapproving of universal suffrage and of the abolition of aristocratic titles. Upset by extreme republican measures, she favored a "return to the Kingship."[37] Her life in the Barrett household seems to have accustomed her to the admiration of strong men. She was also disappointed by the shifts of power and allegiance among the Italians. She yearned for leaders and heroes: "We want not only a *man*, but men," she cried in a letter to Mrs. Jameson.[38]

She and Robert especially disagreed about Louis Napoleon, whom she defended even after the French action against Rome, which she understood as a move to preempt an Austrian invasion of the city. "It seems to me that he has given proof, as far as the evidence goes, of prudence, integrity, & conscientious patriotism." She admitted that the attack on Rome seemed dishonorable, but she rationalized it: "The French motive has been good, the intention pure,— the occupation of Rome by the Austrians being imminent."[39]

All during the months of revolutionary rumbling, which she followed with intense interest, Elizabeth had an unreliable source of information. Robert could take his daily walk to Vieusseux's and read the Italian and foreign newspapers, but since women were not allowed in the reading room, she was dependent on his bringing home the gist of his reading. Yet Robert was temperamentally unsuited for this task. Whenever he disapproved of a particular political regime, he simply refused to read anything more of its doings. This was especially frustrating for Elizabeth in her thirst for news about France when her questions were met by stubborn dismissal. "M. Thiers' speech— 'Thiers is a rascal; I make a point of not reading one word said by M. Thiers.' M. Prudhon—'Prudhon is a madman; who cares for Prudhon?' The President [Louis Napoleon]—'The President's an ass; *he* is not worth thinking of.' And so we treat of politics," she complained to Mrs. Jameson.[40]

Even so, Elizabeth was alert to all that was going on in the struggles of the Italian states for political freedom, and her intensity of feeling was channeled into a long political poem, *Casa Guidi Windows*, the first part of which she finished in 1848. It begins with a glimpse of a child, a symbol of Italy, who is singing "O bella libertà, O bella!" which inspires the poet to celebrate the legacy of Italy to the world in literature, thought, and art, and to recount the Florentine response in cheers and processions when the grand duke established the Tuscan Civic Guard, "the first torch of freedom lit." The poem continues in a meditation on the need for a teacher and a leader to achieve the union of the Italian states. Would it be Pope Pius IX? Part 1 ends with a call for other nations to come to the aid of Italy in throwing off the Austrian yoke.

Part 2, written two years later, inevitably treats of the deep disillusionment with the duke, the pope, and even with the Florentine people themselves for their failure to fulfill their political destiny. It mourns the heavy peace that followed the widespread failure of the revolutionary movements throughout Italy, and it honors Charles Albert and the dead patriots for their nobility in defeat. The poem ends with a return to the symbol of the child singing of liberty, as the poet then perceives her own child, "my blue-eyed prophet," as an omen: "creatures young / And tender, mighty meanings may unfold" and be God's witness "that the elemental / New springs of life are gushing everywhere." God can be trusted to build on the ruins of defeat that lie all around. The poem was published in 1851.

Among the chance callers at Casa Guidi in late 1849 and the spring of 1850 was Margaret Fuller, who had written perceptive reviews of the poetry of both Robert and Elizabeth for the *New York Tribune*. She had been a fellow member with Hawthorne at the Brook Farm commune and had worked with Emerson as editor of the Transcendentalist magazine, the *Dial*. But she was best known for her pioneering feminist study, *Woman in the Nineteenth*

Century (1845). She had recently married the Marquis Giovanni Ossoli and borne a child, who was about the same age as Wiedeman. She and her husband were in Rome at the time of the siege, he a soldier with Garibaldi's defenders and she a nurse for the wounded. Elizabeth rejoiced in their adventurous marriage as "a romantic proceeding." During several teatime visits with the Brownings, Margaret and Elizabeth were drawn to each other in sympathy for the Italian cause, although Elizabeth did not care for Margaret's socialistic views. Elizabeth described her as "one of the very plainest women I ever saw in my life, & talking fluent Italian with a pure Boston accent. Still she is a woman of undeniable talent & eloquence, with a great deal of generous & womanly goodness in her." What struck Robert was her feminist dominance in the marriage; he observed to Elizabeth that "it was a clear case of 'we keeps a husband,'"—the noble Roman sitting by in meek silence, while she discoursed."[41] The Ossolis called to say good-bye the night before they left Italy to sail to the United States and presented Wiedeman with a Bible as a gift from their own child. But the Ossoli family met with a tragic end when, in May 1850, their ship was wrecked on a sandbar off Fire Island, New York. Elizabeth was devastated by the news, which inevitably brought back memories of her loss of Bro: "I loved her, and the circumstances of her death shook me to the very roots of my heart."[42] Both Brownings contributed a memoir to the two-volume *Memoirs of Margaret Fuller Ossoli* edited by Emerson and others in 1852.

⚛ ⚛ ⚛

News from Wimpole Street in London brought both happiness and remembrances of past anguish. Like some long-suffering Jacob, Capt. Surtees Cook had loyally waited for five years to marry Henrietta Barrett. Elizabeth thought him lacking in resolve and manliness for not taking action the way Robert had, for Cook was a respected cousin of the Barrett family and had a modest income. But Cook suddenly surprised Elizabeth. At the end of April 1850, he formally asked Edward Barrett for Henrietta's hand in marriage, an application that was refused—on the supposed grounds of his High Church leanings and an insufficient income. Further, Cook was warned, "If Henrietta marries you, she turns her back on this house forever." Later that day, Mr. Barrett did not mention this exchange to anyone in the family and displayed "*very good* spirits" in the evening. But Henrietta kept to her room and did not come down to dinner. She was writing him a letter "imploring him not to exact it of her to break [the engagement] off, for she *could* not do it." Mr. Barrett ignored the letter.[43]

Two days passed. Then Arabella was asked to tell those brothers who were at home about Surtees' application, Henrietta's request, and "of their determination to marry." The Barrett brothers, who had always been friendly with Cook, looked kindly on the young couple and regarded their plans as justified. When George arrived home from the court circuit, however, Arabella was summoned by Mr. Barrett to deliver a letter to Henrietta. In the "very harsh letter," he rebuked Henrietta for "the '*insult*' she had offered him in asking his consent when she had evidently made up her mind to the conclusion." He objected to Captain Cook because of "his *tractarian principles* and the want of money." He declared that "if she married, her name should never again be mentioned in his presence."[44]

Rebuffed and hurt, Henrietta and Surtees, nevertheless, acted with dispatch. They were married at 8:30 the following morning. Surtees' brother conducted the marriage ceremony; his sister was a bridesmaid. Bonser, a servant girl sent by Arabella, was the only representative of the Barrett family at the wedding. Arabella was too terrified to attend; the brothers thought the haste "imprudent." The newlyweds planned to live at Taunton in Somersetshire, where Captain Cook had recently secured a military appointment. At breakfast, letters from Henrietta and Surtees were placed on Mr. Barrett's plate, but he paid no attention to them and went cheerfully off to his day in the city.

Elizabeth was swept into a whirl of emotions. The events ripped open old wounds for her; they brought her joy that Henrietta and Surtees were at last joined together; they plunged her into gloom that Arabella was now left alone as the only daughter subject to Mr. Barrett's tyranny. But the emotional bondage that Elizabeth could not escape was still powerful. "I am more anxious now about poor Papa himself," she wrote to her old confidante, Mrs. Martin; "—he will miss Henrietta as it was impossible for him to miss me— and the feeling which he is resolute not to show must cut the deeper—must. Oh, if he were all metal, all rock, I should not love him, Mrs. Martin, though he is my father, nor suffer pain through his refusal to forgive and receive me. The mere flesh and blood tie is not so much—but love is much—and I love him and cling to him in my thoughts—yearn to him forever."[45]

No, not metal, or rock. It took twisted human nature to produce a family tyrant so ego-bound and heartless.

While Elizabeth rejoiced with Henrietta in her marriage, she also charged her to remember "that Arabel belongs to me if any cause should dislodge her from her present home without providing her with another of her own choice—that is a fixed thing."[46]

Chapter 18

Christmas-Eve and Easter-Day

Since Robert Browning had published all his finished plays and poems before his sudden departure from England, he did not bring his portfolio with him to Italy. Any notes, fragments, or undeveloped ideas for further poems, he left behind with the portfolio itself. He was determined to take a new direction in his career, to give voice to his own personality in a work, perhaps "R. B. a poem," as Elizabeth had urged him to do. But content in his new life, settling into new routines and surroundings, he postponed this project and instead thought vaguely for a while of a joint publication with Elizabeth in a book of poems about Italy. When this new plan evaporated, he set about revising his published work for a hardcover edition, convinced that the *Bells and Pomegranates* pamphlets with their double columns of small print were detrimental to his standing as a poet whom the public should take seriously. He seemed reluctant to turn in the new direction that Elizabeth had encouraged him to go.

"I should not altogether wonder if I do something notable one of these days," he wrote with a lackadaisical air to Fanny Haworth. He even had trouble expressing his inner conflict clearly, for he continued his assertion about doing something with the confusing words "all through a desperate virtue which determines out of gratitude—(not to man and the reading public, by any means)—to do what I *do not* please." Something was interfering with his creative will.[1] He went on to say, "I could, with an unutterably easy heart, never write another line while I have my being"—he paused—"which would surely be very wrong considering how the lines fall to poets in the places of this world generally. So I mean to do my best whatever comes of it."[2]

Underlying his joys and sorrows and slackenings of creative purpose between 1845 and 1855 was a reexamination of his faith. His courtship of and marriage to Elizabeth, the birth of his son, and the death of his mother, had made questions about his beliefs both pressing and immediate. He had thought deeply about such questions, but now the answers to them had more than a merely intellectual bearing on his life. He worked through some of these issues in *Christmas-Eve and Easter-Day*, published in 1850, and the extent to which he found answers can be judged by his finishing "Saul," which he had published as a fragment in 1845 and which he completed for the 1855 *Men and Women*. The topics with which he struggled are central Christian beliefs—the Incarnation and the Atonement—but his focus was on the human responses to those doctrines: the acts of loving and choosing.

"Saul" might be considered a dramatic monologue, since David is the speaker of the poem, but Browning uses as his title the name of the listener rather than the speaker, and when Edmund Gosse asked him to pick "'Four poems, of moderate length, which represent their writer fairly,'" Browning chose "Saul" as representative of the "lyrical."[3] By that adjective Browning is perhaps indicating that the poem is not the exploration of the psychology of an individual character but rather the expression of universals in human nature, of (what he calls in the essay on Shelley) "the primal elements of humanity." Hence he replaced the "evil spirit" from which the biblical account says Saul is suffering (in 1 Sam. 14) with a common affliction: a sense of failure, a loss of purpose, and a loss of faith, all of which result in the torpor sometimes labeled *accidie*. The "primal element" in David is love, and this "lyrical" monologue presents the struggle of love with accidie. In the first nine sections of the poem as published in 1845, David attempts to restore Saul by expressing "How good is man's life, the mere living!" (78) and by reminding him that a king is in a privileged position for "High ambition and deeds which surpass it, fame crowning them" (95): "all gifts, which the world offers singly, on one head combine!" (92)—"the head of one creature—King Saul!" (96). At that point Browning broke off the poem. Readers and critics have sometimes suggested that he did so because he didn't know how to end it, but in fact the ending is implicit in section 4: it is to be a vision of Christ. Saul's posture in section 4 is the key. When David enters the king's tent, going from bright sunlight into darkness, a sunbeam bursts through the roof and illuminates the king, who is fixed in the posture of the Crucifixion—the posture, but without the meaning, which is closed to David but not to Browning's readers. For Browning expects his nineteenth-century readers to use their knowledge of typology, a method of biblical interpretation in which one reads the images, events, and figures of the Old Testament as anticipating the life of Christ. Typology, as George Landow has pointed out, is a system of progressive revelation in which a second event or figure fulfils the promise of a first,[4] and here the crucified Christ will complete the action—the Atonement—prefigured in Saul's posture. Moreover, in the king-serpent simile Browning alludes to a particular typological pattern sanctioned by Christ himself, who drew a parallel between his coming death and the serpent of brass set up on a pole by Moses to deliver the children of Israel from a plague of serpents (Num. 21:4–9):"And as Moses lifted up the serpent in the wilderness, even so must the Son of man be lifted up" (John 3:14). Browning, then, did know how to end the poem, but he seems to have been unable to commit himself to that ending and to the faith it would imply. The "primal element" which makes possible a typological reading is, in Browning's view, love, which he understands as the agent of revelation and the evidence of God within the self. But Browning was not yet ready to make such affirmations.

Christmas-Eve is a dramatic narrative, the story of a dream vision which is a journey of the soul but, like medieval dream visions, firmly grounded in the actual and the here and now. The actual is the Independent chapel in which the narrator takes shelter from the rain on Christmas Eve and which he describes with the eye of a satirist who is a virtuoso in rhyme and its effects.[5] Then, in a dream, he visits the Christmas Eve service at St. Peter's in Rome and the lecture of a higher critic in Germany. His guide is Christ himself, who is fulfilling his promise that, when two or more are gathered together in his name, he will be present—not just in spirit but in the flesh: he is here the incarnate Christ, "He himself with his human air" (432). The speaker is not merely an observer: at every stage in the journey he responds to and interprets what he sees (like Bunyan's Christian in the House of the Interpreter). And although he is himself responsible for his views and is working out his own salvation, he is not entirely on his own. The attitudes of his guide are crucial: when the narrator is in error, he sees only the back of Christ or holds only the hem of his garment; when he is moving toward truth, he sees Christ's face. His most dangerous moment comes when he reaches a stage of genial tolerance and "mild indifferentism" (1148), which is in fact the avoidance of a choice. Then he experiences again "the horrible storm" (1158) and the receding vesture—at which point he awakes in the Independent chapel, comes to the full realization of the need to commit himself, and says, "I choose here!" (1341).

That choice has provoked much debate among Browning's readers, who want to identify the narrator with Browning himself and so wonder why the poet would choose a congregation so unlike the one in which he grew up.

But Browning is making a point about a "primal element" in human nature, the growth of the soul: such growth depends upon choice, and though the choice may be the wrong one, not choosing at all is even worse. Moreover, Browning is making a point parallel to that learned by Carlyle's protagonist in *Sartor Resartus*, that the whole world and indefinite time are not at one's disposal, and that one's duty lies in one's immediate surroundings, however inadequate; in the here and now, however repellant. In the Incarnation, Christ took on all the limitations and inadequacies of human existence; in the imitation of that being made flesh, men and women choose to act in a limited and inadequate present—and so the narrator of *Christmas-Eve* rightly chooses "here," an adverb which means "in this place," "at this time," and in this particular set of circumstances. Life, Browning will ultimately affirm, is choosing, and when the choice is between good and evil, it is (as the pope in *The Ring and the Book* will affirm) a "terrible choice" which is nonetheless "Life's business" (10. 1237).

While *Christmas-Eve* focuses on the need to make a choice and relates that necessity to the Incarnation, *Easter-Day* focuses on the consequences of a wrong choice and relates that error, appropriately, to the Atonement. Browning treats the Atonement much less frequently than he does the Incarnation (the latter is central to his thinking), but the two are bound up together, as the subtitle of this volume indicates: *Christmas-Eve* and *Easter-Day* are not two narratives but rather *"A Poem."* Still, they differ in dramatic form. *Christmas-Eve* has a single speaker, though one senses a dialogue going on between the speaker and his silent guide; *Easter-Day* also has a single speaker, but he presents a spoken dialogue—he calls it a "parley" (229)— between himself and an unnamed "you" who is "a live actual listener" (355). Their positions blur, however, so that one has a sense that the poem is (to use Matthew Arnold's words) "the dialogue of the mind with itself." The issue debated is the import of the Atonement: if the world gains "at that day's price" (253), should we not conclude that the world is to be rejected? What good is this life, if it must be atoned for? What is its purpose?

The dream vision in *Easter-Day* is of the Last Judgment, when the narrator is suddenly caught in his current situation and with his current choice: "There, stood I, found and fixed, I knew, / Choosing the world" (553), because it was "so near" (566) and because he found it too hard "to renounce it utterly" (574). His judge is Christ, now a dreadful and massive figure, who shuts him out of heaven and gives him as his reward the earth and all its shows. The unspoken dialogue with Christ in *Christmas-Eve* is very much a spoken dialogue in *Easter-Day*, and it too moves toward a choice, when the speaker finally says, "I let the world go, and take love!" (934), and pleads to be allowed to "go on, / Still hoping ever and anon / To reach one eve the Better Land!" (1001–3). His wish is apparently granted, but whether as the punishment he fears or the hope he nurtures he cannot tell. At the end, dawn breaks on Easter Day and the speaker thinks of the Resurrection in relation to his own situation, one of unknowing mixed with hope: "and who can say?" (1040).

Running through both narratives are references to God's love, which both the Incarnation and the Atonement reveal. Such divine love has its counterpart in human love, which Browning came increasingly to understand not just as a powerful emotion but as a faculty which intuits and reveals the love of God, and which is, moreover, God working within each one of us. Hence when Browning returned to "Saul," he made David's love for Saul the agent of the vision of Christ with which the poem ends. In section 10, David realizes he has been offering Saul only "the wine of this life" (130) when he ought to be offering "soul-wine" (175), which is life after death. At first David can sing only of earthly memorials, of Saul's tomb with the king's story fixed in tablets on it, but when Saul looks intently into David's face, David's response is crucial: "And oh, all my heart how it loved him!" (232). That sudden outpouring of love turns David from singer to prophet, as the one-line section 16 indicates. He foretells for Saul a "new life altogether" (235), affirms that the source of that idea is God himself, and confirms its truth through the Incarnation:

> O Saul, it shall be
> A Face like my face that receives thee; a Man like to me,
> Thou shalt love and be loved by, for ever: a Hand like this hand
> Shall throw open the gates of new life to thee! See the Christ
>   stand! (309–12)

The crucified Christ, prefigured in Saul's posture, is completed by the standing Christ, whose erect stance suggests the power, steadfastness, and security of his love.

Such love was no abstraction for Browning. He felt it in the love between himself and Elizabeth, and both of them were conscious of parallels between the effect of the singer-poet in Robert's poem and the intertwining of love and art in their own lives. That complex interchange took a practical form in the influence Robert and Elizabeth had on each other's work. As Mary Rose Sullivan has shown, Elizabeth dwelt on the first (1845) part of "Saul" as she wrote *Sonnets from the Portuguese*; and Robert dwelt on the *Sonnets* as he wrote the last sections of "Saul." They exchanged images and diction, energies and ideas, especially the notion that "human love leads ineluctably to divine love."[6] Of *Christmas-Eve and Easter-Day*, Elizabeth said it had "originality and power"[7]—the manuscript, now in the Victoria and

Albert Museum, is written partly in her hand—but she criticized *Easter-Day* for its "asceticism," as if her husband had "taken to the cilix [hairshirt]." Robert replied that it was only "one side of the question."[8]

Chapman and Hall brought out *Christmas-Eve and Easter-Day* in April 1850, in time for sale during the Easter season. Two hundred copies sold briskly, but by June this early success was checked by the publication of Tennyson's *In Memoriam*, the most widely read religious poem of the century. Thereafter, Browning's book moved sluggishly; Chapman and Hall still had copies in stock as late as 1864. The extent of review notices was likewise limited. Ignored once again by the big quarterlies and many of the influential reviewing organs, Browning nevertheless received notice from several important critical journals, many of which gave lengthy summaries illustrated by excerpts from the poem.

Among the dozen reviewers, two divergent attitudes emerged. The first was that Browning's irregular and grotesque treatment (three reviewers specifically mentioned the manner of Samuel Butler's *Hudibras*) was entirely unsuitable for a serious religious subject. J. Westland Marston was forthright: "The form of doggrel—carried to excess by strange and offensive oddities of versification—is not that in which the mysteries of faith, doubt, and eternity can be consistently treated."[9] The other attitude, found in the majority of the reviewers, expressed surprise that Browning's stylistic idiosyncrasies and realistic approach to his subject provided a successful means for carrying the religious thought in the poem. George Henry Lewes read *Christmas-Eve* three times and "with increasing admiration." He much regretted that Browning was not a "Singer," but he had high praise for the poem. "It is a great theme, powerfully conceived, picturesquely, sometimes grotesquely handled. In distinctness of purpose, pregnancy of meaning, and power of illustration, it shows the masterhand."[10] Lewes and R. H. Hutton[11] were two prominent Victorian intellectuals who joined Forster in defending Browning's metrical ruggedness and commonplace diction. Forster even compared Browning's realism to that of Crabbe and Wordsworth.[12] Browning's work also had two new champions from the Pre-Raphaelite Brotherhood. In a pair of articles, William Rossetti and Frederic Stephens offered unstinting praise for Browning's poems, although their journal, the *Germ*, was discontinued before part 2 of Rossetti's discussion of *Christmas-Eve and Easter-Day* could appear.[13]

Reviewers in two religious periodicals, the *Christian Remembrancer*[14] and the *Monthly Christian Spectator*[15], took a generally favorable view of the poems (after some misgivings about the style) because of their sincere handling of doubts and dilemmas. The anonymous critic in the *English Review*, a High

Church periodical, saw *Christmas-Eve and Easter-Day* as "a wildly fantastic composition, powerful, earnest, in part devotional, yet audacious, and Hudibrastically satirical," and declared it "a great work." Although it was different in essential ways from Tennyson's *In Memoriam*, the critic linked the two works and judged them both to be "destined to an earthly immortality."[16] With the publication of *Christmas-Eve and Easter-Day*, and especially after the critical opinion of the religious journals approved of his work, Browning was placed alongside Tennyson and thereafter regarded by a large segment of the Victorian reading public as a serious religious poet.

Browning's two-volume collected edition of 1849 received even fewer reviews. It contained *Paracelsus* and the contents of all eight issues of *Bells and Pomegranates*, except for three short poems. Since the bulk of the space in the new edition was devoted to the seven plays, this predominance caused some of the critics to see the shorter poems from a new perspective and to comment on their dramatic quality and features. For example, the critic in the *English Review* recognized that Browning's "lyrics were almost all monodramas" and thought them "unlike any thing else we are acquainted with," "by no means easy to understand."[17] Forster, reviewing in the *Examiner*, was perceptive about the compactness and suggestiveness of the dramatic pieces: "Whether he gives vent to the musings of a solitary mind or to reflections struck out by the collisions of assembled minds, he expresses them in address or soliloquy. . . . But with a felicitous and delicate instinct, he gives just so much as his persons would really say; conscious and confident that the words will suggest accompanying actions, the relative positions of the speakers, and the surrounding scenery."[18] The critic for the *Eclectic Review* deplored the present state of the drama in England but looked to the kind of poetry that Browning was writing as a new means of dramatic expression:

> Let our drama, then, develop itself in other, fresh, and genuine forms; as realized by a Chaucer in the fourteenth century, by a Tennyson—by the author of "St. Simeon Stylites," "Ulysses," "Oenone"—in the nineteenth; and by Mr. Browning himself, in so large a proportion of his creative working. . . . In Browning's *un*formal drama, we find the highest success and creative power achieved; in nearly all of his lyrics, so living and deeply suggestive; and in *Pippa Passes.*[19]

One must regret that so few contemporary critics could recognize the change that was taking place or that Browning was the leading exponent of this merging of dramatic objectivity with lyric and narrative poetry.

Chapter 19

London and Paris

In four years of marriage, Robert Browning had never left Elizabeth's side for more than the hour or two he took for his morning walk or his visit to Vieusseux's to read the French and English newspapers. But one day in July 1850 he traveled to Siena by railroad to scout out a summer retreat from the oppressive Florentine heat. It chanced that it was the day of the Palio, the annual horse race around the central piazza in Siena, and there were no return trains to Florence that evening. Distressed at the prospect of being away from his wife's side overnight, he managed to get a ride with two priests in a "halting crazy vehicle" that carried him to Casa Guidi by 3 A.M. At this late hour, Robert was unable to rouse the porter to let him in the entrance gates of the palazzo. Still wakeful and worried, Elizabeth heard his voice under her window calling "Ba!" Elizabeth awakened the servants, who stirred up the porter, and husband and wife were reunited after their unaccustomed separation.[1]

Well might Robert have been concerned to be away overnight, for on July 28 Elizabeth suffered her fourth and most dangerous miscarriage.[2] The doctor told Robert that she lost over one hundred ounces of blood during the first twenty-four hours. She was packed with ice for three days before the bleeding could be stopped completely. So severe was her case that Dr. Harding feared that she would not survive. Not one in five thousand women, he told Robert, could have endured such an ordeal.[3] By mid-August she was somewhat recovered but still could not stand by herself.

When Dr. Harding recommended that Victorian remedy, "a change of air," the Browning family headed for Siena, Robert carrying Ba to the railroad carriage. He rented "Poggio dei venti," a small villa on a hill outside the city, with a *specola* on top that gave magnificent views—in one direction, the russet roofs of all Siena, plus the city's glittering duomo and campanile; in other directions, mountains, vineyards, olive groves. Over the weeks, Elizabeth gathered strength with the help of fresh milk, country bread and eggs, and invigorating hilltop air. She soon could walk "without reeling much."[4] Wiedeman cheered her days. He sang and danced, hopped and jumped, gave incessant hugs and kisses both to Elizabeth and a tolerant Flush. He treated Flush like a sibling; when Flush was scolded, he cried. He crawled on the floor and scratched at the door like Flush. When a saucer of milk was placed on the floor, he got close to it, put his face down, and tried to lap it up.

By September, when Elizabeth could walk a mile or two without fatigue, Robert arranged for a move into Siena for a week so that she could see its rich array of paintings by Pinturicchio, the Lorenzetti brothers, Simone Martini, and especially the *Maestà* by Duccio and the frescoes of St. Catherine by Sodoma. When they at last returned to Florence, her health was so fully restored that she was able to walk all the way up to San Miniato overlooking the city, a daunting climb.

For years now the Brownings had postponed their return visit to England because of straitened finances, for as time passed, Elizabeth's annual income had shrunk to £257, largely because the value of her share in the profits of the *David Lyon* had fallen. Moreover, with the birth of Wiedeman, the Browning household had grown beyond parents, Wilson, baby, and Flush to include Annunciata, the nurse, and Alessandro, a man-servant who did the family cooking. The generous settlement of an additional £100 a year by Mr. Kenyon had not been enough to offset the combined losses and new expenses.

In recent months, the Brownings had seriously discussed a new idea of Elizabeth's, to move their residence to Paris. Paris would then be, for them, a mere two-day journey to London, and she would be able to visit her sisters every summer and perhaps even persuade them to come to her in Paris. In addition, she argued, "Paris is delightful—and one lives in the midst of a brilliant civilization."[5] The cost of living in France would not be much more than what they paid in Florence. The only question to ponder was whether or not Elizabeth could bear a Parisian winter, which, though not as mild as Italy's, was said to be a moderate, temperate season. In the spring of 1851, Robert and Elizabeth decided to give it a try, subletting Casa Guidi for a small profit while they were testing the Parisian weather. When they informed Kenyon of their decision, he offered them £50 to help with the expenses of the move and a further £100 so that Elizabeth could see Rome and Naples before leaving Italy.

After laying out elaborate plans for a leisurely journey through Italy, Switzerland, and France as they approached England, Robert realized that they could not devote two months to Rome and Naples, but he was determined that Elizabeth must see Venice before they crossed the mountains going north. On May 3, 1851, they set out by vettura (a four-wheeled carriage) with Wilson and Wiedeman, leaving Annunciata and the man-servant behind. Traveling with them were their friendly Scottish neighbors, the Ogilvys. They stopped in Bologna to see the paintings of Guercino, Reni, and Pontormo and especially Raphael's *St. Cecilia*. They stayed over a day in Modena and then went on to Parma, where they marveled over the Correggios, particularly the breathtaking *Assumption* swirling up inside the dome of the cathedral. From Parma the party was able to travel across the peninsula by railroad to Venice, where the Brownings took an apartment overlooking the Grand Canal for a month.

Elizabeth was in ecstasies. "Venice has exceeded to me all expectation & all dreams," she wrote to Arabella. "The fantastic beauty of the buildings, the mysterious silence of the waters, St. Mark's piazza by gaslight . . . the moon on the lagunes, & the gondola's passing in & out of the shadows, with their little twinkling lamps."[6] Wiedeman shouted for joy on the first morning he entered the Piazza San Marco, with its flocks of pigeons and brilliant mosaics on the exterior of the basilica.

Robert was pleased to be able to take Elizabeth to the Teatro La Fenice for her first experience of opera. He engaged a box for two nights to see Verdi's *Attila* and *Ernani*. Other nights he took her to the theater, and on two occasions to a matinee. Because of Mr. Barrett's restrictions, she had never seen a play staged before.

The Ogilvys were intelligent, good-humored traveling companions, but Robert and Elizabeth were relieved to have them travel on elsewhere. They agreed that they preferred being alone together in the enjoyment of their travel experiences. By day they glided around in gondolas viewing the palaces and visiting the outlying islands. In the evenings, with Wiedeman safely under Wilson's care in their apartment, they sat quietly in the Piazza San Marco, drinking coffee and reading French newspapers, struck by the fact that they heard no carriage wheels or horses' hooves—only the soothing notes of the musicians in the piazza.

For Elizabeth, Venice was complete enchantment: "For the sake of it, I would give up Florence, & twenty Parises besides."[7] But Robert and Wilson concluded otherwise. Wilson had been frequently unwell with headache and upset digestion, and she dosed herself with castor oil. The usually bouncing Robert had begun to be troubled by "nervous irritability" and occasionally felt "bilious."[8] A future change of residence to Venice was out of the question.

Headed back westward, the little travel group stopped in Padua, Vicenza, and Verona, "lingering in each," and then braved a sixteen-hour, all-night ride by diligence to Milan for a stay of three days. Elizabeth had always claimed that traveling was good for her health, and Robert was happy to see that this summer jaunt seemed to be proving it. She was able to climb 350 steps up to the highest peak of Milan Cathedral. The trip over the Alps was further proof. After luxuriating in the beauty of the Italian lakes, Como, Lugano, and Maggiore, the party traveled to Switzerland by the St. Gotthard Pass. At the height of the mountain passage, above the tree line, with walls of snow on each side of the coach, the former invalid, swaddled in two shawls, felt nothing but exhilaration at the sublimity of the scene: "it was like standing in the presence of God when He is terrible. The tears overflowed my eyes."9 Down, down went the travelers, until they were dropped at Fluellen in Switzerland and taken by steamer across the lake to Lucerne.

Perhaps the reason for Robert's "nervous irritability" in Venice was his concern about the mounting expenses of the trip. Kenyon had neglected to send them their quarterly income payment, nor had it turned up at any of the postal stopovers since they left Florence. The travelers arrived in Lucerne with only ten francs left. But when letters with the long-awaited money met them in Lucerne, Robert's relief allowed him to reflect that the journey was not as expensive as he feared—with income from the tenants in Casa Guidi providing just a little less than the cost of staying in Florence. Even so, worrisome Robert remembered that Kenyon had warned him that the dividends from Elizabeth's "ship money," already declining, would continue to be much reduced in the future because of the fall in shipping rates. He decided they should hold down expenses for the remainder of the journey.

The Browning group made their way by rail to Basle, then to Strasbourg, and finally, in order to save money, they elected to travel twenty-four hours by diligence straight through to Paris, rather than by water and rail on a roundabout route. Robert paid for the whole of the coupé so that Elizabeth could lie down on the floor, a wise decision since the coachman drove his horses six-in-hand, three abreast, at full gallop through the countryside. Everyone endured the long arduous journey well, even Wiedeman, who exclaimed with pleasure when they arrived in Paris on June 30 and passed by the crowded shops of the Parisian scene, while their fiacre took them to the Hôtel aux Armes de la Ville de Paris.

❧ ❧ ❧

During their three-week stay in Paris, Tennyson, who was on his way to Florence, called on the Brownings at their hotel and offered them his house and servants at Twickenham during their stay in England. It was a gracious welcome to Robert, who had not known Tennyson as a friend but had only met him years before at dinner parties. Although he was not able to accept Tennyson's generosity, he became aware that his reputation as an English poet had risen since the publication of his *Collected Poems* and *Christmas-Eve and Easter-Day*, despite his four-year absence in Italy. He became more eager to see his old friends in the literary world, as well as to spend time with Sarianna and his father.

But matters were different for Elizabeth. The closer she traveled toward her old home, the more apprehensive she grew. She had written to her father, telling him her plans to return to London, but had been met with the usual silence. "Ah, if you knew how abhorrent the thought of England is to *me!*" she wrote to Mary Russell Mitford from Venice; "My eyes shut suddenly when my thoughts go that way."[10] She asked Arabella if she could come to meet her on the south coast of England, or better yet, in Dieppe or Calais, traveling with brother Henry, who had promised to renew the family connection. But Arabella could go nowhere without her father's permission.

The momentum of well-laid plans carried them on despite Elizabeth's hesitation. On July 23, the Brownings arrived at Newhaven: Elizabeth stepped off the steamer into a puddle and a fog; she began to cough before they reached London. Arabella had arranged a house for them at 26 Devonshire Street, near John Kenyon—and a short walk to 50 Wimpole Street. Robert had felt uneasy about bringing his wife to meet his father and sister for the first time and to occupy a room now made vacant by the death of his mother. Thus he decided to make his first visit to New Cross by himself on the evening of their arrival, leaving Elizabeth to greet Arabella in a warm, tearful reunion.

The two sisters were together almost every day at one residence or another. "When we sit together," said Elizabeth, "it is like a dream that we ever parted."[11] She was very daring about her presence in London. She sent Wiedeman with Wilson or Bonser to Wimpole Street daily, where he came to know his Aunt "Alibel," and when Arabella went to Devonshire Street to spend the afternoon with Elizabeth, he and Wilson passed the time with Minnie Robinson, the housekeeper, and the other servants. Some days Elizabeth herself went to Wimpole Street, where she took notice of changes in the atmosphere of her former home. Although Arabella's room was cheerful and comfortable, the drawing rooms seemed "smaller & darker, somehow, & the furniture wanted fitness and convenience, and *bachelor-looking* the general effect was."[12] She was viewing it with the critical eye of a mistress of her own household and with a new awareness that it was a male-tainted domain.

Even though the house held many happy memories of family together-ness, she was reluctant to go there because she felt humiliated by the neces-sary secrecy of her presence, and she always felt nervous as the afternoon hours drew to an end. One day when she stayed late with Arabella, she had a heart-twisting shock: Mr. Barrett returned early from the city. While she trembled in Arabella's room, she heard him come upstairs and then go down. For the first time in four years, she heard his voice, talking and laughing. "In a sort of horror of fright and mixed feelings" she slipped past the dining room while the family was at dinner. She walked home with Bonser in a sad, reflective mood. Robert was annoyed with her to have risked a confrontation that would have unnerved her for weeks and destroyed all the pleasure of their return to London.[13]

Henrietta, leaving her baby with Surtees, traveled to London in early August and remained a week in rooms near the Brownings. The two exiled sisters joined Arabella daily, enjoying their love in the shadow of Mr. Barrett's spiteful rejection. The Barrett brothers gradually made their appearance. Henry was a frequent, very friendly caller at Devonshire Street; Octavius came three or four times; Alfred, who was contemplating a marriage of his own, and Septimus each came once to greet her (Stormie was in Jamaica). But George, who, after the death of Bro, had been Elizabeth's favorite, dis-played a mixture of pride and misunderstanding. He wrote to Arabella from the west country, where he was still on the court circuit, informing her that "as Ba never answered his last letter," he would go directly to Wales for his vacation without returning to London.[14] This was an unexpected blow.

Hurt and angry, Elizabeth replied to George,

> explaining for the nine hundred and ninety ninth time, what my reason was for not answering his letter—simply that it ignored the existence of my husband. I added that I always loved him, and did so still, and that only the want of love on his part interposed between us. To which the answer came, that Robert had pertinaciously declined the friendship of my family—that he had taken no notice, for instance, of an affectionate message of Storm's, and had never replied to a letter of Henry's. Absolute misstatements.[15]

In her frustration, she was about to reply, straightening out George's dis-tortions of the matter, when Robert intervened: "I will write," and he sat down and composed "a most kind letter," employing all his verbal skills. But unfortunately this diplomatic letter was returned with an explanatory mes-sage informing him that "the barrister-at-law was no longer on circuit, and left no address."[16]

The London climate was not agreeing with Elizabeth's frail constitution, but the chill breezes from Wimpole Street distressed her more. The hugger-mugger meetings with Arabella and the Barrett brothers and the sight of Henrietta's being unwelcome in the family home made Elizabeth value her life with Robert more fully.

> So far from regretting my marriage, it has made the happiness and hon-our of my life, and every unkindness received from my very own house makes me press nearer to the tenderest and noblest of human hearts, *proved* by the uninterrupted devotion of nearly five years. Husband, lover, nurse—not one of these, has Robert been to me, but all three together. I neither regret my marriage, therefore, nor the manner of it, because the manner of it was a necessity of the act. I thought so at the time, I think so now. . . .[17]

In high contrast to this atmosphere of tension and guarded feelings, Elizabeth was received with great affection at New Cross when she and Robert spent two days there. She was soon bonded in sisterly affection to Sarianna because of her intelligence, her range of learning, and her warm heart. Elizabeth was pleased, too, to see how quickly Wiedeman and his grandfather became devoted to each other.

Bringing additional cheer to Elizabeth's dampened spirits, Robert's friends descended upon the Browning house in Devonshire Street, eager to see the recluse whom they knew only through hearsay or from the printed page. She and Robert were "overwhelmed with kindnesses, crushed with gifts . . . and literally to drink through a cup of tea from beginning to end without an interruption from the door-bell, we have scarcely attained to since we came."[18] They saw Joseph Arnould, who offered them his town house; Fanny Kemble, who presented them with tickets to her Shakespeare readings; John Forster, who gave a magnificent dinner in their honor at Thames Ditton and presided with his usual dominance and charm; Henry Chorley, who had published reams of her work in the *Athenaeum* yet had never set eyes on her; Samuel Rogers, who invited them to a breakfast; Car-lyle, who came for an evening and later invited them to dinner (though at the last minute Elizabeth's cough prevented her from going out); Bryan Procter ("Barry Cornwall"), who called every day he was in town; R. H. Horne, who brought his young wife; and dear "Aunt Nina" Jameson, who rejoiced to see them back in London. Robert was immensely proud of his wife and the court that the London friends paid to her, even though their gracious atten-tions exhausted her. "There's kindness in England after all," she concluded, but added that "the sort of life is not perhaps the best for me and the sort of climate is really the worst."[19]

When Wilson left to spend a couple of weeks in Sheffield with her family, Wiedeman was frantic at the loss of his "Lily," and feared his mother might desert him too. As a consequence, he would not let her out of his sight for more than a moment or two. Elizabeth discovered for the first time the effort and patience that child care demanded. With washing and dressing and feeding and giving constant attention, she had not a moment to herself to satisfy her daily need for writing, except when the child was napping, at which time she would scratch off a hurried letter.

When Wilson returned in September, Elizabeth was ready to leave London, with its inhospitable weather and the tensions of 50 Wimpole Street. But suddenly a bright ray broke through the family cloud. Robert's letter to George had been sent three times to Wales, where George was vacationing. When at last George received it, his feelings were mollified. He returned immediately to London, where a loving reconciliation with Elizabeth took place and friendly relations with Robert began.

Encouraged by this turn of events, Elizabeth finally wrote her father to inform him that she was in town and beg him to see his grandchild. Robert also wrote to him—what Elizabeth called "a manly, true, straightforward letter," "generous and conciliating." He received in reply "a very violent and unsparing letter," accompanied by a packet of all the letters Elizabeth had written to him over the years, unopened. Edward Barrett said that he had been "forced to keep them" because he knew not where to send them for return. Elizabeth resolved never to write again.[20]

At the end of September, Elizabeth said good-bye to the Wimpole Street servants, who were still deeply devoted to her, and when Arabella came to help her pack for departure, the sisters clung in a sad farewell. Robert said his good-bye with an awareness of the firm attachment that had grown between him and the selfless, affectionate Arabella. His parting from his father and Sarianna had been less difficult, for he knew they were considering coming to Paris the next year.

The Brownings' journey to Paris was made more lively by Carlyle, who accompanied them all the way and was "highly picturesque" in his conversation, although he offered no aid to a bustling Robert, who oversaw all the baggage transfers and customs inspections.[21] Robert left London feeling happy and rewarded. It was "pure joy" for him to see Sarianna and his father and to reunite with his literary friends. It had been something of a triumphant return. If Elizabeth's health and spirits could have been equal to the change, he would gladly have settled there. Elizabeth had mixed feelings at departure. "Leaving love behind is always terrible, but it was not all love that I left, and there was relief in the state of mind with which I threw myself on the sofa at Dieppe."[22]

Robert and Elizabeth returned to Paris determined to face the winter months with caution, testing the possibility of a permanent residence there. As soon as she left England, Elizabeth's cough had begun to subside, and she now reveled in the clear, dry air of Paris and the warm October sunshine. They found an ideal apartment on the sunny side of the Avenue des Champs Elysées, with two large bedrooms, drawing room, dining room, kitchen, a study and dressing room for Robert, and a small bedroom for the newly hired *femme de ménage*, Desirée. A small terrace overlooked the avenue, from which Elizabeth could watch her hero, President Louis Napoleon Bonaparte, pass by in his carriage. One day Wilson and Wiedeman, out for a walk, had a clear glimpse of his face as the carriage turned into a courtyard.

Wiedeman was an adaptable international child, joyous wherever he traveled. He was especially attracted to uniforms. In Bologna, he had slipped away to join a group of soldiers and even tried to take hold of an officer's sword. On the train from Lucca, he clutched at the gold button of the railroad conductor. He was drawn to priestly vestments and in Italy had demanded to be taken into churches where he would kneel, cross himself, fold his hands in prayer and roll up his eyes "in a sort of ecstatical state." Robert was amused, saying that it was "as well to have the eyeteeth & the Puseyistical crisis over together."[23] The child loved ritual and ceremony. In the Paris apartment, whenever Robert picked out the notes of a Gregorian chant on the piano, Wiedeman would turn up his eyes to the ceiling, cross himself, pretend to count rosary beads, then pace across the room as if in procession, and bow as if at the altar.[24]

In Italy, he had not begun to talk, for he was adjusting himself to his bilingual home life. Now in Paris, at age two and a half, he began to pick up a third language from Desirée. He understood everything that was said to him in Italian, English, and French, but he spoke a scarcely intelligible, baby-talk mixture of Italian and English with a few French phrases: Elizabeth called it Babylonish. In November he created a new name for himself, Penini, his own way of saying Wiedeman. Penini, Peni, and later Pen, became his family name henceforth.

Robert enjoyed Paris more and more as the weeks went by. For his daily walk, the fashionable boulevards and the crowded narrow streets offered more variety and a sense of the contemporary world of affairs than Florence had done. He had a letter of introduction to Emile Lorquet, an editor of *Le National*, a republican newspaper, and to Garvarni of the satirical journal *Charivari*. He came to know Fraser Cockran, Paris correspondent of the *Morning Herald*. The Brownings received a note from Lady Elgin, widow of Thomas Bruce, Lord Elgin, who had rescued the Parthenon marble reliefs from Turkish neglect and brought them to England. She invited them to one of her Monday-evening receptions for tea and literary conversation. Elizabeth was disappointed with the gathering, for she did not meet any French celebrities. But she did meet Madame Mary Clarke Mohl, wife of Julius Mohl, professor of Oriental (Near Eastern) studies at the Institute of France. Although Madame Mohl was English, she had been educated in France, where she had been an associate of Madame Récamier and frequented her salon. She invited the Brownings to her Friday evenings. Elizabeth seldom left home after dark, but in Paris she insisted that Robert go out for such occasions "because we might as well be at Florence if he shuts himself up here as he does sometimes for days together.... [This] gives him opportunities of social intercourse, which really is good for him, with his temperament."[25] Beginning with their residence in Paris, Robert began now to relax his determination to spend every evening with his wife.

Sarianna and Robert Browning, Senior, visited Paris in November. Since their lease was up at New Cross, they were contemplating a move to Paris. If they made that decision, it would strengthen Robert and Elizabeth's inclination to settle there. Already Elizabeth was enjoying the carpeted warmth of their present apartment more than the icy tiles of Casa Guidi in the cold season, and she spoke frequently in letters to her sisters about the warmth of French houses compared to drafty English homes, even in mild weather. The Brownings appeared inclined to stay on in Paris for good.

Suddenly, national events intruded into their quiet routines. On December 2, 1851, Louis Napoleon carried out a *coup d'état* and seized quasi-dictatorial power. He dissolved the Legislative Assembly, which had failed to approve a constitutional revision allowing him a second four-year term. He issued two proclamations: one justified his actions and outlined a new constitution for the people to vote on in a promised plebiscite; the second called upon the army to carry out orders and save the nation from a political breakdown and reminded the soldiers of the glories of the Napoleonic era at the beginning of the century. Troops were posted all over the city. Seventy-eight opposition leaders and journalists were arrested, including fourteen Deputies of the Legislative Assembly.

As the news spread, resistance began among workers and defenders of the recently established republic, who threw up barricades and for two days fought against the hastily assembled troops in the streets of Paris. But the soldiers crushed the brief opposition, leaving 135 dead among the insurgents and innocent bystanders. Since cannon had been placed in the faubourg close to the Brownings' apartment, they could hear the sounds of the street fighting. Elizabeth, shuddering, found the noise "deafening." Protests in the provinces were likewise put down by military forces, and the arrests mounted. At length, over 26,000 citizens were detained for antigovernment activity, of which 239 were sent to the penal colony in Cayenne, French Guiana, and more than 9,500 deported to Algeria. About 3,000 others were imprisoned and another 5,000 were subject to an extended period of police surveillance. Martial law was declared in thirty-two of the Departments of France until March 31, 1852. Newspapers and journals were shut down. Political clubs were abolished. But surprisingly, the plebiscite of December 20, 1851, approved the coup and the new constitution by a seven-to-one majority. Both the rural masses and the urban bourgeoisie, remembering the workers' uprising of 1848, voted for peace and order. Some older citizens perhaps were guided in their vote by the Napoleonic name and a nostalgia for the days of the empire.

The new constitution set a presidential term of ten years for Louis Napoleon and strengthened his power by establishing an Executive Council and a Senate, members of which were to be appointed by the president. The president also was given the sole power to initiate legislation. The new Legislative Assembly, to be elected by the people, would be allowed only the power to approve legislation, a course that could be negated by the appointed Senate. Despite the elections and the plebiscite, France no longer appeared to be a republic.[26]

As spectators at this upheaval, the Brownings felt that they were at the center of the political universe in Europe. "We are leading the most vivid life possible," Elizabeth wrote in excitement to Arabella. Writing a month later to Mrs. Martin, she mounted her defense of Louis Napoleon's action: "The *coup d'état* was a grand thing, dramatically and poetically speaking, and the appeal to the people justified it in my eyes, considering . . . the impossibility of the old constitution and the impracticality of the house of assembly."[27]

In supporting Louis Napoleon's political excesses, Elizabeth was moved not only by her admiration for him as a decisive leader but also by her fear of socialism. Although a conservative majority of two monarchical parties had controlled the Legislative Assembly, they had been opposed by two very active and combative republican parties whose policies extended from moderate reform to socialist measures. "I love liberty so intensely," Elizabeth had explained earlier to Mary Russell Mitford, "that I hate Socialism. I hold it to be the most desecrating and dishonouring to humanity of all creeds. I would rather (for *me*) live under the absolutism of Nicholas of Russia than in a Fourier machine, with my individuality sucked out of me by a social airpump."[28] Emotionally intense about her political views, she was ready to support extreme measures and uphold the president in his grab for power.

On the day the news of the coup broke, Elizabeth was thrilled to witness Louis Napoleon himself in parade, riding a white horse twenty paces ahead of his military guard, with the cavalry following in procession, their helmets glittering, to the sound of trumpets and the shouts of acclaim from the crowds of people, "Vive Napoleon." "No sight could be grander, and I would not have missed it, not for the Alps," she told Mrs. Martin. From the terrace, Penini shouted "Viva Peone."[29]

Robert was out for a walk when the fighting started. He was turned back by his landlord, "who cried out, 'For God's sake, dont go any farther—A ball whizzed by my head.'" Although he was still curious, Robert returned to the apartment: he had promised his wife he would not go into any dangerous area. The same afternoon, Wilson, with Penini in tow, was warned by a terrified man to get "le petit" back to the safety of his home. For the next two days, they watched from their terrace as the troops rushed by to the sounds of trumpets and shouting.[30]

A few days later, Robert took Elizabeth in a carriage to the area where the street fighting had taken place. Driving down the Boulevard des Italiens, they saw the broken walls, smashed windows, and houses marked by cannon fire. Keyed up by the proximity, Elizabeth was disappointed not to see the barricades, which by now had been removed. In her defense of Louis Napoleon's ruthlessness, she discounted the extent of the casualties when she wrote to Henrietta, "To talk about 'carnage' is quite absurd. The people never rose—it was nothing but a little popular scum, cleared off at once by the troops—Painful of course—very full of pain, of course—for the time!"[31]

Since England was appalled by what had taken place, Elizabeth hastened in all her letters to family and friends to present an apologia for Louis Napoleon in earnest, breathless detail. She urged them not to believe a word of what they read in the *Times*. The coup was not an act of "military despotism"; Louis Napoleon had taken a necessary action; the Legislative Assembly did not really represent the people; "the alternative was between two monarchies and a Socialist republic"; Louis Napoleon's action was "the salvation of

France"; she regarded him as the "legitimate chief of . . . State" because seven and a half million Frenchmen supported him in the plebiscite; the commercial and agricultural interests joined with the army veterans and the peasants in desiring "tranquillity at any price"; she also respected the opinion of the small farmers to whom "the tradition of Napoleon" was a sacred memory; in Paris, too, the tradesmen revered him as "*le vrai neveu de son oncle*"; "no revolution ever took place in France with so little bloodshed & suffering"; the gagging of the press was just "a moment of revolution, & every party, at all such times, has done precisely the same thing"; everything was quiet now; the shops had reopened; people were going about their daily business.[32]

Robert, with totally opposite views of Louis Napoleon and his ambitions, was outraged at the coup d'état and the subsequent repressions. This led to serious quarrels with Elizabeth: "Robert & I fight about Louis Napoleon," she told Arabella, and she referred to their disagreements as "domestic *émeutes* [heated disruptions]."[33] Indeed, he was angrily puzzled that such an intelligent person could defend the president's violations of his oath to uphold the constitution. To express his bewilderment he turned to George Barrett, of all people—George, with whom he had only recently settled the injured feelings of four years' standing. "Is it not strange that Ba cannot take your view, not to say mine & most people's, of the President's proceedings? I cannot understand it—we differ in our appreciation of facts, too—things that admit of proof." But Elizabeth always stood her ground, declaring that the will of the people had been expressed seven and a half million strong in a free vote open to all Frenchmen and that this was the democratic way in a republic. Even Robert himself had been disgusted with the party conflicts in the French Assembly, which he characterized as "stupid, selfish, & suicidal."[34] In reality, neither of them had full information on what was happening throughout France. Aside from government reports, they were dependent for news on the English newspapers and on word-of-mouth accounts from their friends because the French press had been silenced.

This opposition in their political opinions about Louis Napoleon would become the source of recurring conflict—indeed, one of two serious problems in their domestic life. Elizabeth insisted to Arabella that she and Robert really agreed on "the *principles* of things:—& therefore it is, that what you used to call 'our quarrelling' is an element of our loving one another, & a very important element too."[35] Nevertheless, differences in their two passionate natures would continue to emerge as their marriage went on and as each expressed, both in personal interchange and in literary works, their basic individual selves that had intertwined to form an unbreakable marital bond.

The International Life

French political turmoil in later 1851 did not distract Browning from writing when he had a responsibility to meet or a creative need to fulfill. In mid-October, as soon as he had moved his family into the new apartment, he settled down to write an introductory essay to a collection of Shelley's letters that Moxon was planning to publish: he finished it at the end of November.[1] It and the 1842 essay on Chatterton were his two essays in literary criticism, but the essay on Shelley has been the one more widely read and used. In a letter to Carlyle, Browning indicated his indebtedness to him: "I have put down a few thoughts that presented themselves—one or two, in respect of opinions of your own (I mean, that I was thinking of those opinions while I wrote)."[2]

The principal idea in the essay is the distinction between two kinds of poetic creation. In the first, the "objective poet" is described as a maker, one who creates his works out of the objects of the external world, although he sees "external objects more clearly, widely, and deeply, than is possible to the average mind." In the second, the "subjective poet" is a seer, one who attempts to express ideal Platonic concepts, "not what man sees, but what God sees"—absolute ideas, although the poet perceives them imperfectly, presents them through "the primal elements of humanity," and finds them within himself. The objective poet, in dealing with "the doings of men," produces "what we call dramatic poetry," while the subjective poet, "whose study has been himself," employs images—"external scenic appearances"—as the expression of "his inner light and power." There is no reason, Browning asserts, "why these two modes of poetic faculty may not issue hereafter from

207

the same poet in successive perfect works."[3] That combination Browning sees in Shelley, who might be considered a prime example of the subjective poet but whom Browning calls the "whole poet." Readers have thought Browning would consider himself to be an objective poet, but if one considers his portrait of David in "Saul," for instance, David is (to use the labels of the essay) both "fashioner" and "seer," and the model for his creator.[4] The painter Fra Lippo Lippi, too, is both objective and subjective.

Browning's essay did not become a well-known work, for shortly after publication of the book it was discovered that the Shelley letters had been forged, and Moxon withdrew the book from sale. Browning sent a copy to Kenyon and may have sent copies to a few more friends like Forster and Arnould. Such was the extent of his excursion into literary theorizing.

ॐ ॐ ॐ

During the winter of 1851–1852, while the Brownings were testing whether Elizabeth's lungs could withstand the Parisian climate, she followed her usual cold-weather routine of staying indoors, but she urged Robert to go out in the evening from time to time: "we might as well be at Florence if he did not." Since he was reluctant to leave her alone, "I have 'to drive him out with a broomstick,'" she told Arabella, ". . . But really it's good for him, right for him, & right for me to insist on his going."[5] They had their tea at 8 P.M.; then on certain evenings Robert would spend an hour or two at Madame Mohl's or Lady Elgin's and bring back news and gossip.

As their circle of acquaintance widened, they began to have more social interchange with English residents than they liked, "& it's impossible, when people ask if they may call on you, to say brutally, 'no, no,' however you may desire it." Elizabeth became concerned that they risked being drawn into "a regular net of English—'good society'. . . . Not particularly interesting people."[6] After being trapped into an evening of card playing at the Hedleys, Robert rebelled at having to visit her relatives. He believed that social gatherings should be an "association of minds," not an "association of manners."[7]

A happy exception among their new acquaintances was Joseph Milsand, a French critic who had developed a special interest in English literature and culture. He had written a book on Ruskin, *L'Esthetique anglaise*, and a short study of John Wesley and the Methodist movement. He had also recently published a comprehensive critical treatment of Browning's work in the second of a series of articles on contemporary English poets, "*La poésie anglaise depuis* Byron. II, Robert Browning," in the *Revue des deux mondes* that introduced Browning's work to the French literary public.[8] Milsand admired the intellectual curiosity and breadth of view that were exhibited in his two-volume *Poems*, which seemed to show the promise of a future epic poet. Since he was a Catholic who had turned Protestant, he also responded fully to Browning's handling of ideas in *Christmas-Eve and Easter-Day*. Milsand's article was the most serious discussion of Browning's work since R. H. Horne's essay back in 1842, and he thereby won Robert's everlasting gratitude.

Knowing that Milsand would enjoy meeting the Brownings, Fraser Corkran had brought him over to their apartment one evening in mid-December 1851. At this first meeting, poet and critic felt an immediate rapport; it was the beginning of a lifelong friendship. Having found an intelligent and truly sensitive reader, Browning henceforth submitted all his poems to Milsand's judgment before publication and was rewarded with helpful criticism and encouragement.[9]

Since Milsand was modest and withdrawn in his bearing, he did not strike Elizabeth as worthwhile company at first: "a little man, young, & agreeable, though not brilliant."[10] But he soon earned her deep appreciation for an act of kindness and consideration. Elizabeth and Robert had always been obsessed with maintaining their privacy, especially in guarding knowledge of their private life from the general public. In January 1852 Elizabeth was shocked and distressed when she discovered that her friend Mary Russell Mitford had violated her privacy. Without prior warning to Elizabeth, Miss Mitford had published, in late 1851, her *Recollections of a Literary Life*,[11] in which she described Elizabeth's physical frailty, quoted from her letters, and told the story of her grief over Bro's death by drowning. These revelations devastated Elizabeth, especially those about the loss of Bro, even though she was ashamed to be so sensitive about having her griefs aired: "I am morbid, I know," she wrote to Mrs. Jameson. "Like the lady who lay in the grave, and was ever after of the colour of a shroud, so I am white-souled, the past has left its mark with me for ever."[12] Mary Russell Mitford's breach of confidence almost ended their friendship.

When Milsand was preparing an article on Elizabeth's poetry, his editors had recommended that he include the new biographical information about Elizabeth that had been made public, but he doubted the propriety of doing so. In his dilemma, he tactfully approached the Brownings and inquired what their feelings were in the matter. Elizabeth was thus able to forestall any discussion of her personal life in the *Revue des deux mondes*. As a consequence of Milsand's careful consideration of her feelings, her heart opened up to him. She and Robert invited him to visit them every Tuesday, establishing in this way their own private "evening" for him. Soon Elizabeth regarded him as a man of deep intellect with a delicate sensitivity in his relations with everyone.

Eager to have the Brownings meet his literary friends, Milsand invited them to the house of M. François Buloz, the editor of the *Revue*, "where," said Elizabeth with some excitement, "the Parisian literati of the first order are apt to congregate."[13] This was the kind of evening that Robert longed for, meeting the new figures in the literary scene, hearing their views on the latest publications and listening to the political exchanges. Madame Buloz regretted that Elizabeth was unable to attend and urged Robert to bring her to their regular Saturday evenings.

Roy Gridley, in his closely focused study *The Brownings and France*,[14] has speculated that the reason Browning was received so cordially in Paris was that the present generation of French poets prized irony and impersonality in poetry, as well as realism, which they saw pushing aside the idealism and personal lyricism of the Romantic writers of the previous period. French literary figures responded well to Browning's display of an unusual Victorian toughness of mind. Théophile Gautier, Gérard de Nerval, and Ernest Renan were all associated with the *Revue des deux mondes*, and both Charles Baudelaire and Leconte de Lisle were soon to be publishing there. Poets like these, in their manifestos and the example of their work, represented a new spirit calling for a poetry of emotional distance and a concern for sparse, carefully crafted structure, features that were characteristic of Browning's shorter poems. During the next six months, in the Parisian salons and in his reading of current critical commentary, Browning would be absorbing this new spirit as a reinforcement for the kind of poetry he wanted to write and would bring forth in his next publication.

Lady Elgin was trying to arrange a meeting with Alphonse de Lamartine, the aging poet and statesman, who was said to be eager to know the Brownings because of his interest in their poetry ("which he thinks highly of," reported Elizabeth) and also because he had talked briefly with Robert at an evening gathering and was struck by Robert's "elevation of thought," but the press of business prevented him from keeping an appointment to call on them on the designated afternoon.[15]

More important to Elizabeth early in 1852 was the news that George Sand had come to Paris to oversee production of her new play, *Le mariage de Victorine*. For her, this was the opportunity of a lifetime because she regarded George Sand as the first female genius of any country or age.[16] When they had arrived in Paris, the Brownings were carrying a letter of introduction to Sand that had been provided for them by Mazzini, but Robert was at first remiss in getting it presented to her and arranging a meeting. He tried a French intermediary who knew her whereabouts, but this man proved to be ineffectual. Nor would Robert allow the letter to be presented to her back-

stage at the theater, fearful that it might be jumbled together with love letters to actresses and perhaps even end up being read aloud with derision by
some functionary in the green room. As a result, George Sand slipped away,
back to her country house in Nohant, much to the vexation of Elizabeth. In
the midst of what Robert called one of her "flurries" ("I suppose a polite
word for my 'rages,'" she explained to Arabella), she accused him of "coldness
and laxness" toward her desires.[17] When her literary idol returned to Paris
again, she was determined to manage the introduction herself. "I wont die, if
I can help it, without seeing George Sand," she resolved.[18] She wrote a note
to her, had Robert join her in signing it, enclosed the Mazzini letter, and
arranged with a friend to have it delivered into George Sand's very hands.
She was rewarded by a gracious note the next day inviting them to call upon
her the following Sunday. Elizabeth wrapped herself in protective furs and
took her respirator and her muff. Robert arranged for a closed carriage, and
they were at last ushered into George Sand's presence.

She greeted her visitors with quiet dignity and warmth. When Elizabeth
kissed her outstretched hand, Sand protested, "*Mais non, je ne veux pas*," and
kissed her on the lips.[19] They were surprised to find that she was not what
they had imagined—a fading beauty—but was a rather large woman, quietly if fashionably dressed, with her hair plainly parted in the middle and
twisted up behind. She had large dark eyes and a complexion "of the deepest
olive." They wondered what she would look like in men's clothes.[20] Elizabeth
saw "no sweetness in the face, but great moral as well as intellectual capaci-
ties."[21] Two or three young men who were present were very deferential, listening to her opinions with great respect. Robert observed that she "seemed
to be the man of the company, & everybody seemed to know it." The talk was
mostly of politics that revealed attitudes highly critical of the government.
Robert offered to leave with Elizabeth so the group could speak more freely,
but Sand demurred, saying that "she had no political secrets." She had come
to Paris to ask Louis Napoleon for the release of one of her friends from
prison, and she had succeeded. Elizabeth was pleased to hear the great man
had treated her graciously. As they were leaving, Sand kissed Elizabeth, and
asked them to call again the following Sunday. Robert gallantly kissed her
hand. Elizabeth thought that he would have liked a kiss too.[22]

The second visit was a disappointment. George Sand was surrounded by
a circle of seven or eight young men: some were from the theater, others were
political hangers-on among her Socialist associates, all were smoking cigars
and spitting in the fireplace. Elizabeth quailed at the tobacco smoke. Sand
was sitting in the midst of their chatter, occasionally offering a disdainful
remark, especially when she was addressed with obsequious adulation.

"*Caprice d'amitié*," (fancy or whim born of friendship) she remarked with scornful rejection. Surrounded in this way, she seemed to Elizabeth to be their "queen or priestess."[23]

She later sent the Brownings tickets for the opening night of her new comedy, *Les vacances de Pandolfe*, in April, but the cold winds prevented Elizabeth from this enjoyment. Robert saw George Sand six times, including once during his morning walk when she took his arm for a stroll the length of the Tuileries gardens, but he did not arrange for another visit to her lodgings. He disapproved of Elizabeth's return visit "on account of the questionable men," Elizabeth told Mrs. Martin, "and their acts of adoration perpetrated through puffs of cigar smoke and ejections of saliva."[24] The bourgeois restraint of both Brownings prevented them from establishing a true literary friendship, much though Elizabeth, in her heartfelt admiration for George Sand, would have liked to join her in feminine sisterhood. She seemed mesmerized by her personality, even though she could not penetrate that quiet reserve and self-possessed disdain: "I felt the burning soul through all that quietness."[25] In addition, she felt compassion for her. "There is something in her tone & bearing which suggests to me exhaustion after agony. God help her."[26] Sand's power over Elizabeth's sensitivity and imagination would continue for the rest of her career. It shows forth in the verse-novel that she was about to begin, especially in the struggle of her new heroine, Aurora Leigh, to become an artist. George Sand's real name was Baroness Dudevant, and one of her given names was Aurore.

In the spring, Elizabeth had a theatrical experience that thrilled her to the core of her being. Both the Brownings were brought to tears by a magnificent performance of Alexandre Dumas's *La dame aux camélias*. "It almost broke my heart and split my head," Elizabeth told Mrs. Jameson.[27] Later, when Mrs. Jameson asked for her company to a performance, she refused. She could not bear such emotional strain again. The excitement of Parisian salons and occasional meetings with celebrities was quite enough for her.

⚄ ⚄ ⚄

Robert Browning's return to literary work at the end of 1851 might have been an effort to lighten his heart of a burden he had borne since visiting London. Although there is no hint of this problem in the Browning letters until as late as July 1852, when Elizabeth mentioned "some vexation" that they had undergone,[28] Robert's worry went back to the time of their first visit to England, when apparently Sarianna had informed him that their father had been behaving very foolishly. About a year after Mrs. Browning's death, Mr. Browning had become attracted to a certain Mrs. Von Müller, a widow twenty years younger than he, who lived nearby in New Cross. This new interest took the form of his passing by her window every morning as he left for the bank, waving his hand and "looking with great earnestness." He continued waving until he was out of sight, sometimes blowing a kiss toward the window. When a rumor went about that she was going to leave the community, he wrote her an anonymous note dated December 1850, inquiring if the rumor were true, and added, "I do not ask from motives of idle curiosity. Need I mention my name?" Shortly afterward, he met her in the street and asked if he might accompany her home; there he declared "his [marital] intentions."[29] When she later moved to Upton, he entered into an active but peculiar correspondence with her.

How much of this Sarianna knew and was able to tell Robert when he first returned to London, we do not know. But some knowledge of it on Robert's part probably lay behind his attempt to persuade his father and Sarianna to move to Paris and join him and Elizabeth in forming a new family center. When Sarianna and Mr. Browning first traveled to Paris in October 1851, Robert accompanied them around the city to show them the attractions of settling there. He also confronted his father about Mrs. Von Müller and learned that he really did not want to go through with this marriage (or perhaps Robert browbeat him into thinking so). With that accomplished, Robert hotheadedly wrote a forthright letter to Mrs. Von Müller requiring her to break off the correspondence, for it "annoyed" his father, and to cease her "persecution" of him. After Mrs. Von Müller replied, expressing surprise at these reproofs, she then received a letter from Mr. Browning himself, in which he gave his reasons for breaking off the match. He accused her of living a life that was not respectable and charged that "when you married your second husband you knew that your first husband was alive." He further told her that he was informing her brother, her son-in-law, and her physician of his decision. Mrs. Von Müller responded with a lawsuit charging breach of promise of marriage and demanding heavy damages.[30]

The winter in Paris was not turning out well for Robert and Elizabeth either. The weather in January and February 1852 proved not as mild as they had hoped. Although Elizabeth stayed indoors, her lungs suffered severely from the cold, her cough was incessant, she lost her voice for two months, and she was stricken with the "horrible lassitude" that bad weather always brought upon her.[31] Although an early spring helped her to recover, in May she came down with "*la grippe*" which, she told Arabella, "wakened up my cough like a lion, worse than at any time in the winter." She had her "old pain" in her side once more, when she "breathed *long*" or coughed. She was more ill than at any time since her marriage.[32] In deep worry over what the Parisian weather had done to her, Robert would not allow them to begin their summer trip to London until July.

↪ ↪ ↪

The second visit of the Brownings to England was pocked with misfortune. On July 1, 1852, five days before their arrival, the lawsuit had come before the Court of Queen's Bench and was reported in full detail in the *Times* on the following day. The counsel for Mrs. Von Müller charged Mr. Browning with "most cruel cold-blooded cowardice" in his treatment of his client. He read aloud excerpts from about fifty letters from Mr. Browning to her, the earlier ones addressing his client as "My dear Mrs. Von Müller" and later devolving into such salutations as "My dearest, dearest, dearest, dearest, dearest, dearest Minnie." The letters were on various subjects, rambling in manner and inconsistent in attitude, sometimes expressing his doubts as to whether it would be proper for him to marry her because of uncertainty surrounding her second marriage, other times apologizing and returning to endearments. The counsel for Mr. Browning, faced with these embarrassing details and some corroborating testimony from witnesses, tried to make light of Mr. Browning's actions by likening the situation to Dickens's episode of Mr. Pickwick's predicament in the case of *Bardell vs. Pickwick*. He characterized the letters as those of "a besotted old man" and the defendant as "a poor old dotard in love." He asked the jury to bring the case to a quick close by awarding the smallest amount of damages. But the judge in his summary, though he showed some sympathy for the unfortunate position Mr. Browning had got himself into, declared that his conduct toward the plaintiff had been reprehensible, especially his falsely accusing her of entering into a bigamous marriage. The jury decided in favor of Mrs. Von Müller, awarding her damages of £800. (Mr. Browning's annual salary was only £320.)[33]

The publicity given the case was a blight on the Brownings' arrival in London. Robert felt humiliated before his literary friends and more so before the Barretts, who, he imagined, saw Elizabeth as disgraced by her marriage into such a disorderly family. However, his friends were generous in their understanding and welcomed him and Elizabeth to English shores. Later, speaking of evenings with Forster, Dickens, and the Procters, he told Kenyon, "I felt all those spark-like hours in London struck out of the black element I was beset with, all the brighter for it!"[34] Robert and Elizabeth would have paid the court-awarded damages if they could have afforded it, but that was impossible. In mid-July, Robert moved Sarianna and Mr.

Browning to Paris to avoid payment. Kenyon and others agreed with this course of action, and the board of directors of the Bank of England took a helpful view of their longtime employee's predicament and granted Mr. Browning a leave of absence. Later they arranged for him to retire with a pension of two-thirds his annual salary. Sarianna returned to London in August, and she and Robert went almost daily to the elder Browning's house in Bayswater (to which he and Sarianna had moved in the spring), packing the family belongings and arranging to sell the furniture. A large portion of Mr. Browning's beloved books were shipped to Paris.

In the midst of these troubles, Wilson had come to a sudden decision about her future. She had decided to stay in England and to seek employment that would bring her a higher wage. Once before she had asked the Brownings for an increase in her annual salary of £16 a year, but they had refused on the grounds that they could not afford it. Now when she repeated her humble request, asking to be paid twenty guineas a year (£21), she received the same answer. This ungenerous refusal was probably Robert's decision, for he was tightfisted about the family expenditures, despite the fact that the Brownings lived comfortably at a middle-class level. He was unwilling to forgo such small pleasures as renting a piano or hiring a horse for riding or a carriage for Elizabeth's outing in the Cascine. Nor was he willing to cut short their travels or their summer months at Bagni di Lucca. This was his response, seconded by Elizabeth, to the loyal service of the young woman who had left home and proximity to family to accompany them to foreign parts and to render also miscellaneous services that were quite beyond those of a lady's maid. Although Elizabeth thought £16 to be higher than the usual pay for a personal maid, she did not seem to consider that Wilson's duties had doubled in recent years. Wilson not only attended to all of Elizabeth's personal needs, but she also acted as nursemaid for Penini. She washed him, dressed him, fed him his meals, took him for his daily walk, and looked after him whenever his parents were occupied.

This seemingly heartless niggardliness on the part of the Brownings was not unusual among their contemporaries; England's class system divided the population so rigidly that people in any higher class were myopic about the needs and feelings of people whose economic circumstances kept them in lower social standing for generations. It fostered righteous attitudes among members of the upper classes about keeping the lower orders in their place. Someone like Wilson could actually be made to feel guilty about asking for payment commensurate with her required work. In such a system, the Brownings were victims as well as Wilson, although their sensitivity as artists should have broadened their views. If they had been born in the later part of the century when the class system had developed more fluidity, one could hope that their attitudes would have reflected more compassion and understanding.

Wilson's decision came just as she was preparing to return to Nottinghamshire to visit her mother and sisters, and Elizabeth was left to care for Penini herself, which she regarded as a heavy burden. But while Elizabeth was fretting about what steps to take in securing a new servant and mourning the loss of Wilson's genial presence, Wilson came to realize that her love for Penini was so great that she could not leave him. Nor could she break with the Brownings, who had become her new family, and especially with Elizabeth, who had not only become a mother figure for her but who also, with her physical frailties, needed her. She returned to London in September and resumed her arduous duties.

In spite of these distractions, the next three months in England were filled with a stream of visitors and a calendar of social engagements much like the previous summer. W. J. Fox, Robert's early sponsor, was among the first to call at 58 Welbeck Street, the little house the Brownings had leased. The Barrett brothers gradually made their appearance. Florence Nightingale came to see Elizabeth, bringing flowers. Jane Carlyle brought Mazzini to meet the Brownings at last, and they both showed their deep reverence for the old revolutionary. Jane had never cared much for Robert or his work, and this occasion raised him no higher in her opinion, which was "that he is nothing or very little but a 'fluff of feathers.'" Yet she was very taken with Elizabeth: "*She* is *true* and *good*, and the most *womanly* creature."[35]

The Brownings were entertained by Bryan Procter and his gossipy wife at a warm reunion that included Anna Jameson, the Brownings' hovering guide during their honeymoon. They visited Fanny Haworth at Elstree, where Elizabeth was intrigued to meet Lord Stanhope with his crystal ball that allowed him to make prognostications. They also met the Reverend Charles Kingsley, novelist and promoter of "Muscular Christianity." They liked him immensely, but Elizabeth was a little overwhelmed by his vigorous support of Christian Socialism. They were able to meet James Russell Lowell, the American poet, critic, and abolitionist, who had published one of Elizabeth's poems in his magazine, *The Pioneer*, in March 1843, and whose essay on Robert's work in 1848 in the *North American Review* had extended his readership in the United States. They dined with Ruskin and met his young wife, Effie Gray, who was rumored to be restless in her marriage. At John Kenyon's house, they renewed acquaintance with Walter Savage Landor, toward whom Robert had always felt gratitude for the early recognition of his work.

A very important occasion was the day Dante Gabriel Rossetti called to meet the poet whose work he had been reading with enthusiasm for the last five years. Rossetti, an early admirer of *Paracelsus*, had read and transcribed the whole of *Pauline* from the copyright copy in the British Museum and, struck by the style, had written to Browning on October 17, 1847, to inquire whether or not he was the author. Browning replied from Italy on November 10, acknowledging authorship but apologizing for *Pauline* as an example of youthful apprentice work.[36] On meeting Rossetti, Browning was delighted to find that he was a painter as well as a poet. It was the beginning of a long association: Rossetti, his brother William, and the whole Pre-Raphaelite group had recently become the new champions of Browning's work. In the future, they would be instrumental in his coming to know George Meredith and Algernon Swinburne.

Since Elizabeth's chief enjoyment of visiting London was to spend time with Arabella, she begrudged the time given to literary friends and acquaintances. However, she had spent many hours with her sisters on first arrival, for Henrietta, heavy with child, had come to London, where she and Surtees lodged close by Welbeck Street. The three sisters had a full week of soul-refreshing reunion. Later, especially in August as London-dwellers left town to avoid a heat wave ("heavy & strangling," yet welcome to Elizabeth's physical state),[37] she and Arabella passed many afternoons in one house or the other, and Penini gleefully spent the time talking English all day long to his Aunt Arabella and the indulgent servants at Wimpole Street. Although Elizabeth treasured the hours with Arabella, she was reluctant to venture into Barrett territory. She resented the guilty feelings forced on her by Mr. Barrett's obstinate refusal to alter his stern rejection.

"Horribly frightened too, I get about six o'clock," she wrote to Henrietta, and described a recent close call when she was leaving the house and glimpsed Mr. Barrett in the distance coming up the street. She ducked around the corner near Hodgson's shop just in time to escape meeting him. Penini absorbed her fears. "His idea is that a 'Mitaine' [hobgoblin] inhabits the house & comes out about dusk. He was trembling all over yesterday evening while Arabel tied on his hat." In his attempt to understand the peculiarities of his mother's behavior at Wimpole Street, the child had created his own myth to account for the ominous atmosphere that surrounded her former home.[38]

Toward the end of their London stay, Elizabeth decided to appeal once more to her father. She wrote to tell him that she was in London and wanted him to see his grandchild, who, she pointed out, had never done anything to offend him, and humbly asked for a meeting. After years of pleading for forgiveness, she at last received a reply—a shocking, angry refusal. Henrietta, with whom she shared the details, tried to comfort her by suggesting that a written answer was at least better than continued silence. But Elizabeth's aggrieved bitterness at this treatment seemed at last to recognize the true character of Mr. Barrett: "Nothing could be worse than the manner of the written answer," she told her sister; ". . . it was, I confess to you, with a revulsion of feeling that I read that letter—written after six years [of silence], with the plain intent of giving one as much pain as possible. It is an unnatural letter, & the evidence of hardness of heart (towards *me*, at least) is unmistakeable. . . . I have a child myself—I know something of the parental feeling. There can be no such feeling—There never can have been any such—where that letter was produced. Certainly the effect of it is anything but to lead me to *repentance*. Am I to repent that I did not sacrifice my life, and its affections to the writer of that letter? Indeed no—"[39]

🚲 🚲 🚲

The Brownings returned to Paris but did not stay long. They recognized that Elizabeth could not stand another winter there. Kenyon had given an additional £100 so that they might spend the winter in Rome, though, in fact, they would spend it in Florence. They left Sarianna in charge of Mr. Browning, who seemed somewhat depressed and disoriented in Paris, for though he could read French, he could not speak it. Still, he was able to amuse himself by going to the Louvre for some sketching and by prowling among the stalls of the *bouquinists* along the Seine.

In preparation for the trip back to Florence, they consulted a guidebook that tempted them to try a shortcut over the Alps by the Mont Cenis Pass. Since Elizabeth was always fearful of sea travel (still haunted by the memory of Bro), they decided to try going overland by private carriage. They left Paris October 23, traveled by train to Chalon, thence by steamboat to Lyon, and then headed for the Alpine passage via Mont Cenis. But they had been misled by the guidebook, which promised a quick journey to Italy with a stopover at an inn on the summit of Mont Cenis. The trip took two days and one night to reach Turin. The inn was closed for the winter, and they were forced to go straight on without a night's sleep.

It was a horrific ordeal for Elizabeth, because of snow and bitter cold all the way. Sometimes ten horses were required to draw the carriage as it strained up the mountain roads. She coughed continually and became weaker and more frightened as the hours passed and she gasped for breath. She wondered what she had got herself into: "I thought it was all up with me," she wrote later; "I was worn to the bone—miserable to look at."[40] Penini did what he could to encourage her, kissing her and patting her hands. At a stopping place where the horses were changed and fed, they were able to get out and rest on beds in their clothes for five or six hours with fires blazing in the fireplaces. With night fever and cough, "I was nearly extinct before we got to Turin," she reported. "On the Mont Cenis itself, almost suffocation came on."[41] Turin was still too cold to bring her relief. "I shall not forget our descent into Genoa from the mountains in the supernatural moonlight, which touched my brain with all sorts of fantastic suppositions. I remember Robert wondering whether I was mad or not."[42] Although in Genoa the weather was like that of June, it took her ten days to recover. The last two days, however, Robert was able to take her to walk in the city, visiting churches and the palazzo of Andrea Doria.

For Elizabeth, Florence had never been such a welcome sight. Casa Guidi had really become home for her ("I feel myself back in my nest again"), although Robert found it too quiet after the literary intensity of Paris and London. Their former Italian servants greeted them with embraces and cries of delight, but the general populace seemed downcast, "trodden flat . . . under the heel of Austria," which occupied the city.[43] Robert was quite satisfied that their scheme of subletting Casa Guidi had proved profitable: as a result they had earned free rent for six months.

In December, news came from France that Louis Napoleon's desire for a firmer grip on government had culminated in his pressure on the Senate to declare him Emperor Napoleon III and head of a hereditary dynasty. Much to Robert's chagrin and Elizabeth's satisfaction, a plebiscite approved this political aggrandizement by a vote of 7,824,000 to 253,000. They remembered an afternoon just before leaving Paris, when they were visiting the Corkrans' apartment on the Avenue des Champs Elysées. From the terrace they had watched Louis Napoleon, with pompous posturing, parade on horseback, followed by fully caparisoned cavalry (much to Penini's delight). Louis had just returned from a tour of the provinces made to ascertain whether his standing with the people was sufficiently strong for him to reach for further power. Gazing at the scene below, the cheering crowds lining the avenue, Elizabeth could sense the immanence of empire.

Dreamwork

On January 1, 1853, Elizabeth received "an anonymous bouquet" of "the most splendid roses" addressed to the "Olive-eyed prophet."[1] On that same day, Robert Browning, reflecting on the passage of time, was feeling twinges of guilt for not having produced any poetry for three years and made a New Year's resolution to write a poem a day. The splendor of the roses that had been delivered to Elizabeth prompted him to write "Women and Roses," a dream-poem (somewhat incoherent, as dreams so often are) that celebrated womanhood from the classical past up to the fresh, loving women of the present day and on to those yet unborn. In it, the speaker expresses a surprisingly frank wish to possess the woman represented by "the dearest rose to me" in his dream. Reflecting on the image of the probing honeybee, the speaker gives voice to his desire:

> Deep, as drops from a statue's plinth
> The bee sucked in by the hyacinth,
> So will I bury me while burning,
> Quench like him at a plunge my yearning,
> Eyes in your eyes, lips on your lips!
> Fold me fast where the cincture slips,
> Prison all my soul in eternities of pleasure,
> Girdle me for once! (28–35)

But the women, past, present, or future, all elude him. The poem is an expression of sexual frustration, although Browning did not seem to recognize it as such when, years later, in his only recorded comment, he offhand-edly referred to it.[2] Whether he was unconsciously reflecting on his marriage to a physically fragile wife or on his regret at having to leave the excitements of the Parisian boulevards, we will never know. Everything else in his life seems to make abundantly clear his satisfaction in the marital union he had won six and a half years ago.

The next day Browning wrote another poem which, he said, "came upon me as a kind of dream."[3] It was "'Childe Roland to the Dark Tower Came,'" and in it he drew on memories of his reading in childhood and youth and visual impressions that had struck his fancy over the years. Mrs. Orr, who much later talked to Browning about his poems, recorded the information he gave her about his sources: "I may venture to state that these picturesque materials included a tower which Mr. Browning once saw in the Carrara Mountains, a painting which caught his eye years later in Paris; and the figure of a horse in the tapestry in his own drawing-room—welded together in the remembrance of the line from 'King Lear,' which forms the heading of the poem."[4] Other landscape images may have come from one of Browning's favorite childhood books, Gerard de Lairesse's *The Art of Painting*, especially chapter 17, "Of Things Deformed and Broken, Falsely Called Painterlike";[5] the narrative itself, though it takes Roland only to the point of challenging an unseen and unknown foe, has parallels in Malory's story of Sir Gareth.[6] The action and the images in Browning's poem are both riddling and richly suggestive, and generations of readers have speculated on their meaning. Browning characteristically resisted any requests for an explanation. Here is his distinctly unhelpful response when, in 1887, someone offered an interpretation of the poem as an allegory setting forth the despairing situation of a man who suffers the absence of God and asked if the poet agreed. "Oh no, not at all," Browning replied.

> Understand, I don't repudiate it, either; I only mean that I was conscious of no allegorical intention in writing it. 'Twas like this; one year in Florence I had been rather lazy; I resolved that I would write something every day. Well, the first day I wrote about some roses, suggested by a magnificent basket that some one had sent my wife. The next day "Childe Roland" came upon me as a kind of dream. I had to write it, then and there, and I finished it the same day, I believe. But it was simply that I had to do it. I did not know then what I meant beyond that, and I'm sure I don't know now. But I am very fond of it.[7]

The closest Browning ever came to an interpretive comment on "'Childe Roland'" occurred when he was pushed into a vague assent when a friend,

F. W. Chadwick, asked him if the poem could be summarized by the state-ment, "He that endureth to the end shall be saved." Browning answered, "Yes, just about that."[8]

The work is not an allegory, nor can any single interpretation be regarded as exclusively correct. Rather, it is a symbolic narrative and, as such, does not in an allegorical way provide signs that point to a secondary series of mean-ings. Symbolic narrative allows multiple meanings to emerge, the chief guide to interpretation being the generic label Browning provided for the poem: when he rearranged his shorter poems for the collected edition of 1863, he grouped "'Childe Roland'" with the "dramatic romances."

By "dramatic" Browning meant, as he always did, that the speaker in the poem is not the poet himself but rather a character whose mask—*persona*—the poet assumes. It is Roland who tells the story of his quest, and we may infer that he has survived his ordeal and is reliving his experience in the telling of his tale. By "romance" Browning meant not a love story but rather the narrative genre which was one of the two chief kinds of fiction in the Victorian period (the other was "novel"). Sir Walter Scott and Thomas Car-lyle had provided the most influential accounts of the term. Popularly understood as adventure fiction, romance, in Scott's handling of the term (in his 1824 "Essay on Romance"[9]) emerges as the kind of fiction which projects into outward settings and events inner psychological states, and so it is inherently useful for a poet like Browning who wants to explore the inner lives of his characters. The events in romance are improbable when con-trasted with events in the novel, which are realistic, but romance can claim its own kind of truth, because the excitements and frights and improbabili-ties of romance are governed not by things as they are—the novel's chief claim to truth—but by things as they appear to us or as they happen in the light of our wishes and anxieties. Our wishes result in stories in which dreams are fulfilled; our anxieties produce stories about a nightmare world of frustrations, horrors, and fears, the chief fear being that of death. The nar-rative of romance follows a conventional pattern which Scott defined: in chivalric romances, the hero sets out on a journey full of perils and tempta-tions; after a series of preliminary adventures, there is a climactic confronta-tion, usually with death itself in one form or another; after that crucial struggle, the hero returns to enjoy rewards on earth, conventionally a beau-tiful bride, a long and vigorous life, and a prosperous kingdom. Romance did not disappear with the Middle Ages. Thomas Carlyle, who begins his brief history "The Diamond Necklace" (1837) with the memorable line, "The Age of Romance has not ceased; it never ceases,"[10] redefined the genre by making it the key to individual lives—and the key to history itself, history being, in his view, the essence of innumerable biographies. Romance, in his hands, is primarily an internal action, the growth, education, testing, and triumph of the hero, and romance is to be found not in some distant chivalric past but in the "real life" of the present. Robert and Elizabeth both owed a great deal to Carlyle's thinking: Elizabeth subtitled "Lady Geraldine's Courtship" (1844) "A Romance of the Age," and Robert's "'Childe Roland'" is a poem about the forging of the hero.

That hero-making depends upon the action going on within Childe Roland himself. The outer action of the poem—the perilous journey—is conventional enough, and it brings Roland only to the moment of the crucial struggle, so that the poem seems incomplete. The inner action is another matter entirely. In it, the perilous journey and all its deprivations are mental and psychological states; the sight of the dark tower is the crucial moment; and the issuing of the challenge at the end—the blowing of the slug-horn— is the successful completion of the inner change. Browning skillfully plays a complete inner action off against an incomplete outer action, suggesting that the preparation for decisive action is more important than the act itself. For Childe Roland is concerned with his own fitness ("And all the doubt was now—should I be fit?" [42]), and he must "Think first, fight afterwards— the soldier's art" (89). The "soldier's art" is in fact more likely to be unreflecting obedience to orders, so Roland is very much the hero-on-his-own, seeking for means "Ere fitly I could hope to play my part" (88). For the reader, every detail of the outward setting and experiences is a clue to the action going on in Childe Roland himself: his shaping, interpreting, coloring, and distorting of sights and events are all evidence of an inner psychological drama.

First, the "hoary cripple." The figures the questing knight meets in the wasteland are figures who reflect the sterility of the land itself in their age, deformity, and impotence, and the untrustworthy guide is a conventional figure in romance. That convention might account for Roland's response to him—"My first thought was, he lied in every word" (1)—but this guide is apparently not lying, and Roland himself knows that: in the third stanza he says of the "ominous tract" to which the cripple directs him that it is the place "which, all agree, / Hides the Dark Tower" (14–15). So Roland reveals his paranoia: he assumes that the cripple is out to get him. His instinctive distrust of the old man is but one aspect of the crippled understanding which characterizes his mental wasteland. His outlook is limited, too. He conceives of the end of his quest not as a renewal (he could not cope, he says, with the "obstreperous joy success would bring" [22]) but simply as the end of his present state. He remembers his years of wandering, and expects only to fail. Like the man on his deathbed whose friends treat him as dead before he has actually died, Roland seems to be experiencing the results of failure before he has actually failed.

The features of the wasteland are conventional enough: it is a "grey plain" (52) without any distinguishing characteristics; nature is "starved" and "ignoble" (56), and there are not even weeds (though they would be appropriate) since nature seems completely sterile ("a burr had been a treasure-trove" [60]). Roland imputes himself when he makes a "peevish" Nature speak: "'It nothing skills: I cannot help my case'" (64). He imputes himself again in his response to the "stiff blind horse" (76), a creature who ought to evoke sympathy but awakens hatred in Childe Roland, whose explanation reveals his own sense of guilt: "He must be wicked to deserve such pain" (84).

The sight of the "stiff blind horse" is the turning point in the internal action. It marks the first time that Roland tries to do something about his situation: "I shut my eyes and turned them on my heart" (85). His activity here contrasts with his passivity up to this point, when, for instance, in spite of his distrust of the "hoary cripple," he followed his directions "acquiescingly" (15). Now he turns within himself, which (as readers realize but he does not) is the true direction of his quest. His notion is only to escape ("I asked one draught of earlier, happier sights" [87]), but it meets an unexpected reversal: the past is not happy but full of sin and guilt. His memories of Cuthbert and Giles, whose appearances he conjures up so hopefully, lead him to their sins and crimes: "one night's disgrace" (95), unspecified, for Cuthbert, and treachery for Giles, who is hanged for his crime. The reversal forces Roland to choose his current situation: "Better this present than a past like that" (103). That decision makes his perception keener and more active, with the result that the "grey plain," which had had scarcely any distinguishing features up to this point, now presents him with many and varied images which appear when his eyes and ears are straining for sounds and sights along his "darkening path" (104). The first is the "sudden little river" (109). Childe Roland's effort to interpret its significance is not much of an advance over his response to the "stiff blind horse," for he attributes malice to it as he observes its action on the alders and willows which throng its banks: "The river which had done them all the wrong, / Whate'er that was, rolled by, deterred no whit" (119–20). The allusions in stanzas 20 and 21 are to Virgil's account of Aeneas' descent into the underworld in book 6 of the *Aeneid* (especially his meeting with the souls of children and the souls of those who have committed suicide), and the allusions strengthen the reader's sense that Roland is descending and therefore nearing his goal. Reaching it depends upon a continuing active response, as when he sees the "fell cirque" (133), and his advance is indicated by the fact that he is less willing to make statements and more ready to question, to explore possibilities. In fact, he asks four questions about the "fell cirque" (129–31, 134) before he arrives at an answer which "no doubt" (137) is the most likely. There is a similar interpretive struggle with the instrument of torture in stanza 24, which Roland finds himself unable to name, trying out four nouns (140–41) before settling on "Tophet's tool" (143). Moreover, his wishes (as one would expect in romance) start to govern the action. With the sense that he is "just as far as ever from the end!" (157) he longs for a guide, and instantly, "At the thought, / A great black bird" (159–60) appears, its "dragon-penned" (161) wings foreshadowing the dragon who is the conventional opponent in the crucial struggle.

Childe Roland's advance is evident in the sudden appearance of the mountains by which he seems trapped. He had started on a plain which was gray and featureless; then he had seen the river, the cirque, and now the mountains. The progress from a land which is "Nothing but plain to the horizon's bound" (53) to a land with sharply distinguished features is the realization of a psychological truth (and of one of Carlyle's central lessons), that all we need for renewal is directly in front of us, if only we have eyes to see. The journey is bringing Roland closer and closer to himself (though he does not yet know that): he had looked upon the "fell cirque," a scene of imprisonment, as an outsider, but now (in stanzas 28 and 29) he finds himself trapped by the mountains. The moment he realizes he is imprisoned he sees "the Tower itself" (181).

What is the dark tower? Browning would say, late in his life, that everything needful for an interpretation of one of his poems is in the poem itself. Here the description of the tower is crucial. A high tower with a round turret is usually a watchtower, with a comprehensive view of the surrounding countryside, and in romance such a tower is the outward projection of a character's comprehensiveness of perception and understanding. In this poem the tower is "squat"—short and sitting close to the ground—and it is "blind as the fool's heart" (182), so it is the outward projection of Childe Roland's blindness, the darkness within him which is responsible for his present state. Browning himself defines the word "fool" in an important parenthesis in stanza 25: "(so a fool finds mirth, / Makes a thing and then mars it, till his mood / Changes and off he goes!)" (147–49). The fool is changeable in mood, making and discarding images without grasping their significance; the wise man stares fixedly at each image until its meaning reveals itself. No one can hand such wisdom to anyone else; it must be gained through each individual's experience, and that is why Roland insists upon the tower's uniqueness: it is "without a counterpart / In the whole world" (183–84). Roland has been imprisoned by his own limited perception; the moment he recognizes his limitations, he also paradoxically discovers his own powers, both of perception and of moral choice. And so the wise man in him is born out of the fool.

The blind man can now see. The rhetorical questions that begin stanzas 32 and 33—"Not see?" "Not hear?"—indicate his heightened awareness, and the challenge he issues by blowing his slug-horn is a summary of the action which has restored his ability to see and to choose: "'Childe Roland to the dark tower came.'" The line is not just a statement of fact: it describes a past action which enables a future one, whatever its outcome. By treating the line in this way, Browning is building on its use in *King Lear* (for, as the subtitle of the poem indicates, Browning borrows the line from Shakespeare). Edgar utters the line when he is at the nadir of his experience, in disguise as Tom o' Bedlam and in the company of a mad king; he will become the nameless champion who challenges Edmund and finally Lear's successor as king. Those words have power, and their power is further indicated by the fact that a slug-horn was originally not a trumpet or horn at all, but a slogan or war cry, a rallying cry which instills courage. Like the Ancient Mariner, Roland defines himself by telling his story, but unlike his predecessor's haunting and enervating story, Roland's is liberating and enabling. He is now a "fit" champion with name, identity, and mental vigor.[11]

"'Childe Roland'" is as rich and suggestive as *The Rime of the Ancient Mariner* and "The Lady of Shalott," and like those poems, it has entered into the imaginations of generations of readers, not least of whom are the undergraduates who encounter it in introductory courses in poetry or in first-year surveys, where "'Childe Roland'" is a standard text. Critics like Harold Bloom have returned to the poem again and again.[12] A popular writer, Stephen King, has based a whole series of Gothic novels—*The Gunslinger* series—on this Browning text, which he first encountered at the University of Maine (*The Dark Tower*, 1982, is the first in the series); and A. S. Byatt makes a questing Roland the hero of her 1990 novel *Possession* (which is subtitled "A Romance"). This constant rewriting of Browning's text is an indication of the imaginative energy generated by it (like the imaginative energy Browning found in the line from *King Lear*), and is the ongoing life of that poem.

On the third day after his New Year's resolution, Browning composed "Love among the Ruins"; like the poem of the day before, it features a questing male figure and a tower. Browning's first title for the poem was "A Sicilian Pastoral,"[13] and pastoral is a version of romance (though Browning classified the poem as a "lyric") since it presents an ideal setting—a rural landscape and society characterized by the oneness of human beings with nature and with each other—and an ideal state of mind—*otium* or content-ment—which are the goals of the quest. The opposite of such ideals is urban, where the ambitious or aspiring mind creates a society in which human beings seeking glory are at odds with one another and with them-selves. The whole lyric is built upon those opposites. The speaker is appar-ently a shepherd, and he refers to "our sheep" in the quiet of twilight and to an anticipated meeting in a turret with "a girl with eager eyes and yellow hair" (55)—conventional matter for a pastoral. That same green landscape, how-ever, was once the site of "a city great and gay" (7), of which the tower is the last remnant, and its vertical thrust contrasts sharply with the countryside, where not even a tree intersects the horizontal line of the pastures. Readers familiar with the conventions would expect the shepherd to defend the pas-toral as an ideal way of life, and he ostensibly does so, especially when he condemns the glory and the shame of the city that once was, but we sense in him a curious attraction to the city and its values. The poem is much more complex than it at first appears.

For the shepherd is on a quest for a tower where a girl with yellow hair waits for him. Her yellow hair, conventionally indicating vitality, also sug-gests "the gold, / Bought and sold" in the city (35–36), and the tower was once the center of "a burning ring" (45) where chariots raced: it is associated with striving and competition, but also with energy in contrast to the sleepi-ness of the pastoral landscape. The girl, curiously, seems lifeless, because she is "breathless, dumb / Till I come" (59–60), and "When I do come, she will speak not" (67), but they will embrace and "extinguish sight and speech / Each on each" (71–72), as if the meeting were with death rather than life. The contradictions are summed up in the exclamation in the final stanza, where the shepherd defines his inner state: "Oh heart! oh blood that freezes, blood that burns!" (79). What freezes his blood? The shepherd thinks it is the city and its "whole centuries of folly, noise and sin!" (81), but those same things make his blood burn; and the girl with the yellow hair may make his blood burn, but she may also be a siren figure, like Coleridge's Life-in-Death in *The Rime of the Ancient Mariner*, who "thicks men's blood with cold." In the midst of such contradictions, the shepherd's final assertion, "Love is best," rings hollow. In the manuscript of the first draft of the poem, that final line is "This is best," the pronoun gesturing toward the shutting in of those sin-ful centuries. The commonplace that Browning later substituted makes the shepherd's choice even less convincing.

The sense of things at odds is reinforced by the unusual stanzaic form. Each stanza has twelve lines arranged in couplets, hexameters alternating with dimeters. The effect of an unusually long line in contrast to an unusually short line is that of a mismatch, as if the speaker were allowing himself to be expansive and then reining himself in by a quick return to the rhyme word. The dominant foot is the trochee, and its apparent excessive regularity has led Paul Fussell, who knows as much about meter as any critic, to condemn the effect with the question, "Dancing, anyone?"[14] But Browning wants that sense of something excessively regular with something unbalanced and truncated (hence his use of catalexis in the final foot of each line), and he thought well enough of the poem to place it first in *Men and Women* in 1855.

Browning was no better than anyone else at keeping New Year's resolutions. His poem-a-day resolution did not last long, but it produced one masterwork and two poems of great interest.

Chapter 22

Withdrawal into the Creative Life

The Brownings settled down for the winter in Florence, for Elizabeth did not wish to leave Casa Guidi for the warmth of Rome, even in the colder months. In writing to her friend Isa Blagden, who had left Florence for the winter in Rome, she reported her contentment after so much stress in London and Paris, and in the Alpine journey: "We have been living the most happy life this winter, never stirring from our own fire-side and keeping the olive-wood in a blaze . . . there is poetry in my life—the ideal overflowed into life when I least hoped for it. But there is always poetry in life—is there not?—when there is love."[1] Blagden, their best-loved member of the Anglo-American colony in Florence, had become very close to Elizabeth. She was a lively, olive-skinned little woman of obscure origins. It was rumored that she came from India and was the illegitimate daughter of a native woman of that country and an English officer. In her villa at the top of Bellosguardo, which looked out over Florence, she lived modestly with her friend Louisa Alexander but entertained frequently on her slender means. She was drawn to the Brownings because of her literary inclinations: she wrote poetry and, as time went on, published five novels.

Robert had not gone out in the evening since his and Elizabeth's return. Friends interested in literature and the arts who were part of their small circle of English and American residents sometimes dropped by for tea. Among them were old friends like Hiram Powers, the American sculptor, and Seymour Kirkup, the white-bearded old antiquarian, whose fascination with the occult had intrigued Robert, who was always curious about eccentrics. There was quiet, shy Frederick Tennyson, brother of the laureate, also a poet, who had married an Italian woman and chosen Florence as his new home. He was a lover of music and often arranged concerts at his villa for friends. A somewhat newer friend of the Brownings was Thomas Trollope, brother of Anthony and son of Frances, a vigorous and prolific novelist, who lived with Tom when she was not traveling. When the Brownings had first come to Florence, Robert, in an overprotective mood, resolved beforehand that Elizabeth should not be exposed to Mrs. Trollope, who was said to be a pushing, domineering woman, but when she later called at Casa Guidi, they found her an agreeable, intelligent person. Friendship developed more firmly, however, with Tom, who was their own age.

Newer to the community were two sons of renowned fathers, one British, the other American. Robert Lytton, a newly appointed attaché to the court of Tuscany, was the son of the novelist and playwright Edward Bulwer-Lytton, with whom Browning had been acquainted in London. Although the aging dandy Bulwer-Lytton was a literary figure of high standing in England, he looked with scorn upon his son Robert's desire to be a poet, which he regarded as an "effeminate" tendency, and insisted that he make a career in the diplomatic service.[2] Young Lytton was a captivating young man, blue-eyed, clean-shaven, with dark curly hair. He had taken a villa on Bellosguardo near Isa Blagden, who soon became his intimate friend. Since he was an ardent admirer of Browning's poetry, he paid a call at Casa Guidi as soon as he arrived in Florence, bearing a letter from John Forster, who had been helping him toward a literary career. Robert welcomed him and encouraged him in the poetry he published under the name "Owen Meredith."

Lytton happened to be a friend of a young Bostonian, William Wetmore Story, whom he had met in Washington, D.C., when he was on the diplomatic staff of his uncle, the British ambassador to the United States. Story had met the Brownings in Florence briefly in 1848[3] and cemented his friendship with them when Lytton brought him to Casa Guidi. Story was a genial, dark-bearded young man, the son of an associate justice of the United States Supreme Court, Joseph Story, and like his father had followed a career in law. Although he became a brilliant lawyer who published books on contracts and property law, he was also a poet and a self-taught sculptor. In midcareer he had abandoned the law and settled in Italy with his wife and children in order to develop his art. This bright, vigorous polymath became Browning's closest friend during his Italian years.

Another American couple newly arrived in Florence were William B. and Elizabeth Kinney. Mr. Kinney was the American ambassador to the Kingdom of Sardinia (now centered in Piedmont in its capital, Turin). Mrs. Kinney was a poet and journalist whose son from an earlier marriage, E. C.

Stedman, became a renowned American critic and anthologist. They met the Brownings in Florence in July 1853 and shortly afterward became members of the Anglo-American circle of artists and writers when William Kinney retired. Elizabeth Kinney's observant eye allows us a brief look at the middle-aged Brownings as they appeared to their friends at this time. Robert is described in her journal as a man below medium height but broad-shouldered with a large, round head. He had "a profusion of coarse, waving black hair" sprinkled with gray. "His eyes were gray, large and expressive; his beard was long, thick, and grayer than his hair. His manner was impulsive; his movements were constant, and as wiry as a cricket's. Taking him for all in all, he was a very entertaining man, full of anecdote and wit, seldom really ill-natured. . . . No one would have taken *him* for a poet."[4]

Elizabeth is seen appearing "many years older than her husband" because of her poor health. Her voice seemed hoarse, and she spoke with difficulty above a whisper. "She was of medium height, or would have been had she stood erect," but her shoulders were stooped. "She was thin to emaciation, which of course made her look older than her age [forty-seven]. Her mouth, being large, would have been the noticeable feature of her face, had not her great dark soul eyes, with their heavy black lashes, at once drawn attention to the upper part of her face. This was veiled by the peculiar way in which she wore her abundant black hair, straight down from the crown of her head on each side to her rather high cheek-bones" where it curled down in a loose fashion. If she had dressed her hair "somewhat back from her face," she would have appeared "younger and better-looking. . . . Those wonderful eyes of hers,—windows . . . through which one looked into her soul,—redeemed her face from its ugliness; while her kindly smile, her gentle, even caressing manners, drew one to her after the first impression had passed." Mrs. Kinney is the first person to leave any record about the effects of the morphine upon Elizabeth's behavior. She observed that when she had recently taken her draught, "she would appear more lively and cheerful than when she had been nearly her full time without it. But at no time, nor under any circumstances, did I ever know her to be ill-natured, nor disagreeable toward any one about her; nor did I ever hear her speak unkindly of any person."[5]

In their happy togetherness in Casa Guidi during the quiet winter months of 1852–1853, both Brownings benefited. Elizabeth's health improved because of the mild climate and her determination to restore her former weight and stamina. She took her two tablespoons of cod-liver oil daily with a tumbler of ass's milk to help her to get it down. For breakfast every day, they had eggs and cold meat; for dinner they dined on chicken, duckling, or turkey, which she preferred to red meat. For tea they had plenty of buttered toast and tea, and occasionally Robert persuaded her to share a chop or a turkey leg.

For Robert, the next two years were among the most creative periods of his whole career. His resolve at the beginning of 1853 to "write something every day" was carried on for two weeks, Mrs. Orr tells us.[6] Winter nights by the blazing fire and freedom from the distractions of Paris or London allowed his literary imagination to awaken. By now his habits of work had become so disciplined that he could work rapidly. At some point early in the year, he began to realize that a new collection of poems was taking shape. Since he had been disappointed with the sparse and specialized reception of *Christmas-Eve and Easter-Day*, he began to prepare a book of poems more like *Dramatic Romances and Lyrics*, which had met with much greater critical success than any of his previous publications. As early as February 24, he told Milsand, "I am writing a sort of first step toward popularity (for me!) 'Lyrics' with more music and painting than before, so as to get people to hear and see—something to follow, if I can accomplish it."[7] He longed to have the broad and diverse audience that Tennyson commanded. He was trying to make his style a little less elliptical and his meters a little less rough. "I shall mend my ways, I assure you," he promised his new friend Elizabeth Kinney, "get as smooth as I can, and as plain as I can."[8]

During these early months, he secluded himself almost daily in his little study off the dining room with the "Tintoretto" angel hovering over him on the ceiling. We have only an occasional hint as to which poem he was composing at any specific time. In March, Elizabeth commented to Arabella that in this new "collection of Lyrics" Robert "will assert himself as an original writer I dare say—there will be in them a good deal of Italian art . . . pictures, music."[9] In April she remarks that in his reading he has been "digging at Vasari."[10] It appears then that some of the earliest poems he created for the new book were probably "Fra Lippo Lippi," "Andrea del Sarto," and "A Toccata of Galuppi's." As the months went by, he began to accumulate the most significant body of shorter poems of his entire career. By the end of April, Elizabeth reported to Arabella that Robert had "nearly enough lyrics to print."[11]

At the same time, Elizabeth, with no political conflicts to distract her, had begun composition of the "novel-poem" that she had been comtemplating even before she met Robert. The scope and contemporary focus were what she had determined as long ago as 1846: "the novel or romance I have been hankering after so long, written in blank verse, in the autobiographical form; the heroine, an artist woman—not a painter, mind," as she described it to Mrs. Jameson. "It is intensely modern, crammed from the times . . . as far as my strength will allow."[12] Again, to Arabella: "It is a poem of the times & for the times, & I mean everything to be found in it."[13]

In the spring, Helen Faucit, now in her marriage Lady Martin, the actress who had brightened the productions of *Strafford* and *A Blot in the 'Scutcheon,* wrote Robert to ask permission to produce *Colombe's Birthday* in London. Browning, a good distance away from any oversight, agreed to allow the play to be cut as necessary for performance. Although he himself affected indifference about its success, Elizabeth urged her brothers to attend the first performance and form a claque, and she eagerly requested they send reviews as soon as possible. The play had seven performances at the Haymarket Theater and met with mild praise from critics. Later, Lady Martin took it to Manchester for an uncertain number of performances. But this, his most actable drama, was destined never to have a sustained success on the stage.

෪ ෪ ෪

The Brownings lacked the money, and probably the will, to travel to London in the summer of 1853, but the heat in Florence, which seemed so hard on Elizabeth's delicate constitution, drove them once again to Bagni di Lucca. They formed "a stiff resolve of not calling nor being called upon," and Elizabeth informed Mary Russell Mitford that "we mean to buy our holiday by doing some work."[14] They rented Casa Tolomei, a large house in the second village, Bagni alla Villa, with four bedrooms, a study, a drawing room, and a kitchen as well as servants' quarters. They were accompanied by both Wilson and Ferdinando, their new manservant, who prepared the meals. The servants had both a sitting room and dining room of their own. The house had a row of plane trees in front and a view of the mountains behind, as well as a garden and an arbor. Nearby was a rushing river, surrounded by chestnut woods with sheep walks and goat walks. On the peaks of adjacent mountains were other small villages. Elizabeth's romantic heart responded to it as a "fresh, unworn, uncivilised, world-before-the-flood."[15] Ferdinando and Penini took Flush for a swim (his bath) in the river every morning. Fearless Peni was ready to swim too and had to be restrained.

They were surprised to find that the Storys had taken a house at the highest village, Bagni Caldi, with their children, little Joe, age five, and Edith, age eight. The Brownings' resolution to hold to their writing and avoid social exchanges was soon relaxed. Elizabeth and Emelyn Story began visiting back and forth, drinking tea and gossiping. Some days Elizabeth, on donkeyback with Robert holding the reins and walking alongside, would ride all the way up to Bagni Caldi. Their children played happily together. Peni, at only four, no longer talked Babylonish but instead could speak fluently in both English and Italian, and he fell in love with Edith.

Robert Lytton came for two weeks, staying in the Brownings' spare bedroom, and the group of friends, including children and servants, with Wilson on donkeyback holding Peni, went for picnic excursions from time to time, some of them quite long. On one occasion, they went six miles up in the mountains to Prato Fiorito, along a narrow path atop a perpendicular cliff. The guides had to hold the donkeys' halters as the picnickers rode along these dangerous heights or climbed up steep mountain rises "like riding up a wall," and later passed over mountain torrents on narrow wooden bridges with loose planks.[16] Elizabeth returned exhausted and bruised by the ride, but she was proud of her stamina. During the summer she grew as close to Emelyn Story as Robert was to William. "She is kind and pretty, fresh and innocent, and intelligent enough besides."[17]

Robert did not spend all summer on weekend excursions and social interchange, for he managed to create some poems that were to figure prominently in *Men and Women*. Apparently the stage production of *Colombe's Birthday* awakened some latent yearning in him to try once more to write a play. The result was his composition of an abbreviated tragedy in blank verse of 920 lines, *In a Balcony*, with a romantic hero who bears some resemblance to Valence in *Colombe's Birthday*.[18] At the center of the play are Norbert, a young prime minister whose diplomatic efforts have just brought about the joining of two principalities and an additional crown for his queen, and Constance, a young cousin of the queen, whom Norbert loves and wishes to marry. Complications develop because the queen herself has long harbored a love for Norbert.

In the course of the action, the queen mistakenly thinks Norbert had proposed marriage to her, although he has been asking for the hand of Constance. When the truth emerges, the queen falls into a fury of rejection. At the close of the play, as the lovers cling together, the heavy footsteps of the palace guards are heard ominously approaching. As the guards enter, the play abruptly ends. Despite the ambiguity of the ending, there are clear hints in Norbert's final speeches of tragedy to come: references to "end" and "death" suggest that the guards will take them to their execution.

This romantic tragedy is the most compact of Browning's plays, with a clear structural development, even though as a closet drama it has many long declamations in the dialogue. In fact, teetering among its improbabilities, the text is like the libretto of an opera; it has opportunities for arias and duets rather than the reasonable conflict of character that is found in a verse tragedy. Yet Browning was very fond of it because of its hero and the stance he takes declaring his love for Constance, despite the conflict with the queen. Browning named him among the six most admired characters in *Men and Women* in the volume's epilogue, "One Word More." Norbert's crucial speech expressed for him an authentic statement of Browningesque romantic love:

> I love once as I live but once . . .
> You did not know this, Constance? now you know
> That body and soul have each one life, but one:
> And here's my love, here, living, at your feet. (869, 877–79)

Browning gave *In a Balcony* a unique place in the midst of the monodramatic poems of *Men and Women*. In the rearrangement of his poems in the collected edition of 1863, he placed it with "Tragedies and Other Plays." In the collected editions of 1868 and 1888, it stood alone rather than as part of any group of poems.

ℛ ℛ ℛ

Another work associated with the autumn of 1853 is a major love poem, "By the Fire-Side," that has many personal associations for Robert Browning. The poem begins and ends with a scene in which a husband sitting by the fireside meditates on the occasion that led to his marriage, while his wife, Leonor, sits quietly reading by his side, with "that great brow / And the spirit-small hand propping it" (113–14; a clear picture of Elizabeth Barrett Browning). The poem took its rise from the serene winter period of closeness that the Brownings experienced after the two years of intense literary and social activity in Paris and London. The principal action in the poem draws upon scenes reminiscent of the area around Bagni di Lucca, which the speaker describes from memory. Two young lovers take a walk in the chestnut woods in early November, along a path by a gorge to "the straight-up rock" (46) of a mountainside—a walk that ends in the critical moment that determines their life together.

In "By the Fire-Side" we find Browning's first use of his concept of the "infinite moment," a phrase he would continue to employ in later poems to describe the heightened sense of mutual discovery in love, a feeling that "two souls . . . mix as mists do" (127–28).[19] There is a great deal of subtle symbolic action in the poem as the lovers respond to the natural scene around them, cross a bridge to explore an ancient chapel,

> Then cross the bridge that we crossed before,
> Take the path again—but wait!

> Oh moment, one and infinite!
>   The water slips o'er stock and stone;
> The West is tender, hardly bright:
>   How grey at once is the evening grown—
> One star, its chrysolite!
>
> We two stood there with never a third,
>   But each by each, as each knew well:
> The sights we saw and the sounds we heard,
>   The lights and the shades made up a spell
> Till the trouble [i.e., agitation] grew and stirred.
>
> Oh, the little more, and how much it is!
>   And the little less, and what worlds away!
> How a sound shall quicken content to bliss,
>   Or a breath suspend the blood's best play,
> And life be a proof of this! (179–95)

The speaker's recounting of the remembered day turns into a commentary on the nuances of the genuine love experience. The beloved must completely banish any hindrance to the absolute giving of self.

> Had she willed it, still had stood the screen
>   So slight, so sure, 'twixt my love and her:
> I could fix her face with a guard between,
>   And find her soul as when friends confer,
> Friends—lovers that might have been. (196–200)

Further, the lover must not be precipitate in reaching for the consummation of the eternal moment (Browning employs the metaphor of shaking the last leaf from the tree). Rather, one must wait for the leaf to loosen and fall naturally: "Be your heart henceforth its dwelling-place" (214). Nor should the beloved set too many conditions or requirements, which might prevent the two souls from fitting together completely.

> If two lives join, there is oft a scar,
>   They are one and one, with a shadowy third;
> One near one is too far. (228–30)

But this remembered experience had been a full and mutual giving of self that had lifted them to a new level of being: the natural forces surrounding them had operated upon them and swept them into their new state.

But we knew that a bar was broken between
    Life and life: we were mixed at last
In spite of the mortal screen.

The forests had done it; there they stood;
    We caught for a moment the powers at play:
They had mingled us so, for once and good. . . . (233–38)

The poem echoes and expresses Browning's own sense of a personal decisive occasion, the act of joining with Elizabeth Barrett to abandon their London lives and establish a new life in Italy. The speaker in "By the Fire-Side" declares what that meant for him:

I am named and known by that hour's feat;[20]
    There took my station and degree;
So grew my own small life complete,
    As nature obtained her best of me—
One born to love you, sweet! (251–55)

He was to revisit and develop further his idea of the infinite moment in many poems up to his very last published book, *Asolando,* which he beheld in its dark rose binding as he lay on his deathbed.

Spirits from the Vasty Deep

Although 1853 had been full of contentment and creativity for the Brownings, clouds had begun to accumulate that would occasionally darken their days. These troubles were brought on by Elizabeth's increasing fascination with some recently popularized forms of occult thought and practice that had arisen in England and America, specifically mesmerism, divination by means of a crystal ball, the writings of Emanuel Swedenborg, and finally spiritualism, a semireligious movement that involved attempts to communicate with the spirits of the dead.[1] Her belief in a busy spiritual world that swirled around human beings and could be penetrated by them is understandable. She was a deeply sensitive, religious woman who because of her precarious health had lived close to death for many years in her young womanhood, and her father's attitudes and his lugubrious nightly prayers, said while holding her hands, had led her (and her family) to prepare for her imminent death. Further, her deep grief over her mother's early death and her hysterical reaction to the death of her brother Edward (Bro) kept the presence of these lost loved ones fresh in her memory. Beyond this, she openly confessed her predilection for supernatural questions and suppositions. "I always believed in a spirit-world & in the possibility of communications," she told Mary Russell Mitford, ". . . & I believed long ago in the fact of such communications having taken place in Germany & elsewhere . . . so I have less to get over than persons of a less speculative tendency."[2] Stimulated by both verbal and written reports from a variety of sources, many of them from respected, well-educated men and women, she eagerly grasped at any chance of being in touch with the spirits of those who had occupied a prominent place in her emotional life.

The Spiritualist movement had begun in 1848 in America in upper New York State, when two daughters of a family named Fox had declared they were able to communicate, by means of rapping noises, with what they claimed to be the spirit of a murdered peddler. Later when these two young women moved to Rochester, New York, they asserted to others that they were able to summon the spirits of dead relatives or prominent historical figures. They had found that, by pointing to or calling out letters of the alphabet, they could ask a spirit to respond by rapping and thus convey messages. These procedures, carried out with small groups of people trying to communicate with the dead through a "medium" who presided over the "spirit session" (or séance, as it came to be called), soon spread widely because of a recently growing interest in mesmerism, the belief that a person in a hypnotic trance had access to sights and information beyond normal human powers.[3] In England in 1852, there began to be spiritualistic gatherings engaged in the phenomenon of "table turning," in which a group of friends would place their hands on a table and call for a spirit to indicate its presence by moving or tilting the table. Also they would ask the spirit to respond to questions, yes or no, by rapping or tilting the table, or to spell out messages by tilting the table in response to letters of the alphabet.[4]

Soon American and English mediums were traveling to Europe and developing other demonstrations, such as inviting spirits to ring handbells or play musical instruments; to appear in darkened rooms as moving lights or as hands, arms, or whole bodies; or to speak in strange voices through the mouths of the mediums. Another practice was involuntary writing, in which a spirit would supposedly answer questions by causing the hand of the medium, or some interested person, holding a pencil, to write a message.

Elizabeth's curiosity about supernatural manifestations began in the fall of 1851 when she was reading Swedenborg, probably *Heaven and Hell*, his most frequently translated and best-known work. In midlife this brilliant physicist and engineer had a mystical experience in which he claimed that God spoke to him, telling him that he was to be the prophet of a new revelation about the correspondences between the spiritual world and the natural world and that he was to make known to all people the conditions of life after death. Swedenborg stated that he had been allowed to visit the spiritual world, talk with spirits, and learn about their life together in communities much like those in the earthly world. Over the years, he set forth all of this privileged knowledge in several published books.[5] Elizabeth reported that she was "drawn" and held spellbound by Swedenborg's revelations.[6]

As early as February 1852 she had heard about "rapping spirits" and was eager to know more.[7] By April, she had heard stories about spirit sessions in

America from Hiram Powers and from the American abolitionist George Thompson, who was visiting Florence—reports about spirits moving tables and chairs and playing on guitars.[8] In July of that year, as we know, she visited Fanny Haworth to meet and observe a man who reported visions that he could see in a large crystal ball. In December, she told Arabella about Robert Lytton's fascination with the "rapping spirits" and his account of his uncle Sir Henry Bulwer-Lytton's experiences at spirit sessions in America. Another American, James Jackson Jarves, an art collector recently settled in Florence, gave her an abundance of news about spirit happenings in America, which he received in weekly letters from his mother. She and Robert also spent a curious evening in Florence when a Mrs. Bionti invited the Brownings, Robert Lytton, and Hiram Powers to a demonstration of clairvoyance, when her daughter was put under a spell of "animal magnetism" by a Bolognese savant. The young woman then answered questions while in her hypnotic state. Unfortunately, to the disappointment of the assembled guests, forty-nine out of fifty answers were "as wrong as possible." Robert denounced it all as a "humbug." But as they sat in a circle, Elizabeth began to drift into a hypnotic state herself, so that afterward the Bolognese hypnotist asked her to be a subject. She hastily refused. Robert thought it was only one of her fainting fits.[9]

Elizabeth continued to write to various correspondents about her attraction to the new manifestations of supernatural activity, and from friends in Florence and elsewhere she received reports that encouraged her belief. Hiram Powers's American friend Mr. Coale offered his testimony about table moving—a table that was "wrenched" from his and his brother's restraining hands and another table that glided around the room like a skater, in S-shaped curves.[10] William Story wrote from Rome about table lifting and spirit writing. Seymour Kirkup told a story of a medium who called up a man from the dead to get his secret formula, "a mode of preserving anatomical preparations by petrification."[11] Longfellow's brother-in-law, Thomas Appleton, told Elizabeth of a woman friend's attendance at a séance at Lamartine's house in Paris where the spirit of Henry Clay, the Kentucky statesman, was summoned. Apparently Clay had learned French in the spirit world, for he told the group, "J'aime Lamartine."[12] Newspapers reported that Louis Napoleon of France, the queen of Holland, and the czar of Russia all consulted spirits. Even some of the Barrett brothers—Alfred, Sette, and Occy, plus a friend—met for a table-moving session, and when they succeeded, they had to run in pursuit of it.[13]

Still, nothing worked when Elizabeth and her indulgent husband tried spirit experiments. On one occasion, the Brownings, the Storys, and Frederick Tennyson had no luck at table turning even though they waited for twenty minutes with their fingers carefully poised on the tabletop. Robert was blamed for keeping off the spirits because he had laughed and joked, "playing Mephistopheles," during the solemn silence of the others.[14]

More details are available about a confused and disappointing séance the Brownings held at Casa Guidi in November 1853, which Elizabeth described in a long letter to Arabella.[15] She had prevailed upon Robert to allow her to invite friends for a spiritualistic "circle" presided over by Mrs. Shaw, an American medium. On the appointed evening, the Brownings, the Storys, Robert Lytton, Hiram Powers, Mr. and Mrs. Shaw, and a Miss Silvestre, a thirteen-year-old, gathered around a small table with their hands alert for table moving. After fifteen minutes of silent tension, the table began to turn slowly round and round, indicating a spiritual presence. When Mrs. Shaw asked if any friends were there, the table tilted "Yes" and, following the alphabet, spelled out "Robert." Since there were two Roberts in the group, Robert Browning, who had been standing aside, was called to the table, and a "yes" tilt identified him as the friend. When he requested the spirit's name, "Eliza Flower" was spelled out. Robert then asked for verification of the identity of the spirit: it was to spell out her sister Sarah's second name.[16] No movement of the table. But after prodding questions by Mrs. Shaw, the reluctant spirit agreed to have Mrs. Shaw, as medium, write out the word. When Mrs. Shaw held a pencil to the paper, her hand moved compulsively, writing one word, then another below it. Robert, reading, pronounced it to be the wrong name and proceeded to "upbraid the spirit as being untrue, & not giving the promised proof of identity." When the perplexed medium asked if the spirit would communicate on another day, Wednesday was named.

After the Shaws and others left, Elizabeth and the Storys wanted to try again, since they had attracted a spirit. They sat around the table with Robert, while Lytton waited across the room with pencil at the ready to take any messages. They assumed a respectful demeanor, waited, hands on table, then asked if "a communication" could be received. "Table tilted violently . . . never tilted so violently before." Is it to me? asked each person. The table tilted toward Robert. He asked, "Dear Eliza Flower, give me proof of your identity. Will you give it?" The table tilted "Yes." By the tilting? "No." By writing? "Yes." "May Mr. Story write?" "No." "May my wife write?" "Yes." Elizabeth took paper and pencil. Nothing happened. After some frustrated consultation, they tried the alphabet. As Lytton, sitting across the room, recorded the letters, the tilting table spelled out "be earn." Puzzlement. Finally, they guessed, "Do you mean, *Be earnest?*" Table tilted violently. "Hereupon we ended the séance," Elizabeth reported. She thought the spirit was urging Robert to be earnest about the subject and the occasion.

The next day Robert scrutinized the paper Mrs. Shaw had scribbled on and, as Elizabeth said, "became all but convinced that the word he had asked for (that second name) was written really though imperfectly. I myself have no doubt of it. The medium was not equal to the demand made." She surmised that the spirit was having difficulty in the same way that the questioning group exhibited "obtuseness of instrumentality."

On the appointed Wednesday, most of the guests assembled once more. They agreed that the table should tilt toward the person with whom the spirit wished to communicate. The table, taking "much longer before it moved," chose Robert Lytton. This was followed by some spirit writing to determine who the spirit was, and the result looked like "Emily L." Was it Emily Lytton?" "*Yes*." Could Mrs. Shaw be the medium employed? "*Yes*." Might they use the alphabet? "*Yes*." The first letter was F, then L, then "Flower" was spelled out. Surprise and confusion. Elizabeth thought one spirit had pushed itself in front of the other. Robert Browning lost his temper, Elizabeth reported, "reproaching false spirits, & I inveighing against every person present who instead of trying these experiments with humility & reverence, played at sharp-shooting with the invisible world." There was much disjointed talk, with Elizabeth asserting her belief in the presence of the spirits and Robert exhibiting his skepticism, although he could not account for the table tilting. They reexamined the paper and agreed that the writing was so indistinct that it could be interpreted as any word one wanted. They tried getting some new responses by raps, but when everyone removed hands from the table, nothing happened. Mrs. Shaw apologized, saying she was an imperfect medium tonight, perhaps because she had been "in a frivolous & worldly state of mind all day." Elizabeth did not agree. She felt that if everyone had been in "a state of unity with ourselves" about communicating with the spirit world, instead of "objecting to everybody, and aspiring in different directions," the séance would have been successful.

Most of the people closest to Elizabeth's heart were skeptical or downright negative about belief in spiritualism—Arabella, Henrietta, George, John Kenyon, Sarianna, Mrs. Jameson, and Mary Russell Mitford. Her letters to them are filled with arguments that she presented while trying to change their minds or to counter their objections. However, Arabella's piety did not allow her to believe in anything unsanctioned by her Independent Chapel, and Henrietta, with her High Church leanings, thought spiritualism might be the work of the Devil. Yet all of Elizabeth's Florentine friends and the "more cultivated" of their American visitors were on her side.[17] She was distressed that Robert was still a "denier." He said his mind was open, "ready to believe what he shall see & hear himself."[18]

Yet Robert Browning was an uxorious husband. He loved his wife so deeply that he would never interfere in any way with what she wished to do, so long as her health was not affected. He always acceded to her wishes to join their friends at table-turning experiments or at séances with a medium presiding, but he maintained a deep disapproval of her turn of mind in this direction. He was angry that she, as an intelligent woman, could believe that the spirits of the dead, benevolent though they might be in wishing to communicate with their still-living loved ones, would carry out such a limited and peculiar form of communication as rapping on tables, moving furniture about, playing accordions, or appearing as hands to carry lights around the room. He thought that the self-appointed mediums were engaged in parlor trickery and preying upon the bereaved and gullible. "What's to be said," he asked in an exasperated moment, "for a woman . . . who believes in Louis Napoleon and Rapping Spirits?" Elizabeth stood her ground. "Why, that she's open to conviction still."[19]

   ⅎ ⅎ ⅎ

On November 15, 1853, the Brownings set out for their long-postponed visit to Rome. Penini had begged for Ferdinando to go along, so the family had in their entourage during their winter stay a cook who was also a general factotum. The trip to Rome took seven days by *vetturino*, with Peni frequently on top of the coupé with Ferdinando, pretending to be coachman, and with stops on the way at comfortable inns. They stayed in the old Etruscan city of Perugia and were able to view the great works by Perugino and Pinturicchio in the Priors' Palace. A greater enjoyment was the time they spent in Assisi seeing the "triple church," as Elizabeth called it, the Basilica di San Francesco, which displayed Giotto's magnificent frescoes of the life of St. Francis and scenes from the Nativity. In addition, there were frescoes of the last days of Jesus by Pietro Lorenzetti, the most brilliant of Giotto's followers. Two days later they enjoyed an outdoor spectacle at the falls of Terni that tumbled down over giant rock formations.

In Rome, William Story had arranged for an apartment for them in the foreign quarter near the Piazza di Espagna, to which English travelers gravitated. The building was a large structure at 43 Bocca di Leone, with a plaque of Queen Victoria on its corner. Their fourth-floor apartment (quite a climb for Elizabeth) was comfortable but snug, having only three bedrooms (of those, Wilson and Pen slept in one, Ferdinando in another), but with two dressing rooms, plus a dining room and kitchen. Below them was an apartment occupied by someone who was to become a close and respected friend,

William Page, the painter known as the American Titian, with his wife and two children.

A crisis awaited them on their arrival in Rome. They learned that the Storys' youngest child, Joe, age six, was ill. When the Brownings visited them the next day, they discovered that the boy had a serious case of gastric fever (probably typhoid) and was at times in convulsions. William had consulted a homeopathic physician for the child, but Robert now insisted on calling in a real medical doctor. Dr. Pantaleoni found that Joe was too far gone for treatment to save, and the poor child died. The Brownings did what they could to comfort their friends in their shock and sorrow. They had already sent Edith Story, age nine, back to their apartment with Wilson, but when Edith fell ill, Elizabeth was alarmed and sent Penini with Wilson over to stay with Isa Blagden. "I wished myself at the end of the world with Robert and Penini twenty times a day," she told Mrs. Jameson.[20] After Dr. Pantaleoni treated Edith for gastric fever, she was transferred to the Pages' apartment for care, and Penini and Wilson came home.

Robert took care of the funeral arrangements for Joe and for his burial chose a spot in the Protestant cemetery near Shelley's grave. Emelyn Story had woven a garland of violets and white roses for her child's head in preparing him for the casket. Elizabeth was concerned about the Storys because they were Emersonian Unitarians and were thus deprived of the ministrations of a truly Christian church. But the Storys maintained a Unitarian optimism, sure of their child's happiness in the afterlife. Edith had not been able to be moved from the Pages' apartment. Her gastric fever had now turned to Roman fever (probably malaria, though Elizabeth said Roman fever was "not dangerous to life . . . simple fever & ague"). She was a long time in recovering. In April, when the Storys decided to leave Rome for Naples, Edith had a relapse when they had traveled only as far as Velletri. Robert received a panic-stricken letter from Story. Edith had fallen ill with "congestion on the brain & heart & liver" and was frequently losing consciousness. He called for Robert to come "and be with them at the end." Robert left in haste, taking Mrs. Page with him, to rejoin his distraught friend but was relieved to find "things had taken a favourable turn." He stayed up all night with them watching over Edith, who seemed to be completely out of danger. He left in the morning confident that all was well.[21] It was an illuminating example of how Browning was always ready to serve a friend and of how reassured a troubled friend could feel in his presence.

Despite these distresses, the Brownings settled in for the winter months, which gave them, at first, balmy days but turned disappointingly cold in January, keeping Elizabeth indoors. They soon fell into a social routine of the same kind they had followed in Paris; that is, Robert spent many evenings with friends, old and new, while Elizabeth ventured out when the wind and temperature allowed. Besides social life, Rome had many attractions of its own: a vigorous creativity among its artists; great repositories of Italian Renaissance art in its museums and churches; the Vatican complex with its unique galleries and chapels; and the architectural glories and ruins from the ancient Roman past.

Among the first visitors to call upon the Brownings were William Makepeace Thackeray and his two daughters, Anne and Minny, ages sixteen and thirteen. Elizabeth, unresponsive at first, thought Thackeray seemed addicted to the social whirl in Rome, but she changed her mind when she discovered the affectionate nature that he usually hid. "He half won my heart," she wrote to Julia Martin, when he paid kind attentions to Penini, drew pictures for him, and invited him to breakfast.[22] He won the other half when he sat on the bed of the convalescing Edith Story and read to her from his manuscript of *The Rose and the Ring*. Hans Christian Andersen, in his visits to the Storys at the Palazzo Barbarini, came especially to cheer up Edith, too. Some years later, at a children's party that the Storys arranged for her, he read them the story of "The Ugly Duckling." Browning, who was also on hand, suddenly rose to recite "The Pied Piper," which led to a parade of children marching through the Palazzo Barbarini apartment, following William Story playing on the flute.[23]

Thackeray and Browning soon became good companions, attending social events together. Both of the Brownings came to love the Thackeray girls. Elizabeth described them as "frank, intelligent, and affectionate."[24] She soon felt very motherly toward Anne. Two years later Anne recorded in her journal, "I think Mrs. Browning the greatest woman I ever knew in my life." Robert she set down as having "the best and kindest heart in the world."[25] A close association with Robert developed over the years and lasted until the end of his life.

Another early caller who became a close friend to Elizabeth was the multitalented Fanny Kemble, poet, playwright, and outstanding actress on both the American and English stages. Elizabeth was immediately captivated by Fanny: "with such eyes, such a voice!—She has enchanted me."[26] Robert thought her too theatrical in manner, and he may have been a trifle offended that she knew nothing of his poems. After this first meeting, she regularly came to weekly tea and often spent an evening with Elizabeth by the fireside when Robert was out.

When the weather was pleasant, Robert took Elizabeth to see the Colosseum, St. Peter's, and the Vatican chapels. Further, since it was the custom in

Rome as in Florence for visitors to regard artists' studios as open to the public, they not only stopped by William Story's studio but also paid a call on John Gibson, the celebrated English sculptor who had created *Queen Victoria with Justice and Clemency* for the Houses of Parliament. On display in the studio was Gibson's unusual "tinted" Venus, in which the artist had given the marble a flesh-coloring. Elizabeth judged it not "decent"—Venus "has come out of her cloud of the ideal. . . . You have rather a grisette than a goddess."[27] She preferred the more classical works in the studio of the American sculptor Thomas Crawford.

In stopping by the studio of their neighbor William Page, they were struck by his portrait of a commanding figure whom Robert had met in London in 1845, Charlotte Cushman, the American actress, now in Rome. Page later painted a portrait of Robert Browning, which he then presented as a gift to Elizabeth. She thought it the best likeness of him that had ever been done, but Page's experiments with undertoning later caused the picture to darken so much that Robert's features were extinguished.

The Brownings found the social scene in the Anglo-American colony in Rome as busy as the literary interworkings in London. They had Christmas dinner with the Storys. Elizabeth took Penini to a children's Christmas party given by Fanny Kemble and her sister Adelaide (Mrs. Sartoris). Fanny danced around the Christmas tree with Penini. Robert attended a dinner given by the Duke of Northumberland, one of the Catholic peers of England, at which there were many cardinals and Roman princes, all of whom outranked the Duke of Wellington (the victorious duke's son) in taking ladies in to dinner. At a musical evening given by the Kemble sisters, the Brownings met John Gibson Lockhart, the biographer of Walter Scott and editor of the *Quarterly Review,* now wintering in Rome. Lockhart, a white-haired, white-browed, pale-skinned "snow-man," in Elizabeth's phrase,[28] enjoyed Robert's company on frequent occasions. He approved of Browning especially because he was "not at all like a damned literary man."[29] The Brownings had invitations for every evening, although Elizabeth could not accept when the weather grew chill. She made Robert go to "represent" her.[30]

They were intrigued by the bohemian vivacity of a group Elizabeth called "emancipated women" who lived in units of a nearby apartment building. Harriet Hosmer, a refreshing twenty-two-year-old American sculptor who was working under Gibson, became "a great pet of mine and of Robert's," Elizabeth wrote to Mary Russell Mitford. Harriet braved the streets and cafés of Rome alone in a forthright American way and dedicated all her daylight hours to her art. Another occupant was Matilda Hayes, the translator of George Sand, who "dresses like a man down to the waist," with collar, neckcloth, and jacket. She had joined with Charlotte Cushman in a "female marriage," as Elizabeth deemed it. They dressed alike and vowed to live all their lives together in a celibate union.[31] Also in that apartment building was the Brownings' dear friend Isa Blagden, who doted on Penini and invited him and Wilson to dinner twice a week.

As the weather grew milder, Robert could take Elizabeth to outdoor sites and to galleries and churches that had been too cold for her in January. She responded with intense historical enthusiasm to the forum, but she also enjoyed the natural settings of these ancient ruins with the cloudless blue sky above them and the views of hills with umbrella pines in silhouette. She was surprised at the contrast to Florence in the many "leaping fountains and grandiose piazzas."[32] They heard a Miserere in the Sistine Chapel, "very overcoming in its ejaculating pathos," while contemplating Michaelangelo's fearsome fresco of the Last Judgment.[33]

As spring softened the air, they joined friends on picnics and excursions to the environs of Rome. In April they went often with the Kemble sisters, Lockhart, and others to the Campagna and "dined in bosky valleys, and pinewood forests."[34] On one such occasion, the group went for a walk to some nearby place of interest, but since Elizabeth was too frail to accompany them, Robert stayed behind with her. Fanny Kemble, who had often observed Robert's soliticitous care of Elizabeth, said to him, "You are the only man I ever knew who behaved like a Christian to his wife."[35] (Fanny's life in the theater and her unsatisfactory marriage to the American plantation owner Pierce Butler had led her to think little of married men.) Sometimes, Frederick Leighton, a young English painter trained in Italy and Germany, joined the group. In Rome he was at work on his first important painting, *Cimabue's Celebrated Madonna Is Carried in Procession through the Streets of Florence*. The Brownings developed a lifelong friendship with the young painter.

On another picnic with the Kembles, they had a distinguished company: LeComte di Gozze, the Austrian chargé d'affaires; M. Ampère of the French Institute; Mr. Lyons, the British diplomatic representative to the Papal States; and the selfless Dr. Pantaleoni, who had been a member of Mazzini's Legislative Assembly during the revolutionary days. The conversation was so brilliant that it seemed out of place in a bucolic setting, but as Elizabeth remarked, "it harmonized entirely with the mayonnaise & champagne."[36]

There were also excursions to Hadrian's villa, to Tivoli, and to Ostia by the sea. Robert went on fourteen of these springtime outings. Elizabeth joined him for five or six. On the last one, in the Campagna, they encountered the pope, taking exercise on the road as he walked ahead of the papal coach. When he brushed against their carriage, Penini was greatly impressed, as he always was by dignitaries of the world, especially those who were in their uniforms or regalia.

It is likely that at this time, or shortly afterward in Florence, Browning composed "Two in the Campagna," another variation on the subject of the eternal moment, or the "good minute," as he calls it in this poem. It is a dramatic monologue that seems like a soliloquy, for although the speaker addresses his beloved, he is really meditating on his inability to retain the moment of communion in spite of their being together in the Campagna on a serene day in May:

> No. I yearn upward, touch you close,
>   Then stand away. I kiss your cheek,
> Catch your soul's warmth,—I pluck the rose
>   And love it more than tongue can speak—
> Then the good minute goes. (46–50)

They are like the incomplete lovers about whom Browning warned in "By the Fire-Side": "Oh, the little more, and how much it is! / And the little less, and what worlds away!" (191–92). In this poem, the romantic ideal is overshadowed by an awareness of reality that all human beings must understand, even those most intensely in love, and that is that human hearts beat alone. The speaker in "Two in the Campagna" concludes:

> Already how am I so far
>   Out of that minute? . . .
> Just when I seemed about to learn!
>   Where is the thread now? Off again!
> The old trick! Only I discern—
>   Infinite passion, and the pain
> Of finite hearts that yearn. (51–52; 56–60)

Although some commentators have discerned something else in the poem—that Browning was reflecting a disruption in the "perfect love" of Robert and Elizabeth because of their disagreements over spiritualism—one must be careful reading personal revelations into the poems of a mono-dramatic poet like Browning, who presents such a lengthy parade of diverse speakers who reflect an immense variety of values and attitudes.[37]

These diversions in Rome did not turn Elizabeth from her obsession with spiritualism. Soon after they had arrived, she persuaded Robert that they should hold a séance for Mr. Page, who had exhibited an interest in spirit activities. Again Mrs. Shaw, who was now in Rome, was available as a medium. During the session, the group spun a little table around until they were "breathless." Somebody then called, "If spirits are present let the table stop." It did. Elizabeth, who had never been present when the spinning phenomenon took place, was completely convinced that spirits had caused it. Robert had his usual response: "That's perfect humbug, of course."[38]

Wilson had been an outsider to the practice of trying to call up spirits, but she became encouraged by the people at Isa Blagden's apartment to try spirit writing with Elizabeth one day in January 1854. Since Elizabeth had always failed at involuntary writing, she was surprised to find that Wilson's pencil moved automatically and wrote messages from her mother and continued to do so at later trials over several days. Inspired by these astonishing results, Elizabeth asked her at another sitting to request that another spirit identify itself, only to find that the communication came from her own mother. The pencil wrote "Mary" and, after a request for a second name, "Barrett." The question was then put, "What relation?" (since there had been more than one Mary Barrett among the numerous Barrett relatives). The answer came back "Mama." A thrill ran through Elizabeth that almost overcame her, but at this point the session was interrupted.[39]

The next day, when they tried again to communicate, Wilson received a spirit message urging Elizabeth herself to try. When she asked, "Who wants me to write?"—"Then came a beloved name." In her letter describing all this to George, Elizabeth does not reveal the name, but it is evident that she felt herself in communication with Bro, whose name was so sacred to her that she had never spoken it since his death and could not write it now. She took the pencil, poised to write, but nothing came forth. She gripped the pencil for five minutes and then sensed a spiral motion in it and a numbness in her fingers, but no letter or even a mark was produced. Again the session was interrupted.[40] Yet Elizabeth was convinced that communication with spirits of the deceased was possible and that she had momentarily been in touch with her mother and her brother Edward. What Robert thought about all this, we do not know, but he did not think, as Arabella did, that Wilson was engaged in any trickery.[41]

Elizabeth's experience with the spirit messages seemed to buoy her confidence that table turning was also a genuine manifestation of spiritual presence. In a letter to Fanny Haworth she offered a defense that would not have been forthcoming earlier: "As to the 'triviality' and 'vulgarity' of turning tables, I have been twice present during experiments. . . . I never was more deeply impressed . . . than by the quivering and heaving of that dead, dumb wood, and the human emotion and emphasis of expression thrown out, under my own hands and eyes, by it."[42]

Her belief in the presence of spirits was also bolstered by her reading of Swedenborg's accounts of visits to the spirit world and his talks with angels who acted as his guides, touring the different angelic communities where the spirits of the deceased dwelt together with other souls whose moral lives had been like their own. When she applied this reading to her speculations about the supposed behavior of spirits that caused messages to be written in a spirit-writing session or that had been summoned by a medium in a séance, she reasoned in this way: the spirits with whom she and others had been communicating were probably those departed souls who lived in the spirit world but had not yet entered the "interior Heavens" and become part of the "angelic societies."[43]

Even Penini, now almost five years old, was becoming affected by all the spiritualistic discussion in the household. One of the Brownings' friends had presented him with a children's storybook published by the Church of the New Jerusalem, a newly developed Christian religious sect based upon Swedenborgian ideas.[44] He also began to receive a Swedenborgian magazine for children with stories about heaven and the angels. Five-year-old Peni, who had already been given a quite thorough religious upbringing, very much enjoyed these stories about God and the angels. One day, a few months after Elizabeth's experiences with spirit messages, she, Wilson, and some guests were trying again with involuntary writing. Peni was bored because the adults, in their concentration, with pencils poised, were waiting a long time for some movement to take place, and not paying attention to him. He jumped on the table and called out to the "dear little spillet" to write something: "Do please Penini and write *Napoleon*," at which point someone's pencil wrote "*Napoleon*." "Sant you, dear little spillet! If you're a dood beautiful angel, I love you velly much."[45]

In the spring of 1854, when Arabella Barrett wished to raise money at a bazaar to aid the Refuge for Destitute Girls, which she had been instrumental in establishing, she asked Elizabeth and Robert to contribute poems that could be printed in a pamphlet and sold for that purpose. Robert sent "The Twins," which he later included in his forthcoming book. The poem re-creates a fable based on an extract from Martin Luther's *Table-Talk* that develops the theme, "Give and it shall be given to you." The twins are Date and Dabitur, who must always be kept together. Browning's parable, very appropriate for the occasion, is presented with his usual compactness. Elizabeth contributed her "A Plea for the Ragged Schools of London."

During this same season, Bryan Procter solicited poems from the Brownings for *The Keepsake*, a gift annual edited by Margaret Power. Robert sent "Ben Karshook's Wisdom," dated Rome, April 27, 1854. Sometime earlier,

Elizabeth had labeled the nonbelievers in spiritualism "the Sadducees of the age."[46] This phrase may have lurked in Robert's mind when he composed "Ben Karshook's Wisdom," in which a Jewish teacher of an early historical period sharply rebukes one of his pupils, a young Sadducee, who had asked, "Is it so certain we / Have, as they tell us, souls?" Karshook replies, "Certain a soul have I— / We may have none." In later years, Browning referred to the poem as a set of "snarling verses."[47] He perhaps thought the poem too harsh and too trivial for the expression of his theme about the immortality of the soul. He did not include it in *Men and Women*, nor in any collected edition of his work. Elizabeth contributed "My Kate" and "Amy's Cruelty" to *The Keepsake*.

The winter in Rome accomplished its purpose for the Brownings. Elizabeth escaped the cold of Paris and the chill of Florence, and despite the dip in Roman temperature in January, she was able to report to Mrs. Ogilvy at the end of the month, "I have passed a winter like a summer."[48]

But they did not like Rome. The atmosphere of the Papal States, with its restrictions on the press and on book publishing, created an unease. They were not even allowed to bring their King James (Protestant) Bibles within the boundaries. Nor did they approve of the dominance of the higher clergy in the political and social hierarchy. In addition, it was expensive. Living expenses were £3 a week, compared with £2 in Florence. Further, Rome was not as socially comfortable for Elizabeth as Paris or London. Robert was frequently out in the evening, and during the spring was often away on daytime excursions into the country. The closeness that they had maintained in the previous year was impossible in the uprooted life they led from November 1853 through May 1854.

But above all, the death of Joe Story and the illness of Edith had cast a pall over their entire stay in the imperial city and created a constant worry about the health of their child. They feared the "pestilential air" of Rome, and those fears seemed justified in late April when Penini fell ill with fever and diarrhea. On May 24, when they left the city to travel back to Florence by vettura, he was still pale and languid. Robert, writing to Forster after their return, expressed their deep disappointment with Rome, except for the time spent with friends old and new. "The place is ill-starred, under a curse seemingly, and I would not live there for the Vatican with the Pope out of it."[49]

෨ ෨ ෨

Contented to be back in Casa Guidi, no longer "hankering after Rome," as he had been doing since the early 1850s, Browning wrote to W. W. Story, "I am trying to make up for wasted time in Rome and setting my poetical house in order."[50] For the rest of the year, Robert and Elizabeth worked diligently at their poems, not seeing many visitors at all. She had seen only a few of his poems. As she explained, "We neither of us show our work to one another till it is finished," but what she had read was "as fine as anything he has done."[51] She was also giving close scrutiny to these poems and offering her tactful criticism as she had done with *Dramatic Romances and Lyrics*. They did not even go to Bagni di Lucca in the hottest summer months. Elizabeth, whose bodily thermostat did not allow her to bear heat easily, worked at Casa Guidi *en déshabillé*—no gown, no stays, only a short petticoat and a dimity jacket over her underclothes.

She oversaw Penini's lessons every day now. She had been eager to teach him to read early, but Robert had forbade it until he was four. Since he was an alert, intelligent child, he learned to read English quickly and was now, at five, reading his own simple children's books, about twenty pages a day. She began teaching him to read Italian, too, since he was fluent in both languages. She wanted to teach him some Latin verbs, but Robert insisted that they be postponed. Peni also was eager to learn the piano, and although Robert was careful not to push the child too fast, he could read and write music at age six, and even write a simple tune from Robert's dictation and then play it on the piano.

The Brownings had brought up Peni to be a religiously minded child. He was taught early to pray and call down blessings on Papa, Mama, Lily, Flush, and whoever else became meaningful in his life. In his conversation, he talked about God's presence and his impact on their daily lives. He was taught to love "the gentle Jesus" who watched over him and kept him from harm. He soon knew a number of Bible stories and was much taken with the story of "Madam and Eve," but he was horrified by the one about Abraham and the threatened death of Isaac. Nor did he approve of the ram being burnt in the sacrifice. Elizabeth still did not allow him to know about Hell, or the damnation of Judas; she taught him only that bad people could not join the gentle Jesus in the spirit world. Elizabeth was careful to shield him from knowledge of the differences of belief among the Christian sects. She and Robert did not object to Wilson's taking him to visit the Catholic churches or the duomo and watch their ceremonies. He dipped his fingers in holy water, crossed himself, spoke in hushed tones, and prayed. They did not bring him along to their own chapel services; they knew that he should not be subjected to the long, tiresome sermons of their minister, Mr. Hanna.

The first death that touched Peni's life was in Rome when the Storys lost their son Joe. In response to his inquiries, he was taught that Joe went to live with God and the gentle Jesus and the angels. He added Joe to his nightly prayers. All this prepared him for a deeper grief when Flush died in June 1854. Penini cried for hours but was finally comforted by the idea that Flush had gone to join Joe Story. Flush was buried with ceremony in the courtyard of Casa Guidi.

One point of contention in the Brownings' child-rearing was a product of Elizabeth's deep maternal desire to have a girl-child, and when her several miscarriages denied her that wish, she turned some of her need toward Pen. For toys, she tried to interest him in a doll, but he preferred soldiers, drums, and guns. Very early, she dressed him in frocks or in trousers down to his knees and long white gaiters. For outside headgear he had a white felt hat with a decorative feather and white satin ribbons trailing among his long curls. People stopped and stared at him in the street, Wilson reported. "He is much admired" was Elizabeth's interpretation.[52] Penini was often mistaken for a girl, and he resented it. So did Robert. At age six, he still was dressed fantastically—in "very short petticoats" with "short embroidered trowsers" underneath, "deep emboidered collars," and a "low-crowned black-velvet hat" with a white feather. The effect, in Elizabeth's view, was "very picturesque."[53] Although Robert left the choice of attire to his wife, they had strong disagreement, as time went on, over her insistence that Pen's long golden curls should remain until he was twelve. To Mrs. Ogilvy she wrote, "You have a relay of babies. I have but one, & must keep him as long as I can."[54]

The Brownings' differences of opinion over the Crimean War (September 1854 to February 1856) were minimal, for England and France were allies against Russia's attempt to take over Turkish territory in the Mediterranean and Black Sea area. During the war both Brownings were agitated and became especially outraged over Britain's mishaps and mismanagement in the long siege of Sebastopol. Yet while Robert maintained patriotic support for Britain throughout it all, he was explosively angry at the government leaders for allowing Britain to be "disgraced in the face of Europe."[55] Elizabeth took a more extreme position in her criticism, seeing the reverses of the Crimean War as a fitting humiliation for the English nation in its arrogance about its moral and political superiority while the whole corrupt political and military system cried out for reform. "I begin to think," she wrote to Julia Martin, "that nothing will do for England but a good revolution, and a 'besom of destruction' used dauntlessly."[56]

As the summer of 1855 approached, Robert began dictating his poems to a friend who prepared the fair copy for the printer. Able to read through them at last, Elizabeth went over the manuscript daily each afternoon. "Robert's poems are magnificent," she affirmed for Henrietta, "and will raise him higher than he stands."[57] By May 15, he had six thousand lines in final form and the rest completed but not yet copied. Over the months, enough poems had accumulated for two volumes. Elizabeth herself had over six thousand lines of her "poem-novel," which she soon began to call *Aurora Leigh* after its heroine.

The Browning finances worked out well enough that they were able to leave Florence in June for Paris and finally London, to see Robert's poems through the press. Watching their pennies, Elizabeth was willing to risk a sea voyage to Marseilles, where they had an appointment to meet with her brother Alfred, her junior by fourteen years. This was the first time that any of her brothers had arranged to see her outside of London. Alfred was preparing for marriage to his cousin Lizzie Barrett in Paris in August, after which he and his bride expected banishment from the Barrett home, followed by disinheritance. Nothing had softened Mr. Barrett as he aged, not even a serious carriage accident in the autumn that had made him lame for life.

Although Elizabeth's associations with Alfred had not been close, her family affections ran deep. It was emotionally satisfying for her to be reunited with him after almost nine years. Robert was his usual cordial self, and Penini immediately gravitated to Alfred, who took him around Marseilles buying him toys, flowers, and bonbons. He was even allowed to share a glass of the champagne that Alfred had brought to his parents—which made him dizzy. Afterward he told Elizabeth that he liked Alfred "almost as much as you and papa."[58]

The Brownings were traveling with twelve boxes of luggage, but only ten arrived in Marseilles. Elizabeth was grieved that one contained all the new finery she had bought to show off Penini. Later, she discovered that the other contained her manuscript of *Aurora Leigh*. They left for Paris, with Alfred promising to search for the missing boxes.

They had brought Ferdinando and Wilson along on the journey. The servants had been married on June 12 in a Church of England ceremony in the British Embassy in Florence, but since Ferdinando was a Catholic, and since only Catholic marriages were legally recognized for Italian citizens, they were planning to be married by a Catholic priest in Paris, where mixed marriages could be arranged more easily. But even in Paris nothing was easy with the Church authorities, who demanded that Wilson pledge to bring up any future children in the Catholic faith. She pondered this but balked on the grounds that children should be free to choose their own religion. After Robert negotiated with the archevêque, he was able to obtain an agreement "by favor" that Wilson could accept: that if future children chose to turn Catholic, the mother would not hinder them.[59]

Elizabeth had conflicting feelings about the marriage. She and Robert wished to keep the wedded couple in their employ, but she recognized that the time would come when they would leave, as children arrived and the servants' ambitions changed. Penini would be devastated by the loss of his surrogate mother, "Lily," and of his Italian hero and mentor, Ferdinando. Yet Elizabeth realized in the end that there was

> no use looking forward to what may *not* happen—Also, there's no virtue in being utterly selfish, & thinking of everything but of poor dear Wilson herself, who should not, because she has been perfect to one's child & good & kind in every way, be shut out on that account from her own prospects of domestic happiness. Happy I believe she will *be*. A better man, more upright & of a more tender nature, it would be difficult to find, than Ferdinando is. Robert, so opposed in general to mixed marriages, has not a word to say against this—has not a fear for Wilson.[60]

The lost boxes turned up in the Marseilles customhouse, and Alfred sent them on to Paris. The six thousand lines of *Aurora Leigh* did not have to be recopied. Meanwhile, the Brownings enjoyed the company of Mr. Browning and Sarianna and refreshed their friendship with Thackeray and his daughters, the Corkrans, Milsand, Mrs. Jameson, and others. They visited the charming Rosa Bonheur at her studio and admired her paintings. At Madame Mohl's they met briefly Victor Cousin, the philosopher and educator, and Prosper Mérimée, the author of *Carmen* and *Colomba*. It was a short stay. Robert was eager to put his manuscript into the hands of the printer in London.

Troubles in London

The Brownings along with Sarianna reached London on July 12, 1855, which brought little joy to Elizabeth. "There's always a weight on my heart when I arrive," she told Henrietta.[1] Each successive visit sent her into a deeper depression, which began even as they made their first plans. "I dread England," she had confessed to Arabella, "& the moral & atmospheric cold of it."[2] This time she feared that Henrietta would be unable to travel to London because she was in the last months of her latest pregnancy, and she was apprehensive that the pleasure of seeing Arabella, the Barrett brothers, and the servants could not offset the sense of rejection and guilt that Mr. Barrett's invisible presence at Wimpole Street always gave her. Moreover, his troublesome lameness kept him at home much of the time, a situation that would prevent Penini from making his frequent visits to see Arabella and Minny and would reduce the number of times that Elizabeth herself could call.

All this worry and concern preliminary to their travel to London was exacerbated when Henrietta told Elizabeth that she considered making an unannounced visit to Wimpole Street and thus forcing a meeting with her father in order to have him see her son. Elizabeth warned against it and was relieved when Henrietta wrote a letter to him instead. Mr. Barrett's reply was a refusal, and he added that he had given directions to the household that she was not to be admitted if she called. As for Elizabeth's own situation, she had lost any hope of a reconciliation. "I begin to despair—I begin to hate to write about it—I never could have thought such obstinacy possible—such & so long! no! not even in *him*!"[3]

Robert was, no doubt, concerned by Elizabeth's depressed spirits but hoped that they would be lifted by time spent with their literary friends. Very early, they spent an evening with Ruskin. Later Robert called on him a second time, bringing the young painter Frederick Leighton to meet the great art critic and champion of J. M. W. Turner's work. The Brownings were next entertained at Forster's where they also saw Carlyle, who was "in great force, particularly in the damnatory clauses." The Procters twice offered their hospitality, and on one of those occasions, Robert and Elizabeth met with Alexander Kinglake whose book *Eothen*, a chronicle of his travels in the Balkans and the Middle East, Robert had admired in his youth. Also present was the Procters' daughter Adelaide, whose poetry attracted Elizabeth and whose sunny personality drew the praise, "that's a face worth a drove of beauties!" They reunited briefly with the Kemble sisters, who were just leaving London. They were invited to several places in the country but were forced to decline because of Robert's work with his galley proofs, which had begun to arrive. Elizabeth was especially sorry to miss visiting Bulwer-Lytton's estate, Knebworth.[4]

Robert was also able to arrange, through young Robert Lytton, attendance at a séance with the celebrated American medium D. D. Home, whom Elizabeth had longed to meet. Home was staying with Wilkie Rymer, a wealthy solicitor, in Ealing. The Rymers had lost their twelve-year-old son, Wat, and were eager to engage Home to try to communicate with him. Lytton somehow managed to persuade the Rymers to extend an invitation to the Brownings for the evening of July 23. There are three major accounts of the séance. The best and most detailed is Robert Browning's in a letter to Mrs. Kinney;[5] the briefest is Elizabeth's in a letter to Henrietta;[6] the most defensive is Home's written in a memoir[7] years after the event and after the publication of Browning's "Mr. Sludge, the Medium," a fierce satirical dramatic monologue directed obliquely at Home.

When the séance began, a small group of people were seated around a large table in a darkened room. As Browning described it, there "were some noises, a vibration of the table, then an up-tilting of it in various ways." These phenomena were interpreted as communications from Wat. At this point, Home reduced the number of people allowed at the table to ten, including the Brownings. Again the spirit of Wat came among them and touched Mr. and Mrs. Rymer. After additional raps and table tilting, the spirit announced, by means of the alphabet, that it would play the accordion and show its hand to Browning. A hand draped with white muslin emerged at the edge of the table and then another larger hand appeared and picked up a wreath of flowers from the table, carried it over to Elizabeth, and placed it on her head. (She had left Robert's side and gone over to sit by Home to receive it.) Then Elizabeth requested that the wreath be given to Robert. It was carried under the table to him. As this movement took place, he felt several pats on his knee and on his hands. Although he asked to grasp the hand and was told that he might do so, his request was never granted.

At this point, Home took an accordion and thrust it under the table, whence soon came some music, the tune of a well-known hymn. After that demonstration, a hand reached from under the table to seize a handbell from the tabletop and rang it while the larger hand appeared, opened and closed its fingers, and repeated this gesture around the table at places between the guests. Home stated that the hand which placed the wreath on Elizabeth's head was that of a deceased relative of hers, and attempts were made to identify the name by spelling out chosen letters of the alphabet. After many trials, the names spelled out seemed to be several—William, Frank, Charles, Henry, none of which were names of Elizabeth's deceased relatives. "Hereupon Mr. Home went into a trance, & began to address Mr. Rymer, in the character of his dead child—in a sort of whisper, at first, to represent a child's voice, but with Mr. Home's own inflexions, peculiarities, and characteristic expressions." After the voice produced some innocuous remarks about how good and "lovely" God is, Home in his own character stood up, raised his arms, and began to preach (like a dissenting minister, Elizabeth thought). He also said that five spirits had been present, including an old lady named Catherine. There was more table lifting and tilting, during which Home pointed out that the spirits held down the objects on the table to keep them from falling. But Browning remarked that a silver pen rolled on the table: could not the spirits hold that down? Whereupon one of the guests objected to Browning's question and the meeting broke up.

Robert's response to Home's presentation was disgust. "I think the whole performance most clumsy, and unworthy anybody really setting up for a 'medium.'" He thought Home was merely a cheap mountebank and an unpleasant one at that, with his affectations of being a child and his unmanly fawning on the Rymers and other members of the family, kissing them "abundantly." Yet Robert observed the courtesies due his hosts by not making his criticism known to the group.[8] On the other hand, Elizabeth felt "confirmed in all my opinions. To me it was wonderful and conclusive." Still, she did not think highly of the trance that Home affected or the "twaddle" of his preaching. About the spirit who was supposed to be a deceased relative, she "felt convinced in my own mind that *no spirit belonging to me* was present on the occasion."[9] Home himself commented that during the séance Browning declared that he saw nothing "like imposture." Further, he remarked that the Rymer family discerned that Browning was angry and attributed it to his envy that the spirit hand did not crown him with the flowery wreath rather than his wife.[10]

Robert wished to test Home further and tried to arrange another séance at the Rymers and to bring Lady Martin with him as an unbiased witness. Home declined, pleading illness, but shortly afterward called on the Brownings at Dorset Street, bringing Mrs. Rymer and her older son. Robert shook hands with the Rymers but refused to take Home's hand. Elizabeth, observing the tension, stood by "pale and agitated." She then took Home by both hands and told him how sorry she was, adding, "but I am not to blame." After they all sat down, Robert, rather boorishly, blurted out to Mrs. Rymer, "I beg to inform you that I was exceedingly dissatisfied with everything I saw at your house the other night" and wanted to know why his request for another séance was denied. Home interrupted to tell Browning that he should have revealed his dissatisfactions the other night, and an unpleasant interchange erupted. As the group was leaving in a restrained fluster, Robert ordered Home out, while Elizabeth once more took Home's hands, saying, "Dear Mr. Home, I am not to blame. Oh dear! Oh dear!"[11] According to what Browning told William Allingham in 1864, Browning's final words were, "If you are not out of that door in half a minute I'll fling you down the stairs."[12] In the following days, relations between Robert and Elizabeth were strained because of this unseemly show of temper, and spiritualism became "a *tabooed* subject" at Dorset Street. Elizabeth asked Henrietta and others not to mention the subject in their letters for Robert was "a good deal irritated by any discussion of it."[13] Robert's excessive anger at Home arose because, despite the obvious deceptions, Elizabeth's belief in spiritualism was not weakened but strengthened. Beyond this, he felt a personal jealousy: this charlatan had seduced the mind of his wife.

Fortunately, Robert's readiness to explode in a fit of temper about spiritualism did not last. Three weeks later the Brownings were planning to receive some friends in the evening, and Elizabeth prevailed on Robert to invite also Mr. Henry Spicer, the author of *Sights and Sounds*, a book about "spirit manifestations." Even so, she hoped that Spicer would not bring up the subject of spirits, except to her "in remote holes & corners & in low whispers."[14]

By mid-August, Elizabeth had visited Wimpole Street only three times and only when it was safe to do so. But one day Arabella failed to warn her that Mr. Barrett was still in the house; as a consequence, she "was in a continual state of alarm." The day before, Penini himself had unknowingly met the Mitaine in his lair. Elizabeth described it for Henrietta: "George was playing in the hall with him, & he was in fits of laughter. Papa came out of the dining-room & stood *looking* for two or three minutes. Then he called George & went back. 'Whose child is that, George?' 'Ba's child,' said George. 'And what is he doing here, pray?' Then without waiting for an answer he changed the subject. To hear of it thrilled me to the roots of my heart—and there's an end."[15] For Edward Barrett the momentary reawakening of the past must have been startling, for Penini probably resembled one of his own sons at that age. One can only speculate about what he felt. Elizabeth had her own interpretation: "The quietness about Penini proved simply an absolute state of indifference towards me & mine."[16]

Four days later, Mr. Barrett announced that the family would leave London for a holiday of ten weeks at the seaside, although he himself would remain in London. After a search for the best available house to rent, the decision was made to go to Eastbourne, a fashionable resort in East Sussex on the Channel coast. For a few days it looked as if Henrietta might be able to join Elizabeth and Arabella at Eastbourne, but Henrietta became too troubled by the last stages of her pregnancy. Plans also fell through for the Brownings to follow the Barretts to Eastbourne because Robert calculated that the money was lacking.

Elizabeth was distraught. "Everything has gone wrong ever since I touched English ground," she complained to Arabella, "and I shall remember it against England, . . which has grown *wholly* detestable to me, now that you are not here—the one lump of sugar in the cup!"[17] To make matters worse, the Brownings had learned in August that Wilson was pregnant and the baby due in October. At first Elizabeth was shocked and angry. There is very little detail about her response, but when she reported the situation to Henrietta, her first concerns seemed selfish: "It's a great inconvenience & greater vexation—but I am getting over it now."[18] One can discover the reasons for her reaction by looking at her comments on a similar situation in 1843 when Mary Russell Mitford's maid "K"[19] made it known that she was pregnant by the gardener, explaining that they had been secretly married for months. Elizabeth's feelings at that time were that K's situation was not blamable; human beings have been failing to govern their passions for centuries. Yet what she found unforgivable was the deception that K had engaged in—not making the marriage known, if indeed there had been a marriage at all. How could one trust such a servant in the future? As it turned out, Miss Mitford did not take Elizabeth's view and dismiss K but helped out in what way she could and kept both servants in her employ.[20]

Elizabeth's reaction to Wilson's news was probably the same as that she had expressed to Miss Mitford, but she suppressed her feelings and reflected on Wilson's long and loyal service: "Oh—so shocked & pained I have been through Wilson! But after the first, I turn & try to think chiefly of her many excellent qualities & of what she had done for me in affectionate attention and service. Human nature is so full of failures, at its best."[21] For her confinement, Wilson planned to go to her family's house in Nottinghamshire. After the birth, she would leave the child with a wet nurse, to be cared for by her sisters, and then rejoin the Brownings in Paris. Her situation was a bleak reflection on the rigidities of the class system in Victorian England. Although house servants were in the top tier of the working-class hierarchy, a maid, if she were to continue in her position, could not have a child of her own. She would have to marry a man who was a step up in the class structure before she could have a home in which to bring up children. In the meantime, Elizabeth had arranged for a young girl from Arabella's Refuge for Destitute Girls to be her personal maid and travel to Paris with her. This new servant, Harriet, was looking forward to the foreign adventure and to finding a place with another English family in Paris.

Even though events had mounted to spoil thoroughly Elizabeth's return to London, the Brownings became more socially active late in their stay. The evening before Arabella left, they entertained Frederick Tennyson and his wife (now visitors in London), John Forster, the aging W. J. Fox, and Adelaide Kemble Sartoris, recently returned from Paris. The Barrett brothers were also invited but stayed away, feeling obligated to spend the last evening with their father before they took their holiday.

In early September, Browning made preliminary arrangements with J. T. Fields of Ticknor and Fields, the leading Boston publisher, to have his two volumes of poems, now entitled *Men and Women,* published in the United States at the same time that Chapman and Hall issued them in England. Browning was to send a set of Chapman and Hall page proofs on a fast steam packet to America a month ahead of time in order to have an American edition in print long before the American publishing pirates would have received the English edition to copy from. Browning was to be paid £60, and Ticknor and Fields were to be declared his official American publisher. The same arrangement was decided upon for Elizabeth's as-yet-unfinished *Aurora Leigh.*[22]

On September 12, the Brownings celebrated their eighth wedding anniversary. Arabella sent them some grouse for Ferdinando to prepare. Forster dined with them, and Macready was to come but fell ill. The next day Robert went to call on Macready, who was under a doctor's care. He had begun a reconciliation with Macready in September of 1852 when he sent a letter of condolence at the time of his wife's death.[23] The friendship rekindled and was helped along by Forster. Robert was happy "to reknit affection with Macready." Four days after the anniversary, Forster invited the Brownings to one of his lavish dinners; this time Macready was there, meeting Elizabeth for the first time. Later in the month, Forster was again their host. Macready seems to have been one of the party, for the next day he called at Dorset Street, solidifying his friendship with Elizabeth, who thought him a "sensible and gentlemanly" man and grieved over the "sadness of tone" that he still exhibited over the loss of his wife. When Robert said goodbye to him, "we parted," he reported to Kenyon, "old friends and something more." The troubles over the production of *A Blot in the 'Scutcheon* were long forgotten.[24]

Alfred Tennyson came to London from his country house on the Isle of Wight and spent two successive evenings with the Brownings, September 26 and 27. According to Robert, he longed for professional talk. He bid them "as 'brother poets' tell him—as he would tell us,—how we worked, composed, etc."[25] He returned the next day, "dined with us, smoked with us, opened his heart to us (and the second bottle of port)," Elizabeth wrote to Julia Martin, "and ended by reading 'Maud' through from end to end, and going away at half-past two in the morning."[26] Robert set down a perceptive description of the "Tennyson music" for Kenyon. "He read strikingly and peculiarly . . . between a song and a recitation—but very beautiful and impressive in its effect—his tones quite haunt us. . . . In reading, he stopped repeatedly, overcome by his own feeling, tears in his eyes and very voice—this too is worth many travels and pains to have gained."[27] Elizabeth, who had a special taste for sound patterns and rhythm, called it "articulated music"—"The voice hangs in my ear still."[28] "If I had had a heart to spare, certainly he would have won mine," she continued to Mrs. Martin. "He is captivating with his frankness, confidingness and unexampled *naïveté*."[29] Sarianna was equally thrilled. Dante Gabriel Rossetti, with three other members of the Pre-Raphaelite Brotherhood, was also part of the audience and made a sketch of Tennyson in the midst of his reading. Browning, not to be outdone, followed with a reading of the as-yet-unpublished "Fra Lippo Lippi" in his best dramatic manner. Arabella, who had slipped back to London from Eastbourne to comfort Elizabeth with her presence, also heard the performances but preferred Robert's dramatic reading to Tennyson's "voice like an organ," in Elizabeth's simile, "rather music than speech."[30]

When Arabella returned to Eastbourne, she took Penini along for a holiday with his uncles. It was the first time he had ever been separated by any considerable distance from his parents, and without Wilson beside him. As he said good-bye to Robert at the train station, he burst into tears. Elizabeth felt desperate at the parting. To her it was "like throwing my head out of the window after my heart."[31] But Arabella, Peni's favorite, next to Wilson, smothered him with love at Eastbourne, and George, Henry, Septimus, and Occy were lavish with attention. Nevertheless, after a few days, he woke in the night crying out for "Untle Otty" to take him to Mama.

Proofs for *Men and Women* had been coming from the printer all month. Robert went over them "half a dozen times or more" with Elizabeth's help. For general criticism the proofs were sent to Fox, Forster, and Lytton, all of whom, Robert told Kenyon, "take one's breath away with their—not sympathy merely—but anticipation of success—of a 'sale' in short." Kenyon read with a more closely critical eye and made several helpful suggestions for small changes, which Robert adopted, but he was less sanguine about the reception of the general public.[32]

Both Dante Gabriel Rossetti and his brother William called at Dorset Street on September 30, bringing the sketch of Tennyson. Dante Gabriel was preparing a drawing of Robert, preliminary to the painting of his portrait. Kenyon came to visit the Brownings just prior to their departure for Paris. He went over financial details and urged them strongly to visit him on the Isle of Wight next year. Forster was "overwhelming [them] with attentions"[33] during these last days. He still regarded Robert as a protégé whose full potential as a poet was about to be revealed. He arranged a dinner for Robert to spend an evening with his publisher, Edward Chapman, who was confident of a solid publishing success. The last of the page proofs were returned by October 3. Robert had read them with scrupulous attention, making a few last-minute improvements, especially in "'Childe Roland'" and "Old Pictures in Florence."[34] *Men and Women* was published November 17, 1855, in both England and the United States. Since Americans had been more receptive to Browning's work than had his fellow countrymen, he looked with doubled hope on this day as an international literary event.

Men and Women

Browning's *Men and Women* is the most important collection of short poems published in nineteenth-century England since John Keats's *Lamia, Isabella, The Eve of St. Agnes, and Other Poems* in 1820. The two volumes contain fifty-one poems of immense variety and vigor, monodramatic poems that reflect life past and present in England, Italy, Greece, Rome, Palestine, Arabia, Spain, France, Germany, and the imaginary realm of myth and legend. In his new book, Browning displayed his complete command of the monodramatic form, especially in a dozen poems of middle length that allow greater complexity than he had attempted before and result in the full development of some of his most characteristic ideas and the creation of some of his most memorable characters.

Outstanding among them are two poems about art that re-create vividly two painters of the Italian Renaissance, Fra Lippo Lippi and Andrea del Sarto. For these works, Browning was inspired by information he found in Giorgio Vasari's *Le Vite de piu eccellenti architetti, pittori, et scultori italiani,* known commonly in English as *The Lives of the Painters*.[1] He was probably attracted by the contrast in temperament between these two figures, since he had enjoyed pairing poems in his earlier publications.

In "Fra Lippo Lippi" Browning created one of his greatest characters and one whom most critics have accepted as expressing Browning's own ideas about art and life.[2] Those appear when Lippo constructs his apologia for his realism. The prior had taken the view that art must not offer naturalistic representations of human beings: "Your business is not to catch men with show" but rather to "Make them forget there's such a thing as flesh. / Your business is to paint the souls of men. . . ." (179, 182–83). But the prior has difficulty explaining how to do that:

> Man's soul, and it's a fire, smoke . . . no, it's not . . .
> It's vapour done up like a new-born babe—
> (In that shape when you die it leaves your mouth)
> It's . . . well, what matters talking, it's the soul! (184–87)

As an answer to the prior's confused attempt to say how to depict the soul, Browning puts words into Lippo's mouth that reflect one of his own important concepts about art. It is basically a Platonic idea: that the response to physical beauty leads to the perception of beauty of soul. Plato presents the idea in *The Symposium*.[3] Here is Fra Lippo Lippi's version of it:

> Why can't a painter lift each foot in turn,
> Left foot and right foot, go a double step,
> Make his flesh liker and his soul more like,
> Both in their order? Take the prettiest face,
> The Prior's niece . . . patron-saint—is it so pretty
> You can't discover if it means hope, fear,
> Sorrow or joy? won't beauty go with these?
> Suppose I've made her eyes all right and blue,
> Can't I take breath and try to add life's flash,
> And then add soul and heighten them threefold?
> Or say there's beauty with no soul at all—
> (I never saw it—put the case the same—)
> If you get simple beauty and naught else,
> You get about the best thing God invents:
> That's somewhat: and you'll find the soul you have missed,
> Within yourself, when you return him thanks.[4] (205–20)

Lippo concludes the argument with a simply expressed defense of his treatment of human figures in his work:

> For me, I think I speak as I was taught;
> I always see the garden and God there
> A-making man's wife: and, my lesson learned,
> The value and significance of flesh,
> I can't unlearn ten minutes afterwards. (265–69)

What then is the function of art, when actual nature or actual human beings are available? It is to lift the veil of familiarity from the world around us, to reveal its meaning:

> For, don't you mark? we're made so that we love
> First when we see them painted, things we have passed
> Perhaps a hundred times nor cared to see;
> And so they are better, painted—better to us,
> Which is the same thing. Art was given for that.... (300–304)[5]

In contrast to the view of his superiors that art should "instigate to prayer," his view is that art evokes an active response to a world which is to be embraced enthusiastically because it is charged with meaning:

> This world's no blot for us,
> Nor blank; it means intensely, and means good:
> To find its meaning is my meat and drink. (313–15)

Andrea del Sarto presents a sharp contrast to Fra Lippo Lippi: Lippo was a vigorous success; Andrea is a failure, in spite of his reputation (he is, as the ironic subtitle of the poem says, "Called 'The Faultless Painter'"), and his failure extends from his art to his marriage. Browning was probably prompted in this characterization by a contrast that Vasari set up in his *Lives of the Painters*: on the one hand, Vasari wrote, "his figures are simple and pure, well conceived, and flawless and perfect in every particular"; on the other hand, "a timidity of spirit and a yielding simple nature prevented him from exhibiting a burning ardour and dash."[6] From a hint in Vasari, Browning developed the character of Lucrezia, who dominates her husband; Andrea sees her for what she is, an unfaithful, manipulative, money-wheedling woman, and while faithfulness in love might, in another context, be admirable, Andrea's reiterated choice of Lucrezia is clearly a sign of his weakness. But Andrea, in spite of his flaws, voices ideas which critics have identified as those of his creator, especially ideas about the heuristic value of imperfection. The imperfect is literally the incomplete, and imperfect art paradoxically succeeds because it pushes the mind of the viewer to finish it, while perfect (literally complete) art paradoxically fails because it offers everything in itself and shuts off further development. The famous lines, "a man's reach should exceed his grasp, / Or what's a heaven for?" (97–98), sum up the value of imperfection: it prods the viewer to an active response, whereas Andrea's art, "placid and perfect" (complete), does everything for the viewer. Andrea sums up the paradox in the words "less is more" (78). He could, he says, easily correct faults in a Raphael painting (a copy of which Andrea gestures to), "But all the play, the insight and the stretch— / Out of me, out of me!" (116–17). Browning's Cleon voices a line which sums up this central Browning idea: "imperfection means perfection hid" (185).

The idea of the value of imperfection is an ancient one and found even outside the European tradition. The Japanese potter, for instance, will sometimes leave a thumbprint on the glaze of his finished bowl as "the touch of nature." But the valuing of imperfection is more commonly found in northern European literature and art criticism of the nineteenth century. In "The Nature of Gothic" (chapter 6 of the second volume of *The Stones of Venice*, 1853), Ruskin argued that imperfection in art reveals the "soul" of the artist. This view seems to have developed as a reaction to the rise of industrialism and the factory system: machines could turn out perfect products but what is produced by the hand of the craftsman will be imperfect and therefore have greater aesthetic appeal. Browning explored the same ideas in "Old Pictures in Florence," where he links imperfection to moral and spiritual growth, and to Italian politics. "What's come to perfection perishes" (130), he says; what is imperfect makes possible change and growth.

There are twenty-two poems dealing with love or the relations between the sexes that are scattered throughout *Men and Women*. In many of them Browning retains a time-honored Romantic attitude: he asserts that lovers must follow the dictates of the heart, and he thrusts aside reason or the demands of society in favor of love's fulfilment. But in other poems Browning is the realist, ready to see love as a powerful force in human life, but a problematic one bound up with the darker side of human nature. The simplest view, one which has its origin in the courtly love tradition of the medieval chivalric romances, is that love is single and intense in its goal, extreme in its expression, and everlasting in its devotion: the hero of *In a Balcony*, Norbert, is an example of such a lover. Then there is Browning's idea of the "eternal moment," as we have already seen it in "By the Fire-Side," and as Browning developed it in "the instant made eternity" (108) in "The Last Ride Together," a highly erotic poem.[7] "The Statue and the Bust" presents a variation on this theme—but it contains a warning that the lives of lovers who fail to act will lose the illumination that only true love can bestow and so miss the true purpose of their lives. The narrator, anticipating an objection that, had the potential lovers run off together, they would be committing adultery, goes on to argue that a crime will serve as well as a virtuous deed in the game of life: "If you choose to play" (241), he says, do so boldly and with all the skill at your command:

> Let a man contend to the uttermost
> For his life's set prize, be it what it will!
>
> The counter our lovers staked was lost
> As surely as if it were lawful coin:

> And the sin I impute to each frustrate ghost
> Is—the unlit lamp and the ungirt loin,
> Though the end in sight was a vice, I say. (242–48)

This is a bold position for Browning to have taken in the mid-nineteenth century, but it demonstrates the intensity of his belief that in matters of love there should be no hesitation.[8] It is a clear reflection, too, of the determination that lay behind his carrying Elizabeth off to Italy in September 1846, even though it had been a struggle to convince her of the necessity to act. It was, of course, an even more difficult step for her to take, for she gave up much more than Robert did in leaving England. Her place in a tightly knit family, with enough members to constitute a small community, was at stake, as well as her sense of the obligation owed to her father, who had seen her through fifteen years of incapacitating illness. But in the end they both acted. When she read Robert's poem, she did not quibble over the moral dimensions of the narrator's argument.

Over a dozen more poems involving love show a surprising variety of troubles attending the relations between the sexes. Some deal with the problems of married life, a subject treated more commonly by Victorian poets than by their predecessors in earlier periods. Tennyson, Browning, Meredith, Patmore, and Hardy are names that come easily to mind. One pair of poems, in each of which the speaker is a woman, feature married couples: they are "A Woman's Last Word" and "Any Wife to Any Husband." In the former, the woman speaking is making peace after a quarrel as she and her husband lie in bed. The meter, with its truncations and hesitations, brilliantly fits the emotions: Browning uses lines of trochaic trimeter alternating with chopped-off dimeters and punctuated with many dashes. The poem ends with four brief utterances:

> —Must a little weep, Love,
>   (Foolish me!)
> And so fall asleep, Love,
>   Loved by thee. (37–40)

The second poem is a distressing dramatic monologue in which a wife expresses anguish that her husband might remarry after her death. Since their "inmost beings" have "met and mixed," she cannot accept the thought of another woman intruding into their marriage, which she considers immortal. This is a downside of the "eternal moment" that is supposed to solidify true lovers forever; indeed, "Any Wife to Any Husband" follows immediately after "By the Fire-Side" in *Men and Women*. The gamut of emotions in the poem—from earnest plea to unreasonable demand, to accusation of betrayal, to challenge of honor, to grant of freedom, to a boast of her own ability to survive single widowhood if she were left alone, to posing a chivalric trial, to exultation in immortal union, and at last to the anguish of despair—seems only too real, too human.

It is tempting to see in the poem parallels to the Brownings' situation. Certainly, Robert must have imagined various scenarios of his wife's succumbing to her weakened physical condition. But Elizabeth never called upon Robert to remain single in the event of her death, even though he tried to reassure her about his intention not to remarry if anything happened to her. Indeed, she wrote to Arabella in 1854, "I've stopped him twenty times in such vows as never to take another wife, & the like . . . I've held his lips together with both hands . . . I wouldn't have it!"[9] Yet in later letters she twice indicates her disapproval of a person remarrying after the death of a spouse.

Many of the poems in *Men and Women* deal with religious subjects, chief among them the Incarnation, to which Browning imagines contrasting responses, one from an Arab physician, one from a highly cultured Greek artist and intellectual. The success of "An Epistle Containing the Strange Medical Experience of Karshish, the Arab Physician" lies in the gradual disclosure of Karshish's response to an event that lies outside his professional understanding and that evokes unexpected feelings about totally new religious concepts. The character of Karshish, with his reasonable nature and his attraction to these unexpected intellectual possibilities, is very appealing. "Cleon," also an epistle, presents a parallel situation with a contrasting outcome: Cleon too comes in contact with an event which promises to fulfil his deepest desires (for "Some future state . . . / Unlimited in capability / For joy" [325–27]), but unlike Karshish, Cleon is arrogantly confident in his own culture, with its sharp distinction between Hellenes and barbarians: he dismisses the story of "Christus" and the teaching of "Paulus" as something from "a mere barbarian Jew" (343).[10]

The longest poem in *Men and Women*, "Bishop Blougram's Apology," is also one of the most puzzling. What attitude is the reader being asked to take toward Blougram, who is modeled (as Browning admitted during a dinner with Forster and Gavan Duffy one Sunday in 1865[11]) on Cardinal Wiseman, Archbishop of Westminster and head of the reestablished Roman Catholic church in England? Modern criticism presents opposing views. One is represented by F. E. L. Priestley's 1946 reading of the poem, "Blougram's Apologetics";[12] the other finds expression in Susan Hardy Aiken's 1978 essay "Bishop Blougram and Carlyle."[13]

Priestley's argument, mounted to counter the charge that Blougram is a casuist, is a defense of a defense: Blougram, a man of faith, knows he is speaking to a man without faith and, moreover, to a journalist who is unsympathetic to the Church. Blougram speaks not as he would if he had his choice of occasion but as best he can in a difficult situation, and he knows that, if he is to have any chance whatsoever with Gigadibs, he must proceed not from his own premises but from ones Gigadibs will accept: "I mean to meet you on your own premise" (171), he says to Gigadibs, and so he must shape a large portion of his monologue "for argumentatory purposes" (982). He also knows that Gigadibs is (apparently) a lightweight newspaperman preparing to write an exposé about a bishop admitting to lapses in his faith, and he enjoys giving Gigadibs the impression that he—Blougram—is speaking confidentially and voicing his "real" opinions: he has doubts about doctrine and jauntily describes certain miracles, ceremonies, and even vestments in language Gigadibs would use (the miracle of "the Virgin's winks" [699], or the vestments as "the needlework of Noodledom" [426]). His whole apologia proceeds from positions that are commonplace but never thought through, beginning with "Best be yourself" (77). Blougram, knowing that Gigadibs confuses knowledge (which can be proved from empirical evidence) with faith (the affirmations of which cannot be proved empirically)—and knowing also that he confuses knowledge with doubt (the denials of which, like the affirmations of faith, cannot be proved empirically), points out that our actual human experience is a mixture of faith and doubt:

> Just when we are safest, there's a sunset-touch,
> A fancy from a flower-bell, some one's death,
> A chorus-ending from Euripides,—
> And that's enough for fifty hopes and fears
> As old and new at once as nature's self,
> To rap and knock and enter in our soul,
> Take hands and dance there, a fantastic ring,
> Round the ancient idol, on his base again,—
> The grand Perhaps! (182–90)

How then can we make such a mixture "bear fruit to us?" (181). The choice between faith and doubt is not a simple intellectual exercise: "Belief or unbelief / Bears upon life, determines its whole course" (228–29). So Blougram proceeds in his argument, bringing Gigadibs to an understanding of the value of faith (though it is faith largely without dogma) and correcting his conflation of faith and knowledge. Faith goes beyond knowledge and rests rather upon human wishes and aspirations ("the heat of inward evidence," in Tennyson's phrase). The key question about Christianity is this: "It may be false, but will you wish it true?" (628). The very wish is sufficient: "If you desire faith—then you've faith enough" (634). Moreover, limited knowledge has a purpose: it is the condition under which human beings can make choices and so grow and develop:

> . . . when the fight begins within himself,
> A man's worth something. God stoops o'er his head,
> Satan looks up between his feet—both tug—
> He's left, himself, i' the middle: the soul wakes
> And grows. Prolong that battle through his life!
> Never leave growing till the life to come! (693–98)

So Blougram voices favorite Browning ideas, but he has little hope that they will prove effective with Gigadibs, whom he taunts: since he, Blougram, leads such a comfortable life, "why won't you be a bishop too?" (149). Moreover, Blougram has power and influence and fame, while for Gigadibs "the highest honor in your life . . . / Is—dining here" (916, 918). In such a context, Gigadibs's conversion at the end is a surprise.

But what about a reading of the poem which sees Blougram as a less-than-admirable character? Susan Hardy Aiken provides one by linking this dramatic monologue with Carlyle and with all that Browning learned from his longtime friend, especially from *Sartor Resartus*. Carlyle's central metaphor in that book—clothing—is the key, Aiken argues, to "the speciousness of Blougram's apologetics" (324). Clothing, by which Carlyle means every structure of thought and organization through which human beings bind themselves together in society, is the outward and visible manifestation of a divine and energizing spirit, but when clothing no longer embodies that spirit, it becomes worn and needs to be replaced. That need for renewal Carlyle calls (borrowing a term from the French Revolution) "Sansculottism": if clothes "so tailorise and demoralise us . . . can they not be altered to serve better[?]"[14] In the chapter titled "Church-Clothes," Carlyle deals specifically with religion and condemns the church-clothes of his own time: "Meanwhile, in our era of the World, those same Church-Clothes have gone sorrowfully out-at-elbows: nay, far worse, many of them have become mere hollow Shapes, or Masks, under which no living Figure or Spirit any longer dwells" (1. 172). Blougram has much to say about his vestments, in which he is comfortable, and though he protests that he did not choose them, he is not about to change them:

> An uniform I wear though over-rich—
> Something imposed on me, no choice of mine;

> No fancy-dress worn for pure fancy's sake
> And despicable therefore! now folk kneel
> And kiss my hand—of course the Church's hand.
> Thus I am made, thus life is best for me . . . . (332–37)

"My business," he says, "is not to remake myself" (354), and he cannot think that the clothing might function differently: "And thus it could not be another way, / I venture to imagine" (339–40). His challenging of Gigadibs to name his hero, his "pattern man" (435), is Browning's response to Carlyle's lectures *On Heroes and Hero-Worship*, which the poet attended in 1840. Blougram names Napoleon, Shakespeare, and Luther, rejecting Luther (as might be expected) but, significantly for this particular reading of Blougram's character, rejecting the one figure who did retailor the church. And Blougram's enthusiastic embrace of this world and its "creature-comforts" (766) seems to indicate a religious life from which the spirit has departed:

> I act for, talk for, live for this world now,
> As this world prizes action, life and talk:
> No prejudice to what next world may prove,
> Whose new laws and requirements, my best pledge
> To observe then, is that I observe these now,
> Shall do hereafter what I do meanwhile. (769–74)

In governing himself by the standards of this world he seems to have got things backward, and in doing so he fails to recognize the true hero in this dramatic confrontation. It is Gigadibs who, unlike the bishop, "with sudden healthy vehemence" (1007) does cast off his old clothes and remake himself.

The poem sustains both readings, and in its richness and complexity remains evocative and debatable. Of the many articles on it, one stands out because it provides such a wealth of information about the historical context: it is Julia Markus's 1978 essay, "Bishop Blougram and the Literary Men."[15] Browning was always an avid reader of newspapers and journals; Markus identifies the poem's many allusions to contemporary events as they were reported in the papers and periodicals of the day: the reestablishment in 1850 of the Roman Catholic hierarchy in Britain and the appointment of Nicholas Wiseman as Archbishop of Westminster; the opposition to Wiseman by the editor of the *London Globe*, Francis Sylvester Mahony, who wrote under the name Father Prout; the miracle at Rimini in 1850, when an image of the Virgin began to lower her eyes during mass—a miracle widely discussed in the Italian and English press; the Naples liquefaction, when in the cathedral in Naples the blood of St. Januarius (San Gennaro) liquefied on his feast day. The poem, as Markus shows, owes a great deal to the journalism of its day.

Robert dedicated *Men and Women* to Elizabeth. In "One Word More, To E. B. B.," he explores, in Eleanor Cook's phrase, "the mystery of creation," suggesting that the poet is both mage and prophet, and choosing as his metaphor for creation the miracle at Meribah, when Moses struck the rock and brought forth living water (Exod. 17:1–7 and Num. 20:11). In typology, that act foreshadows the life-giving and life-saving flow of water from Christ's side during the Crucifixion: Browning had used the same allusion in *Sordello*, and thus "implies something about the function of poetry in his repeated choice of this miracle as analogy" for its creation.[16] So Robert offers to Elizabeth his fifty "men and women, / Live or dead or fashioned by my fancy" (129–30), whose lives he had entered by imagination and through whom he spoke "from every mouth" (132):

> Take them, Love, the book and me together:
> Where the heart lies, let the brain lie also. (3–4)

Chapter 26

"It is high time that this sort of thing be stopped"

Robert Browning loved and admired his friend Alfred Tennyson, but he secretly envied the critical recognition and the widespread popularity that Tennyson had achieved. Now with the publication of *Men and Women* the time had arrived when he could assume a position in the literary world to equal that of the poet laureate. Yet his hopes were not to be fulfilled. The first review was a devastating attack that appeared in the *Athenaeum* on November 17, 1855. The anonymous reviewer was his friend Henry Chorley,[1] who grieved over the "energy wasted and power misspent" on poems "overhung by the 'seven veils' of obscurity" and who carped at the "Hudibrastic versification in which our author is without a rival." He objected also to the colloquial speech of the speaker in such works as "A Lover's Quarrel." Chorley was not yet attuned to the realistic language of nineteenth-century poetry that Wordsworth had tried to promote as long ago as 1798.

Since the *Athenaeum* was always early in its reviews of newly published works, it had become a trendsetter for literary opinion in England. Knowing this, the Brownings were crushed by the review. Moreover, since Chorley was a frequent reviewer of literature and music for the *Athenaeum*, they guessed uncertainly at his authorship but could not believe their friend would heap such disdain on Robert's book.

The next notice, written probably by John Abraham Heraud[2] for the *Saturday Review* a week later, was even more of a blow. It began, "It is really high time that this sort of thing should, if possible, be stopped." Heraud's was the first review to associate Browning with the school of "Spasmodic Poets" (or "tran-

274

scendental poets," as he called them), and by "this sort of thing" he was referring to the *Poems* of Alexander Smith, Tennyson's *Maud*, and *The Mystic* by Philip James Bailey, all of which had been recently published and were currently in vogue—and much deplored by reviewers of taste. (Tennyson had suffered such quips as that by an earlier critic who remarked that one of the vowels in the title *Maud* should be omitted and it did not matter which one.)[3]

Fortunately, on December 1, Forster came forth in the well-respected *Examiner* to counter this trend. He offered high praise for Browning's poems and admiration for the immense range of the characters who spoke in the dramatic monologues. Since he was a drama critic, he had perceptive appreciation for the monodramatic forms that Browning used. Certain works with greater conflict especially appealed to him: he found that "In a Balcony" and "Bishop Blougram's Apology" "stand out from the rest . . . in striking dramatic power." He came to Browning's defense on two points that other reviewers were resurrecting.

> No doubt there are too many pieces in the volumes to which the objection of obscurity in the meaning and of a perverse harshness in the metres, may be justly urged. It is Mr. Browning's old fault. . . . The robust intellect works actively; and the perceptions of a poet, when applied to thoughts of more than common subtlety, will often necessarily outrun his reader's. Such obscurity proceeds from fullness, not emptiness; and it is not always that a thought which is hard to follow will be found not worth the exercise of mind required for overtaking it.

Further, Forster quoted extensively from the poems in order to "establish beyond dispute that these volumes are not exclusively 'obscure and mystical.'"

An unsigned review that appeared in early December in the *Leader*, a politically and culturally liberal magazine, echoes Forster's judgment. "Robert Browning seems to us unmistakably the most original poet of the day. He stands alone. He writes as if Wordsworth, Shelley, Coleridge, Keats had never been. . . . If any affinities between his poetry and that of his predecessors are to be found, they must be sought in our old dramatists." The reviewer seemed well acquainted with Browning's earlier work, for he saw in these volumes "all Browning's merits and all his old defects." He is recognized for "the same dramatic power of going out of himself, and speaking through his characters; the same reach of knowledge and richness of observation." Yet the old charge of obscurity cannot be avoided; his "manner is not only unusual but abrupt, puzzling, needlessly obscure." The reader is warned "not to give way impatiently."[4]

Some reviewers clearly revealed the limited standards against which they judged Browning's work. The spokesman for the *Critic*, December 1, 1855, sets down the general criterion he brings to his task: "It *was* the object of poetry to turn all things into loveliness: it is the object of poetry . . . to grant us glimpses of the beautiful." Although he can respond to a few of the lyrics in *Men and Women*, he rejects Browning's free range of subjects, most of which are treated too naturalistically for his taste or are "squeezed into all manner of unnatural shapes."[5] The novelist Margaret Oliphant, in an unsigned essay entitled "Modern Light Literature—Poetry" in *Blackwood's*, looks over poems by the Brownings, Dobell, Smith, and Bailey and gives much space condescendingly to Longfellow's *Hiawatha*. "What are we to do with these books?" she asks. "There is no getting through the confused crowd of Browning's *Men and Women*." She confesses that she could "make out" only "very few" poems. She likens him to "the old primitive painters": he had "something genuine in his mind"—in works "marvelous[,] ugly, yet somehow true."[6]

Browning took in the critical response from Paris. He haunted Galignani's bookshop, reading the early reviews, mostly to his disappointment. "I have stopped my ears," he wrote to Chapman in mid-December. "'Whoo-oo-oo-oo' mouths the big monkey—'Whee-ee-ee-ee' squeaks the little monkey and such a dig with the end of my umbrella as I should give the brutes if I couldn't keep my temper."[7]

The notices began to take on a pattern: an attack on Browning's stylistic difficulty and his metrical freedoms and then, at the end of the essay, an acknowledgment of the intellectual power of his work and the brilliance of his characterizations. For example, G. Brimley in *Fraser's Magazine* for January 1856 spends eleven pages sneering at Browning's poetic garden as "a wilderness overgrown with a rank and riotous vegetation." "Odd phrases, startling rhymes, strange arrangements, sudden transitions of thought, all kinds of eccentricities of style, have a fascination for him." And yet in conclusion Brimley says, "Compared with ninety-nine of a hundred volumes of contemporary poetry, these of Mr. Browning's are a treasure of beauty, and sense, and feeling. . . . There is not more than one poet of the present day whose genius is superior to his."[8]

Browning was angry and bewildered by the contradictory quality of the reports. He told Chapman on January 17, 1856, "I have read heaps of critiques at Galignani's, mostly stupid and spiteful, self-contradicting and contradictory of each other."[9] He should have been pleased, for J. T. Fields had sent him newspaper clippings from America with "outrageous praises." One notice from the *New York Daily Tribune* made the distinction between new readers of Browning's work and those who had already become familiar with his "idiosyncratic" style: "Indeed many of his productions appear as crabbed and repulsive to the uninitiated as the flavor of olives to those who taste them for the first time.... In order to enjoy [Browning] fully, one must pass through a preparation like that of learning a new language. But those who have gained the key to his magic treasures will revel enthusiastically in their new-found wealth. He is essentially the poet for poets."[10] Also, Chapman had sent him David Masson's highly favorable review of January 1856 from the *British Quarterly Review*, a Nonconformist periodical. The essays from the monthlies and the quarterlies were now arriving. Those reviewers had more time to read through Browning's volumes and could write lengthy, thoughtful considerations of his work. Some brickbats continued to fly, such as N. J. Gannon's from the *Irish Quarterly Review* for March 1856. His essay "Under a Cloud" deplored the state of poetry at present and worked over Tennyson's *Maud* and offerings by other poets, but Browning received the majority of the abuse, in this manner: "Obscurity is the evil genius that is working the ruin of this poet: Browning is, pre-eminently, the King of Darkness." In these volumes "there are sufficient crudities, contortions and dissections of the language to ruin the reputation of fifty poets."[11]

These longer essays developed fully the opinion expressed by the New York critic that Browning's poems were not for the ordinary reader. David Masson declared that for "power and originality of mind" very few present-day writers are the equal of Robert Browning. This is the "settled opinion" of critics and readers who are "acquainted with his writings, and capable of judging of them."[12] William Morris[13] writing in the *Oxford and Cambridge Magazine* for March 1856 offered advice for casual readers and reviewers: "I know well enough what they ['theory-mongers'] mean by obscure, ... meaning difficult to understand fully at first reading, or, say at second reading, even: yet, taken so, in what a cloud of obscurity would *Hamlet* be!" They regard poetry as "'light literature'; yet ... we must not think it hard if we have sometimes to exercise thought over a great poem, nay, even sometimes the utmost straining of all our thoughts, an agony almost equal to that of the poet who created the poem."[14]

One review, which appeared in the *Rambler*, a Catholic journal and review, especially piqued Browning's curiosity, for he was assured by his friend Father Prout that it had been written by Cardinal Wiseman. Browning was not surprised to find the reviewer annoyed that the caricature of Cardinal Wiseman in "Bishop Blougram's Apology" was so clearly identifiable, but he was astonished by the concluding sentence in the review: "Though much of [the] matter is extremely offensive to Catholics, yet beneath the surface there is an undercurrent of thought that is by no means inconsistent with our religion; and if Mr. Browning is a man of will and action, and not a mere dreamer and talker, we should never feel surprise at his conversion."[15]

Actually the review was written by Richard Simpson, a frequent writer for various periodicals, and it shows a full appreciation of Browning's poetry. Simpson even defends his metrics, which other reviewers had derided as Hudibrastic doggerel. "Modern verses are not read by feet, but by the rules of musical rhythm; not by syllables, but by accents. . . . The application of [these rules] will often solve the problem of an apparently halting verse." Simpson bestows great praise on Browning's "dramatic vigour" and on the realism of his depiction of life. He likens him to Thackeray. "Both throw themselves into a character, and make the character speak, not what we would have it utter, but that they know it would naturally express. Their aim is not abstract beauty, but nature, and the truth of nature. For ourselves, we thank Mr. Browning, sceptical and reckless as he is, for a rare treat in these thoughtful and able volumes." Browning was amazed at these words that he thought came from Cardinal Wiseman. He called it "the most curious notice I ever had."[16] (It was not until 1968 that Simpson was revealed as the author.)[17]

The most satisfying reviews of *Men and Women* came late. Browning's friend Joseph Milsand in the *Revue Contemporaine et Athenaeum Français* in mid-September produced a long, reflective overview of the fifty poems, almost half of which he was translating into French to be published in the *Revue des deux mondes*.[18]

Of all the reviews Browning received, one by George Eliot in the *Westminster Review* in January 1856 was among the most discerning.[19] She demonstrates how to read a poem that has some complexity of thought expressed in language rich in figures of speech and allusions, whether it be by John Donne, John Milton, Percy Bysshe Shelley, or Robert Browning. She begins by distinguishing the ordinary reader from the one who will seek meaning with an active mind. She imagines that the first impression of a Browning poem by a person who is not familiar with his work would be one of "'majestic obscurity,' which repels not only the ignorant but the idle." That reader will not be able to indulge a "drowsy passivity," for he will find "no conventionality, no melodious commonplace, but freshness, originality, sometimes eccentricity of expression; no didactic laying-out of a subject, but dramatic indication, which requires the reader to trace by his own mental activity the underground stream of thought that jets out in elliptical and pithy verse." Eliot is preparing the reader of her review for the right approach to Browning's poetry and also warning away the reader who enjoys relaxing by the fireside with Scott's *The Lady of the Lake* and expects all poetry to provide a similar literary experience. She tries to get the reader ready for Browning's tone and the rhythms of common speech in his verse. The reader will be greeted by "no soothing strains, no chants, no lullabys; . . . he sets our thoughts at work rather than our emotions. . . . his mode of presentation is always concrete, artistic, and, where it is most felicitous, dramatic." She goes on to illustrate why she admires "Fra Lippo Lippi," "Bishop Blougram's Apology," and "Karshish."

Browning received several reviews as thoughtful as this, and despite being sloshed by buckets of bilge from less capable reviewers, he should have been gratified by the overall reception accorded his new collection of poems. It drew over twenty-five reviews in England, many of them long and detailed, plus a great many favorable notices from the United States. But whether these critical assessments praised or denounced his new collection of poems, almost all of them acknowledged that he was among the most important poets of his day. The accumulated opinion held, however, that his poetry was addressed to the few, not the many. His work was, as David Masson put it, "caviare to the general." Yet "if the select and most cultured minds of a time can have a poet all to themselves . . . that is also a great gain to the community."[20]

David Latané in Browning's Sordello and the Aesthetics of Difficulty (1987) has made clear that in the early nineteenth century a division had begun to take place within the poetry-reading public, a gradually widening gap between the casual readers and the more attentive readers who preferred literature that demanded their intellectual and imaginative participation.[21] At the same time, the writers who appealed to a broad readership began to lose respect in the literary world. Browning was a figure of transition in this shift of literary response, and the admiration of a cultural elite was insufficient for his satisfaction. He yearned for "popularity." Moreover, he was deeply hurt by the humiliating maltreatment that his poetry had been given by some irresponsible judges whose critical views lagged behind the times.

The sale of Men and Women was initially brisk—enough to pay the costs of publication within the first three days,[22]—but booksellers were slow to reorder after that early burst of interest. The first edition never sold out, and a decade later some copies were remaindered with a different binding. Mark A. Weinstein has suggested that the reception of Men and Women was tainted by comments in five reviews that associated Browning with the "Spasmodic Poets."[23] A new wave of derision of their work had recently been created when William Edmondstoune Aytoun published a mock-tragedy entitled Firmilian.[24] It parodied the work of Bailey, Smith, and Dobell just fifteen months before Men and Women appeared. Twenty years earlier, Browning's Paracelsus had borne a number of resemblances to the verbosity and extravagance of these later poets, but by 1855 his style had changed completely. It is more likely that since *Men and Women* appealed to a rather select body of readers, its impact in the commercial market was correspondingly small. Furthermore, the last trickle of sales was probably choked off when Chapman published a three-volume edition of Browning's *Poetical Works* in 1863.

In the midst of Browning's distress over some sharp critical stabs came a long letter from John Ruskin that confessed the bewilderment of a literary well-wisher over the new volumes that Browning had sent him. He had sat down of an evening ready to enjoy the poems, only to find them "the most amazing conundrums that ever were proposed to me."[25] The one that he singled out for a series of questions was "Popularity," one of Browning's more esoteric pieces, an oblique tribute to John Keats.

"Popularity" is a baffling poem to most readers because of Browning's allusions, his jumps in imagery, and his habit of elliptical expression. It opens with an allusion to Shelley's "Adonais" in which Keats is likened to a star, and it closes with a reference to "murex," a mollusk that lives in the Mediterranean whose body, when pounded, provides a purple dye (Browning makes his use of "murex" more confusing by referring to its dye as blue). In the poem, the speaker addresses the "true poet" as a star. The star's light is enclosed by God's hand, which will open and release it in the future. At that time its brilliance will be like the best wine that Jesus miraculously produced from water during the wedding at Cana. The speaker would like to draw a picture of the true poet as a fisherman with a net full of the mollusks that yield the famed Tyrian dye. Inferior poets—Hobbs, Dobbs, Nokes, and Stokes (depicted at first as painters)—get some of the blue into their work by imitating the work of the true poet and, as a consequence, will dine well. But "Who fished the murex up? / What porridge had John Keats?"

Ruskin's letter prompted Browning to reply, one of the few occasions on which he set down some defenses of the creative process that took place when he wrote his poetry and of his true feelings about the kind of reader that he wished to address.[26] He begins in a friendly and jocular way, genuinely appreciative of Ruskin's extended comments on the poems, including the perplexities when he tried to read through the two volumes. He points out at once that he and Ruskin "don't read poetry the same way." Ruskin and many others expect a poem to be as clear as a prose statement of fact; indeed, Ruskin demands that it be as exacting as a legal document. However, Browning expects a different kind of reader, one who allows him to express as well as he can the conceptions that his mind holds, as if they were Platonic ideals, "all poetry being a putting the infinite within the finite." He has to employ "various artifices . . . touches and bits of outlines which *succeed* if they bear the conception from me to you." The reader must supply connections between an image and an idea or between one portion of a poem's complete structure and another: "In asking for more *ultimates* you must accept less *mediates*, nor expect that a Druid stone-circle will be traced for you with as few breaks to the eye as the North Crescent and South Crescent that go together so cleverly in many a suburb." Because Browning requires his readers to participate in the development of a poem's meaning, he admits that he does not write for the multitude. In fact, he asks, "Do you think poetry was ever generally understood? . . . A poet's affair is with God, to whom he is accountable, and of whom is his reward. . . . Do you believe people understand *Hamlet?*" The audience misses a third of the play, "with no end of noble things . . . Are these wasted, therefore? No—they act upon a very few, who react upon the rest." Yet in communicating with his readers, Browning says he does his best. "I look on my own shortcomings too sorrowfully, try to remedy them too earnestly." But since it is not a poet's task to tell people what they know already, "I shall never change my point of sight, or feel other than disconcerted and apprehensive when the public, critics and all, begin to understand and approve me."

He no longer needed the reviewers of *Men and Women* to tell him that he could reach only a limited reading audience. What kind of porridge had Robert Browning?

That Little-Seeming Substance

I n December 1856, Dante Gabriel Rossetti wrote to William Allingham describing "one of my delights,—an evening resort [with the Brownings] where I never felt unhappy." He marveled at the discrepancy between their poetry and their physical appearance: "How large a part of the real world, I wonder, are those two small people?—taking meanwhile so little room in any railway carriage, and hardly needing a double bed at the inn." On this occasion he was responding to Elizabeth's *Aurora Leigh*, "an astounding work," he said, and a "wonder."[1] He was not alone in his estimate of Elizabeth's major poem.

For years, Elizabeth had been wanting to write "a sort of novel-poem"[2] which would take as its subject matter "this real everyday life of our age," and which would, she hoped, effect social change by "running into the midst of our conventions, & rushing into drawingrooms & the like . . . & speaking the truth as I conceive of it, out plainly."[3] Inspired by Thomas Carlyle—"the great teacher of the age," Elizabeth said of him to Robert, and "also yours & mine"[4]—she wanted to engage the social issues of the day, like Elizabeth Gaskell, whose *Ruth*, Elizabeth said when it appeared in 1853, "deals in a bold true christian spirit with a detestable state of Christian society," and like Harriet Beecher Stowe, whose *Uncle Tom's Cabin* had evoked Elizabeth's envy as well as admiration for its popularity, which "was really a grand thing & meant much that was good."[5] But she lacked a story. She told Robert in 1845, "I am waiting for a story—& I wont take one, because I want to make one—& I like to make my own stories, because then I can take liberties with them in the treatment."[6] Moreover, she knew (as she admitted ruefully about the unexpected popularity of "Lady Geraldine's Courtship") that "people care for a story," and any reservations she might have had about the appeal of narratives were tempered by her own likings: "I who care so much for stories. . . ."[7] By early 1853 she had her story, for she reported to Mrs. Jameson that she was busy with "the novel or romance I have been hankering after so long," and she told her brother George that she "meant it to be beyond all question my best work."[8] Robert did not read it until early 1856, when it was still unfinished, but he was enthusiastic about it, dating each book in the manuscript as he read it, telling the publisher Edward Chapman that it was "such an admirable poem," and adding to his dating of the seventh book the words "this divine book."[9] Elizabeth completed the ninth and final book in June, sent the manuscript to the printers in early August, worked on proofs when she and Robert were staying with John Kenyon on the Isle of Wight in September, and made last revisions before they returned to Casa Guidi at the end of October. *Aurora Leigh* was published on November 15. It appeared simultaneously in London and New York, sold rapidly, and was widely reviewed.

The story which was so long in coming was the story of the eponymous heroine and her development both as artist and woman. Elizabeth told John Kenyon that the poem was "the autobiography of a poetess—(not me),"[10] but the story of the artist as woman, finding a life and relations of her own choosing, would turn out to be just as important as the story of woman as artist, finding a place for herself in a literary tradition dominated by men. (Elizabeth would say later that "the womans question" "was only a collateral object with my intentions in writing."[11]) Central to Aurora's growth as both woman and artist is her involvement with Marian Erle, and in telling Marian's story Elizabeth proved herself both courageous and daring, for she undertook to write about a subject likely to give offence—"the condition of women in our cities, which a woman oughtn't to refer to"[12]—and, moreover, to write about a woman whom she knew her society would label as "fallen" and whom she defiantly portrayed as chaste. "The intention is *not* licentious," Elizabeth told Arabella, and she defended her story: "I wanted a horrible situation to prove a beautiful verity"; Marian emerges, she insisted, "with a glory of purity & even of moral dignity": "You shall feel the virtue of chastity, in her, more even than in Aurora."[13]

The design of the story is one of opposites and doubles, as a surviving fragment of Elizabeth's notes for the plot indicates.[14] Aurora is the daughter of an Italian mother and an English father, and Italy and England, and the values and culture of each, are constantly juxtaposed. "Education" and "development," "system" and "instinct," and "love" and "philanthropy" are all paired in

Elizabeth's note, but the crucial pairing is that of "Ideal" and "practical," both for the design of the story and for its theme. Elizabeth explained the relation in a letter to John Kenyon: the story "opposes the practical & the ideal lifes," but the important matter is not how "the Real & Ideal" are opposed but how they interpenetrate: the story shows "how the practical & real (so called) is but the external evolution of the ideal & spiritual—that it is from inner to outer, . . . whether in life, morals, or art."[15] In the poem Aurora herself makes a parallel statement which is the motto of the poem: "Inward evermore / To outward,—so in life, and so in art / Which still is life" (5. 227–29). And when she is setting out her theory of the artist, Aurora champions the doubleness that is everywhere in the story: "poets should / Exert a double vision" (5. 183–84), she insists. Aurora's views, if not her story, seem to be those of her creator and flesh out Elizabeth's assertion, in her dedication of the poem to John Kenyon, that the book is "the one into which my highest convictions upon Life and Art have entered."

Aurora Leigh was received enthusiastically, and one must inevitably contrast its reception with that of *Men and Women*. Yet Robert was only pleased for his wife and "happy in the success of the poem," Elizabeth reported to Arabella: "When people write & talk of the 'jealousy' of authors & husbands, let them look at him!"[16] And a success it was. The first printing sold out quickly; there was a second in January 1857 and a third in March of that same year; for the fourth, in June of 1859, Elizabeth made corrections, and there was a fifth reprinting a year later. The book was widely noticed, discussed, and reviewed, both in England and in the United States. Elizabeth took great delight (and found much amusement) in the various responses, gleefully reporting to Mrs. Jameson, for instance, that Aurora was "a brazen-faced woman" and inferring from a comparison with a French novelist a charge of "gross indecency."[17] She was highly amused, too, to learn of the label widely applied to the poem, "Mrs. Browning's *gospel*," and to hear reports of "a party in England, holding up their hands at the scandal of a woman's writing such a book" and refusing to let their daughters read it: "Well the daughters must be very young," Elizabeth responded, "& my comfort is that they will grow older."[18] (Three years later, Elizabeth was still exulting in the "scandal" when she described the poem to Mrs. Jameson as "a very indecent, corrupting book" and offered as evidence "ladies of sixty" of whom she had heard, who had "never felt themselves pure since reading it." That contamination suited Elizabeth's purpose: "it is exactly because pure and prosperous women choose to *ignore* vice, that miserable women suffer wrong by it everywhere."[19]) The major reviews usually acknowledged Elizabeth as "our best living English poetess" (in the words of H. F. Chorley in the

Athenaeum) but were critical of the poem. Even Chorley, an admirer and supporter, voiced two objections which appeared in other reviews as well: that the story, in spite of the poet's intentions, was "unreal" and "its form infelicitous."[20] W. E. Aytoun in *Blackwood's* (which Elizabeth expected would "grind me to powder, I don't doubt, as far as Blackwood can"[21]) also made both points: he commented on the irony of a story which "professes to be a tale of our own times" but is "fantastic, unnatural, exaggerated"[22]; and he insisted that much of the poem was really prose, a point he made by printing passages with continuous lineation and without the metrical divisions. Similarly, John Nichol in the *Westminster Review* attacked passages "in which Mrs. Browning has broken loose altogether from the meshes of versification, and run riot in prose cut up into lines of ten syllables."[23] The one charge which did seem to concern Elizabeth, who had always insisted that she must create her own story, was that of imitation leveled by George Eliot in the *Westminster Review* when she deplored "the lavish mutilation of heroes' bodies" in contemporary fiction: "we are especially sorry that Mrs. Browning has added one more to the imitations of the catastrophe in 'Jane Eyre,' by smiting her hero with blindness before he is made happy in the love of Aurora."[24] Mrs. Jameson had also noted the likeness, and Elizabeth corrected her by setting out, not entirely persuasively, the differences between her hero's fate and Brontë's.[25]

Elizabeth's spirited response to the reception of *Aurora Leigh* and her delight in seeing the work take on a challenging life of its own among its readers soon gave way to sadness. On December 3, John Kenyon died. The Brownings had stayed in his house in Devonshire Place when they had arrived in London at the end of June, and in September they had stayed with him in West Cowes, Isle of Wight, where Elizabeth witnessed with distress the suffering of the dying man.[26] Yet, perhaps because he was close and dear, she was unwilling to admit he was dying, and so the event was for her "a sudden misfortune for which she was all but absolutely unprepared."[27] She suffered "acutely," Robert said, and a month later, he told their publisher, "We have had a sad Christmas time, or indeed existence so far as we are concerned."[28] Kenyon had played a central role in their lives. To Elizabeth, who addressed him in the dedication to *Aurora Leigh* as "cousin" and "friend," he had acted since her marriage as she wished her own father had acted: "These ten years back he has stood to me almost in my father's place; and now the place is empty—doubly."[29] To Robert he had been rather like that character who turns up occasionally in Greek New Comedy, the older man, cultivated and hospitable, himself a bachelor, who promotes the marriage of hero and heroine and watches over their well-being.[30] He is the embodiment of that generous and civilizing power, the comic spirit, presiding over fruitful unions and the happy integration of individuals in their society. Kenyon's final expression of such a benevolent spirit was a legacy of £11,000, of which £4,500 went to Elizabeth and £6,500 to Robert. Though the money would not come to them for a year, it provided them, for the first time in their life together, with financial security. "But oh," Elizabeth exclaimed, "how much sadness goes to making every gain in this world!"[31]

"We have had a black season of it," Elizabeth said of Christmas 1856,[32] and the gloom would not be dispelled. On April 17, 1857, Elizabeth's father died. Arabella had alerted them to that end only the day before his death, and Robert was worried how Elizabeth might respond. In the event, she was "sadly affected at first; miserable to see and hear," he told Mrs. Martin. "After a few days tears came to her relief. She is now very weak and prostrated, but improving in strength of body and mind." Gone now were "all hope of better things, or a kind answer to entreaties such as I have seen Ba write in the bitterness of her heart."[33] Elizabeth herself later told Mrs. Martin that "I believe hope had died in me long ago of reconciliation in this world,"[34] but her immediate response, expressed to Arabella, was an agonized one: "Without a word, without a sign—Its like slamming a door on me as he went out—And yet, if he did not know—he did not mean *that*—."[35] Robert was concerned that Elizabeth might place some of the blame on herself but was optimistic in observing her: "Not that Ba is other than reasonable and just to herself in the matter: she does not reproach herself at all." But Elizabeth herself said otherwise: "There has been great bitterness—great bitterness, which is natural; and some recoil against myself, more, perhaps, than is quite rational."[36] The irrational took the form of the temptation "to lie on the sofa, and never stir nor speak," while "my heart goes walking up and down constantly through that house of Wimpole street, till it is tired, tired."[37] But she did not give up, and Robert's assessment of her reactions was not entirely without foundation: "I drive out for two or three hours on most days, and I hear Peni's lessons, and am good and obedient."[38] Still, she would not go to London that summer: "I couldn't bear it—it would drive me mad, I think."[39]

Instead, they stayed in Italy, going to Bagni di Lucca to escape the summer heat in Florence. The next summer, they went first to Paris and then to Le Havre, where they were joined by Robert's father and sister and by Elizabeth's sister Arabella and her brothers George and Henry and Henry's new wife. Robert and Elizabeth had discussed at length the question of where to spend their winters, even considering Egypt and Jerusalem, but they settled on Rome, leaving Florence at the end of November 1858, and not returning until June 1859. That would be the pattern for the next two winters as well, a pattern that led Isa Blagden to bid them "observe that we pretend to live at Florence, and are not there much above two months in the year, what with going away for the summer and going away for the winter."[40] There was no question of a return to England. Elizabeth, increasingly caught up in the political situation, preferred Italy to England and considered Florence her home. "When all's said and sighed," she told Fanny Haworth in 1858, "I love Italy—I love my Florence. I love that 'hole of a place,' as Father Prout called it lately ... Florence is my chimney-corner, where I can sulk and be happy."[41] Robert, meanwhile, who had turned his attention from poetry to modeling in clay under the direction of W. W. Story, expended much of his energy in socializing, with Elizabeth's encouragement. She was conscious of his robust health, his animal spirits, and his appetite ("At breakfast the loaf perishes by Gargantuan slices," she reported): "He is plunged into gaieties of all sorts, ... has gone out every night for a fortnight together, and sometimes two or three times deep in a one night's engagements. So plenty of distraction, and no Men and Women."[42]

There was another distraction, too, though their responses to it would find expression in poetry. That was the political situation in Italy. Both husband and wife had long supported the Italian nationalists in their efforts to throw off foreign rule and unify the country, a "holy cause," in Elizabeth's view.[43] "The Risorgimento was the grandest and most involving instance of nation-building in this period,"[44] and the Brownings were in the midst of the great events of 1859–1860, following them through the newspapers and bulletins, discussing them in conversations and letters, and witnessing troop movements in Florence, which excited Pen: he "has adorned our terrace with two tricolour flags, the Italian tricolour and the French," the Brownings told John Ruskin.[45] Those great events were the diplomatic and military moves of France and Austria in Italy, and at the center of them, and of all the Brownings' concerns and anxieties and hopes, was the Emperor Napoleon III. Robert and Elizabeth already had strongly divergent views of the emperor, and their differences ran as deeply, and were as troubling, as their divergent views on spiritualism.

On the main points, they were agreed. The Italians must throw off Austrian rule—"We who have lived in Italy all these years, know the full pestilent meaning of Austria everywhere," Elizabeth told Sarianna[46]—and must achieve political union and independence. "I must tell you," Elizabeth wrote to Arabella, "that though Robert, as you know well, sympathizes in general little with me in my 'Napoleonism' so called, thinks entirely with me on this Italian question."[47] Moreover, the Brownings shared in the nineteenth-century understanding of the word *nation* as a people "so closely associated with each other by common descent, language, or history" (in the words of the *OED*) that they are "united by common sympathies"[48] and wish to make their "nation" and the "state" coincide. To Arabella, Elizabeth quoted the words of Massimo d'Azeglio, the former prime minister of Piedmont (who had come to see the Brownings because he valued the work of poets in fostering nationalist feelings): "'Never in the history of the peninsula has the unity of the peoples been so complete'—(We know this from other sources.)"[49] For Elizabeth, *nation* was a key word and the ultimate political authority: "No government ought to stand, against the consent of a nation, —and no treaty ought to hold, against the consent of a nation."[50] In spite of broad agreement with this view, the Brownings took different positions in relation to the Risorgimento: Elizabeth passionately identified with the nationalists; Robert was always a sympathetic but foreign observer.[51]

Piedmont-Sardinia had been the leader of the nationalist movement, and France under Napoleon III was prepared to support the Piedmontese king, Victor Emmanuel, and his prime minister, Cavour, in liberating and unifying Italy. In 1859 France joined with Piedmont-Sardinia in a war against Austria. The conflict lasted less than three months. Though France won a series of victories, including the battles at Magenta and Solferino in June, the emperor, fearing intervention by Prussia and now apprehensive about a strong unified Italy, unexpectedy agreed to a truce which was initially thought to be only a military one but which became a treaty negotiated with the Austrian emperor at Villafranca in July. Under its terms, the Italian states would become a loose confederation with the pope as president, and Austria would continue to be a presence in the north. Italian nationalists were dismayed and reacted strongly throughout the country—"From north to south of Italy," Elizabeth had reported earlier to Arabella, "there is one unity of burning enthusiasm"[52]—with the result that by the end of 1860 Italy (with the exception of Rome and Venice) was united. The Brownings praised the resolve and unanimity of the Italian people and were fond of quoting Massimo d'Azeglio on the successful move to unification: "It is '48 over again . . . but with matured actors."[53]

Elizabeth was a passionate admirer and defender of Napoleon III, describing him as "the only great man of his age" and "the only great-hearted politician in Europe." About his motives she had no doubts. He was "generous and magnanimous" and was "the only man who has it in his head and heart to do anything for Italy." He was "sublime." "He will appear so to all when he comes out of this war (as I believe) with clean and empty hands."[54] Though she was dismayed by the "peace"[55] (the quotation marks are hers) at Villafranca, she continued to believe in the emperor's "great intentions"—he will continue to walk, she insisted, "straight and to unchanged ends"—and she blamed other nations (including England) for forcing him to hide actions and motives, to walk "under the earth instead of on the earth"[56]: "Never was a greater or more disinterested deed intended and almost completed than this French intervention for Italian independence; and never was a baser and more hideous sight than the league against it of the nations."[57] Elizabeth's response to all these events was excitement which too often darkened into agitation and anger. In June of 1859 she said of the political situation, "I feel stirred up to the dregs of me, & go here & there, to hear & talk & look into people's faces for sympathy: I can't rest, I am so excited."[58] She told Isa Blagden that "I pass through cold stages of anxiety, and white heats of rage," and she told Sarianna that she had exhausted herself "with indignation and protestation."[59] When she told Fanny Haworth that "these public affairs have half killed me. You know I *can't* take things quietly,"[60] her strong emotions were posing a danger to her health. Not surprisingly, Elizabeth was seriously ill in the summer of 1859.

Robert's attitude toward Napoleon III, like Elizabeth's, had been formed during the winter of 1851–1852, when the Brownings witnessed the coup d'état by which Napoleon eventually made himself emperor. At that time the disturbances in the street were reflected in *émeutes* (Elizabeth's word) in the Browning household, when "facts" were in dispute between husband and wife, but those *émeutes* were not repeated in 1859–1860, though their disagreements were no less profound. Elizabeth's letters from that later time are full of her views of Napoleon III and Italian politics ("the chief thing with me just now," she told Arabella[61]), and in one of them she insists, perhaps remembering earlier charges, that "Facts have been sacred things with me,"[62] but Robert's letters are full of concern about Elizabeth's health, affected as it was by her passionate responses to the political situation. The way in which they handled their disagreements reveals much about their relationship.

"The peculiarity of our relation is," Elizabeth told Sarianna, "that even when he's displeased with me, he thinks aloud with me and can't stop himself."[63] Years later Robert confirmed such openness when he was remembering "seven distinct issues [which he didn't specify] to which I came with Ba, in our profoundly different estimates of thing and person": "I am glad I maintained the truth on each of these points, did not say, 'what matter whether they be true or no?—Let us only care to love each other.' . . . only to those I love very much do I feel at all inclined to lay down what I think to be the law, and speak the truth."[64] That truthfulness dignified their disputes and made their agreements, when they occurred, sincere and satisfying. In April of 1859 Elizabeth reported to Sarianna that "Robert and I have been of one mind lately in these things, which comforts me much." A month later she told Sarianna that "Robert has taken up the same note, which is a comfort. I would rather hear my own heart in his voice." Her preference, however, was not always gratified. "I would rather not hear Robert say," she began on another occasion, when relating a statement critical of the emperor, and with Isa Blagden she struck a note of uncertainty about their unanimity— "Robert does not dissent, I think"—and then, with just a hint of triumphant vindication, turned the tables on him: "Facts begin to be conclusive to him."[65]

Unlike Robert's socializing, Italian politics did not distract the Brownings from poetry. In March 1860, Elizabeth published her *Poems before Congress*, poems written, she said in the preface, "under the pressure of the events they indicate," and beginning with the ode "Napoleon III in Italy" (the title also used for the pirated American volume). Elizabeth knew, as her preface makes clear, that she would offend "a patriotic . . . English sense of things," and she did. Her opinions, condemned as "utterly unfair to England and English feeling," as Aytoun said in *Blackwood's*, were not, however, the only problem. For Aytoun, who entitled his (anonymous) review "Poetic Aberrations," the chief problem was that she was a woman writing about male concerns, and "We are strongly of opinion that, for the peace and welfare of society, it is a good and wholesome rule that women should not interfere with politics," and should instead be "adorning the domestic circle, and tempering by their gentleness the asperities of our ruder nature."[66] Aytoun's opening paragraphs are a case study in the attitudes about a woman's "sphere" (he actually uses that word) that Elizabeth had been battling in *Aurora Leigh*, but at least he correctly identified America as the target of "A Curse for a Nation," the final poem in the volume. Not so Chorley in the *Athenaeum*, who said *Poems before Congress* "opens with a poean to the Emperor of the French, and ends with a curse to England."[67] Elizabeth wrote to Chorley (who had been an early supporter of hers) to correct the fact, wrote again to protest the way in which the *Athenaeum* made the correction, and wrote a third time in an attempt to renew their friendly relations ("Let us forgive one another our mistakes; and there, an end."). At the same time, she asserted her right to speak as she saw fit: "I never wrote to please any of you, not even to please my own husband."[68] As for Robert, Elizabeth told Isa Blagden that he was "*furious*" at the mistake: "I never saw [him] so enraged about a criticism."[69] Nor was he happy with Elizabeth's handling of it. "Robert is furious still," Elizabeth told Arabella after writing to forgive Chorley, "& comforts himself over what he calls my 'cheap magnanimity' by fancying that it will vex poor Chorley more than if I had been worse-tempered. 'Coals of fire,' thinks Robert chuckling."[70]

Robert too had been writing, "by fits and starts," his usual way during these years, according to Elizabeth: "he has been writing a good deal this winter [1859–1860]—working at a long poem which I have not seen a line of, and producing short lyrics which I *have* seen, and may declare worthy of him."[71] In fact, husband and wife intended to respond together to the events of their time: "Robert and I began to write on the Italian question together, and our plan was (Robert's own suggestion!) to publish jointly." Elizabeth's contribution would have been her "ode on Napoleon," but Robert destroyed his poem, whatever it was, after Villafranca, since what he had written "no longer suited the moment." Elizabeth's response to this change of plan: "I determined to stand alone."[72]

Yet in all essential matters she had Robert's support. His caring for her and watching over her became ever more important in 1860, a sad year for Elizabeth. On March 17, Mrs. Jameson died, and when Elizabeth heard the news at the end of the month, she described the death as "a shock."[73] "It is a blot on the world to me, this loss."[74] Another, and worse, was to come. During the summer she heard, from both Arabella and Surtees Cook, her brother-in-law, that her sister Henrietta, who had "always seemed so strong," had "an internal tumour" which was cancerous. "My first impulse was to rush to England," she told Mrs. Martin, "but this has been over-ruled by everybody, and I believe wisely."[75] Most grievous to Elizabeth was the "acute pain" she had been told Henrietta was suffering, and grievous too was the thought of (what was likely to be) her sister's protracted decline.[76] "I have been very sad, very," she told Fanny Haworth, "with a stone hung round my heart, and a black veil between me and all that I do, think, or look at."[77] All through September and October the Brownings dreaded any communication from England. Robert was "forced to get & inspect all letters before they got to Ba—She had the firmness to desire me to do so."[78] On November 19, they left for Rome, Robert knowing and Elizabeth guessing that Henrietta's death was imminent. "Ba's distress was so acute," Robert told his brother-in-law George "that I thought of no better resource than to hurry our journey at once," giving Elizabeth "six days respite at least from the sad announcement of which I knew your letter was the immediate herald." Henrietta died on November 23, but because of several lapses and crossings of communications the news did not reach the Brownings until December 3, and the days of not knowing were hardly a respite: "the suspense [was] as hard to bear as the ending of it." Of Elizabeth, Robert reported to George that "she has borne it, on the whole, as well as I should have thought possible—but the wounds in that heart never heal altogether, tho' they may film over."[79] Even before Henrietta's death, Elizabeth said that Robert had been "most dear and tender and considerate to me through my trial," but she also said, "I am weak and languid. I struggle hard to live on. I wish to live just as long as and no longer than to grow in the soul."[80] She wanted to withdraw from all social contacts: "I am in a morbid sort of state," she told Arabella, "hating the idea of an old friend, an old association, the face of anyone who ever looked at me in my previous state of being."[81] She was grateful that Robert "kept all the people off," and of a possible summer 1861 visit to France she thought "with positive terror sometimes, less of the journey than of having to speak and look at people." When she sounded a note of hope about the coming year— "by May or June I shall be feeling another woman probably. . . ."[82]—her appended "probably" made the hope halfhearted and suggested world-weariness, increasing physical weakness, and lasting sorrow.

Still sunk in depression, Elizabeth found the journey from Rome at the beginning of June 1861 more exhausting than usual. The day after the Brownings' arrival in Florence, the news of the death of Cavour (whom Elizabeth had praised as "that man of heroic virtue & admirable ability"[83]) dealt her an additional blow. "Ba can only write a word," she scribbled to the Storys. "She has not the heart—in the face of this great calamity . . . I have felt beaten and bruised ever since."[84] To Arabella she wrote, "That death has trampled a great deal of life out of me—."[85] Florence was in the midst of a punishing heat wave, with the brick wall of San Felice sending its scorching reflection into Casa Guidi. Given her weakened condition, Robert canceled their plans to spend the summer in France with Sarianna and his father. Toward the end of June, Elizabeth came down with a cold and a sore throat from sitting in the evening breezes before the opened windows. On June 22, when her cold brought on an extended coughing spell, Robert applied a blister to her chest, which gave her no relief, since she suffered from an accumulation of phlegm that she could not cough up. "For five hours, or six," Robert told Isa Blagden, "she seemed actually strangling."[86] Alarmed, Robert went to fetch Dr. Wilson, a specialist in lung disorders (her regular physician was out of town). After the doctor arrived, Robert helped him apply a mustard poultice to her breast and back and prepare a solution of mustard and water to warm her feet. Listening through the stethoscope, he detected congestion in her right lung. He said that he suspected an abscess had formed and predicted that it would take a long time for Elizabeth to recover. She dismissed their worries, telling them, "This is only one of my old attacks. I know all about it and I shall get better. . . . It was not so bad an attack as that of two years ago." Dr. Wilson stayed all night overseeing her condition. He left about 5 A.M. after assuring them that the worst was over and that sleep would restore her.[87]

Over the next few days, Robert and Annunziata tried to keep her strength up by feeding her strong broth and ass's milk, for she refused all solid food except a little bread and butter. Robert sat up with her during the nights, ministering to her needs during her frequent wakings. Isa Blagden called, offering help and encouragement, although Elizabeth insisted repeatedly that she felt better. By the time Isa had left, Pen had sensed the worry in the household talk. When he went in to say good night to his mother, he asked her three times, "Are you really better?" and was finally reassured by her third answer, "*Much* better."[88]

On the night of June 28, Robert persuaded her to swallow some spoonfuls of gelatinized broth, and she took a slightly increased dose of morphine. Elizabeth dozed fitfully during the night while Robert sat watching over her. During her wakings, her mind seemed to wander. She fancied she was aboard a Channel steamer. At 4 A.M., Robert noticed that her feet were cold and "other disquieting symptoms." He sent the porter for Dr. Wilson and called Annunziata for hot water. They sponged her with the hot water while she smilingly protested, "Well, you do make an exaggerated case of it." Robert asked, "Do you know me?" She replied "Know you! My Robert—my heavens, my beloved—" and kissed him. "Our lives are held by God," she murmured. She was persuaded to take two more saucerfuls of the jelly, although she still felt somewhat disoriented. Asked if she knew where she was, she replied, "Why—not quite." After they exchanged some endearments, she settled into sleep once more.[89]

Later when she began to cough, struggling to spit up some phlegm, Robert took her up in his arms. Her head fell against his, where she rested quietly against his cheek. Robert thought that she had fainted, but after a few minutes, Annunziata exclaimed, "Quest' anima benedetta é passata!" [The blessed soul has passed away.] Elizabeth's lifelong battle was over.

Robert was unbelieving. They had been through many such episodes of respiratory attack in the last fifteen years, but always she had emerged gradually back to her state of smiling invalidism and then asserted her will to be a wife and mother, the voice of kindness in Casa Guidi, a leading English poet, and a distinguished international personality once more. But now, suddenly, she was gone. In his grief, telling Sarianna what had happened, Robert vowed to hold her presence in his life: "I shall live out the remainder in her direct influence, endeavouring to complete mine, miserably imperfect now, but so as to take the good she was meant to give me."[90]

Twelve-year-old Pen bore his loss manfully. He sat all the next day with his arms around Robert, the child comforting the father. On July 1, the funeral services were conducted in the Church of England rooms, "blundered through by a fat English parson in a brutally careless way," according to W. W. Story.[91] On the street alongside Casa Guidi, the shops were closed. For the burial, the funeral cortege wound through the streets of Florence (which was not the usual custom) to the Protestant Cemetery, the coffin crowned with two large wreaths, one of laurel, the other of white roses. Gathering at the cemetery was a small crowd of mourners, Italians as well as English and Americans, the Italian men "crying like children." The Italian newspapers had urged the people "all to go and pay homage to the great poetess, the true friend of Italy."[92] For the funeral services, Robert had chosen the Church of England Order for the Burial of the Dead because of its splendid sixteenth-century language by William Tyndale beginning, "I am the resurrection and the life . . ." taken from the Gospel of John. That evening astrononers were surprised to observe a new comet in the night sky. Robert took it as a tribute to the passing of his beloved Ba.

The Good of Poetry

On August 1, 1861, Browning left Florence; unlike Pen and their traveling companion, the faithful and warmhearted Isa Blagden, he would never go back. Certainly that was his intention while he was preparing to leave, for he told Sarianna that "once away I don't choose to return."[1] But his mind, like the "man's act" in *The Ring and the Book*, was "changeable because alive" (1. 1365), and the next summer, when he had engaged Frederick Leighton to design a tomb for Elizabeth, he told Isa Blagden that "I shall go to Florence whenever the erection takes place of the monument," his plan being to "superintend." While he hid his intention from both Pen and Sarianna, he told Isa that "I *must* go, you under[stand]. If it can be next summer, well—if not, the next."[2] But his thoughts pulled him in contrary directions. "With respect to Florence," he told Isa in September of 1862,

> I cannot tell how I feel about it, so do I change in my feelings in the course of a quarter of an hour sometimes: particular incidents in the Florence way of life recur as if I could not bear a repetition of them—to find myself walking among the hills, or turnings by the villas, certain doorways, old walls, points of sight, on a solitary bright summer Sunday afternoon—there, I think that would fairly choke me at once: on the other hand, beginning from another point of association, I have such yearnings to be there!

He dismissed those yearnings as "foolish fancies" and said he had a "plain duty to do in London," the duty being the rearing and educating of Pen, but the "foolish fancies" would not so easily be dispelled: "I seem as if I should like, by a fascination, to try the worst at once,—go straight to the old rooms at Casa Guidi, & there live & die! But I shake all this off."[3] Still, had the plans for the monument proceeded quickly, Browning might indeed have returned, but there were long delays, questions and worries about the design, more worries about its execution, and feelings of horror at the thought of "strangers' curiosity" intruding on "those dreadful preliminaries, the provisional removement" of Elizabeth's coffin, so that its final resting place, an "arca," or chest held up by six short pillars, might be constructed on the gravesite.[4] In the event, the monument was not finished until December 1865, after others had supervised the construction, and though nearly a year later Browning told his brother-in-law George that "I hope to see it one day," his feelings about returning had, well before then, settled into resolution: "Florence will never be *my* Florence again. . . . As old Philipson said to me once of Jerusalem—'No, I don't want to go there—I can see it in my head.'"[5] So Florence took on its final and true being for Browning: it became a city of his mind. Casa Guidi itself settled into a more prosaic form: Browning had tried to have the drawing room photographed "just as she disposed it and left it," and when that plan failed, he engaged a Greek artist who lived in Florence, George Mignaty, to paint the interior. "The room has not an inch in it without a memory for me, and now that I go away it [the painting] will be invaluable."[6] Browning did not idealize the place in memory. He told John Forster that, on the evening before Elizabeth died, "we talked over our plans, and she was urgent we should take a Villa here 'for three years'—we both of us conceived a sudden dislike for this poor Casa Guidi we had been happy in so long—found it hot, noisy, incommodious."[7] One afternoon's poor light in his new London home evoked "a memory of poor Casa Guidi, which I thought black!" (he meant that his London home was even worse than Casa Guidi).[8] Browning knew that the actual Casa Guidi would go on having a life and history of its own, and he sometimes asked Isa about it—"Who lives in Casa Guidi, I wonder!" "Is Casa Guidi to be turned into any Public Office?"[9]—but whatever happened to it would no longer matter: the painting had fixed it in Browning's memory, and it, like the city itself, had become a mental space charged with emotion.

Browning's plans on leaving Florence were determined enough: "I shall at once go to England, or rather Paris first, and then London," he told his brother-in-law George: "I shall give myself wholly up to the care & education of our child; I know all Ba's mind as to how that should be, and shall try and carry out her desires—I have formed no particular plan as yet, but am certain enough of the main direction my life will take." As for Pen, "I fully

believe that he will do well,—best of all, indeed—with an English education"—a decision with which George concurred.[10] As for himself, Browning
said that he would "never again 'keep house,' nor live but in the simplest manner, but always with reference to Pen."[11] "I shall grow, still, I hope—but my
root is taken, remains."[12]

Pen was now the focus of all the attention and care Robert had lavished on
Elizabeth. "You know," Browning told Fanny Haworth, "I have her dearest
interest to attend to *at once*—her child to care for, educate, establish properly—and my own life to fulfil as properly,—all, just as she would require were
she here."[13] What Elizabeth "would require" seems at odds with the major
change Browning made in Pen's appearance: within days of Elizabeth's death,
Robert reported to his sister that "Pen, the golden curls and fantastic dress, is
gone just as Ba is gone: he has short hair, worn boy-wise, long trousers, is a
common boy all at once: otherwise I could not have lived without a maid. I can
now attend to him completely myself,—so all pins, worked collars and so on,
are gone and forgotten."[14] The quick and radical change seems to suggest that
Robert and Elizabeth had disagreed about Pen's appearance, but Elizabeth's
biographer, Margaret Forster, notes that husband and wife "had spent hours
and hours discussing and deciding how they would bring up Pen" and concludes that "nothing Robert did with Pen during the days following his wife's
death was his own idea."[15] Still, Robert, who distrusted "all hybrid & ambiguous natures,"[16] must have had his own opinion of Elizabeth's compensating for
wanting a girl by dressing Pen as one. Years earlier Elizabeth had hinted at
their divergent views: when Pen was five or six and people mistook him for a
girl, Elizabeth told Mrs. Ogilvy that "we keep the compliments to the 'lovely
little girl' as much as possible in the background."[17] Moreover, Robert must
have considered Elizabeth's wish to keep Pen from growing up for as long as
possible an unrealistic expression of maternal love. But Pen was still wearing
"the velvet tunic & short trousers, the curls & hat & feather"[18] up until the
time of his mother's death, for she had told Mrs. Ogilvy how she had resisted
Pen's desire to wear "long-tailed coats," and she encouraged her friend not to
let *her* son wear jackets. She intended to keep Pen away from "a tunic & cloth
trousers" and to prevent his hair being cut until he was twelve.[19] Pen was in
fact twelve years old when his mother died, so Robert's cutting his hair and
dressing him as a "common boy" at least accorded with the letter, if not the
spirit, of Elizabeth's wishes. At any rate, by July 1861 "the old Peni with the
curls & pretty dresses"[20] was gone for good.

The Brownings—father and son—and Isa Blagden traveled to Paris, and
then Robert and Pen went on to Brittany with Robert, Senior, and Sarianna.
They stayed at St. Enogat near St. Malo, and they would return to Brittany the

following two summers, to Sainte-Marie, Pornic. The area would provide the poet with materials, but its immediate appeal was its contrast with the Tuscan landscape. "The country is solitary and bare enough," Browning told the Storys, "but the sea is everywhere and the land harmonises entirely with it. I like the rocky walks by the sea and complete loneliness."[21] Browning would reiterate his liking for the elemental landscape and its sparse settlement: "the solitude of the bays—any one of many—the sands & rocky islets—& the quiet, pastoral character of the inland with its few inhabitants—are very grateful," he told Isa about St. Enogat in 1861; and he said almost the same about Sainte-Marie the following summer: "This is a wild little place in Brittany something like that village where we stayed last year—close to the sea—a hamlet of a dozen houses, perfectly lonely—one may walk on the edge of the low rocks by the sea for miles—or go into the country at the back. . . . The place is much to my mind; I have brought books, & write."[22] The contrast with the social life he was to lead, and led, in London, was marked: "You suppose I was dull at Ste. Marie," he wrote to Isa, but in fact he stayed longer than planned, and "it was in my scheme to read, walk, & do nothing but think *there*—*here* [in London] my way is to do many other things—among others go out a good deal."[23] The elemental appearance of land and sea, and his bathing daily in the bracing cold of the water, provided the poet with images he would later use in "Amphibian," the prologue to *Fifine at the Fair*, which is set on the Breton coast, but his initial need was for a change from the Florence way of life. Writing from St. Enogat, he told the Storys, "I want my new life to resemble the last fifteen years as little as possible," and though there are nostalgic moments in his letters to Isa Blagden, when he remembers the "winding way" up to her villa, and "the herbs in red flower & the butterflies on the top of the wall under the olive trees," he told the Storys during that first summer near St. Malo that "I only breathe freelier since we arrived at this wild, primitive & lonely place."[24] Sainte-Marie was just as satisfying: "I feel out of the earth sometimes, as I sit here at the window—with the little church, a field, a few houses, and the sea."[25] When, in the summer of 1864, they went further south, to Biarritz and Bayonne and the Spanish border itself, Browning responded to the landscape with different and mixed feelings. He told Isa that "it is very saddening to me to feel the Southern influence again": "the mountains [are] just like the Tuscan ranges, with plenty of oak & chestnut woods," and "there are *cicale* on the trees, and much of the same blue sky as of old." Then the mixed reponse: "No, it is not anything near Italy after all—but dearer for what is like."[26]

In late September of 1861, Browning and his son, having accompanied Robert, Senior, and Sarianna back to Paris, went on to London, staying first with Arabella Barrett and then moving to rented accommodations. In May

1862, father and son moved to 19 Warwick Crescent, which would be Browning's London home for the next twenty-five years and where, in spite of his vow in July 1861, he would again "keep house." The furnishings from Casa Guidi were installed there: "the old books & furniture, her chair which is by mine,—all that is comfort to me," Browning told Isa.[27] And the house itself, which looked out on the Regent's Canal in the area northwest of Paddington now known as "Little Venice," suited Browning. Anne (Thackeray) Ritchie remembered "the house by the water-side" as being in a corner of London "touched by some indefinite romance: the canal used to look cool and deep, the green trees used to shade the crescent; it seemed a peaceful oasis after crossing that dreary Æolia of Paddington. . . . The house was an ordinary London house, but the carved oak furniture and tapestries gave dignity to the long drawing-rooms, and pictures and books lined the stairs."[28] William Allingham, a luncheon guest in the house, remembered Browning's pet owl "on its perch in a corner" and the poet's calling him "'a good man,' petting and stroking him."[29] (Browning, who liked odd pets, said the bird was "the light of our house, for his tameness and engaging ways.")[30] Even in his first year in Warwick Crescent, Browning told Isa that "I find this house very comfortable & shall hope to make it serve my turn till I have done my work here—then I shall go home—not, I think, to establish myself elsewhere, but to wander about the world."[31]

Included in "my work here" was Pen's education. Browning's chief motive in returning to London was to give Pen an English education, and that intention, like his support for the unification of Italy, indicates the extent to which he shared in the nineteenth-century understanding of the words *nation* and *nationalism.* Had Pen been "brought up in England from the first," his father would not have worried so, but Pen's Tuscan boyhood had made his nationality uncertain and, said his father, "I distrust all hybrid & ambiguous natures & nationalities and want to make something decided of the poor little fellow."[32] He intended to engage a tutor as quickly as possible, to prepare Pen for university, and he worried that "if I delay this, as my original notion was, I may lose the critical time when the English stamp (in all that it is good for) is taken or missed." In due time there was a tutor, plus the instruction of the anxious father himself, and early in 1863 Browning reported to the Storys that "I have just succeeded in entering [Pen] for residence at Balliol, Oxford, in 1867, if we live & do well."[33] He chose Balliol because it had a "high standard of scholarship," and because it was "a reading college exclusively—and conferring great honour on those of its inmates who distinguish themselves."[34] One of Pen's sponsors was Balliol's famous master himself, Benjamin Jowett, who would soon become a friend of his father's.

In contrast to the solitude of his summers in France, Browning plunged into a hectic round of social engagements in London. "*I shall go out now*, in earnest, & not in promise," he told Isa Blagden early in 1862,[35] and in his letters he sometimes lists the people with whom he dined, at gatherings that were so frequent that in the summer of 1864 he confessed to Isa, when he was looking back on his winter, that he had been "dining out in a way that looks absurd enough."[36] In spite of his intentions and in spite of his pleasures in all those dinners and the talk and the company, he complained to the Storys, when he was feeling "bilious," about the "continued press of engagements—going out as I do every evening,"[37] and he even suggested to Isa that his social engagements were a kind of addiction that sometimes made him ill: "I went out far too much lately—not being able to help myself—& became unwell."[38] Hence he welcomed the summers, as he did in 1863: "My dinners, & all that, are nearly at an end—to my immense relief."[39] And he told William Allingham in June of 1864 that "if I could do exactly as I liked I should often go to an Opera or Play instead of to a party. I could amuse myself a good deal better."[40] One aspect of his new London life did not evoke such a mixed response. "The infinitely best thing in London to me," he told Isa in 1864, "is the *music*,—so good, so much of it: I know Hallé, Joachim, and others, and make them play at parties where I meet them—the last time I saw Hallé, at his own house, he played Beethoven's wonderful last Sonata—the 32d—in which the very gates of Heaven seem opening."[41]

Browning's social engagements in Florence had distracted him from writing, but dinner parties in London seem to have spurred him into activity, first with the fugitive and unpublished poems Elizabeth had left behind, and then with his own poems, both old and new. For Elizabeth's poems, he had the guidance of a list she had drawn up in June 1861, and to those poems he added translations, the whole making up *Last Poems*, published in March 1862. A year later he oversaw the republication, in one volume, of two essays by Elizabeth which had appeared in the *Athenaeum* in 1842, "The Greek Christian Poets" and "The Book of the Poets." About the same time as *Last Poems* was published, Browning was offered the editorship of the *Cornhill Magazine*, which he turned down, though he was bemused by the offer: "They count on my attracting writers,—I who could never muster English readers enough to pay for salt & bread!"[42]

Browning was nonetheless aware of a shift in his reputation, and his mocking complaint to the Storys indicates what was happening:

> Seriously, now that I care not one whit about what I never cared for too
> much, people are getting goodnatured to my poems. There's printing a

book of "Selections from RB"—(SCULPTOR & poet) which is to
popularize my old things: & so & so means to review it, and somebody
or [other] always was looking out for such an occasion, and what's his
name always said he admired me, only he didn't say it, though he said
something else every week of his life in some Journal.[43]

The *Selections* to which Browning refers appeared in December 1862
(though they were dated 1863) and were edited by John Forster and Bryan
Waller Procter, "two friends" (as they describe themselves in their preface)
motivated by the belief that Browning was "among the few great poets of the
century." In 1863 the publishers Chapman and Hall undertook a more ambitious project, the reissuing of most of Browning's earlier poems. The three volumes of the *Poetical Works* appeared between May and August. "No poem has
been omitted," Browning told Moncure Conway; "and none added to the present edition,—always excepting one very early thing, never known as mine, nor
likely to be remembered by anybody."[44] The "very early thing" was *Pauline*.

The critical response to the *Poetical Works* of 1863, which would finally
lead to the restoration of *Pauline* to the Browning canon, was both the
expression of and the stimulus to Browning's growing reputation, and sales
of the volumes were good enough to delay the publication of his new poems:
"we wait, because there is some success attending the complete edition, and
we let it work."[45] The new volume, titled *Dramatis Personae*, did not appear
until May 1864, and it was a success, selling well and reviewed widely and
favorably. Long afterward Mrs. Orr wrote that "we may fairly credit *Dramatis Personae* with having finally awakened [Browning's] countrymen of all
classes to the fact that a great creative power had arisen among them."[46] The
Athenaeum, for instance, hailed the book as "a richer gift than we shall often
receive at the hands of poetry in our time," and the *Victoria Magazine* said
that "the present volume confirms the verdict which has already placed Mr.
Browning in the foremost rank of modern poets."[47] Though Browning was
amused by some of the comments, as when he asked Isa, "Do you see the
'Edinburg' that says all my poetry is summed up in 'Bang whang, whang,
goes the Drum?'"[48] (a line from "Up at a Villa—Down in the City" in *Men
and Women*), his response to his success was a mixture of gratitude, some bitterness, and ironic detachment. Writing in the summer of 1865 about (in
Isa's phrasing) "'my fame within these four years,'" Browning expressed his
bitterness by saying, "There were always a few people who had a certain
opinion of my poems, but nobody cared to speak what he thought, or the
things printed twenty five years ago would not have waited so long for a
good word"; he expressed his satisfaction in his publisher's telling him that

"'The orders come from Oxford and Cambridge,'" and "all my new cultivators are young men"; and he took up the stance of the *eiron*, detached from received opinion, saying less than he knew, and pursuing in private his own agenda:

> When there gets to be a general feeling . . . that there must be *something* in the works of an author, the reviews are obliged to notice him, such notice as it is: but what poor work, even when doing its best!—I mean, poor in the failure to give a general notion of the whole works,—not a particular one of such and such points therein. As I began, so shall I end, taking my own course, pleasing myself or aiming at doing so, and thereby, I hope, pleasing God.[49]

Browning's charge that the reviewers focused on particular points in the poems and failed "to give a general notion of the whole works" raises the question of what that "general notion" is, and there are hints scattered here and there in the letters and elsewhere which answer that question. Part of the answer is that Browning's imagination was indeed a dramatic one; his imagination and sympathy (which are historically related concepts) worked hand in hand to reveal the inner lives of men and women. Browning was acutely conscious of the differences between his poetry and more fashionable and popular works: "it's one thing to say pretty things about swallows, roses, autumn &c and another to look an inch into men's hearts."[50] He also knew that his style in revealing the inner workings of "men's hearts" had given him the reputation of being difficult and obscure: "I have for thirty years had my own utter unintelligibility taught with . . . public and private zeal," he told Monckton Milnes in 1863.[51] His ultimate purpose, however, went beyond the revelation of character, and Browning alludes to such a purpose in a November 1863 letter to Isa in which he comments on a review of the *Poetical Works*: "That critique was fair in giving the right key to my poetry—in as much as it *is* meant to have 'one central meaning, seen only by reflexion in details'—'our principle,' says the critic—'mine and good' say I."[52] More than a year later, Browning expressed to Isa a fresh confidence in his vocation as poet and a fuller and deeper understanding of the "good" of poetry—without saying exactly what that "good" was: "I feel such comfort and delight in doing the best I can with my own object of life,—poetry,— which, I think, I never *could* have seen the good of before,—that it shows me I have taken the root I *did* take, *well*."[53]

So what is "the right key" to his poetry? What is its "one central meaning, seen only by reflexion in details"? What is its "good"? Browning characteristically kept the answer to those questions hidden, but there is a hint in the

new preface he wrote for *Sordello*, in which he says that "the historical decoration was purposely of no more importance than a background requires;
and my stress lay on the incidents in the development of a soul: little else is
worth study." For Browning believed that each human being does have a soul
which is immaterial and immortal. That belief is likely to be an embarrass-
ment for twenty-first-century critics, who may well think that, if one *must*
believe in the soul, there is not much to make of it, since it *is* immaterial and
reveals little to the observing eye. Browning thought otherwise. The mind,
in his view, is the agent of the soul, and the senses are the agents of the
mind—the five senses, in combination with the mind's awareness of its own
actions, an awareness that Locke labeled "reflection." One can study the acts
of the mind when they manifest themselves in conduct, and especially in
speech, since every statement represents a judgment made by the mind,
which in turn is acting for the soul, for which such acts are crucial. For the
world was for Browning as it was for Keats, a "vale of Soul-making,"[54] and in
it the soul "wakes / And grows" (in the words of Bishop Blougram) when the
mind tries to make sense of experience. The act of interpretation, the judgment of the mind, is central to the soul's growth: the decision becomes the
basis of conduct; the resulting action makes necessary further judgments
and attempts at making sense; and the whole complicated sequence of interpretation, action, reaction, and reinterpretation makes up "the development
of the soul." One begins to understand why Browning says, in the new preface to *Sordello*, that "little else is worth study," and one begins to understand,
too, the motive behind his dramatic monologues: they present speakers' acts
of interpretation which for the reader are both exemplary and cautionary,
though the reader must decide which is which, or—an even more difficult
decision—if the two are mixed. Hence Browning is constructing texts
which are both studies in the development of souls and the site of the development of the reader's soul, the reader being prodded by the dramatic form
of the texts to arrive at his or her own interpretation of them. So the poetic
texts become complete only when readers respond to them, and the act of
reading is an interpretation of an interpretation.

There is yet another hidden dimension to the interpretation the reader
encounters in one of Browning's dramatic texts. Though the poet regularly
insisted that he wrote poetry "always dramatic in principle, and so many utterances of so many imaginary persons, not mine" (Browning frequently quoted
his own 1842 note to *Dramatic Lyrics*), the poet is himself observing and interpreting, like the poet of Valladolid in the 1855 "How It Strikes a Contemporary," and hence every text that he constructs is an incident in the development
of his own soul. At the beginning of their courtship correspondence in 1845,

Robert had told Elizabeth, "I never have begun, even, what I hope I was born to begin and end,—'R.B. a poem.'"[55] But he had indeed begun, and the full nature of the *Poetical Works*, eventually to include even the suppressed *Pauline*, can be guessed at: the "works" are the record of the development of Robert Browning's soul, and the autobiography of which every critical biography must be a representation; their ultimate (but hidden) form is the metaphorical identity of poet and poetry. Writing shortly after Browning's death, Wilfred Meynell, who knew the poet personally, confirmed that one had to go to the works to know the man. The man was open, plainspoken, sociable, and willing to chat about himself—"Never, perhaps, was so great a poet so accessible a man"—but "to reach the real inner Browning his close friends no less than his casual acquaintances had to go to his books. He reserved nothing from those who knew him little to show in secret to those who knew him well."[56]

There were eighteen poems in the original *Dramatis Personae* of 1864, and though the title of the volume suggested more texts like the great dramatic monologues of 1855—"Fra Lippo Lippi," say, or "Andrea del Sarto"—the poet was in fact moving in new directions, shaping material from the Breton coast into the related lyrics of "James Lee" (called later, and more accurately, "James Lee's Wife"), exploring the nature of music in "Abt Vogler," and responding to some of the major theological and scientific issues of the day in "A Death in the Desert" and "Caliban upon Setebos." The poem most like the earlier dramatic monologues was "Mr. Sludge, 'The Medium,'" and in it Browning had the final word on one of the subjects which had been cause for disagreement between himself and Elizabeth, spiritualism, and on the medium about whom they had most disagreed, Daniel Home. Browning's poems were more and more, as we shall see, responses to other texts, but "Mr. Sludge" is a response to the man himself, and Browning told Isa that "I never read Hume's [*sic*] book,—avoid looking at an extract from it."[57] The essence of Browning's objections to spiritualism's main practice of communication with the dead appears in a letter to Isa on the third Christmas after Elizabeth's death, a letter in which Browning begins by expressing his faith in providence and in the future: "this dark tunnel of life" will not last forever; "in many ways I can see with my human eyes why this has been right & good for me—as I never doubted it was for Her—and if we do but re-join any day,—the break will be better than forgotten, remembered for its uses." Then he contrasts his faith and spiritualism: "The difference between me and the stupid people who have 'communications' is probably nothing more than that I don't confound the results of the natural working of what is in my mind, with vulgar external appearances."[58] "Spirit-rapping," Browning called the latter (the label had also been used by Elizabeth); Home himself he called a "dung-ball."[59]

By the 1860s Browning's dramatic interest had turned to the ways in which people interpret the spoken word and the written texts of others, and this interest (plus his own upbringing in the Congregational Church) led him to immerse himself in some major scholarly issues of his day, the questions of the nature of the texts in the Bible and of how to interpret them. The Higher Criticism which dealt with those questions had originated mainly in Germany in the late eighteenth century, and though it was certainly a search for the historical Jesus and a debunking of much that purported to be historical, it was inevitably a study that we would now label the "theory" of texts: their nature, their origin and composition, and the changes they undergo through transmission, commentary, annotation, editing, consolidation, interpretation, and translation; moreover, it was a concern with the people who created and transmitted them in their "testaments" (the word being based on the Latin *testis*, witness). The Higher Critics undermined the idea of verbal inspiration, the belief that God (as the Holy Spirit) dictated the Bible and that the scribes whose names are attached to the various books were only instruments of that Spirit. They also undermined the supposition that the Gospels are eyewitness accounts of the narrated events. Instead, they championed the view that the Bible is a human and fallible response to events, and that it is the product of faith, not the source of it. It is, as Browning says of Half-Rome's monologue in *The Ring and the Book*, "the instinctive theorizing whence a fact / Looks to the eye as the eye likes the look" (1: 863–64). Christians were hardly ready to define their faith as "instinctive theorizing," something that would make it "projection from the mind of man" (in the words of the Higher Critic whom John answers in "A Death in the Desert" [421]), and instead had long assumed that the strength of their faith was its historical basis, which made it objectively "true." The Higher Criticism effected a revolution in that view by suggesting that that history was not Christianity's strength but its weakness. Mark Pattison, one of the authors of the controversial 1860 *Essays and Reviews*, explained why. Because readers assumed they were reading history, they also assumed that the authority of that history rested upon its truth, "the 'Evidences,' or the historical proof of the genuineness and authenticity of the Christian records." Hence "Christianity appeared made for nothing else but to be 'proved'; what use to make of it when it was proved was not much thought about. Reason was at first offered as the basis of faith, but gradually became its substitute."[60] Those fearful of the Higher Critics charged that they were destroying people's faith. In fact, as Pattison and others—including Browning

—recognized, the Higher Criticism was renewing interest in the nature of faith itself, and shifting its center of authority from outward "evidences" to (in Tennyson's phrase from "The Two Voices") "the heat of inward evidence," the acts and motions of the mind as well as the needs and desires of the whole person. Readers may have been skeptical of the claim of David Friedrich Strauss (in his *Life of Jesus* 1835), that "the essence of the Christian faith" was "independent of his criticism," and that, after his casting doubt on nearly every aspect of the historical Jesus, his task is now "to re-establish dogmatically that which has been destroyed critically" ("dogma" being opinion or belief). That "necessary transition," though not undertaken by Strauss himself, would lead to a renewed understanding of faith among Christians genuinely concerned about the grounds of their assent.[61] Browning would contribute to that renewal, especially in one of the major poems of the *Dramatis Personae* volume, "A Death in the Desert."

Browning was well prepared to take part in such contemporary debates, since he had read widely in the Higher Criticism and related texts, as his allusions and references (both in the poems and in his letters) show. The "hawk-nosed high-cheek-boned Professor," the German lecturer whom the speaker satirizes in *Christmas-Eve and Easter-Day*, is clearly Strauss (as the references to "This Myth of Christ" [859] indicate; the couplet "It matters little for the name, / So the idea be left the same" [866–67] is an unsympathetic summary of Strauss's "Concluding Dissertation"). In the 1855 *Men and Women*, Bishop Blougram explicitly names Strauss (577) and rejects him for being "on the denying side" (580). At the end of "Gold Hair: A Legend of Pornic" in the 1864 volume there are references to "our Essays-and-Reviews' debate" (143) and "Colenso's words" (145), Colenso being the author of an 1862 "critical examination" of the first five books of the Old Testament, and the *Essays and Reviews* (1860) being seven pieces by seven different authors (including Benjamin Jowett[62]); the essays (whose publication has since been recognized as " a pivotal moment in ideas and institutional practices"[63]) were controversial, widely discussed, and widely condemned as "a conspiracy of clergymen to blow up the Church from within."[64] Browning had also read an earlier work that influenced the Higher Critics (and which was itself indebted to a still earlier one), Wolf's book on the Homeric texts (*Prolegomena ad Homerum*, 1795); Browning mentions Wolf in his late poem "Development" and was aware of Wolf's attempt to construct a history of the text by examining the nature of its sources and by judging the character of its various "witnesses." The book he read immediately before the publication of *Dramatis Personae* was Renan's *Vie de Jésus*. In a letter to Isa dated November 19, 1863, Browning is critical: "I have just read Renan's book, and find it weaker and less honest than I was led to expect." Interestingly enough, Browning appeals to "the Strauss school" as a corrective: Renan, he says, "admits many points they have thought it essential to dispute—and substitutes his explanation, which I think impossible."[65] Renan appears as one of the speakers in the "Epilogue" to *Dramatis Personae*, but the third speaker (unnamed) concludes with a tercet in which he voices the chief lesson Browning seems to have learned from the Higher Critics: that the apprehension of the incarnate Christ is constantly changing with changing times and places and minds:

> That one Face, far from vanish, rather grows,
> Or decomposes but to recompose,
> Become my universe that feels and knows. (99–101)

The poem from the 1864 volume which clearly owes the most to the Higher Critics and to Renan is "A Death in the Desert."

The death is that of the apostle John, who figures largely in Renan's book as an apologist for Jesus and in Renan's criticism as an unreliable witness writing in his own interest and wanting to show that "he has been the favourite of Jesus" and "that in all the solemn circumstances (at the Lord's supper, at Calvary, at the tomb) he held the first place."[66] Browning simply ignores the interest Renan attributes to John and concentrates instead on John's being "the last surviving eye-witness" to the life of Jesus, a situation which raises the key questions the Higher Critics wrestled with: what privilege can the eyewitness claim? What happens when his testimony is passed on to others who have no immediate experience of the events narrated? John himself voices the question which is the thematic center of the poem: "How will it be when none more saith 'I saw'?" (133). The poem answers, saying, in effect, that eyewitnesses stand in exactly the same relation to events as those who have not seen: for both, interpretation, which changes with changing times and circumstances, is crucial; and events are always mediated, not only for those to whom they are narrated, but by those who actually observe them, since these witnesses bring to the events expectations, patterns of thought and story, and—yes,—faith itself. To define those changing acts of witness, Browning conflates John the author of the fourth Gospel with John of the Epistles and with John of the Book of Revelation. That last John simply listened, "With nothing left to my arbitrament / To choose or change" (143–44): "I wrote, and men believed" (144). John of the letters reasoned from his knowledge: "Friends said I reasoned rightly, and believed" (151). The Gospel, however, was the product of years of reflection which produced "new significance and fresh result": "What first were guessed as points, I now knew stars, / And named them in the Gospel I have writ" (173–75). Browning's concern is with the motions of John's mind that produced the Gospel, and he universalizes those motions by describing "How divers persons witness in each man, / Three souls which make up one soul" (83–84). The three souls he defines as "What Does, what Knows, what Is" (103), and the trinitarian analogy suggests not only that human beings are made in the image of God but that the human mind is a reflection of the nature of the Godhead itself, of the Power and Love which energize and shape our human and physical sight. "In this word 'I see,'" John says,

> Lo, there is recognized the Spirit of both [Power and Love]
> That moving o'er the spirit of man, unblinds
> His eye and bids him look. (223–25)

John thus locates the authority for his interpretation of the life of Christ in the godlike within his own mind. Browning, however, avoids suggesting that the "godlike" is a matter of revelation and instead explores in John's thinking patterns and intellectual powers that are human and ordinary. The poet had already countered spiritualism with "the natural working of what is in my mind"; he would take the same approach to revelation.

Browning's indebtedness to the Higher Criticism is apparent not only in the content of "A Death in the Desert" but in its form. The center of the poem is John's monologue, and at first glance it looks like the monologues of *Men and Women*, but readers soon note that John quotes extensively, mainly from the spoken words of skeptics, critics, and adversaries, all of whom the apostle answers, so that the monologue becomes in effect a dialogue. And while one may quote passages which seem clearly to be an expression of Christian faith, they are in fact John's interpretation of his experience of Christ (like the Gospel itself). Moreover, the form of the poem questions the way in which that interpretation came down to us. In the framing narrative, four men witness John's death: Valens, Xanthus, "the Boy," and the "I" who records the event and John's last words. "Xanthus . . . escaped to Rome, / Was burned, and could not write the chronicle" (56–57); "Valens is lost, I know not of his trace" (648); "the Boy" simply disappears, and "I tomorrow fight the beasts" (652), but he will entrust his memory of the event "to Phoebas" (653). Who, then, wrote the actual manuscript, the "parchment" described at the beginning of the poem? The first twelve lines (yet another frame) do not tell us, and the "I" in those lines says the roll is "Supposed of Pamphylax the Antiochene" (1) and came "From Xanthus, my wife's uncle"

(7). This "I," like the other "I," does not give his name. Hence we cannot determine with any certainty the history of the text nor assess the authority of the witnesses who have contributed to it. Moreover, we are confronted with interpolations and additions: "the glossa of Theotypas" in lines 82 to 104, which give the doctrine of the three souls, a systematizing and universalizing of John's account of his changing responses to the life of Christ; and the additions at the end, by Cerinthus (or by "one" [665] apparently speaking for Cerinthus) and by someone dismissing Cerinthus ("But 'twas Cerinthus that is lost" [687]). The poem thus looks like the kind of work that textual scholarship had gradually revealed to be characteristic of biblical texts: an accretion of stories and records of the spoken word from various sources, with commentary, additions, and interpretations. Trying to determine the facts about all these materials is likely to be frustrating. Hence readers are left, as Browning intended that they should be, with the various witnesses' interpretations of the facts, shapings out of which each reader must make sense, not by determining their history but by assessing their value for the conduct of life itself.

The final lines of the poem, though framed in a way which makes them of doubtful authority, suggest that, while human acts of interpretation go on and on, each attempt to make sense is not without its authority. "That day the world shall end" will reveal that Christ has been the ultimate referent for all words, the ultimate body ("incorporate") for all souls, and the "Groom for each bride" (684)—in short, the ultimate reality of which all human attempts at making sense are only approximations. What looks like nothing more than an addendum at the end of a much annotated and glossed manuscript turns out to be an affirmation of faith.

Fathers, Sons, Books

In 1866, Browning's father, living in Paris with Sarianna, was in his eighty-fifth year and in declining health. Browning went to Paris in April and reported to Isa that "I . . . did *not* find my father well,—far from it."[1] Less than two months later, Sarianna sent an urgent telegram to her brother, who arrived in Paris on June 13 expecting to find their father dead or about to "pass away without knowing me"—but "poor Nonno" rallied "and spoke like his old self." "He told me, with just the usual air," Browning reported to Pen, "that he was perfectly well—and seemed to wonder that we saw anything to grieve about: he is in the full possession of his senses" and "as unconcerned about death as if it were a mere walk into the next room." Brother and sister felt the frustration of loving care: "it is sad indeed to see him lying for hours, half-insensible and breathing heavily, while we can do nothing but look on." Sarianna had been sitting up with her father for two nights; Robert now took his turn. About 2:30 in the morning his father "began to breathe with difficulty." "The suffering was terrible to see," and death came mercifully about six hours later, in the morning of June 14.[2] A Mr. Gardiner eulogized Mr. Browning at the funeral on June 16, but his son's words to Isa were the father's best praise: "So passed away this good, unworldly, kind hearted, religious man, whose powers natural & acquired would have so easily made him a notable man, had he known what vanity or ambition or the love of money or social influence meant." Then the highest praise of all: "He was worthy of being Ba's father."[3] Robert Browning, Senior, had been a loving husband, a foolish widower, and an indulgent father. Books were his passion, and he accumulated them—and the information in them—with unflagging enthusiasm. His lack of critical discrimination may have been what led Robert to tell Elizabeth, in August of 1846, that he and his father had "not one taste in common, one artistic taste" and "the sympathy has not been an intellectual one."[4] Still, what stirred the son's imagination was what spurred the father's enthusiasm: not nature but the printed word; and the aims of both men were encyclopedic ("the whole round of creation," in the words of the son's David). Years later, when Browning was making an ineffectual attempt "to somewhat arrange my books—such a chaotic mass, in real want of a good clearing fire!" he asked Mrs. Thomas FitzGerald, "[H]ow can I part with old tomes annotated by my Father, and yet how can nine out of ten of them do other than cumber the shelves like the dead weight they *are*? Oh that *helluo librorum* [devourer of books] my father, best of men, most indefatigable of book-digesters!"[5]

With their father's death there was no question about Sarianna's future. "Sarianna will arrange matters here," Browning told his son, "and come and live with us as soon as she can." "She will bring her chairs, and Nonno's dear books, and pictures &c and establish herself in the little room which I will make comfortable."[6] For to Sarianna had fallen the lot all too often drawn by daughters: the sacrificing of a life of her own to care for aging parents. There is nothing to suggest that the sacrifice was not a willing and a loving one, for Browning said of his sister that "she has always been perfect in her relation to everyone she was naturally a help to."[7] Hence her father's death was a blow, as Browning told Isa: "You see what she loses,—all her life has been spent in caring for my mother, and, seventeen years after that, my father: you may be sure she does not rave and rend her hair like people who have plenty to atone for in the past,—but she loses very much."[8] Henceforward she became her brother's companion and confidante, and in his letters one catches glimpses of her intelligence, her sympathy, and her independence. She loved Pen and was "immensely kind"[9] to him when he was ill. Though she "came to be friend, comforter, home-maker for her brother" (in the words of Anne Thackeray Ritchie[10]), she did have a life apart from her family: one hears of her traveling, on her own, to Paris in 1867 and 1870, and "to Hombourg—where she has friends,"[11] in 1871. Her friends in France included the Milsands, and she was sometimes in their company when her brother was not; when that happened, Browning ended his letters to her by asking her to convey his love to Milsand.[12] For Milsand had been in Paris when their father was dying, had helped with his care and the watching over him, and had been one of the mourners at his funeral.[13] Hence it is not surprising that Sarianna, like Robert, felt a special affection for him, and visited with him and his family on her own. From St. Aubin in the summer of 1870

Browning reported to Isa Blagden that "Sarianna is out with the Milsands, all three" (the third was Claire, their daughter), and in the summer of 1871, when he and his son were in Scotland, Browning told Isa, "My sister is in France, where the Milsands are,—she will leave in a week or two for Paris."[14] The full story of the relations between Sarianna and the Milsands, and of the role of all of them in Browning's life, has yet to be told. Among the extensive resources in the Milsand Archive, acquired in 2004 by the Armstrong Browning Library at Baylor University, are more than 160 letters between Sarianna and Milsand: the information in them will greatly extend our knowledge and understanding of Browning's later years, and particularly of the poet's relations with his son.[15]

For within days of Elizabeth's death Robert had told Sarianna that "Dear Milsand will be the person for whose help I shall count most presently: he will advise with me about Pen."[16] And from the mid-1860s on, "Pen and his preparation" was a preoccupation of Browning's and a recurring subject in his letters. The "preparation" was for Pen's matriculation at Balliol, and it was the focus of all Browning's paternal hopes and anxieties. A great many of his letters to Isa include heartening comments on Pen's development and anxious assessments of his character, and there is a pattern to these passages: worried observation followed by assurances about Pen's good qualities. For instance, in September 1866, Browning wrote that "he is still, to all intents, growing,—a boy: he seems to me able to do many things for which at present he has little or no inclination." Then the assurances: "but the bases of a strong and good character, on the other hand, are more than indicated,—they are laid: he is good, kind, cautious, self-respecting, and true: I ought to be satisfied with those qualities which are valuable enough."[17] That subjunctive "ought" indicates that Browning thought something was missing, and the something seems not to have been additional virtues but the "inclination" to make the most of the virtues he had. The strengthening of Pen's will—his "inclination"—would be his father's chief concern. (Elizabeth had sensed this deficiency in Pen's character in telling Arabella, when Pen was ten, that though "his very temperament is sunny," "he is a holiday creature overmuch, I sometimes fear."[18]) "A fine little fellow in his way" was the father's assessment in February 1867, but "his way" was no guarantee of future success. "He is strong, healthy, inordinately given to boating, quite a boy still, but good, truthful, *loyal*—I may safely say: all depends on the turn he may take just now."[19]

Browning hoped, and was determined, to make that turn the right one. "Possible advantage to Pen"[20] was his criterion for moves and decisions of his own, particularly those involving his increasing connections with Oxford. In June 1867 the university gave him an M.A. degree by diploma, and in October he was elected an honorary fellow of Balliol. He said of his acceptance of the M.A., "Of course, it is purely for Pen's sake," but a darker purpose lay behind his accepting the second honor: "Well, the good of this to Pen is, that it gives me a natural right to come down to Oxford every now and then, nominally to vote against Dr. Pusey, really to see what the said Pen is about."[21] He had expressed the same purpose about the possibility of his being professor of poetry at Oxford: the post was vacated by Matthew Arnold in 1867, and Browning would have accepted it "to 'stand well' in Oxford" but above all to keep Pen under surveillance: "I should have had a legitimate reason for going down there, and a greater likelihood of hearing the truth of things—how he got on in every way,—more than I should otherwise have."[22] What Pen thought of such an arrangement we do not know, but in 1870 the father would glimpse the son's problem: "His last years have been possibly a sort of battle for his own individuality."[23]

As the date of Pen's matriculation approached—it was to be May 2, 1867—his father's uneasiness increased. "Pen is not nervous at all," Browning reported to Isa in March, but he worked only in the last month, "not before then: in fact, he is immature, and could not realize the nearness of the trial and necessity of preparing for it."[24] Prior to May, Pen visited Jowett, who examined him in Latin and Greek and introduced him to the undergraduates. With them Pen got on well, but Jowett's assessment of Pen's scholarship was not so encouraging: Pen was "up to the mark in Latin, hardly in Greek." "So I got nervous," Browning told Isa, "and wrote to the Master asking leave to delay the matriculation, appointed for May, till the real time of residence, October": "it is now in Pen's own power to do what is wanted or leave it undone."[25]

For some months Pen did seem to do what was wanted. He went to Oxford in the fall of 1867 to prepare for matriculation—now delayed again—and his father's hopes were high: in November Browning told Isa that "he is doing particularly well there, the experiment turning out exactly as I hoped."[26] The new date for matriculation, April 23, 1868, came and went. In June 1868, Pen was home for a holiday, "after which he goes into the country for two months with a Tutor, and then, with Mr Jowett, to Scotland for a month" as part of a reading party.[27] Jowett had told Browning in 1867 that Pen was "deficient in memory," and he reiterated that assessment after the 1868 stay in Scotland, saying also that Pen "is not able to muster more than a certain amount of interest & attention."[28] Still, all that preparation finally was sufficient. On January 15, 1869, Pen did matriculate, but at Christ Church rather than Balliol. His father had written to the dean of Christ Church in October 1868, asking permission for Pen to matriculate there because "I seem to perceive that my choice of a College has been a wrong one": in wanting to prepare Pen for a career in diplomacy he had hoped to combine "strict and complete scholarship," in which Pen would have been trained at Balliol, "with lighter acquisitions and modern languages."[29] Even when Pen had succeeded in entering Christ Church, his father thought, with some disappointment, that Pen might have managed that ideal combination. Of Pen's matriculation he said, "He did it easily & creditably," and he "did all he ought to have done at Balliol."[30]

Getting into Oxford was one thing; continuing there was another, and Pen's admission did not dispel his father's emotional highs and lows. In September 1869, Browning told Isa, "My 'worry' is increased to pretty much the last degree"; in February 1870 he reported, "Pen is *at last* round the corner of his career and fairly with his head in the right way—I do trust!"[31] But the father was to be bitterly disappointed. In June 1870 Pen had to leave Oxford.

In April of that year Browning had received a report from Pen's tutor, who wrote: "I find your son deficient in those parts of his work which depend on application and accuracy; on the other hand, where taste and thought is required, he does well." One sentence must have given Browning pause— "He has been helped too much, and done too little for himself"—but it did confirm Browning's own earlier assessment of the problem, that Pen's "own resources . . . have never been sufficiently relied upon" and that "he has been over-helped, perhaps."[32] Still, Browning commented to Sarianna (to whom he had sent the report) that "it does seem absurd" that the deficiencies might not be overcome "if a will to overcome them is really present."[33] But the will was not there. In June 1870 Browning wrote two bitter letters to his brother-in-law George Barrett, the first beginning in a blunt and abrupt way that revealed the writer's agitation: "Pen has failed again: he did his best in the country, I believe,—but two months of labor were not enough to overcome nine years of idleness. He is obliged to take his name off the books at Ch[rist] Ch[urch]." Browning complained of the cost—"his expenses for the last term of residence (scarcely five weeks) were about £170"—but it was Pen's attitude that made his father so bitter: "He cannot be made to see that he should follow any other rule than that of living like the richest and idlest young men of his acquaintance, or that there is any use in being at the University than to do so." "You see that all my plans are destroyed by this double evil—the utmost self-indulgence joined to the greatest contempt of work and its fruits." Browning (who in 1861 had told George that "I shall give myself wholly up to the care and educating of our child"[34]) was especially bitter about "the last nine years of my life, which have been as thoroughly wasted as if they were passed in playing at chuck-farthing." "The poor boy is simply WEAK," he concluded in the second letter; "he is unfit for anything but idleness and pleasure." All that he had done for Pen's benefit had come to nothing: "I am quite at my wits' end and hopeless of doing anything to the boy's advantage. . . . I am merely the manger at which he feeds."[35]

So the 1860s were for Browning a decade of anxieties, disappointments, worries, and sorrows, feelings he linked with one particular month. "The time of the year always weighs on me,—most of my troubles happen in June," Browning wrote to Isa on July 2, 1870.[36] Pen had been sent down in June; his father, Elizabeth, and his sister-in-law Arabella had died in June. Arabella's death, on June 11, 1868, had been eerily reminiscent of Elizabeth's. Her illness had "seemed not so serious," though Browning, convinced of the gravity of her condition, had called in a second doctor who "saw with the eyes of the first" and said that "there was no immediate danger." "So he went, and, five minutes after, I raised her in my arms where she died presently."[37] One event which caused Browning a great deal of upset (and afterward resentment and anger) happened not in June but rather in September 1869. It was gossip regarding the question of his marrying Louisa, Lady Ashburton.

The possibility of Browning's marrying again was a recurring topic in the poet's social circles, and he was aware of such gossip and angered by it. "Nonsensical reports," he labeled such talk, "more impertinent and intentionally false than merely nonsensical," "stupid and spiteful."[38] "I have plenty of new lady-acquaintances," he told Isa in 1867, "some of them attractive enough, but I don't get intimate with any of them." Still, the gossip persisted. In 1869 Browning reported to Isa, "There is a curious lie flying about *here*—concerning poor me—I am going to marry Miss A. daughter of Ly B. mother also of Ly C. &c. &c. I heard it three times last week. I never even heard there was such a person as any one of the three,—never heard their names even. You will soon have it retailed you as indubitable fact."[39] The gossip which most provoked Browning's anger had its source in one of those ladies herself, and she made no secret of the fact that there had been an actual proposal of marriage.

Our primary source of information about this situation is a letter Browning wrote to Edith Story in 1872, two and a half years after the first incident, when the American sculptress Harriet Hosmer was keeping "that detestable subject" alive. ("I should like to know," Browning wrote, "what business Hatty had with my behaviour to Ly A. in Ly A's house?") Browning describes his conduct in the next sentence:

> I suppose that Lady A. did not suppress what she considered the capital
> point of her quarrel with me when she foamed out into the couple of
> letters she bespattered me with: yet the worst she charged me with

was,—having said that my heart was buried in Florence, and the attractiveness of a marriage with her lay in its advantage to Pen: two simple
facts,—as I told her,—which I had never left her in ignorance about, for
a moment,—though that I ever paraded this in a gross form to anybody
is simply false.[40]

Biographers have read this sentence as indicating that Browning proposed to
Lady Ashburton, but a more likely reading is that she proposed to him, or that
she at least suggested that he remarry and indicated her own interest in that
possibility, initially in September 1869, perhaps more explicitly when Browning was again at Loch Luichart, her home, in October 1871 (and when, in Virginia Surtees's opinion, Browning, in an effort to settle the matter once and for
all, made the statements that were "the worst she charged me with"[41]). That
worst might suggest that he intended (in his own words in that letter of 1872)
"an ambitious or mercenary marriage" (which would be highly uncharacteris-
tic of him); his honest statements suggest instead a firm (even exasperated)
attempt to deal with an importuning woman—and for that honesty Browning paid a price, not only in the anger of a woman scorned, but also in the cen-
sure of twentieth-century critics ready to charge Browning with proposing
marriage in such a way that no woman could accept it.

Louisa, Lady Ashburton, was a wealthy Scotswoman of the Clan
Mackenzie, and she had married wealth in the person of William Bingham
Baring, the second Lord Ashburton (and grandson of the founder of the
banking firm Baring Brothers), a widower twenty-eight years her senior,
who had died in 1864, two years after Browning had first met the Ashbur-
tons in London (and twelve years after Louisa, then Louisa Stewart-
Mackenzie, had met the Brownings in Paris). With impetuous enthusiasm
she collected friends who were artists and writers, among them the Carlyles,
the Ruskins, and some of the Pre-Raphaelites, including Dante Gabriel
Rossetti, who described her as "kind, good, overwhelming Lady A."[42] And
overwhelming she could be. She was entertaining and charming (but impulsive and demanding, asking Rossetti, for instance, "to come down instantly
and meet a sympathising circle"), generous and hospitable (but not to be
counted on to be home when her guests arrived nor to have enough rooms
for all she had invited), and enthusiastic about art and design (but a trial to
the patience of the artists, architects, sculptors, and designers from whom
she commissioned work for her several houses). Thomas Carlyle, who knew
her as well as anyone, enjoyed her hospitality and praised her "genial, effusive
kindness of heart," but marveled at her capacity for complicating all social
plans and every social gathering with her impulses and caprices. "Doing *mis-*

chief with her kindness"[43] was Carlyle's oxymoron for her actions: "nothing can exceed the industry, patience, and continual contrivance of my hospitable Lady Ashburton; and she really has a great deal of sense and substantial veracity of mind,—tho' so full of impulses, sudden resolutions, and living so in an element of 'float.'"[44] One of her failings was a "laxity of purpose as to time and space, whereby much gets *jumbled* daily"—to the consternation and bewilderment of her guests. "The most generous-hearted, but the most tumble-headed" of hostesses was Carlyle's summary of his experience of her hospitality in the south of France during the winter he called "the saddest of my life"—it was the winter of 1866–1867, after Jane Carlyle's death—for in February, Lady Ashburton had left her guests and gone suddenly to Italy. "We were almost glad to see her go," Carlyle reported to his brother, "strange as our circumstances were; such had *her* dubitations and botherings been for weeks past." She was the kind of woman who could not get "the many *lines* of her complex affairs to *intersect* handsomely," wrote Carlyle: "Her situation here is really intricate; and she makes it by her impetuous handling, often enough not *less* so but more so."[45] The most intricate of her situations revolved around the several possibilities of her marrying again. Carlyle's niece, who had come to live with him after Jane's death, thought Lady Ashburton hoped to marry her uncle (Carlyle himself referred to the situation as "that inane and mad affair"), and gossip in Rome had it that Lady Ashburton would marry the wealthy and cultivated Duke of Sermoneta—gossip Lady Ashburton did not contradict and may even have promoted. The situation with Browning was not unique.

Lady Ashburton invited the Brownings and the Storys to her Rosshire estate, Loch Luichart Lodge, in August 1869, when Robert and Sarianna had decided against their usual summer stay in France. At first they were not happy—Browning described the time as "the hideous confusion of three weeks' constant inconstancy, & flitting from bad place to worse"[46]—and, moreover, their hostess was absent when they reached Loch Luichart. Still, on August 28, Browning wrote to Isa saying that he was "at an old friend's" and was "comfortable altogether"—until the proposal which was to come. Had Lady Ashburton kept the matter private, it might have been at an end, but as late as 1872 she let it be thought that Browning was on the point of proposing to her, and she continued to "teaze" him (his word) with her invitations. Browning read them as attempts to set up an opportunity for her to "get handsomely done with it all," with her wanting "to have the air of shutting the door in my face with a final bang" and so rescue herself from a situation that could be damaging to her reputation, but she did "bespatter" him with a "couple of letters" which he kept until the end of his life. Perhaps he had in mind his father's unhappy experience with Mrs. Von Müller and the incriminating letters Robert, Senior, had written; if Browning himself were ever to be charged with breach of promise, he would have Lady Ashburton's letters as proof of his position, and he took the precaution of sending copies of them to the Storys. "Calumnies," he called the contents of the letters fourteen years later, "which Lady A exploded in all the madness of her wounded vanity."[47] Browning pronounced her "contemptible" and said he minded her "no more than any other black beetle—so long as it don't crawl up my sleeve."[48] Her subsequent behavior was a mixture of angry outbursts and gestures at reconciliation.[49]

Another complicated relationship, which caused Browning a different kind of pain, was with Julia Wedgwood, the great-granddaughter of the potter. Browning was acquainted with various members of her family, including her mother and her brother, James Mackintosh Wedgwood, whose death in June 1864 was the subject of their earliest correspondence: the poet offered what comfort he could to the grieving sister. Wedgwood, a well-read woman, novelist, and essayist, initiated their friendship, and she terminated it as well. The cause, ostensibly, was gossip about the poet's visits to her: "I have reason to know," she said in the letter bringing the visits and the correspondence to an end, "that my pleasure in your company has had an interpretation put upon it that I ought not to allow."[50] The relation had seemed fated to such an end from its beginning. "A woman who has taken the initiative in a friendship with a man, as I have done with you, has either lost all right feeling or has come to a very definite decision on the issue of all such friendships," she told him in an early letter, and she warned him that "I have a fine ear for any strain in intercourse."[51] Browning too knew that the strain would come from gossip. "You know the difficulties will begin soon enough," he wrote: "my visits will seem importunate, be remarked on, the usual course of things must be looked for."[52] Still, Browning hoped to defy such talk. "Your friendship has always been precious to me," he told Wedgwood in June 1864, but when she broke it off in March 1865, he told her, gallantly, that "I left you always to decide (as only yourself could) on what length into the garden I might go: and I still leave it to you."[53] But when they resumed their correspondence (but not their visits) in the spring of 1867, the poet confessed that "I underwent great pain from the sudden interruption of our intercourse three years ago: not having the least notion why that interruption must needs be, then or now"[54]; and while she expressed delight "in renewing my acquaintance with your thoughts,"[55] he expressed regret that "we shall never meet again, face to face."[56] The renewal of their letter writing coincided with the preparation of the proofs and the publication of *The Ring and the Book*, and Wedgwood's criticism of the volumes as they appeared, and Browning's defense of his liking for (what he called) "the study of morbid cases of the soul,"[57] are an illuminating debate for all subsequent readers and critics of the poem. But in those same later letters the writers are also concerned with the early years of their friendship, and Browning, who told Wedgwood that he liked "clearly-defined situations and relations,"[58] was discovering that their past relationship, and Wedgwood's reasons for ending it, had been more complicated than they had seemed at the time. She gave a new reason for her decision—"some refracted words of yours"[59]—and he, perplexed, asked "what is this going forward to a quite new piece of information?"[60] She said her loss was greater than his; he said, "There was certainly as great a loss to me as to you."[61] Finally she confessed "how multiform and complex were the influences which impelled me to the surrender of the most prized possession of my life."[62] By the time she wrote that sentence, their correspondence was almost at an end, and we do not know the "influences" to which she referred. In 2004 the Armstrong Browning Library acquired additional letters between the two: perhaps they will illuminate a relationship that has always seemed to need fuller explanation.

The poet's sorrows and cares during the 1860s coincided with the composition of the epic poem which Browning called his "great venture"[63] and which readers have usually considered to be his major work: critical attention to it has far outweighed interest in the poetry published after 1870, even though that subsequent work makes up more than half of the bulk of his collected poems. Browning wrote much of *The Ring and the Book* in 1864 and 1865, at a time when he was expressing fresh confidence in his vocation and a fuller understanding of his aims and techniques. However, he had had the materials, which he usually referred to as his "Roman murder-case," since 1860, when he had bought in Florence "the collection of law-papers,"[64] both printed and handwritten, which he refers to in the poem (and which critics have ever since labeled) as the "old yellow Book" (1. 33), bound documents relating to long-forgotten events in Rome at the end of the seventeenth century. That collection he read at once, according to his account in book 1 of the poem, and he "mastered the contents, knew the whole truth" (1. 117). By "mastering" he meant his judgment of those involved and of their relationships; his treatment of the case and the structure of his epic he would not settle on until much later, probably in the fall of 1864, when he said, of "my new poem that is about to be," "the whole is pretty well in my head."[65] He would fill out the structure between 1865 and 1867, by which time the poem exceeded twenty thousand lines: twice as many as in *Paradise Lost* but, Browning insisted, "the shortest poem, for the stuff in it, I ever wrote."[66] *The*

Ring and the Book appeared in four volumes between November 1868 and February 1869, and it was published by Smith, Elder. Browning had become dissatisfied with Chapman, his previous publisher, who had been not only dilatory and unaccommodating but also reluctant to pay, and Smith, Elder, who brought out Browning's *Poetical Works* in six volumes in 1868, "pay me exactly five times as much for an edition."[67]

Browning's instincts as a poet had always been epic: like his own David, he took as his subject "the whole round of creation," an encyclopedic approach characteristic of that most inclusive of genres. Not so conventional, however, was his attitude toward the story. The epic had always been considered a narrative genre, and certainly Browning does have a story to tell in *The Ring and the Book*, but the story, which is actual and historical, is not his central concern. In this he was very different from Elizabeth, for whom the invention and construction of the story in *Aurora Leigh* were crucial matters. She shapes the narrative in such a way that the reader keeps going to see how things will turn out. Not so Robert, who tells his whole story immediately, and says to the reader, less than one-third of the way through book 1, "You know the tale already" (1. 377). His main concern gradually becomes apparent in his warning the reader that "I may ask, / Rather than think to tell you, more thereof" (1. 377–78) and in his questioning the reader "how you hold" (1. 381) concerning the persons and events. Of the priest's part in the story: "was it right or wrong or both?" (1. 388). Of the slaying of Pompilia's parents, "What say you to the right or wrong of that[?]" (1. 392). For Browning was designing an epic which would embody the "good" of poetry as he had come fully to understand it in the mid-1860s. In the poem, he constantly prods the reader to make moral decisions, to interpret, so that comprehending and judging the poet's interpretation of the historical events becomes an incident in the development of the reader's soul. There will be good, "I fain hope," Browning told Julia Wedgwood, "to who reads and applies my reasoning to his own experience, which is not likely to fail him."[68] The whole complex structure of the poem is designed to elicit the reader's judgment, and there are hints of that purpose in both books 1 and 12. In book 1, for instance, Browning introduces the Pope's monologue as "the ultimate / Judgment save yours" (1. 1220–21), and at the beginning of book 12 he says of Guido, "you have seen his act, / By my power—may-be, judged it by your own" (12. 9–10). The "good" of poetry, for Browning, lies in the reader's struggle with the text, a struggle which is both intellectual and moral, cognitive and conative.

Complicating that struggle is the fact that the text confronting the reader is already an interpretation of events. Hidden behind Browning's "mastering" of them is the fact that his shaping of them is an incident in the development of his own soul. That hidden agenda shows itself at the very end of the poem when Browning states "the glory and the good of Art" (12. 838). Art is, among other things, the revealing of the poet's inner life, in the shapings and interpretations of his materials: "So write a book shall mean, beyond the facts, / Suffice the eye and save the soul beside" (12. 862–63). Then he repeats that last phrase: "And save the soul! If this intent save mine ..." (12. 864). So, in a rare moment, Browning reveals the motive behind his poetry, and he presents himself as a model for his readers. Contrary to their expectations, there is no ur-text which provides pure fact, unadorned and unmediated; even the Old Yellow Book (which, Browning knows, his readers will assume to be fact) is a collection of opinions and judgments, "Pages of proof this way, and that way proof" (1. 239), and his own shaping of that collection is an interpretation of interpretations, a sequence to be continued by every reader of his poem.

What truth can any interpretation claim? Browning forces the reader to wrestle with that question throughout the epic, but especially in the framing books, 1 and 12, where *truth* is a key and repeated word, its meaning bound up with two other repeated words, *fact* and *fancy*. *Truth*, Browning leads the reader to understand, is a combination of both, but he characteristically brings the reader to that realization by indirection on his part and by provoking effort on the reader's part. He knows he is dealing with readers who are recalcitrant and unsympathetic, readers he addresses as "British Public, ye who like me not ... whom I yet have laboured for" (1. 1379–80). Browning is battling prejudice grounded in the empiricist tradition that had, since Locke, dominated English philosophy, and in the poem that prejudice takes the form of the assumption that "facts" alone are true, and anything one does with "facts" creates fiction (from *fingere*, to fashion or form), which is made up and therefore untrue. The faculty which creates fiction Browning calls "fancy," a word which, as a contraction of "fantasy," suggests the illusory or the false. "Fancy" is the poet's faculty, and poetry, so runs the prevailing assumption, is "make-believe" and "white lies" (1. 455–56). "Fact" and "fancy" thus seem opposed, but Browning wants to lead the reader to understand that more than alliteration unites them. There is no "fact" without "fancy," he is teaching his readers, no "fact," that is, which is wholly objective and unmediated, since the very identification of a "fact" requires a mental choice and a context established by the mind. In this view of "fact" Browning has the support of etymology, since the word *fact* is derived from the Latin verb *facere*, to do or to make, so a "fact" is as "made" as a fiction. The question of truth now shifts to the motions of the mind involved in that making: what authority can they claim? One answer, conventionally offered by poets, is that those motions are divinely inspired. Browning's version of that answer is that a human being

> Repeats God's process in man's due degree,
> Attaining man's proportionate result,—
> Creates, no, but resuscitates, perhaps.... (1. 717–19)

Browning's understanding of human sharing in God's creation is unlike the usual understanding of divine inspiration: such creation is not occasional and extraordinary; it is not confined to poets; and it is the support for and stimulus to the ordinary operations of the mind. It makes experience intelligible and useful to us. But Browning only suggests these ideas. If the reader wants to know the true nature of "fancy," he or she must figure it out without the help of explicit statements from the poet. Hence Browning questions the reader about this shaping and interpreting power:

> What's this then, which proves good yet seems untrue?
> This that I mixed with truth, motions of mine
> That quickened, made the inertness malleolable
> O' the gold was not mine,—what's your name for this? (1. 700–703)

Browning leaves the reader to come up with an answer.

Years after the publication of *The Ring and the Book*, Browning told Mrs. Thomas FitzGerald that "poetry, if it is to deserve the name, ought to create—or re-animate something—not merely reproduce raw fact taken from somebody else's book."[69] But he did not mean that one should dispense with fact or make up whatever one liked: "when I comment on a fact," Browning told Tennyson, "a fact I find it and leave it, or what would the comment be worth?"[70] Those two quotations mark the boundaries of interpretation: a "fact" must remain a "fact," and at the same time it must be quickened, given fresh life, and made useful in the present. In *The Ring and the Book*, Browning explores that difficult-to-understand relation between fact and fancy through two sets of metaphors, the ring and the book of the title and the gold and the alloy of the ring. Understood initially and uncritically, book and gold are "fact," ring and alloy, "fancy," but as Browning explores their relations (the subject of much vexed critical commentary), it gradually becomes apparent that the worth of "fact" depends upon "fancy"—and vice versa. The gold ring would not hold its shape without the strengthening alloy, but it would be worth little if it were alloy alone; the significance of a long-forgotten and obscure murder case, by chance surviving in a book of documents, would not be apparent without the ring made by the poet's "fancy," but the ring would be only a shape were its materials not history. So Browning's central metaphors are riddles for the reader, the "British Public, who may like me yet" (12. 831). "My writing has been, in the main, too hard for many," Browning acknowledged in 1868, "but I never designedly tried to puzzle people, as some of my critics have supposed. On the other hand, I never pretended to offer such literature as should be a substitute for a cigar, or a game of dominoes, to an idle man." His audience, like Milton's, was "not a crowd, but a few I value more."[71]

The Ring and the Book is an epic consisting of ten dramatic monologues, each giving a different perspective on the "facts" of the case, and all, together with the frame, giving that comprehensive view characteristic of the epic, except that Browning achieves that comprehensiveness not only through conventional means—allusion and explicit commentary—but also through the range of interpretations, the "voices" which replace the story as the epic's main concern. In spite of the wealth of detail and the complexities created by the different "voices," Browning orders his materials with a sureness of touch and concept. There are several ways of understanding his arrangement.

One simple way is to focus on each speaker's attitude toward Pompilia, the central female character. Then one discovers that the ring of monologues consists of three smaller rings, in each of which there is a speaker *pro*, one *con*, and a third speaker, a *tertium quid*, who is, for one reason or another, detached from her. In the first of the smaller rings, Half-Rome speaks against Pompilia, Other Half-Rome speaks for her, and Tertium Quid refuses to take a stand. In the second ring, Guido speaks against her, Caponsacchi for her, while Pompilia herself, knowing she is soon to die from her wounds, is detached from her situation. In the third ring, one lawyer defends Guido, the other defends Pompilia, while the Pope, whose judgment (we guess) coincides with the poet's, claims truth beyond personal prejudice or interest or professional duty, truth "evolved at last / Painfully, held tenaciously by me" (10. 230–31). He pronounces Pompilia "Perfect in whiteness" (10. 1005) and tropes her as "My flower, / My rose, I gather for the breast of God" (10. 1045–46).

A second way to understand the arrangement of the monologues is to be aware of the sequence of the three inner rings. The labels supplied for that progression by Boyd Litzinger in 1974 are still useful. The first ring of monologues, which Litzinger calls the "Triad of Rumor," is spoken by persons not directly involved in the case but representing public opinion about it. The second ring, the "Triad of Testimony," is spoken by the principals in the case. The third ring, involving two lawyers and the Pope, is the "Triad of Judgement."[72]

A third way of understanding the structure is to examine the literary shape by which each speaker interprets the case and presents its meaning. In using literary shapes or genres in this way, Browning anticipates the argument of historiographer Hayden White in the late twentieth century, who says that historians produce meaning by "emplotment," the shapes of the narrative—the plots—being borrowed from literature.[73] Given the events of the story, one would expect the chief plot to be tragedy, but while Browning does refer to the history as a "tragic piece" (1. 523) and while he uses that shape as his starting point, tragedy, instead of dominating, combines with a range of other plots to give that comprehensiveness characteristic of the epic. Half-Rome, who is afraid his wife is about to cuckold him and tells the story as a warning to her would-be lover, shapes the history as a satire and mounts an antifeminist attack on "the wife's trade," "the sex's trick" (2. 75). Satire will be, in one form or another, the emplotment of the first monologue of each of the three inner rings. Each of the second monologues is a version of romance, that narrative genre the Victorians contrasted with the novel or "realism" because its plots were governed by wish fulfillment or anxieties or fears;[74] the particular version of romance chosen by Other Half-Rome is the saint's legend, which the self-described "sensitive" bachelor combines with a sentimental tale of a cruel husband and a wronged wife. Events in romance are conventionally improbable; "So is the legend of my patron-saint" (3. 1051), says Other Half-Rome as he dismisses those parts of the story that demand a more realistic explanation. The third monologue in each of the inner rings is a *tertium quid,* a third something related to the preceding two books but distinct from both. The third something is a version of comedy which the speaker shapes out of the tragedy, the seminal shape of the historical events. Tertium Quid's plot is a comedy of manners: all his characters (like himself) are motivated by self-interest—that is (in a significant allusion) "the way of the world" (4. 532)—but some have better manners than others, and they know how to present their self-interest in "decent wrappage" (4. 523). He tells a story which doesn't matter to him, since it has no application to his own life; only the telling matters, and the telling, for which he claims "decent wrappage"—the clarity and objectivity of the critical mind—is a performance to advance his own interests in society. In the second of the inner rings, Guido attacks Pompilia; his satiric condemnation of wives parallels Half-Rome's satire in the first triad, but he expands his attack to all those who do not play their proper role in society, and he is a tricky and untrustworthy satirist, since he shifts the standard to which he appeals, sometimes evoking self-sacrifice, sometimes, self-interest. Caponsacchi, who speaks next, explicitly rejects a saint's legend (that of St. George) as parallel to his own story, but he alludes to that genre when he is characterizing Pompilia, and he uses some central conventions of romance to tell of his own responses to Pompilia and to the flight to Rome: the journey is a version of the central narrative of romance, the quest, and the outward physical action is less important than the inner psychological action. Through it Caponsacchi discovers himself and can answer the conventional question posed in romance, who am I? Pompilia's monologue, the third something in this triad, is, contrary to expectations, a version of comedy. Her marriage, which ought to mark the end of a comic action, is in fact the beginning of a tragic one as she descends into a period of illusion and confusion. Three truths sustain her—they are prayer, her "soldier-saint," and her pregnancy— and they become the agents of her deliverance. Her comic plot is the action of successfully freeing oneself from a nightmare world. In the first of the third ring of books, where Archangeli speaks, the elements of satire are present but inoperative. The defense lawyer is also an indulgent father, and his pride in his son ought to lead him to condemn Guido, but he never judges Guido as a father like himself, and he keeps his domestic life separate from his professional life. If Archangeli is a satirist manqué, Bottini, the prosecuting lawyer, is a romancer manqué, saying that in his legal argument he is "sainting" Pompilia, when he is in fact casting her, quite inappropriately, as the heroine of an Ovidian love story to which he brings the sensibility of a voyeur. Where the two lawyers fail in their judgments, the Pope succeeds. In an action parallel to Pompilia's version of comedy, he delivers to justice the men and women of a world in which good and evil are inextricably mixed, but where Pompilia's deliverance made this world seem an insubstantial dream, the Pope's judgment is very much rooted in the solidity of the actual and made "As a mere man may" (10. 1243), without any claim to special insight but with a consciousness of possible dire consequences for himself. If he were to die suddenly and face God's request for "the latest act of thine" (10. 341) as the sum of all the rest, "I must plead / This condemnation of a man today" (10. 344–45).

The one book which does not fit into this careful and complex pattern of three threes is book 11, Guido's second monologue. In introducing it in book 1, Browning contrasts it with Guido's first and calculated performance (which, he told Julia Wedgwood, was all "cant and cleverness")[75]; in his second, "the true words come last" (1. 1281), and insofar as they are the "true words," they confirm, perhaps too neatly, the Pope's judgment. Guido depicts his life as tragedy and romance. He asks the key question in every tragedy: who or what is responsible for the catastrophe? "Whose fault?" (11. 938). His words echo God the Father's question about the fall of Adam and

Eve in book 3 of *Paradise Lost*, and the answer in Milton's epic is that each creature has free will and is responsible for his or her own actions. But Guido, like Milton's Satan, denies such responsibility—the fault is "Not mine at least, who did not make myself!" (11. 939)—and his description of himself as "Implacable, persistent in revenge" (11. 2105) makes him a Satanic figure in an ongoing tragic action that separates him from everyone in his society: "I have gone inside my soul / And shut its door behind me" (11. 2289–90). The sense in which his monologue is a romance is apparent if we compare it with Caponsacchi's. The priest's experience with Pompilia led him on a quest in which his soul developed; Guido's experience with Pompilia took him in the opposite direction, and though he hints at missed opportunities, his story is a story of the devolution of a soul, a cautionary tale of wrong choices and their consequences.

The Ring and the Book was widely read and widely reviewed. Some critics pointed out that the poet's characterization of the "British public" as "ye who like me not" was "scarcely true": "They love him more and more,"[76] and the reviewers spoke of him and Tennyson as the two major poets of the age. Still, judgment of the poem itself varied widely. It ranged from R. W. Buchanan's assessment of *The Ring and the Book* not only as "the supremest poetical achievement of our time" but as "the most precious and profound spiritual treasure that England has produced since the days of Shakespeare" to Alfred Austin's ill-tempered argument that "Mr. Browning is not a poet at all" and is "both muddy and unmusical to the last degree."[77] More mixed were the comments on Browning's characteristic practices as a poet, on (what Buchanan called) "everything Browningish."[78] There was the matter of Browning's style, known to be obscure, crabbed, and downright faulty, though those defects, the reviewers conceded, were less in evidence in the poet's new volumes. There was the "prevailing ruggedness of his versification" and his "persecution of prosody."[79] There was his choice of subject, seen as disagreeable, even repulsive. At the same time, there was his immense intellectual power and energy, his "knitted argumentation," in Buchanan's words.[80] John Addington Symonds said the poem was an "exhibition of prodigious power carefully exerted and marvellously sustained," and Frederick Greenwood described the monologues as "a brilliant demonstration of the human mind, seen under many varieties by one searching light."[81] Though Browning "appears to consider himself still as a comparatively unpopular writer," said one reviewer, "he certainly is not unhonoured."[82]

The poet himself told Julia Wedgwood in March of 1869 that "the British Public like, and more than like me,"—"this week," anyway, he added with the tone of the detached ironist, when he (along with Carlyle and two others)

was invited to meet the queen: "whereupon we took tea together and pretended to converse for an hour and twenty minutes." The gathering was, he
reported bemusedly, the Pentecost of his reputation: "This eventful incident
in my life—say the dove descending out of heaven upon my head—seems to
have opened peoples' minds at last"—"provided the Queen don't send for
the Siamese Twins, the Beautiful Circassian Lady, and Miss Saurin [the
complainant in a widely reported libel case] as her next quartette-party."[83]

Complex Poetry

etween 1871 and 1875, Browning's poetic output was astonishing: six
major poems totaling more than twenty thousand lines. His variety
of purpose and effect was also astonishing, even unnerving. Browning's public, said a reviewer in 1873, "have a right to feel disconcerted. Every
new book is a surprise to them, they never know what to expect of him."[1] "I
have written a good deal of late years," Browning understatedly told John
Forster in December 1875, "and it could hardly be hoped that attempts in
various and opposite directions should always hit the mark."[2] Readers found
the poems long and difficult, and Carlyle's responses to two of them are perhaps typical. William Allingham wrote in his diary for June 24, 1872, that he
had called on Carlyle, who "has been reading *Fifine at the Fair* and saying
every now and again to Browning (though not present), 'What the *Devil* do
you mean?'" A year earlier he had recorded Carlyle's reaction to *Balaustion's
Adventure*: "I read it all twice through and found out the meaning of it.
Browning most ingeniously twists up the English language into riddles—
'There! there is some meaning in this—can you make it out?'" Then came
Carlyle's usual comment about poets: "I wish he had taken to prose."[3] He
didn't, of course, but the six poems from those unusually active and inven-
tive years have been too often neglected or dismissed by critics, though they
are full of interest and will repay careful study. They are *Balaustion's Adventure*
(August 1871), *Prince Hohenstiel-Schwangau* (December 1871), *Fifine at the
Fair* (June 1872), *Red Cotton Night-Cap Country* (May 1873), *Aristophanes'
Apology* (April 1875), and *The Inn Album* (November 1875). Browning's estimate of each was as different as the poems themselves. *Balaustion* he called a

"trifle" and said it was "only . . . a May-month's amusement undertaken, half in fun, at the desire of a singularly pretty & kind person," but *Prince Hohenstiel-Schwangau* he recommended to Isa Blagden as "a sample of my very best work."[4]

In it he returned to a subject which had provoked profound disagreement between him and Elizabeth: Napoleon III. The poem might have been the occasion for Browning to justify his own views and to have the last word, but the monologue Browning gives his prince is both more complex in its analysis of Napoleon and more generous in the attitude it takes toward him. Elizabeth had constantly asserted her belief in the emperor's good intentions and magnanimous motives; Robert had constantly pointed to poor decisions and weak handling of actual situations. Eleven years later, the poem suggests that Robert had come to believe they were both right. That attitude was not a sentimental blurring and softening of their positions; the poem is as much an apologia for Elizabeth's views as it is a reassertion of Robert's realistic approach to the heroic. For Robert, who had his own views of the truly heroic, shared in the attitudes of the realists (like Thackeray and Eliot) who had come to dominate prose fiction in the mid-Victorian period, and who, by analyzing character and by mapping the interaction of character and circumstance, brought about the shift Mario Praz would subsequently label "the hero in eclipse."[5] Hence Robert corrected Edith Story's reading of the poem: "I don't think, when you have read more, you will find I have 'taken the man for any Hero'—I rather made him confess he was the opposite, though I put forward what excuses I thought he was likely to make for himself, if inclined to try."[6] He had told Isa Blagden, aphoristically, in 1867, "it seems ordained that if you believe in heroes you will be sorry for it, sooner or later"—as Elizabeth would have been. In an 1870 letter to Isa he addressed his dead wife: "Oh, oh, Ba—put not your trust in princes neither in the sons of men,—Emperors, Popes, Garibaldis, or Mazzinis,—the *plating* wears through, and out comes the copperhead of human nature & weakness and falseness too!"[7]

The poem was written in August and September of 1871, when Browning was at a shooting lodge in Scotland. Pen enjoyed the shooting; his father disapproved of it and stayed behind. "I am blessedly alone," he told Isa; "I have even a piano, books of course—& I find an impulse to write." That impulse matured into a burst of creativity. "I never at any time in my life," Browning wrote a month later, "turned a holiday into such an occasion of work: the quiet and seclusion were too tempting."[8] He had with him "a little sketch begun in *Rome in '60*." We can only guess at its relation to the poem he destroyed after Villafranca, but *Prince Hohenstiel-Schwangau* at least retains some vestiges of its origin as a companion piece for Elizabeth's "Napoleon III in Italy," for Robert quotes or echoes some of Elizabeth's lines from that poem. His interest in developing what he called in a note on the manuscript those "few lines of the rough draft" of 1860 had been sparked by the Franco-Prussian War of 1870. The Brownings, fearing the advancing Prussian army, had, on the advice of Milsand after the French defeat at Sedan, left Normandy and returned to England, though not without difficulties: finding no passage from Le Havre, they crossed the Channel on a cattle-boat out of Honfleur. Browning had observed with distress the progress of the war— "the sadness of the war & its consequences go far to paralyse all our pleasure" in the summer holiday—and he was apprehensive about the Prussian success: "The effect will be, that we shall all be forced into the Prussian system, of turning a nation into a camp; nothing but soldiering to concern us for the next generation."[9] The defeat at Sedan confirmed Browning's view of the emperor: "he should simply be blotted out of the world as the greatest failure on record." Still, Browning's comments from the autumn of 1871 suggest at least a double perspective which mirrors both his own view of the emperor's weaknesses and Elizabeth's view of his motives. His fate, Browning told Isa, "was only to be nearly a great man," for "the deed was miserably inadequate to what we supposed the will." Browning's comments on the poem itself point to his negotiating of the differences between himself and Elizabeth: "I think in the main, he meant to do what I say, and, but for the weakness,—grown more apparent in these last years than formerly,—would have done what I say he did not. I thought badly of him at the beginning of his career, *et pour cause*, better afterward, on the strength of promises he made, and gave indications of intending to redeem,—I think him very weak in the last miserable year."[10]

Browning's comments point to two crucial elements in the poem's structure: gaps between intention and deed and between time before and time after. Through his handling of these matters, Browning exploits reader response to bring the public to share his and Elizabeth's estimates of the emperor's character and career. Initially the poem seems to be the kind of dramatic monologue Browning's readers had come to expect, with the prince in exile in England, speaking to a woman of doubtful virtue in a room in Leicester Square and offering "Revealment of myself!" (22). Browning's readers in 1871 would know that the emperor was, in fact, an exile in England and would expect Browning's "prince" to offer an apologia for the emperor's life and deeds. And he does. The poem's subtitle is "Saviour of Society," and the prince explains what the word *save* meant for him. "A conservator, call me, if you please, / Not a creator nor destroyer" (298–99), his motto being to "Do the best with the least change possible" (397):

> I like to use the thing I find,
> Rather than strive at unfound novelty:
> I make the best of the old, nor try for new. (266–68)

His policy was not, however, lazy acquiesence in things as they are but rather a balancing of competing aims and claims of the various factions in society: "I rule and regulate the course, excite, / Restrain"—and thus he saved society:

> I think that to have held the balance straight
> For twenty years, say, weighing claim and claim,
> And giving each its due, no less no more,
> This was good service to humanity,
> Right usage of my power in head and heart,
> And reasonable piety beside. (473–78)

Such is the substance of his apologia : "equable / Sustainment everywhere," though such balancing might look like "indolence, / Apathy, hesitation" (1177–80). After twelve hundred lines of such argument, the prince suddenly shifts his perspective, a shift marked by the striking of the clock, the sounds of which are a motif in a poem which manipulates time in such an unexpected way. He turns from the "autobiography" (1220) of the "self-apologist" (1203) and asks his "stranger-friend" and listener to "Hear what I never was, but might have been" (1224). This section of the monologue is Robert's apologia for Elizabeth's views, and it takes the form of an internal dialogue between two allegorical speakers, Sagacity, who is the voice of expediency, and Wisdom, who voices the ideal. The prince consistently chooses the ideal and rejects the "lies" of Sagacity. Sagacity, for instance, advises the prince to annex Nice and Savoy, and to make his son his heir by right of heredity. The prince rejects both courses of action and so proves himself a man devoted to "truth and right" (1865). In this section of the monologue, Browning is making his prince the hero Elizabeth believed Napoleon to be while exploiting the response of his readers, who, because they knew that the emperor had done both things that the fictional prince rejects, were left with the sense of an ironic gap between intention and deed. But there is a final and wholly unexpected turn in the monologue. The clock strikes again, and the prince turns to the present time and place, which is not Leicester Square in 1871 but the "Residenz" in 1860, long before any of the action explored in the first two thousand lines of the poem has taken place—the year of the poem's inception. (Alert readers might have caught the earlier—and, at that point, puzzling—reference in line 511 to "this 'sixty, Anno

Domini.") The feeling provoked in readers by such a shift was unpleasantly double. They recognized that the prince was capable of heroism—and they also knew that the actual historical figure never lived up to that promise. The year 1860 was the crucial point, and Browning ends the monologue with his prince at the moment of a decision, the choice being to send a letter which will launch an "adventure" (a word Browning often uses for an action crucial in one's life) or to keep the letter so that the adventure "never needs to be at all" (2149). The prince hesitates: "The letter goes! Or stays?" (2155). Those are the last words of the monologue; there is "Nothing done and over yet, / Except cigars" (2147–48). The reader judges the fictional prince at the decisive moment as indolent and hesitant and extends that judgment to the historical emperor, mingling a sad sense of what might have been with anger at the man's failures and ineptitude. The tricky, deliberately misleading structure of the monologue is designed to evoke just such a complex response as had troubled the discussions and arguments of the Brownings themselves.[11]

In contrast to Browning's own assessment of *Prince Hohenstiel-Schwangau* as "a sample of my very best work," he spoke of *Balaustion's Adventure* as "my little new Poem,—done in a month,—and I think a pretty thing in its way."[12] But poets are notorious for telling white lies (as Browning himself characterizes them in book 1 of *The Ring and the Book*), and *Balaustion's Adventure* is not "little," and it is more than "a pretty thing"; it, together with its companion piece, *Aristophanes' Apology*, explores the issues involved in an act which was of central concern to Browning, the act of reading and responding to a literary text. Response usually takes the form of reading a work silently and in private, but Browning extends the act to the public sphere by including reciting it aloud, watching it performed on stage, and debating its merits with others. Those multiple responses involve the conventional acts of criticism—understanding, appreciation, and judgment—but Browning identifies those acts not primarily with informed reading but with translation which, as Browning treats it, becomes the paradigmatic act of reader response. Why translation? Because Browning had long considered the problems of rendering Greek texts in English; he had helped Elizabeth with her translation of *Prometheus Bound*; and he was preparing translations of his own. All that work led him to what might be called a theory of translation, the full extent of which was evident in his new poem and in its sequel. In both *Balaustion's Adventure* and *Aristophanes' Apology* there is Browning's actual translation of a play by Euripides, and in both, the play is enclosed in a monologue in which the speaker responds to and interprets the dramatic piece. In that act *translation* takes on a much wider significance than the turning of a Greek play into English: since the word is etymologically *a carrying across*, it refers to the process by which someone responding to a literary text carries across its meaning to his or her own life, and so not only creates a new text but also contributes to the story which Browning insisted was alone worth study: "the development of a soul." The ongoing life of literature depends upon such continuing acts of translation, in Browning's view, and he explores that quickening through the central character of both those major poems, Balaustion, and through the two major dramatic genres with which she is concerned, comedy and tragedy. The development which Browning explores depends upon the act of turning tragedy into comedy and comedy into tragedy, a turning which is not only circular but progressive, a spiraling upward toward greater inclusiveness of seemingly disparate things, progress which Browning links with psychological health and ultimately with salvation itself.

Bound up with that development is a hidden assumption, and that is that no text is ever read in an unmediated way: always there is a responding self-conscious and critical mind which makes the text-as-it-is-in-itself into the text-as-it-is-read. The usual metaphor for such self-consciousness is the frame, and the literary technique which embodies that response is a favorite with the Victorians, the framed narrative in which the storytelling voice is just as important as the story told. (Indeed, in Browning's mind the voices are more important than the story, as we saw in *The Ring and the Book*.) Such a technique is, as David Shaw has pointed out, the revolt of the mind against "the naïve empirical assumption that it is ever possible to mirror an unmediated world of primary facts, plain, exposed, and naked to the eye,"[13] and one might extend Shaw's statement to say that, in Browning's hands, the frame is the celebration of the mind's power to take a text apparently fixed and complete and to give it new life and extended meaning. Every reader actively responding to a text becomes a poet or dramatist in his or her own right, and so Browning anticipates Oscar Wilde's argument, in "The Critic as Artist," that criticism is itself an art and "treats the work of art simply as a starting-point for a new creation."[14] Browning explores that creative critical power by linking it to the two main dramatic genres in the Greek theater: comedy and tragedy. As Browning treats them, tragedy arises when a reader considers a text complete and wants to preserve it in a fixed state; comedy counters such a narrowing and limiting of reader response when the reader feels the energy in the comic text and appropriates it to create his or her own version of the play. Comedy, in the responses of readers and audiences, thus becomes more and more inclusive, and that progressive circling of "the whole round of cre-ation" (in David's words) is a process which brings the human mind and soul closer to God, who is the denouement of all comedy.

In both *Balaustion's Adventure* and *Aristophanes' Apology* there are three texts, the first framed within the second, and both enclosed in a third. In both works, the innermost text is a translation, or "transcript" (Browning's own label), of an Euripides play—the *Alkestis* in one, and the *Herakles* in the other. The *Alkestis* has the narrative shape of a comedy; it is a story of deliv-erance and reunion, and its text saves Balaustion's life: such is the "adventure" she narrates in the 1871 poem. Moreover, Balaustion is so moved by the text and by the theatrical performance of it that she has witnessed that she not only recites the original play but makes a new *Alkestis*. The *Herakles* is a tragedy, and Balaustion presents it as consolation for the tragedy she has suf-fered in her own life, and in the context of a debate with Aristophanes about the rival claims of tragedy and comedy. She recites the *Herakles*, considers it "perfect"—complete, that is,—and is judged wrong by Aristophanes, whose rival text, "Thamuris Marching," is as open-ended and potentially comedic as Balaustion's *Herakles* is closed and finished. Balaustion is reluctant to accept the disruptive, amoral, and apparently natural energy which propels comedy, but she comes to see the value of holding opposites together in works which, like her creator's, are "complex."

Balaustion's Adventure is a text within a text within a text. The innermost play is the *Alkestis*, and it tells the story of a self-sacrificing wife who dies in her husband's place, only to be revivified by the intervention of Herakles. In its narrative shape (though not in its actual treatment by Euripides) the play is a comedy, since it begins as comedies conventionally begin, with a tragic situation—the sentence of death and the separation of spouse from spouse—and ends with a return to life and the reunion of husband and wife, such renewal and coming together being the conventional denouement of comedy. The text which frames that play, Balaustion's story of her "adven-ture," has the same narrative shape. That story, too, begins with potential tragedy, as Balaustion and her companions sail from Sicily to Syracuse, pur-sued by pirates and forced to seek refuge in a hostile port, where they are likely to be made "captives, that pale crowd / I' the quarry" (106–7). But the Syracusans hear Balaustion sing a song of Aeschylus, a song associated with safety and deliverance from a dangerous, even life-threatening situation, and ask if she knows any texts by Euripides. Balaustion, who loves the *Alkestis* and has committed it to memory, saves herself and her fellows by reciting the play. Browning strengthens the links with comedy by having Balaustion make a specific connection between her situation and that of Alkestis—

"For had not Herakles a second time [in her reciting of the play] / Wrestled with Death and saved devoted ones?" (258–59)—and by linking Balaustion's deliverance with her attracting the attention of a young man. He follows her to Athens, and they will, Balaustion tells us, marry—the conventional ending of a comic action.

Balaustion's framing narrative for the Euripidean text is more than just the story of her "adventure"; it is also her account of a performance of the play she once witnessed "at Kameiros" (224). Hers is not a simple description of a theatrical production. Though she tells of the gestures and tones with which the actors brought the lines to life, though she mentions costuming and movement and the blocking of the actors on stage, she indicates from the beginning that she is not only reporting on the decisions of the director and designers but also seeing the production as she would have directed it and designed it. "Plain I told the play," she says,

> Just as I saw it: what the actors said,
> And what I saw, or thought I saw the while,
> At our Kameiros theatre. . . . (246–49)

That formulaic phrasing, "what I saw, or thought I saw," echoes the words of Virgil in book 6 of the *Aeneid*, in which Aeneas descends to the underworld and glimpses Dido in a moment so fleeting that he cannot be sure of what he has seen: "aut videt aut vidisse putat" (either he sees or thinks he has seen [her]). The formula suggests two kinds of repetition: one grounded in actual observations of the world outside the speaker; the other depending upon the shaping and interpreting powers of the mind as it pursues its own ends. The two are the basis of Balaustion's critical reading of Euripides' text and of her review of the production: she both retains and reshapes the original. Its imaginative energy, evoked by her love of the text and its every detail, enables her to turn it and to make her own *Alkestis*.

Balaustion presents (what she calls) "our version of the story" (2661)—"version" is derived from the Latin word for "turn"—and in doing so she sees herself as no different from any engaged reader who sees multiple possibilities in a text ("One thing has many sides" [2402]), indeed, no different from a professional playwright like Sophokles, rumored to be planning his own *Alkestis*. "I think I see," Balaustion says,

> —far from Sophokles,—
> You, I, or anyone might mould a new
> Admetos, new Alkestis. (2413–15)

Her own rewriting of the text she sometimes imagines to be in line with that of Sophokles, as when she says how she would treat the chorus at a particular moment in the action:

> I would the Chorus here had plucked up heart,
> Spoken out boldly and explained the man,
> If not to men, to Gods. That way, I think,
> Sophokles would have led their dance and song.
> Here, they said simply. . . . (1520–24)

With her constant commentary on the Euripidean text and her constant assessment of the theatrical production, she comes at last to make her own *Alkestis*. Having absorbed Euripides' text, she asks, "Could we too make a poem? Try at least" (2433). In her view, the weak character in Euripides is Admetos, who allows Alkestis to die in his place. Herakles, who wrestles with Death for the life of Alkestis, is the hero Admetos ought to be. Balaustion makes a major change in the story: she leaves out Herakles entirely and has Admetos start from the position of moral and spiritual strength which he had attained only at the end of Euripides' play. Thus she begins where Euripides ended: she turns or spins the story, making husband and wife equally self-sacrificing. They, in a fairy-tale ending, live happily ever after— "So, the two lived together long and well" (2652)—and she links that ending with the return of the Golden Age, the ideal version of the new and better community which comedy conventionally establishes.

The outermost frame appears only at the end of this long poem, and in it Browning, the actual translator of the *Alkestis*, extends both Euripides' play and Balaustion's narrative to his own life, so that a more accurate description of the poem is a translation within a translation within a translation. In this personal passage, Browning (his voice now merged with that of Balaustion) celebrates the ongoing creative power of the *Alkestis* as the source of two artworks of great importance to him: Elizabeth's line about Euripides from "Wine of Cypress" ("The Human with his droppings of warm tears"), and Frederick Leighton's painting *Hercules Wrestling with Death for the Body of Alcestis*. The "glory of the golden verse, / And passion of the picture" (2698–99) are both a creative response to Euripides: "It all came of this play . . ." (2704). Browning had earlier put that same line of Elizabeth's in Balaustion's mouth (2412), and that merging of makers' voices suggests that the third frame, apparently so brief, has implications that pervade the whole text. William C. DeVane long ago pointed out that Balaustion is a fictionalized portrait of Elizabeth (350), the shared elements being their love of Euripides and their ability to turn their criticism of him into new works of art. "Implication" is etymologically that which is folded in, and by his quotation from Elizabeth, Browning folds his wife into his model reader of texts, and both of them into his own voice, as hidden translator, hidden narrator, and finally open commentator.

The companion piece to *Balaustion's Adventure*, *Aristophanes' Apology*, is also a text within a text (and, at 5,700 lines, Browning's longest poem after *Sordello* and *The Ring and the Book*—and perhaps the most neglected of his major texts). To speak more accurately, it is a play within a narrative that is also a debate, and Browning, turning his own text as Balaustion had turned the *Alkestis*, begins where he had left off in the earlier poem. *Balaustion's Adventure* had begun, like *The Tempest*, with a tragic action, a ship blown off course and a community threatened with death and destruction. Balaustion's reciting of the *Alkestis* had brought about a reversal, and "so turns to comic what was tragic," as Browning says in one of his later stories ("Pietro of Abano," [62]). *Aristophanes' Apology* reverses that denouement and turns the comedy to tragedy: Athens is defeated by Sparta, the city's defenses are pulled down, and Balaustion and her husband are exiled from their cultural and spiritual home. Browning's continuation of the story anticipates "the view of English comedy of a sagacious essayist" paraphrased but not identified by George Meredith, in his 1877 lecture on comedy, an essayist "who said that the end of a Comedy would often be the commencement of a Tragedy, were the curtain to rise again on the performers."[15] So the text begins with the note of tragedy, the lament of an exile, and then Balaustion tells of the death of Euripides, recounts the debate with Aristophanes, and reads aloud her creator's translation of the *Herakles*. That performance is very different from her reading of the *Alkestis*. Then she had not only repeated the dramatic text but had also integrated it with the theatrical production she had witnessed and with her interpretation of both. Now her reading provides nothing beyond the words of Euripides' text: no staging of it in the theater of her mind, no interpretation of it as she recites it. She introduces the play as "the perfect piece" (3534), and "perfect" means "complete." There is nothing more to be said, since the play is, she insists, "the consummate Tragedy" (3526). The plot of the *Herakles* is a turnaround of the comic romance of the *Alkestis*: the savior there becomes the destroyer here; the man who wrestled with Death, and won, confronts death here but becomes the death-dealer himself. "Reverses are a grave thing" (4923), Herakles says with a grim pun, and tragedy threatens to complete the circle and bring all things to closure. By presenting *Herakles* as "the perfect piece," Balaustion shuts out further possibilities for the genre and for another "adventure." Her reading is followed by a "long silence" (5085) that seems to confirm her claim. It is Aristophanes who breaks the silence: "Our best friend," he mutters, "Lost, our best friend" (5085–86). Who is the friend? Is he referring to the last words of the play, where the Chorus laments the loss of "the greatest of all our friends," Herakles? Or is he referring to Balaustion's friend Euripides, and thereby suggesting that the tragic playwright is the best friend of comedy, because the end of a tragic action is the beginning of a comic one? The text that contains the *Herakles* is Balaustion's account of her debate with Aristophanes. All the intelligence, all the interpretive and quickening powers she had brought to the *Alkestis* but withheld from the *Herakles* she applies to her repeating of the debate. She recounts not only their words but also their looks and gestures, all of which she interprets in terms of motives, feelings, and ideas. Of her reenactment of the debate she says,

> Let us attempt that memorable talk,
> Clothe the adventure's every incident
> With due expression: may not looks be told,
> Gestures made speak, and speech so amplified
> That words find blood-warmth which, cold-writ, they lose? (233–37)

The *Herakles*, merely recited, remains "cold-writ"; it is the debate which Balaustion "amplifies" and, as a result, finds in it "blood-warmth" and, ultimately, renewal. It is (that crucial word again) an "adventure." The subject of the debate is the rival claims of tragedy and comedy, and those claims are bound up with a host of other pairings: "high soul" and "low flesh" (498), virtue and vice, sobriety and drunkenness, laughter and tears, "deity / And dung" (227–28). As Aristophanes and Balaustion come more and more to define their positions, Aristophanes voices a central and damaging charge: that Balaustion and Euripides and the defenders of tragedy have a single perspective, while he and the defenders of comedy champion multiple ways of seeing. Inside the orb—Aristophanes' emblem of the created world— "Euripides hangs fixed, / Gets knowledge through the single aperture / Of High and Right" (5117–19), while "I am movable" (5127) and can "turn all sides with the turning orb" (5115). Aristophanes' answer to Balaustion's reciting of the *Herakles* is his singing of the lyric "Thamuris Marching," and it is his celebration of his powers as a comic writer. Where *Herakles* is "perfect" or complete, "Thamuris Marching" is a fragment and open-ended; where *Herakles* ended with weeping and silence, "Thamuris Marching" breaks off with laughter (5265); where the text of the *Herakles* is, Balaustion insists, a test of "true godship," "Thamuris Marching" is a celebration of an energy which is common to all of creation. That energy is physical and sexual, but it is also imaginative and manifests itself in the animating of inani-

mate things through the trope of prosopopoeia. Everything in nature moves
energetically:

> Each, with a glory and a rapture twined
> About it, joined the rush of air and light
> And force: the world was of one joyous mind. (5221–23)

The antecedent for such oneness is the great Exodus psalm, 114, where "the
mountains skipped like rams, and the little hills like lambs." That psalm is a
celebration of liberation, of an action both epic and comic. The energy
which makes troping possible also makes possible the turning of something
into something else, even into its opposite. In "Thamuris Marching," birds
swim and beasts fly. "How could the creatures leap, no lift of wings?" (5227).
The answer is that they share the same energy, at once both natural and
supernatural, and that energy can transform all things.

  The conclusion of the debate in *Aristophanes' Apology* is one which Aristophanes had suggested almost from the beginning. Both he and Balaustion
come to see the value of holding opposites together in an ideal combination
that Aristophanes calls "complex poetry" (1472),

> Which, operant for body as for soul,
> Masters alike the laughter and the tears,
> Supreme in lowliest earth, sublimest sky. (1474–78)

"Complex poetry," texts which celebrate the play of opposites and the ability
of human beings to keep turning all things, can be understood as Browning's
answer to his critics' charge of obscurity. Even Carlyle thought Browning
ought to be clear. "He liked *Aristophanes' Apology* much" (Browning told
Alfred Domett, who recorded the comment in his diary for December
1875), "but asked Browning why he could not tell it all in a plain straightforward statement? 'As if,' Browning said to me, 'this did not just make all the
difference between a poet's treatment of a subject and a historian's or a
rhetorician's.'"[16] "A plain straightforward statement" would require little
effort on the part of the reader; "a poet's treatment" requires the active
response of every reader who, like Balaustion, takes an earlier text or "adventure" and, by interpreting, creates a new text with its own complexities. That
continuing human action is for Browning the essence of "the development
of the soul," which these two major poems sum up in the view that every
woman must be her own poet, and every man his.

  In the Balaustion poems Browning is working out a theory of literary
influence that had a major impact on Ezra Pound, and those poems are as

important for him as *Sordello*. After his speculations about relations between poets Pound writes, "Just my luck, confounded and delightful, that after I had threshed these things out for myself I find 'Balaustion's Adventure' holds them better said, and said some sooner." What he found in the poem was the idea, in George Bornstein's words, of "a transmission not simply of the work but of the power that produced the work in the first place.... The new work does not threaten the old but rather, since things have many sides, helps make up a part of an ideal order of poetry."[17]

Fifine at the Fair could certainly be considered "complex poetry," both in Browning's sense and in his readers' sense of puzzlement at the difficulties of the poem. For in *Fifine* as in *Aristophanes' Apology*, Browning is exploring the play of opposites and the turning of them in a comprehensive view of human existence. The poem is, at first glance, a dramatic monologue spoken by that most notorious of literary lovers, Don Juan, who appears in modern guise as a self-described "householder," married but tempted to commit adultery (and, at the end of the poem, apparently yielding to temptation). The monologue is Juan's apologia, but Browning complicates matters by presenting Juan in dialogue with his women, and the reader has to struggle to decide if their speeches, to which Juan responds, are actual or attributed. Moreover, Browning makes use of two medieval genres, the *débat* and the dream vision, and he presents the whole in a verse form in which rhythm strains against meter: metrically his lines are rhymed iambic hexameters with a strong medial caesura, but one also hears a four-beat line, the *ictus* coming at the beginning of each of four isochronous units, and the rhyme marking the beginning of every fourth unit. Such tension, such a striving of opposites in the form, mirrors the content of the monologue. Juan's speech is (to borrow a phrase from Matthew Arnold) "the dialogue of the mind with itself," and Juan is like Arthur Hugh Clough's Dipsychus, the man with two souls. In literature a man's soul is conventionally female—his *anima*—and in this poem Browning outers the division within Juan in the two very different women with whom he is involved: Elvire and Fifine. Elvire is Juan's wife, "my queen," he calls her, "Sexless and bloodless sprite" (172–73); Fifine is a gypsy dancer at the fair in Pornic: her body Juan describes with the erotic detail of a blazon (150–68), and her "curtsey, Smile and pout, / Submissive-mutinous" (251–52) are a challenge and a provocation to his sexuality. When one views the poem as a medieval *débat*, one can see that Elvire is the spirit, Fifine the flesh, and the two contend for Juan's soul in a dialogue that is also a psychomachia, or battle within.

Browning's use of the convention whereby a man's soul is made visible in the person of the woman (or women) he loves was a factor in one unfortunate result of the poem's publication: a break in his relations with Dante Gabriel Rossetti, who had long been an admirer and supporter of the older poet. Rossetti had memorably explored the convention of the male *anima* through the 1850 story "Hand and Soul" in which he sets out the agenda for his art: the soul of the painter who is the story's central figure appears to him in the form of a beautiful woman; she presents herself as both his subject and his inspiration. Using that same convention, Rossetti wrote "Jenny," in imitation of a Browning monologue. His speaker, a student, reads like a book the sleeping prostitute who is the subject of his musings, and some version of the formula "In my life, as in hers" (388) is a motif which makes the point that the woman he contemplates is an image of something within himself. That something was "fleshliness," according to the attack made on Rossetti in 1871 by Robert Buchanan. Rossetti replied to "The Fleshly School of Poetry" with his own "The Stealthy School of Criticism," but in the spring of 1872, when Buchanan had published an extended version of his attack, Rossetti's health gave way under physical and mental distress. Impaired judgment led him to view the attack as part of a larger conspiracy against him. Hence, when Browning sent Rossetti a presentation copy of *Fifine at the Fair*, the younger poet's response to it was hardly a sane one: "to the astonishment of bystanders, he at once fastened upon some lines at its close as being intended as an attack upon him, or as a spiteful reference to something which had occurred, or might be alleged to have occurred, at his house." Rossetti's brother, William Michael, called the reaction a "scarcely credible delusion," but it persisted, and the upshot was that "he saw no more of Browning, and communicated with him no more."[18] And Browning, who had been privately critical of Rossetti's 1870 *Poems* and told Isa Blagden that he "hated the effeminacy of his school,"[19] did not try to repair the break.

The *Westminster Review*'s anonymous assessment of the poem was that "we believe that [Browning] has put more substance into *Fifine at the Fair* than into any other poem. But for the ordinary reader it might just as well have been written in Sanscrit."[20] The substance is the play of opposites: law and lawlessness, restraint and freedom, silence and speech, permanence and change, truth and falsehood, action and inaction, spirit and flesh, ideal love and sexual love. All those binaries suggest that Juan is to choose between them, and he does indeed make a choice, beginning with his initial identification with the pennon flying above the fair, "Frenetic to be free" (43), and ending with his leaving Elvire (with a weak excuse for his absence) after their return home from a walk, when Juan goes out a second time, apparently for an assignation with Fifine. But the fleshliness of Juan's choice seems to run counter to his creator's comments on the poem. Browning told his friend

Alfred Domett (who recorded the comment in his diary) that, far from being an exploration of the physical, *Fifine* was "the most metaphysical and boldest [of the poems] he had written since *Sordello*," and hence he was "very doubtful as to its reception by the public."[21] The sense in which the poem is both bold and metaphysical—beyond the physical (according to the sense that the *OED* labels "pseudo-etymological")—becomes apparent if we focus on the action or narrative. Juan and Elvire set out on a walk which is an "adventure" in Browning's sense of the word: they visit the fair, descend to the beach, and at dusk climb the rise above the water where, at the climactic moment of their "tramp of near a league" (2240), they come to a "Druid monument" (2045) which is a menhir, a "huge stone pillar" (2104) in a phallic shape, "once upright, / Now laid at length, half-lost—discreetly shunning sight / I' the bush and briar" (2104–6). During his stay in Brittany in the summer of 1866, Browning had actually seen such a stone. "Croisic," he told Seymour Kirkup months later, "is the old head-seat of Druidism in France, probably mentioned by Strabo: the people were still Pagan a couple of hundred years ago despite the priests' teaching and preaching, and the women used to dance around a phallic stone still upright there with obscene circumstances enough,—till the general civilization got too strong for this."[22] In a manner parallel to Childe Roland's coming to the dark tower, Juan comes to a structure which is clearly physical and sexual in its significance, a connotation strengthened by the other landscape feature Juan describes: a "caverned passage" with a "monstrous door / Of granite" (2054, 2052–53), a "grotto" (2065) which is clearly not Christian, in spite of the cross set up at its end. These images of male and female genitalia Juan interprets by rejecting the teaching of the Curé, who refines "To insipidity" (2144) by insisting that the menhir "points to mysteries / Above our grasp" (2103–4), and by accepting the understanding of "peasant lad or lass" (2070) who not only have no difficulty with the actual and primal energy symbolized by the menhir but also interpret it as a reminder of divine creative energy (people "might forget . . . / Earth did not make itself, but came of Somebody" [2073–74]) and of divine permanence amidst creation's constant change ("remind us, all the while / We come and go, outside there's Somebody that stays" [2081–82]). Folklore thus leads the viewer of the menhir from sex to God, and so the sense in which the poem is both metaphysical and bold becomes apparent. Juan sides with the peasant view: "it seems as they could reach / Far better the arch-word" (2129–30). He does not identify the "arch-word," but Christian teaching makes God one with the Word which is the primary creative energy. In Juan's monologue the Word manifests itself in two mottoes to which Juan keeps returning, both of which point to the intersecting of human and divine, physical and metaphysical. One is a line from Aeschylus' *Prometheus Bound*, "God, man, or both together mixed"; the other is "All's change, but permanence as well." The Word is also the subject of Juan's dream vision. He tells of playing Schumann's "Carnival" and of dreaming about the Carnival of Venice, so that the Pornic Fair expands into the Carnival, and the Carnival, in turn, into the whole of creation. In his dream, he needs only to look to grasp the meaning of the scene; he is able "To see, and understand by sight" (1727). In the waking world, one does not gain "Knowledge by notice" (1762); there one "must reach / As best he may the truth of men by help of words" (1728–29). So the dream brings him to the imperfect human reflection of the divine Word and pushes him back toward actual life. The climactic moment of the dream coincides with the climactic moment of Juan and Elvire's long walk, and the dream, which begins as the opposite of waking life, ends as one with it. Browning manages that converging through architectural images. Juan sees in his dream temples and academies, church and college, all of which are constantly changing; temples, for instance, "subdivide, collapse, / And tower again, transformed" (1913–14). But he also finds "unity in the place / Of temple, tower" (2035–36), and that "common shape" (2040) is the menhir.

Critics often remark that Browning's monologues are exercises in sophistry or casuistry, in which the speaker, himself not very admirable, presents a case for excusing questionable behavior. Certainly one can read *Fifine at the Fair* in that way, but in Browning's "complex poetry" of the early 1870s, the mixing of good and bad, human and divine, physical and metaphysical interested him, and such poetry is (in the words of Aristophanes) "operant for body as for soul." The inclusive view expressed by Juan in *Fifine at the Fair* anticipates the defense of comedy which is the substance of *Aristophanes' Apology*, in which the Greek playwright celebrates the same energy Juan celebrates,

> the Power
> Adulterous, night-roaming, and the rest:
> Otherwise,—that originative force
> Of nature, impulse stirring death to life,
> Which, underlying law, seems lawlessness,
> Yet is the outbreak which, ere order be,
> Must thrill creation through, warm stocks and stones,
> Phales Iacchos. (*Aristophanes' Apology* [2360–67])

Phales Iacchos is "Phallic Bacchus."

In *Red Cotton Night-Cap Country*, Browning spins the elements of "complex poetry" in a different combination. The play of opposites which characterized

Fifine at the Fair is present in the new poem: the subtitle, "Turf and Towers," points to earth and sky, body and soul, fleshliness and spirituality, but to those binaries Browning adds a new one, the colors red and white, and the contrasting cotton nightcaps which are the subject of the debate between the poet and Anne Thackeray, to whom the poem is dedicated. Moreover, the substance of the poem is an "adventure" in which the action parallels that of *Fifine*: the poet and Thackeray undertake a long walk; meet on a Normandy beach which, as "mere razor-edge 'twixt earth and sea" (181), is emblematic of opposites confronting each other; proceed inland to a landscape which is the scene of single combat ("You put me on my mettle. British maid / And British man, suppose we have it out / Here in the fields, decide the question so?" [381–83]); reach a rise which gives them a broad view of the country seat of Léonce Miranda, whose story Browning tells; and end by circling round in a movement which is emblematic of the resolution of their battle and of the comprehensive view from the "little mound" (1018) at which they arrive. Like the Balaustion Browning would soon create in *Aristophanes' Apology*, the poet recounts the debate with Thackeray, and in it he encloses not a translated play but the story of Léonce Miranda. The story is the poet's proof of his own position in the argument, and it is the story of a man like Don Juan, whose mixed heritage has resulted in "a battle in the brain" (1155) and whose "inward strife" (3167) is outered in the two women who contend for his soul: his mother, "French and critical and cold" (1154), and his mistress, Clara de Millefleurs, whose "happy name" (1513) links her with the earth and the bounteous energy of physical nature. Browning complicates the convention of a man's soul becoming visible in the figure of the women he loves by Miranda's devotion to the Virgin, whose local name, "La Ravissante," paradoxically links her with the "enchantress" (3317) who is usually her opposite. Browning used an actual case that had been before the French courts, but (unlike his handling of his "Roman murder-case") he had to change the names of the principals to avoid legal difficulties. Milsand had provided Browning with the legal documents, and Browning had the advantage of contemporary interest in the case: "I collected the accounts current among the people of the neighbourhood, inspected the house and grounds, and convinced myself that I had guessed rightly enough in every respect."[23]

Naming is the subject of the debate between Browning and Thackeray. She wants to characterize the Normandy landscape as "White Cotton Night-Cap Country," on the grounds that the white nightcap is emblematic of the pastoral ideal, *otium*, or contentment of mind: it is a "badge of soul and body in repose" (149). He, borrowing from Carlyle's *The French Revolution*, argues for a red nightcap, which in Carlyle's history is the emblem of revolution, violence, and death, and which in Browning's telling of Miranda's story points to his self-mutilation and to his eventual suicide by a leap from the belvedere, the "tower" of the subtitle; Browning links it with the nightcap by likening it to "a fool's-cap on the roof" (2229). Relatives had gone to court to overturn Miranda's will, in which he left everything to Clara and the Church, and the legal issue was also a question of naming: was Miranda insane or rational when he leaped? The gardener who witnessed the act pronounced his master "mad." Browning, characteristically, objects: "No! sane, I say, / Such being the conditions of his life, / Such end of life was not irrational" (3604–6). In making such a judgment Browning had the backing of the actual court decision, which upheld the will, but the poet's concern is with Miranda's inner life at the moment of his leap. "He thought" (3276), Browning begins, and then breaks off in a parenthesis that defines his interests as a poet:

> (Suppose I should prefer 'He said'?
> Along with every act—and speech is act—
> There go, a multitude impalpable
> To ordinary human faculty,
> The thoughts which give the act significance.
> Who is a poet needs must apprehend
> Alike both speech and thoughts which prompt to speak.
> Part these, and thought withdraws to poetry:
> Speech is reported in the newspaper.) (3276–84)

The poet gives Miranda's thoughts at length but makes the point that they all take place in "a minute's space" (3286), a moment Browning links with a rich and recurring image in the poem, the "flash." The "flash" is like computer software that compresses data, which the poet opens and expands to usable form. The whole four-thousand-line monologue he calls a "moment's flashing, amplified, / Impalpability reduced to speech, / Conception proved by birth" (4236–38).

The debate format which is the governing frame of the story suggests that Browning is arguing for a single point of view, and that he is, in his usual perverse way, defending a man of questionable character. One notes, however, that throughout the story he is critical of Miranda, and at the end he judges him a failure: he "hardly did his best with life" (3997); heart and head were at odds; and "the sense of him should have sufficed / For building up some better theory / Of how God operates in heaven and earth" (4005–7). Browning's central lesson is about the skill needed to negotiate life's opposites. The poem contrasts the whole man (Browning) with the divided man

(Miranda), the true artist who sees things in their entirety (Browning) with the failed artist (Miranda, a jeweler and goldsmith), the man who can hold opposites together (like Joseph Milsand and Sir Thomas Browne, who both figure in the poem) and the man whom opposites destroy. Miranda's story is a cautionary tale which teaches a lesson, though it is not quite the lesson the poet actually voices: "Aspire, break bounds! I say, / Endeavour to be good, and better still, / And best!" (4017–19). Browning's explicit lessons, however acceptable at face value, are often qualified or undermined by the broader concerns of the poems in which they appear. One thinks of the last line of "Love among the Ruins," for instance, which is "Love is best," when the love relation in the poem is obviously problematic, or the "lesson" of *The Ring and the Book*, that "our human speech is naught, / Our human testimony false" (12. 834–35), even though the whole poem has been concerned with the "worth of word" and the truth claims of opinion and testimony. In *Red Cotton Night-Cap Country* the main point is not a theme at all but a method of approaching all things in creation, and that method is the skillful turning of opposites in a comprehensive view that requires all one's intellectual and imaginative energy. Browning's faith makes that human effort a reflection of God's scheme of salvation, as the "march-tune" (401) of the debate with Thackeray suggests. The "march-tune" (for music propels the "adventure" here, though to a much lesser extent than in *Fifine*) is a quotation from the prophet Isaiah, and it defines saving change: "though your sins be as scarlet, they shall be as white as snow; though they be red like crimson, they shall be as wool" (Is. 1:18). Browning reduces the line to "that promise old / *Though sins are scarlet they shall be as wool*" (403–4), but the implication is the same: the human ability to trope (the Greek word means "turn") and to liken or even identify unlike things (such as sins, scarlet, and wool) sustain the hope that must animate all faith because they are signs that God (who can do what human beings only wish they could do) can change things in radical ways. Troping is the central and defining act of the poet, and in *Red Cotton Night-Cap Country* Browning adds to the suggestion in the Balaustion poems that every woman must be her own poet, and every man his: artistry, he says, is "battle with the age / It lives in" (2081–82), and "To be the very breath that moves the age / Means not to have breath drive you bubble-like / Before it" (2086–88). The artist is to be the activist, in Browning's view, and the saving change that he or she brings about anticipates the ultimate change that God alone can effect.

Browning's use of Milsand as a model of the whole man, the man who can hold opposites together, and judge and act appropriately, is an important part of the poem's design. It was Milsand who first told Browning the story of

Léonce Miranda—"the merest sketch of the story on the spot"[24]—and it is Milsand whom Browning presents to Miranda in the poem as the troubled man's "guide" (2890): "There stands a man of men" (2891), Browning says to Miranda; "That man will read you rightly head to foot" (2899). With his understanding he will "teach" (2929), "give / Advice" (2930–31), "supply your crippled soul / With crutches" (2933–34), "help you onward in the path / Of rectitude" (2935–36), and "counsel justice" (2937). When the poet names his friend, he praises him "who makest warm my wintry world, / And wise my heaven" (2945–46). Browning's characterization of Milsand in the poem reflects Milsand's role in the poet's life, for Milsand had as much to do with Browning the father as he did with Browning the poet. Within days of Elizabeth's death Robert told Sarianna that "Dear Milsand will be the person for whose help I shall count most presently: he will advise with me about Pen."[25] The poet relied on Milsand's judgment on issues in French society—"I talked it fully over with Milsand,"[26] he says of one—and he relied on his critical judgment, sending to Milsand manuscripts and proofs for correction. He found his help *"inestimable"*: "I never hoped or dreamed I should find such an intelligence as yours at my service. I won't attempt to thank you, dearest friend. . . ."[27] Browning regularly spent time with Milsand in Paris, and Milsand, who "fulfilled the task of a pioneer, opening for his French readers new regions of English literature, philosophy, and art,"[28] spent several weeks each year in London, staying with Robert and Sarianna in Warwick Crescent. He must have been the ideal houseguest, for Browning invariably expressed his pleasure in these visits. In 1866 Browning reported to Isa Blagden that "Milsand's visit was wholly delightful";[29] "Milsand is staying with me, to my usual delight," he told Isa in 1870: "he goes here, there—sees everything so quietly and effectually." "Milsand was here for a month, to my joy," he wrote later that same year.[30] Browning also expressed regularly the value of Milsand's friendship to him: "a friend that sticketh closer than a brother," he told Mrs. Eckley in 1858;[31] "his friendship," he told Sarianna when Elizabeth died, "remains a most precious treasure to me;"[32] "I know and love Milsand thoroughly," Browning wrote to John Ruskin in 1865, "and his existence to me is proof of innumerable good things which the daily rabble of rascaldom goes near to cast doubt upon sometimes."[33] And in 1872, after Milsand had spent a month at Warwick Crescent, Browning wrote to Isa that "no words can express the love I have for him, you know—he is increasingly precious to me."[34] Unlike Tennyson, who was touchy about the charge that he had called Hallam "dear," Browning, confident in his own sexuality, did not hesitate to address Milsand as "dearest friend" and to refer to him as "dear Milsand." Nor was he shy about embracing him. Mme Blanc (the Milsands' daughter married into the Blanc family) remembered the summer of 1870 at St. Aubin: "Every day the two men could be seen on the beach, the arm of Browning always round Milsand's shoulders, as in the photograph where they are represented admiring the picture of an old woman which the poet's son had painted." Though both men were "short of stature," in Mme Blanc's words, the poet was "vigorous and expansive," while his friend "was thin, nervous, and reserved, with an exquisite sensibility which showed itself in all the lines of his stern and spiritual face."[35]

Red Cotton Night-Cap Country is steeped in Browning's experiences of both the landscape and the company in St. Aubin-sur-mer in the summers of 1870 and 1872. "Sarianna and I passed a short month *brightly* and happily with Milsand at St. Aubyn," he told Isa Blagden about the summer of 1872; "the weather was delightful, the quiet unbroken,—or only pleasantly broken by the neighbourhood of Annie Thackeray at Lion, a few miles off."[36] Thackeray has left us her own account of that summer. For her the landscape was rural, safe, and beautiful, and she saw it with the loving eye which Browning attributes to her in the poem (in line 109); for him "sea-coast-nook-ful Normandy" was also a land on the edge of the sea, and, much as he liked the place, his descriptions suggest something not entirely tamed and humanized. "The wildness, savageness of the place, its quiet and remoteness, suit me exactly," he told Anne Egerton Smith,[37] and that note of something more than pastoral contentment can be heard in his telling Isa Blagden about "this wild little place." "Milsand lives in a cottage with a nice bit of garden, two steps off, and we occupy another of the most primitive kind on the sea-shore—which shore is a good sandy stretch for miles and miles on either side." "Rough," he called the place a month later: "the absolute presence of the sea is more and more attractive, and the solitariness of the spread of sands, at low tide, combined with the fine weather, make it most enjoyable to my taste."[38] Thackeray's memories of the same landscape make it an ideal pastoral setting, "a land flowing with milk and honey," in her words. She tells how Browning appeared at the gates of their chateau, a "broad-shouldered figure . . . dressed all in white, with a big white umbrella under his arm." She records a delightful luncheon with Browning at the Milsands, when "the feast itself was spread out-of-doors on the terrace at the back [of the Milsands' tiny house], with a shady view of the sea between lilac-bushes; the low table was laid with dainties, glasses, and quaint decanters," and the meal was enlivened by a regiment marching past and by the too-late arrival of a "larded capon," which had been sent to the pastry cook's to be roasted. Thackeray walked with Browning back along the path on the high cliff, "the sea-coast far below our feet, the arid vegetation [bordering] the sandy way, the rank, yellow snap-dragons lining the paths." In the house the Brownings were renting, "The sitting-room door opened to a garden and the sea beyond—a fresh-swept bare floor, a table, three straw chairs, one book upon the table. Mr. Browning told us it was the only book he had with him. The bedrooms were as bare as the sitting-room. . . . I heard Mr. Browning declaring they were perfectly satisfied with their little house."[39]

In *The Inn Album*, Browning returned to the dramatic genre he had explored in the Balaustion poems—tragedy—but he said his latest poem was "a tragedy in a new style."[40] By "new" he meant "modern," because he sets the action in the present—1875—and because the poem is full of contemporary references and allusions (including one tongue-in-cheek reference to himself: "That bard's a Browning; he neglects the form: / But ah, the sense, ye gods, the weighty sense!" [17–18]. By "new" he may also have meant that the text is a combination of narrative and dramatic speeches, the "new" element being the fact that none of the characters is named, so that the reader must constantly be on the alert to remember or determine who is speaking. Or he may have meant "new" in another sense entirely: Browning takes a tragic action and makes both its peripeteia, or turning point, and its meaning depend upon rhyme and rhyming.

The rhymes which are the focus of the action are in the book named in the title: the album where guests at a British country hotel record in verse their "gratitude / For breakfast, dinner, supper, and the view!" (2–3). The first comment on the album is about staying within metrical bounds: "Each stanza seems to gather skirts around, / And primly, trimly, keep the foot's confine, / Modest and maidlike" (5–7). Like meter, rhyming is the expression of the tension between restraint and freedom. The tragedy turns on the controlling and confining power of rhyme, which two characters assume (one with evil intent, one innocently) and which the other two characters resist. In the Jules and Phene episode of *Pippa Passes*, Browning had made bad rhyme the revelatory instrument of the marriage-destroying plot of Jules's fellow students, but Jules's response had turned the potential tragedy to comedy. Here the response of the young man and the young woman is also a rejection of the manipulative power Browning associates with bad rhyme, and though their resistance leads to the catastrophe (murder and suicide), the text ends with the promise of renewal in the person of the youngest of the four characters.

In the text, narration and dramatic voices tell of the intertwining of the lives of four characters: the "older man," the "young man," the "young woman," and the "very young woman." The narrator eventually refers to the "older man" as "the Adversary," and since "adversary" in Hebrew is "Satan," the "older man" is clearly the antagonist, the tempter who has ruined the life of the "young woman" and who, attempting the financial fleecing of the "young man," suffers an unexpected reversal: "bent on clearing out / Young So-and-so, young So-and-so cleaned me" (377–78). The "older man" offers the "young man" the "young woman" as payment for his debt: such is the crucial action in the poem. Browning manages the unraveling of the plot in a symmetrical way that suggests (as in rhyme) the bringing together of like and unlike and the resulting tensions between them. The two men speak first; they are alike by being in love with the same woman (although they do not yet know that) but speak of loving "in our different ways" (886). Their references to the promptings of "Reason and rhyme" (791) and to "lines of liking, loving" that "run / Sometimes so close together they converge" (880–81) link their stories to the album and its verses. The two women speak next. With great confidence the "very young woman" offers in album rhyme her reading of the "young woman's" thoughts, verses the "young woman" immediately rejects when she offers her own—unrhymed—lines. "Older man" and "young woman" then confront each other, to be interrupted by the "young man" who, expecting unlikes, "sees, and knows" (2065) that the "older man" who ruined his love and the man who attempted to ruin him at cards are one and the same. The crisis in the action—the "older man's" tempting of the "young man" and his attempted "mastery" (2640) over body and soul of the "young woman"—turns upon the verses which the "older man" inscribes in the album. He thinks, when he sees the two "hand in hand" (2857), that his verses have succeeded, but the "young woman" reads the verses aloud, and her doing so brings about *anagnorisis,* or a moment of recognition, in the "young man." The "older man," anticipating the success of his plot, had suggested that "all three of us contribute each / A line" (2945–46) to the album, and he himself voices not only his own but the others' lines which, with their too-easy and obvious rhyme ("spot," "allot," "shot") indicate his control of the situation. "Young man" and "young woman" reject such mastery of themselves, the "young man" by murdering the "older man," the "young woman" by writing in the album her own unrhymed lines blessing her defender before she herself takes poison.

Reviews of *The Inn Album* were mostly unfavorable, and many reviewers focused on the subject matter, which they found repulsive or terrible, "the raw material of a 'penny dreadful,'" in John Addington Symonds's words, with "all the faults of a melodrama," in the opinion of an anonymous critic.[41] Yet Browning insisted that "there was sufficient motive for the young man killing the old one,"[42] and he would presumably have defended the suicide of the "young woman" on the same grounds, as he also had defended the self-mutilation and eventual suicide of Léonce Miranda in *Red Cotton Night-Cap*

Country. Why did he introduce such horrors into his "complex poetry"? Certainly not for their own sake, "as if" (Domett recorded Browning's saying) "a painter would choose no colours to work in but bloodred and lamp-black. Piling horror on horror in works of fiction served no purpose but to excite disgust."[43] Introducing horrors to counter delights (as Browning did in *Red Cotton Night-Cap Country*) or for certain effects and insights was, however, another matter. In a "long talk" with Domett "as to the admission of 'the horrible' into the drama," Browning defended the inclusion of Hercules' murder of his own children (in Euripides' *Herakles*, which Browning had just been translating) for the "pathos" of the scenes "where Heracles becomes conscious of what he has done, and his passionate comments upon it to Theseus."[44] Browning, like Domett, was conscious of "the dry accounts of similar horrors one reads every other day in the newspapers," sensational accounts which evoke neither pathos nor understanding. Browning's concern, as he wrote in that important parenthesis in *Red Cotton Night-Cap Country*, is with "the thoughts which give the act significance." The expression of such thoughts and the exploration of the significance of all human acts, admirable or horrible, are at the center of his "complex poetry."

Fame and Its Discontents

When he was a young man Browning wanted to be famous. His failure as a playwright modified that ambition to include a more admirable desire for readers and critics, however few, who were willing to make an effort to engage his texts seriously and to see them as the site of honest debate between their minds and the poet's mind. He was frustrated by criticism which simply dismissed his poems as "obscure" and angered by criticism which attacked him as unpoetic or confused or incompetent. Difficult he might be, but he knew what he was doing and why he was doing it. In spite of his expressed indifference to fame, he harbored a lingering resentment over its slowness in coming to him; and in spite of favorable criticism and many engaged and sympathetic readers, in spite even of his publisher's assurance "that it made no sort of difference in the demand for a book of mine whether all the critics praised it or abused it,"[1] he blamed the delay on reviewers who had made his "unintelligibility" "proverbial."[2] In the criticism of a book, Browning remarked to Mrs. Thomas FitzGerald, "the ill word may possibly *shut up* its contents altogether from the reader of the criticism, if he believes it fair and good."[3] One critic in particular evoked his strongest feelings: Alfred Austin, who would become poet laureate in 1896, and who would in that position (Browning would have been gratified to know) be the subject of much derisive laughter and "a target for criticism as barbed and cutting as was ever aimed at any English poet."[4]

The cause for such criticism was Austin's character. In his *Autobiography* he admits to a deficiency in humility, "something mercurial" in his temperament, and "a certain almost fatalistic self-confidence," as a result of which "I have never suffered long from discouragement."[5] What he saw as self-confidence, others saw as egotism. He had abandoned law for poetry, and as early as the 1850s was ambitious to be the laureate. He believed the writing of poetry was mainly a matter of inspiration, and while he composed when his muse moved him, his biographer remarks drily that "far too often he apparently misdiagnosed as the stirrings of the Muse the more mundane phenomena of metabolism."[6] When he was not inspired, he worked as a reviewer and a journalist, and while in 1870 the Brownings were leaving France in distress over the war with Prussia, Austin, then a correspondent for the *London Standard*, was at the Prussian headquarters and entered Paris with the Prussian army, completely in sympathy with its military and political purposes. In 1869 Austin had written a series of articles on contemporary poets for the *Temple Bar*, articles which he gathered together in his 1870 book, *The Poetry of the Period*. The first article, in May, had been on Tennyson; the second, in June, on Browning, and it was an attack on his reputation, his poetry, and, in the final paragraph, on the poet himself. Browning, he said, is "not a poet at all," and he "thinks in prose"; he is "both muddy and unmusical to the last degree," and "his style may fairly be described as the very incarnation of discordant obscurity." Browning would do well, he wrote, to imitate Tennyson, who "has never gone looking for fame," and the reading public would do well to "bluntly forswear Mr. Browning and all his works."[7] Austin said all of this with supreme confidence in his judgment, just as he had unshakable faith in his own abilities as poet. He was an egotistical, cocksure, self-assertive, rather pompous man without a sense of humor and certainly without the ability to see himself as others saw him. And he was little, about five feet tall. His character and his size would be targets of satire when he became laureate; Browning anticipated such attacks in 1876, when in "Of Pacchiarotto, and How He Worked in Distemper" he aimed his satire at a critic who had long angered him.

It is not always easy to sympathize with a satirist. His view of the world is too often ill-tempered, and his techniques, especially exaggeration in the name of truth, seem unfair. The role of satirist is Browning's least admirable, for he shows himself as cranky, "bilious" (his word), and not above the personal attacks he so resented in Austin. The temperament of the satirist appears in an 1870 letter to Isa Blagden, when he tells her how he would like to respond to requests from a Mrs. Kinney (who might "begin by acknowledging humbly that she had been a complete dupe and simpleton") and a Mrs. Bathoe ("would you not tell her something more impolite" than he is about to say to her). "Oh, Isa," he bursts out, "'in this sublunary world,'—as was well observed 'there be marvellous fools!' and I do believe that somehow more than my fair share tumble upon and teaze me."[8] That is the conventional complaint of the satirist, and it found full expression in his attacks upon Austin. Though he had obliquely referred to Austin in *Balaustion's Adventure* as "a brisk little somebody, / Critic and whippersnapper, in a rage / To set things right" (306–8) and in *Aristophanes' Apology* as "Dogface Eruxis, the small satirist" (1674), his attacks were (until 1876) in private letters, and he did not hesitate to use Austin's size. "Little" is his usual adjective, and Austin's diminutive stature, he insists, is a trope for his character: he "seemed the most perfect specimen of the 'little man' I ever met with or imagined," and "he *is* little—physically as well as morally & intellectually."[9] Browning linked him with Dickens's Quilp, the "blackguardly" dwarf in *The Old Curiosity Shop*, and troped him as insect or worse: "my little bug of an Austin," "such vermin as little Austin."[10] Browning had three reasons for his quarrel with Austin. One was Austin's practices as a critic, such as "a trick of 'giving an instance of Mr. Browning's unintelligible stuff' which he makes so indeed by altering my words to his own,—leaving out a whole line, for instance, and joining two broken ends!"[11] A second reason (expressed to both Mrs. FitzGerald and Edmund Gosse) was Austin's claim to be a fellow poet; Browning was scornful of "'poets' who, dropping out of the ranks, condescended to hide behind a wall, throw a handful of mud at their so-called 'rival'; and then slink out and stand by his side as a 'fellow-poet' just as if nothing had happened."[12] A third reason was Austin's conservative social and political views, his attachment to tradition, authority, and the aristocracy. "A filthy little snob," Browning called him, and the poet (with unbecoming glee and some snobbery of his own) exulted in the jealousy his social engagements were arousing in Austin: "it 'riles' such a filthy little snob as Mr Alfred Austin to read in the Morning Post how many dinners I eat in good company." Browning even gave as his motive for eating out more than he otherwise would the fact that "it stings such vermin as little Austin to the quick that I 'haunt gilded saloons.'"[13]

"Of Pacchiarotto" is a narrative poem, the story of a satirist who, knowing that "Things wanted reforming" (28), becomes "the censor of this age" (173), only to suffer a reversal when the members of his own club turn on him, and he is forced to take refuge with a corpse, a "thing fetid and verminous" (317). The story is apt, for Austin, who would be known primarily for his lyrics, was also a satirist: his first important work, *The Season* (1861), was modeled on Byron's *English Bards and Scotch Reviewers*, and in it Austin had attacked the manners of the wealthy and fashionable members of London society to whose interests he would later become so attached. In the poem Pacchiarotto attacks pope and emperor only to shift his position: "lo, he's beside

them, / Friendly now, who late could not abide them" (129–30). Pacchiarotto learns a lesson which is his creator's view of both the function and
limitations of satire: man's work "is to labour and leaven—/ As best he
may—earth here with heaven" (368–69), but the satirist must not "dream of
succeeding" (372) because earth's imperfections are the necessary context for
the development of the soul. So *earth is earth and not heaven* (367) and must
remain so. Pacchiarotto may or may not be Austin, but without question the
final part of the poem is aimed at him. Browning is, in fact, on the point of
naming him (as his "sauced in" rhyme obviously indicates) but breaks off
with a show of restraint which allows him public use of the recurring gibe in
his private letters: "For 'Who would be satirical / On a thing so very small?'"
(The couplet is from an eighteenth-century poem.)

The effective part of Browning's satire is not its content but its form. The
poem is written in rhyming couplets of anapestic trimeter lines, many of
them hypercatalectic and many of the rhymes double and triple. The meter is
vigorous and energetic, the rhymes ingenious. Austin had attacked Browning
as both unpoetic and unmusical, and the form Browning chooses is his
answer to those charges. He had long described himself as a "rhymester" and
had discussed rhyme as one of the defining characteristics of the "poetic"; he
prided himself on his skill with rhymes and on the acuteness of his ear; and
as early as 1845 he threatened to use rhyme as a satiric weapon: when a critic
annoyed him, "I'll be hanged," Browning said, "if I don't rhyme him to death
like an Irish Rat!"[14] (Rosalind in *As You Like It* 3. 2. 173–75, having read
Orlando's verses hanging on a tree, jokes about death by rhyme, the alleged
Irish method of getting rid of rats). Browning had little use for easy or obvious rhymes; he associated them with attempts to control others, as in the
Jules and Phene episode in *Pippa Passes* and in *The Inn Album*. Difficult
rhymes he linked with Austin's other charge against him, that he was unmusical. By "musical" Austin seems to have meant diction which is melodious,
harmonious, and clear, and so he attacked the "discordant obscurity" of
Browning's diction. He could not have understood, as Browning did, that
music in poetry is something other than pleasing sounds. Browning knew
that music in poetry is primarily the organization of beats and rests in units
of equal time, and that rhyme marks the ictus, or beat, at the beginning of
such a unit (the equivalent of the bar in music). The truly "poetic" and the
truly "musical" depend upon the skillful handling of the interplay of
repeated sounds and recurring beats, skill which creates (what Browning
calls in the poem) "true *melos*" (*melos* means song). He contrasts "true *melos*"
with the "music" of his critics, whom he tropes as chimney sweeps whose
idea of measure is only the repetitive thump-thump of "saltbox and bones"

(465), the "rattling" of brushes (482–83), and "the jangle / Of regular drum and triangle" (488–89). Moreover, he links "true *melos*" with content. Austin had asserted that the great poets were also the clearest; Browning answered, "had you to put in one small line / Some thought big and bouncing" (564–65), you would discover that "Clear cackle is easily uttered!" (570). The *Saturday Review* judged the expression "a big and bouncing thought" as "vulgar," preferring instead "a pregnant condensation of wisdom."[15] The *Review*'s insistence on decorum in diction manages to eliminate the connection Austin never understood, between idea ("thought") and movement ("bouncing"), which for Browning is both the energy and the raison d'être of poetry.

There had been an earlier and rather painful moment when Austin impinged on Browning's life. Isa Blagden, the novelist and poet who had long been close to Browning, had died in Florence on January 20, 1873, leaving behind a circle of friends who wished to keep her memory alive. One of them, a Mme Mazini, gathered together her poems and asked Austin to edit them for republication. Austin had met Isa when he visited Italy in 1865, and Isa, who was warm and kind and generous to everyone, had made him a friend, though Browning, writing his regular letters to her, was entirely frank with her in his estimation of Austin's character. The cost of the edition was to be borne by the subscription of Isa's friends. Browning refused Mme Mazini's request, saying he would "be no party to the association of a dearly-loved name with that of Mr Alfred Austin" and promising that, *if* he bought the book, he would "by help of penknife and ink-blotting, purify and render it fit to be read."[16]

Three years later, in writing to his brother-in-law George, Browning showed a better attitude and used a more admirable tone: of "Pacchiarotto" he said, "It was not worth while, perhaps, even to amuse myself for once (first time and last time) with my critics—I really had a fit of good humour—and nothing worse—when the funny image of Austin, 'my castigator,' as he calls himself, struck me in a vision of May-morning."[17] Browning wrote in the same vein to John Gray, who had reviewed the "Pacchiarotto" volume favorably. The poem was, he said, "a moment's amusement," and he conceded that "I may have laid too rough a finger" upon Austin: "But very little of this sportiveness serves its turn, and there shall be no more of it, I promise you."[18]

Browning wrote those words under the distancing and calming influence of the Isle of Arran. For in August of 1876 the Brownings returned to Scotland. "Change" and "health" were their usual vacation motives; they had exhausted the summer pleasures of Brittany and Normandy, and they spent nearly three months on Arran, where they walked for several hours every day, Browning praising "the purity of the air and general sense of pleasantness" which, he said, "ought to do me a world of good, and may really help me through the winter without the usual penalty I pay in the shape of a 'cold.'"[19] But his longings for "change" were turning from north to south, and from sea to mountains. The next summer they traveled south to Haute-Savoie, to La Saisiaz near Geneva, where hiking replaced swimming as the poet's chief physical activity. Strong as was Browning's enjoyment in responding to the Alpine scenery, he would later refer to that summer's vacation as "the disastrous journey."[20] The cause was the sudden and wholly unexpected death of their longtime friend and holiday companion, Anne Egerton Smith.

Miss Smith was a sister of a Florentine friend of the Brownings, Mrs. William Bracken (Bracken's son, Willy, had been a childhood playmate of Pen's and a friend of his throughout their adolescence). Smith loved music and was proficient in it, and music was the bond between her and the poet. During the winters when Smith made her home in London, Browning "was one of the very few persons whose society she cared to cultivate; and for many years the common musical interest took the practical, and for both of them convenient form, of their going to concerts together."[21] She often spent summers near where the Brownings were vacationing. She was with them at Mers-les-Bains in Picardy in 1874; at Villers-sur-Mer in 1875; and in Scotland in 1876. Ten years earlier she and two other women had taken a house near the Brownings in Le Croisic. "I liked her always, and as much now," Browning said at that time: "Miss Smith made the last part of our stay pleasant,—she is my favourite out of the trio."[22]

Browning habitually praised his vacation spots for their "solitude and seclusion," and he did so again when he was describing La Saisiaz for Mrs. FitzGerald: "the peace and quiet move me the most."[23] He responded as strongly to the Alpine setting as he had to the primitive conjunction of land and sea on the French coast: "what wonderful views from the chalet on every side!" Browning exclaimed; "Geneva lying under us, with the lake and the whole plain bounded by the Jura and our own Salève."[24] "Our own Salève" was the mountain four of them—Robert, Sarianna, Anne Smith, and a French friend—planned to climb.

On the morning of the agreed-upon day—September 14, 1877—after Robert had taken his customary plunge in a "delightful bath" supplied by a "live mountain stream,"[25] he and Sarianna looked for the familiar "tall white figure," and when she did not appear, Sarianna went into her room and found her lying facedown on the floor. She "put her arm around her, 'Are you ill, dear?'—then saw that she was insensible."[26] Sarianna called for help. There had been "No premonitory touch," Robert wrote. "As you talked and laughed ('tis told me) scarce a minute ere the clutch / Captured you in cold forever" (109–10)."Warm you were as life" (111) when Robert raised her up, but "all in vain. / Gone you were, and I shall never see that earnest face again / Grow transparent, grow transfigured . . ." (113–15).

La Saisiaz is Browning's elegy for his old friend. Though the poem has major dramatic elements, the poet does not hide behind a dramatic mask: the poem is as personal as the age's other great elegy, *In Memoriam*, and its subtitle, like Tennyson's, consists of its subject's initials and date of death. Also like Tennyson, Browning wrestles with questions of faith in the face of a death which affected him deeply. As he recounts in the poem, he and Smith had been reading Frederic Harrison's essay in *The Nineteenth Century*, "On the Soul and Future Life," and had discussed it on one of their walks, "passing lightly in review / What seemed hits and what seemed misses" (162–63). Now the "hits" and "misses" are no longer matters of playful speculation; "Much less have I heart to palter"—to speak idly, that is, to play fast and loose with the questions Harrison raises—"when the matter to decide / Now becomes 'Was ending ending once and always, when you died?'" (171–72).

The form of the poem is a postmorten dialogue between "I" (Browning) and "you" (Smith), one of several binaries in a poem in which opposites are both close and irremediably separate, like life and death themselves. The poet's dialogue with "you" is also the dialogue of his mind with itself, the question being "How much, how little, do I inwardly believe / True that controverted doctrine [the immortality of the soul]? Is it fact to which I cleave, / Is it fancy I but cherish . . . ?" (209–11). The question, put in that way, suggests that "fact" is true because it is "knowledge" (another key word in the poem) that can be confirmed by the evidence of the five senses, while "fancy," something the mind makes up, is only "surmise" and cannot be proved empirically. The gap between "fact" and "fancy" initially seems as "profound" as that separating Browning alive and Smith dead, but as the poet proceeds he stages in his mind a debate between "the champions Fancy, Reason" (402), a debate which suggests that both are necessary, since knowledge is limited and (without the assumptions of fancy) is an insufficient basis on which to live one's life. The poet begins by presupposing the existence of God and the existence of the soul, presuppositions he calls "facts" not because he can prove them true but because they are assumptions by which he lives. In the debate proper, which starts with the question of the soul's immortality, Fancy "concede[s] the thing refused" (405)—refused by knowledge and its lack of empirical proof, that is—and Reason accepts this "fact" for use in life, finding "it promises advantage, coupled with the other two" (410). So the two voices continue through three more stages, moving from "surmise" through "concession" to "fact" in argumentative iteration that Browning tropes in two ways, as a "circle" (525) and a "chain" (608). In both metaphors ambiguity undermines the elegy's expected (because conventional) consolation. The "full circle" suggests failure, as in "walking in circles": "fancy's footsteps one by one / Go their round conducting reason to the point where they begun" (525–26). That point was the affirmation that God and the soul exist, "facts" that the debate had left unproved. There seems to have been no progress, until one remembers, as Browning does, that, although one must attempt an argument such as that he pursues, one does not live by logic and proof but rather by the emotion of which the two "facts" at the beginning of the argument are the expression. That emotion is hope, one of the two basic emotions of Browning's dissenting religious tradition (the other is fear). "Hope the arrowy" (543), Browning tropes it in the poem, the arrow being part of a conventional cluster of images drawn from archery and associated with thinking (so that the metaphor unites thought and feeling): hitting the bull's-eye signifies correct judgment; missing it indicates an error in judgment (*hamartia*); the launching of the arrow itself means an hypothesis which may or may not hit the mark and prove to be effective. No matter what one's skill, one cannot at the moment of release prove that the arrow will end up in the center of the target, but without hope, there would be no act, no effort, at all. The carefully constructed "chain" of iteration is also double in meaning: it is, the poet says, "flawless till it reached your grave" (608). F. E. L. Priestley long ago commented on the ambiguity of that "till."[27] Did the chain of fancying and reasoning break when confronted with the physical evidence of Smith's death? Or did it extend unbroken all the way to her grave, and remain unbroken even then? The uncertainty is deliberate on Browning's part. He is not in this elegy making a statement of faith, some version of which had provided the conventional consolation in elegies from "Lycidas" to *In Memoriam*; and he presents sardonically the view he imagines readers might have of him: "Why, he at least believed in Soul, was very sure of God!" (604). That view he rejects in his comments on fame, which he attacks because people let the famous do their thinking for them: they believe because "the famous bard believed!" (572). Instead, Browning wants to spur every reader to a serious debate with himself or herself, a debate not to be done by proxy nor to be settled by anyone else. *La Saisiaz* is the model for every such crucial dialogue in one's life.

La Saisiaz raises a question which would later be much discussed by the Browning Society: what *did* Browning believe? For a poet who insisted that he always wrote dramatically, the question could not easily be answered. When, on a visit to the poet on March 29, 1886, John Churton Collins put to him the problem many of his readers were wrestling with—"it would I suppose be erroneous to take the whole mass of your writings and framing from them a body of opinions pronounce them to be the expression of your individual opinion and convictions"—Browning replied, "Yes, yes, most certainly it would. I very seldom write anything which is to be regarded as *my own individual* feeling." Still, on that occasion when "he talked with marked earnestness and sadness about the question of a future state," Browning was remarkably frank: "If you don't accept Revelation, he said, I honestly do not see, after all my thinking and experience, any indication to lead us to suppose that there is a life after this. It is a great desire, that is certain: but I see no reason to suppose that it will be fulfilled." Tennyson "felt positively certain of an extension of individual consciousness after death" but, said Browning, "I can't agree with Tennyson." So Browning came to the same position he expressed in *La Saisiaz*: hope without knowledge. That hope, however, was not without support. To Collins he expressed the radical Protestant position, locating his center of authority within himself: "We have, at least he said, I have, a knowledge of a God within me. I know Him, He is here—pointing to his heart—and it matters little to me what tales you tell me about Him, I smile, I care nothing for any stories you tell me about Him, I know Him." He dismissed aspects of Christianity that others would consider essential—"its historical basis was of no importance," he told Collins, and "a definite religious creed" was "only necessary for people who hadn't the guidance within"—and said rather that the value of Christianity for him lay in the fact that it was "the revelation of that God whom he had felt."[28]

Browning's statements to Collins confirm his own characterization of his faith for Julia Wedgwood more than twenty years earlier: he told her that "my belief is a very composite and unconventional one," and yet it had served him well when put to the test: "I myself am most surprised at detecting its strength in the unforeseen accidents of life which throw one upon one's resources and show them for what they exactly are."[29] "What they exactly are" was a private matter, with complexities and subtleties that were at odds with the robust and seemingly doubt-free affirmations his followers wanted to hear from him, assertions like those recorded by William Sharp in his 1890 *Life of Robert Browning*. Sharp does not date the conversation, but he treats it as recent:

> It seems but a day or two ago that the present writer heard from the lips of the dead poet a mockery of death's vanity—a brave assertion of the glory of life. "Death, death! It is this harping on death that I despise so much," he remarked with emphasis of gesture as well as of speech—the inclined head and body, the right hand lightly placed upon the listener's knee, the abrupt change in the inflection of the voice, all so characteristic of him—"this idle and often cowardly as well as ignorant harping!

Why should we not change like everything else? ... Why, *amico mio*, you know as well as I that death is life, just as our daily, our momentarily dying body is none the less alive and ever recruiting new forces of existence. Without death, which is our crapelike churchyardy word for change, for growth, there could be no prolongation of that which we call life. Pshaw! it is foolish to argue upon such a thing even. For myself, I deny death as an end of everything. Never say of me that I am dead!"[30]

One might hear in such sentences a conventional affirmation of faith in immortality (as many, including Sharp and Moncure Conway, did[31]), but one might also hear, in those words "change" and "growth" and "new forces of existence," a subtler, less orthodox, and far less conventional expression of hope.

On September 19, five days after Smith's death, Browning climbed La Salève, and used the occasion as the starting point of his elegy. He was alone—the sense of an absence and of an impassable gulf between living and dead is the conventional situation of the elegist—and he contrasted his "here" at the summit of the mountain with Smith's "there" behind the "four low walls" of the cemetery in Collonge where she had been buried. The next day Robert and Sarianna, curtailing their planned stay, set out for London, Robert being full of the images and emotions of that September week and feeling the need to make sense of its events: "they impressed me so much" (Browning later told the Reverend J. D. Williams) "that I could proceed to nothing else till I had in some way put it all on paper." The poem was written "in London's mid-November" (606) and was "the only one relating to a personal experience (at least, *directly*) in all my books."[32] Browning published the poem, along with the narrative *The Two Poets of Croisic* and some lyrics, in May of 1878. The reviewers found the subject touching, but one said that the death is "merely used as an occasion for ratiocinative writing," and "ratiocinative poetry is a mistake." Another offered mild approval: "The transition of feelings with which all can sympathize into abstruse and complicated meditation affords a not uninteresting study."[33]

Pen, meanwhile, was finding himself as an artist. His failure at Oxford had left his father first in despair and then resigned to whatever course in life his son would pursue, if indeed he undertook anything at all. From Scotland in 1871 Browning wrote to Isa Blagden saying that his son "has been assiduously labouring in that occupation to which Providence apparently hath pleased to call him,—that is, in shooting, idling and diverting himself"—bitter irony from a father who had a few months earlier told Isa, without irony, that Pen "wants the power of working, & I give it up in despair." But he did not give up on Pen. "I told you," Browning wrote to Isa that same summer, "that, to a certain degree, I am relieved about Pen by knowing the very worst of the poor boy, to-wit that he won't work, or perhaps can't. I shall go on, now, as long as I am able, to do the best for us both, taking the chances of this world." And, as he had before Pen's failure at Oxford, Browning reminded Isa and himself of Pen's good qualities:"He is clever & in the main very good & very conscientious: everybody likes him." And he had potential, in his father's estimation:"his natural abilities are considerable,—and he may turn out a success, though not in the way which lay most naturally before him."[34] That "may" continued to depend upon Pen's will, which showed no sign of strengthening. Alfred Domett, recording in his diary a "long chat" he had with Sarianna when he called at Warwick Crescent and found Browning out, wrote that Sarianna told him "how 'amiable' and 'sensible'" Pen was, and "how popular he was among the Oxford 'men,'" but "she seemed rather to regret her nephew's apparent want of ambition."[35]

A year and a half later, the situation had changed. "Called at Browning's. Miss B. only at home," Domett wrote in his diary for January 16, 1874; "She shewed me some still-life pictures by Pen, praised she said by Millais. . . . Young Browning had just determined to take seriously to painting as a profession."[36] Being serious meant formal training, and after seeking advice and making enquiries, Browning sent his son, soon to be twenty-five years old, to Belgium, to the studio of Jean-Arnould Heyermans in Antwerp. By March his "artist-tutor" reported that "Pen was 'making wonderful progress; was very steady and a *bon enfant* &c.'"[37] By July Browning had received Pen's first composition—"an old man contemplating the old skull"[38]—and in January of 1875 the newly optimistic father told George Barrett that Pen had made "remarkable progress for a student of less than a year's standing." Browning judged that "there wants nothing but a continued application—such as he has shown he can easily manage."[39] A decade earlier "application" had been anything but easy; now Pen really did seem to be working, and by 1878, when Pen was preparing to exhibit at the Royal Academy "and the Grosvenor too," his father could exclaim, "Oh, the blessed thing that Work is!"[40] "You must come and see how pleasantly my sister has brightened up the house," Browning told Mrs. FitzGerald. "We have hung as many of Pen's early works on the walls of my room as will go there,—and very well they really look." Then he added a biblical reference which suggested his readiness to accept his son, whatever his character and motives: "I shall like to raise my eyes from the paper I stoop over, and, like the patriarch, 'taste of the venison of my son that my soul may bless him'—whether he be my true Esau or the supplanter."[41] In 1875, Browning had given a hint that he saw and supported Pen as he was when he called him "the young *Florentine*,"[42] apparently relegating to the past his desire to give Pen an "English stamp" through an English education. In 1881 Browning told Mrs. FitzGerald that "it is clear now that Pen's preference is for a Continental life,—and as he thrives there,—which he never did in England,—thrives morally, I mean, in his love of work,—there is little good in wishing him transplanted."[43]

In 1876 Domett found Browning's "manifest delight in his son's success" "very human (as Carlyle would say) and interesting."[44] There were sales, albeit to friends initially, and requests for portraits. In 1878 Browning could report that Pen "seems happy, full of his art, and regarding it just as I could desire,—aiming at greater work, not stooping to lower considerations or being satisfied with his present success."[45] "He is clearly an artist born," Browning told Mrs. FitzGerald:

> and, in the doing his nature justice, he will find his comfort and reward in life—or nowhere: I have no longer the least doubt about his success,—so far as it may be said to depend on himself: and I contrast, very much to its advantage, his method of study & work with that of other artistic people who are engaged here in what they consider the same pursuit. He is anxious to be back and at the brush again.[46]

While Pen was busy in Antwerp and then in Dinant, his father in London undertook (in his words) to "play showman . . . to Pen's pictures."[47] In March of 1878 he hung one of them at Warwick Crescent and sent friends hand-written notes; the following year he hung several of Pen's paintings in an empty house lent by his publisher in South Kensington and sent out formal engraved invitations. Carlyle was one of the recipients of an invitation in 1878—"a picture by my son will be on view at my house till next Sunday"[48] —and the ancient sage visited Warwick Crescent a few days later, in the company of William Allingham, who recorded the viewing in his diary. Browning received Carlyle "with great emphasis. 'How good and dear of you to come! dear Mr. Carlyle! How dear!' and took him upstairs on his arm." Pen's picture was in the drawing room: "'The Worker in Brass, Antwerp,' intended for the Royal Academy. Old man with hammer and punch finishing a metal dish with rim of dolphins—medallion of Rubens on the floor—pipe on stool— watch hanging on wall." Carlyle's response was noncommittal.

> C., placed in an arm-chair, looked at the picture without speaking; B. went on describing it, from time to time. At last C. said, looking at B., "*Antwerpen*—on the wharf—that is the meaning of the name. It used to be said there was *hand* in it, but that is not so. *On the wharf* is the meaning." C. asked questions about Pen; asked me, is the medallion like Rubens? but said nothing of the Picture.[49]

A month later Sarianna told Alfred Domett that Carlyle had pronounced the picture "'All complete . . . even to the int*aar*lude [interlude] of the pipe!'"[50] The remark was the best she could salvage by way of praise for Pen's art. Still, Pen did exhibit the picture at the Royal Academy, where an MP for Yorkshire paid three hundred pounds for it. "The price was somewhat extravagant, all things considered," Domett wrote in his diary; "the friendship of the artist-assessors for the father had no doubt some influence on their estimate."[51] The father's fame, which (in the words of Wilfred Meynell) "invested [Pen's pictures] with a singular accessory interest of pedigree," was a factor too. "To praise the son was the best compliment which anyone could pay the father," Meynell wrote in his memoir of Browning, and anyone who bought "several of those large canvases . . . must . . . have come near to the heart of the poet."[52]

To Mrs. FitzGerald, Browning professed himself highly satisfied with his son. "He is in high spirits," Browning told her, "and the whole state of the dear fellow is a comfort to me." Moreover, "his letters to me continue to be all I could wish." Not quite all, however. Pen was living his own life in Belgium, but his father's desire to know all about Pen's doings was no less than it had been when Pen was at Oxford. Nor was Pen any more ready to gratify his father's wishes. Hence Browning thanked Mrs. FitzGerald "for the incidental news of Pen" contained in two of her letters: "his reticence is such that I hear less than I like of his doings: and his habitual depreciation of them would mislead me, were I not used to it." Pen's reticence about his art seemed admirable enough—he "never says more of a picture than that he hopes it turns out better than he expected"—but his reluctance to speak about his life was another matter.[53] In 1877 Pen had been on the point of marrying an innkeeper's daughter in Dinant, "a young lady," according to Browning, "of perfectly unexceptionable character and connections." But Browning objected to the marriage. As he explained some four years later to Furnivall, "this occurred at a time when Robert's pictorial career was just begun, and would have seriously affected it: and wholly dependent on myself as he was, with little prospect of becoming otherwise, he had no right so to dispose of his actions in that matter." Browning (forgetting about his own financial situation when he married in 1846) "communicated with the lady's father (who—parenthetically—is wealthy) and the project was dropped on both sides." About Pen's response to his father's intervention we know little, but we may assume that he became more reticent than ever, for his father claimed only "indirect knowledge of past, and present circumstances," and told Furnivall in 1882 that "friends of my son, with vigilant eyes enough, visit him occasionally, and have long ago set my mind at rest."[54] But never entirely. In that same year Browning told Mrs. FitzGerald, "I hope you will not forget that Pen never had the 'pen of a ready-writer.' He writes regularly but briefly to me—speaking about his work as little as possible, though I gather that he has been much occupied with it." So, Browning continues, "if your friends have anything to report, I shall be only too glad to hear it."[55]

℮ ℮ ℮

The emergence of various Browning reading groups and then more formally constituted Browning societies was both an indication of the poet's growing fame and a spur to it. The earliest Browning study group was organized in the United States in 1877 by Hiram Corson, a professor at Cornell University, and the longest continuing Browning Society in the United States (or indeed anywhere)—the Boston Browning Society—was founded in 1885; there would be a great many other such clubs in the United States, where the popular study of Browning flourished more than anywhere else and where Browning's role in late-nineteenth-century literary culture has yet to be examined.[56] By the end of the century there would be hundreds of Browning societies and reading groups in the United States, in Canada, in Britain, and elsewhere, but the most ambitious of the organizations, and the one which attracted the most attention, was the London Browning Society, founded in 1881 by Frederick J. Furnivall and Emily Hickey. Furnivall's prospectus stated the society's aims: "the study and discussion of [Browning's] works, and the publishing of Papers on them, and extracts from works illustrating them. The Society will also encourage the formation of Browning Reading-Clubs, the acting of Browning's dramas by amateur companies," and the publication of scholarly aids to the study of his poetry, including "a Browning Primer" and "a Browning Concordance or Lexicon." The chief activity of the society would be its monthly meetings at University College, London, "for the hearing and discussion of a Paper or Address on some of Browning's poems or his characteristics," and the Society's chief motive, as stated in the prospectus, was the "extension" of the poet's influence and the gaining of "a far wider circle of readers, than he has yet had."[57] Browning credited the society with success in its chief aim. "When all is done," Browning wrote to Nettleship in March of 1889, "I cannot but be very grateful for the institution of the Society; for to what else but the eight years' persistent calling attention to my works can one attribute the present demand for them?"[58] He was grateful, too, for the society's production of some of his plays; in 1888 he told William Allingham that "the acting of my four plays by professionals, *unpaid*, for the Browning Society, is surely one of the greatest and most wonderful honours ever paid to a dramatic writer."[59] He regularly expressed his gratitude to Furnivall, calling his work a "labour of love" and professing himself always aware of Furnivall's "kind intentions": you "who have done so much to serve my poems and myself."[60] Still, Browning's relation with the society and with its prime mover was not an easy one. The principal difficulties lay in Furnivall's personal character and in his limitations as a scholar and critic. The Browning Society was the first literary society devoted to the works of a living poet, and to that study Furnivall brought the editorial and bibliographical practices with which he was familiar—and some uncritical assumptions about having the subject of that study around to answer questions.

Frederick Furnivall's enterprises were deeply involved with his era's major scholarly work in philology, the comparative and historical study of the English language (which, in turn, was a major part of the emerging academic discipline of studies in English language and literature), and philologists needed for their work early texts that existed only in manuscripts or in rare books. That work had been fostered by the Philological Society, of which Furnivall had been honorary secretary, and it found its chief monument in the *New* (now the *Oxford*) *English Dictionary*, which had been promoted by Furnivall as an entirely new dictionary (and not just a supplement to Johnson and Richardson's dictionaries), and in the production of which Furnivall was for eighteen years the "editor" (he superintended the many readers who gathered quotations, with dates, that would make up the history of every word in the language—and he nearly allowed the project to collapse[61]). For that work the editions of the Early English Text Society, which Furnivall founded in 1864, were immensely important, and he extended the production of texts edited and glossed according to modern scholarly standards through the other societies he founded: the Ballad Society (1868), the Chaucer Society (also 1868), and the New Shakspere (as Furnivall insisted on spelling the name) Society in 1873. Furnivall confessed near the end of his life that "I never cared a bit for philology";[62] energy and organizing skills were his chief contributions to the emerging study of England's language as the key to its history (especially, in Furnivall's view, its social history) and national character. To the study of Browning, Furnivall brought some of his scholarly practices: the first publication of the Browning Society was a reprinting of Browning's essay on Shelley, withdrawn from publication in 1852 after the letters to which the essay was a preface turned out not to be genuine, and the second publication was a bibliography of Browning's works and a list of "criticism and notices." When Browning saw all this, he professed himself "startled" at being "brought into prominence after this fashion by the—never mind how partial—judgment of an extraordinarily generous friend," and he told Mrs. FitzGerald that, impressed as he was with the comprehensiveness and detail of the bibliography, "It makes me feel as I look at the thing, as if I were dead and *begun* with"[63]—like the subjects of Furnivall's other societies. But the poet was very much alive, and his presence gave the Browning Society, in Furnivall's view, an immense advantage. To a critic Furnivall replied,

> You've never founded a Chaucer or Shakspere Society, and had to worry and bother over this word and that, this allusion and the other; the man Shakspere's Sonnets were written to, the lady of Chaucer's early love, and all the thousand and one puzzles these poets' works prezent [*sic*]. If you had, you'd never have thought it superfluous, for a set of the contemporaries of each poet to have cleard up all your bothers for you. You'd have blest them every day of your life.[64]

The "bothers," in Furnivall's view (and this view was his major limitation as a critic), were usually factual and biographical rather than interpretive and critical. Browning, aware of the society's efforts "to get behind any plain sense that might be discoverable" in his poems, also thought that Furnivall "strikes me as going to the other extreme; disparaging anything but plain facts."[65] That approach infected other members too. After reading some of the society's papers, their subject exclaimed, "how extraordinary is the 'ordinary' way of considering a poet's method of work. I write, airily, 'quoth Tom to Jack one New Year's Day,'—and one 'student' wants to know who Jack was,—another sees no difficulty there, but much in Tom's entity,—while a third, getting easily over both stumbling blocks, says,—'But—*which* New Year's Day?'" But though the poet was disparaging an obsession with facts, he also understood that the facts were indispensable as a starting point for the serious (and scholarly) study of his works: "Since all this must be done for me by somebody, I congratulate myself on having somebody so energetic as Mr Furnivall to do it."[66] So he responded readily enough to Furnivall's queries between 1881 and 1889, providing facts about occasions, publication, references and allusions, sources, the genesis of poems, and metrics— plus "the list of *real* names and places to be substituted one day for the sham words which saved—problematically—the 'Red Cotton N.[ight] C.[ap] C.[ountry]' from going to grief."[67] His relation with the society, Browning explained to Williams in 1884, was at arm's length, but

> every now and then some question has been put to me through Mr Furnivall, which I made no difficulty to answer. His peculiarities and

defects are obvious—and some of his proceedings by no means to my taste: but there can be no doubt of his exceeding desire to be of use to my poetry, and I must attribute a very great part indeed of the increase of care about it to his energetic trumpet-blowing.[68]

Browning dealt easily enough with Furnivall's requests for facts, but questions of interpretation were another matter. Many of the society's members uncritically thought of Browning as the ultimate authority in all questions of meaning, and since they were reading a poet with a longstanding reputation for difficulty and obscurity, their instinct was to turn to the plain speaking of the man himself as the sure solution to their struggles with his texts. Near the end of his life Browning complained that "I never understood the Society was originally instituted for the purpose of even elucidating dark passages or disinterring deep meanings,"[69] and that was true so far as the society's prospectus was concerned, but Browning also knew, when the society was being formed and he was telling Mrs. FitzGerald about a notice of its organization in a periodical, that the popular understanding of the society's purpose was "the elucidation of the more obscure works of that author!"[70] When Oxford gave Browning an honorary D.C.L. in June of 1882, "the undergraduates lowered down from the gallery a huge cartoon, representing Browning with an immense head and a small body. Before him a group of people, representing the members of the Browning Society, stood with outstretched hands imploring him to explain his poems to them, while Browning waved them off in despair as of one who had no explanation to give."[71] He had none because, as he had said again and again, his poetry was "always dramatic in principle, and so many utterances of so many imaginary persons, not mine." While members of the society struggled with that principle, Furnivall blithely overrode it. His motive for reprinting the essay on Shelley, for instance, was to present the poet himself speaking:

> Browning's 'utterances' here are *his*, and not those of any one of the "so many imaginary persons" behind whom he insists on so often hiding himself, and whose necks I, for one, should continually like to wring, whose bodies I would fain kick out of the way, in order to get face to face with the poet himself, and hear his own voice speaking his own thoughts, man to man, soul to soul. Straight speaking, straight hitting, suit me best.[72]

Browning was of an opposite mind, at least as poet, and his remaining on good terms with Furnivall throughout the remainder of his life is an indication of his tact and forbearance. Furnivall had pressed him to add to his poems explanatory headnotes ("Arguments") which would, among other things, link the texts with stages and occasions in his life (in the same spirit as Furnivall had tried to link the stages of Shakespeare's life with his plays by taking as the main critical purpose of the New Shakspere Society the establishing of the plays' chronology as the key to the playwright's growth and character), and Browning had seriously considered the idea before thinking better of it. In 1887 he told his publisher,

> I have changed my mind about the *notes* I thought of adding to the poems in my own case. I am so out of sympathy with all this "biographical matter" connected with works which ought to stand or fall by their own merits quite independently of the writer's life and habits, that I prefer leaving my poems to speak for themselves as they best can—and to end as I began long ago.[73]

But Browning was inconsistent, and he sometimes did provide an "argument" to his poems when asked. "Browning kept clear of our Society, and we kept it clear of him," Furnivall would later write in his "Recollections of Robert Browning," "but when we couldn't understand a passage or a poem, I either walkt over or wrote to him, and got his explanation of it."[74] The "explanation" was usually a few sentences about the meaning of a poem or passage, a paraphrase of theme or a brief analysis of the motivation of one of his characters. "I should prosaically state the meaning thus" is how Browning begins his answer to one of Furnivall's queries, or he affirms that "the meaning of the passages is much as you say—entirely so, indeed."[75] When, on May 31, 1889, the society heard a paper on "Numpholeptos" and could not reach agreement about the poem, "it was concluded that the Chairman should ask Mr. Browning whether his poem was an allegory only, or meant to represent any type of woman present or past." Browning wrote two paragraphs in reply to Furnivall's inquiry, and they were printed in the society's papers: "Is not the key to the meaning of the poem in its title," he begins.[76] He had helped Mrs. Orr with her *Handbook* in similar ways, providing, for instance, a summarizing prose statement of the beliefs expressed in *La Saisiaz*, paragraphs which she printed *verbatim*. The *Handbook*, published in 1885 and sponsored by the Browning Society, was a fuller and more ambitious version of the primer which Furnivall had named in his prospectus as one of the society's aims. Browning read the whole thing in proof, and while one would be wise not to conclude that he approved of it all, one can at least surmise that he had no serious objections to any part of it. When Furnivall used a "disparaging epithet" for the *Handbook*, Browning defended it, saying that Mrs. Orr was "the dearest woman friend I can boast of in the world" and telling Furnivall that he (Browning) had helped her in the same way as he had him: "I simply answered every now [and] then a question, without the least notion of its exact bearing and purport."[77] And he sometimes deflected queries about meaning by referring the questioner to the appropriate section of the *Handbook*.

Furnivall was not above using (what he considered to be) his inside track to the poet's mind to settle questions raised by papers read at the society. When a Mr. Kirkman had in March of 1882 presented a paper on "'Childe Roland'" in which he had argued that the poem was an allegory, "the sensations of a sick man very near to death," Furnivall began the discussion in his usual confrontational and outspoken way: "MR. FURNIVALL said that he must begin the discussion by applying a charge of dynamite to Mr. Kirkman's theory. With regard to the hidden meaning of the poem, he (Mr. Furnivall) had asked Browning if it was an allegory, and in answer had, on three separate occasions, received an emphatic 'no'; that it was simply a dramatic creation called forth by a line of Shakspere's." Then Furnivall turned to facts supplied by the poet: "Browning had written it one day in Paris as a vivid picture suggested by Edgar's line. The horse was suggested by the figure of a red horse in a piece of tapestry in Browning's house." Other members contributed to the discussion, but Kirkman had the last word, and voiced the central difficulty: "MR. KIRKMAN, in a few words in reply, deprecated Mr. Furnivall asking Mr. Browning the meaning of his poems, and remarked that by so doing there would be no need of the Browning Society."[78]

No wonder then that Browning, for all his openness with Furnivall, often found himself having to restrain his trumpeter's zeal. In April of 1881 Browning had switched the salutation in his letters from "the more formal and un-fellow-student-like style of address" "Dear Mr Furnivall" to "My dear Furnivall,"[79] but the poet could not always maintain the tone of a fellow seeker after enlightenment. Furnivall was obsessed with making Browning's poems widely available in cheap editions, and to one such scheme Browning (who nearly always deferred to the publication plans and business judgment of his publisher, George Smith[80]) responded by abruptly beginning his letter, "Ah, *no*—my dear Furnivall!" Another letter begins "Better not, my dear Furnivall," and still another sounds a note of alarm: "Oh, *no*—emphatically *ny*, dear Mr Furnivall!"[81] For Browning was well aware of Furnivall's belligerent character, his readiness to be intemperate and unwise in speech, and his quarrels with almost everyone. In 1888 (what the poet called) "poor Furnivall's incontinence of tongue"[82] caused Furnivall to lose a libel suit brought against him, and in the 1870s that same failing had led him to quarrel with Swinburne, a verbal battle into which Browning was unwillingly drawn. For

Furnivall had persuaded Browning to become president of his New Shakspere Society in March of 1879, and Browning, who thought the position was an honorary one, soon found himself, much to his dismay, being appealed to by Swinburne and by Halliwell-Phillipps, "the most distinguished Shakespearean antiquary of the nineteenth century" and "the greatest contributor of his age to our knowledge of Shakespeare's life and times."[83] "The very name of Shakespeare," Browning told Charles MacKay early in 1881, "is made a terror to me by the people who, just now, are pelting each other under my nose, and calling themselves his disciples all the while."[84] So Browning's experience of one of Furnivall's societies was not a happy one, and his response to Furnivall's proposal to found a Browning Society was ambivalent at best.

Only a few months after Browning wrote that letter to MacKay, Furnivall and Emily Hickey visited Browning, Furnivall to tell him, characteristically, that there was going to be a Browning Society whether the poet approved of it or not, and Hickey (who had scruples) hoping to learn that Browning did not disapprove and willing to settle for informing him of their intentions, at the very least. Browning "at once laught good-humouredly and talkt about something else," according to Furnivall's account in the *Browning Society Papers* or, according to a later account, "either began talking about something else at once, or did so after saying 'Do as you like.'"[85] From the beginning Browning's feelings were clearly mixed: he knew Furnivall only too well. In the fall of 1881 Browning told a correspondent that the society "was instituted without my knowledge, and when knowledge was, I do not think acquiescence had need of being asked for." He was even more emphatic with Edmund Yates: "I had no more to do with the founding [the Society] than the babe unborn."[86] Yet "I write poems that they may be read," and "exactly what has touched me is the sudden assemblage of men and women to whose names, for the most part, I am a stranger," men and women willing to tackle his texts as best they could, with sympathy and good intentions—"real conscientious criticism," Browning called such reading, as opposed to "mere mopping and mowing and such monkey-tricks"[87] as his reviewers had too often practiced (and as opposed to the partisanship of friends; Furnivall had asked Sarianna for names of friends who might join the society, and she had refused to give them, her brother not wanting "'only a clique—the man's personal following!'"[88]). "As for Dr. Furnivall," Browning wrote, "I am altogether astonished at his caring about me at all," presumably because Furnivall's work had been as an editor and lexicographer: "I think him most warmhearted, whatever may be the mistakes about me of which his head is guilty."[89] Furnivall's bibliography of reviews led Browning to hope that the society would at least improve his reputation. He told Furnivall that "I have a huge shelf-full of reviews of my Father's collecting":

> I assure you I shirked no labour but took down and piled up scores of old dead and gone reviews as stale as the dust on them—"read" them I could not pretend to attempt, so did the sight of their very outsides sadden me. . . . Yourself and those like you [the members of the Browning Society] are the best suffumigators after this old smell: why keep a whiff of it to show how nastily I lived for a long while.[90]

Such was the nature of Browning's earliest gratitude to the society: "I am beginning to enjoy the results of the institution of the 'Society' . . . in the evident annoyance it is giving my dear old critics who have gone on gibing and gibbering at me time out of mind."[91]

Though Browning kept the society at arm's length, he reviewed with interest the readings and interpretations which were the society's chief monthly activities, in the early days usually receiving the "transactions" in proof before they were printed, and later pointedly asking that the papers be sent to him only when "past correction,"[92] to avoid the suspicion that the poet had put his imprimatur on them or was signaling that a reading was the right one. He would like to say, he told J. Dykes Campbell, the society's secretary in 1884, that "I have in no way authorised this intelligence."[93] The papers were as varied as the society's membership. Many of them approached the poet as (to use part of the title of the 1891 book on Browning by Henry Jones) a "philosophical and religious teacher"; many focused on Browning's theology; and many—far too many—paraphrased themes, summarized ideas, and ignored the fact that the texts were poems with the aesthetic interests of organization, tropes, and prosody as well as content. And each paper presented not Browning himself, but the speaker's Browning. The members of the society were aware of that critical problem, and outside observers, then and since, made fun, and have made fun, of speakers who recreated Browning in their own image. None, however, explored the theoretical problems involved in all readings of texts—except Browning himself: a great many of his poems are concerned with the reception of texts and the act of reader response, as we have already seen, and from them one may infer Browning's concept of his ideal reader.

She is Balaustion. To begin with, she knows the texts she receives from Euripides in all their particular and concrete detail because she loves them, and her love of them leads her to see them (to borrow Matthew Arnold's wording) as in themselves they really are. Moreover, the texts matter to her. She holds them dear because they are operative in her ongoing life, for she knows that every act of reading is an act of interpretation, an act which quickens and transforms the original text: she rewrites the text and so creates a new one. Browning's own trope for the original is brickwork; his trope for reading is ivy growing over that structure. He came to value both. He apparently didn't in 1867, when he praised Edward Dowden because "you have so disinterestedly stuck to the business of making my poem speak for itself, and not, as most critics do, diverged and flourished with your own tendrils over my brickwork"[94] but he did so when he used the same images in *Balaustion's Adventure*. Balaustion identifies the *Alkestis* with a temple, her words with ivy festooning porch, pillar, frieze, and roof (348–57). The temple remains the temple, and at the same time it looks forever different because of the ivy, which Balaustion tropes as a parasite. The relation between host and parasite is (as J. Hillis Miller has shown in an influential essay[95]) a reciprocal one. So, complex as were Browning's relations with the society which bore his name, its central activity (and that of every literary society, the reception of texts and reader response to them) was also the activity with which he was centrally concerned in his poems. The society fitted its host, and he it.

Why, in the 1880s, was the more or less organized reading of Browning so widespread and so widely attended to? Arthur Symons, one of the most thoughtful and perceptive members of the society, provides one answer to that question about the society's cultural significance, and it is that Browning was preeminently *the* modern poet and the epitome of the age. Symons gave the reason for that claim in the paper he wrote for the society's meeting of January 30, 1885, a paper entitled "Is Browning Dramatic?" Symons never mentions the pairing of Browning and Tennyson, conventional among reviewers in the 1860s, and instead links Browning and Shakespeare, as many did in the 1880s. "Shakspere, in his objective drama, summed up into himself the whole character of his age; am I rash in saying that Browning also, in his subjective drama, epitomises our age?" Symons argues that the reading of Browning in that way requires a new method, a turning from the drama understood as "character in action" to "a drama of the interior, a tragedy or comedy of the soul" which responds "to the needs of a self-conscious generation."[96] Walter Pater, who reviewed Symons's *An Introduction to the Study of Browning* for the *Guardian* in 1887, reiterated that idea. Browning's work, he argued, "makes him pre-eminently a modern poet—a poet of the self-pondering, perfectly educated, modern world, which, having come to the end of all direct and purely external experiences, must necessarily turn for its entertainment to the world within." "Only the intellectual poet," Pater wrote, "can be adequate to modern demands."[97] The wording of the intentions of the Cambridge Browning Society (founded on November 11, 1881) is more revealing than Furnivall's prospectus for the London society: the founders intend "to develop the society into one for the more thorough study and deeper appreciation of modern literature, making Browning, as *the* representative modern England poet, the centre of the Society's work."[98]

The sense of Browning's modernity helps explain another aspect of the society's cultural impact, its links with women's education. The women in the Browning Society have not enjoyed a favorable reputation: unsympathetic observers readily made fun of them as readers who took themselves too seriously and wanted only to see their own faith reflected in Browning's poems. George Bernard Shaw, who was a mischief-making member of the society, is largely responsible for that view: he famously characterized the group as "a conventicle where pious ladies disputed about religion with Furnivall, and Gonner and I . . . egged them on"; in another letter Shaw added "old" to "pious": "the pious old ladies whose subscriptions kept the [society] going."[99] But Emily Hickey, though a woman of strong faith, had a sense of humor, liked erudite jokes, was an efficient secretary of the society, and was, like her fellows Frances Buss and Dorothea Beale, a teacher and a reformer in education. She taught for eighteen years at the North London Collegiate School for Girls (where Buss, who had founded the school and made it a model of reform in women's education, was headmistress), and she published Browning's *Strafford* as a text for her classroom work, not only providing notes for the play but preparing examination questions on it. (Her examination papers, which Browning saw and praised as putting the play "to such good use,"[100] led to the edition.) Browning helped her with the notes as he had helped Furnivall and Orr, and he read her edition of the play in proof in November of 1883, saying that he had, "besides altering errors, changed a word or two, so as to strengthen the verse a little." He also paid close attention to Hickey's annotation. "Nothing can be better than your Notes," he told her; "and, with a real wish to be of use, I read them carefully that I might detect never so tiny a fault,—but found none—unless (to show you how minutely I searched)"—and he comments on the wording of one passage. As he always did with Furnivall, he expressed his gratitude to Hickey: "I feel all your goodness to me—or whatever in my books may be taken for me."[101] The society was, despite Furnivall's argumentativeness at its meetings, a welcoming place for women. Furnivall, who had taught at Frederick Denison Maurice's Working Men's College and had tried unsuccessfully to have women admitted to its classes, credited Elizabeth Barrett Browning with his views and said that his debt to her was "enormous": "The reading of her books when he was at Cambridge was to him an entirely new revelation of the possibilities and capabilities of woman's nature."[102] Curiously enough, it was the reading of Robert's poems (rather than Elizabeth's) which came to be associated with modern, forward-looking, independent women who resisted conventions both social and literary. In Sara Jeannette Duncan's *The Imperialist* (1904), for instance, the heroine, Advena (whose name indicates that she is the new woman, the woman of the future), not only rejects the domestic and family life embraced by her mother and younger sister, but also asserts her independence by falling in love with the impractical and idealistic young Presbyterian minister fresh from Scotland, Hugh Finlay. During their courtship she and Hugh talk of nothing but books and authors and the "philosophy of life," and they mark their difference from others in Elgin (which is Brantford, Ontario) by reading *Sordello*, which is crucial in their growing toward one another. The fictional Advena, like the actual Hickey, Buss, and Beale, is a secondary-school teacher, and her education at the University of Toronto suggests a web of associations: presumably she came in contact with the actual W. J. Alexander, whose only book, in a long academic career, was *An Introduction to the Poetry of Robert Browning*, published in the year in which Alexander was appointed professor of English in University College, Toronto, 1889. The London Browning Society's meeting of November 29, 1889, was devoted to a discussion of Alexander's analysis of *Sordello*. It was their last session before Browning's death.

At Play in the Land of Souls

A return to Italy had long been in Browning's mind. In 1865 he had written to William Story saying that "I begin to see a pin-point of light out at the end of this London life,—Italy at the end of a few years more, you know!"[1] At that time the focus of his longings was Florence, mainly because of the recent completion of Elizabeth's tomb. He expressed to Isa his expectation, in spite of the closing of the Protestant Cemetery to further interments, that he would be buried beside Elizabeth, "should I die within easy reach,—as my abode is prepared, and not to find."[2] And though he told Isa that "you are really the likelier to see me one fine day at Florence, now this business [the erection of the monument] is over," he also said he would not return to live there. The city was changing—the thirteen-century city walls had been demolished to create a boulevard—and so "Florence will never be her old self now to me . . . but I love her with all my heart: there will be meeting between us yet, I hope, tho' I shall not live there."[3] Browning wavered between "I shall not live there" and "I shall not go there." "The changes seem too violent here [even in distant London]," Browning told Isa; "*you* get used to them little by little, but if I went and found walls levelled, squares where the lanes used to be, and so forth, I could not bear it,"[4] and so the prospect of a visit became associated with pain. "No,—Florence is done with, for me," he told Isa early in 1867, and the pain was not just the result of inevitable changes in the city's appearance. "I don't in the least know—or rather in my fancies I change continually as to how I should feel on seeing old sights again. The general impression of the past is as if it had been pain. I would not live it over again, not one day of it. Yet all that seems my real *life*,—

and before and after, nothing at all: I look back on all my life, when I look *there*: and life is painful."[5] Early in 1868 another possibility presented itself: "How I should like, what is not so unrealisable as most dreams, to go for a little and see Florence, quite unknown by anybody, only seeing the few friends."[6] His model for this dream was Arnold's Scholar-Gipsy. When in 1870 a Miss Regan told Browning that she was returning to Florence, his response was to want to go too, but to hold himself apart: "I felt as if I should immensely like to glide for a long summer's day thro' the streets and between the old stone-walls,—unseen come and unheard go: perhaps,—by some miracle, I shall do so—and look up at Villa Brichieri [one of the villas in which Isa had lived] as Arnold's Gypsy-Scholar gave one wistful look at 'the long line of festal light in Christ Church Hall,' before he went to sleep in some forgotten grange."[7] Wistful Browning was, but also realistic: "Florence would be irritating and, on the whole, insufferable," he wrote in that same letter, "yet I never hear of anyone going thither but my heart is twitched." Other places in Italy, places he had not seen, did not evoke such complex emotions. He expressed regret to Isa that, when he was living in Italy, he had had to follow "the straight line of obligation to get from such a place, in such a time, to such another,—thus I never saw (after fourteen years of intention to see)—Volterra, St Gimignano or Certaldo, Pistoja, and other points of great interest to me,—Ba could not go, I could not leave her."[8] Now he wanted to see such places, though he would not "ever attempt to get into the Florence groove."[9] "If I could dispose properly of Pen, see him advantageously disengaged from me, I would go to live & die in Italy tomorrow."[10]

For Italy was the land of his soul, if the soul be defined as the object of desire and the spur to action, and Browning's linking of Italy and his soul explains the place of Italy in his life. "The Land of Souls," he called it, even "the divine Land of Souls."[11] Elizabeth had used that label for Italy in the book of *Aurora Leigh* that Robert had called "divine," the seventh book, where Aurora says, when she and Marian reach Marseilles on their epic journey, "I felt the wind soft from the land of souls" (7. 467). In 1866 Browning told Isa that "my liking for Italy was always a selfish one,—I felt alone with my own soul there," a feeling he labeled "solitude," which is not loneliness but rather the wholeness which comes of feeling at one (the Latin *solus*) with oneself and one's surroundings.[12] He contrasted his aversion to "ugly London" and "dear ugly old England"[13] with his longing for Italy: "How my whole soul turns to Italy, words are weak to tell you," he wrote to Isa in 1868; "how I wish myself there, out of all this ugliness? If I live & do well, it shall be.'Anywhere, anywhere out of this black rainy beastly-streeted London world."[14] Four years later, when both he and Pen were suffering from colds, when Pen had rheumatism also and his father had "the bile," Browning said that "it comes in the main of this more than ever hateful & to be hated climate, rainy & rainy again, till one is saturated even through brick walls, and by the fireside."[15] If he were to die, it would be "an Italian ending I fancy the fittest—'Et tomber sur le dos sur un beau ciel d'azur'" ("and fall on my back on a beautiful azure sky").[16] In spite of Browning's longings, expressed again and again after his departure from Florence, seventeen years passed before he actually revisited Italy. He had left in 1861; he did not return until 1878.

Even then he was ambivalent about his return. He and Sarianna left London "very unwillingly" and with "the notion of seeing once again *Venice*—and perhaps Asolo,"[17] but their destination was in fact Switzerland and the Alps. They wanted "to pass the main of the heat-season in some mountain quarter,—and then, we may follow our inclinations as far as they point toward the Italian side,—the only part of the world I seem at present to fancy might stimulate me a little."[18] Yet such were the pleasures and satisfactions of the mountains that, Browning wrote in September, Venice and Asolo "seem quite secondary objects now."[19] "We shall certainly stay another week—the fourth—and only then go if needs we must: the scenery is so exquisite, and the weather absolutely life-giving. . . . You would not know either of us with our red faces and elastic limbs, as we come in daily after our morning walk of some five hours." They were staying at the Hôtel Bodenhaus in Splügen, where Browning found "the union of complete silence and solitude with all that is desirable in the way of material comfort."[20] "No pla[ce] ever agreed with me so well,—and henceforth, whether I get it or no,—shall be assured that mountain-air,—and not the sea-bathing,—is my proper resource when fagged at the end of a season." Browning restored himself with a healthy routine: "We walk daily for some four or five hours at a stretch—generally managing seventeen miles about, in that time." Their favorite walk was to Hinterrhein and the source of the Rhine, but another walk was to "the top of the Splügen pass—which gained, you are in Italy." So Browning returned at last to the land of his soul, quietly and without a sense of occasion, on foot and in an unexpected place. He drew no special attention to the moment, but their setting foot on Italian soil determined their course of action. In spite of "good cookery, absolute cleanliness, and *such* quietude" at the hotel, "the end is, we shall stay some ten days longer, and then make for Venice—which I have a yearning to see again. My Sister has never been in Italy at all, and I shall be glad of her enjoyment."[21]

They would go to Venice, but the focus of Browning's feelings and imagination was Asolo. Browning had first visited Asolo in June of 1838, when he explored the cities in Lombardy and Veneto as part of his preparation for writing *Sordello,* and the city, which he called "my very own of all Italian towns,"[22] had a special significance for him. "Properly speaking," he told one of his brothers-in-law years later, "it was the first spot of Italian soil I ever set foot upon—having proceeded to Venice by sea—and thence here." Because "when I got my impression, Italy was new to me," the details of that first visit remained vivid in his memory: in an 1889 letter to Kay Bronson he told her how he had "lodged at the main Hôtel in the square, an old large Inn of the most primitive kind," observed the crack in his bedroom ceiling caused by an earthquake the year before, climbed up to the ruined castle, and "took long walks every day,—and carried away a lively recollection of the general beauty,"[23] which he described for George Barrett:

> The immense charm of the surrounding country is indescribable—I have never seen its like—the Alps on one side, the Asolan mountains all round,—and opposite the vast Lombard plain,—with indications of Venice, Padua, and the other cities,—visible to a good eye on a clear day: while everywhere are sites of battles and sieges of by-gone days, described in full by the historians of the Middle Ages.

In *Pippa Passes,* which Browning sets in Asolo, Ottima, looking out from her hillside house, points out the view to her lover, Sebald, and repeats her creator's experience of the scene:

> Ah, the clear morning! I can see Saint Mark's;
> That black streak is the belfry. Stop: Vicenza
> Should lie . . . there's Padua, plain enough, that blue!
> Look o'er my shoulder, follow my finger! (1. 28–31)

Of the city itself Browning said, "It is an ancient city, older than Rome," and the period in its history which most interested him was the late fourteenth and early fifteenth centuries, when it was "the scene of Queen Catherine Cornaro's exile, where she held a mock court, with all its attendants on a miniature scale,—Bembo, afterwards Cardinal, being her secretary. Her palace is still above us all, the old fortifications surround the hill-top."[24] In one of her lyrics Pippa refers to "Kate the Queen," and Luigi and his mother meet "Inside the Turret on the Hill above Asolo," but it was Bembo's (attributed) turning of the city's name into a verb—*asolare*, "to disport in the open air, amuse oneself at random" (Browning's definition)—which he would use in his last published volume, and which made for him a vital connection between play and the Land of Souls, play being the creative counterpart of solitude: "when I first saw Asolo," Browning would say near the end of his life, "inspiration seemed to steam up from the very ground."[25] Perhaps that was why the city was the subject of recurring dreams the poet experienced in the 1870s. "I used to dream of seeing Asolo in the distance and making vain attempts to reach it—repeatedly dreamed this for many a year," Browning told Kay Bronson in 1889[26]; and in 1876 he had told William Allingham that he had "no dreams worth remembering—no beautiful or clever dreams, 'Except that a few times I have dreamed that I was among the mountains near Asolo . . . and I said to myself, "I have often wished to see Asolo a second time, but now here I am and I'll go and do it"' "[27] On September 28, 1878, he had "done it": he and Sarianna were in the Stella d'Oro hotel, writing letters on opposite sides of a table to Mrs. Thomas FitzGerald. Robert wrote that "I daresay S. . . . has told you about our journey and adventures, such as they were: but she cannot tell you the feelings which which [*sic*] I revisit this—to me—memorable place after above forty years absence." Change there had been—the "old inn" was gone, and the Stella d'Oro was "a much inferior Albergo" where they were "roughly but pleasantly entertained"[28]—but the echo in the "ruined tower on the hill-top," an echo which had been his private discovery—"you can produce it from only one particular spot on a remainder of brick-work"—was still there. Browning found the experience "*too* strange": "it answered me plainly as ever, after all the silence."[29] The sound, one guesses, was the report of his own soul, long mute among landscapes which, however attractive and satisfying, could never be for him "The Land of Souls."

The Brownings would return to Venice in 1879 and 1880, but it was the mountains which renewed their spirits and their health, and they would stay several weeks in the Alps before going on to Italy. In August of 1880, for instance, they were at Lans near Grenoble, and Browning, as usual, praised "this little rural quiet unspoiled" place and the "minute country inn" in which they stayed: "the simplest possible lodging—of perfect cleanliness and *sufficient* comfort—with a capital *cuisine bourgeoise*—more to our taste than Hotel-proper luxuries—and the kindest simplest people we ever met."[30] Browning responded strongly to "the grand mountains which frame in a wonderful vale or plain of pasturage and cornfields," and their walks did not exhaust the beauties of the scenery: "if we chose to clamber, I don't know what fresh wonders we might come upon every day."[31] Browning was not a poet of nature, nor did nature stir his imagination in the way it did that of Wordsworth and Coleridge, for instance. Mrs. Orr tells us that "a friend once said to him, 'You have not a great love for nature, have you?' [to which] he had replied: 'Yes, I have, but I love men and women better.'"[32] That did not mean that he avoided landscape-painting in his poetry. Of Browning's use of landscapes Arthur Symons wrote, "they are never pushed into prominence for an effect of idle beauty" but "are subordinated always to the human interest; blended, fused with it, so that a landscape in a poem of Browning's is literally a part of the emotion."[33] That was Browning the poet. Browning the man responded strongly to landscape, whether spare and elemental, as on the French coast, or eye-filling, as in the Alps or the Veneto.

In 1879 Browning published *Dramatic Idyls*, which he began calling a "first series" after he published a "second series" with the same title in 1880. The poems were narratives, but Browning characteristically labeled them "dramatic" and was as interested in the prosody as he was in the tales themselves. "An idyl, as you know," he wrote to Wilfred Meynell, "is a succinct little story complete in itself; not necessarily concerning pastoral matters." He defined "dramatic" in his usual way: "These [idyls] of mine are called 'Dramatic' because the story is told by some actor in it, not by the poet himself."[34] He used a variety of meters and rhyme schemes, and he drew Meynell's attention to the fact that "all [the idyls] are in rhymed verse; this last ["Pheidippides"] in a metre of my own."[35] Those three sentences define an agenda for critics of Browning's idyls, who must examine the interweaving of story, dramatic voice, sound and movement, and explain the purpose and effects of such a complex conjunction of elements. Browning's handling of those elements might be called "serious play," for he delights in making of his stories thematic, moral, structural, and stylistic puzzles that teach and delight. Browning's critics have certainly had enough to say about his teaching, a critical bias which has obscured his second purpose and the playfulness behind it.

A good example of such aesthetic complexity is "Pietro of Abano" in the 1880 volume. The story is not "dramatic" in Browning's usual sense—"told by some actor in it"—but "dramatic" insofar as much of it consists of dialogue. The narrating voice, anonymous through most of the poem, is in the last four lines explicitly the poet's own, and there he draws attention to the music of the poem. What is the link between sound and story? the reader wonders in retrospect, and that puzzle alerts the reader to the possibility that the music and rhyme of Browning's "rhymed verse" are not merely ornamental but integral to the story and its aesthetic effects. For Browning is exploiting the conventional psychological effects of rhyme—the tension of expectation, the release of recurrence—by embodying in it his plot, which also deals in expectations and resolutions (and some unexpected reversals). The plot is the intertwined lives of his two main characters. One is Peter, the mage whose successes in a variety of professions earn him only "cuffs and kicks and curses" (34); the other is a Greek stranger who prospers from Peter's teaching and becomes first a powerful ruler and then pope. The shifting relations between the two men are the substance of the story: they begin as master and pupil, with pupil petitioning for a favor which master (apparently) grants; pupil then becomes a power in state and church, and master becomes the poor, emaciated petitioner whose request the erstwhile pupil refuses to grant; that reversal is followed by an even trickier reversal back to the initial relationship, when pupil becomes the rejected petitioner. The plot involves opposites which are both like and unlike (both men have great gifts; both lack an essential quality), and the Greek stranger sums up his recognition (*anagnorisis*) of that pattern with the words "cheese at last I know from chalk!" (416). The expression is proverbial and (in the words of the *OED*) concerns "things differing greatly in their qualities or values, though their appearance is not unlike, and their names alliterate." Rhyme too depends upon like and unlike. Once a sound has been voiced at the end of a line, the reader-listener waits with a growing sense of unease and anxiety for the moment of release, when the sound recurs, but the repeated sound is usually in a different cluster of consonants, and so the rhyme word is both like and unlike its original. Browning uses four rhymes in his eight-line stanzas (the basic unit in this narrative poem), and the aesthetic tension and its resolution depend upon the *c* rhyme, which Browning introduces at the end of each fourth line, and which (in that position) frustrates the reader's expectation of a repetition of the *b* rhyme after an *aba* sequence in the first three lines. The *b* rhyme does recur at the end of the sixth line, but in that position it is not a satisfying release, and the reader's sense of aesthetic irritation, now focused on the *c* rhyme, is extended to the very end of the eighth line, when the *c* rhyme at last is heard again after a new and fourth (*d*) rhyme. The lengthy suspension of completion parallels Browning's handling of the time sequence in the story. When the Greek stranger petitions Peter to "Teach me such true magic" (91) and at the same time interprets Peter's inability to drink milk as emblematic of his lack of love, Peter seems to be on the point of granting the petition—"Approach, my calf, and feed!" (172)—and blesses him. The blessing is a "Benedicite," but both the Greek stranger and the reader-listener hear only the first two syllables (at line 173) and must wait until line 408 for the completion of the word. What happens in the interval? The Greek stranger experiences a kind of swoon in which he lives his future life and tells the whole story of it, a lengthy narrative which occurs (readers are asked to believe, or, more accurately, to suspend their disbelief) in the split second between the syllables of Peter's blessing; and reader-listeners experience an act of narrative manipulation which first tries their patience—and then (when they discover what is going on) delights with its cleverness. The reader must hold in abeyance an increasingly complex set of expectations about the decisions and actions of both men, only to be told, finally, about a future that never happened and a present that involves the most obvious of reactions: Peter, trusting no one and fearing the kind of "drubbing" (411) which has been his lot in the past, bangs the door shut on his petitioner. So Browning plays with his readers by allying the psychological effects of his narrative—expectation followed by its fulfilment or frustration—with rhyme's effects of tension, suspension, and release.

But the union of sound and sense in "Pietro of Abano" is still more complex. What is the reader-listener to make of Browning's concluding the poem with eight bars of music of his own composition, the tune being (what he calls) "the lilt" to which his lines are to be voiced or (perhaps more accurately) to be sung? A "lilt" conventionally accompanies movement or dancing and is the singing to a tune of a repeated syllable such as "la, la, la"; in Browning's use of the term, the "lilt" reveals the music of the poem, the bars or units of equal time underlying the poem's complicated stanzaic structure and its intertwined rhyme scheme. It allows the reader-listener to hear a quantitative prosodic pattern in addition to the usual accentual-syllabic scheme. In 1844, when Browning had sent two poems to the editor of *Hood's*, he asked him, "How do you like these?" and then advised him to *"Lilt* them a little, for the music."[36] A twenty-first-century reader can hear the music of "Pietro of Abano" if he or she reads the lines aloud and beats time, remembering always that the stongest beat is at the beginning of each bar, that a bar may have varying numbers of syllables, and that rests count. Try lilting the poem's first two lines, for instance, where there are two bars in each line: *"Petrus Aponensis*—there was a magician! / When that strange adventure happened, which I mean to tell my hearers. . . ." The strong beats are on *"Pe," "en," "*there," and *"gi"* in the first line, and "When," "ven," "which," and "tell" in the second.

What sense might a critic make of Browning's use of that "lilt"? The poet's four-line explanation appears unrelated to the story. He provides the "lilt," he says, "for love of that dear land [Italy] which I so oft in dreams revisit" (442), and so the "lilt" seems only to be the expression of personal emotion. But in the narrative itself there are references to music and singing which suggest a more complex purpose. When the Greek stranger petitions Peter, he asks not for advice or knowledge but for "Leave to learn to sing" (81), and he links singing not only with "leave to make my kind wise, free, and happy!" (84) but also with a fairy-tale transformation of himself from goose to swan. Such magic is possible, he contends, because Greece, which has prepared him for such growth, is the land of his soul, and he contrasts Greece and Padua in the same way his creator contrasted Italy and England:

> I am from a land whose cloudless skies are coloured
> Livelier, suns orb largelier, airs seem incense,—while, on earth—

> What, instead of grass, our fingers and our thumbs cull,
> Proves true moly! sounds and sights there help the body's
>   hearing, seeing,
> Till the soul grows godlike. . . . (67–71)

So Browning's "lilt," sung "for love of that dear land"—Italy—has not only an aesthetic but also a conative effect: it is the music of a growing soul and a stimulus to the growth of the reader-listener's soul, growth which comes about if he or she likes textual puzzles which, like life itself, resist any complete or final explication. The character of Browning's idyls can be summed up in an anecdote told by Wilfred Meynell: "The first time I met him [Browning] was when there was also present the Chinese Minister, in whose suite was a gentleman who brought with him the vague fame of being an author in his own land. Browning had been introduced to him as a brother author. 'I asked him,' said Browning, 'what sort of work his was; and he replied that he composed enigmas. A brother, indeed!'"[37]

Browning's readers too often mistook the nature of the puzzles he presented to them. They thought their difficulties lay in unfamiliar and out-of-the-way materials, sources, references, and allusions, all of which were far too much in evidence, in their view, in the volume which Browning published in 1883, *Jocoseria*. Even Alfred Domett, to whom Browning sent a copy and who ought to have been more understanding, refers in his diary for March 9, 1883—the day of the volume's publication—to "the riddle-writing which Browning is too much given to." "This comes," he continues, "of the practice of exciting surprise by assuming knowledge in the reader which nine out of ten readers will not possess—and the tenth perhaps will not recall in that association." Readers were all too ready to charge Browning with being "wilfully obscure, unconscientiously careless, or perversely harsh"—those are his own sardonic words from the preface to the *Selections* of 1872[38]—and Domett attributes to the poet a similar perversity: "One fancies Browning laughing in his sleeve, occasionally in this book at the surprise of his readers as he taunts their ignorance with quotations in the original Hebrew, flung in their faces without a word of explanation, preface or apology."[39] But wanting to know everything about his sources and references was, Browning told Mrs. FitzGerald, "the exercise of industry in a wrong direction." He advised her to "confine [your attention] to the poems and nothing else, no extraneous matter at all,—I cannot but think you would find little difficulty: but your first business seems to be an inquiry into what will give no sort of help." Even "Jochanan Hakkadosh," with its Hebrew quotations and Talmudic allusions, is, he insisted, self-explanatory: there is "no need to 'know *d'avance* all the Talmudic stories'—which,—such of them as I referred to, are all sufficiently explained in the poem itself—indeed every allusion needing explanation is explained. . . . *Hakkadosh* is explained in the text, and so is *Ruach*." "Years of study in dictionaries" would make readers learned, Browning said, "but not one bit more" understanding of the poem itself. Browning defined the "wrong direction" of many of his readers in his friend's assumption: "I say all this because you imagine that with more learning you would 'understand' more about my poetry—and as if you would somewhere find it already written—only waiting to be translated into English and my verses: whereas I should consider such a use of learning absolutely contemptible." Then comes the sentence quoted earlier in this study: "for poetry, if it is to deserve the name, ought to create—or re-animate something—not merely reproduce *raw* fact taken from somebody else's book." What then did Browning himself consider to be the interest of his poems in this volume, the aspects of them that ought to be the focus of critical attention? In "Adam, Lilith and Eve" it is the shape of the story itself. The poem is a very condensed narrative which, like the far lengthier story of *Paracelsus,* is full of misunderstandings which create the ironic twists and turns in the tale. The narrator does not tell the whole story but, like a Pre-Raphaelite painter who depicts a crucial moment in which is implied a complete action, focuses on a single crucial incident in which is enfolded multiple ironies. "The story," Browning told Mrs. FitzGerald,

> is simply that a man once knew a woman who, while she loved him, pretended that she did not—which pretence, like a man and a fool, he believed, so of course was not married to her—but to a woman who did *not* love him but another though she said she did love him—which, like a man and a fool—he believed; one day as they sat together, each, on a sudden impulse, told him the truth—which, like a man and a fool, he disbelieved. Surely there is nothing so difficult here. . . .

But Mrs. FitzGerald had created difficulties for herself by focusing on the title (which makes particular the generic labels "two women" and "the man" in the body of the poem) and by associating the names with issues the poem does not deal with. She knew that in Talmudic legend Lilith and Eve were both wives of Adam and assumed that "the man" in the poem was a modern Adam and therefore a bigamist. Browning's response: "Now, read the poem and tell me where is the least word about two '*wives*'? Had you let the Title alone and gone on to the subject . . ." So Browning demolished his friend's assumption—the kind characteristic of many of his readers—that "'I cannot understand this till I have learned the whole history of these personages and what marriage is in question.'"[40]

That the stories in the volume were always to be taken seriously—seriously, that is, insofar as they yielded a moral or a weighty idea—was another persistent assumption on the part of Browning's readers, and one he tried to dispel by pointing to the free and lively play of the mind which had been his in creating the poems and which he hoped would be his readers' in responding to them. The title, which Browning called "Dutch Latin, and barbarous,"[41] was borrowed from a sixteenth-century book he had inherited from his father and meant a mixture of jokes and serious things, or, in the poet's own words, "a collection of things gravish and gayish."[42]

That same serious play, or playful seriousness, would characterize the volume Browning published the following year: *Ferishtah's Fancies* appeared on November 21, 1884. To his materials, which yet again were unfamiliar and recondite, he encouraged the same approach he had urged on Mrs. FitzGerald. Writing to Barnett Smith, a reviewer Browning trusted and to whom he sent an advance copy of the volume, he said: "I hope that nothing but an attentive perusal is necessary to the understanding of the book: but there are a few Persian names, and allusions which you might like explained, and I will make a note of these: any question you put to me on particular points requiring elucidation, I will try to clear up."[43] Like *Jocoseria*, the volume was a mixture, a "dish of all sorts,"[44] he told Mrs. FitzGerald, but his shift from "collection"—his word for *Jocoseria*—to "dish" fits with the food metaphors which are so prominent in the 1884 volume, and which account for much of the poems' playfulness. The Persian material was only the clothing in which Browning presented his more central concerns: the lesson of the "Prologue," and the poetic method of the "Fancies" themselves.

First, the lesson of the introductory poem. Members of the Browning Society who focused on his ideas and ignored his images and his prosody would find a corrective in his "Prologue," an elaborate simile in which he likens an Italian meal to "my poem": just as the ortolans are a mixture of tastes and textures—the "luscious lumps" of the birds themselves, skewered "heads by heads and rumps by rumps" with a "toasted square" of bread and "a strong sage-leaf"—so his poems are a mixture of "Sense, sight and song" (30): meaning ("sense") combines with visual imagery ("sight") and prosody ("song") to produce a text which is in its impact cognitive, conative, and affective. Then, with the aforementioned playfulness, Browning states a lesson which has no immediate or obvious link with the poem itself—"'Take what is, trust what may be'"—and calls those words "Life's true lesson." He attributes the quoted words to Gressoney, the Alpine village where he was writing and which supplied plain food—"eggs, milk, cheese, fruit"—in contrast to the Italian meal he was recalling with such gusto: "eggs, milk, cheese, fruit" are just as good "for gormandizing" as the ortolans. So Browning leaves the reader with a puzzle which in its structure points to the method of proceeding in the poems in the body of the volume.

Ferishtah is a Dervish, "a Mohammedan friar," in the words of the *OED*, "who has taken vows of poverty and austere life." Mrs. Orr, drawing on information from the poet himself, wrote that Browning re-created his source when it "occurred to him to make the poem ["The Eagle"] the beginning of a series, in which the Dervish, who is first introduced as a learner, should reappear in the character of a teacher."[45] To that teacher Browning attributes a method which was crucial in his own thinking, a method embodied in the poetic genre called the emblem. Since childhood Browning had been fascinated with that genre, and, as Adrienne Munich has succinctly said of *Ferishtah's Fancies*, "this volume of verse fables is organized around the emblematic use of foods."[46]

The emblems Browning knew best were those by Francis Quarles, published in 1635: "Quarles' *Emblems*, my childhood's pet book" is the phrasing Robert uses with Elizabeth during their courtship.[47] But he knew others from the great age of the emblem, the late sixteenth and early seventeenth centuries: Alciato and Hugo and Wither. And he had another "pet book," the work of the late seventeenth-century Dutch painter Gerard de Lairesse, in whose *The Art of Painting* the emblem figures in a large way. Browning's upbringing as a Dissenter accounts in part for his fascination with the emblem, for though the genre had largely disappeared in the nineteenth century, emblem books continued to be read by Dissenters as spiritual exercises. Browning's mother gave him Quarles's *Emblemes* when he was a child, and over a lifetime Browning found in it the conjunction of two things central to his poetry: the activity of the soul, and something profoundly and essentially literary. Both are bound up with the conventional structure of the emblem, to be seen most clearly in a Wither poem from a volume Browning likely knew, *A Collection of Emblemes, Ancient and Moderne* (also published in 1635).

There are three essential parts to an emblem: the *pictura*, the *sententia*, and the *explicatio*—Italian terms because the genre originated in Italy. The *pictura* is an actual picture, typically an engraving or woodcut, and to the perceiving eye it presents images which, because they are visual and not verbal, are a kind of riddle which the reader must solve. The *sententia*, or motto, which appears, often in Latin, in a circle round the picture or in a line directly underneath the picture, is a concise statement of the meaning of the image or images, but because it is concise, it too is, at least in part, riddling. Only when the reader gets to the *explicatio*, a poem of some thirty or forty lines, does the image's full

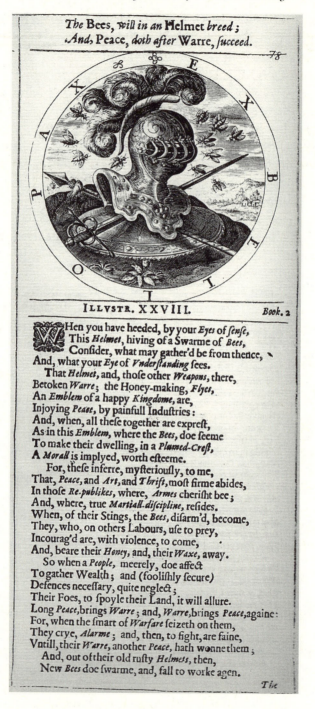

The Bees, will in an **Helmet** *breed ;*
And, Peace, doth after Warre, *succeed.*

ILLVSTR. XXVIII.   *Book.* 2

Hen you have heeded, by your *Eyes* of *sense,*
This *Helmet,* hiving of a Swarme of *Bees,*
Confider, what may gather'd be from thence,
And, what your *Eye* of *Vnderstanding* fees.
    That *Helmet,* and, thofe other *Weapons,* there,
Betoken *Warre;* the Honey-making, *Flyes,*
An *Emblem* of a happy *Kingdome,* are,
Injoying *Peace,* by painfull Induftries :
And, when, all thefe together are expreft,
As in this *Emblem,* where the *Bees,* doe feeme
To make their dwelling, in a *Plumed-Creft,*
A *Morall* is implyed, worth efteeme.
    For, thefe inferre, myfterioufly, to me,
That, *Peace,* and *Art,* and *Thrift,* moft firme abides,
In thofe *Re-publikes,* where, *Armes* cherifht bee ;
And, where, true *Martiall-difcipline,* refides.
When, of their Stings, the *Bees,* difarm'd, become,
They, who, on others Labours, ufe to prey,
Incourag'd are, with violence, to come,
And, beare their *Honey,* and, their *Waxe,* away.
    So when a *People,* meerely, doe affect
Togather Wealth ; and (foolifhly fecure)
Defences neceffary, quite negleCt ;
Their Foes, to fpoyle their Land, it will allure.
Long *Peace,* brings *Warre* ; and, *Warre,* brings *Peace,* againe:
For, when the fmart of *Warfare* feizeth on them,
They, crye, *Alarme* ; and, then, to fight, are faine,
Vntill, their *Warre,* another *Peace,* hath wonne them ;
    And, out of their old rufty *Helmets,* then,
    New *Bees* doe fwarme, and, fall to worke agen.

                                                    The

meaning become apparent. The Wither emblem (reproduced on page 388) has that typical structure. The picture shows a plumed helmet resting on a crossed sword and spear, which in turn rest upon a shield. Bees are flying in and out of the visor. What do these images mean? The motto is *Ex bello pax* (out of war, peace). The *explicatio* elaborates: the helmet and weapons are war; the bees are "a happy Kingdome." The lesson they teach is in the middle of the *explicatio*: "*Peace*, and *Art*, and *Thrift*, most firm abides / In those *Re-pub-likes*, where, *Armes* cherisht bee." In proceeding from *pictura* to *explicatio*, the reader has done several things that are essential to both the creation and the criticism of literature. First, in saying the helmet is war, the reader is creating a metaphor. A metaphor is etymologically a carrying across. Here poet and reader carry across a visual image to an abstract idea, in the characteristic syntactical form of the metaphor, the statement of identity: this is that. In the so-called real world this clearly is not that, and so a metaphor is a fiction, and one wonders what truth it can claim. A metaphor is also a trope, and a trope is etymologically a turn. Here poet and reader turn the word *helmet* from its conventional use as the name of part of a suit of armor and make it refer to something else entirely. That too is a fiction, and again the reader confronts the question of truth. The Wither emblem deals with that question through the crucial verbs *imply* and *infer* and the crucial adverb *mysteriously*, all of which appear in lines 12 and 13 of the *explicatio*.

Those verbs we ordinarily understand as opposites; in this *explicatio* they are synonyms with an implication crucial to Browning's thinking: that the meaning of the images is not to be invented by the reader, but discovered. When Wither says that the moral of the emblem is "implied," he must be aware of the etymology of the word, which means that the moral is literally "folded in" the emblem, and "infer" is not something the reader does (which would make the meaning an invention) but something the images do ("these inferre"), and again etymology indicates that the images "carry in" the meaning, which is then to be unloaded (or in our own time, downloaded) by the reader. The meaning really is there, as objective but hidden truth in the images themselves. For the images "inferre, mysteriously," and a "mystery" is, as the *OED* says, "a hidden or secret thing." Etymologically it is something "closed" (so that the word reinforces the "folded in" etymology of "imply"), and in religion it is a "truth known only by divine revelation." The "mystery" of the emblem explains why the Dissenters valued the genre as a spiritual exercise and why the genre is so central to Browning's poetic thinking. Everything in creation, every image which we receive through one or more of our five senses, is a riddle with a hidden meaning. That meaning is essentially verbal, and behind the human (and therefore tentative) wording of the meaning lies God, who is the Word standing under all words and the supporter and sustainer of (what the Dissenters called in a phrase from the Westminster Confession) the "saving understanding." So the emblem involves an act which is essential to literature—troping—and identifies that act with interpretation, the central act of criticism, and with a "saving understanding," the goal of religion. One reason the human act of interpretation so stirred Browning's imagination is because he saw troping, even when wildly fanciful or willfully self-serving or criminally intent, as a sign of the hope that everything—including human beings after death—can be changed in radical ways. The implications of the "march-tune" that had animated Browning's debate with Annie Thackeray in *Red Cotton Night-Cap Country* receive, in Ferishtah's method of proceeding, their fullest expression.

In lines that might be taken as a motto for *Ferishtah's Fancies* and its gustatory references, Browning's Fra Lippo Lippi sums up the emblem's method: "This world's no blot for us, / Nor blank; it means intensely, and means good: / To find its meaning is my meat and drink" (313–15). The Dervish's usual approach in arriving at his "fancies" is to name an image—a melon slice, the sun, cherries, a garden, a pillar, beans, apples—and to arrive at an interpretation of it—his "fancy"—by telling a story about it. Browning's readers, perhaps accustomed to Tennyson's exploitation of the expressive and affective and suggestive powers of the image, could now better appreciate Browning's exploitation of its cognitive and conative powers. An anonymous critic in the *Saturday Review* asserted that

> Browning's riddles are worth solving, both on account of the meaning which may be eventually disclosed, and for the pleasure of observing the elaborate art with which the puzzles have been constructed. One of the reasons of Mr. Browning's popularity is the activity of mind which he stimulates by insisting on laborious efforts to appreciate his imaginative wisdom. The successful interpreter feels proud of his collaboration with the poet. . . ."[48]

If it is true that every poet must create his or her own audience, Browning was at last succeeding.

Browning's return to Italy in 1878 set the pattern for his travel in the following years: several weeks in the Alps, then on to Asolo and Venice, Asolo for its quiet and its stimulus to Browning's imagination, Venice for its theaters, music, and the "socialities which abound here,"[49] and both cities for the continued interest Browning had in exploring every lane and byway, in searching out every vestige of the past in its streetscapes and buildings and ruins. And always the climate, especially in the autumn, was an attraction. "October is clearly the best month for visiting Venice," Browning told Furnivall in 1883: "the mornings are fresh, not to say cold,—then follows a clear blue sunny noontide, and the evenings are inaugurated by such sunsets as I believe are only to be seen here—when you float between two conflagrations—that of the sky, reflected in the lagune."[50] Writing the same day to Mrs. FitzGerald, he brought the same painterly eye to his account of "the most wonderful sunsets I remember": "Last afternoon, S. and I rowed to the Lido, and returned between two *blazes* of gold and crimson,—the sky and its reflection in the sea."[51] And he provided a frame for his painting, the window where he sat at his letter-writing, its rectangle guiding the eye outward to the blue Venetian sky: "I write at an open window with a cloudless sky and brilliant sun,—having just returned from a two hours' walk under a June or rather June-and-May influence,"[52] though the time was late October. Even in November, Browning reported, "the roses and other flowers are still in bloom, and butterflies abound in the Public Gardens"—reason enough for "our lingering on and unwillingness to return to the fog and cold of which we hear sufficiently."[53] The contrast with London is a recurring theme in Browning's letters: London with its "vile fogs," its "dispiriting fog and cold," its "'filthy air'" (Browning borrows these words from *Macbeth*), its "dolefulness."[54] Still, Venice was not always ideal. October of 1881 brought "unseasonably cold and stormy weather," which Browning described as "cruelly cold and rainy," "abominable and *un-Venetian*."[55] About midmonth Browning reported to Furnivall that "Our weather is mending somewhat, but continues a month behind hand, and very little characteristic of Venice. I walk, even in wind and rain, for a couple of hours on the Lido, and enjoy the break of sea on the strip of sand as much as Shelley did in those days."[56] Not surprisingly, the Brownings cut short their stay and returned to London at the beginning of November. The next year they did not reach Venice at all. "Adverse floods and bridge-breakings"[57] forced them to turn back at Bologna; and two years later an outbreak of cholera made going to Italy "out of the question, as the quarantine was rigidly enforced."[58] Not reaching Venice was a matter of intense regret. "As for the failure to get to Venice," Browning said after the floods of 1882, "we—my sister & I,—have only regretted it once—that is, uninterruptedly ever since."[59] But when the autumn of 1885 turned out to be "one of the worst and most rainy in my Venetian experience," Browning began to look back longingly to "the November of two years ago, which was delightfully sunny without one interruption."[60]

It was sunny in a metaphorical sense as well. The Brownings' hostess in 1883 was Katharine de Kay Bronson, the last of the poet's close women friends. She was a well-to-do and cultivated woman who, as Michael Meredith has written of her, "had all the makings of a Henry James heroine. A wealthy middle-aged American settled in Venice with her daughter, she entertained a cosmopolitan circle of friends in her house on the Grand Canal while her invalid husband retired to Paris to die."[61] Browning's feelings for her are indicated by his cherishing of a token she had given him, "a dear coin, that issued by the Venetian Republic in '48: I had a ring affixed to it, and that again appended to my watch-chain,—the only other token of love there being my wife's ring."[62] Mrs. Bronson's house on the Grand Canal was the Ca'Alvisi, and next to it was "a small courtyard, filled with flowering bushes and trees, which belonged to the ancient Palazzo Giustiniani-Recanati, the remaining portion of which stands away from the canal at the back of the courtyard." Mrs. Bronson rented that truncated palazzo as a guest house. The arrangements were so pleasing and Mrs. Bronson's kindness so "all-embracing"[63] that, for some time afterwards, Browning vividly recalled the sights and sensations of his 1883 visit. The next year, when cholera prevented his return, he remembered their arrival in a nostalgic letter to Mrs. Bronson: "the end of the journey was at the Venice Station when the first blessing was that of Luigi's fat face—lighting the way a few footsteps farther to the more than Friend who had come in the rain to take us and keep us."[64] He remembered "those golden afternoons and evenings through the long Autumn and even longer," and he remembered the days' beginnings and the "daily walking," their "glad and proud companionship immediately available from Palazzo Giustiniani at signal of a whiteness at a window across the Court."[65] And if smell is the most primitive of our senses and the most powerful in evoking past experience, it was the odor of Mrs. Bronson's cigarettes that transported Browning back to the Ca'Alvisi. In 1884 he playfully suggested, after he had been reading the manuscript of one of Mrs. Bronson's plays, "what really good work you might do on a larger scale could one take the cigarette out of the mouth," but the parenthesis which follows indicates his attraction to the smoke: "well,—I don't think I should like *that*, after all."[66] For he had only to recall arriving at Venice and "in a trice I am on the low soft chair in the room over the canal with the delicate cigarette-smoke with which I began to be seduced."[67] Browning's response to Mrs. Bronson's cigarettes confirms the truth of one of Elizabeth's observations, made thirty years earlier when she was defending George Sand's personal habits: "the cigarette is really a feminine weapon if properly understood."[68] "Those two happy months!—and their good stays with me," Browning told Mrs. Bronson from London, "the physical as well as the spiritual good, for, besides the memories, I seem to be living on the strength I stored up there [*sic* for then] and there: I swallow no end of fog and prove unchokable."[69]

House and Shop

With Browning's fame came curiosity about his private life, and that curiosity intensified an inner conflict which had been his from the beginning of his career, a conflict between self-concealment and self-revelation, between reticence and speaking out. He characteristically responded to any intrusion into his personal life, present or past, with such a mixture of determined opposition and resentment that his dramatic imagination, his usual insistence that his poems were "always dramatic in principle, and so many utterances of so many imaginary persons, not mine," must be regarded not just as an innovative and culturally important literary technique but also as a powerful psychological need in the poet himself. Though he had refused, in spite of Furnivall's urgings, to provide "arguments" which would link his poems and his life, though he had told W. J. Kingsland that "I never at any time had the least notion of writing my 'Reminiscences,' nor ever shall do so,"[1] he knew only too well that there would be accounts of his life, and so in the 1880s he paid a great deal of attention to potential biographical materials, destroying much, but providing some through interviews and notes when he was asked. His primary intent was to keep his life and his poetry entirely separate, and he certainly urged that separation on critics and reviewers, but he was too realistic a public figure to think he could enforce that separation and too subtle a thinker to suppose that the separation was absolute. In two poems from the 1876 *Pacchiarotto* volume he explored in a more complex way the links between public and private lives.

The two poems are "House" and "Shop," the titles being middle-class metaphors for life and works, and the pair offer related arguments: the first is that there must be a life behind the works that occupy us daily; the second is that that life must remain hidden behind the works. In "House," Browning tackles Sir Philip Sidney's dictum, "Look in thy heart, and write!" (from the first sonnet in *Astrophel and Stella*) and says in effect "don't!" In "Shop," Browning criticizes a friend whose "shop was all your house!" Some stanzas in "House" express their creator's abhorrence of the personal revelation. He imagines how, with "the whole of the frontage shaven sheer," a "house stood gaping" and open to every passing observer, who reads the images in the exposed rooms and infers the nature of the owner's private life:

> The owner? Oh, he had been crushed, no doubt!
>   'Odd tables and chairs for a man of wealth!
> What a parcel of musty old books about!
>   He smoked,—no wonder he lost his health!
>
> 'I doubt if he bathed before he dressed.
>   A brasier?—the pagan, he burned perfumes!
> You see it is proved, what the neighbours guessed:
>   His wife and himself had separate rooms.' (21–28)

The poem seems to be warning off biographers, but the ninth stanza breaks from that stance and suggests the right way to approach works and life:

> Outside should suffice for evidence:
>   And whoso desires to penetrate
> Deeper, must dive by the spirit-sense. . . . (33–35)

The lines presuppose that critics and biographers will have no inside information—the life—and that "outside"—the works—must suffice, but they do not discourage a move from "outside" to inside if done in the right way, by "the spirit-sense." That double noun, which must be regarded as both invitation and direction to critics and biographers, is richly suggestive. "Sense" is meaning, first of all, and Browning seems to be suggesting that in searching for the link between works and life, one discovers meaning when one brings to bear on the outward evidence of the works all the powers of one's own soul or spirit. "Sense" is also sensation and indicates images, the particulars of the works themselves, here to be apprehended not just with the physical eye (he condemns such limited "optics" in the poem) but with the eye of the soul. Perhaps he hoped that critics using a biographical approach would treat his life as Arthur Symons treated his works: he praised Symons's *Introduction* to his poetry because, he said, Symons had "so thoroughly entered into . . . the spirit in which [the poems] were written and the purpose they hoped to serve."[2] Still, he had no intention of making his life an open book. He came gradually to accept the view that his growth as poet and his mature opinions (and the processes by which he arrived at them) were (to him) acceptable matters of public interest.[3] His purely personal experiences he made every effort to keep private. So, while Browning had, through much of his career, deflected or discouraged any attempt at a biographical approach to his works, he was by the 1880s willing to provide such personal information as illuminated his art and ideas, and the development of them.

He did so for Edmund Gosse, who published in the December 1881 *Century Magazine* the article "The Early Career of Robert Browning, 1812–1846." It "was inspired and partly dictated, was revised and was approved of, by himself."[4] Gosse, a neighbor of Browning's, "had several times ventured to point out to him how valuable would be some authentic account of his life, but he had always put the suggestion from him." Then, in February of 1881, Browning sent him a note inviting him to come round to Warwick Crescent, where the poet said to him, "If you still wish to take down some notes of my life, I am willing to give you all the help I can; I am tired of this tangle of facts and fancies." So, at meetings "for a couple of hours at a time" over the course of several weeks, Gosse tells us, "I sat at his study table, while he perambulated, and I jotted rapidly down the notes of his conversation."[5] In the essay itself Gosse makes a distinction, which was also Browning's, between "personal history" and "literary history": Browning was providing the facts for, and Gosse was writing, the latter. "There are certain facts about the development of a poet's intellect and the direction that it took, the welcome that it received and the reverses that it endured, about which curiosity is perfectly legitimate. For those who desire such a peep through Mr. Browning's window as this, the shutters are at last by his own courtesy taken down."[6] So readers of Gosse's article learned, for instance, that the poet "can hardly remember a time when his intention was not to be eminent in rhyme," and from an early age he was conscious of measure: "His sister remembers him, as a very little boy, walking round and round the dining-room table, and spanning out the scansion of his verses with his hand on the smooth mahogany." Browning also told Gosse about his father's "force and fluency in the use of the heroic couplet, the only metrical form for which he had much taste," a fact not unrelated to Browning's deconstruction of the heroic couplet in *Sordello*, the poem being (Browning told Gosse) an "error," but one undertaken in reaction against the condition of English poetry in 1838, which was "singularly tame and namby-pamby."[7] Gosse also provides a detailed account of Browning's decade-long attempt to be a successful playwright. The information Browning provided in 1881 about his relations with Macready he expanded on in 1888, when William Archer sent him entries from Macready's diary which Browning then annotated with his own memories of such matters as the first meeting with Macready, the supper at Talfourd's house, and the productions of *Strafford* and *A Blot in the 'Scutcheon*.[8]

As the guardian of Elizabeth's memory, Browning applied that same distinction between "personal history" and "literary history" to any requests for information about her. He was willing to answer questions about the latter but far more reticent about the former, and he attributed to Elizabeth his own feelings about self-revelation, though her attitude had in fact been quite different.[9] When in 1882 John H. Ingram was preparing a biographical notice about Elizabeth, Robert told him that "I have neither the right nor the wish to withhold my consent to the appearance of the volume," but he did refuse to "co-operate" with Ingram, insofar as cooperation "implies giving information or allowing letters to be inspected." R. H. Horne had published Elizabeth's letters to him in 1877, but, said Browning, "the correspondence was literary only, between persons who had never seen each other, and before I could pretend to any sort of guardianship." But while he would not supply "any original information," he did promise Ingram "to *correct* any errors which the writer might, or rather would certainly fall into should the performance attempt to be biographical and not critical merely."[10] In one of his letters to Ingram, he does correct statements made in an article in *Tinsley's Magazine*— statements about Elizabeth's father, about the drowning of her brother, and about Browning's first meeting with her. Still, Browning maintained his "determination not to be drawn into furnishing any biographical details on any pretence whatever. What a pressure has been put upon me to break my determination you do not imagine, I am sure,"[11] he told his brother-in-law George at the same time as he was corresponding with Ingram.

Elizabeth's letters were Browning's main concern. "I possess hundreds of letters—besides those addressed to me," he told George Barrett, "those to the Martins, Miss Mitford, Mr Boyd, Chorley, Kenyon, Miss Blagden—and others: and moreover am promised the reversion of other collections when their owners die." How to dispose of them was a matter which "has long been much on my mind": "While I live, I can play the part of guardian effectually enough—but I must soon resolve on the steps necessary to be taken when I live no longer—and I complete my seventieth year next Sunday." His intention was to dip into each letter and "ascertain what should be destroyed, what preserved," and the only criterion he makes explicit for preserving letters is that they contain "nothing to hurt the living or the dead." But he also mentions another "danger," which he does not spell out, but which seems to be a fear of the personal revelation in an age when "the unscrupulous hunger for old scandals is on the increase," and that fear is bound up with letters not in his possession: Elizabeth's letters to her sister Arabella, "desposited in security somewhere," and her letters to her sister Henrietta, "which I am altogether powerless concerning."[12] Five years later, in another letter to George Barrett on the same subject, Browning specified the personal matter he did not want revealed: "the letters to the sisters . . . unfortunately contain besides the inevitable allusions to domestic matters, all the imaginary spiritualistic experiences by which the unsuspecting and utterly truthful nature of Ba was abused." Robert wanted no disclosure of Elizabeth's interest in spiritualism to a "careless and spiteful public, only glad to be amused by the aberrations of a soul so immeasurably superior in general intelligence to their own." Hence he assured George about the correspondence: "*all in my power* is safe, and will ever remain so: and I shall enjoin on Pen . . . to hinder [publication of the letters] by every possible means."[13] He still worried about the letters not in his possession: "The unhappy letters which concern spiritualism I wish with all my heart could be eliminated from those out of my hands, and burnt forthwith—as they ought to be."[14]

Browning did not hesitate to burn his own letters. He told his brother-in-law in January of 1889 that "Two years ago, I spent more than a week in destroying my own letters to my family,—from my earliest days up to the death of my father they had all been preserved." But in spite of his fears about "aberrations" being revealed he would not destroy Elizabeth's letters: "which I could not bring myself to do away with—whatever may be the ultimate disposition of them." And then there were the letters which were the most personal and intimate of all: "the letters to myself,—and for months before our marriage I received one daily,—these which are so immeasurably superior to any compositions of the kind I have any experience of,—would glorify the privileged receiver beyond any imaginable crown in the world or out of it—but I cannot, any more than Timon, 'cut my heart in sums—tell out my blood.'" So he preserved those letters and his own replies to them, never quite facing up to the likelihood that their existence would eventually lead to their publication, but knowing that partial printing of Elizabeth's letters—"just so much of the correspondence as merely relates to literature, politics, theology, description of persons and things"—would not satisfy "this gossip-loving and scandal-hungry world."[15] And while he had destroyed his own letters to his family, he kept his letters to Isa Blagden, which had been returned to him after her death, even though he had reminded her that "these notes are *always private*, you know," and had told her to "remember I read your letters, twice, & then burn them: *mine*, I trust,— earnestly conjure you will never show: but you will not."[16]

It is a curious fact that Browning did not use one common legal instrument—his will—for carrying out his wishes about the letters and his literary manuscripts. He had made his will in 1864, with provisions for Sarianna and Pen, and it remained unchanged throughout the subsequent twenty-five years until his death.[17] As Michael Millgate has pointed out, "No reference was made anywhere in the will to the retention, disposition, or destruction of either Browning's or Elizabeth Barrett Browning's papers and literary remains, nor to any exercise of the duties and responsibilities of a literary executor in respect of those properties: Browning simply bequeathed to Pen 'all my copyrights' along with everything else."[18]

The last of Browning's major poems is a work revealing as much of his life as he considered it appropriate for his readers to know, a work which, he told John Churton Collins, was "more personal more directly from myself than anything which I have yet published."[19] It appeared on January 28, 1887, as *Parleyings with Certain People of Importance in Their Day*, and William Clyde DeVane has accurately labeled the volume "the autobiography of a mind."[20] As such, it belongs with Wordsworth's *The Prelude*, which also is a poet's own account of the growth of his mind and which, like the *Parleyings*, has a dramatic element, since the chief identifying feature of it when its title was "not yet fixed upon" was that it was "addressed to S. T. Coleridge." But where Wordsworth's literary antecedent was epic and his form primarily narrative, Browning's (as one might expect) is dramatic and his form primarily dialogic. The word *parleying* is his name for the genre he is using. The OED defines the word (considered as a verb) as "to grant a parley, or an interview for discussion, to (a person); to hold discussion with, speak to, address," and cites Browning's title as the most recent use of the word since the seventeenth century. In Browning's hands the form is a complex one. Browning, in Mrs. Orr's words, "has summoned his group of men not for the sake of drawing their portraits, but that they might help him to draw his own." The men were "important in their day, virtually unknown in ours," and they are "with one exception . . . men whose works connect themselves with the intellectual sympathies and the imaginative pleasures of his very earliest youth."[21] Now their "personalities," Browning told Furnivall, "serve to strike out some sort of spark from myself."[22] Insofar as these "certain people dead and gone" enable the poet to express his own mature, considered opinions and ideas, the *Parleyings* share in the nature of the *apologia*, that prose genre in which one defends one's positions by explaining how they were arrived at. But six of the seven poems also make use of the dialogue form, for which the model is Platonic, and that form was more challenging than the other chief philosophical form, the complete and systematic arrangement of ideas: it was a teaching form, and required the learner to infer and synthesize rather than simply understand and accept positions already fully worked out. Browning makes the task of inference more difficult still by enclosing the dialogues within a single consciousness—his own—as he had had Balaustion present her debate with Aristophanes. That way of proceeding mimics one's actual experience of a debate—though there are two speakers, each hears the total discussion in his or her own way—but it also makes each parleying a monologue that raises all the problems of response and interpretation so familiar to readers of Browning's earlier dramatic monologues. No wonder reviewers of the *Parleyings* found Browning "harder and darker than ever."[23]

Totally ignored by readers, then and now, is the fact that Browning wrote the *Parleyings* in rhymed verse, though he had pointed out to Furnivall, when he was summarizing the essential features of his new volume, that his "confabulations"—his synonym for "parleyings"—were "all in rhyme, as you know."[24] Browning's ambition from his earliest days was to be (as he told Gosse) "eminent in rhyme," and "rhyme" in that statement is not just a synecdoche for poetry: Browning habitually called himself a "rhymester" and prided himself on his virtuosity in sound repetition, so when he wrote a poem "more personal more directly from myself than anything I have yet published," the rhymes are very much his own voice and style, and merit critical attention. In the *Parleyings* he sometimes writes heroic couplets, characteristically avoiding the clinching effect of the rhymes by using enjambment to make the expectations created by the syntax more powerful than the expectations of a repeated sound. Sometimes he uses an *abab* pattern, and sometimes—often at the ends of sections, to mark the rhythm of his argument—he uses the same rhyme for several lines in a row, and so creates a rising tension which is resolved only when an earlier sound at last reappears in the last word of the section—or, in a variation on this pattern, appears at the end of the half-line which begins the next section of the argument. The question Browning had earlier asked about the French poet Maillard (in *The Two Poets of Croisic*) is the crucial one: "Have people time / And patience nowadays for thought in rhyme?" (559–60). The answer is "Probably not," but still the *Parleyings* are thinner if readers consider them only as "mere grey argument" ("With Christopher Smart," 200); in them rhyme is the living body, the corporeality, of Browning's thought, and a thorough analysis of his rhymes as the realization of his ideas has yet to be done. A starting point would be to link the dialogic nature of the *Parleyings* with the inherently dialogic nature of rhyming, its paired sounds sometimes presenting a contrast, sometimes echoing each other in ways that can embody the give and take of debate. When, for instance, in the first of the *Parleyings*—the one with

Mandeville—Browning summons his opponent, Carlyle, whom he describes as "magisterial in antithesis" (41), he introduces Carlyle's statement with lines (35–43) that have an *abab* pattern, but when he invokes his ally, Mandeville, at the beginning of the dialogue (lines 11–18) he uses rhyming couplets.

Because Browning is speaking with thinkers who, as he said to Furnivall, were once "more or less notable" but are now "dead and gone,"[25] readers are sorely tempted to fall into the error of Mrs. FitzGerald and think that they cannot possibly begin to understand any one of the parleyings without knowing everything about Mandeville or Bartoli, Smart or Lairesse or Avison, but the poet's correction of Mrs. FitzGerald's critical procedure is applicable to this poem too. Not that Browning would discount the value of a thorough knowledge of those men—such a knowledge deepens and enriches our understanding of each dialogue—but the starting point for understanding must be the particular issues raised, and Browning's ally or opponent must be understood not as he was historically but as he has been constructed by Browning in this poem. DeVane's argument, in his 1927 book on the *Parleyings*, that Browning "failed to grasp the true meaning of Mandeville's doctrines,"[26] for instance, misses Browning's point: as the poet told Mrs. FitzGerald, poetry ought to reanimate something, not simply reproduce someone else's book. So the Mandeville of this parleying is Browning's Mandeville, and the Carlyle is Browning's Carlyle, both like and unlike their originals.

As such, they debate an issue central to Browning's thinking: why do human beings have limited knowledge? Browning's purpose in this parleying is to "learn / Man's proper play with truth in part, before / Entrusted with the whole" (14–16). That issue is related to, but distinct from, the paradox which Mandeville had explored in *Fable of the Bees* and which Browning summarizes, that "every growth of good / Sprang consequent on evil's neighbourhood" (112–13). The Carlyle whom Browning summons Mandeville to refute is a Carlyle who, contrary to the sage's actual doctrine of the symbol which both hides and reveals the infinite, thinks "Man, with the narrow mind, must cram inside / His finite God's infinitude" (151–52) and, when that attempt fails, rejects partial knowledge or "a guess at truth" (171). Browning's view is that limited knowledge (like Mandeville's understanding of evil) is the condition of human growth and development and, like the fire that Prometheus brought down to earth, sufficient for human purposes, even though it is not the sun.

There are two more characteristic aspects of this autobiography of Browning's mind, in addition to its dialogic and rhyming features, and the first is its range of artistic and literary concerns. Browning's ambitions had always been encyclopedic. *Pauline* in the 1830s had been part of (what Browning would later call)

> a foolish plan ... which contemplated the assumption of I know not how many different individualities and characters in each of which I was to expatiate and take my pleasure: meanwhile the world was never to guess that "Brown, Smith, Jones, and Robinson" (as our Spelling-books have it) the respective Authors of such a poem, such an opera, such a comedy, such a speech &c &c were no other than one and the same.[27]

"Foolish" or not, those young ambitions motivated a continuing interest in painting and music as well as poetry, and left vestiges of a desire to be an artist and composer as well as a poet. So the parleyings explore issues in painting ("With Francis Furini," "With Gerard de Lairesse") and music ("With Charles Avison") as well as poetry ("With Christopher Smart"), and when one adds the epistemological concerns of "With Bernard de Mandeville," the narrative of "With Daniel Bartoli," and the political argument of "With George Bubb Dodington," there is some justification for thinking the poem epic as well as dialogic in nature. The second characteristic aspect of this poem is that Browning defines himself by books. They rather than nature stimulated his poetic imagination. In 1882 he had told Mrs. FitzGerald that his notion of an earthly paradise was a library. "Have you indeed 'more than 10,000 books'?" he asks her. "You know Pryor's pretty verses beginning 'All in a lonely Study—Where books are in great plenty'—*that* was the Bishop of St David's notion of an Earthly Paradise—and not very far from mine. I bless my lot whenever I can, as last night, find myself at home for the hours between dinner and bed-time,—book in hand, lamp at elbow, and fire not too far from footstool."[28]

Browning dedicated the *Parleyings* to the memory of Joseph Milsand, who had died on September 4, 1886. "My own heart's man-friend,"[29] Browning had described him two years earlier to Mrs. Bronson, and to Isa Blagden he had said, "I never knew nor shall know his like among men."[30] "I have lost our Milsand,"[31] Browning wrote to Mrs. Skirrow two days after his death, and his curious use of pronouns indicates that Milsand was as much Sarianna's as he was Robert's friend. For in June of that year, when Milsand was seriously ill, Sarianna was on the point of going to Paris to be with him, but an "inflammatory attack" kept her in London.[32] Browning also informed Furnivall of his friend's death, and Furnivall, using materials supplied by the poet, wrote a brief obituary which appeared both in the *Academy* and the *Times*. In it he described Milsand as "a country gentleman and owner of vineyards," and as "an accomplished scholar" with "a rare knowledge of English": in 1851

"he was, perhaps, the only Frenchman who then understood and could crit-
icize Mr. Browning." Furnivall's summary of Milsand's character could only
have come from Browning: Milsand was, Furnivall wrote, "a genial companion, a rare judge of character, and full of tact, a firm friend, and a widely cultured man."[33] Two days after the piece appeared in the *Times*, the poet wrote
to thank Furnivall: "You did all I could wish in the way of sobriety and suc-
cinctness as well as adequate recognition and handsome appreciation—
adequate for the 'public'—who will never know what only an intimate of
thirty-five years knows and never will attempt to put into words."[34]

Milsand died at Villers-la-Faye, among his Burgundy vineyards, and he
had had a house in the Paris suburb of Neuilly, which in 1870 he had feared
would be destroyed by the invading Prussians, but his family home was in
Dijon, "a beautiful old house, called the House of the English Ambassa-
dors. . . . It is a jewel of the architecture of the Renaissance," according to
Mme Blanc.[35] Milsand's papers and correspondence survived in its attic
until, at the beginning of the twenty-first century, the whole archive (thousands of letters, and printed pages and manuscript pages numbering in the
tens of thousands) came to the Armstrong Browning Library in Texas.
Browning would be gratified to know that scholars are not about to let the
memory of his best friend die.

English Roses and Florentine Lilies

1887 was a year of changes: Pen at last married; the Brownings were forced out of the Warwick Crescent house; and they did not go to Italy. (They had not gone the previous year either, because Sarianna had been seriously ill; instead, they had gone to Wales for her convalescence.)

In early 1887 Pen was approaching his thirty-eighth birthday and had been leading a peripatetic existence as painter and sculptor, undertaking "hard two months' study of modelling & anatomy in Paris" in 1882,[1] working in Dinant and "painting in the open air" in 1884,[2] exhibiting regularly in Brussels and Paris and London, and taking a studio in Venice in 1885, where he "tries his hand at something different [his father hoped] from the conventional work."[3] In August of 1887, he wrote to his father, then holidaying in St. Moritz, announcing his engagement to Fannie Coddington, a well-to-do American whom he had met some fifteen years earlier when her parents were living in London, to whom he had "proposed" (the quotation marks are his father's) when she was nineteen, and whom he met again "by mere accident at a country house" in July 1887, when "at once the smouldering fire was set flaring,—with the result of a fresh proposal and cordial acceptance."[4] The father responded to the son's choice enthusiastically: "I do approve of your choice with all my heart: there is no young person I know at all comparable to Miss C. She has every requisite to make you happy and successful, if you deserve it—as I believe you will endeavour to do." Browning's objections to Pen's earlier marriage plans had been financial; in that same letter he was explicit about Pen's resources and requirements: "Miss C. has spoken to me with the greatest frankness and generosity of the means she will have of

403

contributing to your support—for my part, I can engage to give you £300 a year: this, with the results of your work—if you manage to sell but a single picture in the year—will amply suffice. Of course, at my death you will have whatever I possess. . . ."[5] Both Robert and Sarianna approved of Fannie. In that same letter, Sarianna (who, Robert said later, has "always been a mother-and-a-half to the fortunate fellow"[6]) wrote to her nephew that she had had a "long talk" with Fannie and found her "very different from the fast American girls who abound here."[7] (But Sarianna would later say, after her brother's death and when her nephew's marriage was breaking up, "From the first Fannie has been of a highly hysteric, excitable nature."[8]) Robert, writing in 1887 to George Barrett, to the Lehmanns and the Skirrows, and to the Reverend J. D. Williams, praised Fannie, saying that no young woman was "more qualified" to make Pen happy. To the Skirrows, Browning said, "Now, it so happens, of all the young persons of my acquaintance, I could not pick out a single one so fitted,—if I can judge at all,—to make Pen, with his many peculiarities, the best of wives—. . . She is a fine handsome generous creature—and honest and good—every inch of her." And she was prepared to be an artist's wife: "This will in no way interfere with [Pen's] sedulous prosecution of his Art—which the Lady is as anxious to further as he can possibly be."[9] To Williams, Browning wrote that "Fannie, my daughter in love and law, is good, true, sympathetic in every way,—a few years younger than Pen,—very pretty, we think, very devoted to him, we know,—and having been an admirable daughter and sister will presumably become as fitting a wife. She has all the ambition for his sake which I could wish, and is eminently distinguished for common sense: so that . . . how can I be other than thankful?"[10] For her part, Fannie could never forget the poet's "affectionate and warm greeting, and his tender expressions in welcoming me" on her first visit to him after the engagement, when he said "He always had wanted a daughter and now he had one!"[11]

The wedding took place on October 4, 1887, at Fannie's cousins' Hawkwell Place, at Pembury, near Tunbridge Wells in Kent. Browning described the occasion for the Skirrows: "the little 'Old Church,'—A.D. 11—,—was decked out with the prettiest of autumn flowers,—and, as nobody had been invited but the few relatives of the Bride,—we saw none but really sympathetic faces, some fifteen or eighteen in all—but the neighbours seemed to share in our satisfaction."[12] The poet, Fannie recorded long afterward, "spoke most feelingly at the weddding-breakfast and gave us his blessing."[13]

"The Couple" or "the young couple"—this is how Browning would habitually refer to Pen and Fannie—sailed a month later for New York, where Fannie would suffer the disappointment of a miscarriage. On their return to

England in the spring of 1888, they went on to Venice and there, Browning reported to his brother-in-law George, "Pen is bent upon settling for some months, in order to paint certain aspects of the city and its inhabitants which he fancies have never been made use of before."[14] But "The Couple's" chief interest took a different direction: the purchase and restoration of a palazzo on the Grand Canal. Browning himself had undertaken such a purchase three years earlier, but the deal had fallen through when the seller backed out of the contract and when Browning himself backed out of the lawsuit he subsequently brought against him because of doubts about the palazzo's foundations. Now Pen and Fannie, in a transaction Browning described as an "advantageous bargain," bought the "huge Rezzonico Palace,—the finest now obtainable in Venice." It took its name from Cardinal Rezzonico, who later became Pope Clement XIII, "whose apartment they [Pen and Fannie] occupy."[15] Though Browning described the palace as "huge," Pen, he said, "does not find [it] at all too vast. He reminds me of the mouse (in a poem of Donne's) who got into the trunk of an elephant—'wherein, as in a gallery, this mouse walked and surveyed the rooms of this vast house.'"[16] While other purchasers of Venetian palaces had turned them into hotels or worse, Pen and Fannie brought "reverent hands" to theirs, and to its statues, pillars, and painted ceilings: Pen "is full of energy, and superintends all the restoration work, . . . and may safely be considered 'the right man in the right place.'"[17] "The treatment of the grand old pile is just what it should be."[18] "The little chapel in their palazzo—once a witness of the daily devotions of Rezzonico—Pope Clement XIII" Pen and Fannie restored and dedicated to the memory of Pen's mother, "putting up there the inscription by Tommasei now above Casa Guidi."[19] The connection with the dead parent was very much a living one. "I believe," Browning told his brother-in-law George, "that Pen's most happy marriage is mainly attributable to his being the son of his mother—whom his wife from her girlhood has all but worshipped." Browning thought the admiration would have been mutual. Fannie, he said, is "a woman of whom I can imagine no greater praise than I imply when I say Pen's Mother would have thoroughly loved and esteemed her."[20]

The Brownings' regular visits to Italy raised for them the question of living there permanently. Browning seems to have thought that he and Sarianna would retire to Italy eventually—but not before they had to. When in November of 1885 he was in the midst of his ultimately unsuccessful attempt to buy the Manzoni Palazzo, he told Furnivall that he was buying the place for Pen, who "will have sunshine and beauty about him, and every help to profit by these: while I and my sister have secured a shelter when the fogs of life grow too troublesome." But he cautions Furnivall, "Don't think I mean to give up London till it warns me away—when the hospitalities and innumerable delights grow a burthen even as we are assured the grasshopper will eventually do in the case of the stoutest of us."[21] A little more than a year later, Browning told Mrs. Bronson that Pen entertained a "strange misconception" about their palazzo hunting, a "misconception on his part that I wanted *any* abode in Venice, and not simply a palace for him which I could occasionally occupy. . . . I am bound by too many ties to London, for such a complete disassociation from it as would be involved by constant residence anywhere else."[22] And though he told the Skirrows that the Manzoni Palazzo would be "a capital retreat" when "the inevitable outrage of Time gets the better of my body," he assured them that "I myself shall stick to London—which has been so eminently good and gracious to me—so long as God permits."[23]

That view had long been in place, and it determined the Brownings' course of action when, in 1882, a bill was passed to allow for the demolishing of the whole of Warwick Crescent in order to build a railway: they would search for a house elsewhere in London, and not in Italy, as their permanent residence. The forced move made Browning face up to his feelings about Warwick Crescent. From the beginning he had considered it a temporary abode, but they had stayed on from year to year to year. Hence when, in the summer of 1881 Browning had, with the help of Mrs. FitzGerald's gardener, "set the little patch of wretchedness called 'our garden' in something like decent order," he told her that "I began by too entirely despising this little house, which has behaved well enough by me for nearly twenty years: I never condescended to consider it as other than a makeshift: but now I ask myself 'what better I deserve'—as Coleridge did, when his tea got cold: and I daresay I shall die here."[24] Six months later Browning expressed himself more bluntly to Mrs. Bronson: "a railway is about to run through my house, just as I had made up my mind that twenty years' occupation of it was proof that I *could* live out my life there!"[25]

But they had no choice. In August of 1882 Browning told Mrs. Skirrow that "That 'Bill' for abolishing our poor little house has finally received Royal assent, and out we must go—where *into* is a mystery, which I shall be troubled to solve on my return [from their autumn vacation in France and Italy]: but we somehow manage to 'fall on our legs' generally."[26] *When* they had to go was also a mystery. In February 1883 Browning reported, "We are still in the same uncertainty as to when they will turn us out here: they can when they please."[27] In December of that year Browning was house-hunting, but in the meantime the railway scheme was postponed, and urgency gave way to waiting in a state of unknowing. It was not until March of 1887 that the scheme was revived, and then there seemed to be no question but that it would proceed. In May of that year Browning told the Storys that "I am turned out of house & home by a Railway, and must get shelter somewhere by the winter."[28] And looking back on (what was now) twenty-five years' residence in Warwick Crescent he reiterated his earlier feelings to Mrs. Bronson: "I was supremely wretched when I entered into possession, and had no other hope than that of getting out of London as soon as possible: how time has slipt away! and but for the menaced invasion of the railroad I might be constant to the old place till I went elsewhere 'for good' it is to be hoped."[29] But, he told Mrs. Skirrow, "A person of my age cannot wait to be turned out by the excavators knocking at his door, and I have not budged till there was a plain necessity."[30]

They settled on "a good freehold property," 29 De Vere Gardens. Browning told Mrs. Bronson about the purchase:

> I have bought a house—Oh, sad descent in dignity—not on *Canal Grande*—the beloved and ever to be regretted—but Kensington—It is a nearly new one, and situated just where I wish: and in consequence of the temporary depreciation of that kind of property, I believe I have done very well. The search for the place was managed by my sister,— and the bargaining effected, with all zeal and abundant intelligence, by my kind and experienced Publisher—George Smith.[31]

They would move in June 1887, but April brought "'the beginning of the end' of poor 19. Warwick Cr," with tapestries removed and sent to Paris for repair, leaving "bare walls—which front me thus exposed for the first time these six and twenty years,"—walls he proposed to cover temporarily "with pictures of Pen, and so avoid unwelcome thoughts."[32] By late June, Browning reported that "we are at least partially installed in the new house"; in December he pronounced it "warm and comfortable, and in that matter . . . we seem to have succeeded beyond our expectations."[33] "Comfortable,—in all but the stairs to climb," Browning told Mrs. Bronson in February of 1889, "and even these are made more tolerable by our Venetian arrangement of lanterns which touch my heart, every step I take past them. Look where we will, there Venice suggests itself,—the curtains and tables and brackets and what not: all go in harmoniously, are fancy, and keep us from caring about the dismal fog outside—too often, not—I am bound to say—this morning."[34]

For in spite of his attachment to London, Browning would more and more frequently complain about its fogs and its unhealthy air, and of the effects of both on his lungs. "I used to boast foolishly that my lungs would outlast my legs and arms," Browning told Mrs. FitzGerald in December 1886, "and it is just these lungs that teaze me." The doctor's diagnosis was "a something very like 'spasmodic asthma'" and his advice was "that I need to guard myself troublesomely when I go out, and, if there be fog in the air, not go out at all." Browning was unable to determine whether his "complaint"—"coughing (not considerable) and wheezing (mainly troublesome at night)"—was "a trifling incommodity or likely to prove an ever increasing plague."[35] In the event, his "spasmodic asthma"—"ugly name," "ugly thing,"[36] Browning called it—would continue to plague him and would be joined by other "complaints": in January 1888 he was shut in for ten days, "attacked by my old spasmodic cough complicated with rheumatism—a quite new experience": "I am forced to give up all old—and refuse all new temptations in the shape of dinner-parties."[37] The three months that he spent in Venice in 1888 were restorative, and on his return he was acutely conscious of the contrast between Venice and London: "The weather was appalling enough when, last week, we exchanged three months of glorious sunshine and cloudless sky for the fog which met us at Dover," he told his brother-in-law: "I suffered not a little and expected to undergo much more."[38] A month later, writing again to George about his concerns over Elizabeth's letters, he reported that "I suffered from the fog, and keep house of an evening all this current month."[39] So "Grim London with its fog and cold" affected him more than usual that winter when, he told Mrs. Bronson, he stayed indoors because of "this dismal weather: it is quite enough to manage living, without adding the wretchedness of being choked by the fog."[40] In mid-January of 1888 he told Pen and Fannie frankly about his health: "My two beloved ones," he begins his letter, "I am far from well,—you shall always have the truth from me as nearly as I can give it,—but I am better,—quite cured of what was a new symptom, the rheumatic pain, and really in the way to get rid of the cough, which is *spasmodic*, not originating in anything worse than my old trouble of the liver."[41]

The Alps and Italy, Browning was convinced, would cure him. From Primiero in the Tyrol in August 1888 he wrote ahead to Mrs. Bronson in Venice, saying that "I am convinced that in London I was slowly dying of asphyxia,—and the mere admittance of fresh air into my exhausted receiver set all to rights at once,—I am absolutely well again." Yet the journey had been a "painful" one, the Channel crossing "the roughest I remember," the long trip by rail "an ugly business enough" in "the hottest of weather."[42] "If I am to get any good out of my visit [to Venice]," Browning had told Mrs. Bronson before leaving London, "I must lead the quietest of lives, and be lulled by the cigarette-smoke of just my friend—not the *chiacchere* [idle chatter] of new acquaintance."[43] The Brownings would stay with Mrs. Bronson for nearly three months, in Ca'Alvisi itself, and after they had returned to London, the poet would look back longingly on that time. "Wonderful" and "memorable" were the adjectives Browning used in describing his vivid memories of that autumn, and he wrote to Mrs. Bronson the following February to say that "I (seriously) believe I shall never have three such perfectly happy months as I had with you,—never again! How good it all was,—the tea and the music, the gondola, the exploration of the labyrinthine city!"[44] He had, Mrs. Bronson would later remember, "never expressed a wish to 'see sights' in the tourist manner"; rather, "because he had known little of the tortuous inner streets of Venice," he had explored those "little Venetian *calli*" with Mrs. Bronson's daughter, Edith, as his guide. "He liked to find himself suddenly in one so narrow as to force him to close his umbrella, whether in sun or rain," and he delighted in discovering "a hitherto unknown bit of stone carving or bas-relief."[45] In January 1889 he said that "I may never see the lovely City again,—but where in the house will not some little incident of the three unparalelled [*sic*] months wake up memories of the gondola, and the stoppings here and there, and the fun at Morchio's [an antiques shop], the festive return home, behind broad-backed Luigi,—then the tea, and the dinner . . . oh, the delightful time!" Before Christmas 1888 Browning had told Mrs. Bronson that "I shall never see the word 'Venice' without a rising of [my] heart at the memory of *you* there,—of the gondola, the Lido, the antichità-shops, all saturated with you."[46] Those memories made him vow: "Oh, my two beloveds [Mrs. Bronson and her daughter, Edith], I *must* see Venice again,—it would be heart-breaking to believe otherwise!"[47]

Browning's attention as poet was occupied at this time by two matters: the preparation of a collected edition of his works, and the writing and gathering of poems for a new volume. In the autumn of 1887 he had discussed with his publisher, George Smith, the issuing of all his poems in a uniform edition of some fifteen or sixteen volumes, the first of which appeared in 1888. The only poem he revised extensively was *Pauline*. At the same time he was writing and collecting the pieces that would make up the volume he entitled *Asolando*, "some thirty pieces great and small," he told J. D. Williams, "of various kinds and qualities—not a few written, and all supervised, in this lovely Asolo—my spot of predilection in the whole world, I think."[48]

In spite of his respiratory problems, Browning enjoyed an extensive social life in London, and in a letter to Pen written in June of 1889 he gives details of all his current engagements, of invitations he accepted and of others he turned down. "Today"—he was writing on June 19—"I have five engagements of one or another kind. On the 25th I go to Oxford; Commemoration next day,— and stay over for the Balliol 'Gaudy'-dinner to the Provost and Fellows of

Eton, on July 1.... By this visit, I escape dinners every day in London, and the wedding of Farrar's daughter—which otherwise I should have liked to attend in spite of the trouble and fatigue."[49] Thoughts of "trouble and fatigue" also affected his plans to return to Italy. "Little as I now like travelling" is one of his asides in that same letter to Pen,[50] and he contemplated a possible return to Italy with mixed emotions. In July he wrote to Mrs. Bronson that "I feel disinclined to leave England this next Autumn that is so soon to overtake us," but later in the letter he exclaimed, "Oh, it will be too hard to keep away from Venice always!"[51] It was the getting there that he dreaded: "the laziness of age is subduing me, and how I shrink from the 'middle passage'!—all that day-and-night whirling from London to Basle—with the eleven or twelve hours to Milan. Milan opens on Paradise,—but the getting to Milan!"[52] By the end of August, however, he and Sarianna had determined to go: he told Furnivall on August 28 that "We start to-morrow for Bale, Milan, Vicenza, and Asolo—where we stay for a month or more—then, go on to Venice."[53]

Browning's last weeks in London were marred by worries about his health and by an unfortunate incident involving the publication of a letter which ought to have remained private. On August 28 Browning wrote to the Reverend J. D. Williams that "the weather has been so cool, not to say cold here, that, by retarding our departure somewhat, I have been able to walk and keep quiet, to the great improvement of my health, so that I do not throw on Italy the whole burthen of making me well again,—so far as 'well' is possible."[54] He was pessimistic, for he had reacted with such anger to the posthumous publication of a letter written by Edward FitzGerald that, he told Pen, he had "really been the worse, physically, for this outrage," while Sarianna wrote of the offending document that "Your papa was quite ill with the pain it gave him."[55] The editor of FitzGerald's letters had allowed the publication of a passage about Elizabeth in which FitzGerald said that "Mrs. Browning's death is rather a relief to me, I must say. No more Aurora Leighs, thank God!" A furious Browning reacted with two stanzas addressed to FitzGerald in the *Athenaeum*, the second of which concluded with the lines,

> How to return you thanks would task my wits:
>   Kicking you seems the common lot of curs—
> While more appropriate greeting lends you grace:
> Surely to spit there glorifies your face—
>   —Spitting—from lips once sanctified by Hers.

Browning wrote a lengthy letter to Lady Tennyson about the matter, knowing that the laureate and FitzGerald had been friends, but saying that "I am unable to regret what I did,—bitterly as I regret having been compelled to do it—on behalf of my son as well as for my own sake."[56] To Pen, Browning wrote that Tennyson "is not the man to sympathize with a poor creature like FitzGerald, whom I punished no more than he deserved—heartily wishing he were alive in the body—not, for the first time, alive in his words which only now go forth to the world: I *did* nothing—only said what I would certainly have done had they been spoken in my hearing."[57]

The Brownings set out from London on August 29. Two weeks earlier Browning had written to Pen to express "my weariness and indisposition to undertake a long journey," and to say that "I *did* fancy that a day's journey only to some quiet place in Scotland, might answer my purpose of getting braced up." But a cold and rainy summer in London turned his thoughts to the south, and he told Pen that he was healthier than he had been the year before: "treating London as the bracing-place, I took plenty of exercise—walking, for the last week two hours daily, and the result is I am in an altogether different condition from this time last year." But in that same letter Sarianna was apprehensive: "Your papa is in good health now," she told Pen, "but he may change," and "I wish he would start at once before waiting till he falls ill."[58]

The Brownings arrived in Asolo on September 4. "We have a valued friend here," Browning wrote to his brother-in-law George, "Mrs. Bronson, who for years has been our hostess in Venice, and now is in possession of a house here (built into the old city wall)—" and called, appropriately, La Mura. Through Mrs. Bronson's "care and kindness, we are comfortably lodged close by."[59] His days began at seven, Mrs. Bronson recalled, when he "took his cold bath, scarcely tempered even in chilly weather, then his simple breakfast, served punctually at eight of the clock, then with his sister—here, as elsewhere, his inseparable companion—he wandered over the hills, seeking and finding such points of view and interest as he had known in his first youth. He recognized a bit of old fresco still left on a house wall, a Gothic window here, a doorway there, the palace where Napoleon slept before the battle of Bassano, the graveled bit of square above the market-place. . . ."[60] Browning told Mrs. Skirrow of his delight in the town: "As for the place itself, it remains what I first conceived it to be—the most beautiful spot I ever was privileged to see. It is seldom that one's impressions of half-a-century ago, are confirmed by present experience but so it is."[61] But there were changes which his delight could not obscure, for the silk industry had moved elsewhere, the castle ruins had deteriorated, and—something he had considered all his own—the echo there was no longer to be heard. "I find the Turret rather the worse for careful weeding—the hawks which used to build there have been 'shot for food'—and the echo is sadly curtailed of its replies."[62] "'I should have thought an echo could never fade,' he said rather sadly."[63]

"'The Poet's age is sad'" are the opening words of the "Prologue" to *Asolando*, and the words might well be Browning's own, but in the poem he assigns them to a "Friend," answers them in his own voice, and concludes by allowing a revelatory "Voice" the final and authoritative word. In this dialogue the "Friend" mourns, as Wordsworth does in his immortality ode, the loss of the kind of imaginative perception which glorifies everything in nature. The poet himself disposes easily enough of that complaint, calling such perception "falsehood's fancy-haze" and opting for sight of "the naked very thing." Then he provides his own account of a change in perception. He likens his first sight of Asolo to Moses' sight of the burning bush, to which his awed response was silence. Beyond that the young poet could not go: revelation (about which Browning always had mixed feelings) curtailed further development and made language—especially poetic language—unnecessary. Now the old poet rejects "the eye late dazed" in favor of the "purged ear," which hears a "Voice" instructing him to recognize each image in nature as a "friend" because, if one apprehends it in an emblematic way, it will ultimately reveal a transcendent God. So, as he privileges hearing over seeing and the thing-in-itself over the thing-as-it-is-perceived, Browning suggests a consolation for the echo he could no longer hear: in contrast to his youthful silence at the sight of an Asolo "palpably fire-clothed," he now voices a "Voice," and his echoing of that "Voice" is, by implication, a reaffirmation of his calling as poet.

If the sights in and around Asolo were no longer "fire-clothed" but now a "naked world," nonetheless "earth, sky, / Hill, vale, tree, flower,—Italia's rare / O'er-running beauty crowds the eye," and Browning continued to respond to those sights. He explored the countryside and nearby towns, the daily drives allowing him to examine towers and walls and fortifications, museums and restaurants and bookshops. The "drive to Bassano was, I think, his favourite," Mrs. Bronson recollected, for they passed the tower of Romano, who figures in *Sordello*, carefully examined the collection in the museum, explored an old bookshop, and ate lunch at a little inn: "The simple food pleased the poet and his sister. Both were always in the highest delight because it was 'Italianissimo.'"[64] Back in Asolo, Browning loved watching the sunsets from Mrs. Bronson's windows: "He never wearied of gazing from the loggia of La Mura at the view over the plain, and of pointing out sites he had kept clear in his mind while writing 'Sordello' and 'Pippa Passes.'"[65] Now he had more poems inspired by that setting.

"This morning"—the letter is dated October 15—"I despatched to Smith the MS. of my new volume,—some thirty poems long and short,—some few written here, all revised and copied."[66] The collection was Brown-

ing's "Indian Summer,"[67] and the poem called "Development" is especially
interesting and attractive because it is not dramatic but personal and
because it is a kind of coda to the *Parleyings* of 1887. Though the poem is a
narrative, the story is of the poet's mind in dialogue with the *Iliad*, and the
theme is the poet's changing perception of that text. The motif, "who was
who and what was what," shifts in meaning as Browning grows. At the age of
five, he takes a "huge delight" (18) in the story; then, as his education proceeds, he progresses, he thinks, from such "make-believe" (26) to the "true
history" (39), first by reading Pope's translation, then by learning Greek and
conning "the very thing itself, the actual words" (42). Then he comes to
Wolf's *Prolegomena ad Homerum*, with its revelation of an unstable and unreliable text characterized largely by accretions and editorial choices, and with
its questioning of the very existence of Homer himself. "Ah, Wolf!" Browning exclaims; "why must he needs come doubting, spoil a dream?" (82–83).
Though the poet does assert that "No dream's worth waking" (84), he does
not settle or provide final views on the issues raised: the sifting of truth from
falsehood, the inferring of moral lessons from the text. Instead, he praises
the wisdom of his father, "who knew better than turn straight / Learning's
full flare on weak-eyed ignorance" (20–21), and he suggests not only that
each stage is a witness of truth, however imperfectly understood, but also
that the process itself—development—is the crucial thing. He confirms
that view in the "Epilogue" to the *Asolando* volume, in lines that would (in
after years) be quoted again and again as an inspiring expression of Browning's optimism: "One who never turned his back but marched breast forward, / Never doubted clouds would break" (11–12). For too many readers
the conventional metaphor of life as a journey—combined with suggestions
of a confident march and a vigorously fought battle—obscures Browning's
affirmation that development, bound up with approaches to truth and uses
of fiction, is the essence of human existence.

On the last day of October 1889 the Brownings arrived in Venice to stay
with Pen and Fannie in the Palazzo Rezzonico. Hiram Corson, then on a
sabbatical from Cornell, visited the poet on November 2, and found him "in
his usual vigor of mind and body" and giving "no impression of old age. His
voice was clear and strong as ever. I thought he had ten years more of good
work in him."[68] When Browning had arrived in Asolo, "a difficulty in his
breathing was very apparent, especially after mounting steep stairs or a hill,"
but, Mrs. Bronson recorded optimistically, "this annoying symptom disappeared after a few weeks."[69] In Venice, Browning continued to enjoy the city,
its public places and theaters and "socialities," but by the last week in
November "his cough was bad,"[70] and when on November 28 he returned

from a performance of *Carmen* "he had great difficulty in breathing, and seemed very tired and used up as he mounted the two long staircases." Browning usually attributed his condition to his liver, but in fact his heart was failing. Dr. Cini said "that he would breathe much better upstairs on account of the high ceilings, and that as his heart was in a very bad condition he should be carried up and on no account do any more stairs himself." He was given digitalis for his heart and linseed poultices for his chest, but the doctors warned Pen and Fannie that "they could give us no hope of his recovery."[71] On the morning of December 12, the day on which *Asolando* was published, Pen told Mrs. Bronson that "he is *quite* clear headed," and—in a report reminiscent of Browning's own report of his father's last hours in Paris in 1866—"is never tired of saying he feels better:—'immensely better—I don't suppose I could get up and walk about—in fact I know I could not, but I have no aches or pains—quite comfortable—could not be more so.'"[72] But by afternoon his respiratory problems were again manifesting themselves, and his heavy breathing gave way to delirium, when "he talked so loudly . . . that we could hear him three rooms off."[73] Then, in Pen's words, "Our Beloved breathed his last as St Marks struck ten—without pain—unconsciously—I was able to make him happy a little before he became unconscious by a telegram from Smith saying 'reviews in all this day's papers most favourable. Edition nearly exhausted—'He just murmured 'How gratifying.' Those were the last intelligible words."[74]

₲ ₲ ₲

In death Browning was honored in both Venice and London. The officialdom of Venice made arrangements for a stately and uniquely Venetian funeral. After a brief funeral service in the first-floor sala of the palazzo, which was attended by a small group of family and friends, a squad of eight *pompieri* in blue uniforms and shining brass helmets bore the coffin down to the canopied black-and-gold funeral barge, which was hung with funeral wreaths. As the sun was setting, the barge, with a golden lion at the prow and propelled by gondoliers dressed in gold-and-black velvet, led the cortege of gondolas down the Grand Canal and out to the isle of the dead, San Michele, where Browning's body was held awaiting burial. Where that was to be was settled when Browning's publisher, George Murray Smith, secured from the dean of Westminster Abbey an invitation for interment in Poet's Corner.[75]

The burial service in London, a large and solemn assembly both of Victorian notables—they included Henry James, Edmund Gosse, Benjamin Jowett, Hallam Tennyson, and Frederick Leighton—and of ordinary people, took place in the abbey on December 31, 1889. The weather was the kind of London weather which had caused physical distress in the poet, for "as midday approached the fog grew denser and darkness brooded over the scene." Inside the great church "the effect [of the gloom] was . . . one of heightened impressiveness and solemnity." The most moving part of the service was the singing of a new anthem composed for the occasion by the abbey's organist, J. F. Bridge, who used the words of Elizabeth's poem "The Sleep." The setting was appropriately dramatic and dialogic:

> It starts with the inquiry, uttered by a boy soprano . . . , "What would we give to our beloved?" the whole of the rest of the anthem being choral. Successively the basses speak of "The hero's heart," the sopranos of "The poet's star-tuned harp," and altos and tenors in a brief martial strain of "The patriot's voice." The whole is rounded off by a lovely phrase to the words "He giveth His beloved sleep," which alike in the poem and the anthem is employed as a refrain.[76]

"The music," Edmund Gosse remembered, "was long-drawn, dreary, delicate, and it floated for an infinite length of time (it seemed) up in the roof of the Abbey. . . . After all was over, Poets' Corner was deserted for a while, and making for it I found the grave open, with the coffin exposed to view, a few flowers resting on the bare wood."[77] In after years the only flowers to be seen would be roses and lilies, fashioned in brass and inlaid in the porphyry and marble over the grave—emblems presenting a not-too-difficult challenge to the thoughtful visitor.[78]

ℜ ℜ ℜ

Why should people at the beginning of the twenty-first century care about Robert Browning's life or read Robert Browning's poetry? When the poet himself was alive, readers wanted to know about the life because they valued the poetry, and that fact still provides the chief motive for a biography and still orders the relation of the life and the works in the right way: we would not have much reason to seek out the details of the poet's personal history if we did not have poems that move us or intrigue us or challenge us to respond to them. Even the story of the Brownings' celebrated courtship and marriage would not have the staying power that it has if husband and wife had not both been poets, famous in their time. But the old reasons for valuing Robert Browning's poetry are no longer compelling: he gives us access to the inner lives of men and women, for instance, or he dramatizes rather than speaking with his own voice, or he can be read as a philosophical and religious teacher. But what can his poetry say to an age in which, in spite of the powerful human wish for certainty and objective truth, we know that all knowledge is interpretation, that meaning rests on meanings already made, and that, in an apparently endless interpretive process, we can never reach a point where we know that "This is the beginning" or "This is the ground" or "This is real." Even language itself seems to be a vast web of referents where we can never find anything of which we can say, "This is itself and not a sign of something else."

Browning, however, welcomes indeterminacy and celebrates its interpretation. For him the making of meaning is the essential and defining human activity, even though he is a realist about its difficulties and lapses and abuses. He does have a theory about the purpose of that activity—it is the development of the soul—but that theory does not have much appeal in an age no longer dominated by ideas of progress and development, an age skeptical about the very existence of the soul. Moreover, he believes that the ground of all knowledge is revealed to us in the Incarnation, for him the central fact of Christianity but for many twenty-first-century readers a no-longer-tenable doctrine. Still, it is perhaps more acceptable when we realize that, for Browning, the Incarnation is not primarily an historical fact, firmly fixed in a dead past, but a living power within himself and in all human beings: that is what he means when he says he finds God within himself. God is the ground of the human ability to make meaning. He is, in our human experience of him, not a guarantor of either truth or right, but he makes interpretation and judgment possible. But Browning does not explicitly teach such ideas. Instead, with his dramatic techniques he provides experiences that suggest those ideas, and he is always prodding the reader to make sense of those experiences in his or her own way. So he is a poet for the twenty-first century, offering for interpretation only suggestions and puzzles and enigmas, for each one of which Childe Roland's imperative for himself is every reader's agenda: "Solve it, you!"

Chapter 1

1. RB, undated letter to Fanny Haworth, quoted in Orr, 103.
2. Mrs. E. F. Bridell-Fox, "Robert Browning," *Living Age*, 184 (1890): 762.
3. Appendix to *Lyrical Ballads* (1802).

Chapter 2

1. The information about Camberwell and the surrounding area is drawn from Douglas Allport, *Collections, Illustrative of the Geology, History, Antiquities and Associations of Camberwell and the Neighborhood* (Camberwell, 1841); William Harnett Blanch, *Ye Parish of Camberwell* (London, 1875); Edward Walford, *Old and New London*, vol. 6, *The Southern Suburbs* (London: Cassell Petter and Gilpin, 1876); Thankful Sturdee, *Reminiscences of Old Deptford* (London: Henry Richardson, 1876); Mary Boast, *Southwark a London Borough* (London: Council of the London Borough of Southwark, 1968).

2. Frederick Rogers, *The Early Environment of Robert Browning* (Privately printed, 1904), Newington District Library, Cuming Museum, library number 17609.

3. Information about the York Street Chapel is drawn from my visit there in 1970 and from Thomas W. Aveling, *Memorials of the Clayton Family* (London: Jackson, Walford, and Hodder, 1867); E. J. Orford, *The Book of Walworth* (Walworth: Browning Hall Adult School, 1925); Rosalyn Dunnico, "A Short History of the Browning Street Church," *BSN* 10 (Dec. 1980): 8–11. The building burned down in 1978 [RSK's note].

4. Blanch, *Ye Parish*, 368.

5. Daniel Hipwell, "Browning's Maternal Ancestors," *Notes and Queries* 11 (Apr. 3, 1897): 261–62. Also Maynard, 27, 31, 360–61.

6. Domett, 212.

7. Rogers, *Early Environment*.

8. RB to EBB [Aug. 26, 1846], *BC*, 13:299.

9. *Collections*, A679 (ABL), A2189 (ABL).

417

10. Ibid., A721 (ABL), A1171 (whereabouts unknown).

11. W. J. Stillman, *Autobiography of a Journalist*, quoted in Griffin and Minchin, 36.

12. Sharp, 25.

13. *RBAD*, 104.

14. Quoted by Miller, 8, from a passage deleted by Leonard Huxley from his volume of Elizabeth's letters to her sister Henrietta.

15. Most of his books at ABL have "Rob Browning" stamped in ink on the flyleaf or title page.

16. "Robert Browning's Ancestors," *BSP*, 3:31.

17. For a detailed challenge to Furnivall's procedure, evidence, and conclusions, and to Julia Markus's more recent speculations in *Dared and Done* (New York: Knopf, 1995), see Richard S. Kennedy, "Disposing of a New Myth: A Close Look at Julia Markus's Theory about the Brownings' Ancestry," *BSN* 26 (2000): 21–47. Some of the preceding sentences and wording have been taken from this article.

18. John Tittle traveled to England, studied for the ministry, was ordained a priest in the Church of England, and returned to Jamaica to become the pastor of two small parishes and a landowner (and also a slaveholder). After his move to St. Kitts, the document trail grows cold, except for two mortgages he signed. Although he had married, there are no records of the birth of his children nor any revealing how his daughter Margaret (Robert Browning's grandmother) and her brother and sister got to England. There is, however, a burial record indicating that John returned to Jamaica in 1758 and died shortly afterward. Jeanette Marks devotes three chapters of her excellent study *The Family of the Barrett* (New York: Macmillan, 1938) to the maternal ancestors of Robert Browning in the West Indies.

19. RB to EBB [Aug. 26, 1846], *BC*, 13:299.

20. Later, Rob Browning moved his family to the northern part of London, Islington, perhaps at the urging of his second wife, Jane Smith, who seemed uneasy with her stepchildren. Shortly before Rob's death, however, father and son reconciled, and Jane even moved back to Camberwell after her husband died.

21. RB to EBB [Aug. 27, 1846], *BC*, 13:304.

22. Mason, 87.

23. Ibid., 80.

24. Ibid., 87.

25. Mentioned in Rob Browning's will when he left no legacy to his son, Robert. The will is published in Furnivall, "Robert Browning's Ancestors," *BSP*, 3:39.

26. *Art Journal*, 1896, quoted by Griffin and Minchin, 8.

27. Orr, 104. See also Maynard, 395, n19. Maynard's research has identified the school and extended our knowledge of the curriculum there.

28. A remininscence of this has found its way into John Kenyon's poem *A Rhymed Plea for Tolerance* (London: Moxon, 1839). The lines are marked in the copy that Kenyon sent Mr. Browning (*Collections*, A1363 [Wellesley]).

29. Orr, 12.

30. Although most of his books are sermons or religious tracts, he owned Quarles's *Emblemes* (1777; *Collections*, A1913 [Berg]); Mandeville's *The Fable of the Bees* (1795; *Collections*, A1534 [Yale]); Milton's *The First Six Books of Paradise Lost* (1773; *Collections*,

A1611 [ABL]), a peculiar edition with a "translation" into prose; Turgenious's *Scots Poems* (1761; *Collections*, A2353 [whereabouts unknown]); Alexander Bower's *Life of Luther* (1813; *Collections*, A286 [Scripps College]); his grandfather's book William Martyn's *The Historie and Lives of Twenty Kings* (1628?; *Collections*, A1556 [ABL]). He is also said to have read Fielding's *Tom Jones* every year (Orr, 4).

31. Griffin and Minchin, 6–7.

32. RB to EBB [Aug. 13, 1846], *BC*, 13:251.

33. Domett, 212–13.

34. *Collections*, A1647 (San Francisco State University); A222 (whereabouts unknown); A1323 (whereabouts unknown); A623 (whereabouts unknown); A1645 (whereabouts unknown); A1259 (Texas); A1689 (whereabouts unknown); A1619 (whereabouts unknown); A1618 (whereabouts unknown).

35. Ibid., A240 (ABL); A2467 (ABL); A769 (Yale).

36. Ibid., A1440 (ABL); A184 (ABL); A774 (ABL).

37. Ibid., A1134 (ABL); A27 (Wellesley); A26 (ABL); A1255 (ABL).

38. Ibid., A2220 (whereabouts unknown); A1176 (ABL); A1183 (ABL); A1926 (whereabouts unknown); A2412 (ABL).

39. Wanley, preface.

40. *Collections*, A2188 (ABL); A2213 (ABL); A2409 (ABL); A1653 (whereabouts unknown); A1442 (ABL); A536 (ABL); A1274 (ABL).

41. Griffin and Minchin, 41.

42. *Collections*, A2496 (Yale).

Chapter 3

1. Orr, 26.

2. Ibid., 27–29.

3. Ibid., 26.

4. The Reverend Edward White, letter to Herbert Stead at the Robert Browning Settlement House, June 5, 1895 (Newington District Library, Cuming Museum).

5. When I visited the building in 1970, it was a theatrical warehouse, but the plaque was still on the wall on the left of the upper gallery [RSK's note].

6. Rogers, *Early Environment*.

7. RB to EBB [Jan. 15, 1846], *BC*, 11:317.

8. RB to EBB [Aug. 25, 1846], *BC*, 13:292–93.

9. W. Boyd Carpenter, *Some Pages of My Life* (London: Williams and Norgate, 1911), 202–3.

10. Orr, 23–25.

11. *Collections*, A940 (ABL), inscribed "Robert Browning 26th July 1819."

12. Ibid., A2430 (ABL), title page missing.

13. Balliol College Library.

14. RB to KB, Sept. 6, 1884, *More than Friend*, 52–53.

15. *Collections*, A1379 (Yale), dated Feb. 13, 1874.

16. Domett, 72.

17. *Collections*, A1978 (whereabouts unknown), notes inscribed on flyleaf. The Lee play, with the note on the title page, is at Balliol College (*Collections*, A1433).

18. Orr, 31.

19. Domett, 73.

20. SB to W. Hall Griffin, Nov. 11, 1902, Griffin Collection VI, 190. However, RB recorded one anecdote that shows Mr. Ready threatening punishment to a boy for a poor translation of a passage in the *Aeneid* (RB to EBB [Jan. 31, 1846], *BC*, 12:36).

21. The book has not survived, but *Collections*, A1213, indicates that EBB studied from the same edition at Hope End.

22. *Collections*, A1217 (ABL).

23. Mason, 13.

24. Kate Lemann to W. Hall Griffin, Nov. 8, 1904 (Griffin Collection VII, 91) speaks of Kate Cole's visit to the Browning household when Robert mentioned Christian in *Pilgrim's Progress*.

25. *Collections*, A1610 (Wellesley).

26. Ibid., A2473 (ABL), title page missing.

27. Ibid., A685 (ABL). There is also a Supplementary Volume (1705).

28. Ibid., A2412 (ABL).

29. When Robert read this abbreviated history of the popes, he got a lurid picture of the Roman Church.

30. Maynard, 181, speculates that Miss Flower may have been one of Robert's music teachers.

31. Edmund Gosse, "The Early Writings of Robert Browning," *Century Magazine* (Dec. 1881): 191.

32. RB letter to Fanny Haworth, Aug. 1, 1837, Orr, 102; Sharp, 30.

33. Hood, introduction, xii.

34. E. F. Bridell-Fox, appendix 2 in Moncure D. Conway, *Centenary History of the South Place Chapel* (London: Williams and Norgate, 1894), 153.

35. A good account of the Flower sisters is found in Richard Garnett, *The Life of W. J. Fox, Public Teacher and Social Reformer* (London: John Lane, 1910). Garnett also suggests that they are depicted in fictional guise in Harriet Martineau, *Five Years of Youth, or Sense and Sentiment* (1831).

36. There is some confusion and controversy over Mrs. Orr's original identification of these two poems as being part of *Incondita* (34). Although other scholars still follow her testimony, I agree with Maynard (427, n40) that they were not poems from *Incondita*. All testimony indicates that *Incondita* was written when RB was twelve or thirteen and that it was Eliza Flower who copied the verses. These two poems were copied by Sarah Flower, who writes about them as something new and gives RB's age as fourteen [RSK's note].

37. This letter, dated May 31, 1827, first appeared in a note by bookseller Bertram Dobell on "The Earliest Poems of Robert Browning" in *Cornhill Magazine* January 1914. Fox's daughter, Eliza F. Bridell-Fox, had sent both the manuscript of *Incondita* and, later, this letter plus "a fragment of verse" to Browning after the death of her father, who had kept the material all his life. Although Browning destroyed the copy of *Incondita* as we have seen, he overlooked the letter and "fragment of verse," which remained among his papers at the time of the Sotheby auction in 1913. They were purchased by

Dobell, who published both the poems and an extract from the letter in his *Cornhill* article. The manuscript of both the letter and the two poems is now held by ABL, *Collections*, E134.

38. From Orr, 33–34, to DeVane, 555.

39. Frederick Pottle, *Shelley and Browning: A Myth and Some Facts* (Chicago: Pembroke Press, 1923).

40. Orr, 40.

41. Probably a pirated edition, for Shelley's privately printed edition of ninety copies was very scarce (Pottle, *Shelley and Browning*, 21). Perhaps this was the book that Sharp refers to (30) in his story of RB first finding a work of Shelley at a secondhand bookstall.

42. *Shelley, Poetical Works*, ed. Thomas Hutchinson (London: Oxford University Press, 1970), 812.

43. Orr, 42.

44. Conway, *Centenary History*, 45–46. Although a Unitarian minister, Fox at this time still believed in the authority of the Bible, a position that he later rejected.

45. Orr, 45–46.

46. Griffin and Minchin, 50, who give as the source "the brother" of the Reverend Edward White, who probably was interviewed by Griffin, for there is no information about this in the Griffin papers.

47. George Clayton, *A Course of Sermons on Faith and Practice* (London, 1839).

48. Douglas Allport, *Collections, Illustrative of the Geology, History, Antiquities and Associations of Camberwell and the Neighborhood* (Camberwell, 1841). Twelve parishioners who were dissatisfied with the minister of St. Giles Church broke off to found Camden Chapel in 1796. It was finally licensed as an Episcopal Chapel in 1830, and Henry Melvill, then a Fellow of St. Peter's, Cambridge, was sent to be its minister. The building, in the shape of a T, held two thousand people.

49. A letter from SB referred to in Rogers, *Early Environment*.

50. *Sermons by Henry Melvill* (London: Rivington, 1833), flyleaf missing (*Collections*, A1583 [ABL]). Four other volumes of Melvill's sermons are in ABL, all with Sarianna's name inscribed.

51. Sermon IX, "St. Paul as a Tentmaker."

52. Sermon VII, "The Power of Religion to Strengthen the Intellect."

53. SB to W. Hall Griffin, Nov. 11, 1902. Griffin Collection VI, 190. She was about ten years old when the family moved there (ca. 1824).

54. Orr, 43.

55. Ibid., 44.

56. See Herbert Eveleth Green, "Browning's Knowledge of Music," *PMLA* 62 (1947): 1095–99, for a convincing discussion of RB's musical ability and technical understanding of music.

57. Maynard (254–57) has tracked down many details about this tutor, including his textbook, *La Gil Blas de la Jeunesse, A L'Usage des Ecoles* (London: Whittaker and Co. and William Pickering, 1835), although Miller (22) had identified the book in 1953.

58. "Prospectus," University College London, *Documents and Notices* I (1825–1829).

59. Quoted in H. Hale Bellot, *University College London 1826–1926* (London: University of London Press, 1929), 67.

60. Quoted from *John Bull* (July 1825) by Negley Harte and John Norte, *The World of UCL 1820–1990*, rev. ed. (London: University College London, 1991).

61. Charles Newman, *The Evolution of Medical Education in the Nineteenth Century* (London: Oxford University Press, 1957); and Zachary Cope, *The Royal College of Surgeons of England, A History* (London: Anthony Blond, 1959).

62. Bellot, *University College*, 65.

63. *Statement of the Council of the University of London Explanatory of the Nature and Objects of the Institution* (London: Longmans, Rees, et al., 1827).

64. University College London (hereinafter UCL), Watson Library.

65. *Statement of the Council*, 1827.

66. Miller, 16.

67. UCL, *Documents*, vol. 1, "Council Meeting, Sept. 30, 1828."

68. Ibid., "Outlines of the Courses of Lectures: Greek Language, Literature, and Antiquities."

69. Ibid., "Warden's Announcement #46."

70. Ibid., "Outlines of the Courses of Lectures: Roman Language, Literature, and Antiquities."

71. Ibid., "Warden's Announcement #46."

72. Ibid., "Outlines of the Courses of Lectures: German Language and Literature"; and Ludwig von Muhlenfels, *An Introductory Lecture Delivered in the University of London, Oct. 30, 1828* (London: John Taylor, 1828).

73. UCL, *Documents*, vol. 1, "Supplement to the Course Outline," 39.

74. Bellot, *University College*, 89.

75. See also Maynard's perceptive discussion of RB's university experience, 270–81.

76. Dec. 13, 1842, and Mar. 5, 1843, *RBAD*, 49, 52.

77. Letter signed W. S., *Times* (London), Dec. 14, 1889.

78. Edmund Gosse, *Robert Browning: Personalia* (Boston: Houghton, Mifflin, 1890), 26.

79. Gosse, *Personalia*, 26; Orr, 49–51.

Chapter 4

1. RB to EBB [May 24, 1845], *BC*, 10:234.

2. John Pettigrew, preface to Pettigrew and Collins, 1:xx.

3. Aug. 9, 1837, *BC*, 3:265.

4. *Collections*, A2173 (ABL), no date. See Thurman Los Hood, "Browning's Ancient Classical Sources," *Harvard Studies in Classical Philology* 33 (1922): 79–180, for a detailed listing of RB's references and allusions to Greek and Latin works in his poems and plays. See also RB's letter to Monclar, Dec. 5–7, 1834, *BC*, 3:112.

5. *Collections*, A885 (whereabouts unknown).

6. *BC*, 12:49 and 4:262.

7. RB explained in a footnote in *Dramatic Lyrics*, 1842: "I had better say perhaps that the above is nearly all retained of a tragedy I composed, much against my endeavour, while in bed with a fever two years ago—it went further into the story of Hippolytus and Aricia; but when I got well, putting only thus much down at once, I soon forgot the remainder."

8. There is a clear record of RB's reading of all the tragedies of Euripides and Sopho-

cles (as well as all the comedies of Aristophanes) during his summer holidays in the 1860s, in notations in his traveling set of Greek classics, 12 volumes, *Collections*, A891 (ABL), but these are likely to have been second readings for pleasure.

9. *Collections*, A61 (whereabouts unknown).

10. Ibid., A874 (whereabouts unknown).

11. Ibid., A49 (ABL); [Pons Aug. in Alletz], *Connoissance des Poetes Latins les plus célèbres* (Paris, 1751–1752).

12. *Collections*, A2147 (whereabouts unknown), 1767?

13. Ibid., A2066 (ABL).

14. Ibid., A1841 (whereabouts unknown).

15. Ibid., A2229 (whereabouts unknown); inscribed by RB, Senior, "R. Browning ejus liber, 1803."

16. RB to Monclar, Dec. 5–7, 1834, *BC*, 3:111.

17. *Collections*, A707 (whereabouts unknown), *Chefs-d'oeuvres de Pierre Corneille*, 4 vols. (1821); and A708 (ABL), *Oeuvres Diverses de Pierre Corneille* (1740).

18. RB comments on seeing a performance of Elisa Rachel in *Phèdre*; RB to EBB [July 16, 1846], *BC*, 13:167.

19. In RB's poem "The Glove" (1845) Ronsard is the speaker; an epigraph from Marot precedes RB's *Pauline* (1833).

20. *Collections*, A1919 (whereabouts unknown), 3 vols., 1820. Also RB refers to Rabelais in "Sibrandus Schafnaburgensis" (1844).

21. *Collections*, A1634 (whereabouts unknown), 1593, a gift to RB from Captain Pritchard.

22. RB cites Rousseau's work in the article in the *Trifler* (Maynard, 381).

23. RB discusses French novelists in RB to EBB [Apr. 27, 1846], *BC*, 12:281–82.

24. RB to EBB [July 16, 1846], *BC*, 13:167.

25. *BC*, 5:356. RB sends the book to Domett, May 22, 1842, adding "I mean to send you more of Hugo's books when I can get them" (*RBAD*, 38).

26. Orr, 32.

27. RB to EBB [Jan. 17, 1846], *BC*, 11:323.

28. See Maynard, 304–6, for a detailed account of Cerutti and his teaching methods.

29. *Collections*, A168 (Balliol College). Cerutti also had his pupils use his *New Italian Grammar*, 2nd ed. (1828); *Collections*, A602 (ABL). Daniello Bartoli, *Dé Simboli Trasportati al Morale* (London: C. Armandi, 1830).

30. On Nov. 16, 1838, RB purchased [Thomas Penrose], *A Sketch of the Lives and Writings of Dante and Petrarch. With some Account of Italian and Latin Literature in the Fourteenth Century* (1790). *Collections*, A1833 (Berg Collection).

31. Although RB described the tragedies to EBB as "coulourless as sallad [*sic*] grown under a garden glass with matting over it" (*BC*, 10:184), he included three volumes of them in his traveling set of Italian masters. *Collections*, A43 (ABL), 1821.

32. Maynard, 34. See also S. G. Pomeroy, *Little-Known Sisters of Well-Known Men* (Boston: Dana Estes, 1912), 143–79, for a summary of Sarianna's life based on the biographies and letters that were published before 1912.

33. *Collections*, A611 (ABL).

34. Ibid., A566 (ABL).

35. Ibid., A2314 (ABL), inscribed "Sarianna Browning from Miss Goodson 1826."

36. Ibid., A14 (ABL) in the Murray's Family Library Dramatic Series, No. 4 (1831), inscribed "Sarianna Browning July 25, 1835."

37. Ibid., A2424 (ABL).

38. *BC,* 12:24.

39. Ibid., 11:207.

40. Ibid., 11:247.

41. *Collections,* A662 (Heydon Collection), 1740.

42. *BC,* 12:160.

43. *Collections,* A2422 (ABL).

44. Ibid., A1318 (whereabouts unknown), 4 vols., 1783.

45. Ibid., A1274, inscribed by RB, Senior, "In Chatterton's works is a Sermon (or Homily) said to have been composed by the fictitious Poet Rowley—every sentence of which was taken from the first (& scarce) edition of these Sermons." RB has added in 1870 "(This note of my Father's refers to the singular discovery I made of this fact, many years before.)"

46. Ibid., A1534 (Yale), 1795.

47. *BC,* 12:280.

48. *Collections,* A2164 (whereabouts unknown), no date.

49. Ibid., A1914 (ABL).

50. In part 2, Quarles presents types of a different sort, weak and weary souls who need God's help.

51. *BC,* 6:221.

52. RB to EBB [Apr. 30, 1845], *BC,* 10:183–84.

53. EBB to RB [July 11, 1845], *BC,* 10:301. EBB accuses RB of reading *Sybil* at unlawful hours.

54. *BC,* 6:353.

55. Orr, 49.

56. Mason, 67, 72. However, there may have been more closeness than Mason indicates, for one of Sarianna's books, *The Contributions of Q. Q. to a Periodical Work* by Jane Taylor (*Collections,* A2258 [ABL]), is inscribed as a gift "from my mother Jany 1827."

57. Mason, 80.

58. W. Hall Griffin first discovered the information on the Colloquials, the research about which is made clear by the many letters in the Griffin Collection, BL Add. Mss. 45558–64. His article, "Early Friends of Robert Browning," *Contemporary Review* 87 (Mar. 1905): 427–46, first described RB's association with the group. John Maynard pursued the research further and developed the fullest treatment of this aspect of RB's life (96–112). He also turned up a copy of *The Trifler* in the Harvard Library.

59. Emily Secretan to Griffin, Oct. 21, 1904, Griffin Collection VII.

60. *Collections,* A1634 (whereabouts unknown).

61. Ibid., A624 (University of London).

62. Frederick Young to Emma Young, Oct. 23, 1904, Griffin Collection VII.

63. Griffin's notes, Griffin Collection III.

64. Emma Young to Emily Secretan, Oct. 21, 1904, Griffin Collection VII.

65. Edward Young was also in business with Frederick Young connected with the dockyard. John Oldfield, the secretary of the group, was from Camberwell. Robert and William Baker lived in Church Row along with the Dowsons and the Youngs. Many of

the members were interrelated by blood or by marriage. Chris Dowson married Alfred Domett's sister Mary.

66. Domett, 166. RB "in young days looked delicate in health" (Domett, 96).

67. Emily (Dowson)Secretan to Griffin, Oct. 21, 1904, Griffin Collection VII.

68. J. Arnould to A. Domett, n.d., *RBAD*, 86.

69. Emily Secretan to Griffin, Oct. 21, 1904, Griffin Collection VII.

70. Maynard, appendix C, 380–82.

71. The National Gallery did not open its doors in Trafalgar Square until 1838.

72. For further information on the gallery see D. G. Banwell, *Allyn's College of God's Gift: 350th Anniversary 1619–1969* (Dulwich, 1969); *A Brief Catalogue of the Pictures in Dulwich College Picture Gallery* (Dulwich, 1953); and *Paintings from the Dulwich College Picture Gallery* (Dulwich, 1954).

73. RB to EBB, Mar. 3, 1846, *BC*, 12:124.

74. The painting by Aert de Gelder was attributed to Rembrandt in RB's time.

75. RB was thoroughly familiar with the work of Brouwer, a pupil of Frans Hals, for Brouwer was his father's favorite painter. In an essay that RB, Senior, wrote on Brouwer, he called him "the greatest painter of the 17th century who followed the line of picturesque figures and conversations" ("Adriaan Brouwer" 15, *Collections*, J60 [ABL]).

Chapter 5

1. Browning's penciled note written at the end of *Pauline*, Victoria and Albert Museum, Forster Collection, 1043 F48D.46.

2. *Robert Browning: Personalia* (Boston: Houghton Mifflin, 1890), 27.

3. Another note written in *Pauline*, Forster Collection.

4. SB to W. Hall Griffin, Griffin Collection VI, 190.

5. Rpt. in *BC*, 3:341–42.

6. [Mar. 4, 1833], *BC*, 3:73.

7. [Mar. 28, 1833], *BC*, 3:75.

8. Rpt. in *BC*, 3:341–44.

9. Quoted in Richard Garnett, *The Life of W. J. Fox* (London: John Lane, 1910), 109. The words appeared in his essay, "Local Logic."

10. (Apr. 6, 1833): 216; rpt. in *BC*, 3:345.

11. (Mar. 23, 1833): 183; rpt. in *BC*, 3:340.

12. (Aug. 1833): 668; rpt. in *BC*, 3:346.

13. Mar. 17, 1835, *BC*, 3:130.

14. [Jan. 15, 1846], *BC*, 11:317. The sheets were later destroyed.

15. F. A. Hayek in *John Stuart Mill and Harriet Taylor* (Chicago: University of Chicago Press, 1951), 43, asserts that the comments "beautiful" alongside certain passages are in a different hand from Mill's, and he declares they are by Harriet Taylor. I did not perceive a difference, but since Hayek was editing the Mill-Taylor correspondence, one must bow to his opinion. Evidently, they discussed the poem together before Mill wrote his review [RSK's note].

16. *Pauline*, Forster Collection.

17. DeVane, 47.

18. RB to Ripert-Monclar, Aug. 9, 1837, *BC*, 3:265.

19. Orr, 48.

20. *Collections*, A224 (Wellesley). RB eventually thought of this as his family Bible, for he recorded genealogical information in it.

21. ABL.

22. Orr, 64.

23. Katharine Bronson, "Browning in Venice," *More than Friend*, 156.

24. Griffin and Minchin, 64–65.

25. *Collections*, A1807 (Heydon Collection).

26. Griffin and Minchin, 69–72.

27. RB to FJF, Oct. 11, 1881, Hood, 199.

28. "The Ironic Pattern of Browning's *Paracelsus*," *University of Toronto Quarterly* 34 (1964): 68.

29. RB to W. J. Fox, Mar. 27, 1835, *BC*, 3:130.

30. The diary is quoted in A. M. W. Stirling, *The Merry Wives of Battersea and the Gossip of Centuries* (London: Robert Hale, 1946), 122. It was found among the papers of Old Battersea House.

31. See Richard Garnett, *The Life of W. J. Fox, Public Teacher and Social Reformer, 1786–1864* (London: John Lane, 1910), for full details about Fox's ideas, his career, and the problems of his personal life; and Moncure Conway, *Centenary History of South Place Chapel* (London: Williams and Norgate, 1894), for further details about him as a Unitarian minister and about his literary circle.

32. Rogers, *Early Environment*. Also C. R. Tracy, in "Browning's Heresies," *Studies in Philology* 33 (Oct. 1936): 616, records a letter from Wallis Mansford, one of the oldest members of the chapel, who states that RB "often attended the Chapel under Fox's ministry." Also, according to the diary of Catherine Bromley, RB regularly attended the South Place Chapel. Diary entries are summarized in Stirling, *Merry Wives*, 119.

33. Eliza F. Bridell-Fox, "Memories," *Girl's Own Paper* (July 19, 1890): 657–61. See also Garnett, *Life of Fox*; and Conway, *Centenary History*, passim.

34. Stirling, *Merry Wives*, 120.

35. Ibid., 121.

36. Ibid., 122.

37. [Apr. 8, 1835], *BC*, 3:133.

38. RB to W. J. Fox, Apr. 16, 1835, *BC*, 3:134.

39. Orr, 52–53.

40. (Aug. 22, 1835): 640; rpt. in *BC*, 3:350.

41. *Paracelsus*, Victoria and Albert Museum, Forster Collection F35. N. 31.

42. *Examiner* (Sept. 6, 1835): 563–65; rpt. in *BC*, 3:350–52.

43. Rpt. in *BC*, 3:352–57.

Chapter 6

1. Eliza F. Bridell-Fox, "Memories," *Girl's Own Paper* 11 (July 19, 1890): 657–61.

2. Nov. 27, 1835, Macready, 1:264.

3. Dec. 7, 1835, Macready, 1:265.

4. Gosse, *Personalia*, 39.

5. Percy Fitzgerald in *John Forster by One of His Friends* (London: Chapman and Hall, 1903) offers a brief, candid portrait of Forster, full of anecdotes. See also James A. Davies, *John Forster: A Literary Life* (Leicester: Leicester University Press, 1983).

6. Feb. 1, 1836, Macready, 1:272.

7. Dec. 31, 1835, Macready, 1:267.

8. Mary Russell Mitford, *Recollections of a Literary Life* (New York: Harper, 1852), 180. For an account of the evening, see also Macready, 1:319–20; and the two earliest biographies (Sharp, 77–78; and Orr, 87–88). Sharp is the source of an anecdote that Wordsworth leaned across the table with an amiable gesture saying "I am pleased to drink your health, Mr. Browning." However, Betty Miller has pointed out in "'This Happy Evening,' the Story of *Ion*," *Twentieth Century* 64 (1953): 57, that Crabb Robinson's diary indicates that he took Wordsworth home before the toasts began. See *The Diary of Henry Crabb Robinson*, ed. Derek Hudson (London: Oxford University Press, 1967), 158. Sharp's anecdote probably came from Sarianna, who sometimes got her details mixed. The gesture of courtesy is not characteristic of the self-centered Wordsworth. It is much more typical of the generous-hearted Landor, who later befriended young Browning in many ways. For a detailed study of the literary relations between Browning and Wordsworth, see John Haydn Baker, *Browning and Wordsworth* (Madison, NJ: Fairleigh Dickinson University Press, 2004).

9. Orr, 88.

10. May 28, 1836, *BC*, 3:173.

11. Feb. 16, 1836, Macready, 1:277.

12. For an account of Strafford's service to the king, his trial, and execution, see C. V. Wedgewood, *The King's Peace* (New York: Macmillan, 1955), 235–429. Helen Clarke in *Browning's England* (New York: Baker and Taylor, 1908), 181–82, summarizes RB's mixture of historical and fictional material in his play. RB drew heavily upon the historical works in his father's library for his sense of the period and its language.

13. Nov. 21, 1836, Macready, 1:361.

14. Nov. 23, 1836, Macready, 1:362.

15. Mar. 30, 1837, Macready, 1:383.

16. Apr. 5, 1837, Macready, 1:385.

17. Apr. 7, 1837, Macready, 1:385.

18. Fitzgerald, *John Forster*, 36.

19. Apr. 12, 1837, Macready, 1:387.

20. Apr. 14, 1837, Macready, 1:387.

21. Apr. 14, 1837, Macready, 1:388.

22. Eliza Flower to Sarah Fox, undated letter, Orr, 91.

23. Macready, 1:392.

24. Frederick Young to Emma Young, Oct. 23, 1904, British Library, Griffin Collection VII, 74.

25. Mar. 19, 1837, Macready, 1:380.

26. *Edinburgh Review* (July 1837): 132–51; rpt. in *BC*, 3:408–15 (see 412).

27. Apr. 5, 1837, Macready, 1:385.

28. Browning's notes on Macready's diary, Hood, 297.

29. Apr. 29 and 28, 1837, Macready, 1:391, 389.

30. *Autobiographic Notes*, quoted in Thomas R. Lounsbury, *The Early Literary Career of Robert Browning* (New York: Scribner's, 1911), 55–56.

31. *Morning Chronicle* (May 2, 1837): 3; rpt. in *BC*, 3:388.

32. *Examiner* (May 7, 1837): 294–95; rpt. in *BC*, 3:400–401.

33. (May 4, 1837): 3; rpt. in *BC*, 3:393–94.

34. May 22, 1837, Macready, 1:396.

35. Eliza Flower to Sarah Fox, undated, Orr, 91.

Chapter 7

1. Garnett, *Life of Fox*, 194.

2. Orr, 37.

3. NS 8 (Oct. 1834): 712.

4. A letter from the rector of Elstree Rectory to W. Hall Griffin (Griffin Collection VII, 117) gives the birth record of Euphrasia Fanny Haworth as May 27, 1802.

5. Griffin and Minchin, 139. She was also a guest at the *Ion* supper and perhaps a source for the account in Sharp and Orr.

6. Orr, 101.

7. RB to Fanny Haworth [July 24, 1838], *BC*, 4:67–68.

8. RB's record of his itinerary, *BC*, 4:xii.

9. But see a different account of his route after leaving Venice in a letter to his brother-in-law GB, dated Oct. 22, 1889, in which he says he went directly to Asolo, "the first spot of Italian soil I ever set foot upon—having proceeded to Venice by sea" (*George Barrett*, 329).

10. RB to EBB [July 13, 1845], *BC*, 10:305.

11. *Sordello*, 6:789–93.

12. *Collections*, A206 (ABL).

13. Bridell-Fox, "Robert Browning," 764.

14. Letter to Mrs. Lance, Sept. 5, 1847, Griffin Collection V. Someone named "Ainslie" was also included in this inner circle. All that is known about him is that he was a member of the firm Dowson, Ainslie, and Martineau, Solicitors, 39 Victoria Street in Limehouse (Griffin Collection III). For full information on Domett and Arnould see Frederic G. Kenyon's introduction to *RBAD*; Domett; and W. Hall Griffin, "Robert Browning and Alfred Domett," *Contemporary Review* 87 (Jan. 1905): 95–115.

15. In time, Domett became a government administrator, then a member of the New Zealand parliament, and eventually prime minister for a brief period. During these years he continued to write verse and later published what has become known as the "epic poem of New Zealand," *Ranolf and Amohia* (1872). See Domett.

16. *BC*, 4:253.

17. Ibid., 3:134.

18. Rpt. in *BC*, 4:416.

19. Rpt. in *BC*, 4:417.

20. Rpt. in *BC*, 4:422.

21. *Autobiography*, quoted in Lounsbury, *Early Literary Career*, 78; and *BC*, 4:326.

22. Sharp, 109–10.

23. Ibid., 110.

24. Ibid.

25. Carlyle to RB, June 21, 1841, *BC*, 5:64–65.

26. BL-KT, Ashley, 247.

27. [May 1840], *BC*, 4:269.

28. Ibid.

29. "Paracelsus; Sordello; Pippa Passes; King Victor and King Charles; and Straf-ford," *Church of England Quarterly Review* (Oct. 1842); rpt. in *BC*, 6:384.

30. [May 1840], *BC*, 4:269.

31. Preface to Pettigrew and Collins, 1:xx.

32. Lecture at the Philadelphia Literary Fellowship, Spring 1965.

33. For example, J. Hillis Miller, *The Disappearance of God* (Cambridge: Harvard University Press, 1963); Thomas J. Collins, *Browning's Moral-Aesthetic Theory 1833–1855* (Lincoln: University of Nebraska Press, 1967); Clyde de L. Ryals, *Becoming Browning* (Columbus: Ohio State University Press, 1983); Stewart W. Holmes, "Browning's *Sordello* and Jung," *PMLA* 56 (1941): 758–96; and, best of all, David Latané, Jr., *Browning's Sordello and the Aesthetics of Difficulty* (Victoria, B.C.: University of Victoria Monograph Series No. 40, 1987), which examines the beginning of a shift in attitude among poets and critics of the early nineteenth century who came to look with some disdain on writers who appealed to a broad reading public and to regard with respect those who found, in Milton's phrase, a "fit audience though few."

34. George Bornstein, "Pound's Parleyings with Browning," *Poetic Remaking: The Art of Browning, Yeats, and Pound* (University Park: Pennsylvania State University Press, 1988), 123, 137, 132.

35. The fullest treatment is found in Mark Weinstein, *William Edmondstoune Aytoun and the Spasmodic Controversy* (New Haven: Yale University Press, 1968). Weinstein declares that Charles Kingsley was the first critic to use the term *spasmodic* in an article, "Thoughts on Shelley and Byron," in *Fraser's*, Nov. 1835. But we should also be aware that a reviewer of *Sordello* in the *Monthly Chronicle*, May 1840, refers back to *Strafford* as a "tragedy in a constant *spasm*" (rpt. in *BC*, 4:421). Aytoun did not begin his attack on the "Spasmodic School" until his review of Longfellow's *Golden Legend* in *Blackwood's*, Feb. 1852. In 1856, he included Browning as a member of the "School of Bailey" in an article in *Blackwood's* (79:125–38), and placed both *Men and Women* and Tennyson's *Maud* in the Spasmodic "family."

36. "The Early Writings of Robert Browning," *Century Magazine* 23 (Dec. 1881): 189–200, later incorporated into *Robert Browning: Personalia* (see page 36).

37. *The Victorian Temper* (Cambridge: Harvard University Press, 1951), 42–43.

Chapter 8

1. *BC*, 4:111.

2. Macready, 1:481–82.

3. *Collections*, A2412 (ABL), page 611.

4. Mrs. Sutherland Orr, *A Handbook to the Works of Robert Browning* (London: George Bell, 1890), 55.

5. Aug. 21, 1839, Macready, 2:22.

6. Browning's historical information came from the *Biographie universelle* and other works. See DeVane, 99–101.

7. Sept. 5, 1839, Macready, 2:23.

8. [July 1, 1837], *BC*, 3:257.

9. Macready, 2:72.

10. June 17, 1840, Macready, 2:64.

11. Aug. 3, 1840, Macready, 2:72.

12. Aug. 27, 1840, Macready, 2:76.

13. Sept. 15, 1840, Macready, 2:80.

14. [July 27?] [1840], *BC*, 4:293.

15. RB to Frank Hill, Dec. 15, 1884, Orr, 119.

16. The acting script of *A Blot in the 'Scutcheon* held by the Beinicke Library, Yale University, shows the cuts that both Macready and Browning made. See Joseph W. Reed, Jr., "Browning and Macready: The Final Quarrel," *PMLA* 75 (1960): 597–603, for a detailed discussion.

17. Quoted in Griffin and Minchin, 115. Dickens's letter, dated Nov. 25, 1842, was too long delayed to play any part in Macready's decision to accept RB's play for production. Perhaps its tardy arrival was the reason Forster never showed RB Dickens's glowing tribute. Griffin interpreted Forster's secrecy as evidence of some conspiracy between Forster and Macready. In any case, RB did not see the letter until it appeared in Forster's *Life of Charles Dickens* (1872).

18. RB to Alfred Domett, May 22, 1842, *BC*, 5:356.

19. RB to Frank Hill, Dec. 15, 1884, Orr, 119.

20. Helen Faucit Martin, "Desdemona," *Blackwood's* 129 (Mar. 1881): 326. She felt that this attitude on the part of the players was chiefly the reason that "a play so thoroughly dramatic failed despite its painful story, to make the great success which was justly its due."

21. The sources for the account of the production of the play are these: Macready; Helen Faucit Martin (cited above); Joseph Arnould to Alfred Domett, *RBAD*, 62–67; RB to Frank Hill, letter quoted in Orr, 118–25; RB to William Archer, Hood, 297–98; Gosse, *Personalia*, 62–69.

22. Feb. 10, 1843, Macready, 2:196.

23. Gosse, *Personalia*, 65–66.

24. Ibid., 66.

25. Yale MS (see n16).

26. Feb. 10, 1843, Macready, 2:196.

27. Feb. 11, 1843, Macready, 2:196.

28. After the first performance, Macready changed the ending to have Tresham retire to a monastery despite Browning's protests. See the review in the *Weekly Chronicle* (Feb. 19, 1843); rpt. in *BC*, 6:403.

29. *Weekly Chronicle* (Feb. 12, 1843); rpt. in *BC*, 6:394.

30. RB to Frank Hill, Dec. 21, 1884, Orr, 124.

31. Mason, 82–83.

32. *RBAD*, 65–67.

33. Feb. 18, 1843, rpt. in *BC*, 6:401.

34. Feb. 13, 1843, rpt. in *BC*, 6:395, 398.

35. Feb. 13, 1843, rpt. in *BC*, 6:399.

36. Feb. 18, 1843, rpt. in *BC*, 6:400.

37. *RBAD*, 64–65.

38. Ibid., 55.

39. [Jan. 11, 1846], *BC*, 11:309.

40. For the widespread prejudice against stage production that was voiced by Romantic drama critics, the fullest discussion is in Janet Ruth Heller, *Coleridge, Lamb, Hazlitt, and the Reader of Drama* (Columbia: University of Missouri Press, 1990). Coleridge's lectures on Shakespeare and Lamb's essay "On the Tragedies of Shakespeare, Considered with Reference to Their Fitness for Stage Representation" were especially influential.

41. Sept. 2, 1835, Macready, 1:246.

42. Apr. 8, 1836, Macready, 1:290.

43. Abraham Maslow, *Toward a Psychology of Being* (Princeton: Van Nostrand, 1968), offers a theory about the creative process: he distinguishes between "primary creativity," which involves the artist's expression of his initial inspiration, and "secondary creativity," which refers to deletions, additions, structural rearrangements, and linguistic revisions and which require critical and analytical powers.

Chapter 9

1. A typescript in the Manor House Library for the Borough of Lewisham summarizing the research of the librarians during the years 1949 to 1956, including information from File 9 of the Deptford Files. I am also grateful to Ms. Patricia Knight, the school historian, for information about the Haberdasher's Aske's Girls School [RSK's note].

2. Letter to W. Hall Griffin, Nov. 11, 1902, Griffin Collection VI, 190. John Coulter, "The Browning House at New Cross," *BSN* 15 (1985–86): 3–19, has an admirable account of the history of the area and surroundings of the house. See also Maynard, 33–34, 66–67. For Sarianna's sketch of the dwelling, see *BC*, 12, frontispiece.

3. Letter to W. Hall Griffin, Nov. 11, 1902.

4. Mason, 88–89.

5. Orr, 19.

6. Griffin and Minchin, 49.

7. RB to Fanny Haworth [Dec. 16, 1841], *BC*, 5:189.

8. *Pippa Passes* was advertised as "nearly ready" on the back pages of *Sordello*, which appeared in Mar. 1840.

9. RB to EBB [Oct. 18, 1845], *BC*, 11:131.

10. Oct. 2, 1841, rpt. in *BC*, 5:396.

11. Dec. 11, 1841, rpt. in *BC*, 5:399.

12. *Spectator* (Apr. 17, 1841); rpt. in *BC*, 5:392.

13. *Atlas* (May 1, 1841); rpt. in *BC*, 5:394.

14. (July 10, 1841), rpt. in *BC*, 5:395.

15. Mar. 5, 1842, rpt. in *BC*, 5:400.

16. Apr. 30, 1842, rpt. in *BC*, 5:403.

17. *Examiner* (Apr. 2, 1842); rpt. in *BC*, 5:401–2.

18. RB to Alfred Domett, May 22, 1842; *BC*, 5:356.

19. Benjamin Willis Fuson, *Browning and His English Predecessors in the Dramatic Monolog*, Humanistic Studies 8 (Iowa City: State University of Iowa, 1948). Fuson's monograph is the most extensive and the soundest study of the history of the form.

20. For example, Oliver Elton, *The English Muse* (London: G. Bell, 1933), 12–13.

21. The review appeared in the *Englishman's Magazine*, Aug. 1831. A reprint appears in Walter E. Houghton and G. Robert Stange, eds. *Victorian Poetry and Poetics*, 2nd ed. (Boston: Houghton Mifflin, 1968), 848–60.

22. For example, see Claud Howard, "The Dramatic Monologue: Its Origin and Development," *Studies in Philology* 4 (1910): 60–61; Robert Langbaum, *The Poetry of Experience* (New York: Random House, 1957), 9–74; Park Honan, *Browning's Characters* (New Haven: Yale University Press, 1961), 107–20; and Michael Mason, "Browning and the Dramatic Monologue," in *Robert Browning*, ed. Isobel Armstrong (Athens: Ohio University Press, 1975), 231.

23. Appendix to *Lyrical Ballads* (1802).

24. Allardyce Nicoll, *A History of Early Nineteenth-Century Drama, 1800–1850* (Cambridge: Cambridge University Press, 1930), 1:58–78.

25. Preface to *Poems* (1853).

26. Langbaum's stimulating study of the "dramatic monologue" has one additional weakness. He approaches the form from the direction of lyric poetry rather than the drama. Thus his idea that the dramatic monologue "derives its special effect from the tension between sympathy and moral judgment" goes wrong because he insists that the reader suspend judgment of the speaker even if he is as much of a villain as the duke in "My Last Duchess" (82–85). H. B. Charlton, "Browning: The Making of the Dramatic Lyric," *Bulletin of the John Rylands Library* 35 (1953): 349–84, has a first-rate discussion of RB's poems, but like Langbaum, he makes no distinction among the kinds of dramatic verse. He holds to the one term, *dramatic lyric*.

27. See A. Dwight Culler, "Monodrama and the Dramatic Monologue," *PMLA* 90 (1975): 366–85.

28. In the 1863 publication of his collected poems, RB regrouped his short poems under the headings *Dramatic Lyrics*, *Dramatic Romances*, and *Men and Women*, but there seemed no clear guiding principle governing each group. (See, however, Lawrence Poston III, "Browning Rearranges Browning," *Studies in Browning and His Circle* 2.1 [1974]: 39–54; and John Woolford, *Browning the Revisionary* [Basingstoke: Macmillan, 1988], esp. chaps. 4 and 5.)

29. In his research, Park Honan could find no earlier use of the term *dramatic monologue* than 1878. John Woolford in *Browning the Revisionary* (St. Martin's Press, 1988), 100, has since discovered that William Stigand suggested this term to describe RB's poems when he reviewed *Dramatis Personae* in *Blackwood's* in 1864. Even so, the term did

not come into common use until late in the century, about the time Tennyson dedicated "this dramatic monologue" ("Locksley Hall Sixty Years After") to his wife. See Ben W. Fuson, "Tennyson's Chronological Priority over Browning in Use of the Dramatic Monologue before 1836," *Studies, Kobe College* 13 (1967): 17. On the other hand, the term *monodrama* is used three times by EBB in her letters of 1845 (*BC*, 10:1, 102, 233), and the second time she qualifies the term by adding, "not a long poem—but a mono-logue of Aeschylus as he sate a blind exile on the flats of Sicily and recounted the past to his own soul. . . ."

30. In a pioneering article, "The Dramatic Monologue," *PMLA* 62 (1947): 503–16, Ina Beth Sessions has offered a prescriptive definition of the dramatic monologue in its most fully developed form: it involves a speaker, an audience (listener), a specific occa-sion, revelation of character, interplay between speaker and audience, and dramatic action that takes place in the present. Although her definition is too restrictive, she is describing the dramatic monologue as it fits several of RB's highest achievements. Going far beyond Sessions in examining the problems of terminology, Park Honan (cited above) provides an excellent scholarly and critical discussion in his chapter "The Solitary Voice," 104–25. The two most important discussions of the dramatic mono-logue since Honan's book are those by Philip Drew and Michael Mason. Drew's discus-sion in *The Poetry of Robert Browning* (London: Methuen, 1970), 12–38, points out all of Langbaum's weaknesses and offers his own argument supporting an essential point: that in a Browning poem "The speaker understands himself and his own situation less thor-oughly than the reader" (32). Michael Mason, in a brilliant, lucid essay in *Robert Brown-ing*, ed. Isobel Armstrong (Writers and Their Background. London: G. Bell, 1974), 231–66, emphasizes the distinctive feature that Browning introduced into the dramatic monologue: that "the speaker *betrays* important aspects of his state of mind rather than *articulating* them" (234).

31. For such a short work, the poem has been the subject of an unusual number of critical discussions, as well as articles attempting to identify the duke, led on by Brown-ing's later supplying the subtitle "Ferrara" to "My Last Duchess" in 1849. See R. J. Berman, *Browning's Duke* (New York: Richards Rosen, 1972).

32. "The Mask of Browning's 'Count Gismond,'" *Philological Quarterly* 40 (1961): 153–55.

33. "A New Reading of 'Count Gismond,'" *Studies in Philology* 59 (1962): 83–95.

34. *BC*, 6:33–34.

35. RB to Fanny Haworth [Dec. 16, 1841], *BC*, 5:189.

36. In *Dramatic Lyrics*, there are no stage directions. For later versions, he added "He sings," "She speaks," and other indications of action.

37. Title later altered to "Rudel to the Lady of Tripoli."

38. Browning actually composed the poem while riding horseback (Domett, 96). The poem expresses the intense purpose of an Arab warrior riding to join Abd-el-Kadr, who was a chieftain long engaged in fighting against the French for Algerian independ-ence.

39. The Harvard copy of the first proof (*Dramatic Lyrics*, Widener 1. 7. 9) has a note, later canceled, which remarks that the lines were written while he was in bed with a fever in 1840 and that they dealt with the recovery of Hippolytus after his terrible accident

and with his love for Aricia. He states that he forgot his planned work after he got well from the fever.

40. An undated note by SB, on display at ABL, states that she showed the poem to Domett, who urged RB to include it in *Dramatic Lyrics.* But Domett was in New Zealand at this time.

41. *Collections,* A2412 (ABL); A685 (ABL); and A1580 (ABL).

42. The detail appears in [Richard Verstegan], *A Restitution of Decayed Intelligence in Antiquities* (Antwerp, 1605), although RB told FJF that he had not seen the book before he wrote the poem ("Notes on Browning's Poems," *BSP,* 1. 159). But Browning as a child must have heard other versions of the story besides Manley's and Collier's. See also Arthur Dickson, "Browning's Sources for 'The Pied Piper of Hamelin,'" *Studies in Philology* 23 (1926): 327–36.

Chapter 10

1. RB to Chris Dowson, Mar. 10 [1844], *BC,* 8:252.

2. Orr, 127.

3. [July 1, 1837], *BC,* 3:257.

4. For critical discussion of the courtly love tradition, see C. S. Lewis, *The Allegory of Love* (Oxford: Oxford University Press, 1936); and D. W. Robertson, *A Preface to Chaucer* (Princeton: Princeton University Press, 1962), ch. 5.

5. William C. DeVane, "The Virgin and the Dragon," *Yale Review* 37 (1947): 33–46; rpt. in Drew, *Essays,* 96–109. DeVane brings a lifetime's knowledge about RB's work to bear upon his use of the Andromeda story as a "private myth." See also Maynard, 150–51.

6. (Oct. 1842): 464–83; rpt. in *BC,* 6:381–88.

7. Sept. 31 [30], 1842, *BC,* 6:89.

8. (Nov. 26, 1842): 756–57; rpt. in *BC,* 6:388–90.

9. (Dec. 20, 1842): 5; rpt. in *BC,* 6:391–92.

10. (Apr. 1843): 357; rpt. in *BC,* 7:395.

11. (Oct. 1843): 430–48; rpt. in *BC,* 7:402–4.

12. *BC,* 7:404.

13. May 22 [1844], *BC,* 8:318.

14. Arthur Symons, *An Introduction to the Study of Browning* (London: Cassell, 1886) first hinted in a phrase that the speaker resembled the Marquise de Brinvilliers. She was a notorious poisoner in the court of Louis XIV who was executed in 1676 (François Bluche, *Louis XIV* [London: Blackwell, 1990], 274–75). Woolford and Karlin (2:218–19) suggest that Browning may have become familiar with her story in the *Biographie Universelle* or in Alexandre Dumas' *Crimes célèbres* (London, 1843).

15. RB to EBB [Feb. 26, 1845], *BC,* 10:99.

16. Donald Thomas, *Robert Browning: A Life within Life* (New York: Viking, 1983), has probed Browning's interest in criminality and insanity most fully in his chapter "The Madhouse and the Shrine." He sees Browning as having a Jekyll-and-Hyde personality.

17. July 31, 1844, *BC,* 9:69.

18. A surviving fragment of a page, *Collections*, E516 (Yale Library); *BC*, 11:189, n3.

19. In the copy of Bartoli in the Balliol College Library, RB has inserted a comment in ink (for Mrs. Orr in the 1880s) which says "Home-Thoughts, from Abroad" was written here in the endpapers of the book, but the penciled lines of the poem have been erased. It is my conjecture that RB was referring to the present poem, which had been published as part 2 of "Home-Thoughts, from Abroad" in *Dramatic Romances and Lyrics*. The poem that had been published as part 1 and was later given exclusively the title "Home-Thoughts, from Abroad" begins, "Oh, to be in England / Now that April's there" would hardly have been written in August. Nor would it have been written in 1838 on the first voyage to Italy, for RB told Fanny Haworth later that he had written only four lines of verse on that first trip. Although both Orr and Griffin accepted an 1838 date for "Home-Thoughts, from Abroad," DeVane, Irvine, and Woolford and Karlin all argue for a spring 1845 date, when RB sent a fair copy of it to EBB to read [RSK's note].

20. "The Ride to Ghent," as RB referred to it in his comment in the Balliol College copy of Bartoli, was written into the book "off the African coast." These penciled lines have also been erased.

21. *Pall Mall Gazette* (Dec. 31, 1889); quoted in Pettigrew and Collins, 1:1087.

22. RB to an unidentified correspondent, Mar. 7, 1884, *New Letters*, 300. For further details see Woolford and Karlin, 2:239–40.

23. RB and EBB discussed some of the likeness to Dick Turpin's ride in Ainsworth's novel *Rookwood*, but she acknowledged that "you have fairly distanced the rider in Rookwood here" by having three riders, each of whom has his particular experience ("EBB's Notes on RB's Poems," Wellesley College Library; *BC*, 11:387). See also Michael Meredith's comments in Woolford and Karlin, 2:240.

24. *Collections*, A1759.

25. Orr, 138.

26. RB to EBB [Nov. 21, 1845], *BC*, 11:188.

27. Orr, 136.

28. *Collections*, H566; these mementos of 1859 are now at Princeton.

29. Canto 4, stanzas 115–27.

30. RB to EBB [July 1, 1845], *BC*, 10:287.

31. *Rome: A Companion Guide* (New York: David McKay, 1865), 334. See also Carlo Faldi Guglielmi, *Roma: Basilica di S. Prassede* (Bologna: Poligraphici Editoriale, no date), the official illustrated guide, which also contains an extensive bibliography on the church.

32. Valery, *Historical, Literary, and Artistical Travels in Italy* (1839); see *BC*, 13:66, n4.

33. RB to EBB [July 10, 1846], *BC*, 13:147.

34. Ibid. [June 22, 1846], *BC*, 13:74.

35. Ibid. [July 31, 1846], *BC*, 13:211.

36. Orr, 137.

37. Joseph Arnould to Alfred Domett, Feb. 26, 1845, *BC*, 10:330.

38. RB to F. O. Ward, Feb. 18, 1845; *BC*, 10:83. For a good example of recent criticism of the poem, see E. Warwick Slinn, "Browning's Bishop Conceives a Tomb: Cultural Ordering as Cultural Critique," *Victorian Literature and Culture* 27 (1999): 251–67.

39. Orr, 104.

40. RB to John Kenyon, May 26, 1837, *BC*, 3:247.

41. Orr, 105; and *BC*, 3:316. See also Meredith R. Raymond, "John Kenyon: The Magnificent Dilettante," *Studies in Browning and His Circle* 14 (1986): 32–62, for a full biographical sketch.

42. EBB to MRM [July 15, 1841], *BC*, 5:75.

43. For example, *BC*, 6:111, 115.

44. EBB to MRM, Dec. 14, 1842, *BC*, 6:226.

45. Ibid., Oct. 15, 1842, *BC*, 6:105.

46. Ibid., Feb. 14, 1843, *BC*, 6:325.

47. Ibid. [July 15, 1841], *BC*, 5:75.

48. Ibid., Jan. 14, 1843, *BC*, 6:289.

49. Ibid., May 4 [1843], *BC*, 7:109.

50. RB to Alfred Domett, Feb. 23, 1845, *BC*, 10:89.

51. RB to EBB, Jan. 10, 1845, *BC*, 10:17–18.

Chapter 11

1. Jan. 11, 1845, *BC*, 10:20.

2. Ibid., 10:18–19.

3. Jan. 13, 1845, *BC*, 10:22.

4. Jan. 25, 1845, *BC*, 10:25–26.

5. Feb. 3, 1845, *BC*, 10:51.

6. EBB to RB [Aug. 25, 1846], *BC*, 13:296.

7. "Glimpses into My Own Life and Literary Character," *BC*, 1:350.

8. EBB to John Kenyon [Aug. 7, 1844], *BC*, 9:81.

9. EBB *Works*, 1:166.

10. Ibid., 1:164.

11. EBB to RB, Jan. 11, 1845, *BC*, 10:19.

12. Jan. 30, 1845, *BC*, 10:41.

13. Jan. 15, 1845, *BC*, 10:26.

14. Feb. 17, 1845, *BC*, 10:79.

15. Feb. 3, 1845, *BC*, 10:52.

16. [Feb. 11, 1845], *BC*, 10:69–70.

17. Feb. 17, 1845, *BC*, 10:79.

18. [Feb. 26, 1845], *BC*, 10:98–99.

19. Feb. 27, 1845, *BC*, 10:102. This monologue in unfinished form was copied out by RB after EBB's death. It was at first mistakenly attributed to him since it existed in his hand. It was first published under the title "Aeschylus' Soliloquy" in *Cornhill Magazine*, NS 35 (1913): 577–81.

20. Feb. 27, 1845, *BC*, 10:102–3.

21. [Mar. 11, 1845], *BC*, 10:118.

22. Ibid., *BC*, 10:120.

23. EBB to MRM, Mar. 18, 1845, *BC*, 10:127.

24. EBB *Works*, 6:309.

25. Elizabeth Moulton to EBB [Mar. 6, 1810], *BC*, 1:3.

26. EBB to Hugh Boyd [Aug. 11, 1838], *BC*, 4:77.

27. MRM to William Harness, July 1836, *BC*, 3:330 (Supporting Document 803).

28. Mar. 2, 1827, *BC*, 2:35.

29. EBB to John Kenyon [July 15, 1838], *BC*, 4:63.

30. [May 13, 1845], *BC*, 10:214.

31. [May 5–6, 1845], *BC*, 10:205.

32. [May 15, 1845], *BC*, 10:216.

33. EBB to Lady Margaret Cocks, Sept. 29 [1837], *BC*, 3:284.

34. EBB to Julia Martin, Dec. 7, 1836, *BC*, 3:203.

35. Ibid., May 26, 1843, *BC*, 7:149.

36. Ibid., Oct. 5, 1844, *BC*, 9:173.

37. EBB to MRM [May 6, 1843], *BC*, 7:113.

38. EBB to RB [Dec. 4, 1845], *BC*, 11:221.

39. Ibid. [Feb. 23, 1846], *BC*, 12:99.

40. Ibid., 12:99.

41. Ibid. [May 19, 1846], *BC*, 12:340.

42. [May 23, 1845], *BC*, 10:232.

43. [May 23, 1845], *BC*, 10:232–33.

44. [May 24, 1845], *BC*, 10:233–36.

45. [May 25, 1845], *BC*, 10:237–38.

46. [June 14, 1845], *BC*, 10:264–65.

47. [June 16, 1845], *BC*, 10:266.

48. *BC*, 10:255, n2.

49. Ibid., 11:378.

50. EBB's criticisms of RB's poems are now in the Wellesley College Library. They were first published in full in the Macmillan edition of *The Complete Poems of Robert Browning* (London, 1914). The best edition, with annotation by Philip Kelley and Scott Lewis, is in *BC*, 11, appendix 4. All of my citations are to this edition [RSK's note].

51. [July 25, 1845], *BC*, 11:3. For a detailed account of the development of "The Flight of the Duchess," see DeVane, 171–76. Important commentary on the poem and on RB's intentions are to be found in Edward Snyder and Frederick Palmer, Jr., "New Light on the Brownings," *Quarterly Review* 269 (July 1937): 48–63; and Fred Manning Smith in "Elizabeth Barrett and Browning's *The Flight of the Duchess*," *Studies in Philology* 39 (1942): 102–17; and "More Light on Elizabeth Barrett and Browning's *The Flight of the Duchess*," *Studies in Philology* 39 (1942): 693–95. DeVane and the other commentators are mistaken, however, in their interpretation that the poem was RB's literary attempt to persuade EBB to escape an oppressive situation in her father's house and settle with him in Italy. At this time, he knew nothing of Mr. Barrett nor of the Wimpole Street household. The most intelligent critical comment on the connection between the poem and the relationship of RB and EBB is the brief treatment by Daniel Karlin in *The Courtship of Robert Browning and Elizabeth Barrett* (Oxford, 1985), 89–94.

52. *BC*, 11:381.

53. Ibid., 11:377.

54. Ibid., 11:376.

55. Oct. 15, 1842, *BC*, 6:105.

56. *BC*, 11:379.

57. For lines 300, 272–74, 324.

58. *BC*, 11:379.

59. *BC*, 11:380.

60. [July 26, 1845], *BC*, 11:5.

61. [July 25, 1845], *BC*, 11:3.

Chapter 12

1. [c. July 18, 1845], *BC*, 10:312.

2. [July 31, 1845], *BC*, 11:10.

3. [Aug. 3, 1845], *BC*, 11:15.

4. EBB to MRM, Mar. 27–28, 1842, *BC*, 5:277.

5. EBB *Diary*, Sept. 10, 12, and 17, 1831, 123, 125.

6. EBB to William Merry, Jan. 8, 1844, *BC*, 8:150.

7. EBB to MRM, Mar. 27–28, 1842, *BC*, 5:278.

8. EBB to RB [July 31, 1845], *BC*, 11:10.

9. EBB to MRM, Mar. 27–28, 1842, *BC*, 5:277.

10. Ibid., Mar. 27–28, 1842, *BC*, 5:279, reflecting Rom. 13:8–9 and 1 Pet. 1:22.

11. Ibid., Oct. 31, 1842, *BC*, 6:129.

12. She had also been baptized privately three days after her birth by the Reverend W. L. Rahm, a family friend (*BC*, 1:xlv).

13. The meaning of the name was "House at the end of the Valley" (scrapbook kept by Mr. and Mrs. John Hegarty, Hope End Country Hotel).

14. The two principal sources for EBB's early life are *Hitherto Unpublished Poems and Stories of Elizabeth Barrett Browning*, ed. H. Buxton Forman (2 vols.; Boston: Bibliophile Society, 1914); and EBB *Diary*.

15. Dr. William Coker to Edward Moulton-Barrett, June 24, 1821, *BC*, 1:326–27. The best account of this early illness is in Margaret Forster, *Elizabeth Barrett Browning: A Biography* (London: Chatto and Windus, 1988), 21–27.

16. Oct. 5, 1843, *BC*, 7:354.

17. "Diagnoses of Elizabeth Barrett's Physicians," appendix 2, *George Barrett*, 341.

18. Edward Moulton-Barrett (Bro) to EBB [Nov. 2, 1822], *BC*, 1:167, 168.

19. Peter Dally, *Elizabeth Barrett Browning: A Psychological Portrait* (London, 1989), asserts that EBB probably had anorexia nervosa caused by distress at the departure of Bro for Charterhouse School in London and resentment at being born a girl. His account is highly selective in its evidence.

20. EBB to H. S. Boyd [July 25, 1832], *BC*, 3:37.

21. In her doctoral dissertation, "The Vision and the Music: Poetic Theory and Conflict in the Poetry of Elizabeth Barrett Browning" (City University of New York, 1994), Jean Newton has an appendix entitled "Elizabeth Barrett Browning's Illness," in which she presents a strong argument that an acute asthmatic condition was the chief cause of

EBB's health problems after her mid-twenties. Clinical reports show that in this condition a patient can suffer severe fits of coughing accompanied by the spitting of blood.

22. EBB to Miss Commaline, Aug. 19, 1837, *BC*, 3:278.

23. EBB to R. H. Horne, May 13, 1841, *BC*, 5:45.

24. EBB to MRM [Nov. 28, 1837], *BC*, 3:298.

25. EBB to H. S. Boyd, May 21, 1839, *BC*, 4:151.

26. Nov. 24 [1839], *BC*, 4:210.

27. EBB to MRM [Nov. 1840], *BC*, 4:298.

28. Letters to B. R. Haydon, Nov. 6, 1842, *BC*, 6:144; to Cornelius Mathews, July 17, 1844, *BC*, 9:53; and to Lydia Sigourney, May 1, 1845, *BC*, 10:191.

29. Edward Moulton-Barrett (father) to Septimus Moulton-Barrett, June 24, 1840, *BC*, 4:365.

30. Edward Moulton-Barrett (father) to Septimus Moulton-Barrett, Sept. 12, 1840, *BC*, 4:367.

31. EBB to Mrs. Martin, Oct. 2 [1846], *BC*, 14:30.

32. EBB to RB [Aug. 20–23, 1845], *BC*, 11:44.

33. Nov. 12, 1841, *BC*, 5:169.

34. EBB to R. H. Horne [Feb. 1841], *BC*, 5:18.

35. EBB to MRM, Nov. 12, 1841, *BC*, 5:168.

36. Ibid. [early Oct. 1840], *BC*, 4:297.

37. EBB to R. H. Horne, June 13, 1841, *BC*, 5:55.

38. May 4 [1843], *BC*, 7:108.

39. EBB to RB [Oct. 31, 1845], *BC*, 11:147.

40. Ibid., Mar. 20, 1845, *BC*, 10:133.

41. EBB to MRM [Feb. 1, 1844], *BC*, 8:180.

42. The door of 50 Wimpole Street to which RB's letters were delivered is now the entrance to the Rare Book and Manuscript Room of the Wellesley College Library.

43. EBB to MRM [June 21, 1845], *BC*, 10:270.

44. EBB to GB [Sept. 3, 1845], *BC*, 11:58.

45. Mr. Barrett's letter is no longer extant. However, the journal of Captain William Surtees, Aug. 25, 1845, records "The Governor consents to poor Ba going abroad but in a way that has left her crying ever since" (quoted in *BC*, 11:59, n2).

46. EBB to RB [Aug. 20–23, 1845], *BC*, 11:44.

47. [Aug. 30, 1845], *BC*, 11:52.

48. [Oct. 24, 1845], *BC*, 11:137.

49. [Aug. 31, 1845], *BC*, 11:53–54. Robert seems to have remembered the last phrase of the letter when he wrote his dedicatory poem addressed to Elizabeth, "One Word More," at the end of *Men and Women*. In offering his love publicly ("Take them, Love, the book and me together: / Where the heart lies, let the brain lie also") he got the last word.

50. [Sept. 2, 1845], *BC*, 11:57—words that RB perhaps unconsciously echoed in *The Ring and the Book*, 7:1447, when Caponsacchi first spoke to the endangered Pompilia and told her "I am yours."

51. [Sept. 13, 1845], *BC*, 11:74–76.

52. [Sept. 16, 1845], *BC*, 11:78.

53. [Sept. 26, 1845], *BC*, 11:100.

54. [Sept. 25, 1845], *BC*, 11:97–98.
55. [Sept. 26, 1845], *BC*, 11:100.

Chapter 13

1. For a detailed discussion of the effects of this grouping, see William E. Harrold, *The Variance and the Unity: A Study of the Complementary Poems of Robert Browning* (Athens: Ohio University Press, 1973).

2. Edward Berdoe, *The Browning Cyclopaedia* (London: Allen and Unwin, 1891), suggests the voice might be Fra Angelico speaking about Raphael. J. B. Bullen, "Browning's 'Pictor Ignotus' and Vasari's 'Life of Fra Bartolommeo di San Marco,'" *Review of English Studies* NS 23 (1972): 313–19, argues that Browning modeled his speaker on Fra Bartolommeo. However, the robustness of Fra Bartolommeo's paintings in no way resembles the work described in "Pictor Ignotus."

3. Giuseppe Mazzini to RB [Nov. 13, 1845], *BC*, 11:169.

4. EBB's notes on RB's poems, *BC*, 11:386. For a reading which argues that the poem is a far less innocent piece, see Ernest Fontana, "Sexual Tourism and Browning's 'The Englishman in Italy,'" *Victorian Poetry* 36 (1998): 299–305.

5. EBB to RB [Oct. 28, 1845], *BC*, 11:145.

6. Probably a reference to the fact that Wordsworth began receiving a government pension in 1842.

7. RB to Rev. Alexander Grosart, Feb. 24, 1875, Hood, 167. For a full exploration and interpretation of the relations of the two poets, see John Haydn Baker, *Browning and Wordsworth* (Madison, NJ: Fairleigh Dickinson University Press, 2004).

8. DeVane (182) reprints Hunt's poem, although he points out that RB may have been familiar with other versions of the story, especially Schiller's *Der Handschuh*.

9. EBB to RB [Oct. 28, 1845], *BC*, 11:145.

10. *British Quarterly Review* (Nov. 1847): 490–509; rpt. in *BC*, 14:397–404.

11. Rpt. in *BC*, 11:361–63.

12. Ibid., 12:377–84.

13. Ibid., 11:366.

14. Ibid., 13:395.

15. Ibid., 11:364–65.

16. Ibid., 11:371–74.

17. Ibid., 13:398–400.

18. *BC*, 11:178, has a reproduction of the original manuscript, which is at Yale University.

19. RB to Edward Moxon [Nov. 19, 1845], *BC*, 11:178. Landor also sent a copy to Forster, but it is more likely that Moxon sent it to the newspaper.

Chapter 14

1. [Aug. 20–23, 1845], *BC*, 11:43.
2. Ibid., 11:42–43.

3. Ibid., 11:43–45.

4. [Sept. 16, 1845], *BC*, 11:78.

5. [Sept. 25, 1845], *BC*, 11:97.

6. Sarah died at age twelve, shortly after Thomas Lawrence had painted her portrait in 1795, the now-famous "Pinkie," which hangs in the Huntington Art Gallery, San Marino, California. It is generally regarded as a companion painting to Lawrence's equally well known "Blue Boy."

7. RB's preface to EBB, *Poetical Works* (1889), 1:vii.

8. Signed by George III, Feb. 21, 1798, three years after the death of Grandfather Edward Barrett.

9. The Sale Catalogue of 1832 (EBB *Diary*, 323–37) gives 472 acres, but Mr. Barrett retained ownership of a portion of the woodland.

10. The only remaining parts are the stables with their minarets. The building has now been converted into a country hotel.

11. EBB to MRM [Jan. 1838], *BC*, 4:5.

12. EBB to RB [Aug. 27, 1846], *BC*, 13:305–6.

13. EBB to RB [Jan. 21, 1846], *BC*, 12:9.

14. He also owned one ship, the *Statira*, that traded in the Mediterranean and the Black Sea. After the death of brother Samuel, individual sons were sent to Jamaica to manage the plantations.

15. EBB to MRM [July 11, 1845], *BC*, 10:302.

16. EBB to RB [Dec. 12, 1845], *BC*, 11:238.

17. Ibid. [Sept. 14, 1846], *BC*, 13:366.

18. EBB to MRM, Apr. 5, 1845, *BC*, 10:149.

19. EBB to RB [Aug. 10, 1846], *BC*, 13:244.

20. Ibid. [Jan. 15, 1846], *BC*, 11:321.

21. Ibid. [Mar. 3, 1846], *BC*, 12:129.

22. [Dec. 12, 1845], *BC*, 11:239.

23. Ibid.

24. RB's headaches have been attributed to various causes. Dr. James B. Carty, Jr., Ophthalmological Surgeon, Bryn Mawr Hospital, believes that, with a different length of vision in each eye, RB's excessive study and writing could account for most of his headaches.

Chapter 15

1. *BC*, 11:212.

2. EBB to MRM [Sept. 13, 1845], *BC*, 11:72.

3. EBB to RB [Oct. 15, 1845], *BC*, 11:128.

4. Ibid., Jan. 10, 1846, *BC*, 11:305; RB to EBB [Jan. 25, 1846], *BC*, 12:20.

5. EBB to RB [Feb. 26, 1846], *BC*, 12:109.

6. Ibid. [May 5–6, 1845], *BC*, 10:203.

7. I am grateful to Dr. Tully Speaker, Temple University School of Pharmacy, for information about opium and its derivatives [RSK's note].

8. EBB to Mrs. Martin [Oct. 7, 1845], *BC*, 11:115.

9. Jan. 20, 1845, *BC*, 5:222.

10. EBB to RB [Aug. 5, 1846], *BC*, 13:229. [RSK estimates that she spent 50 percent of her income on morphine.]

11. [Nov. 12–14, 1845], *BC*, 11:167.

12. [Feb. 6, 1846], *BC*, 12:44.

13. [Feb. 24, 1846], *BC*, 12:101.

14. [July 23, 1846], *BC*, 13:183.

15. The first hint of her work on the *Sonnets from the Portuguese* came on July 22, 1846, when she wrote, "You shall see some day at Pisa what I will not show you now" (*BC*, 13:178).

16. Information about Mrs. Jameson is drawn from Gerardine MacPherson (her niece), *Memoirs of the Life of Anna Jameson* (Boston: Roberts Brothers, 1878); and Clara Thomas, *Love and Work Enough: The Life of Anna Jameson* (Toronto: University of Toronto Press, 1967).

17. [Feb. 14, 1846], *BC*, 12:71.

18. [June 17, 1846], *BC*, 13:63.

19. [Jan. 28, 1846], *BC*, 12:27.

20. [June 17, 1846], *BC*, 13:61.

21. [June 3, 1846], *BC*, 13:18.

22. [June 26, 1846], *BC*, 13:84.

23. [July 29, 1846], *BC*, 13:206.

24. [July 30, 1846], *BC*, 13:208.

25. [Apr. 3, 1846], *BC*, 12:207.

26. [July 22, 1846], *BC*, 13:181. Wilson's annual salary was £16, a remarkable contrast to EBB's annual expenditure of £80 on morphine [RSK's estimate].

27. [Aug. 5, 1846], *BC*, 13:229. Her annual income would be about £380. It would go even further in Italy than in England.

28. [June 12, 1846], *BC*, 13:46.

29. [July 26, 1846], *BC*, 13:194.

30. [July 27, 1846], *BC*, 13:198.

31. [July 22, 1846], *BC*, 13:179.

32. [Mar. 1, 1846], *BC*, 12:118.

33. [Aug. 2, 1846], *BC*, 13:215–16.

34. [Mar. 3, 1846], *BC*, 12:129.

35. [Mar. 4, 1846], *BC*, 12:131. Robert did allow himself to be more outspoken on one previous occasion, when he burst out, "but it is *right*, after all, to revolt against such monstrous tyranny" ([June 12, 1846], *BC*, 13:44).

36. J. Arnould to A. Domett, Nov. 30, 1846, *RBAD*, 133.

37. [June 9, 1846], *BC*, 13:36.

38. [Jan. 15, 1846], *BC*, 11:321.

39. [June 9, 1846], *BC*, 13:35.

40. [Mar. 3, 1846], *BC*, 12:129. Elizabeth had widespread support among friends and relatives who, remembering how her father had stood in the way of her wintering in Pisa last year, were now urging her to be bold and insist on going to Italy this year. Uncle Hedley assured her that he would not cast her off if she was "a rebel & a runaway" ([July

17, 1846], *BC*, 13:171). John Kenyon was always on her side and thought Mr. Barrett subject to "monomania" ([Jan. 21, 1846], *BC*, 12:9). Her cousin Lady Carmichael urged Henrietta "to act for herself" in choosing to marry Captain Cook, and another cousin, Frances Bayford, took a similar view. This was "one of a hundred proofs to show how this case [of overly strict parental rule] is considered exceptional among our family friends" ([May 10, 1846], *BC*, 12:313–14).

41. [Aug. 23, 1846], *BC*, 13:285.

42. [Aug. 15, 1846], *BC*, 13:254.

43. [Aug. 30, 1846], *BC*, 13:314.

44. [Sept. 3, 1846], *BC*, 13:333.

45. Sept. 1 to 7, 1846, *BC*, 13:324–48.

46. [Sept. 14, 1846], *BC*, 13:363.

47. The official marriage certificate is in the collection at the Robert Browning Settlement in Walworth.

48. EBB to AB and HB, Nov. [21–]24 [1846], *BC*, 14:52.

49. EBB to Julia Martin, Oct. 2[2, 1846], *BC*, 14:35.

50. EBB to HB, July 9 [1847], *BC*, 14:242.

51. EBB to AB and HB [Sept. 13, 1847], *BC*, 14:303.

52. [Sept. 13, 1846], *BC*, 13:362.

53. [Aug. 22, 1846], *BC*, 13:280.

54. [Sept. 14, 1846], *BC*, 13:364.

55. [Sept. 1, 1846], *BC*, 13:325.

56. [Sept. 17–18, 1846], *BC*, 14:1–4.

57. [Sept. 18, 1846], *BC*, 14:5–6.

58. Ibid., 13:380.

59. For years, the manuscript of *Sonnets from the Portuguese* has been on permanent exhibition at the British Library (Add. MS 43–487).

Chapter 16

1. EBB to AB and HB, Feb. 8 [1847], *BC*, 14:123.

2. EBB to AB [Sept. 26, 1846], *BC*, 14:9.

3. Anna Jameson to Lady Noel Byron, Sept. 22–23 [1846], *BC*, 14:362.

4. EBB to AB [Sept. 26, 1846], *BC*, 14:11.

5. Oct. 2 [1846], *BC*, 14:19.

6. EBB to AB [Sept. 26, 1846], *BC*, 14:10–11.

7. EBB to AB and HB, Oct. 2, 1846, *BC*, 14:15.

8. Anna Jameson to Lady Noel Byron, Oct. 7–19 [1846], *BC*, 14:364.

9. EBB to AB [Oct. 16–19, 1846], *BC*, 14:27. Almost four lines, presumably about Mr. Barrett's letter, have been obliterated by someone at this point.

10. [Sept. 17–18, 1846], *BC*, 14:1–4.

11. "Browning's Answer," *Cornhill* 68 (Apr. 1930): 426. Jeannette Marks apparently heard a similar family story in 1930 when she visited Brigadier General Edward Alfred Moulton-Barrett, son of EBB's brother Alfred, in Jamaica. The general was seventy-one

at the time. She quotes someone, probably the general, as saying that Henrietta told her father that Elizabeth "had gone off" with Robert Browning and he dropped the book or threw it. Henrietta slipped or fell down the stairs in startled reaction (Jeannette Marks, *The Family of the Barrett: A Colonial Romance* [New York: Macmillan, 1938], 560).

12. EBB to HB, Dec. 19 [1846], *BC*, 14:76; EBB to AB and HB, Oct. 2, 1846, *BC*, 14:15, 13.

13. EBB to AB and HB, Oct. 2, 1846, *BC*, 14:13; EBB to the Martins, Feb. 1, 1847, *BC*, 14:112; EBB to AB and HB, Nov. [21–]24 [1846], *BC*, 14:49.

14. EBB to AB and HB, Oct. 2, 1846, *BC*, 14:14. EBB copied out Kenyon's letter for them.

15. Ibid., 14:16.

16. Anna Jameson to Charlotte Murphy, Oct. 7–9 [1846], *BC*, 14:365.

17. EBB to AB [Oct. 16–19, 1846], *BC*, 14:23.

18. EBB to Hugh Boyd, Nov. 19 [1846], *BC*, 14:45; EBB to AB [Oct. 16–19, 1846], *BC*, 14:24.

19. EBB to Hugh Boyd, Nov. 19 [1846], *BC*, 14:45.

20. EBB to AB [Oct. 16–19, 1846], *BC*, 14:23.

21. Anna Jameson to Lady Noel Byron, Oct. 15 [1846], and Oct. 27, 1846, *BC*, 14:365–66.

22. EBB to AB [Oct. 16–19, 1846], *BC*, 14:26; EBB to Hugh Boyd, May 26 [1847], *BC*, 14:212. Boyd was a change-ringer.

23. EBB to AB, Feb. 24, 1847, *BC*, 14:133.

24. EBB to Julia Martin, Nov. 5–9 [1846], *BC*, 14:42.

25. Ibid., Oct. 2[2, 1846], *BC*, 14:36.

26. EBB to HB, Dec. 19 [1846], *BC*, 14:76.

27. Dec. 12 [1846], *BC*, 14:69–70.

28. Daniel Karlin, "The Brownings' Marriage: Contemporary Representations," *Studies in Browning and His Circle* 21 (1997): 33–52, offers a comprehensive account of the response to the Browning marriage and demonstrates that the literary community regarded it as that of two "poet-souls" drawn to each other and united in marriage.

29. William Wordsworth to Edward Moxon, Oct. 12, 1846, *BC*, 14:365.

30. MRM to Mrs. Ouvry [c. Mar.] 1847, *BC*, 14:370.

31. EBB to AB, Dec. [24–25, 1846], *BC*, 14:90–91.

32. I am grateful to Dr. Toby Eisenstein, professor of microbiology and immunology, Temple University School of Medicine, for this information [RSK's note].

33. EBB to HB, Mar. 31 [1847], *BC*, 14:161.

34. EBB to Hugh Boyd, May 26 [1847], *BC*, 14:213.

35. EBB to AB, May 29–30 [1847], *BC*, 14:216–17.

36. Ibid., 14:216.

37. EBB to Hugh Boyd, May 26 [1847], *BC*, 14:212.

38. EBB to Thomas Westwood, Sept. 11 [1847], *BC*, 14:298.

39. EBB to AB, July 26 [1847], *BC*, 14:252, 257.

40. Ibid., 14:258.

41. EBB to HB, Aug. 2 [1847], *BC*, 14:268.

42. EBB to AB, Mar. [5–]9 [1847], *BC*, 14:141.

43. EBB to Julia Martin, Aug. 7, 1847, *BC*, 14:276.

44. EBB to SB, Aug. 21 [1847], *BC*, 14:284.

45. EBB to AB and HB [Sept. 13, 1847], *BC*, 14:301.

46. EBB and RB to Anna Jameson [mid-]Dec. [1847], *BC*, 14:344–46.

Chapter 17

1. RB to AB and HB, Nov. 25 [1847], *TTUL*, 54.

2. EBB to AB, May 10–11 [1848], EBB *Arabella*, 1:174–75. EBB describes their return to Palazzo Guidi only after an extensive search for suitable quarters. She makes clear that Robert lets her decide which apartment they would rent.

3. EBB to MRM, July 4 [1848], EBB *Mitford*, 3:246.

4. EBB to AB, May 10–11 [1848], EBB *Arabella*, 1:174.

5. Ibid., 1:181.

6. EBB to Eliza Ogilvy, June 25 [1849], EBB *Ogilvy*, 8; and EBB to Anna Jameson, May 4 [1850], EBB *Letters*, 1:448.

7. Many of the pieces described here may be seen in the painting by George Mignaty, 1861, of the Casa Guidi drawing room (Mills College Library, Oakland, CA).

8. This painting has been removed from the church and placed in the local art museum in Fano.

9. The painting (#313 in the Dulwich Gallery catalog) shows an angel holding the hand of a nude infant about two years old and pointing to the sky as if instructing the child about God or his heavenly home. The gallery also holds a painting by Guercino, "The Woman Taken in Adultery" (#281 in the catalog), which Browning viewed many times.

10. EBB to MRM, Aug. 24 [1848], EBB *Mitford* 3:249.

11. Nov. 23–2[4] [1847], *BC*, 14:335.

12. RB to AB and HB [Mar. 9, 1849], EBB *Arabella*, 1:234–35.

13. EBB to Anna Jameson, Apr. 30, 1849, BL-KT.

14. EBB to MRM, Apr. 30 [1849], EBB *Mitford*, 3:269.

15. EBB to Anna Jameson, Apr. 30, 1849, BL-KT.

16. Ibid.

17. EBB to MRM, Apr. 30 [1849], EBB *Mitford*, 3:267; EBB to AB, Apr. 8–16 [1849], EBB *Arabella*, 1:239.

18. EBB to MRM, Apr. 30 [1849], EBB *Mitford*, 3:268.

19. EBB to AB, Apr. 8–16 [1849], EBB *Arabella*, 1:239.

20. EBB to MRM, Apr. 30, 1849, EBB *Letters*, 1:399–400.

21. RB to SB, July 2, 1849, Hood, 23–24.

22. Ibid., 25.

23. RB to Julia Wedgwood [Nov. 1864], Wedgwood, 114.

24. RB to Mary Talbot [1885], published in "Rowland Grey" (Lilian K. Rowland-Brown), "Browning's Answer," *Cornhill* 68 (Apr. 1930): 429–30.

25. EBB to AB, Jan. 12 [1851], EBB *Arabella*, 1:368.

26. RB to Mary Talbot (cited above), 430.

27. EBB to AB, Jan. 12 [1851], EBB *Arabella*, 1:368.

28. There has been some uncertainty about the date and place of Elizabeth's showing Robert the sonnets. Edmund Gosse claimed that Robert told him it happened in

Pisa in 1847 (*Critical Kit-Kats* [London, 1896], 1–3) and pointed to a private printing dated Reading, 1847. But that printing has been proven to be one of the falsified publications by the notorious forger Thomas Wise. One scholar even suspected that Gosse himself was privy to the scheme and was attempting to authenticate the publication. Elizabeth herself, in a letter to her sister Arabella (Jan. 12 [1851]) said that she gave the sonnets to Robert "last spring" (EBB *Arabella*, 1:368), but this was a product of faulty memory. Two letters by Robert Browning have provided the true date and place of this momentous event in his life. In a letter to Leigh Hunt (Oct. 6, 1857, Hood, 48) from Bagni di Lucca, Browning says the sonnets "were shown to me at this very place eight years ago." Elizabeth must have confirmed that information because she wrote a postscript to the letter, in which she did not offer any correction or change to his statement. Another letter to Julia Wedgwood (cited above) is full of detail about the occasion. In it, he tells of first seeing the poems "at Lucca," three years after they had been written. Finally, in an undated letter to Mary Talbot in 1885 (cited above), he mistakenly places that event as "two years" after their marriage, but he gives the full and correct details about the way the poems came to be entitled "Sonnets from the Portuguese."

29. EBB to MRM [July 18, 1849], EBB *Mitford*, 3:273.

30. EBB to SB, Aug. 13, 1849, BL-KT.

31. EBB to MRM, Oct. 2 [1849], EBB *Mitford*, 3:282; and EBB to Anna Jameson, Oct. 1 [1849], EBB *Letters*, 1:422.

32. EBB to Julia Martin, May 14 [1849], EBB *Letters*, 1:405–6.

33. EBB to HB, May 2, 3, 4, 5, 1849, Huxley, 108.

34. EBB to Eliza Ogilvy, June 25 [1849], EBB *Ogilvy*, 4.

35. This overview of Italian history is drawn chiefly from Bolton King, *A History of Italian Unity*, vol. 1 (New York: Scribner's, 1899, rev. 1924); G. F.-H. and J. Berkeley, *Italy in the Making*, vol. 3 (Cambridge: Cambridge University Press, 1940); and Edgar Holt, *Risorgimento: The Making of Italy, 1815–1870* (London: Macmillan, 1970).

36. EBB to HB, Mar. 7–Apr. 1, 1848, Huxley, 81.

37. Ibid., June 24, 1848, Huxley, 87.

38. Aug. 11, 1849, EBB *Letters*, 1:416.

39. EBB to MRM, Aug. 31 [1849], EBB *Mitford*, 3:277.

40. Apr. 2 [1850], EBB *Letters*, 1:442.

41. EBB to HB, Dec. 22 [1849], Camellia Collection, Linton Park, Kent.

42. EBB to Anna Jameson, Feb. 26 [1852], EBB *Letters*, 2:59.

43. EBB to Julia Martin [end of Apr. 1850], BL-KT.

44. Ibid.

45. Ibid.

46. EBB to HB, May 25, 1850, Huxley, 121.

Chapter 18

1. F. R. G. Duckworth, *Browning: Background and Conflict* (New York: Dutton, 1931), also comments on RB's conflict approaching *Christmas-Eve and Easter-Day*, but

he attributes it to a pull between "the poet of action" and the "contemplative poet" as follows: whenever RB tried to "rise to those regions of vision" above the world of action, "the effort produced in him a turmoil and distress" because "the poet of action pulled him back" (210).

2. June 29, 1847, *New Letters*, 43.

3. RB to Edmund Gosse, Mar. 15, 1885, Hood, 235.

4. See George P. Landow, *Victorian Types, Victorian Shadows: Biblical Typology in Victorian Literature, Art, and Thought* (London: Routledge, 1980).

5. For an examination of Browning's satire and its antecedents in this poem, see Barbara R. Ryerse, "Some Aspects of Browning's Satire: Browning, Donne, and Mandeville," Ph.D. Thesis, University of Western Ontario, 1989.

6. Mary Rose Sullivan, "'Some Interchange of Grace': 'Saul' and *Sonnets from the Portuguese*," *Browning Institute Studies* 15 (1987): 55–68. The quoted sentence is on 64.

7. EBB to Anna Jameson, Apr. 2 [1850], EBB *Letters*, 1:441.

8. Ibid., May 4 [1850], EBB *Letters*, 1:449.

9. *Athenaeum* (Apr. 6, 1850): 370.

10. *Leader* 1 (Apr. 27, 1850): 111.

11. In the *Prospective Review* 6 (May 1850): 267, 271–79.

12. *Examiner* (Apr. 6, 1850): 211–13.

13. *Germ* 4 (May 1850): 187–92.

14. 21 (Apr. 1851): 346–70.

15. Quoted in Gertrude Reese Hudson, *Robert Browning's Literary Life from First Work to Masterpiece* (Austin, TX: Eakin Press, 1992), 285–86.

16. 14 (Sept. 1850): 84, 90.

17. 11 (June 1849): 356, 385, 382.

18. (Sept. 1849): 565.

19. 26 (Aug. 1849): 212.

Chapter 19

1. EBB to HB, July 7, 1850, Huxley, 125–26.

2. Elizabeth's third miscarriage had occurred during the winter of 1849–1850.

3. RB to John Kenyon, July 29, 1850, Hood, 28; EBB to Julia Martin, Jan. 30, 1851, EBB *Letters*, 1:475.

4. EBB to IB, Sept. [1850], EBB *Letters*, 1:457.

5. EB to HB, Feb. 20 [1850], Camellia Collection, Linton Park, Kent (published in Huxley, 117–18).

6. June 5 [–6], [1851], EBB *Arabella*, 1:378.

7. EBB to AB, May 16 [1851], EBB *Arabella*, 1:374.

8. Ibid., June 5 [–6] [1851], EBB *Arabella*, 1:378.

9. Ibid., June 26 [1851], EBB *Arabella*, 1:388–90; and EBB to John Kenyon, July 7 [1851], EBB *Letters*, 2:10.

10. June 4 [1851], EBB *Mitford*, 3:323.

11. EBB to Julia Martin [c. Aug. 1851], BL-KT.

12. EBB to HB [Oct. 6, 1851], Camellia Collection, Linton Park, Kent (published in Huxley, 141).

13. Ibid.

14. EBB to Julia Martin [c. Aug. 1851], BL-KT.

15. Ibid. EBB explained George's "misstatements" in detail: "Storm never sent an 'affectionate message' to Robert, but there were one or two words which are interpreted (being always inclined to interpret for the best) into a sort of a kind allusion, and to which I wrote myself as kind a reply from Robert as could be shaped—whereas Henry's letter to Robert was answered instantly by his own hand, as Henry will himself testify" (c. Aug. 1851, BL-KT). Actually, Stormie's letter was more aggravating than Elizabeth indicated to George. Stormie had offered "not a single word of remembrance to Robert." Further, he explained that the reason he had not written before was because "he was waiting for me to be reconciled to Papa!" she told Henrietta. When that happened, "he wd. write often!!. . . My brothers try my love for them too much" (Feb. 20 [1850], Camellia Collection, Linton Park, Kent).

16. EBB to Julia Martin [c. Aug. 1851], BL-KT.

17. Ibid., EBB *Letters*, 2:15.

18. Ibid., 2:13.

19. Ibid., 2:16.

20. Ibid. [Sept. 1851], EBB *Letters*, 2:20.

21. EBB to MRM, Oct. 22 [1851], EBB *Mitford*, 3:331. For details of the trip see *Last Words of Thomas Carlyle* (London: Longmans, 1892).

22. EBB to Anna Jameson, Oct. 21 [1851], EBB *Letters*, 2:23.

23. EBB to MRM, Nov. [1850], EBB *Mitford*, 3:315.

24. EBB to AB, Oct. 21–Nov. 1 [1850], EBB *Arabella*, 1:348.

25. EBB to HB, Dec. 1, 1851, Huxley, 148.

26. This historical account is based on the following works: J. M. Thompson, *Louis Napoleon and the Second Empire* (New York: W. W. Norton, 1955); T. A. B. Corley, *Democratic Despot: A Life of Napoleon III* (London: Barrie and Rockliff, 1961); James F. McMillan, *Napoleon III* (London: Longman, 1991).

27. EBB to AB [Dec. 11–14, 1851], EBB *Arabella*, 1:434; EBB to Mrs. Martin, Jan. 17 [1852], EBB *Letters*, 2:42.

28. June 15, 1850, EBB *Letters*, 1:452.

29. Dec. 11 [1851], EBB *Letters*, 2:37; EBB to HB [Dec. 13–15, 1851] and Jan. 5 [1852], Camellia Collection, Linton Park, Kent (published in Huxley, 149–53).

30. EBB to GB [Dec. 4–5, 1851], *George Barrett*, 156.

31. Dec. 13 and 14, 1851, Huxley, 149.

32. EBB to AB [Dec. 11–14, 1851], EBB *Arabella*, 1:432; EBB to Julia Martin, Feb. 22, 1852, BL-KT; EBB to AB [Dec. 11–14, 1851], EBB *Arabella*, 1:432–34; EBB to MRM, Feb. 15 [1852], EBB *Letters*, 2:51; EBB to AB, Dec. 25–26 [1851], EBB *Arabella*, 1:440–43; EBB to Anna Jameson, Dec. 10 [1851], EBB *Letters*, 2:33; EBB to GB [Feb. 28, 1852], *George Barrett*, 172; EBB to AB [Dec. 11–14, 1851], EBB *Arabella*, 1:432–34.

33. EBB to AB, Dec. 25–26 [1851] and [Dec. 11–14, 1851], EBB *Arabella*, 1:444, 433.

34. RB to GB, Feb. 4, 1852, *George Barrett*, 169.

35. EBB to AB [Dec. 11–14, 1851], EBB *Arabella*, 1:433.

Chapter 20

1. EBB to HB, Dec. 1, 1851 ("Robert has finished and is sending off his Shelley"), Huxley, 149. The fair copy that he mailed to Moxon is dated "4 Dec. 1851."

2. [Oct. 1851], Hood, 36.

3. All quotations from the essay are taken from Pettigrew and Collins, 1:1001–13.

4. On these issues, see Philip Drew, "Browning's *Essay on Shelley*," *Victorian Poetry* 1 (1963): 1–6; and Thomas J. Collins, "Browning's *Essay on Shelley*: In Context," *Victorian Poetry* 2 (1964): 119–24. The distinction between the objective poet and the subjective poet was a commonplace in the literary commentary of the nineteenth century, as M. H. Abrams points out in *The Mirror and the Lamp* (New York: Oxford University Press, 1953). It had its origins in the theoretical discourses of Schiller and the Schlegel brothers and was disseminated in England by Coleridge, De Quincey, Henry Crabb Robinson, and Carlyle. See Thomas J. Collins, *Robert Browning's Moral-Aesthetic Theory 1833–1855* (Lincoln: University of Nebraska Press, 1967), for a thorough discussion of RB's essay as it relates to his religious ideas and his creativity. See also Philip Drew, *The Poetry of Browning: A Critical Introduction* (London: Methuen, 1970), for an accurate close reading of RB's stylistically difficult essay.

5. EBB to AB [Dec. 11–14, 1851], EBB *Arabella*, 1:435.

6. These are some of the people EBB listed: Miss Fitton, an old woman who knew Kenyon; the Shores, a large family; Mrs. Stuart Mackenzie and her daughter (the future second Lady Ashburton), "who is pretty"; Mr. and Mrs. Carré—he was an "angel" (bishop) in the Irvingite church; Major and Mrs. Carmichael-Smith; Miss Williams Wynn, a cousin of Gladstone; Aunt Jane Hedley, who also brought a Mrs. Stre[a]tfield, an English widow with several children. EBB felt "surrounded" (ibid., 1:436).

7. Ibid., Dec. 25–26 [1851], EBB *Arabella*, 1:445.

8. NS 11 (Aug. 15, 1851): 661–89.

9. Th. Bentzon (Marie T. de S. Blanc), "A French Friend of Browning—Joseph Milsand," *Scribner's* 20 (July 1896): 108–20.

10. EBB to AB [Dec. 11–14, 1851], EBB *Arabella*, 1:435.

11. EBB had first encountered the revelations in a review of the book in the *Athenaeum* in Jan. 1852, which had quoted all these biographical details as if they were the most important feature of the book.

12. Feb. 26 [1852], EBB *Letters*, 2:58.

13. EBB to HB, Apr. 1, 1852, Huxley, 158–59.

14. (London: Athlone Press, 1982), 133–38.

15. EBB to HB, Apr. 1, 1852, Huxley, 158.

16. A summary of her statement to Henry Chorley in Jan. 1847, as quoted in EBB *Works*, 2:379.

17. EBB to AB [Dec. 11–14, 1851], EBB *Arabella*, 1:436.

18. EBB to MRM, Feb. 15–[16, 1852], EBB *Mitford*, 3:347.

19. EBB to John Kenyon, Feb. 15, 1852, EBB *Letters*, 2:55.

20. EBB to AB [Feb. 18, 1852], EBB *Arabella*, 1:464.

21. EBB to John Kenyon, Feb. 15, 1852, EBB *Letters*, 2:56.

22. EBB to AB [Feb. 18, 1852], EBB *Arabella*, 1:464–65.

23. EBB to MRM, Apr. 7 [1852], EBB *Mitford*, 3:353; and EBB to AB [Feb. 24, 1852], EBB *Arabella*, 1:470.

24. Apr. 27 [1852], BL-KT.

25. EBB to John Kenyon, Feb. 15, 1852, EBB *Letters*, 2:57.

26. EBB to AB, Mar. 23 [1852], EBB *Arabella*, 1:480.

27. EBB to Anna Jameson, Apr. 12, 1852, EBB *Letters*, 2:66.

28. EBB to Julia Martin [July 1852], BL-KT.

29. *Times* (London), July 2, 1852.

30. Ibid.

31. EBB to AB, Feb. 11–12 [1852], EBB *Arabella*, 1:454.

32. Ibid., May 25 [1852], and May 29–30 [1852], EBB *Arabella*, 1:490, 495.

33. The foregoing account is from the *Times* (London), July 2, 1852.

34. RB to John Kenyon, Jan. 16, 1853, Hood, 39–40.

35. Jane Welsh Carlyle to John A. Carlyle [July 27, 1852], *The Collected Letters of Thomas and Jane Welsh Carlyle*, Duke-Edinburgh Edition, ed. Clyde de L. Ryals and Kenneth J. Fielding (Durham: Duke University Press, 1999), 27:190.

36. *BC*, 14:329. See also Mark Samuels Lasner, "Browning's First Letter to Rossetti: A Discovery," *Browning Institute Studies* 15 (1987): 79–90.

37. EBB to Mrs. Ogilvy [Aug. 5, 1852], EBB *Ogilvy*, 81.

38. EBB to HB [Sept. 25, 1852], Camellia Collection, Linton Park, Kent.

39. [Sept. 16, 1852], Camellia Collection, Linton Park, Kent.

40. EBB to Julia Martin, Apr. 13, 1853, BL-KT.

41. EBB to Mrs. Ogilvy, Jan. 24 [1853], EBB *Ogilvy*, 90.

42. EBB to W. W. Story [Dec. 1852], in Henry James, *William Wetmore Story and His Friends* (Boston: Houghton Mifflin, 1903), 1:283.

43. EBB to AB [Nov. 13–15, 1852], EBB *Arabella*, 1:518.

Chapter 21

1. EBB to AB [Jan. 15–17, 1853], EBB *Arabella*, 1:539. The sender was Jane Wills-Sandford, a "devoted reader" of EBB (EBB to AB, Dec. 21, 1852, EBB *Arabella*, 1:525).

2. See below in the discussion of "'Childe Roland.'"

3. Quoted by Lilian Whiting, *The Brownings, Their Life and Art* (Boston: Little, Brown, 1911), 261.

4. Orr, *Handbook*, 274, n1.

5. DeVane, 230–31; Browning's copy of Lairesse's book is now at Yale (*Collections*, A1379).

6. See Lionel Stevenson, "The Pertinacious Victorian Poets," *University of Toronto Quarterly* 21 (1952): 239–45. For parallels with other chivalric romances, see Harold Golder, "Browning's *Childe Roland*," *PMLA* 39 (1924): 963–78.

7. Quoted by Whiting, *The Brownings*, 261.

8. Quoted by DeVane, 231 (from the *Christian Register*, Jan. 18, 1888). Ian Jack reminds us that Chadwick was quoting Matthew 10:22 (*Browning's Major Poetry* [Oxford: Clarendon Press, 1973], 194, n62).

9. Walter Scott, *Essays on Chivalry, Romance, and the Drama* (London: Frederick Warne, 1837), 65–108.

10. *Critical and Miscellaneous Essays* (New York: AMS, 1969), 3:324.

11. Among the many readings of "'Childe Roland'" the reader may find the following useful: Robert Langbaum, *The Poetry of Experience: The Dramatic Monologue in Modern Literary Experience* (New York: Random House, 1957), 192–99; John W. Willoughby, "Browning's 'Childe Roland to the Dark Tower Came,'" *Victorian Poetry* 1 (1963): 291–99; Eugene R. Kintgen, "Childe Roland and the Perversity of the Mind," *Victorian Poetry* 4 (1966): 253–58; Susan Hardy Aiken, "Structural Imagery in 'Childe Roland to the Dark Tower Came,'" *Browning Institute Studies* 5 (1977): 23–36; and Stefan Hawlin, *The Complete Critical Guide to Robert Browning* (London: Routledge, 2002).

12. See, among other works and essays, *The Ringers in the Tower: Studies in Romantic Tradition* (Chicago: University of Chicago Press, 1971); "How to Read a Poem: Browning's 'Childe Roland,'" *Georgia Review* 28 (1974): 404–18; and *A Map of Misreading* (New York: Oxford University Press, 1975).

13. Houghton Library, Harvard University, Lowell 1243. 16 C. 111. 4. 20.

14. Paul Fussell, *Poetic Meter and Poetic Form*, rev. ed. (1965; New York: Random House, 1979), 91–92.

Chapter 22

1. Richard Kennedy gives as a reference for this quotation "EBB to IB [Winter 1852–53], EBB *Letters*, 2:99." The quotation does not appear there, and I [Hair] have been unable to locate it. Kennedy may be quoting from the full text of the original letter in the Fitzwilliam Museum, for which Kelley and Hudson supply the date "[Nov 1852]" (item 52:136 in *Brownings' Correspondence: A Checklist* [Arkansas City, KS: Browning Institute and Wedgestone Press, 1978]).

2. For a full treatment of Lytton's life and career, see Aurelia Brooks Harlan, *Owen Meredith: A Critical Biography of Robert, First Earl of Lytton* (New York: Columbia University Press, 1946).

3. James, *William Wetmore Story*, 1:96.

4. Ronald A. Bosco, "The Brownings and Mrs. Kinney: A Record of Their Friendship," *Browning Institute Studies* 4 (1976): 62–63.

5. Bosco, "The Brownings," 62. Mrs. Kinney also records later an escapade in which EBB, Mrs. Kinney, and madcap young Harriet Hosmer disguised themselves with wigs and costumes as young Italian male pages in order to visit an art collection in a monastery that did not allow women visitors. It all went awry when Elizabeth, having taken an extra dose of morphine, grew giddy and wandered off from the group and risked arrest by the town police, much to Robert's irritation; RB then refused to continue the plan (Bosco, "The Brownings," 115–17).

6. Orr, 383.

7. W. Thomas, "Deux lettres inédites de Robert Browning à Joseph Milsand," *Revue Germanique* 12 (1921): 251, 254–55.

8. RB to Mrs. William Kinney, July 25, 1853, Hood, 41.

9. EBB to AB [Mar. 2, 1853], EBB *Arabella*, 1:542.

10. EBB to Julia Martin, Apr. 13, 1853, BL-KT.

11. EBB to AB, Apr. 30 [–May 1, 1853], EBB *Arabella*, 1:575.

12. Apr. 12 [1853], EBB *Letters*, 2:112.

13. EBB to AB [Mar. 2, 1853], EBB *Arabella*, 1:542.

14. July 15 [1853], EBB *Mitford*, 3:388.

15. EBB to Henry Chorley, Aug. 10 [1853], EBB *Letters*, 2:130.

16. EBB to SB [c. Sept. 16, 1853], BL-KT; and EBB to GB, Oct. 7 [1853], *George Barrett*, 199.

17. EBB to HB, Aug. 30, 1853, Huxley, 193.

18. Mrs. Orr (261) regarded the play as incomplete. She considered that RB had planned to return to it in the same way that he later completed "Saul." See Elmer Edgar Stoll, *From Shakespeare to Joyce* (Garden City, NY: Doubleday, 1944), 328–38, for a discussion of reconciling the improbabilities in this play.

19. RB's idea of two souls mixing into one probably had its source in John Donne's great love poem, "The Extasie," though in a Victorian treatment of the idea he had to de-emphasize the sexual component.

20. Altered to "that moment's feat" in 1865 and subsequent editions. RB had perhaps slipped into being too autobiographical in writing "hour's."

Chapter 23

1. The most comprehensive treatment of EBB's interest in the occult is Katherine H. Porter, *Through a Glass Darkly: Spiritualism in the Browning Circle* (Lawrence: University of Kansas Press, 1958).

2. EBB to MRM, May 20 [1853], EBB *Mitford*, 3:385.

3. Elizabeth's acquaintance with mesmerism went back before 1843. Her sister Henrietta had been hypnotized by their friend Mary Minto in a daring but harmless experiment. Her benefactor John Kenyon had reported to her a startling case of a hypnotized subject who displayed clairvoyant knowledge of the private activities of other people. Both Henrietta and George had dined with two physicians who had witnessed surgical operations performed on a hypnotized subject without anesthesia. Her literary correspondent Harriet Martineau had claimed to have been cured of cancer by hypnosis. Yet only against her will did Elizabeth believe the testimony she had heard. As she told Mrs. Jameson, "I will confess, then, that my *impression* is in favour of the reality of mesmerism to some unknown extent. I particularly dislike believing it, I would rather believe most other things in the world; but the evidence of the 'cloud of witnesses' does thunder and lightning so in my ears and eyes, that I believe, while my blood runs cold" ([end of Dec. 1844], EBB *Letters*, 1:228).

4. For the history of modern spiritualism, see Geoffrey K. Nelson, *Spiritualism and Society* (London: Routledge, 1969). Of additional interest are Russell M. Goldfarb and Clare R. Goldfarb, *Spiritualism and Nineteenth-Century Letters* (Madison, NJ: Fairleigh Dickinson University Press, 1978); and Ruth Brandon, *The Spiritualists: The Passion for the Occult in the Nineteenth and Twentieth Centuries* (London: Weidenfeld and Nicolson,

1983), which provides explanations of the tricks and devices which lay behind the phenomena that the "medium" presented.

5. Signe Toksivic, *Emanuel Swedenborg, Scientist and Mystic* (New Haven: Yale University Press, 1948). For *Heaven and Its Wonders and Hell, from Things Heard and Seen*, see the edition first published in Latin in London 1758, now translated into English by J. C. Ayer, and issued by the Swedenborg Foundation, New York, 1960.

6. EBB to Fanny Haworth, Sept. 24, 1851, EBB *Letters*, 2:21.

7. EBB to GB, Feb. 2 [1852], *George Barrett*, 165.

8. EBB to AB, Apr. 28 [1852], EBB *Arabella*, 1:485.

9. Ibid., Dec. 21, 1852, EBB *Arabella*, 1:525–26.

10. EBB to GB, July 16, 17, 18 [1853], *George Barrett*, 191.

11. EBB to HB, July 26, 1853, Camellia Collection, Linton Park, Kent.

12. EBB to IB, Aug. 24, 1853, BL-KT.

13. EBB to SB [Autumn 1853], BL-KT.

14. EBB to AB, Apr. 30 [1853], EBB *Arabella*, 1:572; EBB to John Kenyon, May 16 [1853], EBB *Letters*, 2:117.

15. EBB to AB, Nov. [12–14] [1853], EBB *Arabella*, 2:34–38. The material in this paragraph and in the next three paragraphs is drawn from this letter.

16. The name Robert was asking for was Fuller. As Scott Lewis, the editor of EBB's letters to Arabella, points out, "her middle name was known only by a few as she went by Sarah Flower Adams" (EBB *Arabella*, 2:42, n11).

17. EBB to MRM, May 20 [1853], EBB *Mitford*, 3:385.

18. EBB to AB, Apr. 30 [1853], EBB *Arabella*, 1:572.

19. EBB to Julia Martin, Apr. 13, 1853, BL-KT.

20. Dec. 21, 1853, EBB *Letters*, 2:147.

21. EBB to AB, Apr. 3 [1854], EBB *Arabella*, 2:72–73; RB to John Forster, Apr. 2, 1854, *New Letters*, 73; EBB to MRM, Jan. 18, [1854] EBB *Mitford*, 3:401.

22. [c. Mar. 1854], BL-KT.

23. James, *William Wetmore Story*, 1:285–86.

24. EBB to HB, Mar. 4, 1854, Huxley, 203.

25. Journal, Sept. 21, 1855, *Letters of Anne Thackeray Ritchie*, ed. Hester Ritchie (London: John Murray, 1924), 73–74.

26. EBB to AB, Dec. [16–]19 [1853], EBB *Arabella*, 2:51.

27. EBB to Anna Jameson, Dec. 21, 1853, EBB *Letters*, 2:148.

28. EBB to MRM, Jan. 18 [1854], EBB *Mitford*, 3:402.

29. EBB to AB, Apr. 3 [1854], EBB *Arabella*, 2:75.

30. Ibid., Feb. 1–2 [1854], EBB *Arabella*, 2:62.

31. EBB to HB, Dec. 30, 1853, Huxley, 196; EBB to MRM, May 10 [1854], EBB *Mitford*, 3:409; EBB to AB [Oct. 22, 1852], EBB *Arabella*, 1:506.

32. EBB to Fanny Haworth, Feb. 12 [1854], BL-KT.

33. EBB to W. W. Story [c. Apr. 1854]; James, *William Wetmore Story*, 1:283.

34. James, *William Wetmore Story*, 1:283.

35. RB to Mrs. Thomas FitzGerald, July 15, 1882, *Learned Lady*, 142.

36. EBB to MRM, May 10 [1854], EBB *Mitford*, 3:409; and EBB to AB, May 24 [1854], EBB *Arabella*, 2:80.

37. William Sharp mentions this supposition:"I have been told that the poem . . . was as actually personal as . . . 'Guardian Angel'" but rejects it (159). Betty Miller, always ready to see the worst in both Brownings, is more forthright, declaring that the poem reflects the "hiatus" in their married life (183).

38. EBB to AB, Dec. [16–]19 [1853], EBB *Arabella*, 2:53.

39. EBB to GB, Jan. 10 [1854], *George Barrett*, 212–14.

40. Ibid.

41. EBB to AB, Apr. 3 [1854], EBB *Arabella*, 2:73–74.

42. Feb. 12, 1854, BL-KT.

43. EBB to AB, Feb. 1–2 [1854], EBB *Arabella*, 2:61.

44. The Church of the New Jerusalem began as the Theosophical Society in London in 1783, which led to the founding of the church in 1787, and spread from London and Manchester throughout England and Scotland and eventually to the United States in Philadelphia, Boston, New York, and westward. Its present headquarters in America and its cathedral are in Bryn Athyn, Pennsylvania. It has many congregations throughout the United States. I first heard of the church from Joan Kreible, one of my students, whose family were members of a congregation in Pretty Prairie, Kansas [RSK's note].

45. EBB to AB, Aug. 22 [1854], EBB *Arabella*, 2:90.

46. Ibid., Apr. 1[–2] [1853], EBB *Arabella*, 1:552.

47. RB to FJF, Sept. 15, 1881, Hood, 196.

48. Jan. 24 [1854], EBB *Ogilvy*, 111.

49. RB to John Forster, June 5, 1854, *New Letters*, 77.

50. June 11, 1854; James, *William Wetmore Story*, 1:288.

51. EBB to Henry Chorley, Aug. 10 [1853], EBB *Letters*, 2:131.

52. EBB to HB [Nov. 2, 1851], Camellia Collection, Linton Park, Kent (published in Huxley, 146).

53. EBB to Mrs. Ogilvy, Mar. 6 [1855], EBB *Ogilvy*, 132.

54. Mar. 6 [1855], EBB *Ogilvy*, 132.

55. EBB to SB, June 12, 1855, EBB *Letters*, 2:203.

56. EBB to Julia Martin, Apr. 20, 1855, EBB *Letters*, 2:193.

57. EBB to HB, Apr. 27, 1855, Huxley, 216.

58. EBB to AB, June 25 [1855], EBB *Arabella*, 2:157.

59. Ibid. [July 8, 1855], EBB *Arabella*, 2:163.

60. Ibid., May 15 [1855], EBB *Arabella*, 2:142.

Chapter 24

1. EBB to HB, July 13, 1855, Huxley, 218.

2. EBB to AB, June 11–12 [1855], EBB *Arabella*, 2:148.

3. EBB to HB, Feb. 12 [1855], Camellia Collection, Linton Park, Kent.

4. EBB to Anna Jameson [July–Aug. 1855], EBB *Letters*, 2:210.

5. RB to Elizabeth Kinney, July 25, 1855, in William Lyon Phelps,"Robert Browning on Spiritualism," *Yale Review* NS 23 (1933): 129–35.

6. Aug. 17, 1855, Huxley, 219–21.

7. Daniel Douglas Home, *Incidents in My Life*, second series (New York: Holt and Williams, 1872), 105–6.

8. July 25, 1855, Phelps, "Browning on Spiritualism," 129–35.

9. EBB to HB, Aug. 17, 1855, Huxley, 220–21.

10. Home, *Incidents*, 106.

11. Ibid., 107.

12. William Allingham, *A Diary*, ed. H. Allingham and D. Radford (Harmondsworth: Penguin, 1985), 101. On June 30, 1864, Allingham recorded a brief summary of what RB told him of the séance and its aftermath. RB's blustering acccount is not only inaccurate but also highly exaggerated compared to his letter to Mrs. Kinney written a few days after the séance nine years earlier.

13. EBB to HB, Aug. 17, 1855, Huxley, 219.

14. Ibid. [Sept. 6, 1855], Camellia Collection, Linton Park, Kent.

15. [Aug. 17, 1855], Camellia Collection, Linton Park, Kent.

16. EBB to HB, Aug. 30 [1855], Camellia Collection, Linton Park, Kent.

17. EBB to AB [Sept. 6, 1855], EBB *Arabella*, 2:167.

18. [Aug. 21, 1855], Camellia Collection, Linton Park, Kent.

19. Her full name was Kerenhappuch.

20. See EBB to MRM, Apr. 1, 1843, *BC*, 7:41–42 and *passim*; and EBB's comments on the secret marriage of her own maid, Crow, Mar. [29], 1844, *BC*, 8:283–84.

21. EBB to HB [Sept. 6, 1855], Camellia Collection, Linton Park, Kent.

22. The Browning letters to Fields, Sept. 6 to Oct. 26, about American publication are in Ian Jack, "Browning on *Sordello* and *Men and Women*: Unpublished Letters to James T. Fields," *Harvard Library Quarterly* 45 (1982): 185–99.

23. RB to Macready, Sept. 23, 1852, *New Letters*, 55.

24. RB to John Kenyon, Oct. 1, 1855, Autograph File B, by permission of the Houghton Library, Harvard University.

25. Ibid.

26. EBB to Julia Martin [Oct. 1855], EBB *Letters*, 2:213.

27. RB to John Kenyon, Oct. 1, 1855, Autograph File B, by permission of the Houghton Library, Harvard University.

28. EBB to HB, Oct. 3, 1855, Huxley, 230.

29. [Oct. 1855], EBB *Letters*, 2:213.

30. EBB to Julia Martin [Oct. 1855], EBB *Letters*, 2:213.

31. EBB to AB [Oct. 1, 1855], EBB *Arabella*, 2:175.

32. RB to John Kenyon, Oct. 1, 1855, Autograph File B, by permission of the Houghton Library, Harvard University.

33. EBB to AB [Sept. 20, 1855], EBB *Arabella*, 2:173.

34. A bound set of page proofs is in the Huntington Library. "Old Pictures in Florence" was still entitled "Opus Magistri Jocti."

Chapter 25

1. Vasari's *Vite* was originally published in two volumes in 1550. Browning used the edition of 1846–1857, edited by Gaetano Milanesi and others, for he owned a copy of

this edition in thirteen volumes (*Collections*, A2379). These volumes, sold at the Sotheby auction in 1913, have disappeared. RB also had a copy of the 1550 edition (*Collections*, A2378), but he did not acquire it until the late 1850s or early 1860s, for it was a gift from Walter Savage Landor, whose close association with RB in Florence developed during these years. This copy, signed by Landor in both volumes and later inscribed by RB to Pen, is now in the Temple University Library.

2. Susan Hackett and John Ferns, "Portrait of the Artist as a Young Monk: The Degree of Irony in Browning's 'Fra Lippo Lippi,'" *Studies in Browning and His Circle* 4 (1976): 105–18, survey thirteen critical commentaries that disagree on whether the ideas about art that are set forth in the poem can be regarded as RB's views. They cautiously conclude that RB maintained his detachment from Lippo's theorizing about art.

3. Glen Omans, in a well-argued article, "Browning's 'Fra Lippo Lippi,' A Transcendental Monk," *Victorian Poetry* 7 (1969): 129–45, traces the origin of the idea to Kant, whose transcendental view of the phenomenal world had widespread influence in the nineteenth century, and points to René Wellek, *Immanuel Kant in England 1793–1838* (Princeton: Princeton University Press, 1931) for evidence. Omans speculates that RB picked up the idea from Carlyle's *Sartor Resartus* and *On Heroes, Hero-Worship and the Heroic in History*.

4. RB's good friend, Mrs. Anna Jameson, in her *Memoirs of the Early Italian Painters* (London, 1845) identifies Fra Lippo Lippi with the beginning of a Naturalist movement in Italian painting. She describes these artists in a statement that Lippo echoes in his defense of realistic painting. These painters, she says, were "profoundly versed in the knowledge of the human form, and intent on studying and imitating the various effects of nature in color and in light and shade, without any other aspiration than the representation of beauty for its own sake" (84; quoted from the Houghton Mifflin edition, Boston, 1898). David DeLaura, "The Context of Browning's Painter Poems: Aesthetics, Polemics, Histories," *PMLA* 95 (1980): 367–88, argues that she absorbed these ideas from the French critic Alexis François Rio's *De la poésie chretienne . . . Forme de l'art* (translated as *The Poetry of Christian Art*, 1854).

5. See M. H. Abrams, *Natural Supernaturalism: Tradition and Revolution in Romantic Literature* (New York: Norton, 1971) for a full discussion of this new way of seeing, creating "the sense of novelty and freshness, with old and familiar objects."

6. Vasari, *Lives of the Painters*, 2:303.

7. Only recently has the eroticism of "The Last Ride Together" been given notice. Russell Goldfarb, "Sexual Meaning in 'The Last Ride Together,'" *Victorian Poetry* 3 (1965): 255–61, was the first to publish a sexual interpretation of the poem, although he allegorizes his commentary too much and thus pushes his reading of the poem into absurdities of detail in seeking correspondences with sexual intercourse. Barbara Melchiori (in *Browning's Poetry of Reticence* [New York: Barnes and Noble, 1968], 168) remarks on the "sexual rhythm" of horseback riding. Students in classroom seminars readily perceive the suggestiveness of the poem.

8. Irked by RB's attitude about taking action in response to love, no matter whether society regarded that action as good or bad, George Santayana wrote a famous attack on RB in which he objected to his glorification of "the irrationality of the passions." See "The Poetry of Barbarism" in *Interpretations of Poetry and Religion* (New York: Scribner's, 1900), 188–216.

9. EBB to AB, Apr. 3 [1854], EBB *Arabella*, 2:70.

10. For work which enriches a reader's response to "Cleon," see Antony H. Harrison, *Victorian Poets and Romantic Poems: Intertextuality and Ideology* (Charlottesville: University Press of Virginia, 1990); and "'Cleon' and Its Contexts," in *Critical Essays on Robert Browning*, ed. Mary Ellis Gibson (New York: G. K. Hall, 1992), 139–60.

11. Charles Gavan Duffy, *My Life in Two Hemispheres* (London: Fisher and Unwin, 1898), 260.

12. *University of Toronto Quarterly* 15 (1946): 139–47; reprinted in *The Browning Critics*, ed. Boyd Litzinger and K. L. Knickerbocker (Lexington: University of Kentucky Press, 1965), 167–80.

13. *Victorian Poetry* 16 (1978): 323–40.

14. Thomas Carlyle, *Sartor Resartus in The Works of Thomas Carlyle*, Centenary Edition, vol. 1 (New York: AMS Press, 1969), 1:47.

15. *Victorian Studies* 21 (1978): 171–95.

16. Eleanor Cook, *Browning's Lyrics: An Exploration* (Toronto: University of Toronto Press, 1974), 229–38.

Chapter 26

1. Philip Kelley has identified all the reviewers of both Brownings in this magazine, "The *Athenaeum* and the Brownings," *BSN* 24 (May 1997): 79–81. Chorley was following the editorial policy established by Charles Dilke that reviews should be "free from the warping influences of politics, religion, business, and so far as possible, from the bias of personal friendship or enmity" (Leslie A. Marchand, *The Athenaeum: A Mirror of Victorian Culture* [Chapel Hill: University of North Carolina Press, 1941], 98).

2. Merle Bevington, *The Saturday Review, 1855–1868* (New York: Columbia University Press, 1941), 332–33, identifies the reviewer as "Arnould(?)," the name marked in the Columbia University file that identifies three-quarters of the authors of articles and reviews in eighteen numbers of volume 1 of the magazine, and he suggests that it was Joseph Arnould, the close friend of Browning's youth. Since Arnould was an enthuasiastic supporter of Browning's work, I speculate that Bevington may have misread the name in the file and that the reviewer was Heraud, a longtime critic for English periodicals [RSK's note].

3. Charles Tennyson, *Alfred Tennyson* (New York: Macmillan, 1949), 286.

4. Dec. 1, 1855, continued in the Dec. 8, 1855, issue.

5. 14 (Dec. 1, 1855): 581–82.

6. 79 (Feb. 1856): 135–37.

7. RB to Edward Chapman, Dec. 17, 1855, *New Letters*, 85.

8. *Browning: The Critical Heritage*, ed. Boyd Litzinger and Donald Smalley (London: Routledge, 1970), 165, 172, 173.

9. RB to Edward Chapman, Jan. 17 [1856], *New Letters*, 87.

10. Undated [early 1856] clipping in ABL (*Collections*, A1739).

11. 6 (Mar. 6, 1856): 121–28.

12. 23 (Jan. 1856): 151–80.

13. Morris and his friend Edward Burne-Jones, recently graduated from Oxford, were soon to be disciples of Dante Gabriel Rossetti. They regarded Browning as "the greatest poet alive" (J. W. Mackail, *The Life of William Morris* [London: Longmans, 1899], 1:108).

14. *Browning: The Critical Heritage*, 195–96.

15. 5 (Jan. 1856): 71 (inclusive page numbers are 54 to 71).

16. RB to FJF, Aug. 29, 1881, Hood, 195.

17. Esther Rhodes Houghton, "The Reviewer of Browning's *Men and Women* in the *Rambler* Identified," *Victorian Newsletter* 33 (Spring 1968): 46.

18. 27 (Sept. 15, 1856): 511–46; EBB to HB, Nov. 15, 1855, Huxley, 233.

19. NS 9 (Jan. 1856): 290–96.

20. *British Quarterly Review* 23 (Jan. 1856): 180.

21. *Browning's* Sordello *and the Aesthetics of Difficulty* (Victoria, BC: University of Victoria Press, 1987), chap. 1.

22. EBB to HB, Nov. 15, 1855, Huxley, 233.

23. *William Edmonstoune Aytoun and the Spasmodic Controversy* (New Haven: Yale University Press, 1968), 183–87. The five reviews appeared in the *Saturday Review* 1 (Nov. 24, 1855): 69–70; *Fraser's* 53 (Jan. 1856); 105–16; *Blackwood's* 79 (Feb. 1856): 125–38; *Christian Remembrancer* NS 31 (Apr. 1856): 267–92; and *North British Review* 28 (1858): 231–50.

24. Aytoun published under a pseudonym, T. Percy Jones, *Firmilian: or The Student of Badajoz. A Spasmodic Tragedy* (Edinburgh: Blackwood, 1854).

25. John Ruskin to RB, Dec. 2, 1855, in David DeLaura, "Ruskin and the Brownings: Twenty-Five Unpublished Letters," *Bulletin of the John Rylands Library* 54 (1972): 324–27.

26. Dec. 10, 1855. The letter is printed in W. G. Collingwood, *The Life and Work of John Ruskin* (London: Methuen, 1893), 1:199–202.

Chapter 27

1. Dante Gabriel Rossetti to William Allingham, Dec. 18, 1856, *Letters*, ed. Oswald Doughty and John Robert Wahl, 4 vols. (Oxford: Clarendon Press, 1965–67), 1:309.

2. EBB uses the phrase twice in letters: EBB to MRM, Dec. 24, 1844, *BC*, 9:293; and EBB to RB, Feb. 27, 1845, *BC*, 10:102.

3. EBB to MRM, Dec. 30, 1844, *BC*, 9:304; and EBB to RB, Feb. 27, 1845, *BC*, 10:102–3.

4. EBB to RB, Feb. 27, 1845, *BC*, 10:101.

5. EBB to Mrs. Ogilvy, Sept. 9, 1853, EBB *Ogilvy*, 107. Four years later EBB said of Stowe, "she above all women (yes, and men of the age) has moved the world—and *for good*" (EBB to Anna Jameson, Apr. 9, 1857, EBB *Letters*, 2:259).

6. EBB to RB, Feb. 27, 1845, *BC*, 10:103.

7. EBB to MRM, Dec. 30, 1844, *BC*, 9:304.

8. EBB to Anna Jameson, Apr. 12, 1853, EBB *Letters*, 2:112; and EBB to GB, Oct. 7, 1853, *George Barrett*, 200.

9. RB to Edward Chapman, Feb. 6, 1856, *New Letters*, 88; and William Irvine and Park Honan, *The Book, the Ring, and the Poet: A Biography of Robert Browning* (New York: McGraw-Hill, 1974), 346.

10. EBB to John Kenyon [Mar. 1855]; *Aurora Leigh*, ed. Margaret Reynolds. Norton Critical Edition (New York: Norton, 1996), 330.

11. EBB to Julia Martin, May 14 [1858]; *Aurora Leigh*, ed. Reynolds, 347.

12. EBB to Julia Martin, Feb. 1857, EBB *Letters*, 2:254.

13. EBB to AB [Oct. 4, 1856], EBB *Arabella*, 2:257.

14. "Fragmentary Notes on the Plot," *Aurora Leigh*, ed. Reynolds, 348–49.

15. EBB to John Kenyon [Mar. 1855]; *Aurora Leigh*, ed. Reynolds, 331.

16. EBB to AB, Dec. 10 [1856], EBB *Arabella*, 2:273.

17. EBB to Anna Jameson, Dec. 26, 1856, EBB *Letters*, 2:245.

18. EBB to AB, Dec. 10 [1856] and Jan. 25 [1857], EBB *Arabella*, 2:275, 279.

19. EBB to Anna Jameson [early 1860], EBB *Letters*, 2:364; EBB to W. M. Thackeray, Apr. 21, 1861, EBB *Letters*, 2:445.

20. *Athenaeum* 1517 (Nov. 22, 1856): 1425.

21. EBB to HB, Jan. 10, 1857, Huxley, 265.

22. *Blackwood's Edinburgh Magazine* 81 (Jan. 1857): 32.

23. *Westminster Review* 68 (NS 12) (Oct. 1857): 400.

24. Ibid., 67 (NS 11) (Jan. 1857): 306–7.

25. EBB to Anna Jameson, Dec. 26, 1856, EBB *Letters*, 2:245–46.

26. Forster, *Elizabeth Barrett Browning*, 312–13.

27. RB to Mrs. Kinney [Dec. 7, 1856], *New Letters*, 98.

28. RB to Edward Chapman, Jan. 5, 1857, *New Letters*, 99.

29. EBB to Julia Martin, Dec. 29, 1856, EBB *Letters*, 2:248. EBB had used almost the same words to Anna Jameson on Dec. 26, 1856: "He has been to me in much what my father might have been, and now the place is empty twice over" (EBB *Letters*, 2:247).

30. One example of such a character is Periplectomenus in Plautus's *The Swaggering Soldier*. Prospero in Shakespeare's *The Tempest* is a descendant. Kenyon was twice married and twice a widower, living life as a single man from 1835 on (*DNB*).

31. EBB to Anna Jameson, Dec. 26, 1856, EBB *Letters*, 2:247.

32. EBB to HB, Jan. 10, 1857, Huxley, 264.

33. RB to Julia Martin, May 3, 1857, EBB *Letters*, 2:263–64.

34. EBB to Julia Martin, July 1, 1857, EBB *Letters*, 2:265.

35. EBB to AB [29?] [Apr. 1857], EBB *Arabella*, 2:298.

36. RB to Julia Martin, May 3, 1857, EBB *Letters*, 2:264; and EBB to Julia Martin, July 1, 1857, EBB *Letters*, 2:264.

37. EBB to Julia Martin, July 1, 1857, EBB *Letters*, 2:265; EBB to HB, May 13, 1857, Huxley, 272.

38. EBB to Julia Martin, July 1, 1857, EBB *Letters*, 2:265.

39. EBB to HB, June 2, 1857, Huxley, 274.

40. EBB to SB [Sept.–Oct. 1859], EBB *Letters*, 2:342.

41. EBB to Fanny Haworth, July 23, 1858, EBB *Letters*, 2:285.

42. EBB to IB, Jan. 7, 1859, EBB *Letters*, 2:303.

43. EBB to RB, Sr. [May 1859], EBB *Letters*, 2:315.

44. Matthew Reynolds, *The Realms of Verse 1830–1870: English Poetry in a Time of Nation-Building* (Oxford: Oxford University Press, 2001), 38.

45. RB and EBB to John Ruskin, June 3, 1859, EBB *Letters*, 2:317.

46. EBB to SB [Apr. 1859], EBB *Letters*, 2:311.

47. EBB to AB, Mar. 29 [–31] [1859], EBB *Arabella*, 2:400.

48. Reynolds, *Realms of Verse*, 25.

49. EBB to AB, Mar. 29 [–31] [1859], EBB *Arabella*, 2:400.

50. Ibid. [Apr. 30, 1859], EBB *Arabella*, 2:405.

51. For the substance of this sentence I am indebted to Reynolds, *Realms of Verse*, 158 [DSH's note].

52. EBB to AB [Apr. 30, 1859], EBB *Arabella*, 2:404.

53. EBB to IB, Mar. 27, 1859, EBB *Letters*, 2:308. EBB uses the same quotation to AB, Mar. 29 [–31] [1859], EBB *Arabella*, 2:400.

54. EBB to Julia Martin, Mar. 27, 1858, EBB *Letters*, 2:278; EBB to SB, Feb. 1, 1859, EBB *Letters*, 2:307–8; EBB to SB [May 1859], EBB *Letters*, 2:314.

55. EBB to Anna Jameson, Aug. 26, 1859, EBB *Letters*, 2:324.

56. EBB to SB [July–Aug. 1859], EBB *Letters*, 2:320; EBB to Fanny Haworth, Aug. 24, 1859, EBB *Letters*, 2:323.

57. EBB to Anna Jameson, Aug. 26, 1859, EBB *Letters*, 2:326.

58. EBB to AB [June 27, 1859], EBB *Arabella*, 2:417.

59. EBB to IB, Mar. 27, 1859, EBB *Letters*, 2:308; EBB to SB [May 1859], EBB *Letters*, 2:313.

60. EBB to Fanny Haworth, Aug. 24, 1859, EBB *Letters*, 2:323.

61. EBB to AB, Mar. 29 [–31] [1859], EBB *Arabella*, 2:401.

62. EBB to GB, Apr. 18, 1860, *George Barrett*, 226.

63. EBB to SB [Mar. 1861], EBB *Letters*, 2:435.

64. RB to IB, Sept. 19, 1867, *Dearest Isa*, 282.

65. EBB to SB, Apr. and May 1859, EBB *Letters*, 2:312–14; EBB to John Forster, May 1860, EBB *Letters*, 2:385; EBB to IB, Sept.–Oct. 1859, EBB *Letters*, 2:341.

66. W. E. Aytoun, "Poetic Aberrations," *Blackwood's Edinburgh Magazine* 87 (Apr. 1860): 490–91.

67. *Athenaeum* 1690 (Mar. 17, 1860): 371.

68. EBB to H. F. Chorley, May 2, 1860, EBB *Letters*, 2:381, 379.

69. EBB to IB [Mar. 1860], EBB *Letters*, 2:366–67.

70. EBB to AB, May 7 [1860], EBB *Arabella*, 2:462.

71. EBB to SB [Mar. 1861], EBB *Letters*, 2:435; and EBB to Fanny Haworth, May 18, 1860, EBB *Letters*, 2:388.

72. EBB to SB [Mar. 1860], EBB *Letters*, 2:368–69.

73. EBB to IB [Mar. 1860], EBB *Letters*, 2:365–66.

74. EBB to AB, Apr. 5 [1860], EBB *Arabella*, 2:456.

75. EBB to Julia Martin, Aug. 21, 1860, EBB *Letters*, 2:401.

76. EBB to GB, Sept. 6, 1860, *George Barrett*, 239.

77. EBB to Fanny Haworth, Aug. 25, 1860, EBB *Letters*, 2:405.

78. RB to GB, Dec. 3, 1860, *George Barrett*, 251.

79. Ibid., 251–52.

80. EBB to Fanny Haworth [autumn 1860], EBB *Letters*, 2:410.

81. EBB to AB, May 25, 1861, EBB *Arabella*, 2:532.

82. EBB to Fanny Haworth, Jan. 1861, EBB *Letters*, 2:423.

83. EBB to AB, Feb. [c. 28]-[c. Mar. 3, 1859], EBB *Arabella*, 2:396.

84. June 13, 1861, Hood, 58.

85. EBB to AB, June 15 [1861], EBB *Arabella*, 2:540.

86. RB to IB, June 23, 1861, *Dearest Isa*, 79.

87. RB to SB, June 30, 1861, Hood, 58–60; RB to GB, July 2, 1861, *George Barrett*, 271.

88. RB to John Forster, July 1861, *New Letters*, 138.

89. RB to SB, June 30, 1861, Hood, 61–63; RB to John Forster, July 1861, *New Letters*, 139–40. There is more than one reading of the letter to Sarianna. I have used a manuscript copy of the original in the British Library for the material in this paragraph and the following paragraph [RSK's note]. The expressions of love were crucial for the bereaved Browning, and though he told others about them, he kept their substance private: they were "unrepeatable things" (RB to Fanny Haworth, July 20, 1861, Hood, 64). To Sarianna he said "I only put in a thing or two out of the many in my heart of hearts" (RB to SB, June 30, 1861, Hood, 62) and for Macready he included a parenthesis: "(from much I cannot write)" (RB to W. C. Macready, July 18, 1861, Hood, 64). To Fanny Haworth, Browning was slightly more explicit about Elizabeth's final words: "Then came what my heart will keep till I see her and longer—the most perfect expression of her love to me within my whole knowledge of her—always smilingly, happily, and with a face like a girl's—and in a few minutes she died in my arms, her head on my cheek" (RB to Fanny Haworth, July 20, 1861, Hood, 65).

90. RB to SB, June 30, 1861, Hood, 58–62.

91. W. W. Story to Charles Eliot Norton, Aug. 15, 1861, in James, *William Wetmore Story*, 2:67.

92. RB to John Forster, July 1861, *New Letters*, 139.

Chapter 28

1. RB to SB, July 13, 1861, *New Letters*, 134.

2. RB to IB, Aug. 18, 1862, Sept. 19, 1862, Aug. 18, 1862, *Dearest Isa*, 116, 126, 117.

3. RB to IB, Sept. 19, 1862, *Dearest Isa*, 122–23.

4. Ibid., Sept. 19, 1863, *Dearest Isa*, 175.

5. RB to GB, Oct. 19, 1866, *George Barrett*, 285; RB to IB, Jan. 19, 1865, *Dearest Isa*, 204.

6. RB to SB, July 22, 1861, *New Letters*, 140.

7. RB to John Forster, July 1861, *New Letters*, 137.

8. RB to IB, Oct. 18, 1862, *Dearest Isa*, 127.

9. Ibid., Sept. 19, 1862, and Jan. 19, 1865, *Dearest Isa*, 125, 204.

10. RB to GB, July 2, 1861, and Sept. 30, 1861, *George Barrett*, 271–72, 273.

11. RB to SB, July 5, 1861, *New Letters*, 133.

12. RB to Fanny Haworth, July 20, 1861, Hood, 65.

13. Ibid.

14. RB to SB, July 5, 1861, *New Letters*, 133.

15. Forster, *Elizabeth Barrett Browning*, 369.

16. RB to the Storys, Aug. 20, 1861, *American Friends*, 76.

17. EBB to Mrs. Ogilvy, Jan. 24, 1854, EBB *Ogilvy*, 113.

18. RB to IB, Sept. 17, 1861, *Dearest Isa*, 92.

19. EBB to Mrs. Ogilvy [Oct. 31? 1859], June 8 [1854], Mar. 6 [1855], EBB *Ogilvy*, 146–47, 121, 132.

20. RB to the Storys, Nov. 10, 1861, *American Friends*, 85.

21. RB to the Storys, Sept. 13, 1862, Hood, 70.

22. RB to IB, Aug. 22, 1861, and Aug. 18, 1862, *Dearest Isa*, 83, 116.

23. Ibid., Oct. 18, 1861, *Dearest Isa*, 130.

24. RB to the Storys, Aug. 20, 1861, *American Friends*, 77, 75; RB to IB, Sept. 19, 1862, *Dearest Isa*, 126.

25. RB to IB, Aug. 18, 1862, *Dearest Isa*, 119.

26. Ibid., Aug. 19, 1864, *Dearest Isa*, 190; the quotation about the mountains is from RB to Mrs. Story, Aug. 22, 1864, *American Friends*, 146.

27. RB to IB, Nov. 19, 1862, *Dearest Isa*, 133.

28. *Records of Tennyson, Ruskin, Browning* (New York: Harper, 1893), 185–86.

29. Allingham, *Diary*, 151.

30. RB to IB, Feb. 19, 1866, *Dearest Isa*, 230.

31. RB to IB, Nov. 19, 1862, *Dearest Isa*, 137.

32. RB to the Storys, Aug. 20, 1861, *American Friends*, 76.

33. Ibid., Mar. 5, 1863, 117.

34. RB to IB, Mar. 19, 1863, *Dearest Isa*, 156; RB to the Storys, Mar. 5, 1863, *American Friends*, 117.

35. RB to IB, Feb. 6, 1862, *Dearest Isa*, 95.

36. RB to IB, Aug. 19, 1864, *Dearest Isa*, 190.

37. RB to the Storys, Mar. 5, 1863, *American Friends*, 116.

38. RB to IB, Dec. 19, 1862, *Dearest Isa*, 142.

39. RB to IB, July 19, 1863, *Dearest Isa*, 168.

40. Allingham, *Diary*, 102.

41. RB to IB, Aug. 19, 1864, *Dearest Isa*, 191.

42. RB to the Storys, Mar. 19, 1862, *American Friends*, 101.

43. Ibid.

44. RB to Moncure Conway, Sept. 17, 1853, *New Letters*, 157.

45. RB to IB, Nov. 19, 1863, *Dearest Isa*, 180.

46. Orr, 280.

47. *Athenaeum* (June 4, 1864); *Victoria Magazine* (July 1, 1864); both quotations are in *Browning: The Critical Heritage*, 221, 229.

48. RB to IB, Oct. 19, 1864, *Dearest Isa*, 196.

49. RB to IB, Aug. 19, 1865, *Dearest Isa*, 220.

50. RB to IB, Aug. 19, 1863, *Dearest Isa*, 173.

51. RB to Richard Monckton Milnes, July 7, 1863, *New Letters*, 150–51.

52. RB to IB, Nov. 19, 1863, *Dearest Isa*, 180–81. The critic may be Richard Holt Hutton, who wrote a brief review of the *Poetical Works* for the *Spectator* in Sept. 1863 and a longer piece for the *National Review* a month later. Browning may have been quoting from memory, for the quotations do not appear in Hutton's texts. Hutton does say, however, in the *Spectator* review (Sept. 5, 1863) that "it is Mr. Browning's characteristic that there are

so few parts of any of his poems which will impress the reader at all adequately if severed from the whole" ("Mr. Browning's Poetry," *A Victorian Spectator: Uncollected Writings of R. H. Hutton*, ed. Robert H. Tener and Malcolm Woodfield [Bristol: Bristol Press, 1989], 75), and a month later he wrote that if one is to read a Browning poem, one must remember "this characteristic of his, that the whole must be fairly grasped before any of the 'component parts' are intelligible" ("Mr. Browning's Poems," *National Review* 47 [Oct. 1863]: 418). Browning's later reference (in that same letter to Isa) to the charge that he "never delineate[s] the quieter female character" fits with Hutton's assertion of "the far superior character of his masculine than of his feminine sketches" (*National Review*, 425) because his women are always shown in extreme situations.

53. RB to IB, Dec. 19, 1864, *Dearest Isa*, 201.

54. John Keats to George and Georgiana Keats, Feb. 14–May 3, 1819.

55. [Feb. 11, 1845], *BC*, 10:69.

56. "The Detachment of Browning," *Athenaeum* 3245 (Jan. 4, 1890): 18.

57. RB to IB, Apr. 19, 1863, *Dearest Isa*, 160.

58. RB to IB, Dec. 19, 1864, *Dearest Isa*, 201.

59. RB to IB, Nov. 19, 1862, and Dec. 19, 1863, *Dearest Isa*, 135, 183.

60. Mark Pattison, "Tendencies of Religious Thought in England, 1688–1750," *Essays and Reviews* (London: Parker, 1860), 259–60.

61. David Freidrich Strauss, *The Life of Jesus Critically Examined*, trans. George Eliot (1846, London: Sonnenschein, 1906), xxx, 757.

62. Jowett's essay was entitled "On the Interpretation of Scripture." David Shaw argues that "Jowett's theory of biblical interpretation exercises an important influence on Browning," an influence particularly evident in *Balaustion's Adventure* (*The Lucid Veil: Poetic Truth in the Victorian Age* [Madison: University of Wisconsin Press, 1987] 198–202).

63. Victor Shea and William Whitla, eds., *Essays and Reviews: The 1860 Text and Its Reading* (Charlottesville: University Press of Virginia, 2000), ix.

64. Basil Willey, *More Nineteenth Century Studies: A Group of Honest Doubters* (London: Chatto and Windus, 1956), 137.

65. RB to IB, Nov. 19, 1863, *Dearest Isa*, 180.

66. Ernest Renan, *The Life of Jesus* (London: Trübner, 1863), 15.

Chapter 29

1. RB to IB, Apr. 19–22, 1866, *Dearest Isa*, 235.

2. RB to Pen, June 13 and 14, 1866, Hood, 94–96.

3. RB to IB, June 20, 1866, *Dearest Isa*, 240–41.

4. Aug. 13, 1846, *BC*, 13:251.

5. RB to Mrs. FitzGerald, Dec. 4, 1886, *Learned Lady*, 193.

6. RB to Pen, June 15 and June 17, 1866, Hood, 97, 98.

7. RB to Seymour Kirkup, Feb. 19, 1867, Hood, 106.

8. RB to IB, June 20, 1866, *Dearest Isa*, 241.

9. Ibid., Aug. 9, 1870, *Dearest Isa*, 341. The information in the following sentence is from *Dearest Isa*, 267, 333.

10. *Records of Tennyson, Ruskin, Browning* (New York: Harper, 1893), 166.

11. RB to IB, Apr. 25, 1871, *Dearest Isa*, 357.

12. RB to SB [Apr. 15, 1870], and [Aug. or Sept. 1875], *New Letters*, 194, 228.

13. RB to Pen Browning [June 13, 1866], and [June 17, 1866], Hood, 95, 98.

14. RB to IB, Sept. 19, 1870, and Aug. 19, 1871, *Dearest Isa*, 346, 365.

15. For information on the Joseph Milsand Archive, see the ABL's website, www.browninglibrary.org.

16. RB to SB, July 5 [1861], *New Letters*, 134.

17. RB to IB, Sept. 24, 1866, *Dearest Isa*, 247.

18. EBB to AB, Oct. 7–8 [1859], EBB *Arabella*, 2:424.

19. RB to Seymour Kirkup, Feb. 19, 1867, Hood, 107.

20. RB to IB, Feb. 19, 1867, *Dearest Isa*, 254.

21. RB to IB, June 18, 1867, and July 19, 1867, *Dearest Isa*, 269, 271–72.

22. RB to IB, Feb. 19, 1867, *Dearest Isa*, 253–54.

23. Ibid., Feb. 24, 1870, *Dearest Isa*, 331.

24. Ibid., Mar. 21, 1867, *Dearest Isa*, 258.

25. Ibid., Apr. 23, 1867, *Dearest Isa*, 263. Gertrude Reese prints Jowett's Apr. 1, 1867, report to Browning in "Robert Browning and His Son," *PMLA* 61 (1946): 789.

26. RB to IB, Nov. 19, 1867, *Dearest Isa*, 284.

27. Ibid., June 16, 1868, *Dearest Isa*, 297.

28. Jowett to RB, Dec. 22, 1867, and Oct. 8 [1868], printed in Gertrude Reese, "Robert Browning and His Son," *PMLA* 61 (1946): 790, 791.

29. RB to Henry George Liddell, Oct. 17, 1868; Maisie Ward, *The Tragi-Comedy of Pen Browning* (New York: Sheed and Ward, 1972), 158.

30. RB to IB, late Jan. 1869, *Dearest Isa*, 307–8.

31. Ibid., Sept. 19, 1869, and Feb. 24, 1870, *Dearest Isa*, 324, 331.

32. RB to Pen's tutor, the Reverend Reginald Broughton; quoted by William Whitla, "Browning and the Ashburton Affair," *BSN* 2. 2 (1972): 23.

33. RB to SB, Apr. 15, 1870, *New Letters*, 192n, 192.

34. RB to GB, July 2, 1861, *George Barrett*, 271.

35. Ibid., June 17 and July 1, 1870, *George Barrett*, 292–95.

36. RB to IB, July 2, 1870, *Dearest Isa*, 337–38.

37. Ibid., June 19, 1868, *Dearest Isa*, 298.

38. Ibid., Aug. 19, 1865, *Dearest Isa*, 219.

39. Ibid., July 19, 1867, and Feb. 19, 1869, *Dearest Isa*, 274, 312–13.

40. RB to Edith Story, Apr. 4, 1872, *American Friends*, 169–72.

41. Virginia Surtees *The Ludovisi Goddess: The Life of Louisa Lady Ashburton* (Salisbury, Wiltshire: Michael Russell, 1984), 145.

42. Rossetti to William Allingham, Feb. 28, 1870, *Letters of Dante Gabriel Rossetti to William Allingham 1854–1870*, ed. George Birkbeck Hill (London: T. Fisher Unwin, 1897), 288. The next quotation is from the same letter.

43. Quoted by Surtees, *The Ludovisi Goddess: The Life of Louisa Lady Ashburton*, 150.

44. Carlyle to Dr. John Carlyle, Feb. 6, 1867, *New Letters*, ed. Alexander Carlyle (1904; Hildesheim: Georg Olms, 1969), 2:244.

45. The four preceding quotations are from unpublished letters quoted by Surtees, 154, 128. For the situations with Carlyle and the Duke of Sermoneta, see Surtees, 159, 163.

46. RB to IB, Aug. 28 [1869], *Dearest Isa*, 322. The next quotations are from the same letter.

47. RB to W. W. Story, June 19, 1886, *American Friends*, 186.

48. Ibid., June 9, 1874, 175.

49. For a detailed account of the Lady Ashburton affair, see William Whitla, "Browning and the Ashburton Affair," *BSN* 2. 2 (1972): 12–41. See also Surtees, *The Ludovisi Goddess*.

50. Julia Wedgwood to RB, Mar. 1, 1865, Wedgwood, 132.

51. Ibid., June 25, 1864, Wedgwood, 27–28.

52. RB to Julia Wedgwood, July 25, 1864, Wedgwood, 45.

53. Ibid., undated, Wedgwood, 135.

54. Ibid., May 17, 1867, Wedgwood, 140–41.

55. Julia Wedgwood to RB, Jan. 30, 1869, Wedgwood, 174.

56. RB to Julia Wedgwood, Feb. 1, 1869, Wedgwood, 177–78.

57. Ibid., Nov. 19, 1868, Wedgwood, 158.

58. Ibid., undated, Wedgwood, 135.

59. Julia Wedgwood to RB, Good Friday, 1869, Wedgwood, 197.

60. RB to Julia Wedgwood, Mar. 29, 1869, Wedgwood, 199.

61. Ibid., Mar. 8, 1869, Wedgwood, 194.

62. Julia Wedgwood to RB, Apr. 7, 1869, Wedgwood, 202.

63. RB to IB, Aug. 19, 1865, *Dearest Isa*, 220.

64. RB to Fields, Osgood, July 19, 1867, Hood, 114.

65. RB to IB, Sept. 19, 1864, *Dearest Isa*, 193. He made the same statement to Julia Wedgwood, Oct. 3, 1864, Wedgwood, 95.

66. RB to Fields, Osgood, July 19, 1867, Hood, 114.

67. RB to IB, Dec. 31, 1867, *Dearest Isa*, 286.

68. RB to Julia Wedgwood, Nov. 19, 1868, Wedgwood, 159.

69. RB to Mrs. Thomas FitzGerald, Mar. 17, 1883, *Learned Lady*, 157.

70. RB to Alfred Tennyson, Aug. 7, 1880, *The Brownings to the Tennysons: Letters from Robert Browning and Elizabeth Barrett Browning to Alfred, Emily, and Hallam Tennyson 1852–1889*, ed. Thomas J. Collins (Baylor Browning Interests 22; Waco, TX: ABL, 1971), 43. I am indebted to Thomas J. Collins for first juxtaposing these two quotations.

71. RB to W. G. Kingsland, Nov. 27, 1868, Hood, 128–29.

72. "The Structural Logic of *The Ring and the Book*," *Nineteenth-Century Literary Perspectives: Essays in Honor of Lionel Stevenson*, ed. Clyde de L. Ryals (Durham: Duke University Press, 1974), 105–14.

73. See *Metahistory: The Historical Imagination in Nineteenth-Century Europe* (Baltimore: Johns Hopkins University Press, 1973); and *The Content of the Form: Narrative Discourse and Historical Representation* (Baltimore: Johns Hopkins University Press, 1987).

74. For a fuller account of romance in the Victorian period, see Donald S. Hair, "Romance," in *Encylopedia of the Victorian Era*, ed. James Eli Adams and Tom and Sara Pendergast (Danbury, CT: Grolier Academic Press, 2004), 3:328–29.

75. RB to Julia Wedgewood, Nov. 19, 1868, Wedgwood, 161.

76. *Spectator* 12 (Dec. 1868); *Browning: The Critical Heritage*, 292.

77. *Athenaeum* (Mar. 20, 1869); *Temple Bar* (June 1869); *Browning: The Critical Heritage*, 317, 340, 346.

78. *Athenaeum* (Dec. 26, 1868); *Browning: The Critical Heritage*, 293.

79. J. H. C. Fane, *Edinburgh Review* 130 (July 1869); John Doherty, *Dublin Review* (July 1869); *Browning: The Critical Heritage*, 334, 326.

80. *Athenaeum* (Dec. 26, 1868); *Browning: The Critical Heritage*, 293.

81. *Macmillan's Magazine* (Jan. 1869); *Cornhill Magazine* (Feb. 1869); *Browning: The Critical Heritage*, 309, 314.

82. *Saturday Review* (Dec. 26, 1868); *Browning: The Critical Heritage*, 296–97.

83. RB to Julia Wedgwood, Mar. 8, 1869, Wedgwood, 195–96.

Chapter 30

1. G. A. Simcox, *Academy* 4 (June 2, 1873), 201–3; *Browning: The Critical Heritage*, 379.

2. RB to John Forster, Dec. 2, 1875, *New Letters*, 230.

3. Allingham, *Diary*, 209, 205.

4. RB to IB, Oct. 1, 1871, and Aug. 19, 1871, *Dearest Isa*, 367, 364.

5. Mario Praz, *The Hero in Eclipse in Victorian Fiction*, trans. Angus Davidson (London: Oxford University Press, 1956).

6. RB to Edith Story, Jan. 1, 1872, *American Friends*, 167.

7. RB to IB, Nov. 19, 1867; July 19, 1870, *Dearest Isa*, 284, 341. "Ba" is McAleer's reading of Browning's handwriting; Hood had earlier read the same word as "Isa."

8. RB to IB, Aug. 19 and Oct. 1, 1871, *Dearest Isa*, 365, 367.

9. Ibid., Aug. 19, 1870, *Dearest Isa*, 342, 344.

10. Ibid., Oct. 19, 1870, Jan. 23, 1871, Dec. 29, 1871, *Dearest Isa*, 347, 348, 356, 371.

11. The work of Leo Anthony Hetzler is the best guide to *Prince Hohenstiel-Schwangau*. See "The Case of Prince Hohenstiel-Schwangau: Browning and Napoleon III," *Victorian Poetry* 15 (1977): 335–50, an essay based on Hetzler's 1954 M.A. thesis at the University of Toronto.

12. RB to IB, July 19, 1871, *Dearest Isa*, 362.

13. *The Lucid Veil: Poetic Truth in the Victorian Age* (London: Athlone, 1987), 49.

14. *Intentions* (1891), in *The First Collected Edition of the Works of Oscar Wilde 1908–1922*, ed. Robert Ross (1908. Rpt. London: Dawsons, 1969) 8:148.

15. George Meredith, "On the Idea of Comedy and of the Uses of the Comic Spirit" (1877), in *George Meredith's Essay* On Comedy and *Other* New Quarterly Magazine *Publications: A Critical Edition*, ed. Maura C. Ives (Lewisburg, PA: Bucknell University Press, 1998), 117.

16. Domett, 161.

17. George Bornstein, "Pound's Parleyings with Browning," *Poetic Remaking: The Art of Browning, Yeats, and Pound* (University Park: Pennsylvania State University Press, 1988), 127–29.

18. William Michael Rossetti, *Dante Gabriel Rossetti: His Family-Letters, with a Memoir* 1895 (New York: AMS, 1970), 1:308.

19. RFB to IB, June 19, 1870, *Dearest Isa*, 336.

20. *Browning: The Critical Heritage*, 377.

21. Domett, 52–53.

22. RB to Seymour Kirkup, Feb. 19, 1867, Hood, 106.

23. RB to T. J. Nettleship, May 16, 1889, Hood, 309.

24. Ibid.

25. RB to SB, July 5 [1861], *New Letters*, 134.

26. RB to IB, Aug. 18, 1862, *Dearest Isa*, 117.

27. RB to Joseph Milsand, May 13, 1872; quoted in Th. Bentzon (Mme. Blanc), "A French Friend of Browning—Joseph Milsand," *Scribner's Magazine* 20 (1896): 111.

28. Bentzon, 110.

29. RB to IB, Nov. 26, 1866, *Dearest Isa*, 251.

30. RB to IB, Feb. 24, 1870, and Mar. 22, 1870, *Dearest Isa*, 331, 333.

31. RB to Mrs. Sophia Eckley, Aug. 19, 1858, *New Letters*, 110.

32. RB to SB, July 13, 1861, *New Letters*, 136.

33. RB to John Ruskin, Feb. 24, 1865, *New Letters*, 166–67.

34. RB to IB, Mar. 30, 1872, *Dearest Isa*, 376.

35. Th. Bentzon (Mme Blanc), "A French Friend of Browning—Joseph Milsand," *Scribner's Magazine* 20 (1896): 116–17. Clyde de L. Ryals reproduces the photograph in his *The Life of Robert Browning: A Critical Biography* (Oxford: Blackwell, 1993), 192 (plate 12).

36. RB to IB, Sept. 19, 1872, *Dearest Isa*, 384.

37. RB to Anne Egerton Smith, Aug. 4, 1870, Hood, 140.

38. RB to IB, Aug. 19 and Sept. 19, 1870, *Dearest Isa*, 342, 346.

39. Anne [Thackeray] Ritchie, *Records of Tennyson, Ruskin, Browning* (New York: Harper, 1893), 173–78.

40. Quoted by Pettigrew and Collins, 2:1030.

41. *Browning: The Critical Heritage*, 404, 413.

42. Domett, 162.

43. Ibid., 177.

44. Ibid., 100.

Chapter 31

1. RB to Mrs. Thomas FitzGerald, Sept. 4, 1880, *Learned Lady*, 89.

2. RB to Norman MacColl, Jan. 1, 1878, Hood, 183.

3. RB to Mrs. Thomas FitzGerald, Nov. 20, 1880, *Learned Lady*, 104.

4. Norton B. Crowell, *Alfred Austin, Victorian* (London: Weidenfeld and Nicolson, 1955), 24.

5. *The Autobiography of Alfred Austin, Poet Laureate, 1835–1910*, 2 vols. (London: Macmillan, 1911), 1: 43–44; 1: 153.

6. Crowell, *Alfred Austin*, 53.

7. *Browning: The Critical Heritage*, 340, 339, 346–47, 352.

8. RB to IB, Dec. 30, 1870, *Dearest Isa*, 352–53.

9. RB to Mrs. Thomas FitzGerald, Aug. 28, 1876, *Learned Lady*, 36; on Aug. 19, 1876, Browning made a similar comment ("physically as well as morally and intellectually a dwarf") to Edmund Gosse (Hood, 175).

10. RB to GB, May 25, 1875, *George Barrett*, 300; RB to IB, May 21, 1871, *Dearest Isa*, 359.

11. RB to GB, May 25, 1875, *George Barrett*, 300; see also Hood, 175.

12. RB to Mrs. Thomas FitzGerald, Aug. 28, 1876, *Learned Lady*, 36; see also letter to Edmund Gosse, Aug. 19, 1876, Hood, 175.

13. RB to IB, Mar. 22, 1870 and May 21, 1871, *Dearest Isa*, 332, 359.

14. RB to Edward Moxon, Nov. 19, 1845, *BC*, 11:178.

15. *Browning: The Critical Heritage*, 426.

16. *Dearest Isa*, xxvi-xxvii.

17. RB to GB, Aug. 12, 1876, *George Barrett*, 303.

18. John Miller Gray, *Memoir and Remains*; 2 vols. (Edinburgh: David Douglas, 1895), 1:39–40.

19. RB to Mrs. FitzGerald, Aug. 28, 1876, *Learned Lady*, 36.

20. RB to Mrs. FitzGerald, Aug. 24, 1878, *Learned Lady*, 57.

21. Orr, 304.

22. RB to IB, Sept. 24 and Oct. 19, 1866, *Dearest Isa*, 246, 249.

23. RB to Mrs. FitzGerald, Aug. 17, 1877, *Learned Lady*, 44–45.

24. RB to Mrs. FitzGerald, Aug. 17, 1877, *Learned Lady*, 45.

25. RB to Mrs. FitzGerald, Aug. 17, 1877, *Learned Lady*, 44.

26. Domett, 210.

27. See F. E. L. Priestley, "A Reading of *La Saisiaz*," *University of Toronto Quarterly* 25 (1955): 47–59.

28. L. C. Collins, *Life and Memoirs of John Churton Collins* (London: John Lane, 1912), 80–82.

29. RB to Julia Wedgwood, June 25, 1864, *Wedgwood*, 29.

30. Sharp, 195–96.

31. Sharp quotes Moncure Conway on "Browning's 'orthodoxy'" in a note on page 193.

32. Thomas J. Collins, ed., "Letters from Robert Browning to the Rev. J. D. Williams, 1874–1889," *Browning Institute Studies* 4 (1976): 14.

33. *Browning: The Critical Heritage*, 447, 449, 454.

34. RB to IB, Aug. 19, July 19, and Oct. 1, 1871, *Dearest Isa*, 367, 364, 362.

35. Domett, 55.

36. Domett, 115.

37. Domett, 119.

38. Domett, 154.

39. RB to GB, Jan. 20, 1875, *George Barrett*, 299.

40. RB to Mrs. Thomas FitzGerald, Aug. 9, 1878, *Learned Lady*, 55.

41. RB to Mrs. Thomas FitzGerald, June 9, 1878, *Learned Lady*, 49.

42. RB to Mrs. Lippincott, June 28, 1875, *New Letters*, 227.

43. RB to Mrs. Thomas FitzGerald, Aug. 6, 1881, *Learned Lady*, 120.

44. Domett, 169.

45. RB to Mrs. Thomas FitzGerald, Sept. 7, 1878, *Learned Lady*, 62.

46. RB to Mrs. Thomas FitzGerald, Oct. 12, 1878, *Learned Lady*, 71.

47. RB to Mrs. Thomas FitzGerald, June 19, 1880, *Learned Lady*, 80.

48. RB to Thomas Carlyle, Mar. 26, 1878, Hood, 183.

49. Allingham, *Diary*, 263–64.

50. Ibid., 213.

51. Ibid., 215.

52. Wilfred Meynell, "The 'Detachment' of Browning," *Athenaeum* No. 3245 (Jan. 4, 1890): 18.

53. RB to Mrs. Thomas FitzGerald, June 19, 1880; Oct. 12, 1878; Sept. 19 and 4, 1880, *Learned Lady*, 81, 71, 93, 87.

54. RB to FJF, Jan. 5, 1882, *Browning's Trumpeter*, 45–46.

55. RB to Mrs. Thomas FitzGerald, Sept. 16, 1882, *Learned Lady*, 154.

56. See, however, the first chapter of Patricia O'Neill's *Robert Browning and Twentieth-Century Criticism* (Columbia, SC: Camden House, 1995). For a history of the London Browning Society, see William S. Peterson, *Interrogating the Oracle* (Athens: Ohio University Press, 1969).

57. *BSP*, 1:19–20.

58. RB to T. J. Nettleship, Mar. 10, 1889, Hood, 304.

59. *Diary*, 373.

60. RB to FJF, Oct. 2, 1881; Aug. 29, 1882; Jan. 29, 1884, *Browning's Trumpeter*, 28, 58, 90.

61. See Simon Winchester, *The Meaning of Everything: The Story of the* Oxford English Dictionary (Oxford: Oxford University Press, 2003), 67–69.

62. Quoted by William Benzie, *Dr. F. J. Furnivall: Victorian Scholar Adventurer* (Norman, OK Pilgrim Books, 1983), 7.

63. RB to FJF, Aug. 29, 1881, *Browning's Trumpeter*, 21; RB to Mrs. Thomas FitzGerald, Sept. 6, 1881, *Learned Lady*, 124–25.

64. *BSP*, 1:2.

65. RB to T. J. Nettleship, Mar. 10, 1889, Hood, 303.

66. RB to J. D. Williams, Sept. 24, 1884; *Browning Institute Studies* 4 (1976): 38–39.

67. RB to FJF, Dec. 9, 1882, *Browning's Trumpeter*, 61–62.

68. RB to J. D. Williams, "Letters from Robert Browning to the Rev. J. D. Williams, 1874–1889," ed. Thomas J. Collins, *Browning Institute Studies* 4 (1976): 38.

69. RB to T. J. Nettleship, Mar. 10, 1889, Hood, 303.

70. RB to Mrs. Thomas FitzGerald, Aug. 6, 1881, *Learned Lady*, 119.

71. W. Boyd Carpenter, *Some Pages of My Life* (London: Williams and Norgate, 1911), 201.

72. "Foretalk," *BSP*, 1:3.

73. RB to George Smith, Nov. 12, 1887, *Browning's Trumpeter*, 198, n10.

74. *Browning's Trumpeter*, 195.

75. RB to FJF, Mar. 2, 1889; Feb. 23, 1889, *Browning's Trumpeter*, 154.

76. *BSP*, 2:338.

77. RB to FJF, Nov. 19, 1885, *Browning's Trumpeter*, 123.

78. *BSP*, 1:21–26.

79. RB to FJF, Apr. 7, 1881, *Browning's Trumpeter*, 18.

80. See Michael Millgate, *Testamentary Acts: Browning, Tennyson, James, Hardy* (Oxford: Clarendon Press, 1992), 10–12.

81. RB to FJF, Oct. 3, 1881; Oct. 15, 1883; Feb. 17, 1884, *Browning's Trumpeter*, 31, 81, 92.

82. RB to Mrs. Charles Skirrow, Feb. 8, 1888, *New Letters*, 356.

83. *Browning's Trumpeter*, 167; Marvin Spevack, *James Orchard Halliwell-Phillipps: The Life and Works of the Shakespearean Scholar and Bookman* (New Castle, DE: Oak Knoll Press, 2001), ix.

84. RB to Charles MacKay, Mar. 2, 1881, *Browning's Trumpeter*, 188.

85. *BSP*, 1:1; "Recollections of Robert Browning," *Browning's Trumpeter*, 195.

86. RB to Miss West, Nov. 12, 1881; Griffin and Minchin, 269; RB to Edmund Yates, c. 1881, Hood, 212.

87. RB to FJF, Dec. 8, 1881, *Browning's Trumpeter*, 41.

88. RB to E. Dickinson West, Nov. 12, 1881, Hood, 202.

89. Griffin and Minchin, 269–70.

90. RB to FJF, Aug. 29, 1881; Dec. 8, 1881, *Browning's Trumpeter*, 22, 41.

91. RB to FJF, Jan. 12, 1882, *Browning's Trumpeter*, 46–47.

92. RB to J. D. Williams, Sept. 24, 1884; *Browning Institute Studies* 4 (1976): 38.

93. RB to J. Dykes Campbell, Mar. 15, 1884, Hood, 227.

94. RB to Edward Dowden, Dec. 13, 1867, Hood, 123.

95. "The Critic as Host," *Critical Theory Since 1965*, ed. Hazard Adams and Leroy Searle (Tallahassee: Florida State University Press, 1986), 452–68.

96. *BSP*, 2:3–4.

97. Walter Pater, "Browning," in *Essays from 'The Guardian.' Works*, Library ed. (London: Macmillan, 1910), 10:43, 47.

98. Quoted by Benzie, *Dr. F. J. Furnivall*, 232.

99. Quoted by Benzie, *Dr. F. J. Furnivall*, 251; quoted by William S. Peterson, *Interrogating the Oracle* (Athens: Ohio University Press, 1969), 129.

100. RB to Emily Hickey, Mar. 24, 1883, *New Letters*, 284.

101. RB to Emily Hickey, Nov. 30, 1883; Feb. 15, 1884, *New Letters*, 291, 297–98.

102. *BSP*, 2:339.

Chapter 32

1. RB to W. W. Story [Oct. 15, 1865], *American Friends*, 156.

2. RB to IB, Sept. 19, 1865, *Dearest Isa*, 229.

3. RB to IB, Dec. 19 and Oct. 19, 1865, *Dearest Isa*, 229, 227.

4. RB to IB, Mar. 19, 1866, *Dearest Isa*, 232.

5. RB to IB, May 22, 1867, *Dearest Isa*, 267.

6. RB to IB, Feb. 20, 1868, *Dearest Isa*, 293.

7. RB to IB, Feb. 24, 1870, *Dearest Isa*, 330.

8. RB to IB, Oct. 1, 1871, *Dearest Isa*, 367–68.

9. RB to IB, July 19, 1871, *Dearest Isa*, 362.

10. RB to IB, Oct. 1, 1871, *Dearest Isa*, 368.

11. RB to IB, Aug. 7, 1866; May 19, 1866, *Dearest Isa*, 244, 239.

12. RB to IB, Aug. 7, 1866; May 19, 1866, *Dearest Isa*, 244, 239.

13. RB to Annie Egerton Smith, Aug. 4, 1870, Hood, 140; and RB to IB, Oct. 19, 1865, *Dearest Isa*, 226.

14. RB to IB, Jan. 19, 1868, *Dearest Isa*, 289–90.

15. RB to IB, Jan. 19/25, 1872, *Dearest Isa*, 372.

16. RB to IB, Oct. 19/ Nov. 8, 1871, *Dearest Isa*, 369–70.

17. RB to Mrs. Thomas FitzGerald, Sept. 7, 1878, *Learned Lady*, 61.

18. RB to Mrs. Thomas FitzGerald, Aug. 9, 1878, *Learned Lady*, 54.

19. RB to Mrs. Thomas FitzGerald, Sept. 7, 1878, *Learned Lady*, 61.

20. Ibid.

21. RB to Mrs. Charles Skirrow, Sept. 12, 1878, *New Letters*, 248–49.

22. RB to KB, July 17, 1889, *More than Friend*, 97.

23. RB to KB, June 10, 1889, *More than Friend*, 94.

24. RB to GB, Oct. 22, 1889, *George Barrett*, 329. However, RB's own record of his itinerary in 1838 indicates that he was in Venice for more than two weeks before travelling on to Asolo (*BC*, 4:xii–xiii).

25. RB to KB, Aug. 24, 1889, *More than Friend*, 102.

26. RB to KB, June 10, 1889, *More than Friend*, 94; Mrs. Bronson gives a full account of these recurring dreams in her "Browning in Asolo" (1900), reprinted in *More than Friend*, 127–28.

27. Allingham, *Diary*, 248.

28. RB to KB, June 10, 1889, *More than Friend*, 94.

29. RB to Mrs. Thomas FitzGerald, Sept. 28, 1878, *Learned Lady*, 68.

30. Ibid., Aug. 17, 1880, *Learned Lady*, 85.

31. Ibid., Aug. 17 and Sept. 4, 1880, *Learned Lady*, 86, 87.

32. Orr, 316.

33. Arthur Symons, *An Introduction to the Study of Browning* (London: Dent, 1906), 24.

34. Clyde Ryals points out that, in the "first series," "'Martin Relph' alone fits Browning's description" of the "dramatic" (*Browning's Later Poetry 1871–1889* [Ithaca: Cornell University Press, 1975], 168.

35. RB to Wilfred Meynell, Apr. 10, 1879; *Athenaeum* No. 3245 (Jan. 4, 1890): 18.

36. RB to Frederick Oldfield Ward [May 24, 1844], *BC*, 5:75.

37. Wilfred Meynell, "The 'Detachment' of Browning," *Athenaeum* No. 3245 (Jan. 4, 1890): 18. Browning told this same story in 1885 to Hiram Corson, who repeats it in his 1908 "A Few Reminiscences of Robert Browning," reprinted in *Browning Institute Studies* 3 (1975): 70–71.

38. Rpt. by Arthur Symons, *An Introduction to the Study of Browning* (London: Dent, 1906), 259.

39. Domett, 248–49.

40. RB to Mrs. Thomas FitzGerald, Mar. 17, 1883, *Learned Lady*, 156–57.

41. RB to FJF, Feb. 4, 1883, *Browning's Trumpeter*, 65.

42. Ibid., Jan. 9, 1883, *Browning's Trumpeter*, 63.

43. RB to Barnett Smith, Oct. 6, 1884, *New Letters*, 310.

44. RB to Mrs. Thomas FitzGerald, Sept. 9, 1884, *Learned Lady*, 183.

45. Orr, *Handbook*, 331.

46. "Browning's Hieroglyphic: The Emblem Tradition and Poetic Vision in the Poetry of Robert Browning" (Ph.D. dissertation, City University of New York, 1976), 143.

47. RB to EBB, Aug. 19, 1846, *BC*, 13:269.

48. *Saturday Review* (Dec. 6, 1884); *Browning: The Critical Heritage*, 489–90.

49. RB to FJF, Oct. 25, 1881, *Browning's Trumpeter*, 38.

50. Ibid., Oct. 9, 1883, *Browning's Trumpeter*, 80.

51. RB to Mrs. Thomas FitzGerald, Oct. 9, 1883, *Learned Lady*, 167.

52. Ibid., Oct. 29, 1883, *Learned Lady*, 171.

53. Ibid., Nov. 8, 1883, *Learned Lady*, 172–73.

54. RB to KB, Jan. 30, 1882, *More than Friend*, 11. RB to KB, Dec. 17, 1882, *More than Friend*, 18. RB to KB, Jan. 6, 1884, *More than Friend*, 33.

55. RB to FJF, Oct. 2, 8, and 21, 1881, *Browning's Trumpeter*, 29, 32, 37.

56. RB to FJF, Oct. 11, 1881, *Browning's Trumpeter*, 35.

57. RB to KB, Nov. 10, 1882, *More than Friend*, 16.

58. RB to Mrs. Thomas FitzGerald, Sept. 9, 1884, *Learned Lady*, 181–82.

59. RB to KB, Nov. 10, 1882, *More than Friend*, 16.

60. RB to Mrs. Thomas FitzGerald, Nov. 5, 1885, *Learned Lady*, 187.

61. Michael Meredith, introduction to *More than Friend*, xxiii. The sentence about the Palazzo Guistiniani is also Meredith's, from page xxxii.

62. RB to KB, Sept. 6, 1884, *More than Friend*, 53.

63. RB to Mrs. Thomas FitzGerald, Oct. 22, 1883, *Learned Lady*, 169.

64. RB to KB, Sept. 16, 1884, *More than Friend*, 54.

65. Ibid., Feb. 9, 1884, *More than Friend*, 40.

66. Ibid.

67. Ibid., Jan. 30, 1882, *More than Friend*, 11.

68. EBB to MRM, Apr. 7 [1852], EBB *Mitford*, 3:352.

69. RB to KB, Jan. 6, 1884, *More than Friend*, 33.

Chapter 33

1. RB to W. J. Kingsland, June 15, 1888, Hood, 294.

2. Quoted by Symons in his preface to the second edition of *An Introduction to the Study of Browning*, x.

3. Browning's 1852 essay on Shelley, an introduction to some of Shelley's (supposed) letters, had raised similar questions about the relations of a poet's life and works. The value of letters, Browning wrote then, was "towards a right understanding of [the] author's purpose and work," and especially for the "objective" or dramatic poet "we covet his biography," not because of curiosity about his private life, but because "we desire to look back upon the process of gathering together in a lifetime, the materials of the work

we behold entire." Nonetheless, readers may finally dispense with such details: "The man passes, the work remains. The work speaks for itself . . . and the biography of the worker is no more necessary to an understanding or enjoyment of it, than is a model or anatomy of some tropical tree, to the right tasting of the fruit we are familiar with on the market-stall." In the work of the "subjective" poet, however, "we necessarily approach the personality of the poet": "Both for love's and for understanding's sake we desire to know him, and as readers of his poetry must be readers of his biography also" (Pettigrew and Collins, 1:1001–2).

4. Gosse, *Personalia*, 4.

5. Ibid., 5–6.

6. Ibid., 17–18.

7. Ibid., 19–20, 49–50.

8. RB to William Archer, June 29, 1888, Hood, 295–98.

9. See Philip Kelley and Ronald Hudson, "The Poets' Attitude towards Publication," *BC*, 1:xxxiv–xxxviii.

10. RB to John H. Ingram, May 5 and May 22, 1882, Hood, 210–11.

11. RB to GB, May 2, 1882, *George Barrett*, 304.

12. Ibid., 304–6.

13. RB to GB, Nov. 5, 1887, *George Barrett*, 309.

14. Ibid., Jan. 21, 1889, *George Barrett*, 320.

15. Ibid.

16. RB to IB, June 19, 1862, and Aug. 18, 1862, *Dearest Isa*, 108, 117.

17. FJF printed the will in *BSP*, 3:37–38.

18. Michael Millgate, *Testamentary Acts: Browning, Tennyson, James, Hardy* (Oxford: Clarendon Press, 1992), 21.

19. *Life and Memoirs of John Churton Collins* (London: John Lane, 1912), 82.

20. *Browning's Parleyings: The Autobiography of a Mind* (New Haven: Yale University Press, 1927).

21. *A Handbook to the Works of Robert Browning* (London: G. Bell, 1913), 339.

22. RB to FJF, Jan. 8, 1887, *Browning's Trumpeter*, 143. The first phrase in the next sentence is from this same letter.

23. From an unsigned notice in the *Westminster Review*, Apr. 1887, *Browning: The Critical Heritage*, 498.

24. RB to FJF, Jan. 8, 1887, *Browning's Trumpeter*, 143.

25. Ibid.

26. William C. DeVane, *Browning's Parleyings: The Autobiography of a Mind* (New Haven: Yale University Press, 1927), 8.

27. RB to Monclar, Aug. 9, 1837, *BC*, 3:265.

28. RB to Mrs. Thomas FitzGerald, Jan. 14, 1882, *Learned Lady*, 133–34.

29. RB to KB, Apr. 13, 1884, *More than Friend*, 47.

30. RB to IB, Aug. 19, 1870, *Dearest Isa*, 344.

31. RB to Mrs. Charles Skirrow, Sept. 6, 1886, *New Letters*, 336.

32. RB to W. W. Story, June 19, 1886, Hood, 250.

33. *Times*, Sept. 10, 1886, page 3.

34. RB to FJF, Sept. 12, 1886, *Browning's Trumpeter*, 137.

35. Th. Bentzon (Mme Blanc), "A French Friend of Browning—Joseph Milsand," *Scribner's Magazine* 20 (1896): 116.

Chapter 34

1. RB to GB, May 2, 1882, *George Barrett*, 304.

2. RB to the Skirrows, Sept. 13, 1884, *New Letters*, 309.

3. RB to FJF, Sept. 7, 1885, *Browning's Trumpeter*, 116.

4. RB to the Skirrows, Sept. 30, 1887, *New Letters*, 348.

5. RB to RBB, Aug. 19, 1887, Hood, 265–66.

6. RB to the Skirrows, Oct. 5, 1887, *New Letters*, 350.

7. SB to RBB, Aug. 19, 1887, Hood, 267.

8. Quoted by Michael Meredith, introduction to *More than Friend*, lxix.

9. RB to the Skirrows, Sept. 30, 1887, *New Letters*, 348–49.

10. RB to J. D. Williams, Oct. 21, 1887; Collins, "Letters . . . to Williams," *Browning Institute Studies* 4 (1976): 48.

11. Fannie Barrett Browning, *Some Memories of Robert Browning* (Boston: Marshall Jones, 1928), 9–10.

12. RB to the Skirrows, Oct. 5, 1887, *New Letters*, 350.

13. Fannie Barrett Browning *Some Memories*, 11.

14. RB to GB, Mar. 28, 1888, *George Barrett*, 312.

15. RB to GB, Dec. 21, 1888 and Feb. 24, 1889, *George Barrett*, 317, 322.

16. RB to GB, Dec. 21, 1888, *George Barrett*, 318.

17. RB to GB, Feb. 24, 1889, and Dec. 21, 1888, *George Barrett*, 322, 317.

18. RB to GB, Apr. 16, 1889, *George Barrett*, 328.

19. RB to GB, Mar. 29, 1889, and Oct. 22, 1889, *George Barrett*, 325, 329.

20. RB to GB, Mar. 29 and Feb. 24, 1889, *George Barrett*, 325, 322.

21. RB to FJF, Nov. 17, 1885, *Browning's Trumpeter*, 121.

22. RB to KB, Jan. 14, 1887, *More than Friend*, 72.

23. RB to the Skirrows, Nov. 15, 1885, *New Letters*, 321.

24. RB to Mrs. Thomas FitzGerald, Aug. 6, 1881, *Learned Lady*, 120.

25. RB to KB, Jan. 1, 1882, *More than Friend*, 8–9.

26. RB to Mrs. Charles Skirrow, Aug. 30, 1882, *New Letters*, 278.

27. RB to KB, Feb. 20, 1883, *More than Friend*, 21–22.

28. RB to the Storys, c. May 1887, *American Friends*, 192.

29. RB to KB, June 20, 1887, *More than Friend*, 75.

30. RB to Mrs. Charles Skirrow, late June 1887, *New Letters*, 346.

31. RB to KB, Feb. 28, 1887, *More than Friend*, 73.

32. RB to Mrs. Thomas FitzGerald, Apr. 2, 1887, *Learned Lady*, 194.

33. RB to KB, June 20, 1887, *More than Friend*, 75; RB to GB, Dec. 21, 1888, *George Barrett*, 318.

34. RB to KB, Feb. 7, 1889, *More than Friend*, 90.

35. RB to Mrs. Thomas FitzGerald, Dec. 4, 1886, *Learned Lady*, 192–93.

36. RB to the Martins, Dec. 5 and Dec. 28, 1886, *New Letters*, 337, 338.

37. RB to Mrs. Charles Skirrow, Jan. 24, 1888, *New Letters*, 354.

38. RB to GB, Dec. 21, 1888, *George Barrett*, 318.

39. RB to GB, Jan. 21, 1889, *George Barrett*, 320.

40. RB to KB, Dec. 15, 1888, and Jan. 4, 1889, *More than Friend*, 86, 88.

41. RB to Pen and Fannie Browning, Jan. 14, 1888, Hood, 281.

42. RB to KB, Aug. 21, 1888, *More than Friend*, 81.

43. RB to KB, Aug. 8, 1888, *More than Friend*, 80.

44. RB to KB, Feb. 7, 1889, *More than Friend*, 91. The quoted adjectives are on pages 92 and 95.

45. Katharine Bronson, "Browning in Venice," *More than Friend*, 162, 153.

46. RB to KB, Dec. 15, 1888, *More than Friend*, 86.

47. RB to KB, Jan. 4, 1889, *More than Friend*, 88.

48. RB to J. D. Williams, Oct. 14, 1889; "Letters to . . . Williams," ed. T. J. Collins, *Browning Institute Studies* 4 (1976): 56.

49. RB to Pen Browning, June 19, 1889, *New Letters*, 378–79.

50. *New Letters*, 381.

51. RB to KB, July 17, 1889, *More than Friend*, 97–98.

52. RB to KB, Aug. 8, 1889, *More than Friend*, 100.

53. RB to FJF, Aug. 28, 1889, *Browning's Trumpeter*, 162–63.

54. RB to J. D. Williams, Aug. 28, 1889, *Browning Institute Studies* 4 (1976): 54.

55. RB to Pen Browning, July 13, 1889, Hood, 312. SB to Pen Browning, July 17, 1889, Hood, 315.

56. RB to Emily Tennyson, July 21, 1889, *The Brownings to the Tennysons*, 49.

57. RB to Pen Browning, Aug. 16, 1889, Hood, 317.

58. RB and SB to Pen Browning, Aug. 16, 1889, Hood, 316–18.

59. RB to GB, Oct. 22, 1889, *George Barrett*, 329.

60. Katharine Bronson, "Browning in Asolo," *More than Friend*, 130.

61. RB to Mrs. Charles Skirrow, Oct. 15, 1889, *New Letters*, 383.

62. RB to Mrs. Thomas FitzGerald, Oct. 8, 1889, *Learned Lady*, 202.

63. "Browning in Asolo," *More than Friend*, 140.

64. Katharine Bronson, "Browning in Asolo," *More than Friend*, 132.

65. Ibid., 129.

66. RB to Mrs. Charles Skirrow, Oct. 15, 1889, *New Letters*, 384.

67. The metaphor is Richard S. Kennedy's. For critical commentary on the poems in the volume and for an account of the context in which they were written, see his *Robert Browning's* Asolando: *The Indian Summer of a Poet* (Columbia: University of Missouri Press, 1993).

68. Hiram Corson, "A Few Reminiscences of Robert Browning," *Browning Institute Studies* 3 (1975): 75.

69. Katharine Bronson, "Browning in Asolo," *More than Friend*, 135.

70. Fannie Barrett Browning, *Some Memories*, 24.

71. Ibid., 25, 27, 28.

72. Pen Browning to KB, Dec. 12, 1889, *More than Friend*, 111.

73. Fannie Barrett Browning, *Some Memories*, 28.

74. Pen Browning to KB, Dec. 12, 1889, *More than Friend*, 112.

75. Most of the sentences in this paragraph are drawn from Kennedy, *Robert Browning's* Asolando, 3–4.

76. *BSP,* 3:14, 18.

77. Quoted by Joanna Richardson, *The Brownings: A Biography Compiled from Contemporary Sources* (London: Folio Society, 1986), 274.

78. For an account of the issues surrounding Browning's burial, see Samantha Matthews, "Poets' Corner, Browning, and the Hero as Poet," in *Poetical Remains: Poets' Graves, Bodies, and Books in the Nineteenth Century* (Oxford: Oxford University Press, 2004), 222–55.

Index